(From the original front cover flap)

339th FIGHTER GROUP
100 AIR VICTORIES IN 100 MISSIONS

Man needs to stand out as an individual and at the same time, to be part of a winning team. The 339th Fighter Group filled this need for us.

The record of the men of the 339th Fighter Group is described in readable form, but in sufficient depth to assure our place in the history of air warfare during World War II. This book is also a personal and living memorial. It is dedicated to all of our comrades who have passed on and especially to those who, in 1944-1945, fell from the sky into the arms of God.

The 339th F. G. was forged into a combat ready team in the California desert, under the command of Colonel John B. Henry, Jr. The results of our year of operations justified the faith in assigning this Group to the Eighth Army Air Force in England. The 339th flew its first mission two weeks after the first Mustangs were delivered to our base at Fowlmere. During our first month, the 339th F. G. flew 28 missions and recorded 39 air victories. The Group went on to achieve 100 air victories in our first 100 missions.

DUST JACKET

       Design – Harry R. Corey
       Combat Stills – Richard C. Penrose
       Art Work – Harold J. Kotora

339TH FIGHTER GROUP

TURNER PUBLISHING COMPANY

TURNER PUBLISHING COMPANY
Publishers of Military History

Chief Editor: G. P. Harry

Copyright © 339th Fighter Group & Turner Publishing Co. This book or any part thereof may not be reproduced without the written consent of the publisher.

The materials for this publication were compiled using available information; the publisher regrets it cannot assume liability for errors or omissions.

Library of Congress Catalog Card No.: 91 075227

ISBN: 978-1-68162-267-5

First Printing 1991

CONTENTS

Introduction	6
Acknowledgement	7
Prayer for the 339th Fighter Group	8
Prologue	9
Combat Narratives	11
Roster of Pilots	57
Pilot Articles	
503rd Fighter Squadron	60
504th Fighter Squadron	76
505th Fighter Squadron	97
Memoriam	132
Killed in Action, Killed, not in Action, Evaded Capture/Interned & POW's	133
General Roster of Group Personnel	134
Ground Articles	
339th Headquarters	146
503rd Fighter Squadron	155
504th Fighter Squadron	175
505th Fighter Squadron	199
1786 Ordnance Supply & Maintenance Company (AVN)	214
Biographical Sketches of Group and Squadron Commanding Officers	218
Epilogue	221
Tables	
1. Missions of the 339th Fighter Group	223
2. 339th Fighter Group-Credits for Enemy Aircraft	228
3. 339th Fighter Group-Enemy Aircraft Types Destroyed (Air)	239
4. 339th Fighter Group-Original and Replacement Pilot Assignments	239
5. 339th Fighter Group-Compilation of Pilot Casualties	247
6. Enemy Aircraft Destroyed by Eighth Air Force Fighter Groups	252
7. Enemy Air Force Fighter Squadrons	253

503RD

504TH

505TH

503RD FIGHTER SQUADRON INSIGNIA

504TH FIGHTER SQUADRON INSIGNIA

505TH FIGHTER SQUADRON INSIGNIA

INTRODUCTION
By Jim Starnes

The purpose of this book is twofold. First, it is to save the 339th Fighter Group's story for posterity. Secondly, it is to provide an accessible compilation of the record for future generations to read and know the contribution that this dedicated group of men and women made in the rescue of the American way of life that was so gravely threatened by our nation's ruthless enemies during the Second World War.

The collection of material for this publication is timely almost to the point of being too late. While much has been taken from United States Air Force Archives, it also includes many accounts of personal experiences and remembrances. To have delayed much longer would have risked losing many of these human interest stories and exciting combat dramas as the aging characters fade away. These pages are radiant with the luster of the brilliant record and heroic deeds performed by members of the 339th Fighter Group and its support units. It is intended that this book will preserve the glow of that luster for all time to come.

For each member of this group the war experience was one of stress, hardship, privation and danger. For all, it was the most important and memorable period of their lives. The vast majority were men who had no prior military service and were in uniform to fulfill what they considered to be their patriotic duty. After the war some remained and made a career in the military service. Most returned to civilian life where they achieved varying degrees of upward progression and success in the professional and business world.

When most of us reflect back on those days, it brings into sharp focus the memory of the faces and figures of many brave and dedicated Americans. Most were just young men standing on the threshold of life whose dreams and aspirations for the future were interrupted by the urgent task at hand. Each believed in the cause for which he was fighting and was determined to prevent the towns of America from ever being subjected to the brutal assault and suffering he saw inflicted upon the villages of Europe. In accomplishing this, their untiring efforts and courage were awe inspiring. Each member of this fighting team was indispensable in his or her role, and each performed as expected with honor, dignity and unswerving determination.

Each mission day brought examples of exceptional effort, bravery and self-sacrifice along with sadness and tragedy that were an inevitable part of war. Yet these youthful defenders of freedom were unflinching. One can only wonder what it was in the mores of American life that instilled such a strong sense of courage and patriotic obligation in men so young.

Many of these men, barely beyond their teens, did not return from combat missions. To these men who so bravely paid the supreme price in the defense of their country's freedom, we will forever be indebted for the good life they gave us to enjoy. Also, we shall always remember with solemn pride and reverence those who survived to return home. So much could be said for the joy and sorrow, but here we will merely say that each one who served on the 339th Fighter Group team deserves our nation's undying admiration and eternal gratitude.

To the memory of all the men and women of the 339th Fighter Group and its support units who fought this country's grizzliest war with such distinction, and to the mothers, fathers, wives and sweethearts who waited for their return, this book is affectionately dedicated.

ACKNOWLEDGMENT
By G. P. Harry

In the course of compiling the material for this book, I am indebted to many people.

The editors did an outstanding job. They are:

Steve Ananian	Sal Carollo	Sterling Conley
Harry Corey	Dale Fitzgerald	Steve Fletcher
Earl Gertz	Walter Knox	Jack Mitchell
Richard Penrose	James Starnes	Harry Ziegler

In a sense, this book is a composition of the Group's history which has been collected by our news letter editor, Colonel James R. Starnes. His tireless efforts over the years have been the bond holding the 339th Association together. His record as one of our fighter aces was an early indication of his dedication to the 339th . . . past and present.

Steve Fletcher, although not a "339er," contributed many hours in researching the combat narratives. Not only the editors, but the Association members came through in great fashion with material and photos for the book.

To these people and many others who rendered assistance, my thanks.

A PRAYER FOR THE 339TH FIGHTER GROUP

By Reverend Dr. Henry Opperman

Dear God, Heavenly Father, it is with gratitude in our hearts that this history of the 339th Fighter Group has been written.

In it we give thanks to Thee for the memories that are ours—memories of the days we served our country during World War Two—memories of our comrades—of the pleasant associations that were ours, together with the friendships we hold so dear. Above all we are mindful of Thy care, Thy love and the comfort which Thou gave to us in the days when we needed them.

We also pay tribute through this history to those of our comrades who sacrificed their lives and are no longer with us, but whose personalities will always remain a living memory in our hearts.

So, gracious God, we invoke Thy blessing upon us. May Your grace and guidance continue to be a reality in our lives and in the lives of those who read this history.

Such is our prayer, O God.

PROLOGUE
By John B. Henry, Jr.

The 339th Fighter Group began its existence at Hunter Field, Savannah, Georgia, on 10 August 1942 as the 339th Bombardment Group (Dive). The Group moved at reduced strength on 6 February 1943 to Drew Field, Tampa, Florida. In the next few months personnel and equipment were assigned to bring the Group up to strength while flying A-24 and A-25 aircraft. On 3 July 1943 the 339th moved to Walterboro, South Carolina, and began conversion to a fighter bomber group. Dive bomber pilots were transferred out and replaced by fighter pilots, and P-39 aircraft began to arrive.

On 12 August 1943, I, John B. Henry, then a lieutenant colonel, received orders to proceed to Walterboro to assume command of the group. On that day I fell into more good luck than I deserved. I was about to have the privilege of being a part of one of the best flying organizations in the U.S. Army Air Forces. I was told of the Group's conversion underway, and the bottom line was that we had three weeks to complete the manning, equipping and organizing of various squadrons and support elements. We would then move all of it to the California desert to provide air support to ground troops training in the Army's Desert Maneuver Area. When I heard we were expected to be at Rice Field, California, in thirty days, I had grave misgivings about being able to accomplish such a gargantuan task. To move a well established group from east to west coast in thirty days might have been a reasonable task, but for one that was still converting to fighters, it seemed questionable. Nevertheless, we had no choice but to do our best to comply.

I was announced as commander of the 339th Bombardment Group (Dive) on 17 August 1943 and the 339th changed its name to 339th Fighter Bomber Group on 20 August 1943 with three redesignated squadrons — the 503rd, 504th and 505th Fighter Bomber Squadrons. I will be grateful always to the commanders of units from which the pilots and aircraft came. I could not have done better if given the privilege of making the selections. We received 65 top notch pilots, including the five bomber pilots who remained to fly fighters. I saw no substandard officers or "hangar queen" aircraft being passed to the 339th. Through the super-human efforts of a group of highly motivated people, many of whom were working together for the first time, we made it. The ground elements departed by rail and 49 P-39 aircraft flew out on 10 September 1943, arriving at Rice Field on 17 September 1943.

The 85th Fighter Bomber Group to which I was assigned previously had spent six months on the California Desert in the same role we were getting, so I knew what to expect. I knew from the 85th's experience that the air support requirements for Army Desert Training were minimal. This meant that we would need to fill a significant amount of slack time with other activities. We would need to develop a flying training program to improve the skills of our pilots and to prevent the boredom that stems from idleness. Therefore, I took with me a copy of the training materials used by the 85th to train individual combat pilot replacements. The use of this material, along with the knowledge and expertise we had in our squadron commanders and operations officers who had come from fighter groups in Florida, enabled us to develop a well balanced and meaningful combat pilot training curriculum. This kept us busy when we were not responding to the infrequent calls to provide aircraft to support Army troop maneuvers.

The California Desert Maneuver area was commanded by a major general who also commanded the army division that was in training at the time. In our case it happened to be Major General Alexander Patch. He had priority on our flying activities, and we were to respond to any and all demands that he levied upon us at whatever place and time that he designated. The 339th had been transferred literally out of the Army Air Forces to the command of the Desert Maneuver Area which had the same status as an overseas theater of operations. Aside from assuring that we kept enough aircraft in commission to satisfy the Army troop training needs, they were not concerned with how we occupied our time. Thus, we could pursue our own training program without outside interference. With the flight line force and the Group's supply section pulling together, we were able to maintain a high aircraft flyability rate despite the low supply priority granted by Army Air Forces. No small part of this achievement was due to the old American ingenuity and determination to overcome obstacles on the part of all concerned.

The pilots entered seriously into the spirit of this training and in so doing developed a high level of skill in gunnery, formation flying, bombing and other flying requirements that make up a good combat pilot. Three things contributed directly to the success of this program. One was the rigid stability of our personnel and aircraft. War Department regulations prohibited the transfer of a single individual or aircraft from the group throughout its tour in the maneuver area. This stability for six months had a very favorable effect. Secondly, our isolated location forced all personnel to live on base full time, which assured maximum personnel availability at all times. Thirdly, there was abundant good flying weather — every day was a fair weather day with unlimited potential for flying, enabling the squadrons to pile up training accomplishments in rapid fashion. However, the good weather served us badly for what was in store in that it did not prepare us for the eternally inclement British weather we would have to endure a few months later.

About six weeks before our tour on the desert was to end, an Inspector General team from Third Air Force came to Rice to determine the general condition of the 339th. They remained three days and departed without leaving an exit report. I thought that was rather brief but assumed the inspectors had seen enough to make their findings in a later report. My concern was that we may have been judged deficient to the extent that they saw no point in delving further. However, we never received a report of that team's findings, orally or in writing.

Ten days later a rather large group of officers headed by a full colonel arrived unannounced. My initial reaction was one of alarm—that the previous team had found serious problems. That fear was short-lived. The team leader, Colonel John E. Barr, informed us that his team was to give us an Operation Readiness Inspection (ORI) with a view of sending the 339th overseas directly from Rice Field. This was a tremendous morale boost and generated great enthusiasm among our personnel. For eight days this team examined in minute detail our training, supply, administration and medical records. They inspected personal and technical equipment and noted shortages that would have to be filled for overseas readiness. The operations segment of the team put us through every phase of combat operational flying, culminating in a maximum effort group formation with all aircraft of three squadrons in the air and assembled in a group formation on a timely basis. The exit briefing informed us that we had passed an excellent ORI and would be recommended for filling a Third Air Force obligation to the Eighth Air Force in England. Assignment to the prestigious Eighth Air Force was a tremendous surprise—one that exceeded our dreams. Enthusiasm ran high!

Soon we began receiving equipment that was to accompany the group overseas. Other equipment on the overseas Table of Allowances was shipped directly to the port of embarkation. The 339th left Rice Field in early March 1944, and arrived at Camp Shanks, New York, on 12 March 1944. One week later we boarded the *HMS Sterling Castle* along with several other fighter groups, arriving at Liverpool thirteen days later. The group went by rail to Fowlmere, England, on 5 April 1944 to be equipped with about 75 P-51 Mustangs in the next three weeks.

Many original members of the 339th Fighter Group believed that the plan from the beginning was for the group to train in the California desert for six months and then proceed to an overseas location. However, the intent was strictly to fill an obligation to support Army Desert Training Area activities, after which we would likely have other stateside training responsibilities or else be broken up for assignment as replacement personnel. Fortunately, our story had a very happy ending. The moral to this story is that a group of conscientious young men who were in the Army to fulfill their patriotic duty to their country in time of peril were recognized and rewarded for their hard work, zeal, self-discipline and talents. The group's brilliant record of combat harvest will fill the pages that follow with the luster of sparkling crystal.

339th Fighter Group Combat Narratives

30 April 1944 to 21 April 1945

FOREWORD

By Steve Fletcher

The combat narrative for the 339th Fighter Group was compiled from a number of sources, the main source being the official records kept by each squadron and the Group as it happened on a day-to-day basis.

These records were copied from the microfilm files at Bolling Air Force Base, Washington, D.C. Over 3,400 pages covered the history of the 503rd, 504th and 505th Fighter Squadrons, Group Headquarters and all other units that contributed to the operations and success of the 339th Fighter Group. Additionally, several hundred encounter reports were found and copied at the Suitland Records Center, Suitland, Maryland.

Numerous reference books and other unit histories were checked and some information used. A number of Group pilots were also contacted to clarify certain items. Ranks and squadron assignments are as of the mission listed. Any quotes attributed to a specific pilot were taken directly from the records or from that pilot himself. Anything not taken from the records is so noted. The excellent newsletter put out by Jim Starnes was an outstanding source from which to add to, change, correct and update the "official" records.

Each mission is listed by date. Times shown are usually for the first aircraft off and for the final aircraft landing and is meant to be representative of the mission flown. Mission number shown is the Group's mission number. A problem with these numbers arose and is explained in the "comments" section following the 8 August 1944 mission narrative. The F/O number shown is for the Field Order for that mission.

Claims for enemy aircraft, either airborne or on the ground were very detailed and very complete. Other claims were not so well documented. The Group destroyed tremendous amounts of ground targets besides aircraft, especially locomotives and rail targets. These claims were not always totaled or credited to individual pilots. Though there is no intention to down-play the significance of this destruction, it is not listed in the day-to-day narratives as it was usually too vague and too general to be of use.

This narrative covers from Mission No. 1 flown on 30 April 1944 through Mission No. 264 flown on 21 April 1945.

APRIL 1944

30 April '44
No. 1   W#59   (1615-1815)

The 8th Air Force dispatched nearly 300 heavy bombers, escorted by 644 fighters, to attack targets in the south central area of France and the Pas de Calais. Another force of fighters flew fighter-bomber, dive-bomber, and support missions against several airfields in the Tours/Bricy area.

The 339th flew its first combat mission when they sent 52 aircraft on a fighter-sweep ahead of these attacks. They made landfall at Dunkirk and almost immediately suffered their first battle damage when moderate flak damaged two aircraft. The sweep was completed without further incident, and all aircraft returned safely. The mission was regarded a general success.

The 339th had gone to war.

Losses/damaged:
- Major Scruggs (CO, 503), slight damage by AA fire
- Lt. Folwell (503), slight damage by AA fire

MAY 1944

1 May '44
No. 2   F/O#322   (0840-1109)

Over 700 bombers and fighters were dispatched to attack CROSSBOW targets (Vl sites) in the northern area of France. The Group sent 36 aircraft on a sweep to the Belgium coast for orientation. Inaccurate and moderate flak was encountered in the vicinity of Utrecht and Nijmegen, but the main problem was the haze and poor visibility which caused the Group to break up. All aircraft eventually returned safely.

1 May '44
                              (1701-1806)

The 503rd sent eight aircraft on a "practice" escort mission over East Anglia, England. No bombers appeared, so everyone returned home. Upon landing, one aircraft's landing gear collapsed causing it to belly-in. All others returned safely.

Losses/damaged: Lt Wyatt (503), landing accident, unhurt.

1 May '44
                              (1750-1915)

Lt. Harte (503) and Lt. Knott (503) were sent off under 66th Wing verbal orders. They were to perform Air/Sea Rescue patrol, but both were forced back early due to radio failures.

Comment: no mission credit or combat time given.

2 May '44
No. 3   F/O#324   (1100-1302)

The 339th was the only P-51 group operating this day when they sent 52 aircraft to escort 2nd BD B-24s attacking CROSSBOW targets in the Pas de Calais area. Inaccurate, moderate flak was encountered. Visibility was 9/10. All returned safely.

3 May '44
No. 4　　　　F/O#325　　　　(1500-1730)

Again the 339th was the only P-51 group operating when they again escorted 2nd BD B-24s on a CROSSBOW mission to St. Omer, France Although heavy, inaccurate flak was encountered in the target area, the bombers flew a good formation, and concentrated hits were seen on the objective.

4 May '44
No mission flown.

5 May '44
No. 5　　　　F/O#327　　　　(0755-0945)

For the third time, the 339th was the only P-51 group operating, and again, they escorted 2nd BD B-24s attacking a CROSSBOW target at Wizerness, France. The bombers were picked up over the Channel, but the boxes were widely separated, and with the cloud conditions, the escort was very difficult. A number of pilots lost contact with the bombers, but they swept the target area before returning to base.

The mission, as a whole, was only a fair success.

6 May '44
No. 6　　　　F/O#328　　　　(0910-1112)

The Group again escorted 2nd BD B-24s attacking CROSSBOW targets in the Pas de Calais area. Although the bombers were late, off course, and in a very straggled formation, they were still escorted to the target. 9/10 and 10/10 cloud cover persisted in the target area, and the bombing results could not be seen. No flak or fighters were seen.

7 May '44
No. 7　　　　F/O#329　　　　(1025-1410)

The Group flew its deepest penetration mission to date when they provided escort for B-17s returning from Berlin. The bombers were picked up near Celle amid heavy flak, but all told, there was surprisingly weak German reaction. The bombing was done visually with very poor results.

In the Hannover area, the Group suffered their first combat loss when Lt. Luper (505) was hit by heavy flak. All else returned safely.
Loses/damaged:
- Lt. Gerard (503), minor damage from AA fire - F/O Steier (503), operational, parachuted safely - Lt. Arch B. Luper (505), AA fire, KIA

"... Lt. Luper had been damaged by a 'first burst' flak hit through a solid deck of clouds in the Steinhuder Lake area. Tried to return, but his aircraft finally caught fire. He was last seen by his wingman, Lt. Perry (505). Lt Luper was trying to parachute when he disappeared into the clouds. Lt. Perry followed him down, but lost him in the cloud cover. Lt. Luper's body was later found with his unopened chute very near his crashed plane at Gees, Holland...."

"... F/O Steier (503) aborted when he lost his blower over the Channel. While preparing to land at Fowlmere, he came in at about 400 feet and peeled up. He blacked out in the process and his ship zoomed up to about 2,500 feet, rolled out and fell into an inverted, nose-down spin. He regained consciousness and tried to pull the ship out. Failing in this, he jettisoned his cockpit cover and bailed out. His chute opened almost instantaneously at approximately 300 feet. He landed unhurt. The aircraft was completely destroyed . . . . "

7 May '44
No. 8　　　　F/O#330　　　　(1741-2045)

Escorted 2nd BD B-24s to attack a railway marshalling yard (M/Y) southwest of Liege. Meager to heavy inaccurate flak was encountered at Knocke. Bombing results were unobserved.

8 May '44
No. 9　　　　F/O#331　　　　(1046-1415)

The Group provided withdrawal escort to bombers returning from Berlin. Heavy to moderate accurate flak was encountered. On the return, the 503rd left the escort and dropped to the deck to strafe on their way home. Several barges and rail targets were attacked. All returned safely.

9 May '44
No. 10　　　　F/O#333　　　　(0751-1100)

The Group provided support for bombers attacking targets in southwest Belgium and France. At 0950 near Vouziers, enemy fighters were seen for the first time and the Group scored their first air-to-air victories, shooting down two Me-109s. All our aircraft returned safely, including Capt. Aitken (504) who was attacked by four P-38s!
Claims: 2/0/1 air
- 1 Me-109E shot down, 1 Me109E damaged/air - Lt. Everett (505)
- 1 Me-109F shot down - Lt. W. A. Jones (505) Lt. Harold M. Everett (505), who scored the Group's first victory reported, "... I was flying on Lt. Farmer's (505) wing escorting B-24s. We were cruising at about 25,000 feet when I noticed approximately 15-18 Me-109s with bright yellow tails. I picked out one and gave him a rather short burst. No hits. We both started down for the deck. He took violent evasive action and at about 3,000 feet he gradually started pulling out, leveling at approximately 50 feet, his right wing striking a row of trees . . . I immediately overshot and zoomed up to about 7,000 feet ... A minute later, I saw another 109 and damaged it before losing it at low level . . . ."

10 May '44
No. 11　　　　F/O#334　　　　(0916-1230)

The Group was to provide penetration escort for bombers attacking a target northeast of the Ruhr Valley. Weather forced the recall of the bombers and most of the 339th. Major Scruggs, Lt. Wyer and Lt. West (all 503) did not hear the recall, however, and flew on. They broke into the clear near Namur, and since no other aircraft were seen, they swept as far as Coburg before returning home.

11 May '44
No. 12 F/O#335 (1304-1610)

The Group was to provide penetration escort to bombers attacking targets deep in France. Enroute to the bombers, the 503rd was sent to investigate several different groups of aircraft. They all turned out to be "friendlies," but due to the time involved, they could not meet the bombers and returned home. The rest of the group completed the escort. The mission was flown in poor visibility with heavy to moderate, accurate flak over Orleans. All aircraft returned safely.

12 May '44
No. 13 F/O#337 (1031-1342)

This was a Group escort mission into Germany. The bombers were met south of Brussels and taken to Frankfurt. Experienced heavy, intense, accurate flak in the Frankfurt/Koblenz area. Otherwise, an uneventful mission.

12 May '44
(1543-1734)

...The second flight of the day was not planned. It was a scramble to assist returning bombers and stragglers. Forty-plus aircraft took off and met the bombers over the Channel. Several orbits were completed from Mons to Charleroi. No bandits were seen, and all aircraft returned safely. No mission credit or combat time given.

13 May '44
No. 14 F/O#338 (1149-1700)

The Group used wing tanks for the first time. The mission was to provide target support for the deepest penetration into Germany to date. Targets were in the Posen area northwest of Berlin.

Numerous aircraft were forced back, mainly with problems with the new tanks. The rest picked up the bombers north of Hamburg and completed the mission. Heavy, intense, accurate flak was encountered along most of the escort. Ten miles southeast of Lubeck, several FW-190s were seen and attacked. All our aircraft returned safely.
Claims: 0/1/0 air
- 1 FW-190 probable shot down - Capt. Larson (505) Comment: the P-51 carried 279 gallons of fuel internally. Two 75-gallon wing tanks added another 150 gallons.

14 May '44
No mission flown.

15 May '44
No. 15 F/O#339 (0813-1029)

On a fighter sweep into northwestern France, even though no flak or enemy aircraft were seen, we still suffered a loss. An operational problem caused the loss of an aircraft and made Lt. Wyer (503) the Group's first POW. All others returned safely.
Losses/damaged: Lt. Albert L. Wyer (503) had been a spare, but stayed on to fly the mission. He suffered a coolant leak and was forced to parachute over Belgium. Captured, POW.

16, 17, 18 May '44
No mission flown.

19 May '44
No. 16 F/O#342 (1200-1720)

The Group provided target escort for bombers attacking in the Berlin/Brunswick areas. They met the bombers at Havelberg and took them to Berlin. The Group then left the bombers and dropped to the deck to hunt for air and ground targets on the way home.

Several aircraft were shot down as well as the first claims made for aircraft destroyed on the ground. Numerous other ground targets were destroyed or damaged, but this mission cost the Group two more pilots.
Claims: 3/0/0 air 3/0/10 ground
- 3 Do-217s damaged/ground - Capt. Carter (503)
- 3 Do-217s damaged/ground - Lt. Whitelaw (503)
- 3 Me-109s damaged/ground, 1 biplane trainer damaged/ground - Lt. Folwell (503)
- 2 Ju-52s destroyed/ground - Lt. Crockett (503)
- 1 T/E transport destroyed/ground - Lt. Wolfort (503)
- 1 FW-190 shot down - Lt. O'Sullivan (504)
- 1 FW-190 shot down - Lt. E. M. V. Johnson (505)
- 1 FW-190 shot down - Lt. E. M. V. Johnson (505)/ Lt. Starnes (505)
Losses/damaged:
- Lt. Folwell (503), damaged by AA fire, returned unhurt.
- Lt. James R. Crockett (503), strafing a train, killed.
- Lt. Walter R. O'Sullivan, Jr. (504), dogfight, POW.

"...Lt. Crockett (503) strafed and destroyed two Ju-52s on an airfield near Ludwiglust...then strafed and destroyed a nearby locomotive...." Lt. Wolfort (503) reported, "...at 1530 hours I was flying on Lt. Crockett's wing while strafing a train.

As I started down to make a second pass, Lt. Crockett was firing on the train...It appeared to me as he started to pull up from this pass he either mushed into the train or misjudged and flew into it. I thought I saw a piece of his airplane fly through the air. It appeared to be part of its tail. I was unable to see anymore due to the steam from the locomotive. I did not actually see him hit the locomotive, but was unable to contact him on the radio after this, and just prior to the second pass we had perfect communication...."

Whatever happened, Lt. Crockett was killed. Lt. O'Sullivan (504) reported, "...Just after I shot down a FW-190, two Me-109s got on my tail, and after a brief dogfight, I ended with four 20mm's thru the wing and thru my hip. I started spinning and lost my oxygen mask and passed out. I woke up around 12,000 feet and hit the silk."

Comment: Lt. O'Sullivan had just scored the 504th's first air-to-air victory when he became the Group's first air-to-air loss. He parachuted over Lubeck, Germany, and was very lucky to be captured almost immediately.

He had lost much blood and would spend his entire time in hospitals. By January 1945, he was repatriated to the States due to his wounds.

20 May '44
No. 17   F/O#343-A   (0856-1145)

The Group provided target and withdrawal support for B-17s attacking targets north of Orleans, France. The bombers were picked up east of Paris. Experienced heavy, intense, accurate flak. All returned safely.

Losses/damaged: Lt. Graham (504), slight damage by AA fire.

21 May 44
No. 18   F/O#344   (1050-1630)

The Group took part in the first "Chattanooga" attack. These were planned strafing attacks against railway rolling stock and grounded aircraft. Nearly all heavy bombers "stood down," and all fighters were sent out. Each Group was assigned a specific area to attack. The 339th area was to be between Dresden and Leipzig with five airfields assigned: Groszenhain, Riesa, Oschatz, Mockau and Polenz. Claims were high as numerous air and ground targets were destroyed. The cost was also high: four pilots lost and six aircraft returned with damage. Three had flown through trees, cables, or high tension lines!

Claims: 14/0/3 air   10/0/13 ground
- 1 He-111K shot down, 1 Ju-88 damaged/ground - Lt. Wright (503)
- 2 Ju-88s damaged/ground - Lt. Price (503)
- 3 Ju-88s damaged/ground - Lt. Harte (503)
- 1 Ju-88 damaged/ground - Lt. Stephenson (503)
- 1 Me-110 destroyed/ground, 1 Ju-88 damaged/ground - Lt. Fiorito (503)
- 1 U/ITE A/C damaged/ground - Lt. Whitelaw (503)
- 1 U/ITE A/C destroyed/ground - Lt. Reynolds (503)
- 1 U/ITE A/C destroyed/ground - Lt. Erickson (503)
- 1 U/ITE A/C destroyed/ground - Lt. Lowery (503)
- 1 U/ITE A/C destroyed/ground, 2 U/ITE A/C damaged/ground - Lt. Dearey (503)
- 2 U/ITE A/C destroyed/ground - Lt. Bryan (503)
- 2 Ju-88s destroyed/ground, 1 Ju-88 damaged/ground - Capt. Carter (503)
- 2 Me-109s shot down - Capt. Routt (504)
- 1 S/E tricycle fixed-gear A/C damaged/air, 1 Ju-87 damaged/ground - Lt. Harry (504)
- 1 FW-190 destroyed/ground - Lt. Eisenhart (504)
- 1 Ju-88 shot down - Lt. Everett (505)/Lt. Mudge (505)
- 2 biplanes shot down - Lt. Hanseman (505)
- 1 Ju-88 shot down - Lt. Hanseman (505)/Lt. Reid (505)
- 1 Ju-88 shot down - Lt. Reid (505)
- 1 S/E trainer shot down - Lt. Hanson (505)/Lt. Starnes (505)
- 1 biplane shot down - Lt. Hanson (505)
- 1 biplane shot down - Lt. Strong (505)
- 1 Do-217 shot down, 1 S/E trainer shot down - Lt. Lynch (505)
- 1 Do-217 shot down - Lt. Lynch (505)/Lt. G.F. Perry (505)
- 1 liaison A/C damaged/air - Lt. Farmer (505)

Losses/damaged:
- Capt. Walter T. Carter (503), shot down by AA, POW
- Lt. Robert F. Mulvey (503), KIA - probably by AA fire
- Lt. Arthur H. Steier (503), KIA - probably by AA fire
- Lt. Floyd P. Heneghan (505), KIA - probably by AA fire
- Lt. Lowery (503), damaged by AA fire, returned unhurt
- Lt. Harte (503), damaged by AA fire, returned unhurt
- Lt. Bryan (503), damaged by AA fire, returned unhurt
- Lt. Fiorito (503), hit cable, returned unhurt, but aircraft damaged beyond repair
- Lt. Harry (504), damaged by AA fire and flew through a tree—and high tension lines—returned unhurt.
- Lt. Everett (505), flew through high-tension lines - returned unhurt, but aircraft damaged beyond repair.

Comment: None of the pilots lost were seen to go down.

. . . Capt. Carter (503) was badly wounded in his right leg by shrapnel from a 40mm flak burst from Polenz airfield. He parachuted from very low level, hit his tail, but survived. Captured, spent over two months in hospitals. POW . . .

. . . an unknown call was heard, thought to be Lt.. Heneghan (505), said he was wounded and bailing out over the Channel near the French/Belgium border. Not heard from again; KIA . . . .

. . . Lt. Everett (505), on his last strafing pass on a train, ran through some high-tension lines. He reported, "I had to pull up and broke off as I had about 300 feet of wire and crosstie dangling off my left wing. I landed at Framingham, England, to get gas and inspect the damage as the wing began to vibrate halfway home. The spinner was chewed up and the prop damaged, plus the air scoop was flattened. I returned to my home base after having it checked by their engineering section . . . ."

A pilot who will remain anonymous reported, " . . . We went down to minimum altitude for a strafing run . . . I saw a herd of cattle and test fired my guns . . . ."

21 May '44
Annex to Mission Report VIII F.C. F. O. 334 Chattanooga
J. Claims (AIR)
0/0/2   (In Air) SE
5/0/0   (In Air) TE
7/0/4   (On Ground) SE
0/0/9   (On Ground) TE
7 Locomotives destroyed   14 Locomotives damaged

In Air
-1 He - 111K destroyed - Lt. Wright - (503)
-1 Me - 109 destroyed - Capt. Routt - (504)
-1 Me - 109 destroyed - Capt. Routt, Lt. Showker and Lt. Harry - (504)
-2 Ju - 88 destroyed - Lts. Reid and Hanseman - (505)
-1 Se Trainer destroyed - Lt. Strong - (505)
-2 Se Trainers destroyed - Lts. Hanson and Starnes - (505)
-2 Se Trainers destroyed - Lt. Hanseman - (505)
-1 Me 410 destroyed - Lts. Everett and Mudge - (505)
-1 Se Trainer destroyed - Lt. Lynch - (505)
-1 Do 217 destroyed - Lts. Lynch and Perry - (505)
-1 Se UIA damaged - Lt. Harry - (504)
-1 Se Trainer damaged - Lt. Farmer - (505)

On The Ground
-1 ME 110 destroyed - Lt. Fiorito - (503)

-6 Te UIA destroyed - Lt.s Bryan, Lowery, Deary, Whitelaw, Reynolds and Erickson - (503)
-3 Te UIA damaged - Lts. Bryan, Lowery, Deary, Whitelaw, Reynolds, and Ericson - (503)
-1 Ju 88 damaged - Lt. Wright - (503)
-1 Ju 88 damaged - Lt. Fiorito - (503)
-2 Ju 88 damaged - Lt. Price - (503)
-3 Ju 88 damaged - Lt. Harte - (503)
-1 Ju 88 damaged - Lt. Stephenson - (503)
-1 Fw 190 damaged - Lt. Eisenhart - (504)
-1 Ju 87 damaged - Lt. Harry - (504)
-1 Fw 190 damaged - Capt. Larson, Lt. Knight - (505)
-1 Te UIA damaged - Capt. Larson, Lt. Knight - (505)
-2 Locomotives destroyed - Lts. Bryan, Lowery, Deary, Whitelaw, Reynolds, and Ericson - (503)
-1 Locomotive destroyed - Lts. Thistlewaite and Brownshadel - (504)
-2 Locomotives destroyed - Lts. Everett and Mudge - (505)
-1 Locomotive destroyed - Lts. Hanson, Everett and Mudge - (505)
-1 Locomotive damaged - Lts. Bryan, Lowery, Deary, Whitelaw, Reynolds, and Ericson - (503)
-2 Locomotives damaged - Lts. Price, Harte, and Stephens - (503)
-2 Locomotives damaged - Lt. Brownshadel - (504)
-3 Locomotives damaged - Lt. Eisenhart - (504)
-2 Locomotives damaged - Lt. Starnes - (505)
-1 Locomotive damaged - Lt. Reid - (505)
-2 Locomotives damaged - Lt. Hanseman - (505)
-1 Locomotive damaged - Lt. Farmer - (505)
-1 Locomotive damaged - Lts. Jones and Sawicki - (505)
-4 Flak Towers destroyed - Lts. Showker and Wilcox, Capt. Routt - (504)
-1 Flak Tower destroyed - Lt. Harry - (504)
-1 Flak Tower destroyed - Lt. Mudge - (505)
-2 Gas Storage Tanks destroyed - Lt. Craigo - (504)
-2 Gas Storage Tanks damaged - Lt. Craigo - (504)
-1 Fuel Refinery damaged - Lts. Stockman and Thibert - (504)
-2 Barracks destroyed - Capt. Routt, Lts. Showker and Wilcox - (504)
-1 Railroad St. damaged - Lts. Stockman and Thibert - (504)
-1 Factory damaged - Capt. Larson and Lt. Knight - (505)
-1 Factory damaged - Lt. Lynch - (505)
-1 Factory damaged - Lt. Farmer - (505)
-1 Factory damaged - Lt. Sawicki - (505)
-1 Factory damaged - Lt. Ewing - (505)
-1 R.R. Switch House damaged - Lt. Hanson - (505)
-1 Airdrome Hanger damaged - Capt. Larson and Lt. Knight - (505)
-1 He-111K destroyed - Lt. Wright - (503)

22 May '44
No. 19   F/0#346   (1025-1245)
The Group flew an escort mission into northwestern France. Over the target at St. Pol, there was meager to heavy inaccurate flak. No damaged suffered.

23 May '44
No. 20   F/0#348   (0753-1155)
The Group flew an escort mission deep into French territory to near the Swiss border. The bombers were picked up at Chalons, and the mission went without incident.

24 May '44
No. 21   F/0#349   (0835-1400)
The Group flew a penetration, target, withdrawal, support mission (P.T.W.S.) for B-17s attacking the Berlin area. Experienced heavy, intense, and very accurate flak. Near Bradenburg, a large number of German fighters attacked the bombers and a huge dogfight developed.
Claims: 8/1/7 air   1/0/0 ground
- 1 FW-190 shot down - Major Scruggs (503)/Lt. Whitelaw (503)
- 1 FW-190 shot down - Lt. Bryan (503)/Lt. Graham (503)
- 1 Me-109 shot down - Lt. Brown (503)/Lt. Wolfort (503)
- 2 Me-109s damaged/air - Lt. Brown (503)
- 1 Me-109 damaged/air - Lt. Wolfort (503)
- 1 Me-109 shot down - Lt. Griffith (504)
- 1 Me-109 probably shot down, 2 Me-109s damaged/air - Lt. Stevens (504)
- 1 Me-109 damaged/air - Lt. M. R. Ball (504)
- 1 FW-190 shot down - Lt. E. M. V. Johnson (505)
- 2 Me-109s shot down, 1 FW-190 shot down, 1 FW-190 damaged/air - Major Larson (505) (He would later receive a Silver Star for this mission.)
- 1 Me-109 destroyed/ground - Lt. Lynch (505)
Losses/damaged:
- Lt. Joseph Wolfort (503), damaged by AA fire, seen to parachute - reported KIA
- Lt. Graham (503), damaged by AA fire, returned unhurt - Lt. Stevens (504), damaged by fighters, returned unhurt.

24 May '44
No. 22   F/0#61(66FW)   (1803-2135)
The second mission of the day was a late bombing mission against a bridge east of Soissons, France. All aircraft were armed with one 500-1b. demolition bomb.
The 503rd made a low level glide-bombing attack with excellent results. The 504th tried skip-bombing from 50 feet; results were poor and the pilots thought dive-bombing would have been better. The 505th's results were not known.
After the attack, air and ground targets were attacked on the way home. There was heavy, intense flak in the area.
About this same time, three 505th pilots were escorting a P-38 photo-reconnaissance aircraft near St. Quentin when they were bounced by a large number of FW-190s. One pilot was shot down, but the P-38 got away safely.
Claims: 5/0/0 air   0/0/1 ground
- 1 Me-109 shot down - Lt. Knott (503)/Lt. Shake (503)
- 1 Me-109 damaged/ground - Lt. Stephenson (503)/Lt. Knott (503)/Lt. Shake (503)
- 2 Me-109s shot down - Lt. Hanseman (505)
- 2 FW-190s shot down - Lt. Everett (505)

Losses/damaged:
- Lt. Harold M. Everett (505), shot down, wounded, POW Lt. Everett reported, "...We were escorting a P-38 photo ship to Soissons. We formed a box around the P-38 with Lt. Price (505) on the right, Lt. Tower (505) to the rear, and myself to the left. Approximately 10 minutes from the target I saw 50-plus enemy aircraft about 2,000 feet above us at 4 o'clock. I called them in and broke into the formation. Four peeled off from the main group to attack us. I picked the first e/a (enemy aircraft) and gave him a burst from about 80 or 90 degrees of deflection. He burst into flames and rolled over for the deck.

"At the same time, I incurred several 20mm hits which exploded my left gas bags. I was hit by more 20mm's, and the radio and armor plating came into the cockpit breaking my shoulder and shattering the instrument panel. I was also hit by a 7.9mm shell which barely entered my left ankle.

"I don't remember how I shook them off my tail, but a few moments later I was alone and headed for England.

"Approximately two minutes later I ran into 30-plus enemy aircraft, all FW-190s with brilliant red crosses on their wings. About half of them peeled off to engage, so I broke into them, getting into a Luftberry. About halfway in the turn, a 190 crossed my sights, and I fired until he burst into flames and broke out of the circle. I saw the pilot bailout safely after dumping his canopy.

"I incurred more hits and, as I had no more ammunition, broke down to try to run for home. They followed me, still shooting until my engine was hit and began to burn. I dumped the canopy and left as my aircraft started to spin. I landed in an orchard approximately 150 feet from my plane which had ceased burning. Somehow I got over to it and set off the incendiary bomb on the gun camera..."

Lt. Tower (505) reported, "...I saw Lt. Price with two e/a on his tail. Lt. Everett was on the tails of these FW-190s with two more on his tail. I took on the two e/a on Lt. Everett's tail... with e/a behind me, but not close enough to do damage...." Lt. Tower confirmed Lt. Everett's first victory, then lost sight of him. Lt. Tower and Lt. Price returned separately.

Comment: Lt. Everett had a quick and violent war. On 9 May he scored the 505th's and the Group's first air-to-air kill; on 21 May he flew through high-tension lines while strafing; and now, on 24 May he was shot down, badly wounded, parachuted, captured, and made a POW. He was in hospitals until September (1944) when he was rescued as the Germans evacuated their hospitals in France.

25 May '44
No. 23   F/O#350   (0735-1142)
The Group provided target and withdrawal support for B-17s attacking Blainville, France. After leaving the bombers, the Group strafed their way home. Numerous rail targets were destroyed or damaged despite heavy, intense, inaccurate flak.
Claims: 1/0/0 air
- 1 FW-190 shot down - Lt. Mudge (505)/Lt. Hrico (505)
Losses/damaged:
- Lt. Lynch (505) was damaged by " four red-nosed P-47s"

Comment: The "P-47s" persistently attacked Lt. Lynch near Metz before he finally got away and returned unhurt. The 56th Fighter Group, operating in the same area, flew "red-nosed" P-47s.

26 May '44
No mission flown.

27 May '44
No. 24   F/O#351   (1044-1500)
The Group flew a free-lance fighter sweep to the Manheim-Stuttgart-Strasbourg areas. They then dropped down to strafe on the way home. The 505th found an aerodrome near Frankfurt. Encountering no flak, they made four passes before heading home.
Claims: 7/0/12 ground
- 1 Fieseler Storch destroyed/ground, 1 He-111 destroyed/ground, 1 Fieseler Storch damaged/ ground, 1 U/ITE A/C damaged/ground Capt. Thury (505)
- 1 Fieseler Storch destroyed/ground, 1 U/ITE A/C destroyed/ground - Lt. Ewing (505)
- 1 Fieseler Storch destroyed/ground - Lt. Rohm (505)
- 1 Fieseler Storch destroyed/ground - Lt. Sawicki (505)
- 1 Me-109 destroyed/ground - Lt. Olander (505)
- 5 training gliders damaged/ground - Capt. Thury (505)/ Lt. Ewing (505)
- 5 training gliders damaged/ground - Lt. Rohm (505)/ Lt. Sawicki (505)

27 May '44
At approximately 1907 hours, a four-man orientation flight from the 503rd, Harte-Amerman-Ammon-Dickens, were returning to Fowlmere at low level. They flew over an airfield as an A-20 was taking off. Dickens flew into it; both aircraft crashed on the field.
Losses/damaged: Lt. Robert L. Dickens (503), killed, accident

28 May '44
No. 25   F/O#352   (1222-1700)
The Group was off to provide penetration and target escort to the oil refinery at Lutzendorf near Halle. Experienced intense, accurate flak in the target area, otherwise it was an uneventful mission.

29 May '44
No. 26   F/O#353   (1030-1545)
The Group provided the longest penetration escort to date. The target was an aircraft assembly plant beyond Berlin near the Polish border. Flak was heavy, intense and accurate. Claims: 2/0/0 air
- 1 FW-190 shot down - Capt. Thury (505)
- 1 FW-190 shot down - Lt. Starnes (505)

Losses/damaged:
- Lt. Gordon F. Perry (505), killed
- Lt. James L. Lynch (505), killed
- Capt. Routt (504), midair collision
- Lt. M. R. Ball (504), midair collision

Comments:
- Lt. Perry and Lt. Lynch were lost due to an apparent navigational error. They missed England to the south on their return and were last heard from south of the Isle of Wight when they requested a steer from ground control. Their radio transmissions were very weak, and they did not acknowledge the new heading. It is believed they flew out over the Atlantic until their fuel was exhausted. Neither was seen or heard from again.
- Capt. Routt and Lt. Ball had a "slight" midair collision. Both returned and were forced to belly-land at Woodridge, England. Both aircraft were damaged, but neither pilot was injured.

30 May '44
No. 27   F/0#354   (0902-1320)
This was an escort mission to Oschersleben near Magdeburg. The bombers were picked up over the target. Heavy to moderate, inaccurate flak was encountered over Brunswick and south of Nienburg. Near Magdeburg, enemy fighters attacked and quickly shot down two 504th pilots while others attacked the bombers. A dogfight from 25,000 feet down to the deck followed.
Claims: 5/2/1 air
- 2 FW-190s shot down - Lt. Bryan (503)
- 2 FW-190s shot down - Lt. Stevens (504)
- 1 FW-190 shot down, 1 FW-190 damaged/air - Major Gravette (504)
- 1 FW-190 probably shot down - Capt. Peter (504)
- 1 FW-190 probably shot down - Lt. Eisenhart (504)
Losses/damaged:
- Lt. Paul M. Meyer (504), shot down by FW-190s, aircraft exploded, KIA.
- Lt. Edward A. Thistlethwaite (504), shot down by FW-190s, forced to parachute, captured, POW
- Lt. Stockman (504), damaged by a FW-190, returned unhurt.

31 May '44
No. 28   F/0#355   (0935-1220)
Was to provide bomber escort to Colmar near the Swiss border. Due to extremely bad weather, picked up bombers near Antwerp and attacked targets in the Brussels area instead.

JUNE 1944

1 June '44
No mission flown.

2 June '44
No. 29   F/0#358   (1044-1425)
The Group went on a Type 16 Control fighter-sweep to Evreux, France, where the bombers were operating. The assigned area was patrolled without incident. No enemy aircraft were seen, and only meager, inaccurate flak was experienced. All returned safely.
Comment: "Type 16 Control" was a mission flown under radar observation from England.

3 June '44
No mission flown.

4 June '44
No. 30   F/0#367   (1338-1615)
Bomber escort into northwest France. Uneventful.

4 June '44
No. 31   F/0#368   (1824-2107)
Bomber escort into northwest France. Uneventful.
Comment: Capt. Routt (504) was the first pilot in the Group to attain 100 combat hours.

5 Jun '44
No. 32   F/0#369   (0815-1122)
This was a bomber escort into northwest France. The bombers hit various coastal targets between Cherbourg and Le Havre. The Group patrolled inland an uneventful mission. Comment: ... All personnel were restricted to the post ... Line personnel were given orders on short notice to paint the planes with black and white stripes—"invasion stripes."

6 June '44
No. 33   F/0#371/FULLHOUSE   (0548-1206)
"D-Day" started shortly after midnight. The Group's first part was an area patrol and support from south of St. Albans Head almost to the Channel Islands. A dense overcast forced some early returns and probably caused a 504 pilot to spin out of formation and crash. All others returned safely. Although no ammunition was expended or needed, it still was a very grueling patrol.
Losses/damaged:
- Lt. Elton J. Brownshadel (504), crashed, killed on take-off.

6 June '44
No. 34   F/0#371/STUD   (1354-1815)
The Group flew dive-bombing and strafing attacks against targets behind the beachhead. Half the aircraft carried two 250-lb. bombs each, and half acted as escort. A marshalling yard at Sable was hit with very good results. East of St. Brieuc, a railway bridge was hit with good to excellent results. A truck convoy southeast of Fourgeres was also attacked. All returned safely.

6 June '44
No. 35   F/O#372B   (1810-2230)

The Group's third mission flown produced the only air-to-air claims for "D-Day". Two pilots of the 505th became separated from the rest of the squadron while climbing through the overcast. They found and joined several 355th Fighter Group P-51s and flew patrol with them. They then strafed several trains near Orleans. At about 2045 near Janville, France, they saw P-51s of the 357th Fighter Squadron, 355th Fighter Group, attacking a squadron of Ju-87s near the deck. They joined in and shot down three.
Claims: 3/0/0 air
- 2 Ju-87s shot down - Lt. McMahon (505) - 1 Ju-87 shot down - Lt. Mudge (505)

Comment: On 7 June '44, the Group flew several P-51Ds on combat missions. One of the main changes was armament. The "B" and "C" models had four .50-caliber machine guns with a total of 1,260 rounds. They had 350 rounds for the inboard gun and 280 rounds for the outboard gun in each wing. The "D" model had six .50-caliber machine guns with a total of 1,880 rounds; i.e., 400 rounds for the inboard gun and 270 rounds for both the center and outboard guns in each wing.

7 June '44

The 503rd sent 18 aircraft to dive-bomb Laval Airfield. Takeoff was at 0426 in darkness and through a low, dense overcast. Because of this and the resulting difficulty getting into formation, the mission was cancelled. One pilot overshot the runway trying to land and crashed. He still had two 250 lb. bombs on the aircraft. They did not explode, but the aircraft was destroyed. All others were back safely by 0521. No one received combat time for this flight. The mission was rescheduled for later in the day. Losses/damaged:
- Lt. Folwell (503), crashed on landing, aircraft destroyed, pilot unhurt.

7 June '44
No. 36   F/O#373   (0700-0945)

The 504th flew a dive-bombing and strafing attack to Laval, France. Each aircraft carried two 250-1b. bombs. After bombing a marshalling yard with very good results, they saw and shot down two FW-190s right on the deck. Nearby, they found an airfield with a number of FW-190s parked under camouflage netting. Only one light AA gun was firing so eight passes were made, destroying five aircraft. Claims: 2/0/0 air 5/0/0 ground
- 1 FW-190 shot down - Capt. Peter (504)
- 1 FW-190 shot down, 1 FW-190 destroyed/ground - Lt. Atteberry (504)
- 1 FW-190 destroyed/ground - Lt. Caldwell (504)
- 1 FW-190 destroyed/ground - Lt. Stevens (504)
- 1 FW-190 destroyed/ground - Lt. Waters (504)
- 1 FW-190 destroyed/ground - Lt. Corbin (504)

7 June '44
No. 37   F/O#375   (1029-1549)

Area support mission to Laval, France.

7 June '44
No. 38   F/O#376   (1737-2140)

Area support mission to Nantes. Experienced heavy, intense flak in the area, but all returned safely.

8 June '44
No. 39   F/O#377-1   (0425-0740)

The Group dive-bombed targets to the rear of the beachhead. Each squadron was assigned a different target. The 503rd attacked oil storage and a railroad station near Chateaubourg and Betton. An airfield at Rennen was seen, but so heavily defended the strafing attack was called off when three aircraft suffered minor damage. All returned. The 504th became separated in the darkness and overcast, but most continued. After attacking a marshalling yard and strafing trains, several aircraft were seen and shot down. Flak was very intense.
Claims: 3/0/0 air
- 1 Do-217 shot down - Lt. Tower (505)/Lt. Opitz (505)
- 1 FW-190 shot down - Lt. Tower (505)
- 1 Me-109 shot down - Lt. Starnes (505)
Losses/damaged:
- Lt. Ammon (503), slight damage by AA fire, returned - Two 503rd aircraft slightly damaged by AA fire.

Comment: Lt. Ammon (503) reported on this mission, " . . . I outmaneuvered a Me-109 and finally forced him into the ground. I did not fire my guns, but the Jerry crash landed at approximately 300 mph and skidded along the ground for about 40 yards . . . I claim one (1) Me-109 destroyed . . . ." The claim was resubmitted on 22 July '44. This time the "Victory Credits Board" " . . . after reassessment have awarded a damaged . . . ." Later in the day, Lt. Ammon would submit another claim that would not be downgraded.

8 June '44
No. 40   F/O#377-2   (0957-1325)

The Group took off on a combination dive-bombing and bomber escort to Rennes. Over the Channel, the Group was ordered to escort the bombers through their target before delivering their own bombs. Marshalling yards at Vitre and Ploermel were then attacked with very good results. There was light flak in the area.
Losses/damaged:
- Lt. Phillip H. Ewing (505), damaged either by flak or by his own bomb blasts. Parachuted in the vicinity of Alençon, France, evaded capture and was later returned.

8 June '44
No. 41   F/O#378   (1511-1820)

The Group participated in dive-bombing missions to

targets of opportunity in the vicinity of Rennes. The weather was very poor—4/10 overcast. The squadrons broke up before attacking various targets: bridges, trains and a motor convoy. Bombs carried were as follows: 503rd - one 500-1b. bomb each; 504th - two 250-1b. bombs each; 505th - two 100-lb. bombs each. While strafing, FW-190s attacked and individual dogfights broke out.
Claims: 8/0/0 air
- 1 FW-190 shot down - Lt. Ammon (503)
- 1 FW-190 shot down - Lt. Whitelaw (503)
- 1 FW-190 shot down - Lt. Ball (504)
- 1 FW-190 shot down - Lt. W. A. Jones (505)
- 1 FW-190 shot down - Lt. Jaaskelainen (505)
- 1 FW-190 shot down - Lt. McMahon (505)
- 1 FW-190 shot down - Lt. McMahon (505)/Lt. Starnes (505)
- 1 FW-190 shot down - Lt. Olander (505)/ Lt. Sirochman (505)
Losses/damaged:
- Lt. Zeine (504), crashed on takeoff w/two 250-1b. bombs on aircraft; no explosion; aircraft damaged; pilot unhurt.
- Lt. Robert C. Smith (503), shot down by FW-190s, KIA - Lt. Joseph F. Sawicki (505), shot down by FW-190s, KIA - Lt. William A. Jones (505), damaged by FW-190s; able to return to Friston, England; parachuted safely

9 June '44
No mission flown.

10 June '44
No. 42   F/O#379   (0740-1111)
This was a combination area support patrol and strafing mission to Le Havre/Laigle, France. Very low overcast prevented bombing results from being seen. After patrol, targets of opportunity were attacked. Intense flak damaged some aircraft, but all returned safely...eventually.
Claims: 2/2/0 air 0/0/1 ground
- 1 Me-109 probably shot down - Lt. Stockman (504) - 1 Me-109 probably shot down - Capt M. R. Ball (504) - 1 Ju-52 shot down - Lt. Reid (505)/Lt. E. M. V. Johnson (505) - 1 Me-109 shot down, 1 Ju-88 damaged/ground -Lt. Hanseman (505)
Losses/damaged:
- Lt. Rutan (504), during strafing attack, damaged by AA or by ricocheting bullets . . . smoke in cockpit, radio out, landed on a field near the beachhead that was still being graded, checked out his aircraft and decided to fly home. Brought "souvenirs" back. First 339th pilot to land in France and fly his own aircraft home.

Comment: When Lt. Chris J. Hanseman (505) shot down the Me-109, he became the 339th's first "ace". He also became the youngest American "ace" ever. He was still 54 days from his 20th birthday. Unfortunately, he did not live to celebrate his birthday on 2 August.

10 June '44
No. 43   F/O#381   (1356-1727)
This was a dive-bombing mission against railway traffic near Rennes. Not only was the weather unfavorable, but there was heavy, moderately accurate flak in the target area.

Losses/damaged:
- Lt. Hetzel K. Boden (504), forced to parachute over the Channel. No known cause. Last seen in a dinghy; later reported as a POW.

10 June '44
No. 44   F/O#381-3   (1938-2232)
Dive-bombed railroad installations at Chartres, a railroad bridge and a marshalling yard at Courtalain. Poor weather made for poor results. Experienced intense, light to heavy flak near Evreux and Rouen. All returned safely.

11 June '44
No. 45   F/O#382   (0547-0909)
Flew area support patrol south of the beachhead. Weather was very poor.

11 June '44
No. 46   F/O#382-3   (1256-1528)
Dive-bombed a marshalling yard and rail targets in the vicinity of Alençon. Bombing results were excellent. Only light flak experienced. All returned safely.

12 June '44
No. 47   F/O#383   (0735-1137)
Flew area support in the vicinity of Rouen.

12 June '44
No. 48   F/O#384-2   (1906-2152)
Flew an escort mission into northern France.

13 June '44
No. 49   F/O#386   (0840-1004)
Flew area support and patrol mission for bombers attacking Evreux Airfield, northern France. Bombing generally good. Upon return to England, one pilot was forced to parachute near Epping. All else returned safely.
Losses/damaged:
- Lt. William R. Opitz (505), forced to parachute from his spinning aircraft; badly injured; expected to recover, but lost to the Group

13 June '44
No. 50   F/O#387   (1805-2205)
Provided area support for P-47 and P-38 fighter bombers attacking Loire River bridges at Angers and Saumur. Bombing results were generally poor due to the impenetrability of the targets. Enroute home, ten FW-190s were seen, but broke away when attacked. One pilot was lost; cause unknown. All else returned.
Losses/damaged:
- Lt. Jack E. Shively (504), flying his first mission was lost; not seen to go down; killed.

14 June '44
No. 51   F/O#388   (0608-0937)
Flew area support in northern France near Orleans.

15 June '44
No. 52   F/0#390   (0538-0930)

Flew escort mission to Tours, France. At Montiers the formation was attacked by enemy aircraft. After a quick fight, the bombers were escorted through the target and back to St. Valery.

Claims: 4/0/0 air
- 1 FW-190 shot down - Lt. V. M. Meyer (503)
- 1 FW-190 shot down - Capt. Wyatt (503)
- 1 Me-109 shot down - Lt. Fiorito (503)
- 1 Me-109 shot down - Lt. Waymire (504)

Comment: Lt. Waymire did not fire his guns. "... I attacked the German at speeds in excess of 500 mph... Several pieces broke off his aircraft, and he bailed out before I could fire...."

Losses/damaged:
- Lt. Richard W. Montell (504), last seen during the dogfight; later learned he had been killed.
- Lt. Craigo (504), waiting to take off when a 505th aircraft taxied into his tail; both aircraft damaged; neither pilot injured.

16 June '44
No. 53   F/0#393   (1556-1804)

Flew bomber escort to northeast of St. Pol. 10/10 overcast. No flak, no fighters — uneventful.

17 June '44
No. 54   F/0#394   (1131-1500)

Flew escort mission south of Paris. Bombing was good to excellent, otherwise, the mission was uneventful.

17 June '44
No. 55   F/0#395   (1912-2228)

Dive-bombed rail installations in northern France. A marshalling yard at Courtalains was attacked with good to excellent results.

Losses/damaged:
- Lt. Walter M. Armistead (505), on his third combat mission suffered engine trouble near Orleans; forced to parachute; POW.

18 June '44
No. 56   F/0#396   (0727-1150)

This was the Group's first mission over Germany in two weeks — a bomber escort to Hamburg. Experienced meager to heavy inaccurate flak. It was an uneventful mission.

19 June '44
No. 57   F/0#399   (0722-1142)

Provided bomber escort deep into southern France. Three pilots were lost due to extremely severe weather. All else returned.

Losses/damaged:
- Lt. Robert B. Brown (503), weather, killed - Lt. Ralph H. Dearey (503), forced low by weather, damaged by AA fire, parachuted - POW - Capt Nathan T. Folwell (503), weather, killed.

Lt. John J. Hauff (503) filed this report, "... We took off at 0719 hours and formed over the field; Capt. Folwell was leading with Lt. Dearey flying his left wing. Lt. Brown was element leader, and I was his wingman, flying his right wing. We circled the field and then set course, climbing through a 1,000 foot layer of clouds; breaking out at about 2,500 feet. We proceeded as briefed, climbing to an altitude of 12,000 feet. The weather kept getting worse, but it did not seem to be bad enough to turn back. We tried to climb above the overcast, but when we reached 18,000 feet, we hit snow, sleet and icing conditions. We leveled off and started to let down to our previous altitude. At this time we were about 15 minutes inside France. Lt. Brown dropped back and disappeared. I started to close on Capt. Folwell, but taking a quick glance at my own instruments, I noted that the ball was all the way over to the left, the needle to the right, and the gyro horizon had exceeded its limit. I looked back and saw Lt. Dearey veer suddenly off to the left and disappear in the clouds followed almost immediately by Capt. Folwell. I immediately went on my own instruments and finally leveled off at 18,000 feet, still in the overcast. I tried to contact Capt. Folwell by radio, but could get no answer. I returned to base.... "

20 June '44
No. 58   F/0#402   (0635-1128)

Provided bomber escort to Hamburg. After escorting the bombers to the target, the Group then continued north of Hamburg for patrol. The bombing was excellent.

Losses/damaged:
- Major Routt (504), test hop of a new P-51D in England; couldn't get gear down; crash landed at Fowlmere; aircraft damaged; pilot unhurt.

20 June '44
No. 59   F/0#404   (1901-2146)

Flew a fighter-sweep to the Rouen/St. Quentin area.

21 June '44
No. 60   F/0#407   (0650-1230)

This was the first escort to Berlin in almost a month. The bombers were picked up at Schaal Lake. Between Neubrandenburg and Stettin, 25-plus aircraft attacked. Our fighters either engaged them in combat or drove them off, then stayed with the bombers through the target area. Ground targets were attacked on the way home. All returned safely.

Claims: 3/1/2 air
- 1 Me-410 shot down - Lt. West (503)
- 1 Me-410 shot down - Lt. Bryan (503)
- 1 Me-410 probably shot down - Lt. Bryan (503)/Lt. Talcott (503)
- 1 Me-109 shot down - Lt. Thibert (504)
- 1 Me-109 shot down - Lt. Hunter (504)
- 1 Me-410 damaged/air - Lt. E. C. Ball (505)

22 June '44
No. 61　　　F/O#410　　　(1034-1315)

Provided area support over Pas de Calais. Area patrolled without incident from enemy aircraft or flak. On the way home, ground targets were attacked at Denain, France. Heavy, moderately accurate flak encountered there.
Losses/damaged:
- Lt. Arthur L. Lowery (503), killed by AA fire - Lt. Corbin (504), damaged by 20mm AA fire, returned safely

22 June '44
No. 62　　　F/0#41　　　(1711-2055)

Escorted bombers to Paris. Huge fires and clouds of smoke observed after bombing. Heavy, moderately accurate flak. All returned safely.

23 June '44
No. 63　　　F/0#413　　　(1106-1645)

This was a combination area support and strafing mission northeast of Paris. Patrolled ahead and east of the bomber formation, then looked for targets to strafe. Mission was unsuccessful due to heavy overcast. All returned safely.

23 June '44
No. 64　　　F/0#414　　　(1710-2058)

Twenty-five aircraft patrolled the skies above Paris. There were still heavy fires in the area. Mission was uneventful.

24 June '44
No. 65　　　F/0#415　　　(0640-1011)

Escorted bombers attacking a bridge on the Loire River at Saumur. Bombing results were poor.

Comment: Lt. Rodney C. West (503) was killed in a jeep accident at Fowlmere, England.

25 June '44
No. 66　　　F/0#417　　　(0629-1233)

Participated in a deep penetration mission into southern France. An airfield near Gien was bombed. Some of the B-17s dropped crates by parachute into fields near the target. These were probably supplies for the French Underground. As there were no enemy aircraft and no flak, all returned safely.

25 June '44
No. 67　　　F/0#418　　　(1744-2105)

Escorted bombers to Paris. Milk run.

26 June '44
No mission flown. This was the first day off since the 9th of June. The Group had flown 26 missions in the last 16 days.

27 June '44
No. 68　　　F/0#420　　　(1727-2045)

Participated in area support and dive-bombing missions in northern France. East of Paris, rail targets in the vicinity of Méru were attacked with good to excellent results. All aircraft carried two 250-1b. bombs. Several enemy aircraft were seen and shot down. All returned safely.
Claims: 2/0/0 air
- 1 FW-190 shot down - Lt. Thury (505)
- 1 FW-190 shot down - Lt. Farmer (505)/Lt. Fish (505)

28 June '44
No. 69　　　F/0#421　　　(0555-0933)

Performed escort mission into northern France. Weather forced recall of the bombers that the Group was to escort. Picked up other B-17s at Tourlaville. After one hour the Group left the bombers and strafed their way home, attacking rail and other targets. All returned safely.

Comment: Today, a VI rocket hit 500 yards southwest of the control tower at Fowlmere. No one was injured; little damage was done.

29 June '44
No. 70　　　F/0#422　　　(0645-1230)

Provided escort to Leipzig, Germany. Picked up the bombers near Lingen. Several flights of enemy aircraft attacked the bombers in the vicinity of Eisleben and Naumburg. Most of the Group became separated during this engagement and came home, but some flights did stay with the bombers until Dummer Lake before heading back. Various ground targets were strafed.
Claims: 8/0/4 air, 0/0/1 ground:
- 2 FW-190s shot down, 2 FW-190s damaged/air - Lt. Col. Scruggs (HQ, flying with 503rd)
- 1 FW-190 shot down - Lt. Knott (503)
- 1 FW-190 shot down, 1 Me-109 damaged/air - Lt. V. M. Meyer (503)
- 1 Me-410 shot down - Lt. V. M. Meyer (503)/unknown
- 1 FW-190 damaged/air - Lt. Fiorito (503)
- 1 Me-109 damaged/air, 1 Ju-88 damaged/ground - Lt. Wright (503)
- 1 FW-190 shot down - Lt. Eisenhart (504)
- 1 Me-109 shot down - Lt. E. M. V. Johnson (505)/Lt. Sirochman (505)
- 1 Me-410 shot down - Lt. E. M. V. Johnson (505)/Lt. Graham (505)
Losses/damaged:
- Capt. Richard S. Whitelaw (503), killed, probably due to AA fire, not seen to go down - Lt. V. M. Meyer (503), slight damage by AA fire, unhurt - Lt. Stockman (504), slight damage by a Me-109, unhurt

30 June '44
No. 71　　　F/0#424　　　(1242-1608)

Participated in a combination escort and dive-bombing mission into northern France. After leaving the bombers, a marshalling yard at Lille was attacked. Experienced poor results due in part to poor weather. All returned safely.

JULY 1944

1 July '44
No mission flown.

2 July '44
No. 72   F/0#426   (1149-1456)
Flew area patrol in northern France and the Pas de Calais. Inaccurate flak. Uneventful mission.

3 July '44
No mission flown.

4 July '44
No. 73   F/0#427   (0608-1040)
Group flew escort mission to Tours, France. Uneventful mission except for one 505th pilot experiencing engine failure.
Losses/damaged:
- Lt. Carl H. Bundgaard (505), on his first operational mission; engine failure; bailed out near Authon, France; evaded capture; returned to England 22 days later.

Comment: The Group had been testing the new "G-suits"; wore them for the first time on a combat mission; excellent results.

5 July '44
No. 74   F/0#430   (0709-0911)
The Group flew an escort mission for bombers attacking the Gilze-Rijer aerodrome in Holland. There were three different takeoff times as all three squadrons picked up the bombers at different points on the way to the target. Weather was very bad along the route. As there were no enemy aircraft or flak, all returned safely.

6 July '44
No. 75   F/0#432   (0735-1215)
Flew escort mission to Kiel, Germany. Practically 80% of the trip was over water. Uneventful except for moderate to heavy, fairly accurate flak over Kiel and Flensburg. All returned safely.

6 July '44
No. 76   F/0#435   (1800-2123)
This was an escort mission to Saumur/Tours, France. A good concentration of hits was seen on the target including a bridge over the Loire River near Tours.

7 July '44
No. 77   F/0#436   (0643-1145)
Participated in a maximum effort escort mission to Leipzig. The mission was uneventful until reaching the target area. There, a large number of Me-410s, attempting to attack the bombers, were driven off. We then attacked the Me-410's escorting fighters. There was also heavy, intensely accurate flak in the target area. All returned safely.
Claims: 6/0/1 air:
- 1 Me-109 shot down - Lt. Bush (503)/Lt. Wyatt (503)
- 1 Me-109 damaged/air - Lt. Ammon (503)
- 2 Me-109s shot down - Lt. Caldwell (504)
- 2 Me-109s shot down - Lt. Wilcox (504)
- 1 Me-109 shot down - Major Routt (504)

Comment: Major Routt (504) reported, "... I saw 50-plus Me-410s swinging into position to attack our bombers. I led 7 P-51s into attacking position and started to go down on the Me-410s. At this time I looked above us and saw four groups of 25-each fighters. I changed the pass on the Me-410s into a feint to drive them away from the bombers and then broke into the fighters diving on us...." Two other fighter groups, the 55th and the 355th benefited the most as they were able to attack the Me-410s, shooting down 18 of them.

8 July '44
No. 78   F/0#437   (0532-0800)
Flew escort and area support patrol northeast of Paris. Both bombers and fighters turned back because of intolerable weather conditions. All returned safely.
Losses/damaged:
- Lt. Erickson (503), slight taxiing accident, aircraft damaged, pilot unhurt - Lt. Cozad (503), slight taxiing accident, aircraft damaged, pilot unhurt - Lt. E. V. M. Johnson (505), giving a new P-51 a "very vigorous" test flight over the base when a wing buckled and collapsed, aircraft destroyed, pilot parachuted safely.

Comment: The Group started receiving the new K14 gunsight on 8 July 1944.

9 July '44
No. 79   F/0#438   (0549-0938)
Flew escort mission to Tours, France. Heavy, accurate flak over La Maillerge sur Seine. The bombers did not hit the assigned targets and bombed Chateaudum airfield instead with apparently poor results. All returned.

10 July '44
No mission flown.

11 July '44
No. 80   F/0#441   (1018-1535)
Flew escort mission to Munich, Germany. Heavy accurate flak in the target area. After leaving the bombers, the Group dropped to the deck to head for home. Few targets seen. One pilot lost; all else returned safely.
Claims: 1/0/1 air, 1/0/0 ground:
- 1 Me-110 damaged/air - Capt. Stephenson (503)
- 1 S/E biplane trainer destroyed/ground - Lt. Starnes (505)/ Lt. Olander (505)

- 1 training glider shot down
  - Major Thury (505)/Lt. Olander (505).

Losses/damaged:
- Lt. Peter J. McMahon (505), killed, cause unknown, not seen to go down.

Comment: Major Thury reported, "... I dropped to about 4,000 feet and saw a glider somewhat below 1,000 feet. I made one pass and observed hits on both wings. Lt. Olander then shot at him and the glider started to burst into flames. I made another pass at him and observed a few more hits as he crashed into the ground...." Air Force policy did not allow credit for a victory over a glider. A hand written note on the encounter report said, "... no victory credit allowed for gliders...." yet several post-war reports, including Air Force Study #85, do give Thury and Olander credit. A letter written by Thury after the war did not appear to claim credit for it. It is credited as an air-to-air victory by both the 505th and Group records.

12 July '44
No. 81   F/O#442B   (1132-1650)
Provided escort to Munich. Uneventful except for heavy flak at Munich and Donauworth. 9/10 and 10/10 clouds most of the way. All returned safely.

13 July '44
No. 82   F/O#444   (0746-xxxx)
Provided escort to Saarbrucken. Uneventful except for heavy flak in the target area. Weather 10/10.

14 July '44
No. 83   F/O#446   (0635-1227)
Flew deep penetration into southern France and provided cover for bombers apparently dropping materials to the French Underground. Uneventful. Strafed on the way home.

15 July '44
No mission flown.

16 July '44
No. 84   F/O#450   (0728-1220)
This was originally to be a Penetration, Target and Withdrawal Support (P.T.W.S.) mission to Munich. Severe weather forced the bombers to go to Stuttgart instead. Even with an almost solid overcast, there was heavy flak along the way.
Losses/damaged:
- Lt. Wesley G. Fish (505), damaged by AA fire near Nancy, flew to Verdun, forced to parachute, captured, POW - Lt. Penrose (504), emergency downwind landing at Fowlmere, forced to "nose-up" aircraft to miss other aircraft, aircraft damaged.

17 July '44
No. 85   F/O#451   (0810-1213)
Flew escort mission into eastern France, almost to the Swiss border. Broke off escort to assist a training box of bombers until their P-47 escorts arrived, then flew area patrol. Flak heavy from Mulhouse to Colmar. All returned safely.

17 July '44
No. 86   F/O#453   (1902-2215)
Flew a "Type 16 Control" area patrol mission into northern France. Uneventful.

18 July '44
No. 87   F/O#454   (0645-1235)
Flew escort to Griefswall Bay, northeast Germany. Experienced heavy flak. 3/10 to 4/10 (clouds) over target, but bombing results were excellent. All returned safely.

19 July '44
No. 88   F/O#456   (0710-1215)
This was a P.T.W.S. mission to targets in south and southwest Germany: Munich, Mannheim and Ulm. Very little flak in the target area. All dropped to the deck to look for targets on the way home. All squadrons destroyed or damaged ground targets, but the 505th led the scoring. All pilots returned safely.

"...Thury led the 505th escort to Kempten... headed home, spotted an airfield 10 miles southwest of Augsburg... took his section down to strafe... he and his wingman each destroyed one aircraft, but flak was intense, so he held off the rest of the squadron...Thury was hit twice in the wingroot left of the cockpit... Again headed home, but stayed below the cloud cover to search for targets... clouds 4/10 to 5/10... saw an airfield in the vicinity of Heilbronn... took squadron down at 400 mph... They destroyed three aircraft on their first pass.... Received no flak so they established a traffic pattern around the field and made four additional passes which left a total of 12 Ju-188s and 2 other aircraft burning."
Claims: 14/0/0 ground (includes two gliders)
- 1 Ju-188 destroyed, 1 FW-190 destroyed - Lt. Mudge (505)
- 1 Me-109 destroyed, 1 U/ITE A/C destroyed - Major Thury (505)
- 1 Ju-188 destroyed - Lt. Krauss (505)/Lt. Knight (505)
- 1 glider destroyed - Lt. Krauss (505)
- 1 Ju-188 destroyed - Lt. Olander (505)/Lt. Graham (505)
- 1 Ju-188 destroyed, 1 U/ITE A/C destroyed - Lt. Hanseman (505)
- 1 Ju-188 destroyed - Lt. Sirochman (505)/Lt. Tannous (505)
- 1 Ju-188 destroyed - Lt. Hanson (505)
- 1 Ju-188 destroyed - Lt. Ball (505)/Lt. Starnes (505)
- 1 Ju-188 destroyed - Lt. Tower (505)
- 1 glider destroyed - Lt. Stewart (505)
Losses/damaged:
- Major Thury (505), slight AA fire damage, returned safely.

20 July '44
No. 89 F/O#457 (0906-1345)

Flew escort to Gotha and Erfurt. There was heavy, intense and accurate flak over Bonn as Lt. Hurley (504) can testify. He was at 21,000 feet when a burst knocked off his canopy and badly damaged his horizontal and vertical stabilizers. Although slightly wounded, he was able to return safely. The bombing of an aerodrome at Giesen was excellent.
Losses/damaged:
- Lt. William T. Hurley (504), WIA by AA fire, aircraft badly damaged, returned safely

21 July '44
No. 90 F/O#458A (0737-1200)

Scheduled to escort B-24s to Kempten, but met the bombers earlier and in a different area than briefed. Then, due to bad weather, the bombers turned back and bombed secondary targets. 10/10 clouds made identification impossible. We provided top cover.

22, 23 July '44
No missions flown.

24 July '44
No. 91 F/O#461 (1046-1415)

Flew support for bombers operating over the Normandy beachhead in the Caen area. Routine.

25 July '44
No. 92 F/O#462 (0946-1300)

Flew a "Type 16 Control" mission into northern France. Twenty miles east of Rouen, six enemy fighters were seen and attacked. A quick fight over Etrapagny and Beauvais claimed five of them. We had slight damage to one aircraft, but all returned safely.
Claims: 5/0/0 air:
- 1 FW-190 shot down - Major Reynolds (503)
- 1 Me-109 shot down - Lt. Stephenson (503)
- 1 Me-109 shot down - Capt. Wyatt (503)
- 1 FW-190 shot down - Lt. Beavers (503)
- 1 Me-109 shot down - Lt. Holloway (505).
Losses/damaged:
- Lt. Holloway (505), damaged by a Me-109, returned safely.
- Lt. Reuter (503), "nosed-up" on landing, minor damage to aircraft, pilot unhurt.

Comment: Lt. John G. Holloway (505) reported, "...I got into range again going straight down and gave him another burst. At about 8,000 feet his canopy flew off and he dove straight into the ground. The pilot did not get out. I would say that I was about 200 yards from him when his canopy came off and hit my aircraft. I could feel the impact and knew that both the prop and tail had been hit. It took a little nick out of my prop, put a small hole in the left wing and also dented the leading edge of the wing. The left horizontal stabilizer had about a foot torn off. The plane flew okay on the way home...."

25 July '44
Lt. John W. Cozad (503) was killed during a training flight over England.

26, 27 July '44
No missions flown.

28 July '44
No. 93 F/O#469 (0715-1230)

Flew escort to Leipzig, Germany. 9/10 to 10/10 clouds at target. Flak was heavy around Antwerp/Leipzig/Frankfurt. Only one aircraft was seen and that quickly shot down. All Group aircraft returned safely.
Claims: 1/0/0 air:
- 1 Ju-52 shot down - Major Larson (505)

29 July '44
No. 94 F/O#470 (0800-1245)

Flew a P.T.W.S. mission to Merseburg, Germany. Shortly after the bomb run, 30-plus fighters attacked and a dogfight started. At least five were shot down, but the action cost two 504th pilots. On the way home, several airfields were strafed. Two more aircraft were destroyed on the ground, but this cost the Group another pilot.
Claims: 5/3/1 air, 2/0/0 ground:
- 1 FW-190 shot down - Lt. Atteberry (504)
- 2 Me-109s shot down - Lt. Rutan (504)
- 1 Me-109 shot down, 1 Me-109 probably shot down, 1 Me-109 damaged/air - Lt. Stockman (504)
- 1 Me-109 probably shot down - Lt. Trester (504)
- 1 Me-109 probably shot down - Lt. Winkleman (504)
- 1 Me-109 shot down - Lt. Starnes (505)/Lt. Krauss (505)
- 1 Ju-52 destroyed/ground - Lt. Mudge (505)
- 1 Ju-52 destroyed/ground - Lt. Jones (505)/Lt. Hrico (505).
Losses/damaged:
- Lt. Ray N. Atteberry (504), shot down by fighters, parachuted, captured, POW- Lt. Frederick B. Rutan (504), shot down by a FW-190, parachuted, captured, POW- Lt. Chris J. Hanseman (505), strafing, crashed, killed.

Comments: - ...Lt. Rutan (504) led Lt. Atteberry (504) down from 25,000 feet after several Me-109s... lost them in the overcast... broke out of it at about 4,000 feet.... Rutan then attacked and shot down two Me-109s.... Rutan was then damaged by a FW-190 that Atteberry then shot down.... Rutan tried to fly back, but was forced to parachute... captured almost immediately... saw his aircraft on the ground—it had bellied-in without him—Atteberry was also shot down by fighters, parachuted and captured.....
- Lt. E. C. Ball (505) reported, "... We had just broken up an attack on the bombers and ended up below the overcast. We spotted two Ju-52 transports on the ground about four miles northwest of Naumburg parked in a meadow along a row of fairly high trees. We went down to strafe them and on the first pass, Lt. Hanseman evidently carried his pass too far, catching a wing in the ground and cartwheeling over the trees into

a field. His plane caught fire and scattered over a wide area . . . ." The crash site was 15 miles northeast of Erfurt, Germany.

30 July '44
No. 95   F/0#471   (1634-1957)

Flew a "Type 16 Control" fighter-sweep into northern France. The mission was not too successful; only a few ground targets strafed. Light flak; all returned safely. Losses/damaged: Two minor accidents on takeoff, slight damage two aircraft, neither pilot hurt.

31 July '44
No. 96   F/0#472   (1051-1640)

This was the fifth escort of the month to Munich. Though bombing was not observed due to cloud cover, there was heavy flak over Munich. On the way home the 505th strafed three airfields.

The first field attacked was a large, well established grass airfield near Holzkirchen with over 50 aircraft of all types on the ground. There was only light flak on the first two passes, but as many unmanned gun positions were seen, a third pass was called off.
Claims: 0/0/1 air, 15/0/11 ground:
- 1 Ju-88, 1 FW-190 and 1 Me-110 all destroyed/ground - Lt. Mudge (505)
- 1 U/ISE A/C, 1 FW-190, both destroyed/ground - Lt. Staggers (505)
- 1 FW-190 destroyed/ground, 1 FW-190 damaged/ground - Lt. Starnes (505)
- 1 Me-410 destroyed/ground - Lt. Powell (505)
- 1 U/ITE A/C destroyed/ground, 1 U/ISE A/C damaged/ground - Major Thury (505)
- 1 Me-410 destroyed/ground - Major Thury (505)/Lt. Graham (505)
- 1 U/ISE A/C damaged/ground - Lt. Nay (505)
- 1 U/ISE A/C destroyed/ground - Lt. Stewart (505)
- 1 FW-190 destroyed/ground - Lt. Jackson (505)
- 3 U/ISE A/C damaged/ground - Lt. Farmer (505).

The squadron left Holzkirchen and went to rejoin the bombers. They saw two more airfields at Kaufbeuren. The first field had few aircraft on it, but a S/E trainer was seen circling the field and it was attacked. Only a single pass by one flight was made on this field.
- 1 S/E trainer damaged/air - Lt. Mudge (505)
- 1 U/ITE A/C destroyed/ground - Lt. Starnes (505)
- 1 S/E trainer damaged/ground - Lt. Olander (505).

A third airfield, one mile south of the second, was also attacked. Ten to fifteen aircraft were on it. There was only light flak.
- 1 U/ISE A/C destroyed/ground - Major Thury (505)
- 1 U/ISE A/C damaged/ground - Lt. Mudge (505)
- 1 U/ISE A/C damaged/ground - Lt. Graham (505)
- 1 U/ISE A/C damaged/ground - Lt. Powell (505)
- 1 U/ISE A/C damaged/ground - Lt. Stewart (505).

All returned safely with only a few suffering minor damage. Major Thury reported, ". . . a great deal of success is due to the incendiary ammo in two guns of the P-51D . . . ."

AUGUST 1944

1 August '44
No. 97   F/0#473   (1155-1751)

Escorted bombers to target in southern France and then part way home. The Group split into two parts: an 'A' group and a 'B' group. The 503rd sent half its aircraft to fly with the 504th and half to fly with the 505th. Experienced moderate to heavy, fairly accurate flak over Dijon. All returned safely.

2 August '44
No. 98   F/0#475   (1745-2210)

Flew a combination support and strafing mission into northern France. After the patrol, dropped to the deck toward Paris. Locomotives and goods wagons plus various other targets were destroyed. Very accurate flak over Compiègne and Chauny.
Losses/damaged:
- Lt. Lewis H. Schneider (504); AA fire; parachuted near Chauny, France; killed- Lt. Winkelman (504), damaged by AA fire, large hole in aircraft's tail, returned home safely.

3 August '44
No. 99   F/0#476   (1247-1745)

The Group sent 51 aircraft on an escort to Strassbourg, Germany. Excellent bombing. The bombers were left at Liart, and the Group strafed their way home. Three airfields were attacked by the 505th. All returned safely.
Claims: 5/0/1 ground:
(first airfield - 6 miles west of Strasbourg)
- 1 Do-217 destroyed - Major Larson (505) - 1 Do-217 destroyed - Lt. Graham (505). (second airfield - vicinity of Benestroff) - 1 U/ITE A/C destroyed - Lt. Sirochman (505).
(third airfield - south of Metz, much light flak, only the lead flight made one pass) - 1 FW-190 destroyed - Major Larson (505) - 1 FW-190 destroyed - Lt. Shaw (505) - 1 U/ITE A/C damaged - Lt. Sirochman (505).

4 August '44
No. 100 F/0#478   (1046-1520)

This was a P.T.W.S. mission for B-17s attacking oil refineries at Hamburg, Germany. At approximately 1300 hours the Group went down on the deck to chase bandits and strafe airfields. During the next thirty minutes, dogfights went on from south of Hamburg to the Ulzen/Celle area. An airfield 20 miles east of Celle was strafed during the air fighting with very good results. Several pilots took part in air-to-air fighting, then strafed ground targets, then more air-to-air. There were many good claims for air and ground targets, but it cost the Group three 505th pilots.
Claims: 9/0/0 air, 6/0/1 ground:
- 1 FW-190 shot down - Lt. Fiorito (503)
- 1 Me-109 shot down - Lt. Holloway (505)
- 1 Me-109 shot down - Lt. Tongue (505)
- 1 Me-109 shot down - Lt. Tongue (505)/Lt. Muller (505)
- 1 Me-109 shot down - Lt. Tongue (505)/Lt. Powell (505)
- 1 Me-109 shot down - Lt. Powell (505)
- 1 Me-109 shot down - Lt. Starnes (505)

- 2 Me-109s shot down, 1 Me-410 destroyed/ground - Major Larson (505)
- 1 Ju-88 destroyed/ground - Lt. Strong (505)
- 1 Ju-88 destroyed/ground - Lt. Rohm (505)
- 1 Ju-88 destroyed/ground - Lt. Sirochman (505)
- 1 Me-410 destroyed/ground - Lt. Muller (505)
- 1 Ju-88 destroyed/ground - Lt. Shaw (505)
- 1 Ju-88 damaged/ground - Lt. Slovak (505)

Losses/damaged:
- Lt. Robert F. Burns (505), midair collision, POW- Major Donald A. Larson (505), midair collision, KIA - Lt. Roland W. Strong (505), AA, parachuted, POW.

Comments: - As the 100th mission approached and claims of the 505th rose, Major Larson wanted his squadron to destroy 100 enemy aircraft (air and ground) in 100 missions. The day's claims brought their total to 104, but Major Larson did not live to see it. Major Larson led his squadron over an airfield at about 20 miles east of Celle. He set fire to a Me-410, then broke up as enemy aircraft were seen in the area. Lt. Malarz (505) made the following report, " . . . on the deck we strafed an airfield in the vicinity of Dedelstrof. After leaving the airfield I pulled up and joined Upper Red Flight. Two Me-109s came out of the clouds in good formation . . . . Red Leader (Major Larson) closed range and fired on the first e/a (enemy aircraft) . . . . The pilot bailed out of the 109 and his plane crashed into the ground . . . . After this combat we rejoined and strafed two locos that were end-to-end on the line from Celle to Ulzen. After my pass I saw Upper Red Leader chasing a Me-109. He closed and gave the e/a a short burst. The pilot bailed out almost immediately, and the plane crashed into the ground. All the fighting took place at about 500 feet. I claim two Me-109s destroyed by Major Larson . . . . We then went after another 109 which was turning into two P-51s. As the two P-51s were closing on the e/a they collided. One P-51 crashed immediately, and the pilot did not bail out. The other stood on its tail, and the pilot bailed out . . . . We rejoined and headed home . . . ."
- Lt. Starnes (505) became the Group's first pilot to pass 300 combat hours. He immediately requested 50 more.

5 August '44
No. 101   F/O#483   (1054-1535

Shortly after takeoff for an escort to Brunswick, Germany, the 503rd suffered a three-aircraft midair collision. One pilot was killed, one pilot injured, two aircraft destroyed and one aircraft damaged.
Despite this start the Squadron completed the mission. Near Hamelin, twenty-plus German fighters were attacked and three shot down. All our aircraft returned safely.
Claims: 3/0/1 air
- 2 FW 190s shot down - Major Aitken (503)
- 1 FW-190 shot down - Capt. Bryan (503)
- 1 Me-109 damaged - Lt. Graham (503).
Losses/damaged:
- Lt. Edward C. Flaherty (503), midair collision; parachuted but chute did not open in time, killed - Lt. Frank M. Stillwell (503), midair collision; parachuted, broke foot, sent to hospital, did not return to Squadron- Major Reynolds (503), midair collision; tail surfaces damaged but able to land safely.

Comment: On takeoff while trying to form up, Lt. Flaherty crossed under and hit Lt. Stillwell's aircraft in the lower section with his prop. His aircraft then struck Major Reynolds' aircraft in the tail.

6 August '44
No. 102   F/O#487   (0848-xxxx)

Flew support penetration escort mission for bombers going on a 'shuttle mission' to Russian bases. The 339th and the 55th Fighter Groups escorted the 3rd BD B-17s to the target, flying the longest fighter mission to date: 1,592 miles in 6 hours and 35 minutes. The bombers were picked up at Cuxhaven and taken to Muritz where the Group turned back. They then attacked thirty-plus Me-109s south of Scheriner Lake.
Claims: 7/0/0 air
- 1 Me-109 shot down - Capt. Stephenson (503)
- 1 Me-109 shot down - Lt. Fickel (503)
- 1 Me-109 shot down - Lt. Behrend (503)
- 1 Me-109 shot down - Lt. Penny (504)
- 1 Me-109 shot down - Lt. Winkleman (504)
- 1 Me-109 shot down - Lt. Wood (504)
- 1 Me-109 shot down - Lt. Zeine (504).
Losses/damaged:
- Lt. Victor W. Meyer (503), shot down by Me-109s, parachuted north of Juist Island; Air/Sea Rescue could not get to him, broadcast his position on international frequency for Germans to find him, but they too could not find him; lost at sea.
- Lt. Franklin D. Talcott (503), coolant problem, forced to fly to Sweden, interned.
- Lt. Arthur E. Tongue (505) was killed while climbing out through overcast after his element leader had to abort the mission.
- Lt. Penny (504), returned and landed with both wings and fuselage "buckled". He reported, ". . . at approximately 20,000 feet I observed a Me-109 at 15,000 feet . . . . I half-rolled and dropped on his tail. He rolled, slipped and skidded to evade. I was able to follow him to 3,000 feet in a vertical dive, firing short bursts all the way down. My ship fluttered at approximately 600 mph causing my shots to disperse around the entire area of the 109. At 3,000 feet we leveled out and I fired two bursts that went short. I was overtaking him very fast and sprayed his ship as I went by, observing hits . . . . The Me-109 went over on its back . . . trailing smoke; dove straight into the ground . . . ."

Comment: Lt. Talcott (503) was forced to fly into Sweden due to a coolant problem and was interned. The Swedish Air Force used interned American pilots to relocate interned aircraft inside Sweden. On 7 October 1944, Lt. Talcott was flying a P-51B that had belonged to the 359th Fighter Group. While flying in northern Sweden, he crashed and was killed.

7 August '44
No. 103   F/O#490A   (1023-1425)

Flew a "Type 16 Control" mission to the vicinity of Èvreux, France. Moderate to heavy, fairly accurate flak was experienced over Dieppe. Uneventful mission.

8 August '44
No. 104   F/O#494A   (1111-1555)

This was an escort mission to the Paris area with the bombers taken to and from the target area. Experienced moderate to heavy, inaccurate flak at Paris, Amiens and Rouen. Strafed on the way home as flak became more accurate.
Losses/damaged:
- Lt. Edwin C. Ball (505), hit by light flak while strafing a train near Roulers, Belgium, forced to paracute, KIA.

Comment: Mission numbers - "Officially" the 339th flew 264 combat missions: Mission #1 on 30 April 1944, mission #100 on 4 August 1944, mission #200 on 15 January 1945, and mission #264 on 21 April 1945. The Group kept numbers for the missions they assigned, and each Squadron kept the number of missions for which they flew. Although all Squadrons usually flew together, this was not always the case. Consequently, each Squadron might have different mission numbers for the same date, or in the case of 8 and 9 August 1944, two missions on two separate days seem to have been given the same number. "Officially" 28 missions were flown during August 1944; in actuality 29 missions were flown. Two missions, one on 8 August as well as one on 9 August, were both designated "Mission #104." In summary, all missions prior to 8 August and all after 9 August have a "correct" number if it is recognized that missions on those two dates carry the same #104.

9 August '44
No. 104   F/O#496   (0832-1315)

This was a P.T.W.S. mission to Nurnburg, Germany. Very bad weather forced most of the bombers to return, so the Group picked up and escorted other bombers home.

10 August '44
No mission flown.

11 August '44
No. 105   F/O#503   (1014-1315)

Flew escort to Paris. Moderate to heavy, inaccurate flak in the target area. Bombing appeared to be very good on airfields in the target area.
Losses/damaged:
- Lt. Van Cleave (504), forced to return with fuel problems/engine cutting out; crash-landed near Luton, England; aircraft badly damaged; pilot suffered cuts on face and head.

12 August '44
No. 106   F/O#506   (0615-0945)

Flew a bombing and strafing mission with each squadron attacking separate targets: the 503rd to Virton, the 504th to Luxemburg, and the 505 to Strasburg. Most aircraft carried two 250-1b. bombs. Many rail targets were destroyed. All returned safely.

12 August '44
No. 107   F/O#507B   (1024-1450)

Escorted bombers returning from Italy. Uneventful.

12 August '44
No. 108   F/O#506A2   (1212-1510)

This was a dive-bombing mission on the Diekrich marshalling yard. Four 503rd aircraft flew with sixteen 504th aircraft. Each carried one 500-1b. bomb. All returned safely.

12 August '44
No. 109   F/O#508   (xxxx-1952)

The 503rd sent eight aircraft on a bombing/strafing mission to the Amiens area. Uneventful mission. All aircraft returned safely.

Comment: Totals for the four missions (93 sorties) flown on 12 August from 0615 to 1952 hours were: 25 locomotives destroyed, 200-plus box cars destroyed, 5 round houses destroyed, 100-plus tank cars destroyed.

13 August '44
No. 110   F/O#511A   (1606-1854)

This was a bombing and strafing mission, each aircraft with two 500-1b. bombs. A rail/highway intersection just southwest of Beauvais, France, was attacked with excellent results. Heavy secondary explosions and many fires resulted from this attack. All returned safely.

13 August '44
No. 111   F/O#511B   (1714-1950)

Flew bombing and strafing attacks north of Paris. Most aircraft carried two 250-1b. bombs. Marshalling yards at St. Quentin, Fonguenias, Beauvais and St. Omer were attacked with very good results, but this action cost the Group two pilots and damage to two additional aircraft.
Losses/damaged:
- Lt. Myer R. Winkelman (504), last seen starting a bombing run at Fonguenias, probably lost to AA fire, KIA - Lt. Andrew Sirochman (505), strafing a train when it exploded, aircraft badly damaged, forced to parachute. Found by French Underground, later returned to Group.

14 August '44
No. 112   F/O#513   (0842-1305)

Forty-two aircraft took part in a P.T.W.S. mission to the south of France. Two marshalling yards in the vicinity of Anyoulone were attacked with excellent results.

15 August '44
No. 113　　　F/O#516　　　(1044-1328)

This was a P.T.W.S. mission escorting R.A.F. Lancasters hitting airfields in the vicinity of Volkenburg, Holland. Bombing was excellent. Heavy flak experienced near the Hague, but all aircraft returned safely.

16 August '44
No. 114　　　F/O#518　　　(0825-1330)

Flew bomber escort to the vicinity of Chemnitz, Germany. 10-plus Me-109s were seen and attacked near Gotha/Muhlhausen. A quick fight claimed half of them, but cost the 504th one pilot. The bombers were then left near Dummer Lake. Experienced heavy, intense flak.
Claims: 5/0/1 air:
- 1 Me-109 shot down - Lt. Gerard (503)
- 1 Me-109 shot down, 1 Me-109 damaged - Maj. Routt (504)
- 1 Me-109 shot down - Lt. Hunter (504)
- 1 Me-109 shot down - Lt. Penrose (504)
- 1 Me-109 shot down - Lt. Stockman (504)
Losses/damaged:
- Lt. Charles M. Hunter (504), last seen circling the chute of a Me-109 pilot he had just shot down, probably getting gun-camera proof; lost, cause unknown, killed.

Comments: - "... quite a few victory rolls over the field on return...."
- "... in 1986, Dick Penrose (504) researched this fight using German records. He found confirmation for all these claims, including the names and units of the German pilots involved. A full account was published in the March 1986 Newsletter . ..."

17 August '44
No. 115　　　F/O#519　　　(1520-2018)

The Group split into an "A" and a "B" Group. The "A" Group was a P.T.W.S. mission to support experimental bombers hitting La Rochelle, France. Briefing and takeoff for the mission occurred from an advance base. Three 503rd aircraft were damaged while landing there. The rest completed the mission, taking the bombers to Bayeux. Bombing results were not known.

Meanwhile, "B" Group dive-bombed nearby targets. Most aircraft carried two 500-1b. bombs. A marshalling yard was hit with good results, but one pilot was lost there.
Losses/damaged:
- Lt. William J. Pastor (504), last seen in the target area beginning a dive-bombing run; probably lost to AA fire; KIA.
- Lt. Reynolds (503), landing, brake trouble; unhurt - Lt. Coe (505), landing, damaged tail wheel; unhurt.
- Lt. Mayer (503), "cracked-up" on landing, damaged right gear, wing and prop; unhurt.

18 August '44
No. 116　　　F/O#520　　　(0817-1129)

Conducted a "Type 16 Control" mission, patrolling the vicinity of Amiens. Uneventful except for Lt. Wells (504) who lost his aircraft to "friendly forces!" All else returned safely.
Losses/damaged:
- Lt. Arlen W. Wells (504), had engine trouble, landed behind the beachhead at an airfield in the vicinity of Caen. ... Unhurt, but "... it now seems that every ship from the 8th Air Force that lands at a 9th Air Force base is immediately under the jurisdiction of the 9th Air Force and remains in their possession!..." "... and to add insult to injury, his ship just had a new K14 gunsight installed the day before!...."

18 August '44
No. 117　　　F/O#522　　　(1408-1700)

The Group took part in bombing and strafing attacks against rail targets in the area north of Paris. The Group split up at Lille, each squadron searching for its own targets. Most aircraft carried 100-lb. bombs. Marshalling yards at Beaumont and Gisors were attacked with good to excellent results. 175-plus box cars were destroyed, 300-plus box cars damaged. All returned safely.

19, 20, 21, 22, 23 August '44
No missions flown.

24 August '44
No. 118　　　F/O#527　　　(0925-1525)

Flew a P.T.W.S. mission to Dresden. Lost one aircraft shortly after takeoff and another in the target area. Experienced heavy, accurate flak in the target area.
Losses/damaged:
- Lt. Ermy L. Beadle (504), had engine trouble shortly after takeoff, but had to wait until the rest of the mission had all gotten off - too late - engine failed completely on final approach, hit runway with such force that landing gear gave way; aircraft burst into flames, leaving trail of burning gasoline several hundred feet long; Lt. Beadle badly burned (still in hospital by October 1944).
- Lt. Bernell V. Shaw (505), lost coolant, forced to parachute near Oelsnitz, Germany; POW.

25 August '44
No. 119　　　F/O#529　　　(0938-1530)

Flew a deep penetration mission into Germany with part of the Group again going to an experimental airfield near Moritz Lake and the other part going to an oil refinery in the vicinity of Dresden. Both targets hit with excellent results. Despite heavy flak, the mission was a milk run. All aircraft returned safely.

26 August '44
No. 120　　　F/O#532　　　(0845-1255)

Flew area patrol over the Brest Peninsula. Lost one aircraft due to operational problems. All else returned safely.
Losses/damaged:
- Lt. Ely N. Van Cleave (504), operational problem, forced to parachute into the Channel, rescued after four hours by Air/Sea Rescue.

Comment: This was Lt. Van Cleave's second accident. He had crash landed on 11 August, destroying his aircraft but surviving unhurt.

26 August '44
No. 121   F/O#533   (1615-1930)

This was a P.T.W.S. mission for targets in northern France and Belgium. 10/10 overcast made observation impossible. All returned safely. Mission uneventful.

27 August '44
No. 122   F/O#535   (1115-1530)

Forty-five aircraft took part in an escort mission to Berlin. Severe weather forced the mission to be aborted. Although no enemy aircraft were seen and there was no flak, the Group still lost a pilot. All else returned safely.
Losses/damaged:
- Lt. John M. Carothers (503), about 1400 hours over Cuxhaven, had engine trouble, headed back to England; not seen again, killed.

28 August '44
No. 123   F/O#538   (0733-1115)

Flew a strafing and bombing mission to Nancy, France. Marshalling yards were attacked and a well-camouflaged airfield near Saverne was hit. Intense light flak was experienced in the area. One pilot was lost; two other aircraft damaged.
Claims: 3/0/0 ground:
- 1 Ju-88 destroyed - Lt. Bush (505)
- 1 Ju-88 destroyed - Major Reynolds (505)/Lt. Young (505)
- 1 Ju-88 destroyed - Lt. Marts (505)
Losses/damaged:
- Lt. Russell W. Wilcox (505), forced to parachute in mid-Channel, probably due to AA damage; chute fouled, killed.

29 August '44
No mission flown.

30 August '44
No. 124   F/O#542   (1414-1815)

Flew bomber escort to Bremen, Germany. Weather was very bad with heavy but inaccurate flak in the Hamburg/Bremen area. All aircraft returned safely.

31 August '44
No mission flown.

SEPTEMBER 1944

1 September '44
No. 125   F/O#543   (0834-1205)

Bomber escort to Frankfort, Germany, was intended, but a weather front west of Paris forced the entire 8th Air Force to abort. Targets west of Chartres were attacked instead. No results were seen, but all returned safely.

2, 3, 4 September
No missions flown.

5 September '44
No. 126   F/O#550   (0838-1445)

Flew escort mission to Stuttgart, Germany. Bombers were taken to and from the target with heavy, intense, inaccurate flak encountered near the target. Two 503rd pilots picked up a B-17 of the 390th Bomb Group. It had two engines out and was trying to get to Switzerland. Near Uberlinger on Lake Constance on the Swiss border, however, the bomber pilot changed his mind and headed west and back towards France. Ten minutes later, three Me-109s were seen headed towards the B-17. They were intercepted and two quickly shot down. It was later learned the Me-109s were flown by Swiss pilots.

Ground targets, including railways and airfields, were strafed on the way home.
Claims: 2/0/0 air, 0/0/3 ground:
- 1 Me-109 shot down - Lt. Ostrow (503)
- 1 Me-109 shot down - Lt. Ostrow (503)/Lt. Erickson (503)
- 1 Me-410 damaged/ground - Lt. Johnson (505)
- 1 Me-410 damaged/ground - Lt. Graham (505)
- 1 Me-410 damaged/ground - Lt. Bundgaard (505)
Losses/damaged:
- Lt. Martin W. Nay (505), damaged by 20mm AA fire while stafing a marshalling yard; fractured jaw while crash landing; evaded capture - spent 73 days on the ground before being rescued.

Comment: The Swiss Me-109s should have been marked with "red and white" neutrality stripes similar to our invasion stripes. It is unknown if they were correctly marked or not. Regardless of markings, our pilots reacted correctly by protecting any B-17 from any Me-109s. The B-17 did however land in Switzerland where it and its crew were interned.

6, 7 September '44
No missions flown.

8 September '44
No. 127   F/O#556   (0915-1415)

The Group provided bomber escort to Mainz, Germany, taking the bombers to the target and back to mid-Channel. Experienced heavy but inaccurate flak over the target area. All returned safely.

9 September '44
No. 128   F/O#559   (0913-1413)

The Squadrons flew bomber escort to Dusseldorf, Ruhr Valley, then broke up to escort stragglers home. Experienced heavy, intense flak in both the target area and over Calais. All returned safely.
Losses/damaged:
- Lt. Wright (503), WIA/damaged by AA; returned safely

Comment: Lt. Wright (503) returned safely due largely to Lt. Stockton (503). They had been detached to escort a straggler home. The bomber had been brought out to safety when Wright was damaged by AA fire and lost his oxygen system. Forced to fly even lower, he was hit again over Calais by AA fire. This time he was wounded in the left shoulder and left eye by pieces of his canopy which was practically blown away. His windshield was "cobwebbed" so badly he could not see out. With most of his instruments also knocked out, he had to depend on Lt. Stockton to "talk" him home. They returned and landed at Manston. Wright's canopy was so badly jammed, they needed a crowbar to get him out of the aircraft!

10 September '44
No. 129   F/O#561   (0850-1400)

This was an escort mission to Nurnburg, Germany. Bombers were picked up near Heilbronn and taken to the target and back. There was moderate to heavy, accurate flak at Nurnburg and Karlsruhe, however, bombing results were good. After the escort, the Group broke up and each Squadron came home separately, strafing on the way. Various ground targets were hit. The 505th found and attacked three airfields. At the first field, Weiszenburg, a "... veritable hell of 20mm and 40mm flak ... " shot down one pilot and damaged Major Thury (505). When Major Thury was forced to take his section home, Captain Tower took over and led the 505th to attack two more airfields.
Claims: 26/0/32 ground:
(first airfield near Weiszenburg - 5/0/2 ground)
- 1 Ju-88 destroyed - Major Thury (505)
- 1 Me-109 destroyed - Lt. Jones (505)/Lt. Stewart (505)
- 1 Ju-88 destroyed - Lt. Muller (505)
- 1 He-111 destroyed - Lt. Jackson (505)
- 1 FW-190 destroyed - Lt. Rich (505)
- 1 Ju-88 damaged - Lt. Krauss (505)
- 1 Ju-88 damaged - Capt. Mitchell (505)
(second airfield northeast of Munich - 4/0/4 ground)
- 2 Ju-88s destroyed - Lt. Stewart (505)
- 1 Ju-88 destroyed, 1 Ju-88 damaged - Capt. Tower (505)
- 1 Ju-88 damaged - Lt. Malarz (505)
- 1 Ju-88 destroyed, 1 U/ISE damaged - Lt. Jackson (505)
- 1 U/ISE damaged - Lt. Tannous (505)
(a dispersal area along both sides of an autobahn southeast of Munich - 17/0/26 ground; no gun positions observed, so a gunner pattern was established; between 75 and 125 planes in the area, well camouflaged, and all types).
- 1 U/ISE destroyed, 1 Me-410 destroyed, 5 U/ITEs damaged - Lt. Tannous (505)
- 2 Me-410s destroyed, 1 Ju-88 damaged, 2 He-111s damaged, 1 U/ITE damaged - Lt. Marts (505)
- 1 Me-410 destroyed, 1 Ju-88 destroyed, 3 He-111s damaged - Lt. Malarz (505)
- 1 He-111 destroyed, 3 U/ITEs damaged - Lt. Jackson (505)
- 1 U/ISE destroyed, 1 Ju-87 destroyed, 2 He-111s damaged - Lt. W. A. Jones (505)
- 1 Ju-52 destroyed, 2 He-111s damaged - Capt. Tower (505)

- 1 Me-410 destroyed, 1 Do-217 destroyed, 4 U/ITEs damaged - Lt. Powell (505)
- 1 U/ITE destroyed - Lt. Farmer (505)
- 1 Ju-88 destroyed - Lt. Moore (505)
- 3 U/ITEs destroyed - Lt. Young (505)
- 3 Ju-88s damaged - Lt. Stewart (505).
Losses/damaged:
- Lt. Raymond F. Reuter (503), coolant leak; forced to parachute in the vicinity of Saarburg, evaded capture, rescued by the French Underground and returned to England.
- Major John R. Reynolds (505), shot down by flak near Weiszenburg; seen to parachute safely; later reported killed.

11 September '44
No. 130   F/O#563   (0928-1455)

Performed escort mission to Brimma, Germany. Bombers were picked up 40 miles west of Frankfurt. Several Me-109s attacked. Though they were driven off, they were not followed as the Group was the only escort for this wing which was still 35 miles from the target. Near Annaburg, 100-plus German fighters attacked the bombers. The 503rd intercepted them, and a major dogfight developed. Shortly before this, the 505th had been detached to attack the same dispersal area they had attacked the day before southeast of Munich. By day's end, the Group had destroyed more aircraft on a single mission (up to this date) than ever before. Two pilots were lost.
Claims: 14/2/4 air, 24/0/26 ground:
- 1 Me-109 shot down, 1 FW-190 damaged/air - Major Aitken (503)
- 3 Me-109s shot down, 1 FW-190 shot down, 1 Me-109 damaged/air - Lt. Gerard (503)
- 1 FW-190 shot down, 1 FW-190 probably shot down - Lt. Erickson (503)
- 1 FW-190 shot down - Lt. Coe (503)
- 1 FW-190 shot down - Lt. Coe (503)/Lt. Graham (503)
- 1 Me-109 shot down - Lt. Graham (503)/Lt. McClish (503)
- 1 Me-109 shot down - Capt. Robinson (503)/ Lt. McClish (503)
- 1 FW-190 probably shot down - Lt. McClish (503)
- 1 FW-190 shot down - Lt. Price (503)
- 2 Me-109s shot down - Lt. Mayer (503)
- 1 Me-109 shot down - Capt. Cloud (503)
- 1 FW-190 damamged/air - Lt. Stockton (503)
- 1 Me-410 destroyed/ground, 2 Ju-88s destroyed/ground, 1 Ju-87 destroyed/ground, 1 He-111 destroyed/ground, 2 Ju-88s damaged/ground - Capt. Tower (505)
- 2 Me-410s destroyed/ground, 1 Ju-88 destroyed/ground, 1 Me-110 destroyed/ground, 3 Me-410s damaged/ground Lt. Krauss (505)
- 1 Me-410 destroyed/ground, 2 U/ITEs destroyed/ground, 1 Me-410 damaged/ground - Lt. Rich (505)
- 1 Me-110 destroyed/ground, 1 Ju-88 destroyed/ground, 1 Me-110 damaged/ground, 1 He-111 damaged/ground, 1 Ju-88 damaged/ground - Lt. Staggers (505)
- 2 Ju-88s destroyed/ground, 1 Ju-88 damaged/ground, 1 Me-109 damaged/ground, 1 Me-410 damaged/ground, 1

He-111 damaged/ground - Major Thury (505)
- 2 Ju-88s destroyed/ground, 3 Ju-52s damaged/ground - Lt. Bundgaard (505)
- 1 Me-410 destroyed/ground, 1 U/ITE destroyed/ground, 2 Me-410s damaged/ground - Lt. Slovak (505)
- 1 Ju-88 destroyed/ground, 1 He-111 damaged/ground - Lt. Jaaskelainen (505)
- 1 U/ITE destroyed/ground, 2 U/ITEs damaged/ground - Capt. Olander (505)
- 1 Me-410 destroyed/ground, 1 Do-217 damaged/ground, 1 Me-410 damaged/ground, 1 Ju-88 damaged/ground Lt. Graham (505)
- 1 Ju-88 destroyed/ground, 1 Ju-88 damaged/ground, 1 Ju-52 damaged/ground - Lt. W. A. Jones (505)
Losses/damaged:
- Lt. Theodore R. Staggers (505), damaged by AA fire while strafing; started home; over Munich hit by heavy flak and wounded; crash landed and captured almost immediately - POW - Lt. William A. Jones (505), slightly damaged by AA fire while strafing; headed home, but attacked by a Me-262 and shot down over Stuttgart; parachuted; captured - POW - Lt. Stockton (503), aircraft damaged during a dogfight due to high speed; returned home safely.

Comments: - This was to have been Lt. William A. Jones's last mission as he started the day with 297 combat hours! Instead, he was shot down by a German fighter for the second time. On 8 June he had been damaged by a FW-190 and bailed out safely over England.
- The day was extremely memorable for various reasons: the Group's first pilot to shoot down four aircraft during a single mission - Lt. Gerard (503); the Group's first pilot to destroy five aircraft on the ground during a single mission - Capt. Tower (505); the Group's first pilot (and probably the first 8th Air Force P-51 pilot) to be shot down by a German jet fighter - Lt. William A. Jones (505) by a Me-262.
- Lt. Stockton (503) reported, "... I started firing at the second of two FW-190s ... I observed hits on his left wing as he broke down in a rolling dive, but my ship started to disintegrate due to the excessive speed. We were going straight down, and the left rear panel of my canopy blew out; I was holding the sliding bubble closed with my right hand but managed to pull out ..." "... both wings buckled and almost ripped the tail off ...." He was still able to return to the base safely.
- Major Aitken (503) reported, "... at this time, I would like to mention the Berger 'G' suit. Having never used it before in contact with the enemy, I hadn't given it a fair test. I have noticed before, though, that it lessens flying fatigue. In the combat I have described above, I must have turned with five or six enemy planes, never blacking out, and out-turning all except the couple I was going too fast to turn with. No one in the Squadron blacked out today and no one was lost during the attack. One pilot, Lt. Mayer (503), was diving straight for the deck on the tail of a 109. This 109 went straight into the ground, so he began pulling out at 600 mph which he did without even graying out. Another pilot, Lt. Stockton (503), was pulling out of a dive and buckled both wings, blew the canopy off and almost ripped the tail off, but never once blacked out. I heartily recommend that these suits be made available to all combat fighter pilots...."
- Lt. Gerard (503), who shot down four fighters, finished his report with, "... my G-suit was invaluable, and I never want to fly combat without one...."

Comment: For the two missions flown on 10 and 11 September 1944, the Group would be awarded a Distinguished Unit Citation.

12 September '44   No. 131
F/O#565   (0806-1350)
Flew escort mission to Magdeburg, Germany. Bombers were taken to the target and back to Ostend. Heavy to moderate, inaccurate flak was experienced at Cuxhaven and Magdeburg. A small number of enemy fighters were seen and driven off.
Claims: 3/0/0 air:
- 1 Me-109 shot down - Capt. Harte (503)
- 1 Me-109 shot down - Capt. Stevens (504)
- 1 Me-109 shot down - Capt. Olander (505).

13 September '44
No. 132   F/O#566   (1147-1700)
Forty-eight aircraft took off for a maximum effort fighter-sweep and strafing attack to Munich. Several airfields were to be strafed, including the same one attacked by the 505th on the 10th and 11th of the month. This time the entire Group was ordered to go back for one more attack. As predicted, the flak was heavy, intense and accurate. Major Thury (505), who was leading the mission, reported, "... left two squadrons as top cover and went down to finish the job.... We dropped our wing tanks in the target area to spray gas around and help the fires along ... Jerry had moved in 20 to 30 guns ... flak became SO intense I called off the entire attack.... We lost two pilots on the first pass...."
Claims: 5/0/3 ground;
- 1 Ju-88 destroyed - Major Aitken (503)
- 1 Ju-88 destroyed - Lt. Stockton (503)
- 1 FW-190 destroyed, 1 U/ITE destroyed - Lt. Caldwell (504)
- 1 Ju-88 destroyed - Lt. Powell (505)/Lt. Moore (505)
- 1 Do-217 damaged - Lt. Mitchell (505)
- 2 U/ITEs damaged - Lt. Hrico (505).
Losses/damaged:
- Lt. William R. Slovak (505), hit by AA fire on the first pass; aircraft crashed - KIA - Lt. William R. Moore (505), hit by AA fire on the first pass; stayed in air for ten minutes, then parachuted from a low level; captured - POW.

14, 15, 16 September '44
No missions flown.

17 September '44
No. 133   F/O#575   (0833-1243)
This was an area patrol in southern Holland in the vicinity of Arnheim. The mission was uneventful. All re-

18 September '44
No. 134   F/O#578   (1140-1700)

Flew area support and patrol over airborne operations in Holland. Light, meager, inaccurate flak was experienced. Visibility was very poor.

Losses/damaged:
- Major Hathorn (HQ), returned with AA damage (did not think flak was inaccurate).

19 September '44
No. 135   F/O#579   (1128-1612)

Participated in a P.T.W.S. mission to the north and west of the Ruhr Valley. A weather front forced the bombers to abort and attack targets of opportunity on the way home. Experienced moderate flak near Wiesbaden. The Group also flew a 30-minute patrol over airborne operations going on in Holland. All returned safely.

20 September '44
No. 136   F/O#580   (1518-1900)

This mission consisted of 52 aircraft split into "A" and "B" Groups flying area patrols in support of airborne operations in Holland. Though there was heavy flak over Rotterdam and Venlo, all returned safely.

21 September '44
No mission flown.

22 September '44
No. 137   F/O#583   (1111-1615)

This was a P.T.W.S. mission to Kassel, Germany. Took bombers from Liege to the target and back to Ghent. Flak was heavy and intense, but inaccurate. Experienced a very low ceiling, thick haze and very poor visibility upon return to Fowlmere.

Losses/damaged:
- Lt. Coe (503), overshot field on landing; crashed, aircraft demolished; pilot unhurt.

23 September '44
No. 138   F/O#585   (1406-1820)

Participated in Operation "Market Garden," aerial invasion of Arnheim, Holland, by flying an area support mission. Over Walcheren, in 8/10 clouds from 2,000 to 8,000 feet, up to 40-plus FW-190s were seen and attacked. A quick, vicious fight cost the Luftwaffe at least seven aircraft and a loss of three pilots to the Group.

Claims: 7/1/1 air;
- 2 FW-190s shot down - Lt. Ammon (503)
- 1 FW-190 shot down - Lt. Marsh (503)
- 1 FW-190 shot down - Lt. Beavers (503)
- 1 FW-190 shot down - Lt. Mayer (503)
- 1 FW-190 probably shot down - Lt. Cernicky (504)
- 1 FW-190 shot down, 1 FW-190 damaged - Lt. Tannous (505)
- 1 FW-190 shot down - Lt. Powell (505)

Losses/damaged:
- Lt. Alfred O. Manke (503), shot down by a FW-190; POW - Lt. Hauff (503), damaged by a FW-190; returned to base (required a wing and prop change) - Lt. Ammon (503), buckled both wings in pullout during dogfight; returned unhurt
- Captain Raymond M. Mitchell (505), shot down by a FW-190, parachuted; captured - POW - Lt. James B. Muller (505), shot down - POW - Lt. Tannous (505), buckled both wings in pullout during dogfight; returned unhurt.

Comments: - Lt. Beavers (503) reported, "...I opened fire at 60 degrees from 500 yards and saw strikes and smoke...."
"...K14 sight, which I used for the first time, is an excellent instrument and is far superior to our old sights...."
- Lt. Tannous (505) reported, "...my ammunition doors opened and my wings buckled...was forced to make a hard pullout...."

24 September '44
No mission flown.

25 September '44
No. 139   F/O#586   (0838-1328)

This was a P.T.W.S. mission to Frankfurt. The bombers were taken from Aachen to the target and back to Brussels. Experienced heavy, intense flak over Darmstadt and Frankfurt. Uneventfull mission—all returned safely.

Comment: On 25 September 1944, the 505th was conducting a training flight over England to practice formation flying. Lost two aircraft and one pilot to a midair collision.

Losses/damaged:
- Lt. Carl R. Stewart (505), midair collision; parachuted and broke leg when he hit the ground; lost to his Squadron.
- Lt. L. M. Stoudt (505), midair collision; parachuted; unhurt.

26 September '44
No. 140   F/O#588   (1334-1800)

Provided bomber escort to Bremen. Picked up the bombers north of East Frisan Island, escorted them to the target and back to mid-Channel. Heavy to moderate, inaccurate flak.

Losses/damaged:
- Lt. Paul D. Fickel (503), coolant trouble; forced to parachute southwest of Wilhelmshaven, Germany; struck the aircraft's tail, but unhurt; captured - POW.

27 September '44
No. 141   F/O#590   (0738-1245)

Flew a P.T.W.S. mission to Ludwigshafen, Germany. Escorted bombers from Namur to target and back to Murlenbach. Experienced heavy but inaccurate flak at Ludwigshafen and Wiesbaden. Several jet propelled aircraft were seen in the vicinity, but too far away. Very poor weather, but all returned safely.

28 September '44
No. 142   F/O#591   (0906-1415)

Flew a P.T.W.S. mission to Merseburg, Germany. Escorted bombers from Merseburg to Koblenz. Experienced heavy flak along the entire way. German fighters attacked the bombers southeast of Brunswick. All returned safely.
Claims: 2/0/0 air:
- 2 FW-190s shot down - Lt. Ammon (503)

29 September '44
No mission flown.

30 September '44
No. 143   F/O#592   (1113-1528)

Flew escort mission to Bielefeld, Germany. Picked up bombers at Antwerp, escorted them to the target and back to Ijmuiden. Bombing results were excellent. Experienced heavy but inaccurate flak along the way. All returned safely.

OCTOBER 1944

1 October '44
No mission flown.

2 October '44
No. 144   F/O#593   (0906-1445)

This was a P.T.W.S. mission to Kassel, Germany. Bombing results were excellent. Uneventful mission.

3 October '44
No. 145   F/O#596   (0848-1435)

Flew bomber escort to Kitzingen, Germany. Flak ranging from heavy to moderate was encountered from Nurnburg to Sarrebourg. "... bombing not too hot... bombs appeared to fall into a clump of trees..." All returned safely.

4 October '44
No mission flown.

5 October '44
No. 146   F/O#598   (0952-1345)

This was a P.T.W.S. mission to Munster. Bombers were picked up at Ijmuiden and escorted back to the Zuider Zee. The Group then went back to pick up stragglers. One aircraft was lost to AA fire.
Losses/damaged:
- Lt. Stephen Ananian (505), aircraft damaged by a single burst of AA fire; parachuted into the Channel about 40 miles from Alderburgh; survived.

Comment: When Lt. Ananian landed in the water, he could not get out of his harness, and the wind began to pull him through the sea. Lt. George T. Rich (505) flew low over Ananian and collapsed the chute with his prop wash. After an hour in rough water, a R.A.F. Walrus (amphibian aircraft) landed and picked him up. The Walrus could not take off and waited for and transferred Ananian to a British minesweeper. The Walrus had to be sunk and its crew taken back also. Lt. Ananian was back flying within a few days.

6 October '44
No. 147   F/O#599   (0918-1437)

Participated in a P.T.W.S. mission to Berlin. The bombers were picked up near Helgoland. Near Oranienburg, a straggling wing of B-17s called for help when 75-plus German fighters hit them. The 503rd went back to help, but arrived too late. Fourteen B-17s had been shot down, including an entire squadron of eleven aircraft of the 285th Bomb Group.

Meanwhile, bombing at the target appeared to have been excellent. All 339th Fighter Group aircraft returned safely.

Comment: Several of the Group's pilots reported, "... six to seven solid-black P-51s in the area... appeared to be enemy operated. They had white invasion markings... "

7 October '44
No. 148   F/O#600   (0926-1425)

This was a P.T.W.S. mission to Leipzig. The bombers were met, but they were in a very confusing formation. In spite of this, they were escorted to the target and back to Osnabruck. Although heavy flak was experienced at Leipzig, all returned.

8 October '44
No mission flown.

9 October '44
No. 149   F/O#603   (1251-1705)

Flew an escort mission to Frankfurt. The bombers were met south of Malmédy and accompanied until Ostend. A solid overcast prevailed over the entire route, but heavy moderate flak was still encountered over the target. All returned safely.

Comment: - F/O#603 was the last Field Order from the disbanding VIII Fighter Command. Field Orders would now be from the VIII Air Force.

10, 11 October '44
No missions flown.

12 October '44
No. 150   F/O#1235A   (0936-1420)

Provided bomber escort to Bremen, Germany. Bombers were taken from Hemel to the target and back to mid-Channel. Experienced heavy, moderate, inaccurate flak at Bremen. Bombing results were excellent. All returned safely.

13 October '44
No mission flown.

14 October '44
No. 151 /0#1239A (1036-1530)

This was a P.T.W.S. mission to Cologne with a Group record of 62 aircraft participating. Bombers were picked up and returned to Namur. The Group then went back to near the target area to look for stragglers, but found none. All returned safely.

15 October '44
No. 152 F/0#1240A (0736-1128)

Again flew a P.T.W.S. mission to Cologne. The bombers were badly scattered. Consequently, rendezvous was not made with the correct bombers until they were entering the target area. Flak was heavy, intense and varied from accurate to inaccurate over Cologne and Walcheren. No wing tanks were carried, and numerous ships were forced to land elsewhere for fuel. All eventually returned safely.

16 October '44
No mission flown.

17 October '44
No. 153 F/0#1245A (0748-1248)

This was an area support mission between Limburg and Siegen. Uneventful mission. All returned safely.

18 October '44
No. 154 F/0#1246A (0907-1455)

Flew an escort mission to Kassel, Germany. The bombers were covered to the target area and back to the south of Liege where they were left. Part of the Group then hit the deck to strafe northwest of Koblenz. Various rail targets were attacked at the cost of three more pilots. Twenty-four other pilots were forced to land in France for fuel.
Losses/damaged:
- Lt. Raymond D. Mayer (503), strafing a train at Ludwigsau, Germany; hit electrical wires, aircraft flipped over - KIA.
- Lt. William D. Stockton (503), probably lost to AA fire - killed, buried at Ghent.
- Lt. Valdee Wyatt (503), badly injured by AA fire; parachuted behind British lines and spent two weeks with the British - returned to the U.S.A. by Christmas '44.

19 October '44
No. 155 F/0#1249A (1117-1526)

Flew a P.T.W.S. mission to Ludwigshafen. Heavy, moderate flak was experienced in the target area and at Kaiserlautern. All eventually returned safely.
Losses/damaged:
- F/O Kuhlman (504), forced down in France with engine trouble; returned later.

20, 21 October '44
No missions flown.

22 October '44
No. 156 F/0#1254A (1226-1630)

Flew escort mission to Munster. Bombers were escorted from mid-Channel to the target area and back to mid-Channel. Heavy, meager, inaccurate flak was experienced over Osnabruck and Munster. A solid overcast extended over most of the journey.

23 October '44
No mission flown.

24 October '44
No. 157 F/0#1261A (1318-1730)

This was a strafing mission to the area around Dummer Lake. Experienced heavy, intense and accurate flak over Bremen at 17,000 feet—several ships slightly damaged. Although a 10/10 overcast existed from the deck to 3,000 feet, one hole was found and the Group went down. The 504th shot down twenty barrage balloons northeast of Dummer Lake.
Claims: 0/0/0 - no credit given for balloons.
Losses/damaged:
- Lt. Stillwell (503), damaged by AA fire - returned safely.

25 October '44
No mission flown.

26 October '44
No. 158 F/0#1264A (1332-1650)

Flew bomber escort to Hanover, Germany. Experienced a heavy overcast with heavy to moderate, inaccurate flak over the target area.

27 October '44
No mission flown.

28 October '44
No. 159 F/0#1269A (1033-1353)

This was an escort mission to Hamm, Germany. The bombers were late, and the weather was very poor. The first Luftwaffe aircraft seen during the month — two Me-410s — were met in the target area. One of the Me-410s "attacked" Lt. Stiles (505) and three other 505th pilots! This "hot-shot" was chased but got away safely. All 339th Fighter Group pilots returned unhurt.

29 October '44
No mission flown.

30 October '44
No. 160 F/0#1273A (1024-1418)

Flew an escort mission to Merseburg, Germany. The bombers, however, were forced to abort due to weather. The Group still patrolled an area between Osnabruck and Hanover, experiencing inaccurate flak over both areas. All returned safely.

31 October '44
No mission flown.

NOVEMBER 1944

1 November '44
No mission flown.

2 November '44
No. 161　　　F/0#1281A　　　(0950-1515)
Flew an escort mission to Merseburg. Experienced intense, accurate flak near the target. Only two enemy fighters were seen, and both were quickly shot down. All returned safely.
Claims: 2/0/0 air;
- 1 FW-190 shot down - Lt. Ray F. Herrmann (504)
- 1 Me-109 shot down - Lt. Donald E. Penny (504)

Comment: Lt. Penny (504) did not have to shoot down his Me-109. "... The pilot bailed out without my having to fire at him ...."

3 November '44
No mission flown.

4 November '44
No. 162　　　F/0#1286A　　　(0946-1442)
This was a P.T.W.S. mission to Hanover, Germany. Heavy, intense, accurate flak at Hamburg and Hanover. All returned safely although one aircraft was lost over England.
Losses/damaged:
- Lt. Becker (505), unknown reason, forced to belly-land at Kessingland, England; aircraft damaged; pilot unhurt.

5 November '44
No. 163　　　F/0#1288A　　　(0916-1423)
This was a combination bomber escort and strafing mission. Heavy low clouds canceled the strafing part of the mission, so the Group provided P.T.W.S. to Ludwigshafen.

6 November '44
No. 164　　　F/0#1291A　　　(0845-1345)
Flew a P.T.W.S. for 3rd BD B-17s to Neumunster, Germany. Meager, inaccurate flak experienced. Mission was uneventful.

7 November '44
No mission flown.

8 November '44
No. 165　　　F/0#1296A　　　(0909-1450)
This was an escort mission to Merseburg, Germany. Experienced heavy, intense and inaccurate flak in the target area. Weather was 10/10, and persistent contrails prevailed. Strafed on the way home, destroying and damaging numerous rail targets as well as destroying eight barrage balloons. All returned safely.

9 November '44
No. 166　　　F/0#1299A　　　(0807-1233)
Conducted an escort mission to Saarbrucken. Although the weather was 8/10 overcast and heavy to moderate flak was experienced, all returned safely.

10 November '44
No. 167　　　F/0#1301A　　　(1024-1455)
Flew an escort mission to Wiesbaden, Germany. Experienced heavy to moderate, accurate flak in the target area, but all returned safely.

11 November '44
No. 168　　　F/0#1306A　　　(0953-1400)
This was a P.T.W.S. mission of 3rd BD B-17s to Coblenz. Except for a V2 rocket contrail seen near Karlsrude, the mission was routine.

12, 13, 14, 15 November '44
No missions flown.

16 November '44
No. 169　　　F/0#1314A　　　(1140-1605)
Flew escort for medium bombers attacking targets in the Aachen-Duren-Erkelanz triangle. The Group then conducted strafing of rail and transportation targets between Siegen and Marburg. Although all returned safely from the mission, two aircraft had been lost on takeoff.
Losses/damaged:
- Lt. Hill (503), crashed on takeoff, aircraft burned and demolished; pilot only slightly burned on forehead - Lt. Haidle (503), crashed on takeoff; pilot uninjured; aircraft sent to depot for repair.

17 November '44
No mission flown.

18 November '44
No. 170　　　F/0#1317A　　　(1032-1445)
The scheduled mission was to be a strafing attack against oil targets in the Neuburg area, but before reaching the target area, several groups of Me-109s attacked. Dogfights ranged from 20,000 feet to the deck; from Mannheim to Dachau to Neustadt. A number of enemy aircraft were shot down without a loss to the Group. Following this encounter, everyone (in separate flights and elements) went to the deck to strafe their way home. Various ground targets were claimed, but three pilots were lost to ground fire.
Claims: 7/1/1 air;
- 1 Me-109 shot down - Capt. Shafer (503)
- 1 Me-109 shot down - Capt. Beavers (503)
- 1 Me-109 shot down - Lt. Marsh (503)
- 1 Me-109 probably shot down - Lt. Stillwell (503)
- 1 Me-109 shot down - Lt. Mead (504)
- 1 Me-109 shot down, 1 Me-109 damaged - Capt. Johnson (505)
- 1 Me-109 shot down - Lt. Malarz (505)/Lt. Rich (505)
- 1 Me-109 shot down - Lt. Bundgaard (505).

Losses/damaged:
- Lt. Vincent J. Spaziano (503), flying low over "friendly" ground troops, mistaken for an enemy aircraft and shot down by "a terrific barrage of fire" - killed.
- Lt. Allen D. Young (505), shot down by heavy AA fire near Metz; forced to parachute; captured - POW - Lt. Laird D. Travis (505), shot down by AA fire near Kaiserlautern - KIA.

Comment: Lt. Spaziano (503), a former enlisted member of the 19th Bomb Group in the Philippines early in the war, received the Silver Star and a DFC for actions there.

19 November '44
No mission flown.

20 November '44
No. 171   F/O#1320A   (1035-1417)
Took off for a strafing attack, but shortly after takeoff, the Group was ordered to escort bombers recalled because of weather. After the bombers were brought back to Flushing, the Group again broke off for strafing. A 9/10 overcast made this impossible, so the mission was abandoned. All returned safely.

21 November '44
No. 172   F/O#1323A   (1010-1430)
An escort to Merseburg was changed because of bad weather, and the bombers were forced to hit targets east of the Ruhr instead. A large airfield northeast of Munster was attacked. One aircraft on the ground was strafed and destroyed. Suddenly heavy AA fire opened up and shot down two of our aircraft and damaged another of the lead flight. The attack was immediately broken off. Several airborne enemy aircraft were then seen and attacked.
Claims: 2/0/0 air 1/0/0 ground;
- 1 Ju-88 destroyed/ground - Lt. Jackson (505)
- 1 Me-109 shot down - Capt. Dowell (505)/ F/O Palmer (505)
- 1 Me-109/Me-309 shot down - Lt. Rich (505)

Comment: Lt. Rich (505) reported, "... the plane encountered had the fuselage of a Me-109 with the same tail and scoops under the wings, but had a narrow eliptical wing. Just like the Spitfires, except more narrow ... the e/a (enemy aircraft) then pulled into an extremely tight turn to the right, pulling dense streamers. I turned with him, but mushed out.... I couldn't turn with this e/a, partly due to my higher rate of speed. But, in my estimation, he would have out-turned me decisively, all factors being equal...."
Losses/damaged:
- Lt. Boyd O. Jackson (505), shot down by AA fire; went down in flames - KIA - Lt. Leland M. Stoudt (505), shot down by AA fire - KIA - Capt. Charles W. Dowell (505), damaged by AA fire during strafing attack; took part in a dogfight helping to shoot down a Me-109; later forced to bail out near Munster - KIA.

Comment: Captain Johnson (505), reported, "... northeast of Munster we crossed an airfield with 50 to 75 Ju-88s and 50 to 70 FW-190s parked ... Lt. Jackson (505) decided to make a pass on this field, so we let down and spaced our flights for the pass ... I saw Lt. Jackson shooting and observed an explosion followed by dense, black smoke erupting from the parking area. Then, the worst concentration of light and medium flak I have ever experienced was thrown up. I observed another explosion, but just at this point, I broke off the attack due to flak...."

22, 23, 24 November '44
No missions flown.

25 November '44
No. 173   F/O#1333A   (0948-1515)
Flew escort mission to Merseburg, Germany. Heavy, intense accurate flak was experienced in the target area despite an 8/10 overcast. All returned safely.

26 November '44
No. 174   W-496A   (1035-1437)
Fifty-six aircraft took off for a routine escort mission to Hanover, Germany, but returned with their largest claim of air-to-air victories on a single day. The Group did not rendezvous with a particular box of bombers, but generally covered the target area between Osnabruck and Hanover. At approximately 1300 hours, the 2nd BD B-24s reported they were under heavy fighter attack southeast of Dummer Lake. When the Group arrived, perhaps 200 FW-190s were attacking the bombers in "gaggles" of 30 to 40 aircraft each. A huge fight developed from 26,000 feet to the deck. The FW-190s were unusually aggressive and were fighting instead of running away. One pilot reported, "... the enemy aircraft were not flying together, but seemed to be pursuing a policy of 'every man for himself....' " This policy was to cost him heavily.
Claims: 29/1/4 air:
- 3 FW-190s shot down, 1 FW-190 probable, 1 FW-190 damaged - Lt. Marsh (503)
- 3 FW-190s shot down - Capt. Johnson (503)
- 2 FW-190s shot down - Lt. Col Henderson (503)
- 2 FW-190s shot down - Capt. Beavers (503)
- 2 FW-190s shot down - Capt. Edens (503)
- 2 FW-190s shot down - Lt. Wilson (503)
- 1 FW-190 shot down - Lt. French (503)
- 1 FW-190 shot down - Lt. Coe (503)
- 1 FW-190 shot down - Lt. Petitt (503)
- 1 FW-190 shot down - Lt. Stillwell (503)
- 1 FW-190 damaged - Lt. Allen (503)
- 1 FW-190 damaged - Lt. Gokey (503)
- 1 FW-190 shot down - Lt. Bates (504)
- 5 FW-190s shot down - Lt. Daniell (505)
- 1 FW-190 shot down - Lt. Phillippi (505)
- 1 FW-190 shot down - Lt. Phillippi (505)/Lt. Loveless (505)
- 1 FW-190 shot down - Lt. Stiles (505)
- 1 FW-190 shot down, 1 FW-190 damaged - Lt. Bundgaard (505)

- 1 FW-190 shot down - Lt. Girzi (505)
Losses/damaged:
- Lt. Ely N. Van Cleave (504), last seen during the dogfight - KIA - Lt. Bert Stiles (505), last seen diving after and shooting down a FW-190; both crashed - KIA (Lt. Stiles was a well known author and an ex-B17 pilot flying a tour with the Group.)

Comments: - Lt. Van Cleave (504) had already experienced two close encounters with fate and survived only to be lost during this mission: 11 August, he had crash landed in England, suffering face and head cuts; and on 26 August he had parachuted into the Channel due to an operational problem, but had been picked up within four hours by Air/Sea Rescue.
- This was one of the biggest days of the air war. 1,137 heavy bombers, escorted by 668 fighters, were sent; over 500 German fighters were airborne. Thirty-four heavy bombers were lost, including 15 B-24s of the 491st Bomb Group shot down by German fighters over Hanover. Nine U.S. fighters were lost this day. The U.S. fighters and bombers claimed 124/11/36 air-to-air.
- The 18 aircraft shot down by the 503rd were the most claims for a single squadron in the ETO (European Theater of Operations) for a single mission. This record would stand for one day! The next day, 27 November '44, the 362nd Fighter Squadron, 357th Fighter Group, would shoot down 19 aircraft.
- The Group gave much of the day's credit to the performance of the wingmen and to the K14 gunsight. Many reports were similar to the one filed by Lt. Marsh (503), " . . . I wish to commend Lt. French (503) for staying with me through the most violent and complicated maneuvers. He covered my tail in such excellent fashion that I was able to give all my attention to shooting . . . ." Captain D. W. Johnson (503) said, ". . . I couldn't miss with the K14 though and kept getting hits all the time . . . . All my shooting was done at 300 yards or less and with the K14 it was easy . . . . " Captain Johnson was so close to his last kill that he got oil all over his windshield and was forced out of the fight because he couldn't see!

27 November '44
No. 175   F/O#1343A   (0949-1440)
A combination escort and strafing mission was to hit an underground oil storage depot at Derben, Germany. The Group was to escort P-47s of the 78th Fighter Group. For unknown reasons, the targets were not bombed. The Group then broke off to attack ground targets. Locomotives, goods wagons, and other targets were hit. The cost was two pilots lost.
Losses/damaged:
- Lt. Felix J. Girone (503), missing, unknown cause - KIA - Capt. Edward H. Beavers (503), damaged by AA fire; parachuted over Belen, Germany - killed.

28 November '44
No mission flown.

29 November '44
No. 176   F/O#1348A   (1047-1533)
Flew an escort mission to Hanover, Germany. Bombers were taken to and from the target. Weak flak was experienced over Egmond and Hanover. It was, however, an uneventful mission.

30 November '44
No. 177   F/O#1354A   (1031-1556)
This was an escort mission to Merseburg, Germany. Milk run!

Comment: During November 1944, Lt. Alan F. Crump (503) crashed in England during a training flight.

DECEMBER 1944

1, 2, 3 December '44
No missions flown.

4 December '44
No. 178   F/O#1370A   (1128-1629)
Flew escort mission to Wiesbaden. Good concentration of bomb hits in the target area. Heavy, moderate, inaccurate flak. One operational loss.
Losses/damaged:
- Lt. Richard C. Cain (505), engine failure; forced to parachute near Trier - POW.

5 December '44
No. 179   F/O#1374A   (0822-1353)
The Group provided close escort, sweeping ahead of bombers attacking Berlin. Experienced very poor weather: heavy clouds at all levels plus a solid undercast. Many small groups of enemy fighters were seen and chased through the clouds. Two 339th pilots were lost.
Claims: 0/0/1 air:
- 1 FW-190 damaged - Capt. Shafer (503)
Losses/damaged:
- Lt. Col. Harvey E. Henderson (503), shot down by FW-190s; parachuted 25 miles north of Berlin - POW - Lt. James A. Baker (505), engine failure; parachuted west of Steinhuder Lake - KIA.

Comment: Lt. Col. Henderson (503) and Lt. Francis (503) went to investigate several fighters below their squadron. They bounced several German fighters at 20,000 feet and chased them to 7,000 feet where they lost them in the clouds. Henderson and Francis started back up, but at 17,000 feet between two layers of clouds, three FW-190s dropped out of the clouds, shot up Henderson and then disappeared into the lower clouds. Henderson's aircraft was badly damaged and last seen upside down in the clouds. He did manage to bail out and was captured as soon as he hit the ground.

6 December '44
No. 180 F/O#1383A (0942-1443)
Flew an escort mission to Merseburg, Germany. Experienced heavy, inaccurate flak. All returned safely.

7, 8 December '44
No missions flown.

9 December '44
No. 181 F/O#1397A (1020-1521)
Flew an escort mission to Stuttgart, Germany. Routine.

10 December '44
No. 182 F/O#1404A 0923-1248)
This was a P.T.W.S. mission for 3rd BD B-17s attacking Koblenz, Germany. The weather was very poor, and the mission was uneventful.

11 December '44
No. 183 F/O#1408A (1013-1415)
Conducted an escort mission to Giessen, Germany. While the mission was militarily uneventful, the Group lost one aircraft on the return flight.
Losses/damaged:
- Lt. John W. Gokey (503), aircraft caught fire over Frinton, England (reason unknown); forced to parachute - unhurt.

12 December '44
No. 184 F/01412A (0952-1451)
Flew an escort mission to Merseburg, Germany. For a change we were late and the bombers were early, finally picking them up near the target in a 10/10 overcast. Experienced heavy, moderate, inaccurate flak. This was considered a routine mission, but the Group still lost a pilot.
Losses/damaged:
- Lt. Harry G. Loskill (504), unknown operational problem - POW.

13, 14 December '44
No missions flown.

15 December '44
No. 185 F/O#1422A (1021-1433)
This was an escort mission to Hanover, Germany. Though the weather was very poor—10/10 most of the way—the mission was uneventful overall.

16 December '44
No. 186 F/O#1426A (1021-1545)
Conducted a P.T.W.S. mission for 3rd BD B-17s attacking Stuttgart, Germany. Again, the weather was very poor, but all returned safely.

17 December '44
No mission flown.

18 December '44
No. 187 F/O#1430A (1130-1541)
Flew an escort mission to Wiesbaden, Germany. Uneventful.

19, 20, 21, 22, 23, 24, 25, 26, 27 December '44
No missions flown.

28 December '44
No. 188 F/O#1458A (1053-1540)
After nine days, the longest non-flying time for the Group during the war, the weather finally cleared enough for a mission — a bomber escort to Koblenz, Germany. The Group sent an "A" flight and a "B" flight. Routine mission.

29 December '44
No. 189 F/O#1463A (1045-1503)
This was a bomber escort mission to Frankfurt, Germany. Experienced heavy, moderate, inaccurate flak in the Frankfurt/Koblenz area. One pilot was lost due to mechanical troubles.
Losses/damaged:
- Lt. Charles M. Mead (504), mechanical trouble; forced to parachute - KIA.

Comment: During the mission, "... a mysterious crystalline ball suspended from a balloon was observed in the vicinity of Malmedy, at 1324 hours, at 27,000 feet...."

30 December '44
No. 190 F/O#1467A (1035-1512)
Flew an escort mission to Kassel, Germany. 10/10 cloud cover most of the way with only minor flak. Uneventful.

31 December '44
No. 191 F/O#1471A (0901-1342)
This was an escort mission to Hamburg, Germany. For the first time in over three weeks, the Luftwaffe reacted. Small groups of enemy fighters were seen and attacked south of the target area. At least one of our two losses can be attributed to several Me-262 jet fighters that were seen.
Claims: 6/0/2 air:
- 1 FW-190 shot down - Capt. Bryan (503)
- 1 FW-190 shot down - Lt. Allen (503)
- 1 FW-190 shot down, 1 Me-262 damaged - Capt. Hawkins (503)
- 2 FW-190s shot down - Lt. Herrmann (504)
- 1 FW-190 shot down - Lt. Allers (504)
- 1 FW-190 damaged - Lt. Barto (504).
Losses/damaged:
- Lt. James A. Mankie (503), became the second 339th pilot to be shot down by an Me-262; never saw it; parachuted, hit the ground, dragged by his chute, dislocated shoulder; captured within minutes - POW.
- Capt. Anthony G. Hawkins (503), first 339th pilot to damage a Me-262; hit the one that shot down Lt. Mankie, followed it down, not seen again - KIA.

JANUARY 1945

1 January '45
No. 192   F/O#1476A   (1056-1504)

The Group flew a number of different assignments. Most escorted 3rd BD B-17s to Hanover. The bombers were late, but were still taken to and from the target. On the return, two different formations, one of B-24s and another of B-17s, were seen without escort. They were both picked up and taken out.

Meanwhile, the 504th was escorting an "Aphrodite" mission to Ijmuiden. Heavy, moderately accurate flak was encountered over the Hague, Ruhr Valley and Cologne. All returned safely.

Comment: "Aphrodite" was the overall code name for 8th Air Force experimental operations with radio or television controlled aircraft or bombs.

2 January '45
No. 193   F/O#1479A   (0927-1337)

The Group escorted 3rd BD B-17s to Metz, Germany, to attack targets in the Siegfried Line defenses. The 505th also supplied two four-plane flights to Saarbrucken/Mannheim and Stuttgart/Strasbourg. Encountered flak in most areas, but it proved to be no problem. A city south of Frankfurt, possibly Worms or Darmstadt, was smoking to heights of 6,000-7,000 feet and showed evidence of having been badly bombed.

3 January '45
No. 194   F/O#1485A   (0923-1435)

This was a Group escort to Fulda, Germany. A 10/10 overcast over the entire route made observations impossible. Contrails of six V2 rockets were the only enemy activity seen. The mission was uneventful until the return to Fowlmere and trying to land in very strong winds. Part of the Group was forced to land at Duxford when two accidents closed down the Fowlmere runway.

Losses/damaged:
- Lt. Howard (505), landing accident due to cross winds; aircraft destroyed, pilot unhurt - Lt. Carr (505), landing accident; aircraft destroyed, pilot unhurt.

4 January '45
No mission flown.

5 January '45
No. 195   F/O#1491A   (1122-1530)

Flew a Group P.T.W.S. mission to Trier-Murlenbach-Ruten, Germany. The bombers flew very good formations, but results could not be seen due to 4/10 clouds and a solid undercast up to 7,000 feet. Large fires were seen in the vicinity of Neunkirchen. Four 503rd aircraft were also sent to escort a photo-recon mission, but it was aborted when the photo ship lost an engine. One 505th pilot did land with engine trouble at Merville, France, but all else returned safely.

6 January '45
No mission flown.

7 January '45
No. 196 F/O#1499A   (0938-1458)

The Group flew as an "A" group and a "B" group Fifty-two aircraft flew a P.T.W.S. mission for 3rd BD B-17s to Ruthen, Germany, while the 503rd sent four aircraft as escorts for a P-38 photo-recon mission, and the 505th sent eight planes to escort two B-17s on a weather scouting mission.

A 10/10 overcast prevailed over the Continent. There was a solid undercast up to 12,000 feet, then an overcast starting at 28,000 feet. Visibility was good in between.

Heavy, meager, inaccurate flak was fired by the enemy in the target area. At Calais, the flak was fired by unfriendly allies! It was more accurate than the enemy flak, but still, all returned safely. One 504th pilot did land in France due to mechanical difficulties, but returned later.

8 January '45
No. 197   F/O#1503A   (0958-1405)

The Group flew a fighter-sweep to Aachen-Cologne-Munich. The weather was very bad with a 10/10 cloud layer over most of the Continent. Some flak was seen plus three V2 rocket contrails, but all returned safely.

9 January '45
No mission flown.

10 January '45
No. 198   F/O#1508A   (1001-1445)

Groups "A" and "B" took off for an escort mission to Cologne, but shortly after takeoff, it was changed to an area patrol to the vicinity of Giessen. Bombing results appeared very good with two bridges destroyed at Bonn and the approaches to a bridge at Koln seen burning. Various bombers were picked up and taken out. Most of the 503rd landed on the Continent for fuel and did not return until 1730.

Losses/damaged:
- Lt. Blizzard (504), crash-landed shortly after takeoff in an open field near Fowlmere; aircraft damaged, pilot unhurt.

11, 12, 13 January '45
No missions flown.

14 January '45
No. 199   F/O#1515A   (0945-1520)

Although one 504th pilot crashed shortly after takeoff, groups "A" and "B" took off for an escort mission to Magdeburg. Encountered heavy, intense but inaccurate flak over the target. Good to excellent bombing—saw many fires and pillars of smoke over Magdeburg. Intense smoke screens were observed at Hamburg, Wilhelmshaven and Kiel. The 503rd also sent aircraft to escort an R.A.F. Spitfire during a photo-recon to Hamburg.

Several jets were seen—two Me-262s and one Me-163—

but none attempted to attack the bombers. After leaving the bombers, the Group dropped down to strafe. Mainly rail targets were attacked, but Lt. Haslam (504) and Lt. Barto (504) found barrage balloons at 6,000 feet over Dortmund and claimed 5/0/3. One pilot was lost during the mission, but all else returned safely.
Losses/damaged:
- Lt. Kunz (504), caught fire shortly after takeoff, put down at Arrington, England; minor burns, but flying again by end of the month.
- Lt. Lawrence J. Powell (505), already destroyed three locomotives and was attacking a fourth when he flew through high tension wires near Nauen; aircraft badly damaged; crash-landed near Ibbenburen, between Osnabruck and Rheine; quickly captured - POW (was on his second tour).

15 January '45
No. 200   F/0#1519A   (1032-1535)
Fifty-nine P-51s flying "A" and "B" groups escorted 3rd BD B-17s to Kempton, Germany. Despite 10/10 weather, the bombers flew good formations. "A" group broke escort west of Stuttgart and looked for targets to strafe, but not much worthwhile was found. The 504th again found barrage balloons, this time over a dam at Kehl, and claimed 6/0/0. All eventually returned safely.

16 January '45
No. 201   F/01521A   (1048-1513)
Fifty aircraft took off for a fighter-sweep to Zwolle and Dummer Lake. The main story was the weather. Six aircraft returned early when they could not form up. As the mission progressed, England "closed in." The remaining forty-four aircraft were all forced to land on the Continent, either at St. Trond, Beaumont or Le Bourget. Most landed safely and returned on the 17th, but some remained in France until the 18th.
Losses/damaged:
- Lt. Allers (504), landing accident at St. Trond; pilot unhurt and returned later; aircraft abandoned Comment: 362 fighters spent the night in France!

17 January '45
No. 202   F/0#1525A   (1004-1500)
Since most of the Group was still in France, a small number of aircraft were sent on an area patrol to Dummer Lake. Meanwhile, Capt. Bryan (503) led ten aircraft from St. Trond, France, at 1230 hours and gave withdrawal support to bombers on their way home. This was the Group's first mission from France to England. The rest of the Group headed home and began strafing targets around Dummer Lake. Two pilots were lost to a heavily defended train near Lippstadt.
A train was spotted and a flight from the 505th went down on it. As they came within range, they saw the train was composed of a locomotive, 25-plus goods wagons, of which at least six mounted light flak batteries, and a caboose. A terrific barrage came up and badly damaged two aircraft. One crashed nearby, while the other was last seen in heavy clouds and lost while trying to get home. The train was only slightly damaged.
Losses/damaged:
- Lt. Waldon E. Howard (505), AA fire; parachuted - KIA -
Capt Richard B. Olander (505), AA fire; badly damaged; tried to get back, but last seen in dense clouds and icing conditions - killed.

18 January '45
No mission flown.

19 January '45
No mission flown. The Fowlmere runways were badly in need of repair, so the Group moved to nearby Bassingbourn, a bomber base, and operated from there for a short time.

20 January '45
No. 203   F/0#1535A   (0838-1226)
Groups "A" and "B" made up of 56 aircraft flew an escort mission to Steckrode, Germany. 7/10 clouds caused bomber formations to be poor and straggled. Only one enemy aircraft was seen, a Me-262, and that was quite far away. Other bogies turned out to be 30-plus R.A.F. Typhoons over Antwerp. Experienced heavy, meager, inaccurate flak. All returned safely.

21 January '45
No. 204   F/0#1539A   (0952-1510)
The Group took part in a Ramrod to Mannheim, Germany. Experienced 10/10 clouds with some breaks. The rail yard at Durlach was bombed with very good results. Encountered heavy, intense flak from Rastatt to the target. Four B-17s were seen to go down, but all our aircraft returned.

22, 23, 24, 25, 26, 27, 28 January '45
No missions flown.

29 January '45
No. 205   F/0#1566A   (0935-1420)
This was the first mission flown after seven days downtime due to weather, the second longest non-mission period during the war. Although the bombers were late, the Group provided escort to Kassel, Germany. Encountered 10/10 cloud cover most of the way, but CAVU (Ceiling and Visibility Unlimited) in the target area. Individual bomb groups flew good formations, but overall, the formations were too spread out for effective escort.
The Group looked for targets to strafe on the way home, but found very little. Some rail traffic in the vicinity of Bad Lauterburg was strafed. Although three pilots landed on the Continent due to mechanical problems, all pilots eventually returned safely.
Claims: see under "Comment"
Losses/damaged:
- F/O Cohen (504), mechanical problems, landed on the Continent; took off to return home, but forced back to the

Continent a second time; left aircraft and returned later.

Comments: - At the end of this mission, Lt. Jay Marts (505) claimed the destruction of two enemy operated P-51s. He made his report, and it and his gun camera films were taken to Wing Headquarters for disposition and confirmation. He was told not to discuss the mission, and heard no more about it at that time.
- In 1981, Roger A. Freeman published the excellent Mighty Eighth War Diary. On page 431, he mentioned in a footnote to the 29 January 1945 mission, "... one P-51 MIA believed shot down in error by a 339FG P-51...." This is not correct.
- The only American Groups to lose P-51s that day were the 355th and the 359th Fighter Groups. The 355th pilot, "... reported rising engine temperatures and dropped below the undercast to try to reach Allied lines. He was hit by enemy flak near Geldern and was badly burned before bailing out. Captured, POW...." The 359th lost three aircraft (not one as listed in Mighty Eighth), all in the 368th Fighter Squadron. One of these was lost to American fire as one pilot inadvertently strafed a U.S. troop position near Inguiller. He made three passes in spite of warnings from the ground troops. They finally opened fire. He crashed and was killed near Bauxviller. Another pilot had operational problems and was forced to parachute near St. Genis de Saintogne, returning to his Group after a time in the hospital. The third pilot parachuted near Exeter, England, on his return and was unhurt.
- In May 1990, Jay Marts (505) was contacted about this mission and supplied the following information:

"... My wingman (Gerald Palmer?) and me had become separated from the rest of the Squadron. We approached two P-51s slowly from the rear and below. They were heading north at approximately 24,000 feet. We slid into a 3rd and 4th position on their right side. I signaled the lead P-51 pilot to use the general radio channel but received no response. Both pilots just continued eyeballing us.

I knew something was wrong as their planes were all silver without any markings on the nose, wings or tail, and not even squadron nor manufacturing serial number on the sides. The pilots wore helmets and goggles that were unlike any I had seen before. I called my wingman to fall back behind the second P-51, and I started to ease myself behind the leader. They both flipped over violently into vertical dives. As I rolled over with them, I flipped on my gun camera switch and fired a three to four second burst. My bullets hit the lead P-51 about three feet behind the cockpit causing the fuselage to tear apart from the explosion that almost engulfed me as I was no more than 40 feet behind him, but also in an inverted position. I went through the debris and saw the second P-51 below me, pulling away, going straight down. In my attempt to catch him, I pushed the throttle full forward and dove after him. At about 18,000 feet I caught him, but was unable to move the stick to aim my guns as I was in compressability. I would have collided with his tail had I not chopped the throttle, which threw me to the side of him. I slowed down slightly, but the vibration and porpoising continued and increased. I remember using the elevator trim tab hoping to lift the nose, but it did not start to affect the dive before I was down to maybe 11,000 feet. I glanced at the airspeed indicator. It was still on the peg-off scale. We both went through the broken overcast about 5,000 feet, but were in the clear an instant later. I remember thinking I was going to hit the ground like the German pilot below me was going to do. He never slowed down, but went straight in. My pullout was very slow. I did not have the strength to pull the stick back any harder, but fortunately, the trim tab became increasingly effective. I cleared the ground no more than 300 to 500 feet." Old "JUNIOR" had held together.

"My wingman who had spiralled down finally rejoined me. We both headed for home. My claim for two (2) enemy aircraft destroyed was submitted. One blew up, and I drove the other into the ground...."
- Neither pilot got out. Lt. Marts (505) never saw his gun camera films nor received credit for these two claims. At that time, it might have been feared that the P-51s were flown by American pilots, but all losses on that date have been accounted for.
- The Luftwaffe admitted to using captured aircraft for training purposes. The Versuchsverband Oberbefehlshaben der Luftwaffe toured fighter bases instructing German fighter pilots in the fine points of combating the Mustang, but have always officially claimed to never have used them operationally against American aircraft.

30 January '45
No mission flown.

31 January '45
No. 206   F/O#1573A   (0935-1140)
This was to have been an escort mission to Bremen, Germany. Extremely severe weather forced recall of the mission. Returning pilots landed at various bases in England before returning safely to Fowlmere.

FEBRUARY 1945

1, 2 February '45
No missions flown.

Comment: During February, it became standard policy for each squadron to send one or two flights down to strafe after each mission... weather permitting.

3 February '45
No. 207   F/O#1586A   (0845-1502)
The Group sent up a record number of aircraft for a single mission when they dispatched 62 planes for an escort to Berlin: 503rd - 22; 504th - 21; 505th - 19. The bombers flew very good formations, and each squadron was able to furnish unusually close escort. Despite a solid overcast up to 10,000 feet, the flak at Berlin was heavy and accurate—25 of 1,437 bombers dispatched were lost. Although no enemy aircraft were seen, eight V2 contrails were witnessed.

The first sighting of the Russian Army was made by Major Long (503) and Lt. Boychuck (503). They reported seeing the flashes of Russian artillery fire. It was also reported, "... roads were jammed with refugees fleeing north from Berlin. The move was orderly, with people, horse-drawn and hand-drawn vehicles on both sides of the road ...."

Military ground targets were attacked—mainly rail transportation. One train attacked had a bonus as 25 of its flat cars each held two and a half-ton trucks. Although several pilots landed on the Continent on the way home, everyone did return safely.

Comment: The following is a direct quote from the mission report filed as soon as the pilots landed; "... perhaps everyone felt to some extent that so-called "comradeship in arms" for here was our first mission that literally linked us up with our great Russian allies...."

4, 5 February '45
No missions flown.

6 February '45
No. 208   F/O#1595A   (0848-1410)

Again, the Group sent 62 aircraft on an escort to Leipzig. 8/10 to 10/10 solid overcast was experienced for most of the way. The bomber formation was only fair as too much space separated the boxes. Flak was heavy, moderate, and fairly accurate, especially at Ijmuiden. Although the flak was normal and no enemy aircraft were seen, the weather still claimed three pilots. All else returned safely, though several pilots were late as they landed in France for fuel or due to the weather.

Losses/damaged:
- Capt. Robert W. Bloxham (505), weather, killed; aircraft found later during low tides in the sands off the Isle of Wight.
- Lt. Kessler O. Thomas (505), weather, killed; found in his aircraft, crashed in the south of England.
- Lt. Gerald W. Palmer (505), weather, killed; found in his aircraft crashed on the Isle of Wight.

7 February '45
No. 209   F/O#1598A   (1144-1314)

The Group was scheduled for an escort to Gladbeck, Germany. The mission was recalled due to weather when a solid front closed in from 22,000 feet.

8 February '45
No mission flown.

9 February '45
No. 210   F/O#1605A   (0928-1505)

Fifty-seven aircraft were sent in "A" and "B" groups for escort to Leipzig. Six aircraft were forced back when they had trouble with the new English drop tanks—unable to draw fuel from them over 24,000 feet. The Group found three unescorted boxes of 1st BD B-17s and took them to the target. Just south of Meiningen, several Me-262s attacked the bombers. There, and at Fulda, the Group made their first air-to-air claims since 31 December and also the first confirmed Me-262 shot down by the 339th. Flak was heavy, moderate and innacurate at Greiz and Altenburg. Something new was reported: "... flak had the appearance of an inverted umbrella and burst at both ends...." Numerous stragglers (bombers) were picked up and taken out.

Claims: 1/0/1 air:
- 1 Me-262 damaged - Lt. Sainlar (504)
(damaged and drove off a Me-262 attacking two straggling B-17s)
- 1 Me-262 shot down - Lt. Ananian (505).

Comment: Lt. Ananian (505) reported, "... fired at one Me-262 at extreme range but missed ... then went after another and ended up on his tail at a range of 2,400 feet (probably the maximum range for the K14 gunsight) and gave him a three-second burst with little hopes of hitting him. However, I was surprised to notice strikes along the wings and around the left engine ... followed him down, hitting him until he burst into flames, and he fell out of control...."

10, 11, 12, 13 February '45
No missions flown.

14 February '45
No. 211   F/O#1622A   (1009-1600)

The Group flew an escort to Chemnitz, Germany. Experienced 8/10 to 10/10 low clouds, 2-3,000 feet in the target area, and 10/10 cirrus clouds at 21-25,000 feet. The bomber boxes were inter-mixed and the general stream snafued coming out of the clouds. Finally found our groups, the 96th and the 390th Bomb Groups, far south and off course. Took them to Frankfurt. No enemy aircraft were seen, but one V2 contrail was seen near Zwolle. Transportation targets were strafed in the vicinity of Weimar and Fulda. So much strafing was done that when the 504th found two airfields, their ammo was already expended. All the Group returned safely.

15 February '45
No mission flown.

16 February '45
No. 212   F/O#1631A   (1127-1602)

Provided area patrol to Hamm, Germany. Weather was 4/10 to 10/10 with haze up to 26,000 feet along the entire route. Bombing was visual and appeared excellent.

Lt. Boychuch (503) led a four-plane escort for a photo-recon aircraft to Frankfurt. Two Me-262s attacked, but our aircraft and the photo plane got away by diving into the clouds. All returned safely—with photos.

Losses/damaged:
- F/O Cohen (504), crash-landed at Coltishall on return; aircraft damaged (cat. "AC"), pilot unhurt.
- Lt. Hendricks (504), nosed over on landing; slight damage to aircraft, pilot unhurt.

Comment: "... a bomber believed to have exploded in the vicinity of Bury St. Edmunds ... brilliant flash and huge black cloud of smoke observed at top of overcast around 3,000 feet at 1550 hours...."

17 February '45
No. 213   F/0#1634A   (1018-1530)

The Group was scheduled for a P.T.W.S. mission to Frankfurt, however, severe weather forced recall of many of the bombers. The Group did find bombers of the 100th, 486th, 94th and 47th Bomb Groups and took them from Koblenz to Frankfurt and back to Koblenz. Flak was heavy, intense and accurate in the target area. The 503rd went back north of Fulda to strafe, but were driven off by intense, light, accurate flak. All returned safely.

18 February '45
No mission flown.

19 February '45
No. 214   F/01638A   (1203-1600)

The Group flew escort to Osnabruck, Germany. Weather was 10/10 over most of the route, three layers solid undercast over the Continent with the top layer at 23,000 feet. Bomber formations were very poor too spread out with stragglers on each box. They did tighten up for the bomb run, but results are not known. Experienced heavy, meager, inaccurate flak over the target. Several V2 contrails were seen in the Zuider Zee area, but all aircraft returned safely.

20 February '45
No. 215   F/0#1642A   (1032-1645)

Flew "A" and "B" Groups for an escort to Nurnburg, Germany. A solid overcast in layers up to 30,000 feet covered most of the route. Even so, and despite poor, spread-out formations within boxes plus many stragglers and heavy, moderate, accurate flak over Stuttgart, the bombing results were very good.

The 503rd sent four aircraft as escort for a photo-recon mission to the target area, but this proved completely uneventful. Two other flights of the 503rd broke escort and strafed rail targets near Wurzburg. Light, intense and very accurate flak damaged four aircraft (all cat. "A" damage), but all returned safely.

The 504th lost two aircraft to a midair collision while strafing. One pilot parachuted; the other was forced to crash land.

Captain Starnes (505) veered off the bomber stream near Nordlingen and led three flights on a strafing spree, working from Regensburg into Czechoslovakia, south of Pilzen and along the Czech border to the vicinity of Precatitz, destroying/damaging locomotives and other rail targets. This was the first attack by 8th Air Force pilots into Czechoslovakia. On the way home, a 505th pilot was lost after he reported suffering from vertigo.
Losses/damaged:
- F/O Cohen (504), midair collision; crash landed, unhurt; returned to the U.K. by 24 February.
- Capt. Wells (504), midair collision; parachuted, unhurt; returned to the U.K. by 24 February.
- Lt. William M. Beecher (505), vertigo; crashed in the vicinity of Valenciennes, France - killed.

21 February '45
No. 216   F/0#1647A   (0819-1425)

Again, flew "A" and "B" Groups for an escort to Nurnburg, Germany. Weather was very poor: 7/10 - 10/10 most of the route; 6/10 - 8/10 over the target. Bombers were thirty minutes late, and by the time they reached the target, they were over an hour late. Lt. Col Thury (505) reported, ". . . the target was finally hit from 24,000 feet R.A.F. style, with bombers seemingly approaching the target from all directions . . . . " No results were seen due to the undercast. " . . . flak at Hausach was a bright red and different from any flak yet observed . . . . "

The 505th also flew a photo-recon to the target area. All squadrons then strafed rail traffic in the area of Schweinfurt-Meiningen-Bad Kissingen. Two aircraft were damaged by light, intense and accurate flak, but all returned safely.
Losses/damaged:
- Capt. Bryan (503), slight AA damage (cat. "A"), unhurt - Lt. Farrell (503), AA damage (cat. "AC"), unhurt.

22 February '45
No. 217   F/0#1650A   (0850-1530)

Group flew a P.T.W.S. mission to Eger, Hof and Saalfeld. The weather was very poor with a haze to 10,000 feet and 10/10 clouds from 11-12,000 feet. Bombers straggled very badly and most bombed by instrument from various altitudes. No results seen; no flak seen; no enemy aircraft seen. Escort broke at Sélestat, and all squadrons strafed their way home. Much rail traffic was claimed, but not without cost. The Group lost two pilots and had several other aircraft damaged. ". . . flak, light, intense, accurate at Crailsheim, Coburg and Geislingen . . . a train near Crailsheim carried three cars of 20mm and 50-caliber flak guns . . . . " A grass aerodrome at Ganacker was attacked, but, ". . . the field was just too hot to handle . . . . "
Losses/damaged:
- Lt. Farrell (503), damaged a second time in two days when he hit a tree while dodging flak from a train; returned unhurt; aircraft required a new wing.
- Capt. Ray F. Herrmann (504), damaged by AA fire in the vicinity of Coburg - killed (only a Captain since 11 February).
- Capt. Robert T. Wood (504), last seen over Crailsheim; probably lost to AA fire - killed.

23 February '45
No. 218   F/0#1654A   (0845-1500)

Flew "A" and "B" groups for escort/support to the Neustadt area. 1/10 undercast on penetration and withdrawal, but CAVU in the target area. Bomber formations were excellent as were the results. Flak was heavy, moderate, accurate at Feiburg and Hausach. Several aircraft were damaged while strafing, but all returned.
Losses/damaged:
- Lt. Krauss (503), airborne for three hours; engine failure; returned and crash landed at Debden; aircraft only slightly damaged (cat. "A"), pilot unhurt.
- Lt. Caywood (505), slight damage by light flak near Regensburg; returned unhurt.

24 February '45
No. 219   F/O#1658A   (1032-1520)

Group flew an escort to Bremen, Germany. Completely uneventful. The bomber formation was good, and there was normal flak over the target and Osnabruck. The Group broke escort and strafed from Wilhelmshaven to Wessermunde. The 505th while strafing, "... unexpectedly encountered an aerodrome near Oldenburg and received a very warm reception in the form of light, intense, very accurate flak... runways were black top... there was one four-engine aircraft very strongly resembling a B-17 on the drome which was given a squirt and damaged...." Captain Bline (505) reported, "... I'll be damned if it didn't look like a B-17, but we didn't hang around long enough to find out!...." All returned safely.

Claims: 0/0/1 ground:
- 1 four-engine aircraft damaged - Capt. Bline (505).

25 February '45
No. 220   F/O#1662A   (#854-1525)

The Group provided escort to Munich, Germany. Bombers flew good, close formations, and bombing results were excellent. While it was CAVU most of the way, the group experienced heavy, intense and accurate flak at the target area and at Hausach. Part of the escort stayed with the bombers while the rest broke off in the vicinity of Heilbronn to attack rail targets. One pilot crash landed in France, and several others just landed for fuel. All returned later.

Losses/damaged:
- Lt. Moreland (503), coolant problem; crash landed in the vicinity of Sedan, France - unhurt.

26 February '45
No. 221   F/O#1665A   (0949-1605)

Flew escort to Berlin. Weather was 10/10 throughout the mission. Bomber formations were snafu from the start: boxes were loosely formed; many combat groups were out of stream. The only enemy activity seen were two V2 contrails. The only danger occurred when a 100th Bomb Group gunner fired on the 503rd when they joined up! Fire was not returned. All returned safely.

27 February '45
No. 222   F/O#1607A   (1039-1715)

This was a Group escort to Leipzig. Weather was 10/10 throughout up to 7,000 feet, but CAVU above that. Most of the Group stayed with the bombers for the entire mission. Those that did try to strafe were stopped by weather conditions. Though several pilots landed in France for fuel, all returned safely.

28 February '45
No. 223   F/O#1675A   (1148-1725)

The Group flew a P.T.W.S. mission to Kassel, Germany. Although the clouds were 10/10, the 3rd BD B-17s flew a very good formation. Large gusts of smoke came up through the undercast as the bombs were dropped. It appeared that the target had been well hit. The Group broke escort in the vicinity of Wurzburg. Rail and road traffic was almost non-existent, however, a marshalling yard was attacked, "belly-tanked" and strafed, but with minimal results. Flak was minimal, also. All returned safely.

MARCH 1945

1 March '45
No. 224   F/O#1679A   (1111-1700)

This was an escort mission to Ulm, Germany, giving cover for 3rd BD B-17s. The bomber stream was straggled, but individual boxes were in good order. Weather was 10/10 over the target while flak was heavy, meager but inaccurate. After the escort, rail traffic was strafed, and the 505th discovered a dispersal area holding nine twin-engine aircraft. They were well dispersed in a clump of trees off the autobahn south of Munich. Lt Col Thury (505) reported, "...no AA fire, so we set up a right hand traffic pattern and made passes out of the sun....dropped belly tanks on the area, helped set two Ju-88s afire...a picnic...some hard to set afire, but all blazing at the end...." All returned safely.

Claims: 9/0/0 ground
- 2 Ju-88s destroyed - Lt Ananian (505)
- 1 Ju-88 destroyed - Lt Irion (505)/Lt Biggs (505)
- 1 Ju-88 destroyed - Lt Irion (505)/Lt Booth (505)
- 1 Ju-88 destroyed - Lt Bundgaard (505)
- 1 Ju-88 destroyed - Lt Ziegler (505)
- 1 Ju-88 destroyed - Lt Marvel (505)
- 1 Ju-88 destroyed - Lt Col Thury (505)
- 1 Do-217 destroyed - Lt Woolery (505)

2 March '45
No. 225   F/O#1683A   (0739-1300)

Flew escort to Ruhland, Germany. The day started badly as, "...escort practically impossible because of 25 to 50 mile interval between each group...individual boxes befuddled, off course and struggling...." Encountered 6/10 to 8/10 clouds to 9,000 feet. It was clear above that. And then it happened the biggest Luftwaffe reaction since November. Fifty-plus enemy fighters were seen forming up to attack the bombers, but we attacked first. Thirty of the Me-109s "...were beautiful: a vertical red band on the fuselage just forward of the tail section, a white spiraled spinner and colored a gunmetal blue..."

A huge dog-fight developed. The 505th started it just east of Magdeburg, claiming four Me-109s. As the fight moved, the 503rd joined in, claiming 10/2/7, but losing one pilot. Five U/I "blow-jobs" (jets) and two Me-309s attacked a force of R.A.F. bombers over Osnabruck and shot down two before the 505th could drive them off. The 505th then strafed their way home, claiming 11/0/3 on the ground, but at the cost of two more pilots.

Claims: 14/2/8 air   11/0/3 ground

- 1 Me-109 shot down - Lt Gokey (503)
- 1 FW-190 shot down, 1 Me-109 shot down, 1 FW-190 damaged/air - Major Bryan (503)
- 1 FW-190 probably shot down, 1 Me-109 damaged/air - Lt Butler (503)
- 1 Me-109 shot down, 1 Me-109 damaged/air - Lt Chetneky (503)
- 1 Me-109 damaged/air - Capt Behrend (503)
- 1 Me-109 damaged/air - Lt French (503)
- 1 Me-109 damaged/air - Lt Frisch (503)
- 2 Me-109s shot down, 1 Me-109 damaged/air - Lt Gerard (503)
- 2 Me-109s shot down, 1 FW-190 shot down - Lt Poutre (503)
- 1 FW-190 shot down, 1 FW-190 probably shot down - Lt Preddy (503)
- 2 Me-109s shot down - Lt Marts (505)
- 1 Me-109 shot down, 1 Ju-88/FW-190 "pick-a-back" damaged/ground - Capt Starnes (505)
- 1 Me-109 shot down - Lt Ziegler (505)/Lt Withers (505)
- 1 Me-309 damaged/air - Lt G. W. Jones (505)
- 3 Do-217s destroyed/ground, 2 Do-217s damaged/ground - Lt Biggs (505)
- 3 Do-217s destroyed/ground - Lt Burch (505)
- 3 Do-217s destroyed/ground - Lt Howard (505)
- 2 Do-217s destroyed/ground - Lt Conners (505)

Losses/damaged:
- Lt Esteban A. Terrats (503), last seen during dogfight with enemy fighters - KIA - Lt Bertis A. Conner (505), wounded; captured - POW - Lt Harvey F. Howard (505), crashed while strafing a dispersal area in the vicinity of Mockern; captured POW

Comments: - Captain Starnes (505) had shot down one Me-109 off the tail of a 78th Fighter Group P-51 and was chasing another Me-109 on the deck when he saw the first "pick-a-back" planes seen by the Group. These were a bomber with a fighter plane mounted on its back. The bomber would be filled with explosives and flown/controlled by the fighter to a target where the bomber would be cut loose to crash into the target. This one was a Ju-88 with a FW-190 mounted on it. Captain Starnes only had time for two quick passes before being forced to leave.
- Lt Gerard (503) had just shot down one Me-109 when, "...I next bounced a single 109, but the pilot was a real hot-rock, and I broke off to attack another; there were lots of them around, the hot boy had a big lead, and I didn't want to waste time...." He then attacked twelve 109s and shot down their leader. "...I flew instruments in the clouds for about one minute before I popped out again. When I broke out I saw two aircraft that I thought were 109s, silhouetted against the sun, and fired a 90 degree deflection burst at the leader. Luckily I missed him because it was my element leader and his wingman. We joined up and came home...."
- Captain Behrend (503) had a difficult time attacking a Me-109. "...I closed in again when five or six P-51s cut me out....I then thought I had him, but I was again cut out by P-51s....finally managed to damage it, but it got away...."

3 March '45
No. 226 F/0#1690A (0748-1250)

This was an escort mission to Dallberger, Germany. Bomber formations were generally poor, and the weather was 5/10. Experienced heavy, moderate but inaccurate flak in the target area. A number of Me-262s attacked the bombers before they were driven off.

The 503rd also flew a four-plane escort for a photo-recon to Hanover/Berlin. They were attacked by three Me-262s. All got away and returned safely.

The 504th broke escort and strafed rail traffic in the Hilgesheim-Celle-Lippstadt area. One pilot was lost to flak.

The 505th chased Me-262s east of Magdeburg, then found and attacked a field in the vicinity of Mockern. The field held over 50 aircraft: Ju-88s, Do-217s and Ju-88/FW-190 "picka-backs". The field was defended by at least six .30-caliber guns and one 40mm position. Although two pilots were shot down on the first pass, the rest made numerous passes and destroyed ten aircraft.

The day wasn't over for the 505th. On their return to England they crossed the coast between Canterbury and Deal at an altitude of 10,000 feet and were fired at by English gunners with 25 bursts of heavy flak! No damage done.
Claims: 0/0/1 air 10/0/2 ground
- 1 Me-262 damaged/air - Lt R. G. Johnson (503)
- 3 Ju-88s destroyed/ground, 1 Do-217 destroyed/ground, 1 Ju-88 damaged/ground - Lt Col Thury (505)
- 1 Ju-88 and 1 FW-190 "pick-a-back" destroyed/ground - Capt Starnes (505)
- 1 Ju-88 and 1 FW-190 "pick-a-back" destroyed/ground - Lt Jones (505)
- 1 Ju-88 destroyed/ground - Lt Thiene (505)
- 1 Ju-88 destroyed/ground - Lt Ziegler (505)
- 1 Ju-88 damaged/ground - Lt Withers (505)

Losses/damaged:
- Lt Otis A. Kurth (504), last seen strafing rail targets; probably lost to AA fire - KIA - Lt George W. Jones (505), damaged by AA fire while strafing; tried to parachute below 200 feet; chute only partially opened - KIA
- Lt Harry D. Ziegler (505), damaged by AA fire while strafing; "bellied in" (making a beautiful landing according to Lt Col Thury); captured - POW

Comment: Lt R. G. Johnson (503) had attacked a Me-262 at 14,000 feet, damaged it, and chased it to the deck. "...the Me-262 then landed at Fassburg airdrome and rolled into a hangar...." Before Lt Johnson could do anything about it, he was driven off by intense flak.

4 March '45
No. 227 F/0#1697A (0721-1305)

This was scheduled as an escort mission to Nurnburg, Germany. Due to the weather, the rendezvous was not made. The Groups made a couple of 360s (circles) in the rendezvous area, then proceeded to the target area. As the weather was 9/10 to 10/10 in the target area, most of the bombers had already been recalled. Experienced heavy, moderate but inaccurate flak south of Strasburg. All returned safely with most forced

to land at Duxford when an accident closed Fowlmere.
Losses/damaged:
- Lt Rawls (503), brakes locked on landing; aircraft damaged and airfield closed for a short time; pilot unhurt

5 March '45
No. 228   F/O#1704A   (0720-1400)
This was an area patrol to Ruhland, Germany, very close to the "Eastern" front. Weather was 10/10 with heavy flak at Leipzig and Dresden. A number of aircraft landed on the Continent for fuel. One aircraft was lost when landing for fuel. All returned later.
Losses/damaged:
- Lt Gauger (503), crash landed at "B83" on the Continent; aircraft destroyed, pilot unhurt

6, 7 March '45
No missions flown.

8 March '45
No. 229   F/O#1721A   (1208-1740)
The Group flew a combined area sweep and escort mission to Munster, Germany. Although the weather was 10/10, the bombers flew good formations. Encountered heavy, moderate, inaccurate flak in the vicinity of Dortmund. All returned safely.

9 March '45
No mission flown.

10 March '45
No. 230   F/O#1731A   (1031-1506)
The Group flew an "A" and "B" escort mission to the Dortmund area. There was a 10/10 undercast. While the bomber formations were fair going in, there were numerous stragglers after leaving the target. As there was no visual contact made with the briefed bombers throughout the mission, general support — sweeping up and down the bomber stream was flown. B-17s and B-24s inter-mixed on withdrawal, and this cost the Group one aircraft. The 504th sent a pilot down to check on the identity of a group of B-17s, and they shot him down! All else returned safely.
Losses/damaged:
- Lt Sainlar (504), shot down by B-17s; parachuted near St. Trond, rescued unhurt

Comments: - Lt Sainlar (504) reported, "...I was ordered to go in and observe the markings on the box of B-17s on our left....I pulled ahead and close enough to the bombers to observe the red tips on their tails, but could not observe the letters. I started to skid the plane broadside towards the B-17s when they began firing at me....I felt about 10 hits...2 of which went straight through the canopy at 90 degree angles....I immediately split away and dropped my tanks...vicinity of St. Trond the aircraft caught fire and I was forced to bail out...."
- The 8th Air Force had four P-51s shot down this date, none by the Luftwaffe, but all by other Americans! The 339th lost Lt Sainlar to the B-17s, and the 359th Fighter Group had three of its P-51s shot down by American AA fire near the Remagen Bridge. Two pilots were killed and one rescued unhurt.

11 March '45
No. 231   F/O#1738A   (1035-1525)
Flew escort to Hamburg, Germany. Weather was 10/10. Individual boxes flew good formations, but the combat groups were strung out. Experienced heavy, intense but inaccurate flak over Hamburg and Bremen. Mission was uneventful.

12 March '45
No. 232   F/O#1742A   (0907-1530)
This was an escort mission for 3rd BD B-17s to Swinemunde on the Baltic coast. Bomber formations were good within their respective boxes, but the boxes were strung out. Weather was 10/10 over the target area. Flak was meager to moderate and fairly accurate. A small number of Me-109s seen over an airfield at Hellevad, Denmark, produced the only air-to-air claims for the entire 8th Air Force on this date. AA fire from the field appeared to be indiscriminately fired at both Me-109s and P-51s. Neither suffered any damage.
Claims: 4/0/1 air
- 1 Me-109 shot down - Capt Farmer (505)
- 1 Me-109 shot down - Capt Farmer (505)/Lt Carr (505)
- 1 Me-109 shot down, 1 Me-109 damaged - F/O Coker (505)
- 1 Me-109 shot down - F/O Pesanka (505)
Losses/damaged:
- Lt Richard C. O'Brien (505), unknown reason; belly landed behind Russian lines; later returned unhurt Comment: F/O Coker (505) had a difficult time during the dogfight: "...my trigger had fallen out of the stick about thirty minutes before we encountered the enemy aircraft. I wasn't sure that my guns would fire so I placed my fingers in the hole where the trigger had been. Feeling a metal tab, I figured that by pressing up on the tab the necessary contact for firing the gun would be made...." Everything worked as he shot down one Me-109 and damaged another.

14 March '45
No. 233   F/O#1742A   (1153-1645)
The Group flew "A" and "B" groups on a P.T.W.S. mission to Hanover. Although the 3rd BD B-17s flew good formations, intervals between boxes became too lengthened at times to assure close escort. Experienced a low, thick haze in the target area as well as heavy, intense yet inaccurate flak. Only one Me-262 was seen. All returned safely.

15 March '45
No. 234   F/O#1761A   (1214-1750)
This was a P.T.W.S. mission to Oranienburg. Although one aircraft was lost on takeoff, the mission was continued. Bomber formations were good; bombing results were excellent. Barrage balloons were seen at 5,000 feet, protecting a railway bridge just south of Brunswick. The 504th claimed 10/0/0 of them.
Losses/damaged:
- Lt Rawls (503), lost a wing tank immediately after takeoff; crashed, aircraft destroyed, pilot unhurt

16 March '45
No mission flown.

17 March '45
No. 25   F/O#1774A   (0903-1505)
Flew an escort mission to Ruhland, Germany. Weather was 10/10 with bomber formations as good as could be expected because of the adverse weather. Flak was heavy, meager and inaccurate over the target to Frankfurt. The first AR-234 jet bomber was seen and chased over Torgan, but it got away. All returned safely.

18 March '45
No. 236   F/O#1779A   (0829-1405)
Flew patrol mission to Brandenburg. Low clouds persisted over the entire area. Twenty-plus "long-nosed" FW-190s were encountered over the Dummer Lake region. A quick fight claimed a number of them, but most got away by diving through the clouds. One FW-190 stayed long enough to damage and force one 503rd aircraft to crash land. All else returned safely.
Claims: 4/0/2 air
- 1 FW-190 shot down - Capt Gerard (503)
- 1 FW-190 shot down - Lt McElwee (503)
- 1 FW-190 shot down, 1 FW-190 damaged - Maj Shafer (503)
- 1 FW-190 damaged - Lt Poutre (503)
- 1 FW-190 shot down - Lt Ballard (504)
Losses/damaged:
- Capt Gerard (503), damaged by a FW-190; almost bailed out but able to crash land safely at St. Trond Comment: The FW-190 claimed by Captain Gerard was "shot down" without firing. As soon as Captain Gerard got into firing range, the enemy pilot bailed out.

19 March '45
No. 237   F/O#1785A   (1041-1625)
Performed an escort mission to the Leipzig area. Flak was heavy, meager and inaccurate in the Bad Nauheim and target areas. Weather was 10/10, perhaps aided by smoke screens over the target area and especially heavy in the Remagen area. This was an uneventful mission, and all returned.

20 March '45
No. 238   F/O#1794A   (1405-1845)
Flew area patrol to the Bremen/Hamburg area. The only enemy aircraft seen in the air were Me-262s. Thirty-plus were seen flying singly or in pairs, attacking B-17s over Hamburg. At least ten B-17s were hit or trailing smoke, but only four were lost. Four R.A.F. Mosquitoes were also attacked by the Me-262s.
The Group split up to intercept the Me-262s, and all three squadrons made claims. One 504th pilot was lost to AA fire while chasing a 262 over its airfield. Most of the 504th chased a single 262 with five pilots getting close enough to fire before one pilot finally hit it, causing it to explode. The 504th then saw and straffed Heilgenhafen near Grossenbrode, Germany. They dropped their wing tanks first in the area of several buildings, then strafed.
Claims: 2/0/3 air   3/0/3 ground
- 2 Me-262s damaged/air - Lt Hill (503)
- 1 Me-262 shot down - Lt Barto (504)
- 1 Me-262 damaged/air - Lt Berguson (504)
- 1 Me-262 shot down - Lt Irion (505)
- 1 U/ITE destroyed/ground, 1 He-lll damaged/ground - Lt Col Clark (504)
- 1 He-lll destroyed/ground - Lt Barrett (504)
- 1 FW-200 destroyed/ground, 1 Ju-52 damaged/ground - Lt Kuhlman (504)
- 1 Ju-52 damaged/ground - Lt Chenez (504)
Losses/damaged:
- Lt Jerome J. Ballard (504), hit by AA fire while chasing a Me-262 across the airfield at KaltenKirchen; tried to parachute, but chute did not open properly; reported to have survived and eventually returned to the U.S. after the war

21 March '45
No. 239 F/O#1801A   (0703-1225)
The Group flew a P.T.W.S. mission to Ruhland, Germany. Again, the only enemy aircraft seen in the air were jets. The 1,353 heavy bombers were directed primarily against jet fighter bases. The bombers were attacked southeast of Wittenberg by 18 Me-262s. Group aircraft dropped their tanks and attempted to break up these attacks, but were handicapped by the bombers flying just below the overcast. This made it nearly impossible to give them top cover. The "blow jobs" were finally chased away, but not until they destroyed three B-17s without a loss to themselves. Others (enemy aircraft) were attacked and one shot down. Six Me-163s along with four Me-262s were seen on the runway at Liepzig, but they did not try to takeoff.
Claims: 1/0/0
- 1 Me-262 shot down - Lt Greer (504)

22 March '45
No. 240   F/O#1810A   (0958-1510)
The Group performed an escort/patrol mission to Ruhland, Germany. The 505th lost one aircraft on takeoff, but the rest completed the mission. North of Dresden, two flights of Me-262s and one flight of Me-163s (four aircraft to a flight, flying line abreast) attacked the bombers and shot down two. They were reforming for a second attack when the Group drove them off. Experienced heavy, intense flak in the target area.
Losses/damaged:
- F/O Rice (505), crashed on takeoff; aircraft destroyed, pilot unhurt

23 March '45
No. 241   F/O#1819A   (1042-1625)
The Group flew an area support patrol to Dortmund, sweeping the area from Giessen to Kassel to Fulda. The weather was perfect, but the Group encountered heavy, moderate, very accurate flak twenty miles southwest of Giessen. Bomber formations were excellent; bombing was excellent. The Group returned safely.

24 March '45
No. 242   F/0#1828A   (xxxx-xxxx)

Flew in "A" and "B" groups with staggered takeoff times to keep a continuous force over the patrol area of SiegenGerleburg. "A" group flew from 0538-1200 hours; "B" group from 0936-1533. Much rail and road traffic — everything from locomotives and buildings to individual soldiers and motorcycles was destroyed or damaged. Experienced light, moderate, inaccurate flak. All returned safely.

Losses/damaged:
- Capt Perry (503), "slight" midair collision on takeoff, returned unhurt
- Lt Frisch (503), "slight" midair collision on takeoff, returned unhurt
- Lt Preddy (503), landed at Duxford and nosed over; aircraft destroyed, pilot unhurt - Lt Clifton (504), nosed over due to runway conditions; aircraft damaged, pilot unhurt

25 March '45
No. 243   F/0#1838A   (0713-1235)

Flew an escort mission to Brunswick. 2nd BD B-24s were late, forcing the Group to circle 30 to 40 minutes. When the bombers finally arrived they were flying very good formation, and close escort was maintained throughout. Bombing results were excellent. Weather was CAVU with only a slight haze. Me-262s were met in the target area. One 262 was seen to shoot down a 352nd Fighter Group P-51. Four other 262s tried to attack the bombers, but were driven off. Claims: 0/0/1 air
- 1 Me-262 damaged - Major Shafer (503)

26 March '45
No. 244   F/0#1843A   (1109-1640)

This was a P.T.W.S. mission to Plauen. Again, the 503rd had a "slight" midair collision shortly after takeoff, but the mission continued. Weather was CAVU. Captain Farmer (505) reported, "...excellent formation flying...all squadrons of the 34th Bomb Group...packed like sardines in a can except when they loosened up to bomb by individual squadrons...." Several Group pilots landed in France for fuel, but all eventually returned.

Losses/damaged:
- Lt C. I. Ferrell (503), nosed up when landing on the Continent; needed a new propeller before returning - Capt Edens (503), "slight" midair collision; needed new wing tip
- Lt Gauger (503), "slight" midair collision; needed a new rudder

27 March '45
No mission flown.

28 March '45
No. 245   F/0#1857A   (0901-1406)

This was an escort mission to Hanover, Germany. Despite a major accident on takeoff and losing another aircraft shortly after takeoff, the Group completed its mission. Experienced heavy, meager, inaccurate flak at Hanover.

Lt Col Clark (504) reported, "...attempted to pick up and escort the bombers coming off the target, but all seemed to have sufficient fighter escort...." Several pilots landed in France for fuel. All returned safely.

Losses/damaged:
- F/O E. E. Hupp (505), hit prop-wash on takeoff, ground-looped; aircraft burst into flames, pilot survived
- Lt Guyton (505), suffered power failure shortly after takeoff; "bellied in" at Colchester; aircraft damaged, pilot unhurt

Comment: After F/O Hupp crashed and with his aircraft in flames, "...the medical enlisted personnel, despite exploding ammunition, were on scene and helped to drag Hupp from the cockpit in complete disregard to their personal safety...." Hupp had just joined the 505th five days earlier. He was back flying in a few days.

29 March '45
No mission flown.

30 March '45
No. 246   F/0#1863A   (1125-1600)

The Group flew a P.T.W.S. mission to Hamburg. The escort was uneventful until the bombers entered the target area where heavy, intense but inaccurate flak was encountered. Coming off the target, fifteen-plus Me-262s attempted to attack the bombers. The Group broke up to drive them off. The 503rd chased two 262s to 20 miles southwest of Rendsburg. One jet started to turn, and the Squadron was robbed of a certain kill when a 361st Fighter Group P-51 split-essed down and picked off the Jerry! Lt McElwee was closing fast at this time and did not see the German pilot bail out. He riddled the enemy aircraft which then crashed in flames. (Full credit was given to the 361st pilot; no claim submitted by Lt McElwee.) The 504th chased and shot down another jet at Lubeck, then shot down one of two Me-262s taking off from Kaltenkirchen airfield. The 505th meanwhile was busy with various Me-262s. One Me-262 made a hit-and-run pass, shooting down a 339th pilot, the third 339th pilot shot down by a jet. Four 262s "flying an American-style formation" attacked a group of B-24s near Wangerooge Island off Bremen. They were driven off.

Claims: 2/1/3 air
- 1 Me-262 shot down, 1 Me-262 damaged - Lt Bennett (504)
- 1 Me-262 shot down - Capt Sargent (504)
- 1 Me-262 probably shot down - Col Henry (Hq)
- 1 Me-262 damaged - Capt Rich (505)
- 1 Me-262 damaged - Lt Ananian (505)

Losses/damaged:
- Lt Evergard L. Wager (505), shot down by a Me-262; parachuted northeast of Hamburg; chute failed to open properly

31 March '45
No. 247   F/0#1874A   (0643-1215)

This was a P.T.W.S. mission to the Zeitz area. The bomber formation was very poor, and the combat groups were not in proper sequence. This made proper escort impossible. Fortunately there were no attacks by enemy aircraft. It was surprising that the bombing results were excellent. Oil storage tanks in the vicinity of Erfurt were well hit. The only danger on the mission was when three 390th Bomb Group aircraft opened fire on the 505th. No damage was done.

Lt Col Thury (505) reported, "...Pattons army packed the autobahn running north from Frankfurt for about 30 miles. Motor transports of all types, bumper to bumper..." Losses/damaged:
- F/O Joseph R. Coker (505), oil leak, forced to crash land near Flauen; captured - POW

APRIL 1945

1 April '45
No mission flown.

2 April '45
No. 248   F/O1845A   (1334-1812)

Flew escort to Grove Nidenmark, Denmark, to attack airfields. Weather forced a recall, and the escort was broken half way back across the North Sea. All returned safely.

Meanwhile, the 505th was escorting a photo-recon aircraft when, north of Arnhem, they were "attacked" by a R.A.F. Spitfire. Lt Col Thury (505) was not too impressed: "...his marksmanship was as poor as his recognition abilities...." They all returned safely, also.

3 April '45
No. 249   F/0#1887A   (1500-2005)

This was a P.T.W.S. mission to Kiel, Germany, One 503rd aircraft crashed on takeoff, but the rest of the Group continued on the mission. Bomber formations were good. Experienced heavy, intense but inaccurate flak at Kiel. Losses/damaged:
- Lt Moreland (503), engine failure on takeoff, crashed; aircraft destroyed, pilot unhurt

Comment: Major Bryan (503) completed his second tour with this mission.

4 April '45
No. 250   F/0#1896A   (0705-1252)

Sixty-three aircraft took off for an area patrol to the jet airfield at Parchim, Germany. Air-to-air visibility was excellent. As the Group approached Parchim, seven Me-262s were seen taking off. These were attacked and several shot down. A number of airfields were then strafed: Wismar, Tarnewitz and Schneverdinger. Intense, heavy and light flak was encountered at all three, but all Group aircraft returned safely.
Claims: 4/0/1 air   6/0/1 ground
- 1 Me-262 shot down - Capt Everson (504)/Lt Croker (504)
- 1 Me-262 shot down - Capt Greer (504)
- 1 Me-262 shot down - Lt Havighurst (504)
- 1 Me-262 shot down - Capt Corey (505)
- 1 Me-262 damaged/air, 1 U/IME destroyed/ground - Lt Col Clark (504)
- 1 U/IME damaged/ground - Lt Col Clark (504)/ Lt Carter (504)
- 2 Me-410s destroyed/ground - Maj Tower (505)
- 1 Me-410 destroyed/ground - Lt MacClarence (505)
- 1 Do-217 destroyed/ground - Capt Rich (505)
- 1 Ju-88 destroyed/ground - Lt Ananian (505)
Losses/damaged:
- F/O Steiger (505), damaged by debris from a Me-262; returned safely

Comment: F/O Steiger (505) reported, "...in fact, as Capt Corey finished off the Me-262, I caught some of the flying debris which damaged my canopy and knocked off my goggles although somehow I managed to escape unhurt...."

5 April '45
No. 251   F/0#1903A   (0832-1442)

This was a P.T.W.S. mission to Frankfurt. The bomber formation was only fair; i.e., they were flying in small groups and were too spread out at times. The escort was broken and squadrons swept the area from Regensburg to Weiden looking for jet aircraft. Several airfields containing Me-262s were patrolled, waiting for them to take off. One did, and he was immediately attacked.
The 262 got away with only a few strikes on his wings as he "...took quite a lot of evasive actions, ducking behind trees and houses until he was out of range...."

6 April '45
No. 252   F/0#1909A   (0711-1305)

Flew a P.T.W.S. mission to Gera, Germany. Bombers flew good formation on penetration, but were scattered in the tarqet area and on withdrawal. They did not fly the briefed course which, when added to the weather conditions, made escort very difficult. Experienced heavy, moderate but inaccurate flak at Leipzig and Gera. All returned safely. Comment: All Squadrons reported, "...there was music on 'C' channel on withdrawal...."

7 April '45
No. 253   F/0#1914A   (1008-1450)

Conducted an escort mission to Hamburg, Germany. Bombers were taken from the Zuider Zee to Hamburg and part way back. The formations were too spread out in that the first box of bombers were too far ahead of the other boxes. Heavy flak was meager, and the light flak was moderate; both inaccurate.

For the first time in three weeks, conventional fighters were encountered in large numbers. Twenty-five-plus Me-262s were seen and attacked. Running fights from Steinhuder Lake to Celle and Hamburg accounted for at least twelve enemy aircraft. There were no losses to enemy fire, but the Group lost its second pilot to American B-17 gunners.

The 503rd reported, "...tactics went by the board as the Jerries carried out what might be called 'patriotic' although wholly uncoordinated attacks. In some instances, fanatical and literally suicidal passes were made....a number of bombers were rammed...."

Claims: 12/2/7 air
- 1 FW-190 shot down, 1 Me-262 damaged - Lt Petitt (503)
- 1 Me-109 shot down - Lt Krauss (503)
- 1 Me-109 shot down - Lt Poutre (503)
- 1 FW-190D shot down - Lt Poutre (503)/ Lt R. G. Johnson (503)
- 1 Me-109 shot down, 1 Me-262 damaged - Lt Carter (504)
- 1 FW-190 shot down, 1 Me-109 damaged - Capt Guernsey (504)
- 1 Me-109 shot down - Capt Everson (504)
- 1 Me-109 shot down, 1 Me-109 damaged - Lt Cresswell (504)
- 1 Me-109 shot down - Lt Hermansen (504)
- 1 Me-262 probably shot down - Maj Hathorn (504)
- 1 Me-262 probably shot down, 1 Me-262 damaged - Lt Blizzard (504)
- 1 Me-262 damaged - Lt Mason (504)
- 1 Me-109 shot down - Lt Barto (504)/Lt Kunz (504)
- 1 FW-190D shot down - Capt Bline (505)
- 1 Me-109 shot down - Lt Col Thury (505)/Lt Biggs (505)
- 1 Me-262 damaged - F/O Rice (505)
Losses/damaged:
- Lt David A. MacKenzie (503), shot down and killed by B-17 gunners
- Lt Paul (505), landing accident; ran off runway, aircraft flipped/destroyed - pilot unhurt (back flying in two days)

Comments: - The following report was filed by Lt Kunz (504) and Lt Barto (504), "...as the Me-109 broke away from us, he split-essed and crashed into the rear fuselage of a straggling B-17. There was a terrific explosion and both planes crashed to the ground. The enemy pilot did not get out of his plane. The e/a (enemy aircraft) undoubtedly did not see the B-17. The evasive action of the e/a when we broke into him was the direct cause for his destruction...." Although this ramming appeared accidental, others that day were not.
- After the war, it was learned that the "Sonderkommando Elbe", the Luftwaffe unit specially formed and trained to ram enemy bombers, flew its only known operation against the 8th Air Force on this date. Seventeen heavy bombers were lost, and at least eight were known or suspected lost through ramming tactics. At least two other bombers were rammed by fighters, but were able to return.
- On a lighter note, Capt Bline (505) reported in relation to chasing a FW-190D near the bomber stream, "...closed to about 600 yards when the pilot bailed out....since I was closing fast, at 450 mph, I clobbered the e/a from 400 yards to 300 yards range just for the hell of it...."

8 April '45
No. 254 F/0#1918A (0832-1445)

The Group split into "A" and "B" groups, flying a P.T.W.S. mission to Eger, Germany. The bomber boxes were so far apart that Lt Col Shafer had to split up the groups even more to try to cover them. Fortunately, no airborne enemy aircraft were seen, and the flak was inaccurate. Bombing, however, was excellent.

9 April '45
No. 255 F/0#1929A (1310-1935)

This was a P.T.W.S. mission to Munich, Germany. Experienced heavy, meager and accurate flak at the target. Several B-17s were seen to go down. Two 503rd and two 504th pilots escorted a P-38 on a photo-recon mission to Eiseleben where they were attacked by two Me-262s. Both enemy aircraft were damaged and driven off, and all our pilots and the P-38 returned. Several pilots landed on the Continent, but all returned safely.
Claims: 0/0/2 air
- 1 Me-262 damaged - Lt Hunt (504)
- 1 Me-262 damaged - Lt Orcutt (504)
Comments:
- Lt Col Thury (505) was not pleased by something he saw on the mission. "...about 50 Mustangs trespassing on the 505th private range about seven miles south of Munich, at 1715 hours, 20 fires were observed raging in the dispersal area and one P-51 seen to go down while strafing...wanted to know if fighters had been released to strafe conventional airfields...NUTHOUSE, on penetration, specially instructed Upper Squadron to prang jet fields only...."
- The 4th Fighter Group reported for 9 April '45, "...the 335th Fighter Squadron broke escort early... sweeping over Munich...Brunnthal airdrome, they found crammed with enemy aircraft....claimed 14 a/c destroyed at the cost of two pilots...."

10 April '45
No. 256 F/01936A (1245-1800)

The day began as a P.T.W.S. mission to Neuruppin. By the end of the day, the Group would be the first in the 8th Air Force to destroy over 100 aircraft on the ground during a single mission.
Overall Claims:
503rd   6 / 0 / 6 ground
504th   36 / 0 / 39 ground
505th   63 / 0 / 33 ground
Total 339th   105 / 0 / 78 ground
(Total 8th AF 309 / 0 / 235 ground)

Lt Col Propst (503) reported, "...this squadron had been ordered to remain with the bombers and did so, even though the other two squadrons in the Group were setting new records of e/a destroyed...." However, Lt Col Shafer (503), flying with a K25 camera and escorted by Lt. Frisch (503), took pictures of the bombing and found the dispersal area near Neuruppin "crammed with various types of aircraft." He called in other squadrons for the kill. While waiting, he and Frisch made seven strafing runs on one dispersal area. Claims: 6/0/6 ground
- 1 Me-109 destroyed, 1 Ju-88 destroyed, 4 Ju-88s damaged - Lt Col Shafer (503)
- 4 Ju-88s destroyed, 1 Ju-88 damaged, 1 U/IME damaged - Lt Frisch (503)

Major Julian (504) reported, "...chased several Me-262s, both evaded; squadron somewhat split up...we arrived at the target, a dispersal area northwest of Neuruppin...over 100 e/

a seen dispersed around ten acres in this area...Upper Squadron already at work...joined the traffic pattern and entered into the fun; it was all too easy...only one 30-cal. flak gun within reach of our traffic pattern and it was completely ignored...over the A/D itself was a thick concentration of 20 and 40mm for anyone who wandered too near, but this was seldom necessary...few of the e/a seemed to contain enough gas to explode quickly, but evidently were serviced with oil for they burned nicely once started. Eventually the whole area became so clouded with smoke that it was exceedingly difficult to find targets....first pass at 1535. Last pass at 1610 hours...averaged 10 passes per man.

Claims: 36/0/39 ground
- 3 Me-410s destroyed, 2 Me-410s damaged - Major Julian (504)
- 3 Me-410s destroyed, 2 Me-410s damaged - Lt Bennett (504)
- 3 Me-410s destroyed, 2 Me-410s damaged - Lt Kunz (504)
- 2 Me-410s destroyed, 2 Me-410s damaged - Lt Blizzard (504)
- 3 Me-410s destroyed, 2 Me-410s damaged - Lt Mason (504)
- 3 Me-410s destroyed, 3 Me-410s damaged - Lt Hermansen (504)
- 3 Me-410s destroyed, 4 Me-410s damaged - Lt Croker (504)
- 3 Me-410s destroyed, 2 Me-410s damaged - Capt Sargent (504)
- 2 Me-410s destroyed, 1 Me-410 damaged - Lt Allers (504)
- 2 Me-410s destroyed, 2 Me-410s damaged - Lt Chenez (504)
- 1 Me-410 destroyed, 1 Ju-88 damaged - F/O Smith (504)
- 3 Me-410s destroyed, 7 Me-410s damaged, 3 Me-ll0s damaged - Capt Everson (504)
- 1 Me-410 destroyed, 1 Me-410 damaged - Lt Krueger (504)
- 2 Ju-88s destroyed, 1 Ju-88 damaged - Lt Barto (504)
- 2 Ju-88s destroyed, 3 Me-410s damaged - Lt Barrett (504)

Lt Col Thury (505) reported, "...we left the 'big friends' just before target time. I split the squadron into two task forces, taking 11 aircraft with me and sending 8 with Major Tower (505)....We discovered a huge dispersal area which ran north from Neuruppin a/f for almost two miles....we started a traffic pattern...accomplished 10 to 15 passes, leaving only when our ammunition was very low....whenever we made our pass too close to the a/f, accurate 40mm flak was tossed up at us. However, none of our 11 planes suffered battle damage....As we left, I counted about 35 large fires and 20 smaller ones....The smoke curled up to about 6,000 feet and blanketed an extensive area. It was truly a wonderful sight!...again, I attribute our remarkable success in strafing e/a to the fact that all Upper Squadron aircraft fire incendiary-type ammunition from two guns...we initiated our attack as the bombs began to fall on the airdrome which gave us perfect cover since most of the personnel had gone underground...."

Claims: 26/0/14 ground
- 3 U/ITEs destroyed, 1 Ju-88 destroyed, 1 He-lll damaged, 1 U/ITE damaged - Lt Col Thury (505) - 3 Me-410s destroyed, 1 Me-410 damaged - Lt Marvel (505)
- 2 Do-217s destroyed, 1 Do-217 damaged - F/O Rice (505)
- 1 Do-217 destroyed, 3 Do-217s damaged - Capt Starnes (505)
- 1 Do-217 destroyed, 1 Do-217 damaged - F/O Hupp (505)
- 1 Ju-88 destroyed, 2 Ju-88s damaged - Lt Withers (505)
- 1 Ju-88 destroyed, 1 Do217 destroyed, 2 Me-410s damaged - Lt Carr (505)
- 2 Ju-88s destroyed - Capt Farmer (505)
- 4 Ju-88s destroyed - Lt Caywood (505)
- 3 Ju-88s destroyed - Lt Phillippi (505)
- 3 Ju-88s destroyed, 2 Ju-88s damaged - Lt MacClarence (505)

Meanwhile, Major Tower (505) spotted Wittstock airfield. "...we picked out a dispersal area...set up a gunnery pattern on about 30 e/a parked in the woods....e/a were also parked in front of approximately five hangars and also inside the hangars. I estimate that at least 30 aircraft were parked wing tip to wing tip in the area east of the hangars....We made between 12 and 15 passes and stopped only when we had expended nearly all of our ammo....of my section of 8 aircraft, five of us were hit by light flak; there were no tracers so we weren't able to find the guns and eliminate them. All of my section returned home safely...it was a merry day and I wish there might be more like it...."

Claims: 37/0/19 ground
- 2 Ju-88s destroyed, 2 Me-410s destroyed, 2 Do-217s destroyed, 2 Hs-129s destroyed, 1 Ju-88 damaged, 1 Do-217 damaged, 1 Me-410 damaged - Major Tower (505)
- 2 Ju-88s destroyed, 2 Me-410s destroyed, 2 Me-ll0s damaged, 1 Ju-88 damaged - Lt Irion (505)
- 4 Ju-88s destroyed, 2 Ju-88s damaged - Lt Biggs (505)
- 4 Ju-88s destroyed, 1 Ju-88 damaged, 1 FW-189 damaged, 1 Ju-52 damaged - Capt Corey (505)
- 2 Ju-88s destroyed, 3 Do-217s destroyed, 2 Ju-52s damaged - Lt Paul (505)
- 3 Do-217s destroyed, 2 Ju-88s destroyed, 3 U/ISEs damaged - Lt Murphy (505)
- 2 Ju-88s destroyed, 1 Do-217 destroyed, 1 Ju-88 damaged - Lt Guyton (505)
- 4 Me-ll0s destroyed, 1 He-lll destroyed, 1 Me-ll0 damaged, 1 U/IME damaged - Lt Burch (505)
Losses/damaged:
- Major Tower (505), slight damage due to AA fire; returned unhurt
- "Several" 504th aircraft - slight damage due to AA fire; all returned safely
- Four 505th aircraft - slight damage due to AA fire; all returned unhurt

Comment: Lt Col Shafer reported, "...those red-nosed P-47s gave a very good exhibition on indiscriminate and dangerous strafing...called them on 'C' channel...no response...they did not join our pattern or set up one of their own, but fired from all angles and even 180 degrees to each other...did not pick targets, rather sprayed a whole line of enemy aircraft...." Note: "red-nosed" P-47s were the 56th Fighter Group.

11 April '45
No. 257   F/0#1944A   (1023-1607)
This was a P.T.W.S. mission to Ingolstadt, Germany. Weather was CAVU. Bombers "clobbered" the target. No enemy aircraft were seen, nor was there any flak. Escort on withdrawal (from the target area) was very difficult as our stream of bombers was flanked by streams of bombers on either side. The three parallel streams were flying a very close formation.

12, 13, 14 April '45
No missions flown.

15 April '45
No. 258　　　F/O#1989A　　　(1147-1645)

Flew an escort mission to Ulm, Germany. This was the Group's first time as escort for the 9th Air Force. Picked up B-26s at Ulm and brought them back to Selestade. Experienced 6/10 weather. Flak was heavy, meager and accurate over Hausach.

Losses/damaged:
- Lt Roland E. Gousie (505), engine failure; forced to parachute in the vicinity of Herrenburg - POW

16 April '45
No. 259　　　F/O#1997A　　　(1203-1828)

Sixty-two aircraft took off for a fighter sweep/area patrol/strafing mission to the Regensburg area. During the mission, the Group broke its own record for aircraft destroyed and became the only 8th Air Force Group to destroy over 100 aircraft on the ground on two separate missions.

Overall Claims: 503rd　31 / 0　18 ground
504th　　　　　　48 / 0 / 13 ground
505th　　　　　　39 / 0 / 7 ground
339th Totals　　118 / 0 / 38 ground
(8th Air Force Totals 724 / 0 / 373 ground)

To accomplish this, each squadron split off to attack separate targets. The 503rd found and attacked five airfields. Three were abandoned because of intense light flak, but two others were aggressively strafed. One flight tried fields at Pilzen and southeast of Prague, but both were too hot to tackle. They then saw some 78th Fighter Group aircraft over Krulupy airfield and joined their gunnery pattern though the field was already badly beat up when they got there. They made 8 or 9 passes.

Claims: 4/0/10 ground
- 1 U/ITE destroyed, 1 U/ITE damaged - Lt Hill (503)
- 1 Do-217 destroyed, 3 U/ITEs damaged - Lt Gokey (503)
- 2 FW-190s destroyed, 1 FW-190 damaged, 1 Me-109 damaged - Lt Haidle (503)
- 1 Me-109 damaged - Lt Frisch (503)
- 1 FW-190 damaged - Lt Boyd (503)
- 1 U/ITE damaged - Lt Preddy (503)

Captain Ammon (503) was leading a single, four-aircraft flight when they spotted Prague/Kbely. There he would set the all time record for an 8th Air Force pilot when he destroyed eleven aircraft on the ground, while the other three destroyed sixteen more.

He reported, "...I was leading a flight...my first pass over the edge of the field to draw flak, and shot up a He-lll as I went by....spotted two flak positions...we shot these positions up on our second pass and set up a 180 degree traffic pattern...we really went to work on the parked e/a, and I counted 24 fires before a Duxford Squadron (78th FG) came in and started shooting up everything in sight. They did not ask to join us or try to join our pattern, but came in from all directions. They forced me to break off two passes and endangered my whole flight....we finally got the traffic reorganized and made about three more passes before I got hit. My cockpit filled with smoke, so I called off my flight and headed for home...."

Claims: 27/0/9 ground
- 4 Me-109s destroyed, 2 FW-190s destroyed, 3 Ju-88s destroyed, 2 He-llls destroyed, 2 FW-190s damaged, 2 JU-88s damaged - Capt Ammon (503)
- 3 Me-109s destroyed, 2 Ju-88s destroyed, 1 He-lll destroyed, 1 Me-109 damaged, 2 Ju-88s damaged Lt Chetneky (503)
- 4 Ju-88s destroyed, 2 FW-190s damaged - Lt Ferrell (503)
- 4 Ju-88s destroyed, 1 FW-190 destroyed, 1 Me-109 destroyed, 1 Ju-88 damaged - Lt Byers (503) Lt Col Clark (504) had compass trouble and reported,

"...we proceeded to Klatovy airfield, found 25-plus fighter aircraft there...no flak...set up strafing pattern...seeing we had more aircraft than needed, I reassembled part of the squadron...proceeded to a large airfield at Bedejovice where we found at least 500 e/a of all types. These e/a completely covered the whole field. Quickly planning an attack to check for flak we came in low from the south with the sun at our backs. The aircraft destroyed on this field burned quickly after a very few rounds being fired...just as I was passing over an e/a it exploded blowing the (German) crew chief, who was in the cockpit, over my left wing. A large piece of this FW-190 hit my wing on the left side. By this time the flak was very heavy so I called the section and told them not to make any more passes as the flak was too thick. Because of the flak only four e/a were destroyed on this field....found another field near Platting with a great number of aircraft dispersed around it...going down to check for flak...we destroyed a number of Me-109s and FW-190s...flak was too heavy, so I quit the field...south of the town found another dispersal area...again heavy flak...made one pass at Straubling a/d and then headed home...."

Claims: 48/0/13 ground
- 5 FW-190s destroyed, 2 Me-109s destroyed, 1 Ju-52 destroyed, 1 Me-109 damaged - Lt Col Clark (504)
- 1 Me-109 destroyed, 1 FW-190 destroyed - F/O R. W. Smith (504)
- 3 Me-109s destroyed, 2 Me-109s damaged - Lt Aldrich (504)
- 2 FW-190s destroyed - Lt Hunt (504)
- 2 Me-109s destroyed, 1 U/I transport destroyed, 1 FW-190 damaged, 2 U/ITEs damaged - Lt Creswell (504)
- 1 Me-109 destroyed, 3 Me-109s damaged - Lt Allers (504)
- 4 Me-109s destroyed - Lt Blizzard (504)
- 3 Me-109s destroyed - Lt Chenez (504)
- 3 FW-190s destroyed - Capt Everson (504)
- 2 Me-109s destroyed, 2 Me-109s damaged - Lt Carter (504)
- 2 FW-190s destroyed, 1 Me-109 destroyed - Major Hathorn (504)
- 2 Me-109s destroyed, 1 FW-190 destroyed - Lt Clifton (504)
- 1 U/I transport destroyed, 1 Me-109 damaged, 1 FW-190 damaged - Major Julian (504)
- 1 Me-109 destroyed, 1 FW-190 destroyed - Lt Krueger (504)
- 1 Me-109 destroyed - Lt Barto (504)
- 1 Me-109 destroyed, 3 FW-190s destroyed - Lt Hudson (504)
- 2 Me-109s destroyed - Lt Hermansen (504)
- 1 FW-190 destroyed - Lt Kunz (504)

The 505th also split up to cover more area. Lt Col Thury

(505) took nine aircraft to hit Prien airfield on the southwest tip of Lake Chien, and dispatched eight other aircraft to hit others. He reported, :...Prien field was all grass...Jerry had excellently camouflaged his planes and dispersed them in wooded areas...didn't help...found a total of 20 e/a there, and we destroyed them all...two light guns were firing throughout the attack and four of our aircraft sustained minor battle damage...."
Claims: 20/0/0 ground
- 1 Me-109 destroyed, 1 U/ISE destroyed - Lt Col Thury (505)
- 1 FW-190 destroyed, 1 U/ISE destroyed - Lt Floyd W. Smith (505)
- 2 U/ISEs destroyed, 1 FW-190 destroyed - Lt Woolery (505)
- 1 U/ISE destroyed - Lt Pesanka (505)
- 4 U/ISEs destroyed - Capt Corey (505)
- 1 U/ISE destroyed, 1 U/ITE destroyed - Lt MacClarence (505)
- 1 Me-109 destroyed, 1 Ju-88 destroyed - Lt Marvel (505)
- 1 Me-109 destroyed, 1 Ju-88 destroyed - Lt Guyton (505)
- 1 Ju-88 destroyed, 1 U/ITE destroyed - Capt Farmer (505)

Lt Carr (505) reported, "...led two other aircraft to a permanent type airfield near Wallersdorf, but very few planes on it...directly across the Isar River was a small grass field that held about 40 Me-109s and one Ju-52...made one pass... claimed two aircraft there before 88mm and 40mm opened up... found another field outside of Passan...Jerry now fully alerted...one pass, only, because of all the 20mm flak...field lit up like a Christmas tree...all returned safely...." Claims: 6/0/2 ground
- 1 Me-109 destroyed, 1 Ju-88 destroyed, 1 U/ITE destroyed - Lt Biggs (505)
- 1 Do-217 destroyed, 2 Me-109s damaged - Lt Carr (505) - 1 Ju-52 destroyed, 1 Ju-88 destroyed - Lt Burch (505)

Captain Loveless (505) reported, "...took five aircraft to check out several fields...all looked like flak traps and were left alone....found an airfield across the Inn River not shown on the map...found the 353rd Fighter Group working it over...joined their pattern since there were lots of grounded Jerries to be shot up...." All returned safely.
Claims: 13/0/5 ground
- 3 FW-190s destroyed, 1 Ju-87 damaged - Capt Loveless (505)
- 3 FW-190s destroyed - F/O Steiger (505)
- 3 Me-109s destroyed, 1 U/ISE destroyed, 1 Me-109 damaged, 2 Ju-88s damaged - Lt Caywood (505)
- 2 Me-109s destroyed, 1 Ju-88 destroyed, 1 Ju-88 damaged - F/O Rice (505)
Losses/damaged:
- Lt Col Clark (504), damaged by pieces of an exploding FW-190 - returned unhurt
- Lt Aldrich (504), damaged by AA fire near Budejovice; canopy damaged, glass slivers in face - able to return safely

Comment: Three other 8th Air Force Groups also scored over 100 ground kills on this date, but none without loss as did the 339th. The 4th Fighter Group paid the most. They destroyed 105 aircraft, destroying 61 aircraft at Praha aerodrome, Czechoslovakia, but losing eight aircraft to flak. Two were KIA; six were POWs.

17 April '45
No. 260   F/O#2006A   (1135-1800)
Fifty-five aircraft took off for a bomber escort/fighter sweep to Pilzen, Germany. The escort was broken near Selbat as each squadron went to an assigned area, breaking into flights there. One Me-262 was seen and shot down, but again, it was a big day against grounded aircraft.
Overall Claims: 1/0/0 air
503rd   5 / 0 / 0 ground
504th   23 / 0 / 0 ground
505th   39 / 0 / 9 ground
339th Totals   67 / 0 / 9 ground
(Total 8th AF claims 286 / 0 / 113 ground)

The 503rd "...attacked Klatovy airfield which had been hit by another group...destroyed four e/a there...Eisendorf airfield which was littered with burned-out aircraft was also strafed for one destroyed...two hangars burned...four other fields investigated, but extremely intense, light and accurate flak forced withdrawal...one Me-262 shot down southeast of Rokycany...."
Claims: 1/0/0 air   5/0/0 ground
- 1 Me-262 shot down - Lt Campbell (503)
- 1 Ju-88 destroyed/ground - Lt Potthoff (503)
- 2 Ju-88s destroyed/ground, 1 Me-262 destroyed/ground - Lt Frisch (503)
- 1 Me-109 destroyed/ground - Lt French (503)

The 504th "...proceeded to an area south and west of Praha...went back to Klatovy where we had hit the day before...four Fieseler Storches, not there then, were immediately destroyed along with 4 Me-109s...reformed and proceeded to airfields in the vicinity of Amberg...fields had been well worked over...several aircraft were found and destroyed along with a number of Ju-88s parked in some woods...."
Claims: 23/0/0 ground
- 6 Me-109s destroyed, 2 Ju-88s destroyed - Lt Orcutt (504)
- 1 Me-109 destroyed, 2 Ju-88s destroyed, 1 Storch destroyed - Lt Clifton (504)
- 2 Me-109s destroyed, 1 Ju-88 destroyed, 2 Storchs destroyed - Capt Everson (504)
- 1 Me-109 destroyed, 1 Ju-88 destroyed, 1 FW-190 destroyed, 1 Storch destroyed - Lt Hunt (504)
- 1 Ju-52 destroyed, 1 Storch destroyed - Lt Barrett (504)

Lt Col Thury (505) reported, "...with eighteen aircraft, we discovered and hit a dispersal area just southwest of Pocking...50-plus e/a in the area, dispersed among clumps of trees and excellently camouflaged. Jerry had done an even better job of camouflage than on the Prien a/f we hit on 16 April...Some of the e/a exploded, but most started to burn very slowly at first before developing into raging fires...we counted claims only after observing positive fires. When we left there were 25 hugh fires and 14 smaller ones, and smoke from the e/a was curling up to 6,000 feet...I'm convinced that some of our claims would not have caught fire were it not for the fact that all my ships have two guns firing incendiary ammo. Unfortunately, we used the last of our incendiary ammo during the strafing on 17 April and are unable to procure any more...there were two 20mm guns and one

40mm gun firing at us during the attack...Lt Irion (505) knocked out one 20mm position...the remaining gunners weren't too eager after that...(claims here: 39/0/8 ground)...went to Ort dispersal across the Inn River from Pocking...Capt Loveless (505) made a test pass, damaged one Ju-88...flak was too intense so we called it a day...all returned safely...."
Claims: 39/0/9 ground
- 2 Me-109s destroyed, 2 U/ISEs destroyed, 1 Ju-88 destroyed, 1 U/ISE damaged - Lt Col Thury (505)
- 1 Ju-88 destroyed, 1 Me-109 destroyed - Lt. F. W. Smith (505)
- 1 Ju-88 destroyed, 1 Me-109 destroyed, 1 Me-109 damaged - Lt Woolery (505)
- 1 Me-109 destroyed, 1 He-111 destroyed - Lt Pesanka (505)
- 2 Me-109s destroyed, 2 Ju-88s destroyed - Capt Bline (505)
- 1 He-111 destroyed, 1 Me-109 destroyed, 2 Me-109s damaged, 1 Ju-188 damaged - Lt Murphy (505)
- 1 He-111 destroyed, 1 U/ITE destroyed, 1 Me-109 destroyed - Lt Marvel (505)
- 1 Ju-188 destroyed - Lt Paul (505)
- 1 Ju-188 destroyed, 1 He-111 destroyed, 1 Ju-88 damaged - Lt MacClarence (505)
- 1 Do-217 destroyed - F/O Hupp (505)
- 1 Ju-88 destroyed - Lt Biggs (505)
- 1 Ju-88 destroyed, 1 Me-109 damaged - Lt Carr (505)
- 2 Do-217s destroyed - Lt Bunch (505) - 2 Ju-188s destroyed, 1 Me-109 destroyed - Capt Corey (505)
- 1 Do-217 destroyed, 1 U/ITE destroyed - Capt Diefenbeck (505)
- 4 Do-217s destroyed, 1 Me-109 destroyed, 1 Ju-88 damaged, 1 Do-217 damaged - Capt Loveless (505)
- 1 Me-110 destroyed - Lt Irion (505)
Losses/damaged:
- Capt Raymond F. Reuter (503), missing, unknown cause (flying with Preddy)
- Lt William R. Preddy (503), missing, unknown cause - Lt Potthoff (503), slight damage from AA fire; returned
- One 503rd aircraft, slight damage from AA fire; returned

Comments: - Lt Preddy was killed this date. He is buried at St. Avold, France, alongside his brother, George E. Preddy, Jr., fighter ace with the 352nd Fighter Group who was killed by American AA fire on 25 December 1944.
- Lt Col Thury (505) did not have to worry about the lack of incendiary ammunition because, unknown to him, this was their last major strafing mission of the war.

18 April '45
No. 261   F/O#2017A   (1003-1640)
This was a P.T.W.S. mission to Kolin, Czechoslovakia. Weather was 3/10 to 7/10. 3rd BD B-17s were 14 minutes early. The bombers apparently had some difficulty finding the target as some made a second run before dropping. The results, however, were excellent. Several jets were seen in the area, and the Group's last air-to-air combat (with German aircraft!) took place.
Claims: 1/0/1 air
- 1 AR-234 shot down - Lt Col Shafer (503)
- 1 Me-262 damaged - Lt Col Thury (505)
Losses/damaged:
- Lt Hill (503), bellied in on final approach; slight damage to aircraft, pilot unhurt Comment: The last air-to-air victory scored by the 339th was the only jet bomber they shot down, an AR-234. Lt Col Shafer (503) wasn't very impressed with it. "...During this engagement I did not drop my wing tanks, but was easily able to overtake the jet... seems to lack the speed and maneuverability of the Me-262...however...takes a lot of punishment because I saw at least thirty strikes while I was firing...."

19 April '45
No. 262   F/O#2024A   (0730-1415)
Flew a freelance patrol to Dresden, Germany. Met Russian fighters for the first time, and the last "almost air-to-air combat" took place. Lt Col Propst (503) reported, "...met some LAGG-5s at Dahme...very quick triggered boys and fired at Capt Ammon (503) when he went down to investigate... no damage done...no fire returned...." Capt Sargent (504) reported much the same, "...Lt Langohr (504) jumped by a thick wing S/E, probably a YAK. Russian aircraft made a pass at him and, two turns were made before the Russian broke off into the clouds...." The rest of the mission was uneventful. Many small towns between Berlin and Dresden were burning.

20 April '45
No. 263   F/O#2039A   (0728-1250)
This was a P.T.W.S. mission to Neuruppin, Germany. 3rd BD B-17s did not fly the briefed course. Formations within boxes were good, but distances between boxes were too great. No enemy aircraft or flak. Mission was uneventful, and all returned safely.

21 April '45
No. 264   F/O#2053A   (0813-1445)
Fifty-five aircraft took off for an escort/area patrol/freelance strafing mission to Nordlingen/Munich/Stuttgart. The 505th lost one aircraft on takeoff, but the rest made it off safely. Picked up 1st BD B-17s in very bad weather conditions. Our bombers had bombed and left the area before we reached the target. Experienced heavy, moderate and inaccurate flak in the target area. All aircraft returned safely, but were forced to land at Bassingborn due to heavy cross winds.
Losses/damaged:
- One 505th aircraft, engine failure on takeoff, crashed; aircraft destroyed, pilot unhurt
- One 505th aircraft, slight damage on landing due to cross winds; pilot unhurt

Comment: It was unknown at the time, but this was to be the the last combat mission flown by the 339th Fighter Group.

The war was over for the 339th.

Summary of Operations

The 503rd, 504th, and 505th Fighter Squadrons of the 339th Fighter Group flew their first combat mission on 30 April 1944, a shallow fighter sweep into France. Their final combat mission would be flown on 21 April 1945, a strafing mission deep into southeast Germany. In between, over 262 more combat missions would be flown over Belgium, Holland, France, Germany, Denmark and Czechoslovakia.

Besides providing escort for 8th Air Force bombers, they also flew escort for the 9th and 15th Air Forces, and for R.A.F. Lancasters and Spitfires. Other type missions flown were: fighter sweeps, strafing, area patrols, photo-recon, dive bombing, glide bombing, radio relay, air/sea rescue, weather, etc.

During these missions, they would shoot down or destroy almost every type aircraft the Luftwaffe had - from gliders and bi-planes to jet fighters and jet bombers. These included: AR-234s, Do-217s, Fiedler Storches, FW-190s, FW-200s, He-111s, Hs-129s, Ju-52s, Ju-87s, Ju-88s, Ju-188s, Me-109s, Me-110s, Me-309s, Me-262s, Me-410s, "pick-a-back" Ju-88s/FW-190s, plus other unidentified types.

Besides aircraft, every conceivable type of ground target was attacked: from locomotives, rolling stock and railway yards to factories and bridges; from flak positions and hangars to barges; from truck convoys to single motorcycles and cars; and from troop concentrations to individual soldiers.

The cost of this success would be heavy, as losses would exceed their total original strength. At least 63 pilots would be killed on operations; 16 more were lost in training accidents or on the ground; 29 other pilots were captured and became POWs; 7 others went down, evaded capture and returned safely.

Pilots and aircraft were shot down by German aircraft and German anti-aircraft fire. More would be lost to engine failure, to midair collisions, to accidents on takeoff or landing, on training flights over England, to weather, to navigational errors, to vertigo, to flying into trees or power lines, or just disappearing. Still others would be shot down by American aircraft or by American anti-aircraft fire.

Although in combat for less than one year, the 339th would set many Group, Squadron and individual records for the entire 8th Air Force:

- Most enemy aircraft destroyed, air and ground, by a Group in its first year of combat in the ETO - 653 plus

- Most enemy aircraft destroyed on the ground by a Group in its first year of combat in the ETO - 423.5 plus - Most enemy aircraft destroyed, air and ground, by a Group during one month- 286.5 in April 1945 - Most enemy aircraft destroyed on the ground by a Group during one month-269.5 in April 1945 - Of the thirty-five 8th Air Force pilots to destroy at least 10 aircraft on the ground, six were 339th. Lt Col Thury (505) was No. 2 with 25.5 ground claims.

- Of the thirty-nine 8th Air Force pilots to destroy at least 5 aircraft on the ground during a single flight, ten were 339th.

- Most enemy aircraft destroyed, air and ground, by a Squadron in its first year of combat - 352 by the 505th - Most enemy aircraft destroyed on the ground by a Squadron in its first year of combat - 267.5 by the 505th

- Most enemy aircraft destroyed on a single mission by a Squadron - 60 on the ground by the 505th on 10 April 1945

- Most enemy aircraft destroyed on a single mission by an individual pilot - 9 on the ground each by Captain Robert H. Ammon (503) on 16 April 1945 and Lt Leon Orcutt (504) on 17 April 1945

- 339th pilots among the first Americans to witness and report artillery action between Russians and Germans east of Berlin - 3 February 1945

- 339th pilots among the first fighter groups to operate extensively in Czechoslovakia - 20 February 1945 - 339th pilots flew on the first 8th Air Force mission giving fighter support to bombers of the 15th Air Force - 22 March 1945

The Group received a Distinguished Unit Citation for its action on 10-11 December 1944. This award, those records set, the combat narrative, and the various charts show the 339th Fighter Group's contribution to the war. They did their share and much more.

339th Fighter Group Roster of Pilots

Pilots of the 339th Fighter Group Headquarters

Allman, Johnnie M.	2/Lt
Clark, William C.	Lt Col
Dowell, Charles W.	Capt
Goldenberg, Carl T.	Lt Col
Hager, Rose F.	Major
Harry, G. P.	1/Lt
Hathorn, Vernon B., Jr.	Major
Henry, John B., Jr.	Col
Long, Robert D.	Lt Col
McPharlin, Michael G.H.	Major
Oliver, Bernard J.	Capt
Propst, John R.	Lt Col
Scruggs, Harold W.	Lt Col
Smith, Robert H.	Capt
Wight, Carroll H.	Major
Wright, Ellis E., Jr.	Capt

Pilots of the 503rd Fighter Squadron

Aitken, John	Major
Allen, Bernie A.	1/Lt
Ammon, Robert H.	Capt
Beavers, Edward E.	Capt
Behrend, William W.	Capt
Boychuck, Alec	Capt
Boyd, William H.	1/Lt
Brown, Robert B.	1/Lt
Bryan, William E., Jr.	Major
Bush, Jerry P.	1/Lt
Butler, Frederick	Capt
Byers, John R.	1/Lt
Caler, Rollin C.	1/Lt
Campbell, John C.	1/Lt
Carothers, John M.	1/Lt
Carter, Walter T.	Capt
Chetneky, Steve J.	1/Lt
Clark, Jack W.	2/Lt
Cloud, Carl E.	Capt
Coe, Charles S.	1/Lt
Connors, Arthur F.	2/Lt
Cozad, John W.	2/Lt
Crockett, James R.	1/Lt
Crump, Alan F.	2/Lt
Cunnick, John W.	1/Lt
Deary, Ralph H.	2/Lt
Dickens, Robert L., Jr.	2/Lt
Edens, Malcomb B.	Capt
Erickson, Wayne R.	1/Lt
Farrell, Joseph G.	Capt
Ferrell, Clarence I.	1/Lt
Fickel, Paul D.	1/Lt
Fiorito, Leonard J.	Capt
Flaherty, Edward C.	2/Lt
Foard, William W.	1/Lt
Folwell, Nathan T.	Capt
France, James L.	F/O
Francis, Luther B.	1/Lt
Fratello, Tom C.	F/O
French, Carl H.	1/Lt
French, Lloyd J.	Capt
Frisch, Robert J.	1/Lt
Ganer, Seymour	2/Lt
Gauger, Henry W.	1/Lt
Gerard, Francis R.	Capt
Girone, Felix J.	2/Lt
Gokey, John W.	Capt
Gordon, William R.	F/O
Grad, Carl E.	F/O
Graham, Ethelbert H., Jr.	1/Lt
Grothendieck, Carl W.	F/O
Haidle, Elmer E.	1/Lt
Harte, Allan S., Jr.	Capt
Hauff, John J.	1/Lt

339th Fighter Group Roster of Pilots

Hawkins, Anthony G.	Capt	Steier, Arthur H.	F/O	Dey, Russel C.	2/Lt
Haynes, Harry E.	Capt	Stephenson, Enoch B.	Major	Dunn, John W.	1/Lt
Henderson, Harvey E.	Lt Col	Stevens, Bradford V.	Capt	Dunn, Robert	1/Lt
Hill, Ralph S., Jr.	1/Lt	Stillwell, Frank M.	Capt	Eisenhart, Lee D.	Capt
Hubbell, William R.	2/Lt	Stockton, William D.	1/Lt	Everson, Kirke B., Jr.	Capt
Hull, James F.	2/Lt	Talcott, Franklin D.	2/Lt	French, Bernard J.	2/Lt
Hutton, John E., Jr.	2/Lt	Terrats, Estaban A.	1/Lt	Fulton, Jospeh O., Jr.	2/Lt
Johnson, Allen D.	2/Lt	Titus, Robert D.	1/Lt	Garland, Edgar L.	F/O
Johnson, Donald W.	Capt	Warren, Don W.	1/Lt	Gilbert, Kenneth L.	Capt
Johnson, Raymond, G.	1/Lt	West, Rodney C.	1/Lt	Gooch, William D.	F/O
Johnson, William G.	2/Lt	Wells, Richard G.	F/O	Gordon, William R.	F/O
Johnstone, George J.	2/Lt	Whitelaw, Richard S.	Capt	Gravette, Edgar B.	Lt Col
Keim, Paul T.	1/Lt	Wilson, John P.	Capt	Green, Claude W.	F/O
Kelly, George P., III	1/Lt	Wolfort, Joseph	1/Lt	Greer, Nile C.	Capt
Kernisky, George	2/Lt	Wright, Lyle M.	1/Lt	Griffith, Walter B.	1/Lt
King, John B.	2/Lt	Wyatt, Valdee	Capt	Guernsey, Frank D.	Capt
Knott, Clarence W.	Capt	Wyer, Albert L.	1/Lt	Gustke, Richard N.	F/O
Krauss, Richard E.	1/Lt			Haslam, Frederick C.	1/Lt
Leitner, Frank W.	1/Lt			Havighurst, Robert C.	1/Lt
Lettus, Andrew N.	F/O			Hendricks, Charles J.	2/Lt
Linger, Claude D.	1/Lt			Herrmann, Ray F.	Capt

Pilots of the 504th Fighter Squadron

Lowery, Arthur L.	1/Lt			Hermansen, Cephas	2/Lt
MacKenzie, David A.	1/Lt			Hoffman, William R.	1/Lt
Manke, Alfred O.	1/Lt			Hudson, Will M.	1/Lt
Mankie, James A.	2/Lt			Hunerwadel, Hugh P.	2/Lt
Marsh, Lester C.	1/Lt			Hunt, Harlan F.	1/Lt
Mayer, Raymond D.	1/Lt	Aldrich, Richard T.	1/Lt	Hunter, Charles M.	1/Lt
McElwee, Francis E.	1/Lt	Allers, Lorne W.		Hurley, William T.	Capt
McNally, Richard M.	2/Lt	Arnold, Merlin A.	2/Lt	Julian, William H.	Lt Col
McClish, Donald E.	Capt	Atteberry, Ray N.	2/Lt	Kernisky, George	2/Lt
Mele, Raymond R.	F/O	Ball, Melville R.	Capt	Kerrigan, John S.	2/Lt
Meyer, Victor W.	1/Lt	Ballard, Jerome J.	1/Lt	King, James G.	2/Lt
Miller, Harold	1/Lt	Barrett, L. Jack	1/Lt	Knapp, Frank J.	2/Lt
Moreland, Kenneth E.	1/Lt	Barto, Vernon M.	1/Lt	Knight, George	1/Lt
Morrow, Ralph E., Jr.	1/Lt	Bates, Arthur W., Jr.	1/Lt	Knipper, Robert R.	2/Lt
Mulvey, Robert F.	1/Lt	Beadle, Ermy L.	2/Lt	Krueger, Donald F.	2/Lt
Ostrow, Nathan	Capt	Bennett, Carroll W.	1/Lt	Kuhlman, Robert M.	Capt
Perry, William W.	Capt	Berguson, Kenneth V.	1/Lt	Kunz, Leonard A.	1/Lt
Petitt, Philip E.	Capt	Blizzard, Robert V.	1/Lt	Kurth, Otis A.	1/Lt
Porter, George W.	1/Lt	Boden, Hetzel K.	2/Lt	Langohr, Bill E.	1/Lt
Potthoff, John P.	1/Lt	Bradner, Robert H.	1/Lt	Larson, Duane S.	1/Lt
Poutre, Lawrence	Capt	Brownshadel, Elton J.	2/Lt	Loskill, Harry G.	1/Lt
Preddy, William R.	1/Lt	Cabanne, William C.	1/Lt	Mason, Clair M.	Capt
Price, Jack B.	1/Lt	Caldwell, Merle F.	1/Lt	McLure, James M.	Capt
Rawls, Dennis B., Jr.	1/Lt	Carter, Lyle M.	1/Lt	Mead, Charles M.	1/Lt
Reuter, Raymond F.	Capt	Cernicky, Melvin L.	1/Lt	Montell, Richard W.	1/Lt
Reynolds, Gardner H.	Capt	Chenez, Gordon H.	1/Lt	Myer, Paul M.	1/Lt
Riggs, Gaston H.	1/Lt	Clifton, Frank A.	1/Lt	Nowlin, Louis E.	
Robinson, James G.	Capt	Cohen, Gilbert G.	F/O	Orcutt, Leon M., Jr.	1/Lt
Sams, Thomas G.	Capt	Cole, Douglas P.	1/Lt	O'Sullivan, Walter R., Jr.	1/Lt
Shafer, Dale E., Jr.	Lt Col	Corbin, Luther L.	1/Lt	Ott, Maurice D.	1/Lt
Shake, Charles E.	2/Lt	Craigo, Cecil E., Jr.	Capt	Pastor, William J.	2/Lt
Smith, Linwood P.	2/Lt	Creswell, Ray	1/Lt	Penny, Donald E.	1/Lt
Smith, Robert C.	1/Lt	Croker, Robert C.	1/Lt	Penrose, Richard C.	Capt
Spaziano, Vincent J.	1/Lt	Degner, Ralph M.	2/Lt	Peter, Lewis S., Jr.	Major

339th Fighter Group Roster of Pilots

Rosen, George J.	1/Lt	Burns, Robert F.	2/Lt	Marts, Jay F.	1/Lt
Routt, Bill C.	Major	Byrd, Cecil L.	1/Lt	Marvel, Thomas W.	1/Lt
Rutan, Frederick S., Jr.	1/Lt	Cain, Richard C.	1/Lt	McMahan, Bruce D.	1/Lt
Sainlar, Jerome J.	1/Lt	Carr, Vernon D.	1/Lt	McMahon, Peter J.	1/Lt
Saleem, Albert	2/Lt	Caywood, Herbert L.	1/Lt	McMullen, James P.	2/Lt
Schneider, Lewis H.	2/Lt	Coker, Joseph R.	F/O	Miller, Robert C.	Capt
Sargent, Robert F.	Capt	Conner, Bertis A.	1/Lt	Mitchell, Raymond M.	Capt
Shively, Jack E.	1/Lt	Corey, Harry R.	Capt	Moore, William R.	1/Lt
Showker, Fred S.	Capt	Daniell, J. S.	1/Lt	Mudge, William F., Jr.	1/Lt
Siegel, Gordon J.S.	Capt	Decourcy, James L.		Muller, James B.	2/Lt
Smith, Lee W.	2/Lt	Diefenbeck, James S.	Capt	Nay, Martin N.	1/Lt
Spriggs, Alfred G.	1/Lt	Evans, Frank T.	1/Lt	O'Brien, Richard C.	1/Lt
Stachura, Robert M.	F/O	Everett, Harold M.	1/Lt	Olander, Richard B.	Capt
Stapp, Glen E.	F/O	Ewing, Philip H.	1/Lt	Opitz, William R.	2/Lt
Stockman, Hervey S.	1/Lt	Farmer, Owen P., Jr.	Capt	Palmer, Gerald W.	2/Lt
Smith, Roland W.	F/O	Fish, Wesley G.	2/Lt	Paul, Robert H., Jr.	1/Lt
Sutton, John L.	1/Lt	Frink, James P.	2/Lt	Perry, Gordon F.	2/Lt
Talley, Vernon B.	1/Lt	Gelpke, Robert E.	F/O	Pesanka, John	1/Lt
Thibert, Henry G.	Capt	Gilbert, Kenneth C.	1/Lt	Petticrew, Stanley S.	F/O
Thistlethwaite, Edward A.	2/Lt	Gilmer, Harry U.	2/Lt	Phillippi, William R	1/Lt
Thompson, Ralph P.	1/Lt	Girzi, Henry E., Jr.	1/Lt	Powell, Lawrence J.	1/Lt
Trester, John R.	1/Lt	Gousie, Roland E.	1/Lt	Reid, Langhorne, Jr.	Major
Van Cleave, Ely M.	1/Lt	Graham, Gerald E.	1/Lt	Rice, John J.	2/Lt
Waters, Frank T.	1/Lt	Gregory, Vincent L.	2/Lt	Rich, George T.	Capt
Waymire, Harvey R.	1/Lt	Guyton, William R.	Capt	Rohm, Richard A.	1/Lt
Welch, Roger	Capt	Hanseman, Chris J.	1/Lt	Sawicki, Joseph F., Jr.	2/Lt
Wells, Arlen W.	Capt	Hanson, James R.	1/Lt	Shaw, Bernell V.	2/Lt
Weller, Richard E.	Capt	Heneghan, Floyd P.	2/Lt	Shepherd, George W.	F/O
Wilcox, Richard H.	1/Lt	Holloway, John G.	Capt	Sirochman, Andrew	1/Lt
Winkelman, Myer R.	2/Lt	Howard, Harry F.	1/Lt	Slovak, William R.	2/Lt
Wood, Robert T.	Capt	Howard, Waldon E.	1/Lt	Smith, Floyd W.	1/Lt
Zeine, Donald A.	1/Lt	Hrico, George	Capt	Smith, Shirley K.	Capt
		Hupp, Ellis E., Jr.	F/O	Staggers, Theodore R.	2/Lt
		Irion, Robert E.	Capt	Starnes, James R.	Capt
		Jaaskelainen, William	1/Lt	Steiger, James A.	2/Lt
		Jackson, Boyd O.	1/Lt	Steiger, Leroy A.	2/Lt
Pilots of the 505th Fighter Squadron		Jessup, Tom N.	2/Lt	Stevens, Richard C.	1/Lt
		Johnson, Evan M.	Capt	Stewart, Carl R.	1/Lt
		Jones, George W.	1/Lt	Stiles, Bert	1/Lt
		Jones, William A.	2/Lt	Stoudt, Leland M.	2/Lt
		Knight, George	1/Lt	Strong, Roland W.	1/Lt
Ammerman, Roy W.	1/Lt	Karhuma, Karl O.	2/Lt	Tannous, Richard H.	1/Lt
Ananian, Steve	1/Lt	Knighton, Ralph M.	2/Lt	Thieme, Richard G.	1/Lt
Armistead, Walter M.	1/Lt	Kotora, Harold J.	2/Lt	Thomas, Kessler O.	1/Lt
Baker, James A.	2/Lt	Kovar, Robert J.	2/Lt	Thury, Joseph L.	Lt Col
Ball, Edwin C.	1/Lt	Krauss, William H.	Capt	Tongue, Arthur E., Jr.	2/Lt
Becker, Leo H.	1/Lt	Lanfer, William A.	2/Lt	Tower, Archie A.	Major
Beecher, William M.	2/Lt	Larson, Donald A.	Major	Travis, Laird D.	2/Lt
Biggs, Oscar K.	1/Lt	Laverick, John H.	2/Lt	Wager, Evergard L.	1/Lt
Bline, J. Brooks	Capt	Lawes, Bayard F.	2/Lt	Wark, Raymond D.	2/Lt
Bloxham, Robert W.	Capt	Loveless, Philip M., Jr.	Capt	Wilcox, Russell W.	2/Lt
Booth, Billy B.	1/Lt	Luper, Arch B.	1/Lt	Withers, John C.	1/Lt
Brock, Thomas C.	F/O	Lynch, James L.	1/Lt	Woolery, James C.	1/Lt
Bungaard, Carl H.	1/Lt	MacClarence, William R.	1/Lt	Young, Allen D.	1/Lt
Burch, Hal	1/Lt	Malarz, Chester	Capt	Ziegler, Harry D.	1/Lt

339th Fighter Group

Pilot Articles

Rememberances By Men Of The 503rd Fighter Squadron

Bloody Sunday

by Nip Carter

I'm gonna be a little short of fuel when we get back to Fowlmere...and I'll be damned! They've shot up my hydraulics, and I'll have to shake the gear down.... These thoughts were running through my mind as I did evasive, uncoordinated turns while departing Polentz Airdrome near Leipzig on that fateful 21st of May '44, "Bloody Sunday" when every hired gun in Eighth Fighter command was area strafing to knock out transportation in Germany.

But let's do this by the numbers as we were taught in the good ole days and start at the beqinning of "Operation Chattanooga Choo Choo." Briefing was early, and it was cold. This was going to be a mission different from any we had flown in our brief three weeks of combat experience.

Operation Chattanooga Choo Choo was a special fighter sweep by all fighter groups in Eighth Air Force on 21 May '44, and the bombers stood down that day. The P-51 groups were given low level sweep sectors in eastern Germany, whereas the P-47 and P-38 groups swept sectors closer to England because of their more limited radius of action. The 4th Fighter Group had the rectangular sector from Berlin to the Baltic Sea. Our area encompassed Dresden, Leipzig and Magdeburg below Berlin.

After making notes on our knee clip boards at the briefing, we picked up E & E gear, chutes, dinghies, etc., and went out to our Mustangs. Mine was "Mon Petite," an affectionate term for my wife, Marie. I checked Mon Petite over with the crew chief and armorer before starting the engine. Enroute to takeoff position I saw Major Hal Scruggs pulled off on a revetment checking his aircraft. He indicated "thumbs down" meaning he'd have to abort. If memory serves me well, he was group lead that day and Don Larson of the 505th Squadron had to take over. Our mission for the day was to knock out German transport, rail engines (#1 priority), trucks, tug boats or anything that could move men and material. Our tactics for this ground attack mission were to hit our targets from the east on a "one-pass" basis to eliminate repeat passes and to emphasize surprise attacks, continuing to the west on our way back to Fowlmere as we covered the targets in our assigned sector. We proceeded to our sweep area of responsibility at high altitude, letting down through clouds in the easternmost part of our area, then fanned out to sweep on a westerly heading with squadrons and flights in a loosely line-abreast type formation. That gave us flexibility of movement and avoided making one big target for all that flak in our area. The flak map for Leipzig-Dresden was mostly red because Germany's synthetic fuel production and storage was concentrated there.

We began breaking out of clouds at 4 to 5,000 feet with scud all the way down to 1,500 feet. I could feel the adrenalin flow as we searched for transport of any type. Very soon we saw a canal with numerous tugs and barges on it. A slight turn to the right, down with the aircraft's nose, smooth out ball in center, line up sight and fire a short burst into the engine compartment. The ole 50-calibers struck, and I saw sparks, dust and wood hunks flying as I swung back to the left and pulled up to get back on course and to improve my field of vision. Railroad tracks coming up—no trains, damn it—wait now, off to the left a mile or so, an engine puffing away and pulling a long string of boxcars. Turn left, roll out smooth, drop nose while checking wingman and element—all okay—line up on the engineer's Compartment. Boy! My heart pounded as I started firing. My rounds hit a little low—up a little, fire again—most rounds slammed into the tender behind the cab. As I started my pull-up, my wingman really put a load into the engine. Steam and sparks were flying, and I was so pleased he'd gotten a good lick.

After we pulled up and back on course, I wagged my wings to close up the flight a bit since I was about to lose sight of my element. We leveled off about 2,000 feet, in and out of the scud. Checked course while searching for a new target. I really needed to hit one dead center this time. We dropped down a little for better visibility and...my God! Dead ahead, maybe three miles, was a big city and a BIG airfield. I thought to myself, *Polentz Airdrome at Leipzig!* The runway pattern, taxi strip and everything I saw confirmed Polentz. Aircraft were taxiing and taking off, and there was all sorts of activity and TARGETS.

I could see one JU-88 taking off in the same direction we were headed, one JU-88 taxiing almost at the end of the runway and one at the far end of the taxi strip headed in my direction. This is it, I told myself, and throttled back some to have a try at all three. I nosed over a little more, lined up the sights on one near take-off position, squeezed the trigger with my heart in my throat. The 50-calibers went right where I was aiming and it blew with lots of smoke and fire. Had to line up quickly with the second taxiing JU-88 as I was getting low—slight turn to the right, smoothed out controls as best I could and squeezed off another burst. Helluva deal! One engine started spewing smoke and fire, then it blazed from the wing root area. Now for the JU-88 that was taking off. I started to pull up and swing to the left when things got very noisy in my mustang's cockpit. I could see hits in my right wing. Not unnoticed during the preceding few seconds over the field were those red golf balls filling the air about me, but who has time for evasive action when you're getting your first chance to kill some German aircraft? A few explosions like firecrackers shook my plane, followed by smoke and glass flying from the lower part of the instrument panel. I headed for the deck in a wildly uncoordinated dive and realized I would never get to the JU-88 which had taken off. After terrorizing the locals by flying at rooftops for a couple of miles, I started climbing and hoped to get the flight together for the trip home.

The cloud cover had lifted for the climbout, but I didn't see any of my flight, so I started to assess the damage. That little caper in the cockpit and aircraft had resulted in a wet right wing leaking fuel and the cockpit floor covered with red hydraulic fluid. Meaning? I would have to manually drop the gear and shake it locked. My pants and clothing were smoldering, and when I moved the flight suit, blood spurted out of my right leg just below the knee. The truth dawned on me...that stuff on the cockpit floor wasn't hydraulic fluid. It was ole Nip's blood. I slipped off my scarf and tied a tourniquet just above the bleeding spot and poked the end into the hole in my leg. Still in a climb and looking for my flight, I was unprepared for what happened next: three or four big bursts of flak burst just in front of me. I banked hard to the left and nosed over when all hell broke loose. Got a hit right in the engine—smoke, fire, confusion and the ole Merlin quit. Unbelievable! The prop just stopped turning.

Things were getting hot and it was obvious I had to leave Mon Petite, so I disconnected the oxygen hose, radio, etc., trimmed full nose down, pulled the hatch and off it went. I turned her over and pushed out. Now here's where the excitement really mounted. I wasn't out and the Mustang seemed to be in an inverted flat spin. *What in the world*, I thought. *The dinghy's caught on the lap belt or something.* Somehow I got my feet beneath the instrument panel and pulled myself back into the bird, unfastened my dinghy—*holy mackerel, the ground's getting close*—put my feet on the seat and pushed out again. This time I made it, but hit the tail section. By good luck I hit backwards, and my backpack chute helped to protect me. When clear of the P-51 I pulled the rip cord, felt a jolt and saw a canopy above...then passed out, a blessing because I was in great pain.

When I regained consciousness, I was lying in a field on my back with my parachute harness removed. My back hurt and my leg was still bleeding. Things were fuzzy, but I could see a very large, red-faced man standing above me, straddling my legs, a huge club in his hand which he waved menacingly at me. He exhorted the crowd in a loud voice and asked if I had a pistol. I gave him one of my half-dozen German words—"Nein"—and a few well chosen American words as I motioned for him to back off. This increased his intensity with the club and his demands for a pistol. I checked my pockets and realized everything had been removed. Since I was groggy with pain, I again motioned for him to back off and gave him the good ole single digit salute. As he raised the club to deliver a blow, I saw a gray flash between his legs. He jumped from his position over my knees, completely over me with a scream while in mid-air. The gray flash was a Volksturm (home guard) soldier who had his bayonet fixed and had jabbed my assailant in the rear. The soldier retracted the bayonet and, advancing on the crowd of 25 to 30 people, used the rifle's sling to swing it around his head like a club. They retreated rapidly and left the field with old loud-mouth in the lead. The soldier clambered around, and I felt he might have shot someone if the crowd challenged him.

He returned to me and muttered to himself while checking my leg. I indicated that my back was really hurting. While he had me raise my legs one at a time, two more Germans arrived with military type caps on. They talked briefly and left to get a ten-foot-long ladder and a large, wide board. The board was slipped under me and then put on the ladder. I was tied to the board/ladder and carried to the road where we were met by a young German officer. He had them bandage my wound with my scarf, a handkerchief from my pocket and some twine. The soldier and two men left. The officer asked me questions. I answered in French that I didn't speak German. He then spoke to me in French and some English. I was an American, I said, but from loss of blood and shock, I drifted in and out of consciousness. I do remember being on a cart pulled by the soldier and some German men. I wound up in a barn lying in some straw but still tied to the board/ladder stretcher. I stayed like that all night with many curious townspeople coming by to see me. The strangest part was that I never got thirsty, hungry or had any desire to go to the toilet.

The next day I was carried to an auxiliary hospital for foreigners, POWs, etc., and given some warm weak coffee. A French orderly named André dressed the wounded leg, washed and dressed me in a hospital gown. I couldn't move my legs at all by then, and my back pain was exciting, to say the least. (After I was back in U.S. hands, I learned that a vertebra had broken all to hell and I was lucky to have survived.) André was joined by a doctor, Polish or Romanian, who checked me over and had me retied very securely to the board—from my buttocks to my armpits. I stayed that way for three to four weeks. During that time André was my protector and benefactor. He saved my right leg from amputation by stealing sulfa powder and treating my wound which had become gangrenous. He protested to the hospital chief, a German captain, that I'd rather be dead than lose that leg. He secured a crank-type wind-up record player and had a couple of American records from the early '30's which he played for me at "tea time" when he gave me Serbian coffee with black bread and margerine—a real treat since our staple food was thin and tasteless soup...and sometimes black bread.

During this time we were bombed several times during the day by U.S. forces and by the British at night. The patients were carried to a cellar of the hospital where we stayed for one to three hours.

Finally I could travel and was sent to Frankfurt for interrogation by Hanns Scharff. He really knew as much about our group as I did and only wanted me to confirm I was the Captain W. T. Carter from the 339th and not the W. T. Carter from another mustang group in England—I believe it was the 4th Fighter Group at Debden. I tried not to do this, but am not sure I succeeded. Scharff treated me very nicely, didn't threaten me, and got me a new pair of U.S. OD wool trousers.

André had cut off the right leg of my pants when he fixed my leg. I got a lot of dirty looks from Germans enroute to Frankfurt with my leg bandaged and one leg half off my pants. Scharff also got me an OD Eisenhower jacket. After about a week I was shipped off to Stalag Luft III near Sagan in Upper Silesia east of Leipzig. My "one pass" turned out to be about one year in duration, which just increased my desire to get back to U.S. control so I could get on with fighting the war.

Fate's Fickle Finger

by Paul Fickel

Writing about my experience as a POW isn't exactly the subject I would normally pick, as most of it I would just as soon forget. At best the life of a POW is rather grim and apprehensive. I don't think anyone except a former POW will really appreciate what it was like, but here goes anyway. I could have made the article funnier, but it didn't seem right to make light of circumstances that were really tragic to many good men.

26 September '44 started out to be a good day for me. I had just returned from three days leave in Scotland and was scheduled to fly the mission that day. When I arrived at the flight line, our operations officer, Major Stephenson, informed me that I had been selected to lead a flight. It turned out, however, that we had only twelve P-51's ready to fly. I was given the option of leading the second element of the third flight or just sitting the mission out. What a fateful decision that turned out to be! The mission was to Bremen, forty minutes over enemy territory, twenty in and twenty out. I figured it would be a milk run and a good chance to get the feel of things again after having a few days off. Valdee Wyatt was leading the flight with Charles Coe on his wing. James Robinson was flying my wing.

The weather was beautiful—scattered cumulus below 10,000 feet and very thin cirrus layer at about 20,000 feet. Takeoff and run to the target were uneventful and everything was going beautifully. Someone made a wrong turn over the target and the squadron flew through the thickest of flak—and right through the middle of the bombers. We made it through okay, however, and turned north on our way home. Five minutes past the target my engine quit without warning. One second it was running smoothly and the next it quit as if someone had cut the switch. I switched tanks and tried to restart it—no luck. It wouldn't even sputter. After a couple of seconds I smelled coolant and looked back. I was the only mustang drawing a long white contrail.

I knew I'd had it. I kept trying to start the engine, but to no avail. My squadron leader called and asked if I was having trouble. All I could answer was, "Yes." I had a sick feeling in the pit of my stomach and was not in a talkative mood. We were at 27,000 feet when the engine quit, and I decided to glide down to 10,000 feet before bailing out. Just before reaching 10,000 feet I was headed north over the southern edge of Wilhelmshaven Bay and I entered the top of a small cumulus cloud. I could see from my glide angle that I couldn't make the coast and decided I didn't want to bail out over the bay. I turned west while still in the cloud and planned to bail out as soon as I was in the clear, but when I broke out of the cloud I was right over a German airfield at about 5,000 feet. They were shooting light flak at me which was bursting off my wing tips. I could hear the bangs and see the red centers. Not wanting to bail out in all that flak, I made a diving turn to the north and leveled out at 2,000 feet. Since I didn't want to roll the plane over at altitude without power, I climbed out on the wing and let go.

Almost immediately there was a terrific jar. For a second I couldn't figure out what had happened and then realized I was laying on the P-51's tail with one leg and one arm under it while the main part of my body was on top. I pushed myself off and grabbed the ripcord with both hands and pulled. There was another terrific jar, and I thought I'd hit the ground. Couldn't see anything but became aware that I was swinging in the air. The edge of my goggles was across my eyelids. I pushed them up and saw that I was about 50 feet in the air drifting toward some power lines. I had thoughts of dumping air from the chute but decided I was too close to the ground. I pulled up my legs and cleared the power lines by about three feet.

I unbuckled my chute before hitting the ground and rolled over on my right side as I hit. My chute, however, was a good tight fit, and my arm was numb from hitting the tail. I couldn't get the harness off right away and sailed across a pasture on my back, watching the cows go by at about 15 mph. When I finally wiggled free and stood up, I heard a shout and saw a German farmer crossing his barnyard 300 yards away. He was waving a pistol that looked about two feet long. That didn't seem to be the way to go, so I turned and ran in the opposite direction. I was running toward a road with a line of trees along it when I heard shots and, looking closer, saw Germans in uniform. They were shooting at me! Since that didn't seem very sporting with no cover in the open field, I stopped and raised my hands. A German lieutenant and sergeant ran up to me. Of course, one of the first things they said was, "For you, the war is over."

The marines held me in what must have been company headquarters until I was turned over to the Luftwaffe. While there, my pockets were emptied and a list made of everything before putting it into an envelope. They explained it would be returned to me when I reached a prison camp, and I was surprised later when the envelope was returned to me at Stalag Luft I. I was one of few prisoners to reach camp with a wrist watch, pen and pencil set, pocket knife, etc.

I was held overnight at a German air base, probably the one that had been shooting flak at me earlier in the day. Two German guards then put me on a train to Oberursel, near Frankfurt. One was a tall lanky corporal who looked like a college student, and the other was short and stocky and looked like a farm boy. Both looked and acted like civilians recently drafted into the service. The trip took a little over two days. I spent most of the time looking out the window at airplane wreckage which was in almost every open field we passed. With a train full of civilians I tried not to show interest in all the bomb damage along the way.

There were two highlights on the trip. We had to take a bus ride to get around the marshalling yards at Bremen, our target the day before. The bus was crowded with civilians, and in the bomb damaged area, I was aware of angry tones although I didn't understand what was being said. Many turned around and gave me dirty looks, but luckily all damage was in the marshalling yards. Houses only a hundred yards away were untouched, and I was thankful for the accuracy of our bombardiers. The second highlight occurred about dusk as we pulled into a station. There was an air raid, and everyone, including my guards and I, rushed into an air raid shelter. Soon we could hear or feel explosions in the area. Again I became the object of attention, and had I known German, I might have been even more uncomfortable. A German soldier was intent on getting something started, but it was too crowded to do much of anything. Most civilians were satisfied with angry words and looks in my direction. I was relieved when we got out and back on the train.

Toward the end of the second day the tall corporal talked to me in English. He was curious to see what I thought of the war's progress, what life was like in the States and the morale of our troops in the combat zone. He, like the marines I'd talked to, still professed to feel that Germany could win the war even though Patton was practically on their border. They had a secret weapon that would win the war for them if only they could stall the drive in France until spring to gain more time. What surprised me most was their expressed confidence in their officers and the belief that their General Staff was the best in the world. The corporal said I would get no "third degree" type interrogation at Oberursel, but I was apprehensive.

On arrival I was taken to a room and stripped. While they searched my clothes I was taken before an interrogator who asked a few questions and handed me a form which he assured me he had to have completed. I wrote my name, rank and serial number and gave it back. I was given back my clothes and taken to a cell. It was about five by eight feet with a bunk and chair and a window with opaque glass. The first two days I slept almost continuously, but after that the nights were cold and I shivered under two thin blankets made from wood fibers and slept more during the day when it was warmer. I found out that if you're cold long enough, you stop shivering even if you're still cold, but it was a relief not to shiver.

After about a week I was called in for interrogation by Hanns Scharff, their master interrogator. He welcomed me into his office and urged me to sit down as if afraid I was about to fall. Scharff remarked that I didn't look so good and offered me a piece of black bread with some jam on it. All I had been getting to eat was a couple of slices of black bread and a thin bowl of soup a day. The bread tasted like sour sawdust and the soup had an odor that gagged me, so I hadn't eaten much. I hadn't washed or shaved for a week, so his statement on my looks was accurate. Hanns would make small talk and occasionally slip in a question or remark that had something to do with the war. I was surprised at the personal family information he wanted. The interrogations always ended with Hanns shaking his head and saying that his superiors would not let me go without more information. He always sent me back to solitary with the impression that it would be a short while before I would be called back. Then five or six days would pass with nothing to do but wait for the next interrogation. I looked forward to any break in that routine.

Each morning we stood outside our cells while a broom was passed along for us to sweep our cells, and then the guard would inspect it. There was nothing to sweep, but we enjoyed a break from solitary which otherwise was interrupted only by meal time when they brought our bread or soup. I would wonder if the crazy guy I met in the latrine who said he had been in solitary for six months was one of ours or theirs, or if the man in the next cell who coughed all night was for real, as he didn't cough in the hallway during inspection. A captain across the hall sneaked in a word one morning when the guards weren't looking. He said he was getting Red Cross parcels and gave me a cigarette to prove it. I had no match, but took it anyway. I had tried to figure out from private calendars on the wall by former inmates their average length of stay. It was twelve days, but after being there a couple of weeks, I decided there was fallacy in my logic and stopped marking my own private calendar.

The second interrogation went like the first except I was promised a shave and shower by Hanns. He also stated that they had a library and would see if I could get a book. I got the shower and shave but no book. This was after twelve days. About day eighteen I was called in for the third interrogation which went like the others, with the library brought up again. Hanns ended it by saying if I would give him the number off my plane, he thought he could get me released to a camp, which he assured me was much to be desired compared to Oberursel. I was allowed to shave, but saw no books.

On day 21 I went back in for additional interrogation. After the usual preliminaries he asked if I had decided to give him the number of my plane. I had thought it over and decided this might be his best offer, so I gave him the number. Without a word he took the form and started filling in the blanks from a file he pulled from a drawer. He then handed me the form to read. He had filled in the correct squadron, group, base, names of squadron and group commander, chaplain, flight surgeon and other like information. Some of it was out of date, but I handed it back without comment. He probably knew from my expression that he had filled in the right outfit. That evening I went to Dulagluft where POWs were held prior to shipment to a prison camp.

The trip to Stalag Luft I near the Baltic Sea above Berlin was made with thirty or forty other prisoners. There was a train car full of us. The senior officer was a British captain who had been shot down while on a recon flight over Hamburg. He said he got lazy that day and made his run at 35,000 feet instead of 40,000 and the flak got him. Most of the trip was spent trying to convince our guards to give us drinking water. We had been given half of a Red Cross parcel each for food on the trip, and the guards wanted us to trade food for drinking water. This enraged the British captain so that he collected all the Red Cross parcels and kept them in his compartment so no one would be tempted to weaken and make a deal with the guards. At meal time he returned the parcels so we could eat. Without water, however, not much was eaten. After a couple of days the guards gave us some water, but in general, it was a pretty dry five-day trip. As we walked along the road outside the Stalag Luft I enclosure, some prisoners gathered along the fence inside, watching us approach. Suddenly someone called out my name. I looked over to see a couple of buddies I had gone through flying school with and had not seen since. Suddenly the world seemed to be a little friendlier again.

Candy Man
by Bill Knott

It's possible that there are a few folks in the 339th who won't remember Hershel "NMI" McKinley: Executive Officer of the 503rd, the Kentucky colonel, the Teller of Tall Tales, the Encyclopedia of Army Regulations (he could make up a few to suit the occasion) and the Manipulator of the Dice. He seemed to delight in the fact that he had no middle initial, hence, "NMI" McKinley.

This story about McKinley began when we noticed over the course of a week or so that he was "horse trading" cigarettes, etc., for candy. It seemed like he was always acquiring candy from any and all sources. If he couldn't talk you out of it, he'd end up trading for it. We began to wonder about that "sweet tooth" of McKinley.

Almost every evening he would get all dressed up in his Class A's, put his candy-laden musette bag on his bicycle like a saddle bag and take off down the road toward Royston. This went on for awhile, and when our interest was sufficiently aroused, a few of us tailed him out of town trying to ascertain what was with our candy-laden friend.

We weren't too far outside Fowlmere when we came upon a small group of children, all eating candy. Asked where the candy came from they answered, "From Mac." (Can't remember, but they might have said "Uncle Mac", and I wouldn't have been surprised.) All along the road to Royston we'd chance upon small groups of children eating a bit of candy, and always the response was the same: "Uncle Mac gave it to us." A few days later we took off along McKinley's route, but this time, ahead of him. Again, we would come to small groups of children waiting "bus stop" fashion along the side of the road. When queried they would answer, "We're waiting for Uncle Mac." And they could tell you, within five minutes or so, just when he'd be along.

We pedaled on into Royston and visited a couple of pubs. The mention of McKinley's name brought friendly and favorable responses. I'm not sure he used the candy on the pub patrons, but whatever he was doing certainly was the right mixture of blarney, tact and diplomacy. When I think about Fowlmere and the 339th Fighter Group, one of my favorite recollections is of Hershel "NMI" McKinley and his candy for the children on the road to Royston.

An Unforgettable Mission

by Frank Stillwell

August 5, 1944, was a day that will be forever in the deep recesses of my memory. The weather was less than favorable at Fowlmere that morning. The sky was completely overcast, and the ceiling was about 700 feet. When such conditions prevailed, it was standard operating procedure for each flight to join in close formation under the cloud layer and then climb up through the overcast. I was leading the second element that day and Edward Flaherty was flying my wing. The flight leader was Major John R. Reynolds who had been recently assigned as assistant group operations officer. I don't recall who was his wingman.

Major Reynolds and his wingman cleared the runway as Edward Flaherty and I began our takeoff roll. After we became airborne, I immediately started a climbing turn to the left in order to join up with the flight leader as soon as possible. I crossed under his element and moved into close formation on his right wing. Almost immediately the flight leader began to climb up through the cloud layer. We were in the overcast about one minute, and I was concentrating on flying formation on the dim outline of the flight leader. Suddenly I felt a violent jar and saw a large portion of my wing disappear. Beginning with the inboard end of the aileron, there was a jagged diagonal line across to the leading edge of the wing. At the same time, I saw an aircraft disappearing under the flight leader's plane.

The reality of the situation struck me like a thunderbolt. I sensed being in deep trouble. Fortunately, the P-51 did not suddenly become unstable. I lost sight of the flight leader's plane and had to go on my own instruments. By holding quite a bit of right stick pressure, I was able to keep the aircraft level. A quick decision was in order, so I opted to descend down through the overcast to visual flying conditions. I broke out of the clouds at 700 feet and was happy to note that with some extra power the aircraft felt fairly stable. Now the next decision had to be made—should I attempt a landing with this disabled bird? I remembered there was an airfield at Manston which had a real long runway. Perhaps a hot approach and attempt to drop the gear at the last moment before touchdown might be a possibility. I just didn't relish the thought of bailing out of a fighter aircraft under these conditions.

Before I had a chance to call for a steer to Manston, my engine stopped. It's really quite amazing how well your mind functions when you're faced with a life-or-death type situation. I can still remember with distinct clarity that I disconnected the radio jack and the G-suit hose. I reached for and pulled the emergency lever to jettison the canopy. To my dismay, nothing happened. I unfastened my seat belt, raised my body up and gave a good push on the canopy. Finally, it flew off and I felt a sudden rush of air all about me. By this time the plane was beginning to lose altitude and there was really not that much left between me and the ground. I forced myself out the right side of the cockpit. I suspect that when I released the right pressure on the stick, the P-51 snapped into a sharp diving turn to the left. I believe for this reason I was clear of the tail section as I hurtled backward in the slipstream. There was no time to reduce velocity before pulling the ripcord on the parachute.

I recall looking at the "hand hold" at the end of the ripcord, grabbing it and giving a giant pull. I blacked out momentarily when the chute opened. I learned later that one of the panels split as I was probably moving at 200 miles per hour when it opened. When my eyes came back into focus, I was shocked to see the burning remains of my plane directly under me. I was about 400 feet above the ground. At this point I took time out to offer a verbal thanks to God for sparing me. By then it was obvious I was not going to drop into the burning wreckage. The next few seconds were really quite pleasant, and I could see I was coming down in a grain field about 100 feet from the inferno.

There was no time to face the drift, so I hit the ground going sideways. Needless to say, the grain field was very hard, and I hit the ground like a sack of potatoes. I had barely gotten to my feet when a jeep came tearing across the field. I was picked up and transported to an airbase that was located nearby. They took me to the base hospital where I was examined by a flight surgeon. There didn't seem to be anything wrong with my physical being, so they took me back to Fowlmere. By the time I got back to our base, my right ankle was beginning to swell slightly. Doc Stuhlman had some x-rays taken and decided I needed a leg cast for a hairline fracture in the ankle bone. This put me on the disabled list for about six weeks. I hope I never have to use a pair of crutches again.

Upon my return to Fowlmere I was saddened to learn that Edward Flaherty was the other pilot involved in the midair collision, and that he had not survived the crash of his plane. His plane also struck Major Reynolds' P-51. The damage to Reynolds' plane was slight, however, and he was able to return safely to base.

I have often wondered why the engine of my aircraft quit after the collision. As I see it, the propeller of Edward's P-51 chopped through the lower section of my plane's fuselage. Most likely it damaged the cooling system and the engine overheated. Things were happening far too quickly for me to look at the temperature gauge. The really scary part is when I stop to ponder just how close that four-bladed propeller was to the seat of my pants when Edward crossed slightly under me from right to left.

Before closing this story of an unforgettable wartime flying experience, I would like to thank once again the parachute rigger who packed my chute. When I really needed it, that chute worked as advertised.

PILOT ARTICLES

Memories

by Al Wyer

I joined the 339th at Walterboro, SC. I had trained in Florida in P-51As and was delighted by that P-39's tricycle landing gear and *taxiing straight ahead*. And who ever saw doors on cockpits?!? There were occasional sparrings with Corsairs from the nearby Marine base at Beaufort, SC, but I was having a problem in trying to fly close formation. I'd crashed out of a mid-air collision in Florida and was having a tough time getting close to another airplane. I was having nightmares. Ginny was scared half out of her wits every night as I went through that crash again and again.

Soon we were leaving for Rice AAF, CA, and doing our own pre-flights on the trip. Valdee Wyatt was in that Curtiss Helldiver that he so loved to fly. He certainly had more baggage space than the rest of us, and it cruised right along with the fighters. One of the guys put the shock struts of his P-39 through the wings, dropping in over high tension lines at Dallas. As I recall he didn't fly again after that. I had engine problems over the mountains in the El Paso area, and I froze! If the engine hadn't caught again, I'd have ridden it in.

Arriving at Rice, we were greeted by tents and tents and more tents! We had some down-time waiting for the ground crews to arrive...and for the wives who weren't supposed to follow, but did. Johnny and Dottie Hauff and Ginny and I drove to San Bernardino to find a place for the girls. Nothing there, then on up to Crestline. There a real estate lady referred us to the Sans Souci Lodge, a private home that occasionally took in overnight guests. It was owned by a Mr. Springer, retired Chief Salesman for Jantzen on the west coast. He'd built it in the days silent movies were being made up there. He offered to let the girls live there for $1.00 a day with kitchen privileges and trips into San Berdo, and $1.00 a day when the husbands came up. Jan (Mrs. Bob) Brown and Dottie (Mrs. Ralph) Banks also lived there at one time.

The P-39 Air Cobras were soon serviced and back to flying. A bad scene for me. I simply wasn't flying well. I told Capt. Don Larson, 503rd operations officer at the time, about the mid-air collision and the nightmares, the freezing, the formation problems, and he understood. He'd frozen on the side of a mountain once and knew the feeling. Then came the magic pill our flight surgeon, Byron Stuhlman, gave me after breakfast and after the evening meal. I started sleeping again, no nightmares, settling down, thinking again, flying formation again. Flying again! Into dust storms at 10,000 feet and getting silicon fouled plugs! I'll never forget watching tall Brownie taxi out sort of hunched over in the P-39 cockpit and short Enoch Stephenson sort of peeking over the edges. And how about that marvelous hesitation the P-39 had when the slack ran out of the target tow-cable, the sudden drop in speed, then struggling to get that monster to target practice altitude, watching those damned tracers move in toward your wing as the deflection angle narrowed.

Remember flying on the deck over all that marvelous government real estate?...barrel rolls over a string of high tension wires?...the thump of that 37 mm cannon in the nose and those dummy bombs on those circles drawn on the desert? There were strikes on the ground units during the maneuvers. I usually flew Rodney West's wing in Bill Bryan's flight, and that often put me "Tail End Charlie" in the group. When that happened I'd be given the rolled-up streamer with the message attached to drop to the target unit — dropping back, slowing down, rolling down the window and dropping the streamer, then cutting corners like mad to re-join. I experienced loss of power on an early morning strike, weaving around below the mountain tops looking for a place to put it down. I landed on the "enemy" strip at Rice (the 339th was flying off another stip to the south). "Captured!" The only pilot POW taken during our maneuvers. I was out of action for the mandatory three days, then returned with my P-39 covered with very uncomplimentary graffiti. And flying night formation with West's and Bryan's exhausts as my best reference points.

There were occasional weekend visits to Sans Souci—and the mixed emotions at finding out we were pregnant. The girls moved out to the Parker Hotel and waved from the balcony as we flew over Parker, AZ. There were Tommy Dorsey's Boogie Woogie booming every night from a bar down the street and the brains and eggs for breakfast at a little restaurant on Parker's main street. Christmas in Parker: Nip and Marie Carter, Hank and Marge Pence; cockroach clusters in the showers between each pair of rooms. Jack Carson and Dennis Morgan brought a show out to the base at Rice.

I'll never forget training for the combat readiness inspection: full group flights, very beautiful flying; a fine fighter group; flying Tail End Charlie in a 48-plane line winding itself up and over and around those big white cumulus clouds. What a beautiful sight—those P-39s stretching over two or three miles. Gorgeous! Then came the tearful good-byes the morning we thought we were leaving for overseas...and the even more painful good-byes the morning we actually left.

Ginny and I were vacationing in California a few years ago and decided to find the old landmarks. With the help of a filling station attendant we got back to the old base at Rice. It's still there. The old black-top strips have been used for drag-racing and are in bad condition, but they're there. The concrete service area is still intact, plus a few foundation elements from buildings. The Sans Souci, which was isolated in the pines back then, is now a corner house in a mountain community. The Parker Hotel has been boarded up for many years.

It was an amazingly emotional experience for me. I was and still am a bit spooked by it, a real lump-in-the-throat experience. I could almost hear the engines, could almost see the P-39s. The mountains, the wind, the heat—it was all back. I don't think I've ever been hit by anything out of the past quite as hard as that hit me. It triggered an avalanche of memories.

Wyer Behind Wire
by Al Wyer

Yes, I was the first POW from the group, and I've always been a little disgusted about it. It was really unnecessary, you know, as I was flying *SPARE* that day. When no one aborted that mission, I could legitimately have returned to base. It was the 15th of May 1944, a milk-run mission, a fighter sweep over Belgium, and I thought I'd get another mission in. So, I tagged along until I noticed that I seemed to be the only guy pulling contrails that morning. The engine began to overheat, oil pressure dropped and finally the engine seized. I had long since concluded that I had lost my coolant, that I couldn't make it to the North Sea, and that I was going to be walking very soon. It was a bit of luck that I didn't make the open water, as my dinghy tore loose when the chute opened. My flight dropped back with me, so when I waved from the chute, I knew Ginny would be informed that the bailout had been okay.

The drop that morning was utterly quiet, really quite pleasant. I could hear chickens, dogs and other sounds from below the undercast clouds. It was gusty near the ground, and when I was about two shroud-lengths up, a gust caught the canopy and pulled it over about level with me. Thus, I hit the ground like a 150 pound pendulum. I wasn't aware of any injury at the time, but the accident re-visited me several months later.

I didn't have any really good luck that morning. My plane had hit a village and was firing .50-caliber ammunition all over the place, so my arrival was anticipated. A Belgian policeman saw me land, and a large contingent of villagers surrounded me. I was the first Allied pilot to go down in that particular area, and they were curious and very friendly. Most were quite fluent in English. Despite my protestations, they made a three-ring circus of me. A German contingent from the village lost no time in attending the circus and "for me the war was over."

I was taken to a Belgian castle being used as a command post and placed in an underground dungeon which still had manacles attached to one wall. My cell was the precise length of a six-foot bunk installed on one side and was five feet wide. After three days and nights there, I was moved to a Brussels prison. Back into solitary confinement with a peephole in the door, but this time I could hear American voices. One American was being escorted down the hall with his entire head bandaged except for his eyes, obviously terribly burned. In POW camp we saw many burns. If from a cockpit fire, the masked part of the face was often okay; if it was an oxygen fire, the mouth and nose would be burned and the rest of the face could be okay. It appeared to me that German doctors were as attentive to prisoners as to anyone else. The Hippocratic Oath was still operative.

Next I was sent to Frankfurt for interrogation and more solitary. I got a little spooked there because there was no way I could keep track of day and night—disorienting. After going to Dulagluft at Wetzlar for processing, I was sent to Stalagluft III at Sagan, arriving shortly after the famous British escape. There was suspicion of new prisoner purges and possible German agents being planted as phony POWs, so I was incommunicado until I could be vouched for by someone already there. My "certifier" turned out to be a friend from flying school. I was one of the prisoners who caught diptheria in July 1944 and turned out to be violently allergic to the serum. Went into shock after each of nine doses of antitoxin and was brought back with nine adrenalin shots. The "carrier", a pilot from Louisiana named Garaudy who bunked above me, was discovered during a camp-wide program of throat swabs. He never had a sick moment, but it took him six weeks to get a negative culture.

My hospital stay afforded me one highly emotional moment. I heard noises in the adjoining room one night—guys moving around organizing something. The next morning I heard people outside my window. There, in military formation, were 50 RAF officers in Class A uniform. They filed past the adjoining room, and as each passed the window he was handed a cremation can containing the ashes of a British officer killed by Germans after the big escape. I was told they were allowed to bury the remains with full military ceremony. I was one of the most affecting things I've seen and still remains very much a part of me.

Here are a number of quick recalls stuck together to save space: our three decker bunks had nine slats to the bunk and were diligently counted by the Germans on their unannounced inspections; German "ferrets" under the barracks listened to conversations; feelings of guilt at being out of the war in the relative security of a POW camp while the rest were still laying their lives on the line flying combat missions; becoming the official bread slicer for the room—I could consistently get 50-52 even slices from a German bread loaf; toasting the stuff on the stove to drive out the moisture; enough coal briquets for one fire per day in a room; the coded message "Soup's on" indicating that BBC news was ready to be passed on in the latrine (the British were ingenious in importing radio and crystal set components); the constant sorting-out of cooks and bakers in a room and getting the Red Cross parcels and cooking organized; the occasional blood sausage and cheese brought in by the Germans; the discovery that the German camp commander had a son in a prison camp in the States; the guys sitting in the theater and drowning in classical music from records sent to us by the YMCA—attendance was scheduled by barracks; bees swarming in the compound and promptly housed in a jury-rigged hive and put to work; near miracles accomplished in a makeshift medical facility in the compound by a Doctor of Osteopathy (a pilot) and an Osteopathic student (a navigator) (guys sliced by propellers during a bailout were having mobility restored, atrophied muscles toned and joints mobilized—I discovered this miracle factory when back problems from my bailout surfaced); our anger at the news of striking coal miners at home.

We had one big moral issue at Sagan. A talented cartoonist had started a comic strip in the mail room. Its title escapes me, but the two main characters were Nita and her cousin Wanda Leigh. They became increasingly and enjoyably unclothed from episode to episode until finally they were wearing nothing. You could hardly get into the mail room when a new adventure was due. Then a certain conservative element in camp became upset about this public, salacious material...and, by damn, circulated a petition to put an end to that vulgarity. I voted resoundingly against it. Nevertheless, the girls started wearing a modicum of clothing, and that was the beginning of a life-long crusade against any and all CENSORSHIP!!

We had an overly optimistic camp slogan—"Home or homo by Christmas!" As 25 December 1944 approached, mail was saved up and delivered by a Kriegie Santa and Kriegie reindeer on Christmas Eve followed by late lockup. There were caroling groups from various barracks and a little bash of goodies in each barracks for visitors. There was also singing to and with some of the tower guards—"Stille Nacht, Heilege Nacht." We had hoarded jam and margarine for the Christmas bash, and I mashed a pan full of raw potatoes with a fork for potato pancakes. (I still have that fork.) Our rations were supplemented by three kinds of Red Cross parcels—American, British and French—and each had its special goodies: canned bacon in the British, corned beef and garlic in the French, and chocolate, cigarettes and margarine in the U.S. parcels. All three were necessary for a true Kriegie gourmet experience.

By January '45 we could see flashes from Russian artillery at night, and the decision was made to move out. We started preparing sleds, sewing scarves into hoods, getting everything together. I was in a group assigned to unload personal packages from a train stranded in the marshalling yard. They were intended for other camps. As we were sorting stuff into stacks for various barracks, the word came to move out. I simply stuffed my pockets with all the candy and cube sugar I could carry. Later, when really tired, they provided an amazing shot of quick energy.

We marched from Sagan (now a part of Poland) at 12:30 a.m. on 28 January into the blizzard of '45—a terrible winter world wide I learned later. I remember: helping the guys from the South who simply didn't know how to deal with the terrible cold and snow; guys throwing away blankets and extra clothing because they were so tired; German packs and guns on the Kriegie sleds and everyone helping pull; shots from the rear of the column—everyone into the woods; shots if you stuck your head up; finally back on the road, but the last bit of strength drained from some of the guys and from some of the older guards; the "Kriegie Commandoes"—organized in camp and moving tirelessly up and down the line helping those who needed it, keeping guys from lying down and putting their feet flat on the ground during rest periods...lots of frozen feet.

My group had 52 hours of marching, then into a factory in Muskau for sleep. I woke up with feet thawed and swollen. I couldn't get my shoes on. Calluses on the balls of my feet had pulled loose and formed thick blisters underneath. A German orderly with a straight razor the size of a machete pared the calluses away and drained the blisters. Blessed relief. There was also the terrible diarrhea from untreated factory water we'd drunk. Finally, after six days and 62 miles of walking, we were piled into old Forty and Eight (railway) cars. Only a few could sit down at a time. Stopping in a marshalling yard, we heard, "Posten, ein man schissen!" Practically everyone unloaded and dropped their drawers. The presence of German women in a railroad gang didn't inhibit a soul, and a veritable blizzard of paper was left on the ground.

At Nurnberg and into Stalag XIII-D on 4 February 1945-reduced rations, body lice, no baths for six weeks, simply dry the handkerchiefs overnight and use them the next day. Some guys couldn't eat the worms in the grass soup—I loved 'em! More and more guys sick. Constant talking about food. I weighed about 120—down from 150. We made elaborate plans for exchanges of regional delicacies when we got back home. We burned the wood from the wash house and other auxiliary structures. Hitler youths—mean and unpredictable—replaced the old guards who were sent to the fronts. And there were the tremendous air raids on the nearby marshalling yards-dishes crashing in barracks; everyone under whatever was available; Pathfinder flares; no Kriegie injuries, but God, what a show; sweating out the lone Mosquitoes dropping big ones at night.

The order came to move again on 4 April 1945, this time from an Allied offensive. This time the Germans were along more as escorts than as guards. We walked south about 90 miles to Stalag VII-A at Moosburg, about 25 miles northeast of Munich. Spring weather in Bavaria made this move much more bearable—fresh eggs and chickens, sleeping in barns, trading with the Germans. We made "Klim Kan Kookers" of all descriptions and used anything that would burn as fuel. Everyone had turned into a self-sufficient hobo. Guys gained weight and began looking healthy again, although there was some jaundice. American fighters were overhead regularly during the march. I ran into a member of the 82nd Airborne Division (later in college) who said we were watched closely and were to be cut off if marched out of Moosburg. We understood that we might be marched south to Hitler's retreat in the Alps as final negotiation pawns.

We arrived in Moosburg on 13 April. The mass of prisoners saturated the facilities. We were living in tents when Patton's outfit moved through on 29 April (the second anniversary of my commision). Quite a tank engagement, but no Kriegies were hurt. Patton himself was in the liberating unit. We received an issue of American bread and lots of food. Everyone had a bash. I got sick from a Klim Kan of chocolate-flavored oatmeal. I learned a guy had been taking 35 mm photos throughout our POW experience and that another had kept a diary and drawings which he'd lugged with him through everything. Ordered copies of both and got them back in the states. They're now among my cherished possessions.

We were flown out of the airfield at Landshut in C-47s to Camp Lucky Strike and *FOOD*—a ladling spoon of sugar on a mess-kit of oatmeal. We could eat anytime we wanted and we ate *all* the time. From LeHavre our ship went to Liverpool where a number of war brides boarded for the Atlantic crossing. And one final indignity: the well-fed medical people decided our poor systems really couldn't digest any solid food, so we were fed creamed everything on the trip to the States. When in Miami for reprocessing, Ginny and I met Bill and Dee Knott. Bill informed me that I'd been promoted a few days after going down and furnished a set of orders that resulted in a nice back-pay check. I was in fighter refresher training headed for the Pacific when the war mercifully ended.

John Aitken	 Bernie Allen	 Roy W Ammerman
 Robert H Ammon	 Edward A Beavers	 William W Behrend
 Alec Boychuck	 William H Boyd	 William E Bryan
 Jerry P Bush	 John R Byers	 John C Campbell

Steve J Chetneky

Carl E Cloud

Charles S Coe

Earl E Erickson

Joseph G Farrell

Clarence I Farrell

Paul D Fickel

Leonard J Fiorito

Edward C Flaherty

Luther B Francis

Carl H French

Lloyd J French

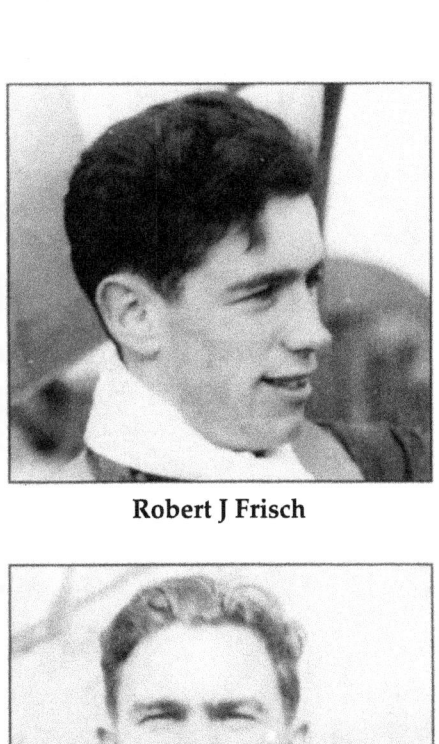
Robert J Frisch

Francis R Gerard

Felix J Girone

John W Gokey

William R Gordon

Ethelbert H Graham

Elmer E Haidle

Allen S Harte

John J Hauff

Anthony G Hawkins

Harvey E Henderson

Ralph S Hill

 John E Hutton
 Allen D Johnson
 Donald W Johnson
 Raymond G Johnson
 William G Johnson
 George J Johnstone
 George P Kelly
 Clarence W Knott
 Alfred D Manke
 James A Mankie
 Lester C Marsh
 Raymond D Mayer

Donald E McClish

Francis E McElwee

Kenneth B Moreland

Robert Mulvey

Nathan Ostrow

William W Perry

Phillip E Petitt

George W Porter

John R Potthoff

Rex L Poutre

William R Preddy

Jack B Price

Dennis B Rawls

Raymond F Reuter

Gardner H Reynolds

James G Robinson

Thomas G Sams

Dale E Shafer

Linwood P Smith

Vincent J Spaziano

Enoch B Stephenson

Frank M Stillwell

William D Stockton

John P Wilson

Lyle M Wright

Valdee Wyatt

David A MacKenzie

ARC CLUB, Fowlmere snack bar and chow line

Rev Apperman, Group Chaplain

Fowlmere from the air

339th with RAF guests

339th Fighter Group

PILOT ARTICLES

Rememberances By Men Of The 504th Fighter Squadron

"Brother Bill"

by Frank Waters

After my brother was shot down and taken prisoner on the 8th of May, 1944, I became obsessed with the idea of buzzing his POW camp if the opportunity arose. It did on 5 August when the 339th went on an escort mission in the Hamburg area.

We were with the bombers at about 25,000 feet. Sighting Hamburg off in the distance, I knew this was the day for me to find Bill's POW camp. I called my squadron leader, told him my engine was rough and that my wingman and I were returning to England. We made a 180-degree turn, dropped our tanks and headed toward the Hamburg-Bremen area. I located the Oste River, found the town of Bremervorde and saw a group of buildings in an area enclosed by a fence with guard towers at the corners. The place looked like a prison camp. Sure enough, this was it! We buzzed in just over the roof tops, pulled around and made two more passes. It must have looked great to the guys below to see a couple of P-51s so close. We could see the men running around, excited, waving and shouting. My only hope was that Bill was there. He couldn't help but know it was me because of the markings on my P-51 and the plane's name, "Brother Bill," painted on the fuselage.

More Memories of the 339th

by Frank Waters

I joined the Air Corps for cadet training on 20 April 1942. Had my pre-flight at Kelly, primary at Corsicana, basic at Randolph and advanced at Brooks. I was in the class of 43-D and had my wings presented by Mrs. Dwight D. Eisenhower, our class sponsor, on 22 April 1943. After flying 0-52s in the Observation Program at Brooks, I went to Thomasville, Georgia, for fighter training in P-39s, then to Thermal, California, for reconnaissance flying and to Rice and the 339th on 23 January 1944. I was assigned to the 504th along with four other pilots who had transferred with me: Brownshadel, Rutan, Whistler and Waymire.

The 339th left Rice for New York and England via the troop ship Sterling Castle and arrived in Fowlmere on 4 April 1944. From that date to 18 October '44, I flew 65 missions and had 270 combat hours. I was credited with one FW-190 during my combat duty. I returned to the States and finished my Air Corps tenure flying P-47s at Bradley Field, Connecticut. My discharge was at the Separation Center at Devens on 3 August 1945.

From Rice to Fowlmere, my ten months in the 504th and 339th brought me many cherished friendships. One interesting experience started in August after returning from a bomber escort mission. Harvey Waymire and I were told that Dr. Tony Kameen wanted to see us. Harvey and I had been together since pre-flight and were feeling blue because a week before, Fred Rutan had been shot down. Only Harvey and I were left of the close-knit five pilots who had reported to the 504th at Rice from the 76th Tactical Reconnaissance Group. Don Whistler had been killed at Rice while dropping practice bombs, and Elton Brownshadel was killed on D-Day when taking off on a mission.

Tony wrote out passes for us, and we took off for Scotland. In Edinburgh we set ourselves up for meals at the North British Hotel. We had a set-to with class distinction, however, on our first time there for dinner. Two other American pilots had joined us when we went to the main dining room. The menu listed lobster, sizzling steak, baked ham, etc. On trying to order, we were informed that they were all out of lobster and steak. We made a fuss because others were being served those beautiful meals. The head waiter, a man of about seventy, came to our table and asked if we would please step out into the lobby. He was very nice and explained that they couldn't serve us those choice meals as they were for nobility. He said he was only doing his job and did not like having to tell Americans this. He gave us a card and directed us to the Grill Room where we were to ask for Mabel. He said that we could get top meals down there.

We went to the Grill Room and met Mabel, a very friendly lady of fifty with pretty reddish hair. She said that she liked Americans and would take good care of us. Through an arrangement with the chef, she could get us the best of meals served family style. We were not to tip her until the end of the week. Well, during the ensuing week we sat at a reserved table enjoying great meals of steak, ham, pot roast, chicken, etc. She even made a reservation for a bus trip to a little harbor town for us to have lobster at the Inn there.

Mabel also organized a tour of Edinburgh Castle, provided girl escorts and sent us to a photographer to have our picture taken in kilts. On our final night at dinner we were served roast turkey and at each place was a sprig of Scottish heather which she said would bring us good luck. The chef came out of the kitchen and wished us well. Mabel, with tears in her eyes, put her hands on her hips and said, "If you have enjoyed the meals and I have been of good service, you may give me a gratuity now." She kissed us all good-bye and went through the doors into the kitchen. We did not see her again.

Needless to say, we left a very good tip for Mabel and the chef. We took the train and rode back to Cambridge, getting to Fowlmere about 9:30 the next morning. We later found Mabel had written our mothers about our stay in Scotland.

During the remaining missions and for many years after, I carried that sprig of heather in my wallet.

PILOT ARTICLES

16 August 1944

by Richard C. Penrose

On 16 August 1944 the Eighth Air Force dispatched 1,090 B-17s and B-124s with a fighter escort of 692 P-38s, P-47s, and P-51s. The aircraft were sent out in four Forces to hit oil refineries and aircraft plants in central Germany. The Luftwaffe sent up some opposition, and the American fighters were credited with destroying two Me-163 rocket planes, three FW-190s, and twenty-seven Me-109s in aerial combat for a total of thirty-two. Groups scoring were:

    4th: 1 Me-109
    20th: 6 Me-109s and 2 FW-190s
    339th: 5 Me-109s
    352nd: 2 Me-109s and 1 FW-190
    355th: 11 Me-109s
    359th: 2 Me-109s and 2 Me-163s

The Eighth Air Force lost sixteen B-17s, eight B-24s and four P-51s.

The Luftwaffe list their losses at twenty-one including two destroyed by the bombers. Their listed losses were:

    I Gruppe, JG-3: 5 Me-109s
    IV Gruppe, JG-3: 2 FW-190s (lost to bombers)
    II Gruppe, JG-5: 2 Me-109s
    II Gruppe, JG-27: 4 Me-109s
    I Gruppe, JG-300: 1 Me-109
    III Gruppe, JG-300: 3 Me-109s
    I Gruppe, JG-302: 2 Me-109s
    I Gruppe, JG-400: 2 Me-163s

The 339th was assigned close escort to the 2nd Force made up of Third Bomb Division B-17s bombing oil installations at Zeitz and Rositz, south of Leipzig. The Group Leader, "Armstrong," was Major Joseph L. Thury who led the 505th. Captain William E. Bryan led the 503rd and Major Bill C. Routt the 504th. The Squadrons took off in that order at 0825 hours and climbed out. Landfall-in was made north of Ijmuiden on the Dutch coast at 0925 hours at 20,000 feet.

At 0957 hours Hauptman (Captain) Moritz of IV Gruppe, JG-3, leading his heavily armored FW-190A-8s from Neu-Ulm, southeast of Stuttgart, sighted the B-17s of the 1st Force near Kassel on their way to bomb Halle, Delitzch, and Bohlen. At 1002 hours these FW-190s and some Me-109s, probably JG-302 based at Erfurt, attacked the B-17s, concentrating on the 91st Bomb Group from Bassingbourn. Two B-17s went down followed by four more as the attacks continued. The bombers shot down the FW-190 of Gerd Kuhn, 15 Staffel, IV Gruppe, JG-3, who bailed out.

Oberleutnant (1st Lt) Ekkehard Tichy, Commander

of 13 Staffel, collided with, or rammed, a B-17 in his FW-190 and was killed. Tichy, an ace with twenty-seven victories, twelve in the West including eleven four-engine bombers, had been shot down five months earlier and lost an eye.

The lst Force fighter escort then entered the battle. About 1000 hours the 20th Fighter Group (P-51s) tangled with the FW-190s of IV Gruppe, JG-3, and the Me-109s of I Gruppe, JG-302, near Kassel. The 20th claimed six Me-109s and two FW-190s destroyed. Also at this time, near Moringen, Captain William F. Hendrian and lst Lt Charles J. Cesky of the 352nd Fighter Group shared in the destruction of a Me-109, possibly from II Gruppe, JG-27. Meanwhile Major Niven K. Crandell of the 359th Fighter Group shot down a Me-109 near Einbeck. The German did not parachute and may have been Oberfaehnrich (Officer Cadet) Heinz Berthold of 7 Staffel, II Gruppe, JG-5.

At 1020 hours in action near Kassel, the 352nd's Captain Alton J. Wallace destroyed a Me-109, and at 1025 hours lst Lt Malcolm C. Pickering claimed a FW-190 - these enemy aircraft apparently from I Gruppe JG-3.

Also about 1020 hours lst Lt Frank 0. Lux of the 359th Fighter Group blasted a Me-109 which then threw its pilot out as it cart-wheeled in flight. The German pilot may have been Leutnant (2nd Lt) Karl-Heinz Muller of 2 Staffel, I Gruppe, JG-302, who bailed out east of Kassel.

By 1005 hours the 339th reached Dummer Lake and turned southeast along the bomber stream. At 1015 hours the 503rd, ahead of the 504th, rendezvoused with the assigned 2nd Force B-17s as the 504th was coming up the left side of the bomber stream at 23,000 feet. About 1020 hours Major Routt, Cockshy Red Leader, at the head of the 504th, reported "Bandits" at ten o'clock. A gaggle of about ten Me-109s of I Grouppe, JG-3, and II Gruppe, JG-27, was approaching at a slightly lower altitude. As the Me-109s passed, Cockshy Red Flight dropped their external fuel tanks and peeled off on the German rear. Routt opened fire and clobbered a Me-109, probably flown by Gefreiter (PFC) Helmut Venohr of 2 Staffel, I Gruppe, JG-3, which dove away and crashed near Stadtoldendorf. Routt switched to another Me-109 of the now disintegrating German formation and scored hits on the aircraft of Unteroffizier (Staff Sergeant) Ullrich Enenkel who evaded further damage as Routt pulled back and up to continue escort of the B-17s. German reports say Enenkel guided his crippled aircraft eastward and bellied-in near Halberstadt where he was strafed and killed by P-51s as he fled the crash site. It may have been that he was attacked by lst Lt Ira E. Grounds of the 4th Fighter Group, escorting the 3rd Force.

As the German formation came apart, lst Lt Hervey S. Stockman, Cockshy Red Three, went after the Me-109 flown by Feldwebel (Technical Sergeant) Richard Karcher of 1 Staffel, I Gruppe, JG-3. Karcher was trailing his 1 Staffel superior, Leutnant (2nd Lt) Hubert Buschmann, in a shallow easterly dive. Stockman's wingman, 2nd Lt Richard C. Penrose, Cockshy Red Four, brought up the rear. Stockman, from dead astern and long range, fired several short bursts at Karcher scoring strikes. The Me-109 began to smoke, and at about 20,000 feet, the wounded Karcher bailed out and was sitting in his parachute when Penrose roared by. The 109 crashed two kilometers north of Negenborn.

Stockman continued on, now in pursuit of Buschmann who proved to be a difficult opponent. At long range Stockman fired a burst and, when the tracers whipped by, Buschmann went into a left turn allowing Stockmann and Penrose to close in a hurry. Buschmann was very elusive. Stockman fired the rest of his ammunition in this dogfight and saw no strikes. Penrose fired a burst for no hits as three guns jammed, leaving one in operation. Penrose continued the battle and scored at least two strikes between the cockpit and the tail on the Me-109. At close range Buschmann chopped throttle, lowered flaps, and rolled out of his turn, forcing Penrose to coast up along side and up. Buschmann dove away and Penrose followed. At several thousand feet altitude Penrose's last gun ran out of ammunition. Soon after, Buschmann jettisoned the canopy, rolled inverted, but didn't fall clear until his aircraft went into an inverted spin. His parachute never streamed, and he fell into the hardwood forest below. The Me-109 crashed in a cultivated field two kilometers north of Lauenstein, east of Hameln.

The 504th's second flight, Cockshy White, did not engage the enemy aircraft and resumed escort of the bombers with Routt. The third flight, Cockshy Blue, led by lst Lt Charles M. Hunter, with 2nd Lt Ray F. Herrmann on his wing and 2nd Lt Melvin L. Cernicky leading the element, singled out a Me-109 and shot up the aircraft of Unteroffizier (Staff Sergeant) Willi Salinger of 7 Staffel, I Gruppe, JG-27. Wounded, Salinger bailed out southeast of Stadtoldendorf. Hunter began making photo passes at Salinger sitting in his parachute. In the confusion the rest of Cockshy Blue Flight mistook another P-51 for Hunter and left the area. Hunter did not return and was later reported as "Killed in Action."

As the 504th bounced the German aircraft, lst Lt Francis R. Gerard, leading Beefsteak Green, the last flight in the 503rd, saw the attack and turned towards it. He soon saw a Me-109 heading after a P-51. In a fast diving turn Gerard closed to 150 feet and opened fire, registering numerous strikes on the engine, wing roots, and cockpit. An explosion sent pieces flying. lst Lt Lester C. Marsh, Beefsteak Green Three, followed the spinning Messerschmidt and watched it crash. The pilot did not parachute. He may have been Unteroffizier (Staff Sergeant) Reinhold Schmutzler of 2 Staffel, I Gruppe, JG-3, who crashed near Polle on the Weser River. Gerard was an original 339th pilot, and this was his first victory. He went on to become top scorer in the 339th with eight destroyed in the air.

Of the 3rd Force fighters escorting the B-24s bombing Magdeburg, Dessau, and Kothen, only the 4th and 355th mixed it up with twenty Me-109s near Brunswick, probably JG-300, and claimed eleven destroyed.

The Biggest Air Battle

by Richard C. Penrose

On 26 November 1944 the 339th had its highest scoring day in aerial combat with the Luftwaffe by destroying twenty-nine FW-190s. On this mission the Eighth Air Force bombers were out to hit rail viaducts, marshalling yards, and oil installations in western Germany. The 339th was to sweep the area and cover bombers hitting oil installations at Misburg near Hannover. The 339th was not assigned to cover any specific bomb group.

The German Air Force put up three counter forces. Force "A" was I and II Gruppen, JG-l; and III Gruppe, JG-6. Force "B" was I, II, and III Gruppen, JG-301. Force "C" was I, II, III, and IV Gruppen, JG-27; II Gruppe, JG-53; and II Gruppe, JG-54. Eighth Air Force fighters recorded 115 enemy aircraft destroyed in combat with these German units. Fighter Groups scoring were: 339th - 29; 361st - 23; 355th - 21; 356th - 21; 78th - 9; 364th - 8; 353rd - 3; and 479th - 1. The Eighth lost nine fighters.

The enemy pilots engaged this day by the 339th were from Force "B", JG-301, operating from bases at Stendal, Salzwedel, Sachan, and Solpke. JG-301 attacked the 491st Bomb Group and shotdown fifteen B-24s. Then the 339th hit the attackers. German records show JG-301 lost twenty-six pilots killed and missing with thirteen wounded from combat with the B-24s and P-51s. Unwounded pilots who parachuted are not included in these figures. A few of these losses were to the southwest of Hannover over Minden and Buckeburg, many to the south of the city over Bad Munder, Einbeckhausen, and Sarstedt, and a few to the southeast at Peine and Brunswick. The 339th lost two pilots, the 504th's lst Lt Ely N. Van Cleave and the 505th's lst Lt Bert Stiles.

The 339th Group Leader, "Armstrong", was Captain Archie A. Tower, leader of the 505th. Lt Col Harvey E. Henderson led the 503rd, Lt Col Edgar B. Gravette the 504th. The Group took off from Fowlmere at 1045 hours, climbed out, and made landfall-in over the Dutch coast north of Haarlem at 1200 hours, 20,000 feet. They swept into the target area around 1300 hours and the battle began. All 339th pilots engaged were fighting almost simultaneously.

The 503rd

At 20,000 feet Captain Edward H. Beavers, leader of the 503rd's second flight, saw a B-24 going down and called it in. Henderson immediately turned the 503rd towards the bombers. FW-109s could be seen attacking the B-24s of the 491st Bomb Group. The 503rd jettisoned their drop tanks and dove in to break up the attack.

At this time, part of 4th Group was climbing up after investigating aircraft on the deck. Above they saw a Me-410 from JG-3 and six Me-109s attacking a straggling B-24. Before 4th Group could get there, the bomber shot down one Me-109 and then it was shot down by another. As the P-51s approached, the enemy aircraft disappeared in all directions. lst Lt Ira E. Grounds, leading the element in Red Flight, made two orbits, spotted a Me-109 and followed it to the deck. As he followed the enemy aircraft through a canyon he hit it hard with gunfire. As Grounds closed on the Me-109 he saw what appeared to be the pilot hanging part way out of the cockpit. He pulled up to avoid colliding. His wingman, Lt Henry A. Ingalls, saw the Me-109 crash into a hill twenty miles west of Magdeburg.

Of all the combat reports examined, this episode comes closest circumstantially to the German report of what befell Unteroffizier (Staff Sergeant) Ullrich Enenkel of I Gruppe, JG-3, whose aircraft had been damaged earlier by the 339th's Major Routt.

At 1045 hours Lt Col John B. Murphy, leading the 359th Fighter Group, and his wingman, 2nd Lt Cyril W. Jones, Jr., went after a Me-163 rocket aircraft flown by Leutnant (2nd Lt) Hartmut Ryll of I Gruppe, JG-400, which was attacking a straggling B-17 southeast of Leipzig. Murphy's fire damaged the jet, but over-ran it. Jones then attacked and scored good strikes on the canopy. The Me-163 plunged earthward in a vertical dive. Murphy spotted another Me-163 five thousand feet below and peeled off on it. He closed and opened fire at seven hundred feet, continuing to one hundred feet. The rear of the jet exploded, sending the aircraft spiraling earthward out of control.

It appears the latter Me-163 may have been that of Feldwebel (Sergeant) Herbert Staznicky. He was shot-up and wounded by gunfire from the 305th Bomb Group and bailed out. It may have been this pilotless Me-163 that was shot down by Murphy.

Some other German casualties were Leutnant (2nd Lt) Herman Faubel of 12 Staffel, III Gruppe, JG-300, missing in action, and the loss of Unteroffizier (Staff Sergeant) Martin Haase of 8 Staffel, III Gruppe, JG-300, near Wernigerode. Also in 12 Staffel, Unteroffizier (Staff Sergeant) Gunther Kortman tried to guide his damaged Me-109 to safety but was forced to bail out south of Helmstedt. His parachute hung up on the tail and he went down with his aircraft. Unteroffizier (Staff Sergeant) Alfred Hanagarth, 6 Staffel, II Gruppe, JG-27, bailed out wounded near Marburg. Unteroffizier (Staff Sergeant) Adolph Knauss and Staffel Commander Alfred Muller, both of 7 Staffel, II Gruppe, JG-27, crashed between Ulsar and Moringen. Both died.

In the number of airmen shot down, including the bombers, the Luftwaffe had the best of it, although they did not prevent the bombing of any target. It must be noted, however, that a higher percentage of German aircraft, airborne in opposition, were shot down than were lost by the Americans.

Pilot Articles

Henderson's scheduled wingman, Lt Luther B. Francis, did not take off as his radio was out. Lt Nathan Ostrow was Beefsteak Red Three; Lt Frederick Butler, Jr., Red Four. Henderson went after a FW-190 starting a pass on the bombers. The German broke it off and dove away. At about 15,000 feet Henderson caught this 190 and scored hits. After a second burst the Jerry jettisoned his canopy. The third burst sent the pilot rolling over the side, but he did not open his parachute in view of his opponent. Soon after, Henderson saw Captain Donald W. Johnson shooting up a FW-190 at the top of a loop and the enemy pilot bail out.

Many P-51s were engaged with 190s and, as Henderson surveyed the situation, a FW-190 made a ninety degree pass. In three turning orbits Henderson was on the German's tail and hit the 190 on the wings. His adversary dove away and a long chase, in and out of clouds, ensued for over ten minutes. Eventually a solid burst of gunfire hit home and dense black smoke poured out of the 190. The chase passed through more clouds, and the P-51 emerged right over the Focke-Wolf. They scissored. Henderson regained control of the fight and hit his foe again. The pilot parachuted. The German pilot may have been Oberleutnant (lst Lt) Rudol Schick, Staffel Commander of 6th Staffel, II Gruppe, JG-301, as German records show he was chased across the Aller Canal and shot down over Boldecker Land.

Captain Beavers, leading Beefsteak White Flight, maneuvered onto a 190's tail, opened fire and saw hits around the engine and cockpit. As Beavers overran his target he saw the pilot bail out and open his parachute. His wingman, lst Lt Carl H. French, was still with him as Beavers attacked another 190 which dove away. He followed, got hits around the cockpit and the canopy came off. The pilot did not appear to make any attempt to bail out and crashed in his aircraft.

2nd Lt John W. Gokey, Beefsteak White Three, watched Beavers shoot down his first 190 but broke right when White Four, lst Lt John P. Wilson, told him a 190 was on his, Gokey's, tail. Wilson broke into this 190 and got on his tail. After several circles the Jerry dove away to circle and dive again. Wilson's gun sight was inoperative. He fired anyway but saw no hits. From 5,000 feet the German dove for the deck, started a sharp pullout, and his aircraft snap-rolled three times to the right and crashed. Wilson pulled out and turned towards the wreckage. It was then that another FW-190, flying at 300 feet, came into view. Wilson attacked, opened fire at five hundred yards, and the Jerry turned into him. Wilson pursued, and they went into a steep turning orbit. Suddenly two FW-190s were seen coming in from above. The Jerry ahead of Wilson pulled his turn in tighter, snapped over on his back and crashed. Beefsteak White Four departed the area at full throttle.

In the meantime, Gokey made several passes on other FW-190s, scored hits on one but had to evade into the clouds after overrunning his opponent.

The third 503rd flight, Beefsteak Blue led by lst Lt Frank M. Stillwell, entered the fray. lst Lts Clarence I. Ferrell was Number Two, Bernie Allen Number Three, and Philip E. Petitt Number Four. Stillwell started after a 190, but another P-51 beat him to it. To his left he saw a Focke-Wolf closing on a P-51 so Stillwell broke onto the Jerry's tail and opened fire from six hundred yards, getting strikes almost immediately. Smoke poured from the engine, the German rolled upside down, started down in a steep dive and disappeared into the clouds below at 3,000 feet.

While Stillwell fought, Allen took on a FW-190 which had just made an attack on the B-24s. After three head-on passes he was able to obtain the advantage and score hits on the fuselage behind the cockpit. The Jerry snapped and spun down, but Allen was unable to follow as other FW-190s were on his and Petitt's tails. They evaded the enemy aircraft by ducking into the clouds.

As Petitt emerged from the clouds he found a FW-190 about twenty degrees off in close flight alignment. Closing fast he fired and saw hits around the cockpit before his superior speed carried him past his target. The 190 fell off on a wing out of control from 1,000 feet or less. Just before the 190 crashed, the 505th's lst Lt Carl H. Bundgaard pumped a few rounds into it.

Captain Donald W. Johnson, Beefsteak Green Leader, took the 503rd's fourth flight into the battle, and they destroyed six FW-190s. lst Lts David A. MacKenzie was Number Two, Lester C. Marsh Number Three, and Lloyd J. French was Beefsteak Green Four. Johnson started after a FW-190 diving away but noticed another slightly higher to the left. Rather than leave this 190 above and behind him, Johnson broke after it. Following the Focke-Wolf into a loop, Johnson hammered it at the top of the loop, and Jerry dropped out of his aircraft. Johnson then took on an enemy aircraft in a slight climb which went into a tight turning orbit. As Johnson out-turned the 190, the German tried a vertical reverse, but halfway through he caught the full fury of Johnson's gunfire. The enemy nosed over and dove away. Johnson followed, firing at intervals until the aircraft crashed. He pulled back up and at 4,000 feet saw a FW-190 pursued by a P-51 pursued by another 190. Johnson attacked the last one which broke off its attack and started skidding and evading. Strikes kept registering on the enemy aircraft as Johnson fired. The canopy came off the 190, but the pilot did not get out before the aircraft crashed.

On Johnson's first attack, his wingman, Lt MacKenzie, broke with him but stalled and spun out. A 190 then went after MacKenzie. Marsh, leading the second element, was to the rear of Johnson and Mackenzie and in position to go after the 190 attacking Beefsteak Green Two. In a tight turning circle Marsh inflicted numerous strikes around the enemy's cockpit. The German aircraft caught fire, flipped over on it back and dove straight in, exploding. Marsh and his wingman climbed back up, and at 15,000 feet, a 190 got on French's tail. Marsh broke hard left and came around on the Jerry's tail but, after a short burst, overran him. French then moved into position behind the

190, but before he could fire, the German bailed out. Marsh then saw two FW-190s attacking a straggling B-24. As he dove in to break it up, he closed rapidly and fired at the rear-most 190 which lost part of its wing and went snap rolling through clouds at 8,000 feet. He then went after the leading Focke-Wolf. After a long fight Marsh got in a good burst and was almost chewing the 190's tail off when the Jerry caught fire, rolled over, and dove straight in. As they were climbing back up they intercepted a FW-190 in a fast, shallow dive. Marsh cut him off, and, after a few short bursts, the aircraft exploded and went down in pieces. Again they started to climb back up but encountered Lt Stillwell fighting the 190 previously mentioned. Marsh gave this aircraft a burst, overran it, and Stillwell shot it down.

The fifth, and last, 503rd flight was Beefsteak Black led by Captain Malcolm B. Edens. His wingman, Lt Ralph S. Hill, Jr., returned early because of high coolant temperatures. The second element was led by 1st Lt Charles S. Coe who had Lt James A. Mankie on his wing. As the 503rd attacked the 190s going after the B-24s, Edens went after one attacking a straggling bomber. He was soon on the 190's tail, and after some short bursts and a few strikes, the Jerry bailed out. Edens then started back towards the bombers but saw two more FW-190s and broke after them. One turned away, but the other went straight ahead and Edens continued after him. He closed rapidly and opened fire from dead astern. Strikes sparked all over the enemy aircraft. It began to burn, and the pilot bailed out. Edens, now alone, climbed to 20,000 feet where he was attacked by three FW-190s. Edens eluded his foes by diving to the deck and heading home at 6,000 feet.

Lt Coe was with Edens on the initial attack but then went his own way. Observing a FW-190 maneuvering to get on the tail of a P-51, Coe fired from ninety degrees off. The 190 broke into Coe's attack, and they went into a circle. Coe was able to out-turn the 190 and pull around into firing position where he got some hits. The 190 broke for the deck, and Coe followed, getting strikes on the way. The canopy came off and the Focke-Wolf began to smoke as it flattened out on the deck. The 190 disappeared over a knoll, and when Coe passed over the rise, he saw it on the ground burning fiercely.

The 504th

Cockshy Squadron heard Armstrong report the bandits. About a minute later the fourth and last flight in the 504th, Cockshy Green, saw a fight in progress to their left. Led by 1st Lt Ely N. Van Cleave, Cockshy Green started in toward the action. Five FW-190s passed through and Van Cleave went after one. Cockshy Green Two, 2nd Lt Lyle M. Carter, was behind Van Cleave. Two 190s came between them. Van Cleave broke sharply, but Carter could not stay with him. Several minutes later Van Cleave called Carter who acknowledged. No more was heard from Van Cleave.

1st Lt Arthur W. Bates was leading the second element in Cockshy Green. He made two firing passes at a FW-190, and it disintegrated. His wingman, 2nd Lt Kenneth V. Berguson, became separated as he was unable to get one of his droptanks to jettison. Two FW-190s then started after him, and Berguson headed for home at full throttle. The 190s could not gain on him, and when the "hung" droptank fell off, he ran away from them.

Van Cleave did not return from this mission. Eventually reports from Germany indicated he crashed in the combat area near Springe, Germany.

The 505th

When the battle started the 505th was the high squadron at 26,000 feet. Although scattered, many FW-190s approached the Squadron from head on. Captain Archie A. Tower, leading the 505th, maneuvered onto the tail of a 190 and squeezed the trigger, but his guns would not fire.

The element leader, Upper Red Three, 2nd Lt Henry E. Girzi, was about to engage a FW-190 below him when another broke in from the left. As the 190 passed, Girzi turned inside of him and fired, getting some strikes. The 190 split-essed from 22,000 feet, and Girzi pursued, firing as he went and scoring hits. The enemy aircraft went straight in.

Leading the 505th's second flight, Upper White, was 1st Lt J. S. Daniell with Lt Harry D. Ziegler on his wing as Upper White Two. 1st Lt Bert Stiles, who had flown a combat tour as a B-17 pilot, led the second element. On his wing as Upper White Four was F/O Gerald W. Palmer. Daniell claimed five FW-190s destroyed on this mission and was awarded confirmation by the Eighth Air Force. Early in the action Ziegler, Upper White Two, was separated from Daniell but managed to join up with him for the trip home.

Over Rethen, Oberleutnant (1st Lt) Vollert, commander of 5th Staffel, II Gruppe, JG-301, attacked a B-24 of the 491st Bomb Group. He was then attacked by the second element of Upper White Flight, Lt Stiles and F/O Palmer. Stiles hit Vollert's FW-190 hard as the German dove away. As Palmer covered, Stiles followed in the dive and scored more strikes. As the plunge neared the deck Palmer pulled out, but Stiles and Vollert continued. Both crashed into a field near Sarstedt. The FW-190 was on fire before the crash and it burned. The P-51 did not burn.

The 505th's third flight, Upper Blue, made no claims. The fourth flight, Upper Green, was led by 1st Lt Carl H. Bundgaard. The name of his wingman is not on record. The second element was led by 2nd Lt William R. Phillippi. On his wing was 1st Lt Philip M. Loveless as Upper Green Four. Upper Green hit the 190s from high and out of the sun. Bundgaard attacked one below and to his right. He scored many strikes, and pieces flew off the 190 as they dove from 25,000 feet to 10,000 feet where the Jerry bailed out. As Bundgaard broke off he saw Lt Petitt of the 503rd shooting down a FW-190. Bundgaard got a short burst into this aircraft as it crashed.

When Bundgaard ended his first encounter, a 190 attacked Upper Green Two from above. Lt Phillippi,

Upper Green Three, broke into this attack and scored hits on the aircraft's wingroots. The enemy aircraft broke left and started down. At 10,000 feet Phillippi shot the tail off the 190, and the pilot bailed out. As Phillippi and his wingman, Lt Loveless, pulled up, they saw a FW-190 to their left. Phillippi got on his tail and fired. Strikes registered on wingroots, fuselage and tail. At about 4,000 feet the Jerry chopped throttle, and Phillippi passed him and broke up to the left. The enemy started to follow, but Loveless was in position on the enemy's tail and hit him with a burst. Descending, the 190 rolled right into a dive at 1,000 feet and crashed.

On the return to Fowlmere the Group made landfall out over the Dutch Islands at 1400 hours at various altitudes, from 10,000 to 23,000 feet. The landing at Fowlmere was around 1430 hours.

26 NOVEMBER 1944
AERIAL VICTORIES BOX SCORE
(all FW-190s)

	Destroyed	Probable	Damaged
503rd Fighter Squadron			
1st Lt Marsh, Lester C.	3	1	1
Capt Johnson, Donald W.	3	0	0
L/Col Henderson, Harvey E.	2	0	0
Capt Beavers, Edward H.	2	0	0
Capt Edens, Malcolm B.	2	0	0
1st Lt Wilson, John P.	2	0	0
1st Lt Coe, Charles, S.	1	0	0
1st Lt French, Lloyd J.	1	0	0
1st Lt Petitt, Philip E.	1	0	0
1st Lt Stillwell, Frank M.	1	0	0
1st Lt Allen, Bernice A.	0	0	1
2nd Lt Gokey, John W.	0	0	1
	18	1	3
504th Fighter Squadron			
1st Lt Bates, Arthur W.	1	0	0
505th Fighter Squadron			
1st Lt Daniell, J. S.	5	0	0
2nd Lt Phillippi, William R.	1 1/2	0	0
1st Lt Bungaard, Carl H.	1	0	1
1st Lt Stiles, Bert	1	0	0
2nd Lt Girzi, Henry E.	1	0	0
1st Lt Loveless, Philip M.	1/2	0	1
	10	0	1
Group Total	29	1	4

Killed In Action
1st Lt Ely N. Van Cleave, 504th
1st Lt Bert Stiles, 505th

The Early Years: From Cadet To Rice

by Ridge Sullivan

Solo

I enlisted in the Army Air Corp on April 13, 1942, the day after my 21st birthday, and was offered duty at Fort Meade or furlough at home until called for aviation cadet training. Since I had been a CMTC soldier at Fort Meade in 1939 and I feared that if I went to Ft. Meade I might miss cadet training for other duty, and as I had a job at GE to fill the time and would still draw Army pay of $21.00 a month, I chose to go on furlough.

I was called up in August 1942 and went to a new replacement depot at Nashville, Tennessee. My recollection of that experience was mud everywhere since the base was unfinished and roads were just a sea of mud. I remember being sick from typhoid shots. From Nashville I was sent to Maxwell Field at Montgomery, Alabama, for pre-flight training which was basic training in military discipline and activities. After that, Hawthorne School of Aeronautics at Orangeburg, South Carolina, was my next stop.

We were to fly Stearman planes, PT-17. These planes, while very safe flying, were known to ground loop if not landed correctly. I had never been in an airplane before, let alone fly one. I had expected my first flight would be sort of an orientation flight—what a surprise to be put right to work. My first flight was just fifty minutes, and during the entire flight, I never saw the ground after takeoff until we landed. After six hours of dual flight training on December 10, 1942, I was allowed to make my solo flight. I made my first landing okay, but on my second landing, I leveled off too high, immediately realizing that I needed to fly off and go around to try again. I pushed the throttle full open, but the plane stalled and dropped to the ground and ground looped at full throttle to the left toward the flight line and hangers. It was like looking out of field glasses the wrong way—things looked far away. I kicked the right rudder and took off again. This time I made a normal landing and returned to the flight line. My instructor told me to go to the clinic for a physical exam. I did so and had no problems, but my fingers on my left hand were treated because I had smashed them in the throttle quadrant as I pushed the throttle open, the reason I couldn't stop the plane as I careened toward the hangers.

I returned to the flight line and was immediately sent up again, this time with the instructor, and shot more landings. I then completed my solo flights. I have a short snorther (a dollar bill signed by my instructor) which attests to the solo flight.

When I returned to the barracks, the other cadets told me that my wing had passed over my flight instructor and that I has missed the nearest airplane by fifteen feet. After hearing this I was a scared, nervous wreck, realizing how lucky I'd been. There was some question, however, whether I should be washed out or not. Ultimately it was decided to allow me to continue training because of my hand being jammed in the throttle. The next day my flight instructor looked at my airplane and said, "There but for the grace of God is your coffin, just as good as new."

I was assigned to Hal Foster for my training, and every flight was a check flight. It was an experience I'll never forget. Errors were corrected by washing out the cockpit with the stick, in other words, the instructor would move his stick in a circle and the student's stick would follow, beating against the student's knees. Of course, there was the usual verbal abuse. In any case, I did move on into basic training.

Incidentally, after I returned from Europe, I applied for membership in the Caterpillar Club since I had bailed out of a plane. I received my certificate signed by Hal Foster who'd received his membership while instructing. Seems he told the student to do a slow roll and he didn't have his seat belt fastened. He fell out of the plane and was saved by his parachute.

Trip to Rice, California, in September 1943

On September 9, 1943, we left Walterboro, South Carolina, flying the P-39Q5 with the 1400hp Allison engine. We flew to Selma, Alabama, and Jackson, Mississippi, finally staying over night in Dallas, Texas. While in Dallas we "partied" since it was Saturday night. I got up early the next morning, found a church, then joined our flight at 9:00 a.m. to continue to California.

We flew to Midland and then on to El Paso. Three of us were ready to quit for the day since we were dog tired from our Saturday night out, but Bill Routt insisted we fly on to Phoenix—he had a buddy at Luke Field. Since he was flight leader, we went on to Phoenix. Three of us landed at Sky Harbor (well out of town in those days) while Bill went on to Luke Field. We stayed at the Westward Ho House. When we went out to dinner, I was so exhausted I literally fell asleep in the middle of dinner.

We rested up the next day and looked around Phoenix. It didn't take too long to see all of downtown Phoenix in those days. There was the main street, and only one block off main street were all private dwellings.

On the 13th we left Phoenix for Rice, only an hour away. When we arrived at Rice Bill Routt ordered us to land, and when we were on the ground, he headed west, radioing that he was on his way to Los Angeles and would see us in a few days. It was too late for us—we were there.

We were the first to arrive. We were met by Major Crowley and driven from Rice to Parker, Arizona. On the way in we were introduced to the dry, absolutely terrible heat of the desert. Opening the windows only made it worse—it was like a blast furnace. And Parker? It looked like a western movie town with just about the same activities.

Paul Meyer's Wedding

On December 13, 1943, we flew from Rice to Las Vegas, Nevada, to attend the wedding of Raymond P. (Paul) Mayer to Ellen. The wedding took place in the post chapel at the bomber base at Las Vegas.

My recollection is that twelve pilots of the 504th Squadron made the trip. As we approached the bomber base our Squadron Commander, Vern Hathorne, radioed that he wanted us to fly down the runway and peel off for a landing with the last plane to land before he turned onto the taxi strip. We landed two abreast, staggered on the runway. I was the last of the twelve to land. The propwash from the other planes bounced me all over the sky. I was scared that I might be dropped unexpectedly onto the runway and I considered going around to land. My pride just wouldn't let me do that. Fortunately I landed without incident. All twelve of us were on the runway at the same time, and the bomber crews were impressed.

I have a photograph of some of those who attended. They were: Mel Ball, Thibert, Weller, Saleem, Hathorne, Tucker, Routt, Gravette, Degner, Peter, and myself. Incidentally, we were not permitted to leave the base so we missed the excitement of Las Vegas gambling and night life.

Paul was a flight leader and was killed in action. Ellen remarried and died a few years ago.

High Tension Wires at Rice

In the middle of September 1943, Fred Showker and I were sent up on an instrument flight. Each of us spent some time under the hood while the other looked out for other aircraft. Before we returned to base, Fred suggested we buzz the 9th Armor Division which was on maneuvers in the area. After a few passes, I pulled up to higher altitude looking for Fred. I radioed to him but no response. As my fuel was running low, I had no choice but to return to base. When I landed I learned that Showker had flown through the high tension electric wires running from Parker Dam to San Diego. Miraculously, he wasn't killed, and even more surprising, he was able to fly the plane back. Both wings were damaged and the propeller was destroyed. Both of us were fined half our base pay ($75.00), he because of the unauthorized low flying and me because I was the flight leader who was responsible for the flight.

While a prisoner of war at Obermassfeld, I ran into a captain from the 9th Armor Division who was on the ground under those high tension wires. He said it was scary because there was lightning jumping all over the desert and the troops were under the wires. It was unbelievable that no one was hurt in the incident.

Blythe Episode

On September 20, 1943, I was sent up on a mission at 6:30 p.m., and after a short time, noticed that while it was still daylight at altitude, it was dark on the ground. When I returned to Rice, I saw that they were trying to move trucks along the runway to light it up so that we could land. The field wasn't lighted for night flying. Since my gas was low, I couldn't wait for the trucks to get into place so I headed south to Blythe Bomber Base. I buzzed the Blythe tower, and they gave me a green light to land. The runway and taxi strip was very long, and I must have taxied several miles. Per tech orders, I parked the P-39 and set the brakes.

That evening after I had dinner I was asked to go on a three-hour B-24 bomber flight. I flew the B-24 for awhile—it was like driving a Mack truck. I tried out the gunnery positions. It felt funny to be in the belly turret hanging out of the bottom of the plane. Eventually I ran out of things to do and sat down in the navigator's compartment. To my embarrassment, I proceeded to get air sick. With great control, however, I didn't throw up. I couldn't stand the thought of the razzing I would get if I did.

The next morning I prepared to fly back to Rice. I released my brakes and opened the throttle. To my surprise and dismay, the left brake locked, and I ground looped into a Cessna airplane. Damage: P-39 - one wingtip; Cessna - an entire wing. The Operations Officer told me I hit the wrong plane—any other plane on the field would have been excusable, but the Cessna belonged to the Base Commander. An hour later the Base Commander came to the flight line, stood me at a brace and said, "If there was a tree on this goddamned desert, I'd hang you from it." Seems he was planning to fly to Palm Springs for R&R.

Later that day the Line Chief drove a new wing tip to Blythe, and I returned to Rice. When I arrived at Rice I taxied to my assigned spot and parked. While I was writing out my paperwork and preparing to get out of the plane and the Crew Chief was taping up the 37mm cannon to keep out sand and dirt, the P-39 next to mine ground looped into my plane. Its prop chewed through to the fire wall while I was still in the cockpit! The brakes had "welded" on Thibert's plane just as mine had done in Blythe. Not realizing just what had happened, Skinney Gravette stormed out of the operations tent, climbed on my airplane and proceeded to chew me out. I explained my engine wasn't even started, and he finally calmed down. Miraculously no one was injured. Quite fortunately, the Crew Chief saw Thibert's P-39 coming and was able to get out of the way. As a result of the brake problems our tech orders were changed, and we no longer set the brakes when we parked.

Maneuvers

We were on the California Desert at Rice to practice combat tactics with ground troops on maneuvers in the area. We were expected to live the same way the ground troops lived; i.e., no cots, "C" rations, pup tents in the field and no other Air Corp pilot amenities. Occasionally, a ground force general would arrive unannounced to be sure we were doing this. It was a rush with shovels to bury the cots in the sand—we had no desire to sleep on the ground with rattlesnakes. At one point we were told to fly wearing steel helmets. Since this was impossible, however, we were ordered to wear the plastic helmet liner when not flying.

Since we were separated from our wives, every so often we would write letters and one of the pilots would fly to Parker, Arizona, and drop the letters from the plane using a streamer message pack. Vern Hathorn tried to see how close he could come to his motel.

The Life and Times of Ralph P. Thompson
by Ralph P. Thompson

I graduated from Luke Field with the class of 42-H as a staff sergeant pilot. From there some of us went to Orlando, Florida, on December 20, 1942, and then Arthur Steier and I went to Fort Bragg, North Carolina, where we instructed Army enlisted men who had some civilian flight time. We flew Cubs and L-5s.

Next Steier and I were transferred December 29, 1943, to Vichy, Missouri, under orders confirmed by one Captain Bruce Gravette, Third Air Force, Tampa, Florida. At Vichy we flew P-43s, P-40s and A-20s on photo recon training flights. Here Steier and I were promoted to Flight Officer, ending questions about why staff sergeants were wearing pilot's wings. Our lifestyles took a decided change.

After Vichy we were assigned to the 76th Tac Recon Group's 23rd Squadron at Statesboro, Georgia, commanded by Captain Harvey Henderson. We were then sent to Jacksonville, Florida, in September for fighter tactics training in P-39s. When we returned to Statesboro, Captain Henderson, Steier and I ferried three P-39s from San Antonio to Statesboro. Later the group was transferred to Thermal, California, where we flew close air support for troops on desert maneuvers.

It was there that we learned that a fighter-bomber outfit was getting ready for overseas assignment and had some pilot vacancies. Eleven of us eager beavers from the 76th Group who had hoped to fly combat requested a transfer. On January 20, 1944, Archie Tower, George Hrico, James Hanson, Frank Evans, Harold Everett, Philip Ewing, Leonard Fiorito, Joseph Wolfort, James McLure, Arthur Steier and I joined the 339th at Rice Air Field. Here, for the first time since primary at Hemet, California, my long-time buddy Art and I were assigned to different squadrons—he with the 503rd and me with the 504th.

Bruce Gravette, now commanding the 504th, Operations Officer Bill Routt and Flight Leader Lewis Peter honed our skills with the P-39s. It wasn't unusual to return from desert forays with props stained green from desert foliage.

After some three months the group was qualified for overseas duty. We left Rice, expecting to fly in the African desert or somewhere hot. Instead we shipped out for England, ending up at Fowlmere.

We wondered what aircraft we would fly and were delighted when the first few P-51Bs arrived. My third hour in a "51" was a "milk run" fighter patrol over France on April 30, 1944. We didn't see the enemy aircraft we'd all anticipated, but we did see our first flak—the first shots fired at us in anger.

During the next few weeks I had some frustrating experiences with English weather. On one mission while trying to stay on my flight leader's wing as he "reached for the sky" at the end of a climb-out, my plane stalled. I recovered on instruments, finally climbed out and rejoined the squadron. Because I wasn't shy about revealing my dislike for needle-ball flying, my reputation was established. While I later flew many hours on instruments, I never lived down that reputation.

The missions that stand out in my memory were the first flight over the channel; the first Berlin run; a low-level fighter sweep across Germany on May 21 in which Art Steier was lost; the mission along the North Sea south of Denmark across the Baltic Sea and then to the Polish-German border to escort the bombers around the German rocket experimental site at Peenemunde; and the D-Day patrol on the flank of the invasion force.

One non-combat episode comes to mind. On final approach returning from a mission, prop wash stood my plane on beam ends. The wing and landing gear picked up 150 feet of wire off the top two strands of the boundary fence at Fowlmere. When I got the plane straightened up, it took three low-level passes across the field to dislodge the pesky wire.

Many memories of my time in the 339th are still vivid. It is especially pleasant to recall some of the pilots I was lucky enough to fly with and the loyal, hard-working ground crews. I don't think there was ever a finer bunch of people than those of the 339th.

First Mission

by G. P. Harry

May 21, 1944, a day I'll always remember. It started out something like this....

The operations phone rang and Flight Leader Bill Routt answered and said, "Briefing in half an hour? O.K." Putting down the phone, he called, "Harry, Saleem, Showker, let's go!"

Routt hadn't finished and I was half dressed while the other pilots who'd had about forty hours of combat took their time. "Hell! Guess it'll be another one of those milk runs, flubbing along at twenty-five thousand feet, escorting the bombers, and not seeing anything but flak," Routt complained. "If they don't give us a good, hot mission soon, we're gonna peel off after 'bombs away' and look for targets of opportunity."

The trucks took us down to the briefing room where we found our designated seats. One of the group leaders stood and said, "This is the type of mission we've been waiting for. The entire Eighth Fighter Command'll be going on a gigantic fighter sweep. Our primary targets'll be the Luftwaffe with locomotives secondary. However, shoot anything that might be of military value. Our particular area is south of Leipzig. Start engines at Ten thirty-two. Take-off at Ten fifty-two. You new pilots stick with your flight leaders because they're not going back to look for you. That's all I have."

The briefing room immediately broke into an uproar. This was the first time we were to see real action - especially myself.

Back at the ready room we tussled into our flight gear and checked all our personal effects such as watches, rings, billfolds, etc., into Intelligence for safe keeping...or mailing home in case we didn't make it back.

Finally, at the planes, we climbed in and waited for the "start engines" signal. I saw Routt's prop turning and I cranked my plane. As Routt taxied by, I slid in beside him for take-off. In the air, we joined the rest of the group, and the leader said, "Setting course in one minute. Close up the formation, and we'll climb through the overcast."

In a few minutes we broke out on top and into the bluest sky I'd ever seen. Looking around, I could well believe the entire 8th Fighter Command was on this mission. The sky was covered with Mustangs, Thunderbolts, and Lightnings.

My fighter proved to be a real gas hog, and I emptied my drop tanks fifteen minutes before anyone else. As I released the tanks safely and saw them go spinning down into Germany, Routt said over the radio, "You gonna have enough fuel?"

"Roger, plenty, no problem." At least I hoped so, but I wasn't about to turn back.

We flew at 17,000 feet for about two hours before the group leader said, "Okay, you guys, follow me down."

Routt lazily turned his fighter on its back and started straight down. I did the same, and we came down from 17,000 feet like a falling brick. As we leveled out over the tree tops, the air speed read 500 mph. For the next few minutes things happened very, very fast. The first thing I saw was some army barracks, so I pushed the nose down and fired a few rounds. When I pulled up there was a ME-109 directly in my gun sight. I gave him a good burst, then passed not fifty feet under him before I could see if my shots were effective. I was still going 350 mph when I looked off to my left and saw an airdrome. Routt banked up and I thought he was going to strafe. I kicked my fighter into a steep bank and started for the airfield, but Routt, the rascal, resumed his heading. I didn't see him until that night in the Officers' Club.

There were Jerry planes buzzing around the field like angry wasps at their nests, but they didn't want to fight. They just wanted to land. I caught one fighter just after he landed. The pilot jumped out of his plane and began running. Unfortunately for him and unintentionally on my part, he ran into my line of fire. I finally got my gun sight lined up on his plane and sent a burst into it. Smoke instantly began pouring from the engine. As I passed over the Me-109, I looked up and saw a Ju-52. There was very little time for a good shot, but I did get a few strikes. About this time, the ground guns were throwing up considerable flak, so I broke off my attack and took up the compass heading for England. Looking around, it was apparent I'd made a mistake by going back to strafe the enemy field since no one else did. They were about 30 miles ahead of me. It was a lonely feeling, plus I'd felt some of the ground fire hit my fighter, and I was a long, long way from home...all by myself. I tried to call my group on the radio, but got no reply.

Pilot Articles

All this time the radio was yakking away. "Let's get that loco....look at the Jerries run....there's a staff car....watch that smoke stack....what happened to number four man?..."

One pilot who'd evidently lost control of his fighter calmly said, "I'm gonna hit that tree."

Another said, "Don't fly behind me. I'm dragging about a hundred feet of telephone wire."

All this was happening from the time we peeled down from 17,000 feet, probably not more than ten minutes of elapsed time.

Five minutes after leaving the German airfield, I caught a liaison plane, but he ducked into the overcast just as I began firing. After that I flew as low to the ground as possible since surprise was important in strafing. I saw a flak tower ahead and pulled up, giving it a long burst. Looking back, I saw two men milling around in the tower, but when I turned and looked forward, there was a huge tree right in my face! It was too late to keep from hitting it, but by rolling my plane over on its side, I did miss the main part of the tree. I felt something hit my face. Hot oil, I thought. The engine's breaking up! Looking down, I saw leaves, twigs and small branches...inside the cockpit. Some of this had hit my face, making me think it was oil. I pulled up to bailout, but the engine never missed a beat. The left wing, however, was bent back about four inches and had a large hole in the leading edge, but after retrimming, the plane flew okay.

I finally decided to concentrate on getting home, so I climbed up through the overcast and broke out at 18,000 feet. Looking around hurriedly, I saw no planes in the sky. I flew for about 45 minutes, and everything was looking good for getting back to England. Then BANG! I thought my engine had blown as a result of hitting the tree. While checking my engine instruments, I smelled gun powder. Strange, I hadn't fired my guns for a long time. Looking outside the cockpit, I discovered the reason for the smell. Flak was coming up thick enough to walk on. The bang I'd heard and the smell of powder was a flak shell exploding. There was a flak hole about four inches in diameter in the wing, but again, the fighter never missed a stroke.

The flak was a surprise in more ways than one. I thought I was over the North Sea, but I was probably over the city of Hamburg. That meant I was still a long way from England, and now my gas burning fighter was presenting a problem. If that was Hamburg, I had to reach England in 85 minutes or I was in for a cold swim. Throttling back as much as possible, I settled back for a ride over which I had no control.

Meanwhile, the radio was still busy. One pilot called in and said, "I've got fifteen minutes fuel remaining. Give me a vector to the nearest land."

The controller answered, "Your nearest land is one hundred and fifty-five miles on a heading of one-four-five degrees." (This was Germany!)

Several minutes later the pilot called, "Mayday, bailing out!" He didn't have time to even reach Germany.

But I wasn't home yet, not by any means. I had about twenty minutes of fuel left at this time. I started down through the clouds knowing if I didn't see land immediately after breaking out of the overcast, I was in big trouble. When I did break out - after an eternity, it seemed - there was nothing in sight except the cold North Sea. A few seconds later, however, a small vessel appeared. At least I could bail out on top of the vessel and possibly have it rescue me. As I started a turn to stay above the boat which looked like a trawler, I took one final look at my original direction and thought I saw something on the horizon. Taking a chance by leaving the boat, I resumed my compass heading and very soon saw the beach. At least I could bail out over England if I had to, but my luck was still holding. There was a R.A.F. airbase just a mile or so from the beach. After landing and cutting the switches, I looked at the clock. I'd been in the air for six hours and fifteen minutes.

Once I'd asked the flight men to gas up my plane, I went into Intelligence and gave my combat report. When I returned to the plane, the men were standing around, and the fighter hadn't been refueled. I asked why, and one of the men responded, "Sir, have you seen all the damage to that plane?" I told him if my plane could bring me 500 miles, it could darn sure take me fifty more miles...gas it up!

The crew chief was waiting when I finally landed at Fowlmere. The damage to my fighter - three large flak holes, two small caliber bullet holes, the left wing bent back and ripped open by the tree I'd hit.

When I walked into the Officers' Club, things got real quiet. "First mission" pilots usually don't make it back when overdue by one hour after empty-tank time.

A Long Time Ago
by Robert M. Kuhlman

A *Bridge Too Far.* One of my most significant experiences happened on my very first mission - the escort of planes and gliders in September '44 for the invasion of Holland. This incident or action has been documented in many movies and is best remembered as "A Bridge Too Far." It boggled my mind to see the gliders coming into the landing areas from all points of the compass. A few months later I met one of the glider pilots in London, and he told me he went from pilot status to infantryman in about 30 seconds after landing when one of our soldiers handed him a "45" and told him to defend himself as best he could.

A "Funny" Thing Happened on the Way to the Fraternity House. One glorious spring morning very near the end of the war, probably in April 1945, we were taxiing out for a mission to some since forgotten target (by this time there were not many left) when all of a sudden we were being fired upon by machine gun fire. There was no question about the type of projectile since we could see the trajectory of the tracer bullets. After our mission some five hours later we went for our debriefing and asked for an explanation for being fired on at our own base. The near catastrophe (no one was hit) was caused by one of the pilots at Duxford checking his gun sight and accidentally pulling the trigger and releasing the brief burst. I remember saying, "If I ever catch that Son of a Barbarian, I'll kill him!" Two years later I was sitting in the basement of my fraternity house in East Lansing, Michigan, (Spartan land) telling this story to two of my fraternity brothers. One of them, Walt Bourque, stood up, a big grin on his face, and said, "Bob, I'm your man." It turned out to be a pretty small war after all.

Strafing German Airfields
by Richard C. Penrose

The first German aircraft destroyed on the ground by the 339th fell to the 503rd on 19 May 1944 when they destroyed three and damaged ten. By early June all three squadrons had destroyed a few enemy aircraft on the ground. After 7 June 1944, airfield strafing was entirely a 505th show until 13 September when each squadron destroyed one or two.

After 13 September there was no airfield strafing until 1 March 1945 except for an abortive attempt by the 505th on 21 November 1944 when they destroyed one aircraft on the ground and lost two of their own at the airfield. On 1 March 1945 the 505th resumed airfield strafing and on 20 March the 504th joined in. In April, with the end of the war near, the number of German aircraft destroyed on the ground rose dramatically. Poorly or undefended aircraft parking areas were strafed at will. On 10 April 1945 the 339th claimed 105 destroyed (officially reduced to 87), 118 on 16 April (reduced to 96), and 67 on 17 April (reduced to 61). Fifty-eight percent of all enemy aircraft destroyed on the ground by the 339th were destroyed on these three missions.

Using 339th records, the Group's units were officially credited with the following enemy aircraft destroyed on the ground:
  HQ 3 (00.7%)
  503rd - 51 (12.0%)
  504th - 102 (24.1%)
  505th - 267.5 (63.2%)
  Total Destroyed - 423.5

No Eighth Air Force comparison based on the average number of enemy aircraft destroyed on the ground per mission by squadron was made as the data was not at hand. The 505th Fighter Squadron, however, is probably tops with 267.5 destroyed in 264 missions (1.013 average per mission).

The top scorers in each squadron for enemy aircraft destroyed on the ground were:

503rd		504th		505th	
Robert H. Ammon	9	Kirke B. Everson	13	Joseph L. Thury	25.5
Steve J. Chetneky	6	Leon M. Orcutt	9	Archie A. Tower	18
Robert. J. Frisch	6	William. C. Clark	8	Oscar K. Biggs	11.5
John R. Byers	5	Robert. V. Blizzard	6	Harry R. Corey	11
Clarence Ferrell	4	Frank A. Clifton	6	Harold W. Burch	10

Who's Superstitious?
by John L. Sutton

With a great many other replacement pilots I was checked out in the P-51 at Goxhill in May 1944. One day I went to a large meeting where assignment to combat groups were made. I was with Frank Stillwell and Dick Tannous, both friends from previous training bases.

At one point the officer directing the meeting yelled, "I need three for the 339th." We had never heard of the 339th, but we looked at one another and nodded. I put up my hand and shouted. Well, for better or worse, that's how assignments were made.

Not long after on a chilly, foggy morning, I was taken by a corporal carrying my B-4 bag to one of those half-buried barrels we knew as quarters. The hut was dark, and all I could see were some lumps in the cots along the wall. The corporal put my bag down in front of one of the cots. When I asked about the clothes hanging there, he said he'd take them away immediately.

Suddenly a head appeared from one of the lumps and a voice asked, "Aren't superstitious, are you?"

I was dumbfounded, speechless to be exact. "You'll be the third in that cot in ten days," grumbled the voice in rather ominous tones.

Not much of a beginning, but the "voice" and I became good friends after that. And the cot? Superstitious or not, I held on to that cot for over six months.

Anybody in the 504th remember the young lady in Cambridge known as the "Kiss of Death"? Seems someone suddenly realized that every pilot who'd know this girl had gone down on a mission soon thereafter. I didn't know her, but I sure made it a point to know her name just in case. One night we had a very young, very new pilot come back from an evening in Cambridge.

During a rather intense interrogation by us wise old veterans who'd been in the 504th perhaps two months longer than this young man, the name of the "Kiss of Death" came up. Everybody in the hut went over and shook the young pilot's hand, giving him the cheerful news that her score was already seven pilots.

Not very funny, you say? Right! Our intrepid young pilot went down a few days later behind the lines in Belgium. He made it back, but the "Kiss of Death" retained her grasp. He went down again, this time in Germany, and became a prisoner of war. Talk about superstition....

PILOT ARTICLES

The Jet War
by Richard C. Penrose

In aerial combat the 339th Fighter Group was officially credited with the destruction of twelve German jet aircraft, the probable destruction of two, and nineteen damaged. This ranks the 339th in fourth place among the fifteen fighter groups in the Eighth Air Force. Only the 357th (18#), the 55th (15), and the 78th (14) surpassed the 339th.

Within the 339th, the 504th Fighter Squadron was tops with seven destroyed, one probable, and eight damaged. The 505th destroyed three and damaged five. The 503rd had two destroyed and six damaged. 339th Headquarters had a probable. The 504th shot down more German jets than each of seven of the fifteen fighter groups. Among the forty-five Eighth Air Force fighter squadrons, the 504th ranks fourth. The top squadron was the 82nd (10) of the 78th, followed by the 364th (8#) and 363rd (8) of the 357th.

The 339th started poorly against the German jet opposition. The Group lost one P-51 to Me-262 gunfire and another had just been shot down before we had a chance to shoot back. Coincidentally, both P-51's appear to have been shot down by the same German pilot, Oberfeldwebel (Master Sergeant) Helmut Baudach of E-Kdo 262 (Me-262 Proving Detachment).

11 September 1944

The 505th's 1st Lt William A. Jones wasn't on the schedule for this day's mission but when he heard the Squadron was going to return to the same German airfield the 505th had strafed the previous day (in which Jones had participated), he asked to go along. At first he was turned down but later put on the schedule. On the return flight to Fowlmere, after the airfield strafing, Major Archie A. Tower, leading the 505th, put the Squadron into a fairly tight "V" formation while still over Germany. A Me-262, probably flown by Helmut Baudach, bounced the 505th, shot up Jones's aircraft, and zoomed away. Jones bailed out of his badly damaged P-51 east of Mannheim, near Eberbach, and became a prisoner of war.

21 November 1944

On an escort mission to Leipzig the 504th saw a Me-262 but was unable to engage.

31 December 1944

The 503rd, led by Captain William E. Bryan, escorted B-17s to Hamburg. Lt Col Carl T. Goldenberg, one-time commander of the 491st Bomb Group (B-24's), led the second flight, Beefsteak White. 1st Lt James A. Mankie flew his wing and 1st Lt Charles S. Coe led the element with 2nd Lt Ralph S. Hill as Number Four. About 1150 hours, in the target area, Goldenburg went into a shallow right turn into Mankie. As he crossed to the other side of the turn, Mankie's aircraft was jolted by a large explosion. He could see a large hole in one wing and lost control of the aircraft. As there was no fire, Mankie fought for control as his P-51 rapidly lost altitude. Unable to regain control, he bailed out and became a prisoner of war. Mankie did not know what shot him down until after the war when Ralph Hill told him it had been a Me-262. German records indicate Helmut Baudach was the pilot of this Me-262.

Two flights to the rear of Beefsteak White was Beefsteak Green led by Captain Anthony G. Hawkins. 1st Lt Bernice A. Allen led the element with 1st Lt John P. Wilson as Number Four. As Baudach approached the 503rd, Allen called him in and Hawkins broke into the Me-262 and fired a short burst as Mankie was being shot down. Strikes hit the Me-262 on the wing and wingroots before it zoomed away and escaped. Ten minutes later Beefsteak Green engaged some FW-190's and Hawkins shot one down. He did not return from this mission and later was reported as killed in action.

14 January 1945

The Group escorted bombers to Magdeburg and saw two Me-262s and one Me-163 which were not observed attacking the bombers.

20 January 1945

On an escort mission to Steckrode, Germany, the Group spotted one Me-262 in the far distance.

9 February 1945

The Luftwaffe launched a major Me-262 assault against the Eighth Air Force bombers using KG(J)-54, a converted bomber unit. Perhaps ten jets were put up and six were lost.

Shortly before noon on a bomber escort mission to Bohlen, Germany, the 505th's Upper Blue Flight, led by 1st Lt Thomas W. Marvel, in the vicinity of Fulda, saw three Me-262's attacking a box of bombers. Upper Blue pursued the enemy jets and Marvel and his element leader, 1st Lt Stephen C. Ananian, opened fire from extreme range but saw no hits. Since Marvel was closer to this jet, Ananian and his wingman, 2nd Lt Harvey F. Howard, went after another Me-262.

Ananian opened fire from eight hundred yards with little expectations, but was rewarded with strikes on the wings and around the left engine. Closing slowly, Ananian fired more bursts, getting more hits in the cockpit area and causing the right engine to catch fire. The Me-262 fell away out of control.

Around noon in the vicinity of Meiningen, east of Fulda, the 504th's 2nd Lt Jerome J. Sainlar, flying as a spare with a four-ship Cockshy flight, saw a Me-262 attacking two B-17's that had dropped out of formation. As the 504th went to the bombers' aid, Sainlar was able to make the best cutoff. He fired from a forty degree angle and registered hits. The jet pulled away in a steady dive and evaded further action.

16 February 1945

A photo reconnaissance aircraft enroute to Frankfurt, escorted by four 503rd P-51s led by 1st Lt Alec Boychuck, was attacked by two Me-262s. The photo aircraft evaded into the clouds.

2 March 1945

The 505th saw five jets attack some British bombers over Osnabruck and drove them off.

3 March 1945

The Germans put up twenty-nine Me-262 sorties, mostly by III Gruppe, JG-7. Near Celle, Germany, on a mission to Dallbergen, the 503rd encountered six Me-262s at 1015 hours. In a brief encounter, only lst Lt Raymond G. Johnson was able to score hits. He dove from 20,000 feet to 5,000 feet before closing within range. The jet entered the landing pattern at an airfield, possibly Fassberg. Johnson fired as the Me-262 turned on his approach and saw strikes. Intense light flak drove Johnson off as the jet completed its landing.

The 504th's Captain Frank D. Guernsey and lst Lt William T. Hurley fired at a Me-262 but observed no hits.

14 March 1945

A Me-262 was seen on an escort mission to Hanover, but not engaged.

17 March 1945

On an escort mission to Ruhland an AR-234 was seen and chased over Torgan, but escaped undamaged.

20 March 1945

The Luftwaffe's JG-7 put up twenty-nine sorties against the Eighth Air Force and lost four. The 339th claimed two destroyed and one damaged as they conducted a fighter sweep in the Hamburg area. First action was engaged at 1530 hours when the 504th's lst Lt Kenneth V. Berguson peeled off on a Me-262 going in the opposite direction and managed to close to eight hundred yards. In a large turning circle Berguson fired a short burst and observed several strikes. The jet evaded below the clouds. Then Berguson, lst Lts Loren W. Allers and Robert C. Croker, and the Flight Leader, lst Lt Jerome J. Ballard, chased a Me-262 over the jet base at Kaltenchirchen where they encountered 20mm and 40mm flak. Ballard's P-51 was hit and caught fire forcing him to bail out. Ballard's parachute did not bloom and he fell into trees which caught the parachute, enabling him to land safely. He was then captured.

At 1620 hours the 505th's Upper White Flight led by Captain Harry R. Corey, flying at 3,000 feet southeast of Hamburg, sighted a Me-262 crossing their path. Upper White broke in behind and fired several bursts from eight hundred to one thousand yards to no avail. lst Lt Robert E. Irion, leading the second element, began to gain slowly when the jet turned slightly to the right. At seven hundred yards he scored a few scattered hits. In another right turn Irion closed to six hundred yards and hit a wing and the fuselage. The jet pulled up steeply and the canopy was jettisoned as the aircraft was being clobbered by Irion's gunfire. The pilot left the aircraft, but his parachute was not seen to open. Circumstantial evidence indicates this German pilot was Unteroffizier (Corporal) Hans Mehn of lst Staffel, I Gruppe, JG-7.

At 1700 hours part of the 504th with Lt Col William C. Clark leading as Cockshy Red Leader was enroute home after strafing the airfield at Heilgenhafen. A Me-262 was spotted coming in from six o'clock. The 504th broke into the jet which continued on in, now head-on. It was fired on by Clark, lst Lts Robert M. Kuhlman, Lawrence J. Barrett, Vernon N. Barto, and 2nd Lt Leonard A. Kunz. As Barto fired, the jet's left engine caught fire, then the right one, followed by a terrific explosion. The Me-262 pulled up over Barto, and as he pulled around to get on the Jerry's tail, the jet rolled upside down and the pilot dropped out. The German pilot was probably Oberfeldwebel (Master Sergeant) Erich Buttner of III Gruppe, JG-7.

During the day's action, lst Lt Ralph S. Hill, Jr., of the 503rd, was able to inflict damage on two Me-262s.

21 March 1945

Thirty-one jet sorties were put up against the Eighth Air Force by the Luftwaffe. The 339th escorted bombers hitting Rhuland, near Dresden. The 503rd called in jets but did not score. Soon after, the 504th's Cockshy Blue Flight, led by Captain Richard C. Penrose with lst Lt Gordon H. Chenez as Blue Two, lst Lt Frederick C. Haslam as Blue Three, and 2nd Lt Will M. Hudson as Blue Four, saw an explosion in a distant bomber formation. A Me-262 was then seen in a shallow dive pursued by P-51's which had no chance.

During withdrawal, Cockshy Green Flight, led by lst Lt. Nile C. Greer, had a Me-262 come in at them from three o'clock high. Cockshy Green broke into the jet and followed it through 270 degrees of turn, never getting within range. The jet pulled away. Greer resumed his course home at 15,000 feet. About 1045 hours Greer spotted a Me-262 being chased below by a P-51 which was not within gun range. Cockshy Green went into a gentle dive and the Me-262, apparently unaware of the P-51's above, went into a climbing turn to Greer's left. Cockshy Green closed and Greer and Cockshy Green Three, lst Lt Billy E. Langohr, opened fire. Strikes were observed on the right wing and engine. As the jet continued in a steep, tight climbing turn, they pounded it with gunfire. Pieces flew off the Me-262 and the right engine burned fiercely. The jet rolled over and dove away, crashing into the ground below. No parachute was seen. The Me-262 pilot may have been Hauptman (Captain) Eberhard Winkel of 3rd Staffel, I Gruppe, KG-51.

22 March 1945

North of Dresden while on an escort mission to Ruhland, eight Me-262s and four Me-163s attacked the bombers and shot down two. As they reformed for a second attack the 339th drove them off.

25 March 1945

The Group escorted B-24s to Brunswick. In the target area a Me-262 was seen shooting down a 352nd Fighter Group P-51. Four others tried to attack the bombers, but were driven off by the 503rd as Major Dale E. Shafer, Jr., damaged one of them.

30 March 1945

Of the thirty-one jet sorties put up by the Germans, the 339th destroyed two plus a probable and one damaged. About 1300 hours, enemy aircraft were reported below the escorting fighters who were at 29,000 feet. As the escort started down to investigate, Col John B. Henry, Jr., the 339th Group Commander, spotted a Me-262 10,000 feet below and climbing steeply. Henry dove on the jet and at 22,000 feet altitude fired a long burst from one thousand to two thousand yards. Strikes flashed on the jet's fuselage. Dark smoke poured from both engines and the Me-262 dove and disappeared into cirrus clouds below at 20,000 feet.

The 505th's Upper Yellow Flight, led by Captain James R. Starnes, pursued some Me-262s but was unable to engage. As they continued on at 2,500 feet northeast of Hamburg a Me-262 bounced Upper Yellow from the rear at 1325 hours. Upper Yellow Four spotted the attacker and called a break but inadvertently used the wrong flight color. As a result, Upper Yellow did not break. The jet hammered Upper Yellow Two with gunfire, tracers whipped by Starnes, and the enemy aircraft zoomed away. Yellow Two's P-51, flown by lst Lt Evergard L. Wager, was set on fire. At 1,500 feet Wager bailed out, but his parachute did not stream until fairly low and never did open. The probable Me-262 pilot was Gefreiter (Private First Class) Heim who, in turn, was killed in action on 10 April 1945.

Shortly before 1330 hours, nine Me-262s passed head on through the 504th. The entire Squadron broke after the enemy aircraft and the chase was on. Captain Robert F. Sargent, Cockshy Green Flight Leader, took several long range shots at two jets but it was ineffective. At 12,000 feet Sargent was joined by Cockshy White Four, 2nd Lt Leonard A. Kunz, and they headed back towards the target area. Sargent then saw two Me-262s taking off from Kaltenkirchen Airfield. Both dove steeply on the jets. At 420 miles per hour Sargent closed easily on the rearmost jet which may have been going 250 miles per hour. As he closed, Sargent fired a long burst getting strikes. One engine poured out white smoke and pieces flew off, including the cockpit canopy. The German pilot bailed out at 300 feet altitude, but his parachute did not have time to open properly before he struck the ground. The jet crashed and exploded nearby. Kunz fired at the diving Me-262 as it crashed. The lead jet was then out of range and escaped. The German pilot bailing out was Leutnant Erich Schulte of I Gruppe, JG-7. German reports indicate they believed Schulte was fired at in his parachute, apparently mistaking Kunz's fire at the crashing jet for fire at Schulte.

Simultaneously with the above action, lst Lt Carroll W. Bennett, leading Cockshy White Flight, broke into the Me-262s and cut two of them off in a right turn and scored several hits on one as they disappeared into clouds at 8,000 feet. Bennett dropped below the clouds and then climbed back up on top. West of Bad Oldsloe, northeast of Hamburg, Bennett saw another Me-262 and chased it to Bad Segeberg and then southeast to Lubeck, making a few hits enroute. Near Lubeck the jet was on fire and dove down into the clouds.

At about 1400 hours the 505th's Captain George T. Rich, leading Upper White Flight with lst Lt Stephen C. Ananian as wingman, dropped down under the cloud cover to 1,500 feet and soon ran across four Me-262s letting down through the overcast. The jets turned and ran, but Rich and Ananian were able to lob in a few hits as the Me-262s pulled away.

4 April 1945

Several books have covered the 504th's action this day and more has been written into it than the official records support. The following, relating to the 504th, is based upon 339th available records.

The Germans put up forty-seven jet sorties and lost eight. This was the 339th's best day against the Me-262s as they destroyed four, damaged one, and fired on others. Lt Col William C. Clark led the 504th, twenty-one P-51s in five four-ship flights plus one spare.

The known flight schedule for the 504th was:
Cockshy Red:
    1, Lt Col William C. Clark
    2, lst Lt Lyle M. Carter
    3, Unknown
    4, Unknown
Cockshy White:
    All positions unknown
Cockshy Blue
    1, Captain Nile C. Greer
    2, 2nd Lt Harlan F. Hunt
    3, Unknown
    4, Unknown
Cockshy Green
    1, Captain Robert F. Sargent
    2, 2nd Lt Robert C. Havighurst
    3, Captain Kirke B. Everson
    4, lst Lt Robert C. Croker
Cockshy Yellow
    All positions unknown
Spare
    Unknown

It is known that the following four pilots were on the mission, but their flight position is unknown:
2nd Lt Cephas Hermansen, fired at a Me-262
2nd Lt Will M. Hudson
lst Lt Donald F. Kreuger
lst Lt Raymond H. Creswell, may have led Cockshy White or Yellow Flight

The 504th took off at 0705 hours on a fighter sweep of the area around the German jet base at Parchim. About 0915 hours, in the vicinity of Parchim, Clark assigned Cockshy White, Blue, Green, and Yellow Flights to positions circling at 8,000 feet above the clouds while he led Cockshy Red Flight on the deck under the clouds towards the airfield.

As Cockshy Red approached Parchim, Luftwaffe Major Rudolf Sinner, Commander of III Gruppe, JG-7, took off, circled the field and formed up seven Me-262s. In formation, they headed out under the clouds. Very soon they passed head-on through Cockshy Red. Clark and his flight broke around after the jets. A burst by Clark scored a few strikes on one Me-262 as the jets disappeared into the overcast.

Sinner soon spotted a hole in the clouds and started up with two others while the other four stayed underneath the clouds for some distance before climbing. As the first three jets appeared above the clouds, Cockshy Blue and Green Flights bounced. Sinner was attacked by Captain Kirke B. Everson, Cockshy Green Three, and lst Lt Robert C. Croker, Cockshy Green Four. Sinner tried to evade into the clouds, but Everson and Croker were able to get in several bursts, hitting the jet's right engine which erupted in flames. The Austrian bailed out at about 900 feet and landed near the burning wreckage of his Me-262. Sinner was placed under additional stress when Everson and Croker strafed his parachute on the ground.

Cockshy Green Leader, Captain Robert F. Sargent, fired on one of the jets but submitted no claims. His wingman, 2nd Lt Robert C. Havighurst, Cockshy Green Two, picked up a Me-262 and trailed it as it headed back towards the airfield, scoring some strikes on the jet's left wing near the engine.

Havighurst then had to evade flak from the airfield. When the jet started up through a hole in the clouds, another burst from Havighurst pounded the fuselage and cockpit. Black smoke poured out of the left engine, and the jet started a forty-five degree climb where, at 2,000 feet, it nosed over. At 1,000 feet, it was going straight down.

On the bounce, Captin Nile C. Greer, Cockshy Blue Flight Leader, and 2nd Lt Harlan F. Hunt, Cockshy Blue Two, closed on two Me-262s. Greer picked the one on the left and fired. The jet flipped over into a reverse turn to the left, and Greer hit both engines and the fuselage behind the cockpit.

As the crippled jet passed through a cumulus cloud, Greer continued to fire. Black smoke poured from both of the jet's engines. When the Me-262's canopy was jettisoned, another burst from Greer sent the pilot over the side in a successful bailout. This pilot was probably Leutnant Franz Schall of III Gruppe, JG-7, who had taken off with Major Sinner.

Around 1000 hours the 505th's Captain Harry F. Corey, Upper Blue Flight Leader, with F/O LeRoy A. Steiger as Upper Blue Two, 1st Lt Thomas W. Marvel as Upper Blue Three, and F/O John J. Rice as Upper Blue Four, was sweeping the Gummerower Lake area at 2,000 feet when a Me-262 was spotted at the ten o'clock position. Corey turned into the jet and fired, observing a few stikes. The enemy aircraft passed over, and

Corey pulled around, getting on the jet's tail. In and out of the clouds and turning, the chase went on. Corey outturned the jet and got in a five-second burst from dead astern. The Me-262 began to lose fuel from the left engine, and pieces flew off the right wing. The jet snap-rolled twice to the left and fell into a flat spin from 1,500 feet, crashed and exploded near Rostock. F/O Steiger had his canopy damaged and his goggles knocked off when he flew through the debris from the disintegrating Me-262 before it crashed.

As a sidelight, one of the jet pilots the Germans lost this day was 209-victory ace, Major Heinrich Ehrler, who was shot down by fighters east of Stendal. This, however, does not appear to have happened because of any 339th action.

5 April 1945

The 505th's Upper White Flight, on an escort mission to Bayreuth, dropped down to 5,000 feet and circled a Me-262 base near Bobirgen, hoping to catch aircraft taking off. Leading the second element was 1st Lt Stephen C. Ananian with 1st Lt William R. Guyton on his wing as Upper White Four. Eventually Ananian spotted a Me-262 taking off and immediately dove after it. He fired a few bursts at 400 MPH and scored strikes on the jet's wing. The jet then pulled away and disappeared into the haze.

7 April 1945

The 503rd's Beefsteak Blue Flight, led by 1st Lt Philip E. Petitt with 1st Lts Carl H. French and George W. Porter flying with him while escorting bombers to Hamburg, had six Me-262s come at them from the rear. The Flight broke into the jets and Petitt hit one of them once or twice. The Me-262s then sped out of danger.

About 1230 hours, the 504th's Cockshy Blue Flight encountered some enemy aircraft. 1st Lt Robert V. Blizzard, Cockshy Blue Three, with 1st Lt Gordon H. Chenez as wingman, started after a Me-262 but pulled off when he saw a Me-262 coming in to attack the bombers. Blizzard and the jet came at each other almost head-on. Blizzard fired a short burst hitting the jet's wingroots. The Me-262 evaded into the clouds below. Blizzard and Chenez resumed flying escort at 13,000 feet. It was not long before two more Me-262s were spotted about five thousand feet below. As Blizzard and Chenez dropped down on the Germans, one jet broke left and the other continued straight ahead. Slizzard followed the one that broke and closed rapidly. He fired several bursts and saw strikes on the wings and cockpit. Smoking, the jet went into a steep dive into the clouds below from about 3,000 feet. Blizzard and Chenez dropped below the clouds but could not locate the Me-262.

Around 1255 hours, 1st Lt Clair M. Mason, 504th, engaged a Me-262 near Ulzen and got strikes on the left wing. The jet was able to avoid further contact.

Flying as part of Cockshy Green Flight, Major Vernon B. Hathorn of Group Headquarters flew in the Cockshy Spare position with Upper Spare on his wing. They made several passes at attacking enemy aircraft for no claims. About 1315 hours the Flight dropped down from 25,000 to 10,000 feet after a Me-262. From there Hathorn continued pursuit alone. The Major closed to two hundred yards at 5,000 feet and let go a long burst, registering strikes on the jet's tail. The Me-262 made a diving turn enabling Hathorn to get even closer. A ten-second burst resulted in many strikes around the cockpit, right wing and engine. The engine caught fire and the aircraft went into a steep spiral to the right and dove into a low cloud layer. Hathorn, flying alone with inconclusive gun camera pictures, received no credit for this action.

About 1320 hours, near Ulzen, the 505th's F/O John J. Rice, Upper Yellow Four, went after a Me-262 which had just made a pass at a bomber at 25,000 feet. Rice fired several bursts from 1,000 yards and saw some hits on the wing roots before the jet outran him.

9 April 1945

The 504th's 1st Lt Leon M. Orcutt and 2nd Lt Harlan F. Hunt escorted a photo reconnaissance F-5 from the 7th Photo Group to the Leipzig area. On the second pass over the target, Hunt called in two bogies at the two o'clock position. They were Me-262s, so the two escorts broke into the attack and started firing. The jets broke away. Orcutt got on the tail of one and fired, getting strikes. The right engine started smoking and the jet went into a steep left turn. Orcutt closed rapidly, firing. The jet's right engine spewed black and white smoke. From 8,000 feet, the Me-262 dove for the deck, and Orcutt broke off his attack as his engine was not running well.

After Orcutt hit the first jet, Hunt went after the other which pulled up sharply, almost colliding with Hunt's P-51. On the jet's tail but with his gunsight obscured by heading directly into the sun, Hunt fired and saw some strikes on the Me-262's fuselage aft of the cockpit. The Me-262 pulled out of range and headed south.

10 April 1945

The 339th escorted bombers to Neuruppin. The 504th chased several Me-262s which evaded.

17 April 1945

At about 1500 hours during an escort mission to Plzen, Czechoslovakia, the 503rd's 1st Lt John C. Campbell, flying the Beefsteak Blue Three position without a wingman, called in two Me-262s which dove by at ninety degrees. Beefsteak Blue fell in pursuit but lost ground to the faster jets. Another Me-262, in a shallow left turn, crossed in front of Beefsteak Blue and was given chase. Campbell pulled six G's in turning to get on the jet's tail. Beefsteak Blue One and Two overshot the enemy aircraft. As it headed for the deck, Campbell opened fire and hit the left engine. The jet leveled off at 200 feet. Further gunfire from Campbell knocked pieces off the left wing and scored strikes on the fuselage. The pilot bailed out, but his parachute did not open.

The 503rd's 1st Lt Clarence I. Ferrell engaged a Me-262 at fairly close range but submitted no claim.

18 April 1945

This was the final day of aerial combat and jet action of the war for the 339th. Lt Col Dale E. Shafer, 503rd Squadron commander, led the squadron on an escort mission. They had just rendezvoused with the bombers at 20,000 feet when he spotted a jet about three thousand feet below at the eight o'clock position. Shafer broke down and to the left. The enemy aircraft, an Arado 234, turned left and began a steep climb. Shafer closed rapidly, firing short bursts as he went which resulted in some strikes. He closed to two hundred yards and, after many hits on the fuselage and center wing section, the Arado 234's right engine began to smoke and caught fire. The pilot jettisoned the canopy about 18,000 feet but didn't bail out until 3,000 feet. The jet exploded just after bailout with pieces falling into a woods below.

German reports state Oberleutnant (1st Lt) Hermann Hoert, Staffel Commander of 1st Staffel, F-1OO (Photo Reconnaissance Group), took off from Lechfeld in an Ar-234 at 1010 hours, climbed out and was attacked by P-51s of the 339th Fighter Group. As his aircraft dove earthward it flew in a steep bank between the school and firehouse at Pichl and crashed on the meadow next to the stream flowing south out of the village center. This was near Aindling, northeast of Augsburg. The pilot died in the crash. Shafer locates the action as being east of Regensburg, somewhat further east than the German location.

Lt Col Joseph L. Thury, leading the 505th in the vicinity of Tabor, south of Prague, Czechoslovakia, at 1305 hours saw a Me-262 below. Thury split-essed from 25,000 feet and managed to register some strikes before the jet disappeared towards Prague. This was the 339th's final action against enemy aircraft in World War II.

Comments:

Some information on the 339th indicates they destroyed many Me-262s on the ground. 339th records show they destroyed only one Me-262 on the ground, that by 1st Lt Robert J. Frisch, 503rd, on 17 April 1945.

A pilot-by-pilot recapitulation of enemy jet aircraft encounters (Destroyed / Probable / Damaged) is provided below.

Jet Encounters Box Score

	Destroyed	Probable	Damaged	Date
Group Headquarters				
Col HENRY, John B., Jr.	0	1	0	30 Mar 45
503rd Fighter Squadron				
1st Lt CAMPBELL, John C., Jr.	1	0	0	17 Apr 45
Capt HAWKINS, Anthony G., Jr.	0	0	1	31 Dec 44
1st Lt HILL, Ralph S., Jr.	0	0	2	20 Mar 45
1st Lt JOHNSON, Raymond G.	0	0	1	3 Mar 45
1st Lt PETITT, Philip E.	0	0	1	7 Apr 45
Lt Col SHAFER, Dale E., Jr.	1	0	1	
			(1)	25 Mar 45
	(1)			18 Apr 45
	2	0	6	
504th Fighter Squadron				
1st Lt BARTO, Vernon N.	1	0	0	20 Mar 45
1st Lt BENNETT, Carroll W.	1	0	1	30 Mar 45
1st Lt BLIZZARD, Robert V.	0	1	1	7 Apr 45
1st Lt CARTER, Lyle M.	0	0	1	7 Apr 45
Lt Col CLARK, William C.	0	0	1	4 Apr 45
1st Lt CROKER, Robert C.	1/2	0	0	4 Apr 45
Capt EVERSON, Kirke B., Jr.	1/2	0	0	4 Apr 45
1st Lt GREER, Nile C.	1 1/2	0	0	
	(1/2)			21 Mar 45
	(1)			4 Apr 45
2nd Lt HAVIGHURST, Robert C.	1	0	0	4 Apr 45
1st Lt HUNT, Harlan F.	0	0	1	9 Apr 45
1st Lt LANGOHR, Billy E.	1/2	0	0	21 Mar 45
1st Lt MASON, Clair M.	0	0	1	7 Apr 45
1st Lt ORCUTT, Leon M. Jr.	0	0	1	9 Apr 45
2nd Lt SAINLAR, Jerome J.	0	0	1	9 Feb 45
Capt SARGENT, Robert F.	1	0	0	30 Mar 45
	7	1	8	
505th Fighter Squadron				
1st Lt ANANIAN, Stephen C.	1	0	2	
	(1)			9 Feb 45
			(1)	30 Mar 45
			(1)	5 Apr 45
Capt COREY, Harry R.	1	0	0	4 Apr 45
1st Lt IRION, Robert E.	1	0	0	20 Mar 45
F/O RICE, John J.	0	0	1	7 Apr 45
Capt RICH, George T.	0	0	1	30 Mar 45
Lt Col THURY, Joseph L.	0	0	1	18 Apr 45
	3	0	5	
Fighter Group Total	12	2	19	

Robert Ammon	Melville Ball	Vernon Barto
Arthur Bates	Jerome Ballard	Kenneth Berguson
Robert Blizzard	Merle Caldwell	Gordon Chenez
Gilbert Cohen	Douglas Cole	Robert Croker

Lee Eisenhart	 Kirke Everson	 Edgar Gravette
 Frank Guernsey	 G P Harry	 Cephas Hermansen
 Ray Herrmann	 Will Hudson	 William Hurley
Donald Kreuger	 Robert Kuhlman	 Otis Kurth

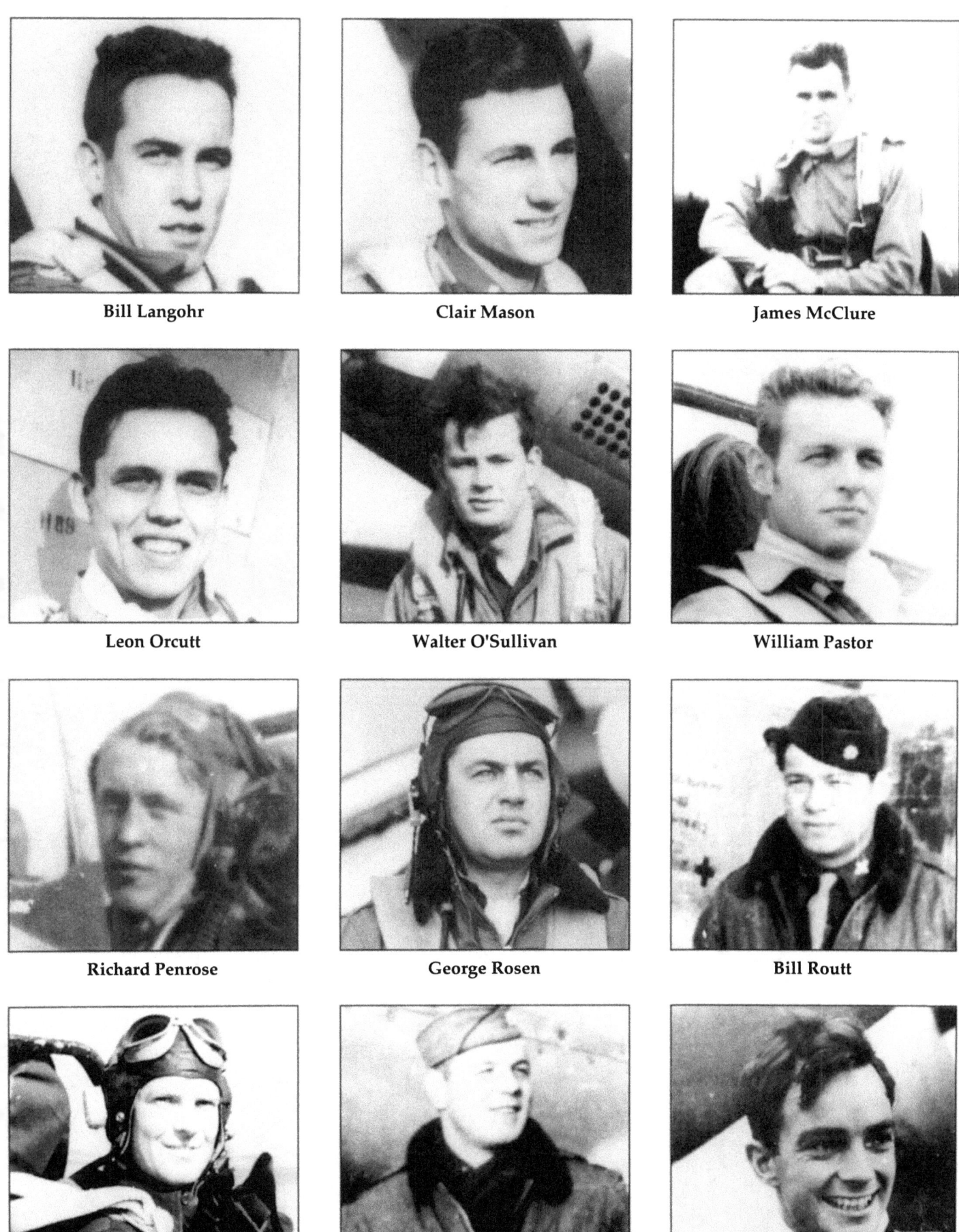

John Trester

Ely Van Cleave

Arlen Wells

Richard Wilcox

Myer Winkelman

Robert Wood

Fowlmere & Steeple Mordeu Baseball Team

339th Fighter Group

PILOT ARTICLES

Rememberances By Men Of The 505th Fighter Squadron

The 339th Goes to War

by Jim Hanson

The war in Europe had been going on for several years as the new year of 1944 dawned. Something drastic had to be done to accelerate the pace and turn the tide. There was that 339th Fighter Bomber Group out in the California desert flying war games. We were getting pretty mean and wild, living in tents, eating sand, and suffering the desert heat and cold. To top it off we were flying the P-39 AirCobra and ready for anything.

At the end of January '44 came the "Preparation for Overseas Movement," along with shots, inspections, physicals, qualifications in aerial gunnery, instruments and related activities. Soon we said goodbye to the old P-39 and boarded an eastbound train. Five days we rocked and rolled, laughed and sang, as the combat fever was building. We arrived at Savannah, Georgia, where we drew new flight gear and saw VD films, then boarded another train northbound for the docks in New Jersey. There we were given one day of freedom — New York City, here we come!

Our transport was a British troop ship, the *Sterling Castle*. Fourteen long days we pitched and smashed against the North Atlantic waves in the March cold. We hung over the rail watching the other ships in the convoy and watching our meals of fish returning to the fish. The trip dragged on boringly except in the middle of one night when we were awakened by sudden silence. All engines had stopped. We slipped into life jackets and proceeded quietly on deck. A submarine had been reported in the area. We all looked forward to daylight, especially after sighting a nearby Escort Carrier with its deck covered with "cocooned" P-51s. Be great if they could be ours, but we didn't know as yet what we would be flying. P-51s, P-47s and P-38s were being flown by the AAF in Europe at the time.

On the fourteenth night, word came down that we were docking at Liverpool. As we were approaching we saw little flickers of light from dock workers' equipment. Otherwise, there was only the outline of blacked-out buildings against the sky. The solid feeling of mother earth felt strange after two weeks at sea. We marched down cobblestone streets to the railroad station as we looked at the sky through the windows of bombed-out buildings, pretty much in awe at seeing war damage for the first time. The railroad station was just a burned out hulk with a spider web of bent girders overhead. While waiting to depart on the train, we were served coffee and doughnuts by the Red Cross girls. Soon a couple of toots from one of those unique train whistles and we were on our way through the darkened English countryside.

About four hours later, still dark, we detrained to board the familiar canvas topped G.I. trucks at a little country station. Our new base was the village of Fowlmere, about six miles southwest of Cambridge.

Our new quarters were six-man Quonset or Nissen huts with a complete flight in each one plus a command hut. The first day it seemed all we heard was "Tanoy test, Tanoy test." Tanoy was the British loudspeaker system on which the important air raid warnings, message calls, etc., were broadcast. Looking over F-378 (our coded station designation), we found it to be a rolling farm with a cement perimeter strip for taxiing, steel matting in the runup areas and wire mesh on the two rolling runways. Each squadron had a cement block building to house operations, communications, armament and maintenance, plus a Quonset work hangar to shelter a couple of planes. Group Headquarters was on higher elevation at the edge of town. The main mess, club area and briefing room were nearby, along with the typical RAF control tower which previously supported Spitfires at Fowlmere.

A couple of miles to the east was Duxford, a more permanent type RAF base housing an Eighth Air Force P-47 Group.

One night shortly after settling in we were awakened by Tanoy "Air Raid Warning Red." We grabbed jackets, helmet and shoes and headed for the sand bag shelters. The night was cold and clear. Off to the south toward London was a sky laced with searchlights. Suddenly we caught sight of an airplane pegged in a cone of lights. Seconds later it burst into flames and spun to earth. While we watched, four more were shot down. One by one the searchlights disappeared, and the world returned to darkness. *The war's really getting close*, I thought.

We started navigation and recognition classes and studied aerial photos of various European landmarks, especially the coastline from Denmark to France. They would often be our best clues for what direction to fly when we left the continent headed for England, our new home. If our fourchannel, pushbutton radio was inoperative and we couldn't get a homing or steer, it was back to basics.

We trucked over to Duxford's swimming pool where we learned to drop out of our parachute harness into the water. Next we were taken up in a C-47 for a familiarization ride around the Cambridge area, Sherwood Forest and The Wash. Soon our brand new P-51s touched down and we knew what we'd be flying. One problem — no one had flown a P-51 or maintained one. We checked ourselves out without even the help of a pilot's manual because none ever arrived. As far as I know, we completed transition without losing anyone. I had two flights in my 6N-Easy before heading out on that first mission on 30 April 1944, a fighter sweep over Belgium and France led by Major Hayes, a combat veteran from another group.

The first umbrella-shaped bursts of flak didn't seem too threatening until on a later mission I saw a B-17 take one in the bomb bay over the target, and there was nothing but a large ball of flame and four engines darting around like fireflies. We learned more about it on 7 May '44 when Arch Luper went down from a high altitude flak burst on our first mission into Germany. On 9 May, Bill Jones and Hal Everett each shot down a Me-109 to even the score. On 13 May, Don Larson, the commander, got a FW-190. We were on the move! On the big Eighth Air Force Fighter Command's sweep of Germany at low altitude, the 505th claimed eleven enemy planes and many other targets. The 24th of May we went back to Berlin with another mission over France in the afternoon where the score again increased.

The Sixth of June — D-Day — arrived and the invasion of France was on. We took off in the black of night, four smudge pots lighting the runway. There were a few layers of low clouds and rain showers most of the way. Our job was to cover the west flank of the invasion fleet crossing the English Channel. I flew 6 1/2 hours on that first mission of the day. While the planes were being refueled and bombs hung under the wings, we grabbed something to eat and got briefed for some bridge "unbuilding" and truck stopping. Some pilots flew twelve hours that day. There was no letup, and the 505th chalked up one hundred enemy planes destroyed in its first one hundred combat missions. Washington had found the right team to help win the air war in Europe — the 339th Fighter Group.

Solo Invasion

by Bill Jones

The mission on 11 September 1944 was escorting bombers, but we obtained permission to leave them before the target for a return engagement in the Munich area — strafing a Luftwaffe dispersal area along an autobahn. We had chanced upon it the day before and, without opposition, destroyed about 25 aircraft on the ground in their revetments.

I had an even better reason to look forward to the mission. After four and a half months of combat flying, I had now accumulated 297 hours and would have comfortably more than the needed 300 hours to complete my prescribed tour. This time, however, we did encounter some ground fire in the area. An unlucky shot knocked Ted Staggers down and another rendered my oxygen system inoperative. Even so, we gave the dispersal area a pretty good beating and destroyed a number of German planes before heading home.

Half an hour later we reached the Stuttgart area, and I was busy thinking happy thoughts about a trip to Philadelphia when a tremendous concussion occurred. Later I learned a German Me-262 jet had hit our formation from the rear and made me the first pilot in any theater to be shot down by a jet. Because of my position as Green Three in the unusual formation we were flying at the time, I assume that he was *not* really trying to hit me. Larry Powell was flying my wing as Green Four or "Tail End Charlie" and should have been the logical target.

My memories of the next few seconds greatly exceed

the time that actually expired. I was keenly aware of the events yet hopelessly confused. One earphone said, "Bail out!" and the other said "Stay with it!" I attempted to throttle back, but the throttle lever in my left hand—indeed the whole throttle quadrant—was no longer attached to the plane. In my decision to bail out, I recalled an earlier bailout on the south coast of England shortly after D-Day. I had done everything wrong but managed to get the chute opened in time. *This time* I would do it right: pull the canopy release, trim forward, roll the plane over, release seat belt and drop free. *But,* something went wrong! Maybe I gave it back trim since the nose quickly pulled through and headed for Germany before I fell free. Speed increased as I flapped along the fuselage in the air stream with my arms over my head, my legs still in the cockpit. Something refused to give.

At last I felt a break, rip or tear and blew free without hitting the tail. I was in a horizontal position with my back to the ground and revolving rapidly like an autumn leaf. I grabbed the rip cord and pulled. Nothing happened. After several more unrewarded tugs on the rip cord, I decided that what had broken loose allowing me to fall free was my chute. Katie would be pretty disgusted if she learned I'd let such a thing happen. Suddenly my chute opened, nearly splitting me in two. Then I knew! I'd forgotten to unplug my "G" suit hose!

The rest of the jump wasn't bad after that hair-raising evacuation from the Mustang. I landed feet first in a hay field, closely observed by two farmers tossing hay with long-tined forks. They asked if I was armed—so I thought as I spoke no German—and I said I had no pistol. That seemed to satisfy them. We were soon joined by a citizens' delegation from town, including a small boy about twelve who spoke excellent English. We walked to town about a half mile away.

I was taken to a small room on the third floor of the town hall where I remained alone for two hours except for several visits by an elderly man in a dark brown uniform with orange piping. I think he tried to question me but let himself get so worked up that all he could do was spit on me. Between visits by the old man I tried to take stock. I found that I had all my parts. There was blood all over my face which seemed to have come from tiny fragments of plexiglass embedded in my forehead and cheeks. The small mirror in the room showed me these were very superficial, but the whites of my eyes were a solid deep red and remained that way for several weeks.

About dusk two husky young men, not in uniform but accompanied my old spitting friend, entered and indicated I was to go with them. We went outside to where a small, four-door, wood-burning auto was parked. I sat squeezed between the two huskies in the rear while a driver and another man took the front seat. As we were about to move out, a commotion arose outside and finally someone stepped through the crowd and deposited a large coil of heavy rope on the floor at my feet. As best I could, I avoided speculation as to the need for the rope.

We finally moved out and proceeded to six or eight small towns in the Stuttgart area. At each one we followed the same procedure. The driver would stop at the town square or town hall. The two huskies would escort me to a place of prominence and hold me by each arm as the front-seat passenger made a vitriolic speech. Several English or semi-English words were discernible. Then the on-lookers were encouraged to pass by and look me over. Curiously, most of them seemed to have a sympathetic look on their faces.

It got dark during all that ceremony and may have been ten o'clock when we parked on a side street off the last town square. The two men from the front seat went inside what looked like a small-town police station, but it probably had something to do with civil defense. The two huskies and I sat in the car for about thirty minutes, but I never learned the purpose for the stop. Next I was taken to a Luftwaffe airfield just outside Stuttgart and turned over to Luftwaffe personnel, joining three B-17 crewmen—a bombardier and two gunners. The bombardier was in poor shape. He and I were taken into Stuttgart to a hospital. A fluoroscope showed a small fragment in my chest but not in my lungs. They dressed the wound but left the fragment where it was. A couple of weeks later it became rather badly infected. After treatment the bombardier and I were taken back to the airfield, but not before we were privileged to sit in an underground shelter in Stuttgart during a RAF bombardment. That was a half hour of pure terror. The following night we managed to hit it just right again. As we arrived in the rail station in Frankfurt, the RAF put on another show. This time the best I could do for safety was pick a large solid-looking arch in the station to stand under. Somehow nothing hit the station that night. The next morning we were taken on foot through Frankfurt to the interrogation center about ten miles out of town. At that point we officially entered the prisoner of war system.

I had really felt all through my combat tour that I would complete it. In a way, I guess I did. I just landed in the *wrong* country.

It'll Never Happen To Me

by Dick Cain

In early December 1944, the winter weather was interfering with our combat operations, and it was not until 4 December that we flew our first mission of the month. Captain Bill Krauss, assistant operations officer, led our squadron on this escort mission to the central German town of Kassell, about 80 miles north/northeast of Frankfurt. It was my 35th mission and, as things turned out, my longest, lasting upwards of six months. On departing the target area my canopy became foggy, and soon thereafter the coolant gauge went through the stops. Great clouds of coolant came through the exhaust stacks and soon it was, "Look Ma...no engine."

I had always felt an extreme distrust of parachutes and had figured to "belly in" if trouble came up. After a quiet, dead-stick glide through the overcast, I was confronted with a beautiful set of wooded mountains. That changed my thoughts in a hurry. I finally got the Mustang inverted, kicked the stick and found myself swinging in the chute at about 700 feet. I had seen a large river shortly before bailing out and thought I had crossed the Rhine into eastern France.

Landing in that rugged forest would have challenged the most skilled parachutist. I brushed through a tree, hit the ground off balance, and cracked my ankle. As I hobbled through the woods, a man waved and shouted from the next ridge. I waved back and continued walking. As he reached me, he yelled, "Deutsch!" and poked a rifle into my ribs. That's when I realized the damn river I'd seen was the Moselle! Actually, I had landed in the staging area for the German buildup for the Battle of the Bulge. There were troops all over the place.

I was taken (carried, finally, as the cracked ankle would no longer permit me to walk) to the command post and transferred that night to a prison in Trier. I can remember waking at night and feeling the building rocking from RAF bombs. Shortly thereafter I was joined in my cell by a P-38 pilot and then a British bomber pilot. When the rail lines were cleared after about a week, we were taken to the interrogation center outside Frankfurt.

Shortly afterwards I recall sharing cheese and crackers with interrogator Hanns Scharff and being taken to a movie, none of which I understood. After being told on a regular basis over the course of about three weeks to go back into the solitary confinement cell to starve and freeze some more, the interrogator evidently figured I didn't know anything anyway and sent me on out. This was the only time I envied bomber pilots, as their tenure at the interrogation center was an average of three days with a whole crew to work on.

While traveling across Germany to Stalagluft I from the interrogation center, I had a firsthand glimpse of the complete devastation of every city of consequence by our bombers. Those who saw this only from 30,000 feet could not imagine the results of their missions. Overshadowing everything for us, of course, was the damp numbing cold of the Baltic coast during that winter and early spring. Together with the all-pervading hunger that was with us until the very end, those memories will continue to color my recollections with a less than rosy glow.

I was among a train-car-load of POWs who had the dubious privilege of spending New Year's Eve '44-'45 in Berlin. It was *not* a gala affair, as we were part of a troop train in the railroad yards that the RAF was bombing. On arrival at Stalagluft I at Barth on the Baltic Sea north of Berlin, the first person I saw when I went to my assigned room was Ted Staggers.

The following are glimpses of life at Stalagluft I:

- All eyes intent on the cook while he filled the food bowls, and the inevitable comment, "That one's short!"
- The day the German sergeant guard drove his right foot from under himself when he clicked his heels together on the ice.
- The small black cat that started across the compound during roll call and only got half way. Meat in the stew that night!
- An unshaven, ragged Kriegie, muffled to the eyeballs, crouched behind the incinerator in a howling blizzard, waiting to club a large crow which had quietly lighted behind him (me).
- The day the German commandant ordered all Jewish POWs to step forward. The whole Kriegie squadron took one step forward.
- The POW (me again) on wood detail under the barracks, industriously pulling out the sub-floor while the guard in the nearby tower tried to figure out where the sounds of breaking wood were coming from. The barracks were ready to collapse when we left.
- Best of all, the morning late in April '45 when we opened the door and saw empty guard towers—no enemy to be seen. The Russians arrived the next day.

Camp Lucky Strike, France, to which we were flown from Germany, was complete confusion. The Medical Corps caused a near riot when they withheld salt and pepper from us with the rather vague and wild reasoning that it was injurious to our stomachs. Needless to say, we swiftly found the seasoning. I have a vivid, satisfying memory of watching General Eisenhower chewing out a colonel for not feeding us lunch by 2:30 p.m. while several Congressmen and ex-POWs cheered. I would probably still be at Camp Lucky Strike if I had not spotted a line moving toward a building. When I learned they were processing to return home, I joined it.

Taken as a whole, this segment of my military career is not one I would care to repeat. In retrospect, however, it *was* an experience I'd never exchange.

Missing Aircrew Report

by Jerry Graham

On 13 September 1944 our squadron went down to strafe dispersed aircraft south of Munich. About 1430 I noticed someone jettison their canopy at about 200 feet, but the pilot was evidently hit by small arms fire. The plane immediately went into a shallow dive, started through the tops of trees, rolled over and crashed into the ground. Lt William R. Slovak was flying P-51D-5, #44-13847

William R. Slovak was killed in the crash of his P-51 on the first pass of this 13 September 1944 mission.

Kriegie Kismet

by Bert Conner

On that fateful day, 2 March 1945, I was to begin a prolonged visit with the Nazis' as well as pick up and carry a souvenir of the trip for the rest of my life.

We embarked on a mission to Berlin flying cover for B-17s. I was leading Green Flight, and Harry Howard was my Element Leader. The mission proceeded without incident until we were somewhere east of Magdeburg when we were bounced by Me-109s. They hit Red Lead Section on the other side first, then splattered through the bombers into us. By then they'd had enough combat and headed for the deck and cloud cover. We followed them down but lost them in the clouds. I thought I would play it cool and fly around just under the clouds. Maybe one would pop out and try to get home. We flew around for awhile, looking, when someone in the flight called my attention to numerous tire marks leading from an autobahn to an open field and disappearing into a grove of trees. Upon closer examination we discovered numerous aircraft parked in the trees. I called the flight and told them to watch for flak while I made a firing pass. Not seeing a sole or a single shot, we set up a regular gunnery pattern. I was making my last pass as a string of tracers from my guns indicated my ammunition was about exhausted. As I pulled up over the trees, the world exploded. I kept wondering why I couldn't get any left rudder until I looked down and noticed that my foot was under the seat. Now, as any pilot knows, you can't fly with your feet under the seat, but it wouldn't come out. I reached under and pulled it out. It then dawned on me that I'd been badly hit. About three inches of my shin was missing. The first thing I thought was to head for home, so I looked at the compass and headed west, shoved the throttle to the wall, then tried to stop the bleeding. At that moment the pain came, nearly overwhelming me, and well it might have, but something else caught my attention—he aircraft was running poorly. I looked up. Smoke was pouring out of the cowling. I looked at the instrument panel and the gauges were all pegged. As I was still at about 500 feet, I thought I'd have to get some altitude before I could bail out.

It occurred to me then that I would snap the leg off when the chute popped and I wanted what was left of that limb. The will to survive—and divine guidance—are powerful forces, and as I looked up again, right in front of me was the only break in a solid forest. In fact, I was lined up with the east-west runway of a German fighter base. I immediately cut all switches and headed just to the right of the concrete runway, bellying in on the grass. All in all, it was as good a landing as I had ever made. Landing beside the runway proved a wise move, as the runway had huge logs lying crossways every two or three hundred feet. When old "Lone Star Lady" came to a stop, I began unbuckling the straps in order to jump out, but the plane did not burn. I put a tourniquet on the leg and gave myself a shot of morphine from the packet on the chute strap.

Suddenly I was aware of someone standing over me. I looked up into the face of a German soldier. He noticed the injury but did nothing until the ambulance and others arrived. They lifted me bodily from the aircraft and placed me on a stretcher, then transported me to a dispensary in the main building. After placing me on the floor, they proceeded to splint the leg while others removed all the goodies from my flight suit. They took my crash bracelet from my right arm and tried so hard to get my ring off that they overlooked the watch on my left arm. I still had my flying jacket (B4) on. After this, they all left the room except one young nurse who stood by.

I began to take stock of my situation and discovered my service pistol in my shoulder holster. I was surprised but pulled it out and tried to get the nurse to keep it for herself or hide it. She hid it all right—under my stretcher. When the others returned, she pulled it out and handed it to the person in charge. He must have thought I'd hidden it because he jumped about four feet in the air and grabbed my holster, jerking it off my shoulder and nearly lifting me straight up. He said in English the only words I'd been able to understand: "You dirty murdering butcher!" After that episode, they locked me in a dark cellar for an undetermined time.

Late in the afternoon they put me in the rear of a pickup truck, about a 1920 model, and took me to Stalag XI-A at a little town called Altengrabau. I arrived after dark and was taken to a dispensary inside the wire. Several people started asking me questions. They spoke very good English, but I thought they were German and said very little. One fellow who seemed to be in charge put his hand on my toes and asked if I could feel it. Since they were already talking amputation, I lied and said I could feel it. He answered that it didn't make any difference because they could always cut it off the next day if the operation didn't work.

Well, they pieced my leg together and put a wheat plaster cast on it. They then took me to a small hut which housed about ten other fellows lying on cots positioned around the room. As I looked around, guess who I saw lying next to me — nobody but Lt Harry Howard.

The French Ejection

by Phil Ewing

We had taken off in the darkness of early 8 June 1944 with a solid overcast sky, breaking out at about 4,000 feet. Our flight of four Mustangs consisted of Lts James Starnes, George Hrico, James Hanson and myself. Our target area was about a 100 miles behind the new invasion beachhead in France. As we neared our target area it was beginning to get light enough to see our wings, and I was anxious to see what my problem was. I discovered that my right ammunition bay cover was not down, about 1 1/2 inches from closing. This made the right wing very heavy, and I had to use left stick to correct the problem with right rudder to control skidding. I didn't know too much about the guns but figured they would fire all right and decided to continue the mission.

In looking for a target, we noticed a line of freight cars off to our right and immediately began an attack. Flames began to spurt up from the left end of a freight car. Suddenly my P-51 received a mortal blow at low altitude. I realized I had to gain altitude and bail out, but my controls were shot up. The windshield was covered with oil, and the engine sounded like a bucket of bolts. I released the canopy, only to get a bath in hot oil which left me able to see just a bit behind me. I called the boys and announced I was bailing out. Must have had about five seconds after the parachute opened to look around before hitting the ground.

After landing I noticed that one foot was numb, but thank the Lord, I could still run, so I headed into the nearest woods. It was so early everyone must have been asleep or I would have been captured. I ran right through the woods into some fields surrounded by thorn hedges.

Still traveling south in the next half hour, I saw a French farmer sowing seed and waited for him to come to one end of the field. I showed him by my language card that I was an American and needed French clothing. He motioned for me to go around the field to his barn. Later he came to the barn pushing a wheel barrow covered with straw. In it he had a set of farm clothes, shoes and leather leggings. The shoes were a mistake as they made my injured foot hurt so much more. I left his farm because I wanted to put as much distance between me and the plane as possible to reduce the likelihood of capture.

From this farm I passed through a wooded area right into a village. I could see women talking to each other, so I tried to walk by as unconcerned as I could in spite of my limp. On and on I walked with the aid of a stick. The pain was becoming unbearable. I finally came to a small river where I "borrowed" a boat, crossed the river and tied it up on the other side. At the next farm, a lady came out.

After I showed her by my language card that I was an American and needed food, she screamed and cried but went after her husband. I later learned he had escaped from a German labor camp. The woman's husband took me to another farmer who gave me food and allowed me to stay in a barn loft, an act of kindness for which I was very thankful. This farmer also brought in a doctor who examined my foot, bound it up and gave me crutches. It was two weeks before I could put any weight on it again.

The night of 8 June '44 was my first night in France, and British bombers came over to finish the job on the freight cars. Some bombs were accidentally dropped on the nearby town of Alençon. Because of this bombing a lot of town people came out to the farm each night to stay. Among those were two girls who spoke English. Each night they brought me food and cider (water was not fit to drink) and news of the war's progress.

After six weeks my foot was getting well and I was preparing to go to our lines with a French boy when Patton made his breakthrough. He was moving so fast I was advised to stay and wait for the Army to liberate me. Within a few days a jeep rolled in with French soldiers using all American equipment. They used the farm house for an observation post, directing artillery fire into the valley. The next day I went to the American Headquarters with the French soldiers. I was taken to an American colonel to be interrogated. I told him about hearing a column of tanks two nights earlier, traveling to the west.

The next day they took me back to General Patton's command post to be verified, and two days later, a soldier took me to the Ninth Air Force base nearby where I was given mechanic's coveralls. *Finally*, I was rid of my French clothing. After one night there, about 55 of us downed airmen were flown to London where we were allowed to send a telegram home announcing that we were well and happy. A few days later we went to our bases. I enjoyed visiting with the old gang of 339ers at Fowlmere before flying back to the States for leave and re-assignment.

Eulogy for Don Larson

by James Starnes

Donald A. Larson of Yakima, Washington, assumed command of the 505th at Rice Field, California, late in 1943 and remained in that position until killed in action near Hamburg, Germany, on 4 August 1944. In my opinion Larson was probably the best pilot in the 505th, having had extensive experience as a P-40 instructor prior to joining the 339th at Walterboro, South Carolina. He never quite lost that flying instructor outlook, and if Don saw someone make an error, it was noted and brought to his attention.

Bill Bryan recalls that while Don was still 503rd Operations Officer at Rice, Nip Carter made a raunchy landing in a P-39. At the next pilots' meeting Larson explained in detail the mistake made until Nip finally said, "Come on, Don, everyone makes a mistake now and then. That's why they put erasers on pencils." He expected his boys to fly the best formation and look sharp for the benefit of ground personnel as they returned for landing at Fowlmere. His air leadership was outstanding, and I would have preferred to engage enemy aircraft behind Larson above any other combat leader. Without question he was the dominant force in the early success of his squadron in combat.

About the only negative we pilots noted under his command was his relatively tight rein on promotions. The 505th arrived in England with pilots as follows: two captains (Larson and Thury), four first Lts (Luper, Olander, Reid and Tower) and the rest second Lts. Luper was lost early in May '44 and Reid made captain late that month. Other pilots made 1st Lt after one to two months of combat experience. Reid, however, was the only pilot promoted to captain under Larson's command. After Thury took over on 5 August '44, four flight leaders made captain within thirty days (Holloway, Johnson, Olander and Tower). Someone wisecracked that when Larson went down the whole squadron got promoted. This was really a joke as we were proud to be under Larson's command and would not have traded commanders with anyone. It was through his aggressive leadership that the 505th destroyed 100 aircraft in the air or on the ground in our first 100 combat missions—a record not achieved by any other fighter squadron during the war.

Don Larson's aerial kill record is as follows:
13 May 44...1 FW-190 (probable)
28 Jul 44...1 Ju-52 Transport
24 May 44...2 Me-109s
4 Aug 44...2 Me-109s, 1 FW-190

His 13 May '44 kill (probable) was the third enemy aircraft shot down by a 339th pilot, being preceded only by the Me-109s shot down by Bill Jones (505th) and Hal Everett (505th) on 9 May '44. It surprised no one that Larson scored early, as we expected him to be top gun. His big mission came on 24 May '44 while leading the group as "Armstrong" escorting bombers to Berlin. His encounter report reads in part, "I saw between 60 and 70 bogies (unidentified aircraft) low and to the right of the bombers as they dropped their bombs on the target. My flight dived on the bogies which proved to be Me-109s and FW-190s. I picked out a No. 4 man in a 109 flight and fired a short burst at very close range. Smoke billowed out with the first strikes and the 109 rolled over to the right and caught fire. It went into a steep dive toward the ground. While I was picking out another 109 the other three P-51s in my flight attempted a pass at E/A which dived down to the right, and I saw no more of them. The second 109 threw out smoke just as dense (as the first) and lots of oil. It also peeled off to the right, and I last saw it 2000 or 3000 feet below in a violent high speed spiral still throwing out smoke and obviously out of control. In clearing my tail I found four 109s positioning for an attack. I pulled up violently and the airplane did several uncontrolled snap maneuvers going upward at a very steep rate of climb. The 109s did not follow. Without support I considered breaking off combat but saw the remainder of the E/A turn toward the bombers so I decided to head them off. I found myself in a good position to attack the 190s which were about 1000 feet above the 109s. After closing I repeated the tactics of the 109s and saw a 190 explode through smoke which became so thick I could no longer fire at it. These flights then broke up, some diving away and others trying to get position to attack me. It is here I believe I destroyed a fourth airplane and I damaged the one for which I make claim. In the confusion I lost track of just what had been done and desire any aid that can be given from assessment of the film taken during firing."

The Confirmation Board awarded Larson 1 Me-109 destroyed, 1 probably destroyed, 1 FW-190 destroyed and 1 damaged. On 28 July '44 he submitted a full legal-length page appeal of the claim downgraded to "probably destroyed." It was endorsed to the board after Major Larson was KIA and later approved by them to give him credit for three destroyed and one damaged on this mission. Don Larson became an ace on 28 July when he downed a Ju-52 three-engine transport at low altitude not far from the Rhine River. He then shot down a Me-109 in an air battle on the deck near Hamburg on 4 August 1944. This occurred as Me-109s bounced the squadron while we were strafing an airfield. Shortly after this sixth kill he was engaged in a dogfight with a second Me-109 when he collided with another P-51. Larson was posthumously awarded the Silver Star for the 24 May mission. As noted by many others, Donald A. Larson will live forever in our memories as an unforgettable American hero.

My Horror Story

by Bill Moore

On 13 September 1944 we were briefed for a strafing mission to the same autobahn near Munich that had been successfully hit on 10 and 11 September '44. On the very first pass William R. Slovak went straight in and my engine was hit by light flak. Oil came out immediately and sprayed all over the plane. The engine was still running, so I headed for Switzerland, hoping my engine would hold out that long. I called my flight leader and explained what happened, but later learned my radio had been shot out as well.

My safest place was to fly low to the ground to avoid more flak. After about ten minutes my engine had heated up so much that the coolant had blown out. When this happened I knew I could no longer remain with the P-51. I released the canopy, unfastened my safety belt and prepared to bail out. I was still on the deck, and the country was so hilly and wooded that I couldn't crash land. Just as I started to gain bailout altitude, my engine quit altogether. I gained as much altitude as possible from momentum, rolled the trim tab full forward and released the stick. This caused the plane to dive suddenly and throw me clear. I was knocked out by the sudden opening of my chute.

When I regained my senses I was hanging in a tree about 200 feet from where my plane had crashed. It made quite a hole in the ground and was still burning. The ammo was exploding, and, at first, I thought someone was firing at me.

Not far away was a farmhouse, and already three farmers had gathered around me. They helped me unfasten my chute and climb down. They then took a good hold of me and took me to the farm house. On the way I managed to ask them if I was in Switzerland. My heart hit my feet when they said, "Nein, Deutschland." I tried to get them to let me go, but it was no use.

One farmer's wife informed me in broken English that the police were on their way to get me. They gave me a drink of water, and soon three German policemen arrived and questioned the farmers. Two went down to the wreck site while the other one and I started walking to town. We did not get far before another policeman came along on a motorcycle. I climbed on back in handcuffs, and we started toward town. Just after passing a small village we had a flat tire. We walked back to a tavern and the policeman gave his gun to the bartender, picked up two glasses of beer, gave me one and went to phone the police station. Soon another policeman arrived in a car and took us to town. At the police station I gave my name, rank, serial number and age. They phoned a Luftwaffe field to pick me up.

About 1800 hours two German officers and an enlisted man arrived. The enlisted man spoke English and told me the officers did not like me and were tired of picking up American flyers. I sat in the back seat beside him, and we proceeded to an airfield near Munich. On the way we passed through a large forest. Just as we entered the forest the officer driving the car turned the engine off. This scared the daylights out of me, as I thought they were going to shoot me. I was relieved to find out he was just saving gasoline while we coasted down a long hill. We stopped at a tavern in a small village. The two officers went inside. In a few minutes a beautiful German girl brought a beer for the enlisted man. I think she just wanted to see a captured American flyer, as the enlisted man was very surprised.

At the airfield I was given two blankets and put into a cell. Later they brought food which consisted of creamed potatoes, barley soup, coffee and dark sour bread which I couldn't eat. Since then I've learned to eat it toasted, as that was all the bread we got. The rest of the meal was good, and I was quite hungry. I hadn't eaten since 0730 that morning. The next morning, breakfast consisted of coffee and bread after which I was again questioned as to name, rank, serial number, time shot down and age. I also had to give them one of my dog tags.

At noon another American and I were taken by five guards by train to Frankfurt, arriving the next day. The train could not proceed into Frankfurt as the British had bombed the city during the night, damaging the tracks. We had to walk the rest of the way. While walking, an elderly German man came at us with his umbrella swinging. Two of the guards held him as we hurried with the other on ahead. We went to Oberursel, the interrogation center.

I was taken into a small room, stripped and searched. They gave me a slip of paper with 19-3 on it, and I was sent wandering down several halls under the watchful eye of many German guards. Finally I arrived at my room and was shoved inside. The private room had one very hard bed, one small table and a barred and blacked-out window. Around 1230 a guard gave me a bowl of barley soup which I quickly consumed. About two hours later a guard came in with a Red Cross form to be filled out. I wrote my name, rank and serial number and handed it back to him. Another two hours passed before I was again confronted. The guard said, "Aus", so I followed him to a different building. We walked down a long hall to a door marked "No. 43," and the guard shoved me through.

Inside was a luxuriously furnished office with a German corporal sitting behind a desk. He arose and said, "Hello! Come right in and have a seat." I sat in a straight backed chair, nervously awaiting the next move. The corporal sat down again behind the desk, hauled out the Red Cross questionnaire and slid it to me. I was amazed to find that he had filled out the entire form in detail. You could have knocked me over with a feather. He asked me to confirm and sign the form. I refused, and he said, "Fortunately for you, Lt Moore, another member of your group has identified you, so we will not keep you around any longer. You will take a shower and leave on a transport train tomorrow morning." He called the guard who had been waiting outside, and I was escorted back to my room.

Back in my room I lay down and daydreamed until around 1800 when the door was unlocked and I was given two slices of bread and a pitcher of weak tea. The door slammed shut and I was left to eat in the darkness. Again I lay down and was about asleep when the guard came in and made me take off my shoes which he placed outside the door. I again tried to sleep and dozed off when a guard said, "Aus!" and gave me my shoes. I then followed him to a hall where there were other American prisoners. On a table were our personal effects taken during the earlier search. Next was a roll call for about forty POWs after which we were taken to another part of the camp and put in a large barracks. The few beds were already filled, so the guards went around taking blankets off sleeping prisoners and made room for us on the floor. More people kept coming in all night, so we didn't get much sleep.

Early the next morning we were given a cup of black, so-called coffee and two slices of bread with jam. The rest of the day we spent telling each other our horror stories. The next morning we all left for the processing center Dulagluft at Wetzlar where the Red Cross furnished us with a kit containing shaving equipment, tooth brush and clothing.

While at Wetzlar for six days I met two pilots I knew in flight training and one 339th pilot from Fowlmere. On 22 September we boarded a train for permanent camp. They gave each POW a Red Cross food parcel and put ten men in a compartment made for six people. We spent four days and nights enroute, playing cards, sleeping and talking to the guards. On Tuesday, 26 September, we arrived at Stalagluft I in Barth, Germany. We were questioned again and searched. Next we got a shower, and our clothes were deloused. Then we got more clothing furnished by the Red Cross and moved into permanent barracks.

The first three months were not bad as life was routine, reporting for roll call twice a day. We spent a lot of our time discussing everything from war to sex or working on craft projects—building a cribbage board from ceiling wood or a chess board with pawns we made of Swan soap which we had in abundance from Red Cross parcels...from which we got most of our food. We had athletic equipment, music instruments and religious material. In November '44, Captain Jack Mitchell from the 505th came over to visit, and we had a long conversation about the 339th, wondering how things were going for the group.

In January 1945 things began to get rough. We had many cold nights with no heat and only one sheet and one blanket. Our food supply dwindled because Allied bombings of railroad targets. We received two Red Cross food parcels during January.

We had very cold weather in February '45 with lots of snow the first few days. When it thawed, the camp became very slushy. Everybody had wet feet. We got only enough coal for cooking — none for heating — and nearly everyone had frost bitten feet and colds.

We knew by then the Russians were driving to cut this area off from the rest of Germany. With the British and Americans closing in from the other side, we had high hopes of being liberated. Late in February we were down to eating one meal per day and very little heat. On 23 February, fifty infantry enlisted men arrived—most were hospital cases. We did not have extra beds for them so they had to sleep on the floor. The needed socks and underwear. Those of us who had anything extra shared it with them.

During March '45 things really got rough as we only got German rations — five slices of bread a day and one small dish of potatoes, usually mashed, no milk or salt in them. We made gravy from pea flour or soup thickening. We got one meal of German meat during this period, two cups of foul German coffee, two meals of dried vegetable stew, a few rutabagas and about two ounces of cheese. Everybody got weak, thin, and our blood pressure hit a new low. I'd never been so hungry for such a long period in my life. Near the end of March they were able to get us some Red Cross parcels, so we were able to eat a bit better.

On 30 April '45, Heinrich Himmler, the Nazi chief, was in camp and sent out his unconditional surrender to the U. S. and Great Britain which was turned down. At this time we got orders to dig slit trenches and stand by for the Russians to arrive. The Germans began blowing up all military installations. On 1 May the Germans left camp at 2330, and we took over. The mayor of Barth surrendered the town to us, and we also took over the airfield. Then we sat tight awaiting the Russians. On 2 May a Russian officer arrived and ordered the fences torn down. We were allowed to go into Barth and watch the Soviet army move through. They had a few tanks, a half dozen trucks and all kinds of horse-drawn wagons. They were a tired bunch and happy to see us, someone they didn't have to fight. Finally, on 13 May, that long awaited day arrived! B-17s came in and flew us to Le Havre, France, where we stayed about four weeks. We went home via Coast Guard ships.

Don't Correct Their Aim

by Jack Mitchell

My fateful mission came on 23 September 1944. With Joe Thury leading our squadron, we took off about noon and were assigned the job of top cover for the paratroopers, gliders and ground support P-47s in the airborne invasion of Arnheim, Holland. I was leading a flight with Jim Muller on my wing and Allen Young and Herky Corey as the second element. As best I recall, not much happened except that we were flying some imaginary patrol corridor from somewhere to somewhere. When we were at the northwest corner, whoever was leading the group that day as "Armstrong" said over the R/T that we would make one more pass and go home. Well, when we got to the southeast corner there was a gaggle of FW-190s, and the fun began. I think we were about 16,000 feet and the FW-190s were about maybe 18,000 to 20,000 feet but definitely above us.

Down they came. I bent that old Peter Five One over and had a clear rear end burst at two of them from close range. The results I'm not sure of, but I don't see how I could've missed. At any rate they disappeared into the clouds about 2,500 feet, and I followed them right on through the stuff. When I came out of the clouds there was no one around but me. The nose came up and I started back up — and there above me were four more FW-190s. I thought to myself, *Just what in the hell am I doing up here by myself*?! but I couldn't resist the temptation to tangle with them and become an ace in one day.

I was going up at about a 45 or 50 degree angle, and they were coming down. I could see the 20mm's winking at me with a slow "boop boop" and I decided I had no business being where I was. The FW-190's aim was not too good, so I shoved the nose down and the throttle to maximum — and corrected his aim! Evidently I pushed the nose right into his

PILOT ARTICLES

line of fire, and a 20mm hit the spinner with maybe seventy inches of mercury in the engine.

Well, with engine parts flying through the air and fire coming into the cockpit, I said, "The time has come!" With that I pulled that little red lever on the right side of the cockpit and jettisoned the canopy. When I did that the flames really came through the cockpit, and I quickly released the safety belt and went over the side. I can remember just as clearly as if it were yesterday that I took my hands and pushed the fuselage away from me as easy as could be. Knowing the cloud cover was about 2,500 feet, I thought there was no reason to pull the chute's rip cord until I got into the clouds. All that worked out fine, and I just drifted down the remaining distance...and almost landed in the cooking pot of some Wehrmacht troops.

The chute's canopy came down over my head, and when I got out from under it there were about a dozen rifles pointed at me. They locked me in a chicken coop and turned me over to the Gestapo the next day. That night the Gestapo locked me in a basement of a castle-like building full of whips and torture instruments. While I might not have been scared to death, my morale was mighty low. The next day the Gestapo walked me to Dusseldorf and put me on a tram to the interrogation center at Frankfort on the Main.

My two-week stay at the interrogation center was probably about par for the course. I was in solitary confinement on bread and water for ten days, and after they decided I didn't know or wouldn't tell them anything, they sent me by train to Berlin and on to Stalag I at Barth.

During my time at Stalag I, I was full of the same frustrations and anxieties as the rest of the 8,000 that were in there. I met some old friends (one was my instructor in primary) and made some new ones.

Sometime in late April (I don't remember the exact date), three of my friends and I were able to get out the front gate and into the woods when Goebbels and his entourage came up from Berlin to establish headquarters for the Third Reich at Barth. We walked into the woods and hitched rides, eventually getting to Paris, but here are some incidents that took place between Stalag I and Paris that might be of interest:

- when our ragged little group entered the town of Rostok, the Burgermeister came out of the City Hall and surrendered the town to us so the Russians wouldn't take over.

- when we came across a German airfield one day and off in a corner revetment I found a perfectly good FW-190, but I never could get it started. Finally gave up and moved on.

- when we came into Rheims, France, on the 8th of May and milled around the military until we hitched a ride to Paris, never knowing that the Armistice was being signed in a building only a few blocks from us.

No one in Paris was too concerned about a 120-pound, ragged POW, and I really didn't know what to do next. Finally someone told me that a boat with POWs was leaving Le Havre the next day and I could get on it. I scrounged up some money, bought a train ticket to Le Havre and got on the boat with no orders, no nothing but the clothes on my back and landed in Boston a couple of weeks later.

Ramrod to Munster

by Steve Ananian

Every fighter pilot remembers his first combat mission. I'll never forget mine....

On 4 October 1944 we were awakened early. Briefing was the usual quick and efficient session. The mission for the day was a "Ramrod" escorting two boxes of B-17s to Munster in the Ruhr Valley. Lots of flak expected, but probably no fighter opposition. Our cruising altitude would be 27,000 feet. There were gale warnings for the North Sea.

I was flying Chet Malarz's Mustang 6N M "Bison Bull." It was a sleek P-51B, and the crew chief told me it was a good plane with a practically new engine. Tom Rich was leading Upper White Flight, and I was flying his wing. At "Landfall Out" I could see white caps on the North Sea below us. It looked cold and gray. Just before we hit the Dutch coast we spread out into battle formation, then rendezvoused with the bombers as we made "Landfall In." Our route was almost straight across the Zuider Zee toward Hamburg, then a 90 degree turn right toward the Ruhr Valley and Munster.

We had nearly crossed the Zuider Zee, flying over some small islands, with the Third Reich straight ahead. All was serene. I couldn't believe this was war and the enemy was below. Then *Bam!* One puff of black smoke with an angry orange center burst nearby. Flak! I lost power.

"Upper White Leader," I called over the radio, "this is Upper White Two. My engine just cut out!"

Tom's smooth voice came back at me, "Upper White Two, this is Upper White Leader. I'll go back with you. Do you know what's wrong?"

I knew I must've been hit, but it didn't make sense. One burst of flak never hit anybody. There was no smoke and no holes. The engine was running, but I just didn't have any power. I checked all the instruments. Oil temperature okay, coolant temperature okay, fuel pressure okay, but oil pressure seemed low. I must've been hit in an oil line or in the supercharger itself. Bad news! Can't go far without oil. Five minutes if I'm lucky.

I was at twenty thousand feet over the Zuider Zee and descending. Everything rushed through my mind all at once. *Bail out here, Steve, and you're a dead duck! If you're lucky, you'll be a prisoner of war. On the other hand, you might be able to make it to the North Sea and bail out over water.* Then I remembered the briefing – storm warnings over the North Sea, no Air Sea Rescue boats patrolling. *No sense worrying about that now. First things first.*

I called Tom Rich. "Let's go on home." Tom's reassuring voice answered, "Good luck, Steve. I'm right with you."

We slowly descended. I was in a flat glide with almost no power, and Tom Rich was "S-ing" back and forth to keep from overshooting me. He was also on the radio alerting

Air Sea Rescue about my predicament. My hands were full trying to get my plane back to Fowlmere.

My manifold pressure gauge was reading ten inches of mercury, the lowest reading on the dial. I had the trim tabs back and the stick in my stomach in an effort to stretch my glide to the sea. I kept looking at my air speed and rate of descent. We hit the coast of Holland, and I was finally over the North Sea. Altitude was 7,000 feet and atmospheric pressure here was enough to keep me aloft. As we hit the coast we were met by two "fat friends", (P-47s) from Air Sea Rescue. They escorted us back toward England. My rate of descent was now reading zero.

Of course I still had a few problems. Oil pressure was now zero, so it was obvious my problem was in the oil system. I looked back and saw Tom Rich. What a comfort! Down below the water was churning. Had to cool the engine somehow. If I could only get the oil in the bottom of the crankcase up on those cylinder walls. I started to rock the plane violently in uncoordinated movements. It worked! The oil temperature started going down.

The radio crackled, and I heard Tom's voice. "What are you doing?"

"Lubricating my engine!" I kept looking ahead for the English coast.

Tom called again, "White Two, I see the coast. We're gonna make it!"

That's when it happened – a runaway prop! While I tried to keep it from changing pitch, all hell broke loose. The coolant boiled over and smoke and oil filled the cockpit. The engine sounded like somebody was pounding it with a sledge hammer. The heat in the cockpit became unbearable. As much as I disliked it, the time had come for me and the aircraft to part company.

"This is it, Tom. I'm bailing out!" I lowered my seat, pulled my goggles over my eyes, lowered my head and released the canopy. I tore off my oxygen mask and detached everything that tied me to the plane. Just before I disconnected the radio plug, I heard Archie Tower's voice on the radio – he must've been monitoring the whole thing back at "Gaspump."

"Say again, Upper Five-four, I didn't understand." Tom broke in, "He said he's bailing out!" For the first time there was a note of concern in his voice. Archie didn't answer.

I raised myself to jump, and the slip stream knocked me back into the cockpit. I rolled the plane over and dropped out, pulling the rip cord at the same time. My oxygen mask went floating past my face as I fell head first, spinning toward the water. Then the chute opened with a pop. I hit the water almost as soon as the chute opened. Once the harness was wet, it was impossible to unfasten. Fortunately for me, when the dinghy floated past my nose in midair, I reached over and pulled the CO_2 inflation cartridge straps and inflated the dinghy. The whole thing took place in a matter of seconds.

After I hit the water, I bounced from the top of one wave to the next. I was skimming off the top of the waves. My chute, aided by gale force winds, was pulling me for a roller coaster ride! I was flat on my back, struggling to dump the air from the chute and swallowing the North Sea like a pint of "Half and Half" at the Checkers! I was in real trouble and on the verge of drowning. A P-51 started to buzz me. It was Tom. He made another pass, and then I understood. He was trying to spill the chute with his prop wash! On his third or fourth pass I suddenly stopped. I think he hit the chute. At any rate, it worked. I don't remember too much after that. I couldn't climb into the raft because the chute went down and started pulling me under. I just hung on to the raft for my life. According to Tom the "fat friends" from Air Sea Rescue dropped their life rafts as soon as I hit the water. This caused confusion. There were now five rafts and five dye markers spreading over several miles of the North Sea. One of them was me. Tom Rich said when they finally located me I looked like a drowning mouse hanging onto a doughnut. I tried to wave once, but nearly drowned. Things were getting worse, and the water was cold.

I prayed aloud, "It's up to you, God. I can't think of anything else I can do."

I knew Tom would be running short of fuel soon. Besides, what else could he do? Tom passed overhead and waggled his wings. He was wishing me well and heading for home. The P-47s were still there, having more fuel, but for how long? I watched them and wondered when they'd have to go home, leaving me alone. Anyway, what more could they do? I became aware of a change. There was a different sound –an airplane engine — and there it was, a Walrus, an Air Sea Rescue flying boat, a twin-wing flying bathtub! He started circling. I knew one thing: that plane could never land in this wind and on this water with ten-foot waves. If this is all they had, I had problems.

I was so numb from the icy water that I must've passed out. Suddenly I was aware of the sound of a plane taxiing on the water toward me. Then, as I rose and fell on wave crests, I caught sight of the Walrus. It had landed! It was coming right at me, and standing up in the hatch was an R.A.F. airman with a big smile on his face.

"Here, Yank, catch this."

He threw me a line. Don't know how I caught it, but I did. He hauled me toward him and grabbed me with a boat hook.

"Don't worry, there're two ships on their way," he said. A few minutes later as we bobbed up and down, I saw the minesweeper. Someone pulled me into a life boat and gave me some rum. It warmed me inside. I was suddenly aware how cold I'd been. A seaman put a blanket around me.

That night I woke up at an R.A.F. hospital on the Thames Estuary. The next day I was back at Fowlmere. I had it made! I knew I was going to live through the war. I don't think I ever thanked Tom for all he did. He called Air Sea Rescue and vectored two P-47s, a Walrus and two ships. When the Walrus arrived at the scene, I'd been in the water about an hour. The pilot realized I couldn't survive much longer and asked permission to land. He knew he'd be lucky to make the landing, let alone a later takeoff. I'd been in the cold water too long, and he felt he had to risk it. Of course Tom's quick thinking and expert flying kept me from drowning on splash-down. All those people risked their lives trying to save me. I'm very grateful.

In all I was in the North Sea for one hour and twenty minutes. I still can't believe I was hit by that one shot of flak. I'll always be indebted to Tom Rich for his great flying and quick thinking. Flying low over the water and deflating a chute is some kind of stunt. Why and how I was able to survive in that cold water and rough seas, I'll never know. To top it all, those brave R.A.F. flyers in Air Sea Rescue, attempting to land under those conditions and making it. Yes, Someone up there loved me!

It'll Never Happen To Me!

by Larry Powell

On 14 January 1945 on my 68th mission, I was leading White Flight and strafing locomotives near Magdeburg, Germany. So intent was I on getting number eleven that day that I failed to clear myself properly before I began the run. It was a beautiful specimen of iron and steam, big like American locomotives. Unfortunately for me, it had stopped under several high tension wires. After coming off my run, I pulled up right into them. I was flipped onto my back. Fortunately, my momentum carried me upward, and I was able to continue the roll to right-side-up. Maintaining full right rudder, aileron and trim, I was able to maintain level flight. My P-51D had been extensively damaged. The outer gun and ammo doors of the left wing were gone. The gun went out right through the wing spar. I could look through a large hole in the wing to the ground. The left elevator and horizontal stabilizer were mostly gone, and worst of all, there was a thin vapor trail of oil coming from the scoop.

Climbing to 12,000 feet with the rest of White Flight (Girzi, Jones, Howard and Caywood), "Happy, Jr." stalled out. She just wouldn't go any higher. It was a constant fight to keep her in the air. About 30 minutes later over Dummer Lake, my engine quit and my role as an Eighth AF combat fighter pilot came to an end.

I couldn't see a thing as coolant steam had covered my canopy, but my last clear vision was of burning airplanes and pilots in parachutes everywhere. Not wanting to bail out and then get run into, I tried to dive away from the flight. I did too good a job, for when I released the canopy, the treetops were slashing by. Boy, what a screw-up! Now I was too low to bail out. Being over a dense forest, I prepared myself for a rough landing in the trees when a nice, long, frozen field appeared ahead. I dumped full flaps, settled to the ground and slid between two farm houses as the prop ticked to a stop. My first thought was, *Should I turn off the Mag switch?* My second thought was, *How in the hell could this happen to me? It always happens to someone else, but NEVER TO ME!*

Leaving the P-51 after failing to set it on fire, the thermite bomb came apart in my hands. I jogged deep into the woods. There were lots of leaves and not too much snow. I covered myself and stayed there until dark and cold forced me to come out. I checked my possessions: two candy bars, two pocket knives and my Escape & Evasion kit. My destination was Holland, so I headed west. The night of 14 January '45 was bitterly cold and by midnight an ice fog had formed. There was no sleep to be had that night. To keep from freezing I had disposed of only my helmet and the British Mae West. I had on my full military uniform and my "G" suit. Because I was frost bitten on my previous mission, Doc Scroggin had ordered me to wear my B-4 jacket and overshoes. That was about the only plus in a day full of "minuses." I could use the roads at night since cold sound travels a long way and I could hear vehicles and even bicycles long before they came near. I would get off the road and hide in bushes until they passed. People simply paid no attention as I walked by.

15 January came clear and cold, so I took to the fields, forests and backwood trails. Later in the morning I broke my first knife trying to dig a turnip out of a frozen field. From then on I used the food in my E & E kit. Water was no problem except, if I used the purification Halizone tablets and the plastic water bottle, it became solid ice before I could drink it. The major obstacle that cropped up that day was the Emms River. I had followed a backwood's path to its edge and now the problem was getting across. Swimming was out of the question, and the bridge upstream had soldiers on it. I went downstream about a mile and found a rowboat chained to a log. As there was no way to work the chain off and I was in no particular hurry, I sat down with my other knife and cut the log in half. It took three hours, half of which was spent taking naps. I rowed across the river, secured the boat and went on my way.

Traveling mostly in the woods, I met several woodcutters chopping firewood. They either smiled, nodded hello or just didn't pay any attention. The second night out I was feeling pretty confident of things. After dark, instead of going around towns, I just went through them. They were mostly small villages. About ten o'clock I was going through a larger town and came to a rack full of bicycles in front of a theater. As I was tired of walking, I decided it would be nice to ride awhile. While I was selecting one, the theater doors flew open, and I was suddenly in the middle of about 200 Germans, all pushing and shoving me around to reach their bicycles and be on their way home. I worked my way to the edge of the crowd and ducked around a corner. It was a real shock, but again, no one paid me the slightest attention.

My second shocker was worse. I had found a nice road that went due west with very little traffic. By 4 a.m when I was very, very cold, I had developed a sort of relaxed walking shuffle, just listening for sounds rather than seeing things. The road ahead made a slight rise and then a dip. As I came to the crest and looked down into the dip, there was a bridge guarded by a soldier with a gun. Since he'd seen me, there was nothing to do but keep on going. The guard was also cold, stamping his feet and blowing on his hands. I went shuffling up to and by him. As I passed him I mumbled and blew on my hands like he was doing. He kept blowing on his hands, mumbled something and turned his back. I kept shuffling along, but sweat was running down my sides.

The road eventually went through an oil field. There were many derricks and some lights, but no people. The further through the field I went the narrower the road became until I passed the last derrick and there was no road at all. There was nothing ahead but a frozen marshland of peat clumps surrounded by ice, or so I thought. Several miles to the north I could see a faint outline of trees. First signs of dawn were appearing, and it was several miles back to another road. I headed for the trees.

Within thirty minutes I was wet from one end to the other. The ice was salt water ice and wasn't solid enough to hold me. Up to now I'd been lucky and made all the right moves, but this was my first wrong decision. It would've been better to go back to a road. I slipped, slithered, splashed, waded, cursed, groaned, crawled and cried my way toward those trees. Fortunately, in the daylight the trees were much closer than they'd earlier appeared. After six tortuous hours, I made it to the trees. They were the narrow tree line along side a cart trail. Other than the trail, all around was more marshland. It was a clear day on 17 January, so I rested in the sunshine and tried to dry my feet and socks. After an hour my feet were warm, but my socks were frozen. I put them on anyway and took off down the trail. I wondered if I might be in Holland, but had no way of telling.

My shuffling gait took me down the trail as it gradually widened into a dirt road. Without my realizing it, I entered a settled area. There were trees, but nothing to hide in. I heard some kids and then I saw them. They were ice skating on wooden shoes. I wondered again if I might be in Holland. As I passed, they quit playing. I didn't look at them, but I did look to see where I was. I was right where I didn't want to be — in a settled area with lots of houses, in the daytime, and no underbrush in the trees. Out of the corner of my eye, I saw one of the boys running up to a house. I kept walking until he was out of sight, then I took to the trees. I ran only a few yards when I heard a shout. "Halt!" I ran harder, then heard a couple of shots. With that I stopped and turned to face an approaching soldier. At least I knew I wasn't in Holland.

I was taken to a Me-109 fighter base where I stayed ten days before being taken to Frankfurt for interrogation at Oberursel. At Oberursel I stayed in solitary for nine days and, having known hunger, readily ate the German food. In my cell was a wooden handle that I lowered when I needed to go to the toilet. This lowered a flag in the hall, and a guard would come and let me out. One of my trips happened to be right after lunch, and I noticed that many prisoners didn't eat their food. When I picked up a few pieces of bread, the guards just smiled. From then on I always had to go just after lunch. One of the guards wanted to trade me three loaves of bread for my white silk scarf. I didn't but later wished I had. They took it away from me at Wetzlar.

From Wetzlar we went by train to Nurnberg and Stalagluft 3A. On the way while passing through Frankfurt there was an air raid alert. The Germans uncoupled our car and left us sitting in the middle of the marshalling yard just in case the target for the day was Frankfurt. Fortunately, it wasn't.

We stayed several weeks at Nurnberg during which time we had several day and night bombing raids on the marshalling yards just outside our camp. No bomb ever fell in our camp. When the American Army crossed the Rhine River, our camp was moved to Moosburg, Stalagluft 7A near Munich. The combining of camps made the prisoner count over 150,000 of all nationalities.

On 29 April 1945 we were liberated by General Patton's Third Army. We had previously dug slit trenches so very few prisoners were hurt in the liberating battle. At 9 a.m. the battle was over, and at 10:30 a.m. General George S. Patton was in the camp. I will never forget his words to us, a small group of officers who happened to be near the gate.

"Gentlemen, I have never in my life seen American officers and men subjected to such humiliating living conditions. You have my word your captors will pay dearly for this horrible state. I welcome you back."

I sobbed softly.

My "Behind the Lines" Adventure

by Martin Nay

I took off in my P-51D on that fateful mission in the early morning hours of 5 September 1944. It was my fortieth mission, and I was Red Two for Major John Reynolds, our recently assigned operations officer. We escorted B-17s to Stuttgart, and the weather was CAVU.

The escort duty was uneventful save for the usual flak which was plentiful and accurate. Upon leaving the target area, Major Reynolds obtained clearance from our group leader, "Armstrong," to break off escort and descend to attack targets of opportunity. With four flights in trail, the 505th descended to about 2,000 feet and attacked an airfield near Rastatt, Germany. We made a single strafing pass and climbed back to 1,500 feet, proceeding northwest for about 100 miles where a marshalling yard was observed. With flights and then single aircraft in trail, Major Reynolds circled the marshalling yard twice at 1,000 feet and decided to attack. While following him down I felt my P-51 shudder as several explosive cannon shells burst near its nose. Pieces of canopy flew about the cockpit. I continued the diving attack and strafed a locomotive. At this point I observed coolant streaming from the left side and, pulling up, I saw the propeller had stopped turning.

I pulled the throttle back and called on the radio, "Red Leader, Red Two here. I'm going in!"

I frantically searched for a reasonably flat place to land, but saw only the hills and valleys of Alsace/Lorraine. I was obliged to select a plowed field with a twenty degree up-slope for a gear-up landing. The Mustang bumped along, fracturing my jaw against the gun sight, and the fuselage ruptured behind the cockpit. I had to use the canopy ejection lever to get out of the cockpit.

Exiting the plane as rapidly as I could, I discarded parachute and dinghy and made for the tall grass about forty yards away. Hidden somewhat by weeds, I tended to a shrapnel gash on my forehead with sulfa powder from my escape kit. When I heard dogs barking nearby, I ran to a nearby stream and quickly made my way down the middle of it. Overhead the roar of P-51s filled the sky as they passed low over my aircraft wreckage. Bleeding profusely from the wound, I stopped running and threw myself on the opposite bank of the stream and hid there until nightfall. As I determined later, I had outrun the German soldiers and their dogs. Nevertheless, I chose to travel only after it was dark.

The nearest village to my downed position was called Kephlich, and I walked into streets empty of traffic. I successfully dodged one or two German vehicles that appeared and passed rapidly through the quiet village. I also dodged strolling German soldiers by hiding behind fences and cement walls. I furtively knocked on some doors, expecting, hoping to meet some pro-Allied partisan. Luckily no one responded. I later found out the place was a beehive of pro-German residents.

I continued on through the village and finally hoisted myself into a small barn. This type of barn, frequently seen in the Alsace region, adjoined the house and fronted on the street in the same manner as the home's front door. With this arrangement, the owner could proceed from barn door to front door by a straight path along the paved sidewalk. This is mentioned so one can understand how a German sentry posted in front of the barn would have to be passed if one exited the barn enroute to the home's front door.

Since the streets were filled with German soldiers during daylight hours, I was able to sneak out only at night to obtain fresh water from a nearby animal trough. I'd been in the barn loft about five days when I finally decided to contact the owner's wife, a woman of about forty who came daily to feed the pigs in stalls below the loft where I slept. I was desperate for solid food. I was also freezing, having left my leather flight jacket at Fowlmere. I had only two escape kit maps to use as blankets.

When she entered the barn that fifth day, I watched her through a hole in the loft floor, a square opening against which rested the ladder to the loft. "Fraulein!" I hissed. My heart jumped as she ran out into the crowded street crying, "Louie...Louie!" My initial thought was, who in the hell's Louie?

Luck was with me that day. Louie arrived wearing a beret and looking for all the world and displaying the same friendly gaze as the then-popular movie actor, Paul Muni.

Louie climbed the ladder and asked, "American?" "Yes, American pilot," I responded hurriedly. "Food, bring me food!"

"Oui," he replied as he clambered down the ladder and quickly darted into the barn owner's house. He was soon back with bread and sausages which I wolfed down. He told me to remain there, that another man would return after nightfall to bring me into the house. It was about an hour after dark that my new contact arrived, another beret-wearing Frenchman calling himself "George."

"Follow me, but say nothing," he ordered as he led me quickly out of the barn onto the darkened street and past the German sentry into the house.

No sooner inside the house than I was drawn into the kitchen and asked my name by both George and Louie while Mrs. Schmisser and her husband (house owners) stood by.

"Nay," I said. "Martin Nay, 1st Lt, U.S. Army Air Force."

"Nay, Nay," they all muttered aloud, almost in unison. "Ney," they repeated, "Le Marshal! Ney Le Marshal!"

They went on to explain in a sort of pidgin German that the famed Marshal Ney of the Napoleonic era had come from this same area and that, for the honor of the town and all its people, I, with the famed "Ney" name, must surely be saved.

"Le Marshal, Le Marshal," they kept crying aloud. Well, there it was. Added to the list of those who God protects — drunks and fools — there must also be inscribed *fighter pilots*.

After all the Hurrahs were done and I'd been properly fed, I was given to understand that a search had been on for me for days by the S.S. It would be best for all concerned that I be taken to a safer hideway. I was immediately led by George (who had me fill a burlap sack with leaves) to a cave in a nearby woods. It was there that I was obliged to remain, alone save for George's short visits every three or four nights to bring food. I slept curled up on the leaf-filled sack while thousands of bats winged their way out over me each night on their nocturnal pursuits. It was cold, dark and increasingly unbearable, so I finally appealed to George to find me another hiding place.

With some trepidation George led me first to one barn and then another – a different barn every night. Each day, each night, it became steadily colder. At this time I was about ten miles from the Moselle River, within earshot of cannonading by advancing American artillery units. Eventually I wound up in a rather large barn belonging to the Schmisser's father, a very elderly gentleman who had no knowledge of my presence. It was here that I began suffering from dysentery, growing weaker and weaker as the days wore on. The barn had a table saw which was used by the Germans while I was hiding and sleeping in the hay-filled loft.

Ill and weak from dysentery, I came close to surrendering to the visiting Germans who daily used the saw to make wood chips for their wood-burning trucks. I was dissuaded from making any overtures of surrender when I noted the death's-head emblem and black uniforms worn by the officers.

It was about this time that George arrived in a state of wild anxiety to tell me that I'd been observed watching the rockets from the barn windows. People were asking, "Who is that man hiding in the barn?" It was clearly time for me to be on the move once more, again with George leading the way.

I was taken to the nearby town of Monneren where I entered the home of Auguste Fousse, the village baker, his wife and two children.

German soldiers were billeted in the building adjacent to and butting against Auguste's home. It had formerly been the local schoolroom and thus lent itself quite well to use as a barracks. It was filled with German troops, yet not once did any of those troops attempt entry through the one shuttered window which opened directly into Auguste's guest bedroom on the second floor where I slept.

While the others operated the bake shop, I remained on the second floor of the house in a small room beneath the attic stairs where I kept abreast of the news with the aid of a small tabletop Philco radio tuned to BBC in London. I also made it my business to observe the movements of S.S. Panzer units passing on the road in front of Auguste's house.

Suddenly the military activity in the area erupted into a crescendo of artillery bursts, late night explosions which lit the sky and nearby mountain tops. The radio spoke of the American Army's river crossings in the region around Thionville. A loud crashing noise woke me one morning. Jumping up, I discovered the wooden shutters on the school/barracks side of my window were banging loosely. The barracks were empty. I threw open the window, climbed over the sill and stood on the barracks floor. All about were military accoutrements, hand grenades, military axes, etc. In the ceiling was a gaping hole, an evident artillery burst of some sort.

I hastened downstairs where Auguste and Eugene stood. They faced me anxiously.

"Your friends are coming, eh, Martin?" asked Auguste nervously.

"Yes, I believe so and I suggest we get into the cellar right now."

Since Auguste had already sent his wife and children to a safer place elsewhere in the village, it remained for us to clamber down into the bakery cellar. Within minutes tank treads were visible to us through the small cellar windows. The ratta-tat-tat of machine gun fire could be heard. Bullets whistled above us. Then suddenly all grew quiet. Over Auguste's and Eugene's protests, I climbed up onto the kitchen floor and made my way to the door. There, about twenty yards away, stood the sweetest sight I'd seen in months a halftrack with a large white American star painted on the side and several G.I.s and a captain, all with rifles and pistols at the ready.

Without a thought I burst through the door with arms upraised. "Hey, I'm an American officer!" I shouted. The soldiers stared at me incredulously. "I'm an Air Force lieutenant."

The infantry captain gave me a quick glance and growled, "Get behind me." Without turning, he added in a more friendly tone, "How the hell did you get here?...and where are the Krauts?"

"I crashed two and a half months ago down the road," I said, "and the Germans are all gone." Slowly the men about me came to a more restful stance.

"You say the Krauts are all gone?"

"Yes," I replied to the captain.

Approaching our location was a long line of tanks led by a colonel. I went through the same questioning from him.

"Okay, I'll make headquarters down the street. See me there," he ordered.

I remained, exchanging greetings with the tank crews as they drove past until, suddenly, the Germans opened up with their 88s. I found myself all alone as tank covers slammed shut as if on command. I found cover under one of the tank turrets before the shelling about twelve rounds stopped. I acquainted the armored column commander with what I knew of the village and enemy troop movements in the area.

I spent that last night in my old bed at Auguste Fouse's home in Monneren. In the morning after a tearful farewell from Mrs. Fouse and the children, Auguste, Eugene and I exchanged handshakes and embraces until I was obliged to jump on board a waiting jeep and leave. It took me to a waiting L-4 which was to fly me on the first leg of my journey back to Fowlmere, England. As I walked across the grassy field a voice called out from somewhere, "Don't go out there, Lieutenant. That field's mined!" I tiptoed back around the tail of the liaison aircraft.

The L-4 pilot laughed. "Hell, we gotta take off that way anyhow!"

I wanted out of the place so bad, I said, "Mined or not, let's go!"

As we eased off the ground I knew the adventure was over. I was back in the air again and enjoying every airborne moment more than I can describe.

We crossed a river and landed in Luxemburg. I was approached by a tall officer wearing an Ike jacket and displaying glistening stars on his collar. His ivory handled pistol caught my gaze — General Patton. He asked about my adventure, my impression of German strength in the region, and then the question of questions, what was my unit? I stood stock still, racking my befuddled brain desperately. For the life of me I couldn't remember. After several agonizing moments, General Patton seemed to know what I was going through.

"Don't worry, Lieutenant, it'll come back to you." With that I was dismissed and taken to the city of Luxemburg. I was introduced to other flying officers stationed in the area and to a British Wing Commander being driven in a staff vehicle to Paris. His invitation for me to come along was gratefully accepted.

In Paris I was taken to an interrogation unit set up especially for such purposes. They sent messages to my unit. Yes, this time I remembered the 339th Group and the 505th Squadron. They also let me roam the streets of Paris for six days before being flown to London. There I had another interrogation before being returned to Fowlmere.

Upon my return to Fowlmere I spent some time gathering my possessions which had been widely dispersed among the lads. I had a particularly difficult time locating my A-2 leather flying jacket.

All's Well That End's Well

by Andy Sirochman

Sunday, 13 August 1944, came with the usual early rising for all who were scheduled to fly that day plus support personnel. Perhaps I was a little more tired than usual, having just returned the previous night from the last England-to-Russia-to-Italy shuttle mission with extra missions from Russia and Italy. I had been selected to fly that shuttle mission with the 357th Fighter Group because of my Russian language fluency, but when asked the status of plane and pilot upon returning to Fowlmere, I replied, "Affirmative." At this time, both pilots and planes were at a minimum in the 505th Squadron.

The mission on 13 August '44 was a search and destroy, and all Mustangs were carrying bombs. Our particular target that morning was a railroad bridge. I should've known it wasn't going to be my day. On my first pass at the bridge, both bombs hung up. Fortunately there had been no enemy fire, so I found the tail end of the bombing string and made a second pass. The results again were poor as only one bomb released and that too missed the target. As I considered a third run during the pull-out, I felt the other bomb release off-target.

In the meantime the squadron had discovered a line of box cars on a siding and was making a gunnery pass hoping for some positive results. I joined in and, on completing the first strafing pass, pulled up over the bridge. In doing so I sighted more box cars alongside what seemed like a "round house." After reaching the bridge on the second run, I turned slightly and made my pass at these untouched railroad cars. My .50-caliber incendiaries started a small fire beneath one of the cars. Just to keep things going, I fired a few more rounds and then proceeded to climb sharply. I was about 250 feet when an enormous eruption – a ball of fire – appeared before me. It was at least 500 feet in diameter. I was in deep trouble! As I flew into that mess, the better part of a box car hurtled up past me along with miscellaneous debris and railroad ties. My instrument flying was okay and I emerged from the explosion with a heavy coat of soot completely covering my canopy. Reaching for the emergency canopy release, I called to see if anyone knew whether or not my Mustang was on fire. When I received no answer, I called once more and was delighted to hear Jim Starnes' reassuring voice.

"No, Rock, you're not on fire."

The soot began to clear from the windshield, and I checked the instruments. Oil pressure suddenly dropped from a normal 70 psi to zero, then back to 30. Still climbing and headed for home, I manually opened both the coolant and oil shutters. Coolant was streaming from the radiator, and most of the fabric was burned off the elevator and rudder. After reaching 10,000 feet, I began a slow descent, hoping to keep the engine cool enough to reach the channel. Strange how even though we flew alone, we never dwelt on the subject, but when the engine suddenly stopped dead, I felt *very much* alone.

I tried priming and restarting the engine unsuccessfully, then released the canopy and prepared to go over the side.

A final message came from a well-wishing Owen Farmer. "See you in thirty days, Rock."

I trimmed the plane and stood it on the side while trying to exit with one hand on the rip cord and the other on the chest strap. Alas, I didn't clear the plane and was still falling with it. Surprisingly, there was no panic. I knew I was getting low as I wiggled, twisted and suddenly cleared. Almost immediately I felt the chute pop open and heard the P-51 hit the ground. After judging the distance to the ground to be about 75 feet, I reached the shroud lines above me and gave a good pull. To my surprise I was sitting on the ground, a freshly plowed field with a Frenchman and his son so close I could almost shake hands!

Those French farmers were as shocked as I was, so I gathered my chute, Mae West and dinghy and placed them in a convenient hay stack.

The boy asked, "English?"

I shook my head, but upon seeing the frightened expression on his face, I quickly added, "American."

With the plane burning nearby I headed for a clump of trees, but stopped abruptly as I heard the boy shout, "No!" He pointed in the opposite direction. I later found out the Germans had a V-1 buzz bomb launching site in those woods. I saw a ravine and trees where he pointed and I *ran*. It took the boy an extra minute to reach my secluded spot. Talk about hospitality! He offered me a sandwich and a huge bottle of beer and signaled me to remain there for ten minutes.

I sat down completely exhausted and was happy to have the food. Sure enough, ten minutes later the boy returned with a change of clothes for me and an escort who was able to take me to a nearby town. Naturally there were some anxious moments such as that first turn in town where I almost bumped into two German soldiers on the sidewalk, or passing the local Gestapo headquarters, guard and all, less than an hour after my plane went down. Upon entering a cafe I was again offered more beer with a fresh egg in it this time. After they prepared some fictitious papers, I was led to my final hiding place — over the cafe. I can't complain about the four-meals-a-day routine featuring excellent French cuisine. With so much beer and wine available, too bad I don't drink. I never did get a drink of water in thirty days.

My admiration goes out to the gallant French family that housed me Pierre Vamberge, his wife and sister. Here were people risking their lives for a complete stranger, yet they never did hesitate to do everything they possibly could. It made me realize that it was a great world after all, and we were fighting a most worthy cause. I remained there until Allied forces pushed through the area.

How to Lose Sixty Ugly Pounds the Hard Way

by Ted Staggers

My final combat mission took place on 11 September 1944, our second day to the autobahn area southeast of Munich. The weather was good, ground fire light, and we were having a ball flying string gunnery patterns. I had two confirmed ground kills in my gun camera and was working on a Me-109 set back in a clearing, but the sucker wouldn't blow, burn or do anything in spite of hits all over. That's when I violated the basic tenets of air-to-ground gunnery. I got greedy and pressed too long on the target. I had to pull up sharply to avoid the trees. I knew immediately my mistake was costly when I felt something hit and saw the coolant streaming out of the engine.

I pulled up to about 1,500 feet and headed west by northwest, pumping away with the primer to keep old 6N U in the air. With my head down in the cockpit I really wasn't watching where I was going. I failed to notice the huge aerodrome just off my right wing on the outskirts of Munich. I can only imagine what went through those German antiaircraft gunners' minds when they saw this lone Mustang wobbling alone at about 150 mph or less, practically on the ends of their gun barrels. Their first burst took off a few feet of my right wing and removed any necessity of dumping my canopy. It disintegrated. I found myself in a steep dive, out of control. After a few seconds I gave up any idea of bailing out at such a low level and concentrated on making a survivable crash landing in a large field. I don't remember much except hard rudder and stick, trying to level out, thinking I wouldn't make it, then nose up at the last second. What a great airplane to perform like that under those circumstances! To this day I'm a staunch advocate of seat belts.

There wasn't much left of my P-51, but I ridiculously tried to set it afire with the thermite cannister gimmick we carried. Couldn't get it to ignite. About that time I saw a buddy buzz over which made me feel good, but it also pointed out a group of German soldiers coming across the field. I ran to the woods nearby and tried to hide in a small depression in the ground since there was almost no underbrush. The soldiers fanned out for a systematic search of the area. It wasn't long before one approached my position and spotted me.

I was taken to a building nearby and made to strip to be searched. The Germans were amused to see my green and white striped pajamas under my olive drab uniform. I had not been scheduled to fly that day and was awakened late to replace someone that was ill. The search found nothing of importance. I was then taken that same afternoon to another location and locked in a basement where I was questioned often and at length by a S.S. officer. After two or three days a Luftwaffe major came in, apologized for my treatment and said they had been looking for me. He took to an airfield near Munich where I received my first food, then turned me over to an old World War I veteran who was to be my escort to the Frankfurt interrogation center.

Walking through Munich at dusk, I recall looking up at the buildings and seeing sky through the empty shell structures. My escort took me into a Munich beer hall, a fantastic marble place with circular balconies up the middle. An orchestra was playing a waltz in the distance as he ordered a beer for each of us. He spoke a little English. Good, because I spoke no German. I told him I liked Munich beer.

When we got to the train station for our trip to Frankfurt, my escort pointed out two other American flyers with their escorts: Major Mike Quirk and Captain Billy Edens of the 56th Fighter Group. Forgetting my rather bloody appearance (minor flak wounds plus a broken nose compliments of the S.S.), I rushed up only to have them back away in horror. I always was ugly, but with my nose pushed sideways, I guess I was even worse than before. I know I sounded funny because I couldn't breathe through my nose. Mike Quirk, bless his soul, gave me the only medical treatment I received by putting his thumb on my nose and moving it back in place... approximately. It hurt, but at least I could breathe.

In Franfurt while waiting to be interrogated, I met "Gabby" Gabreski. We were sitting talking when Tom Underwood, an old friend from the 408th Fighter Bomber Group in the States, came rushing up and said, "Stag, guess who's here? Gabby Gabreski! And guess how he went down? Ran his prop into the ground while strafing! How stupid can you get!" You can imagine the look on Tom's face when I introduced him to Gabreski.

Interrogation was interesting...at least in retrospect. First I got the arrogant captain interrogator, complete with dueling scar, who threatened to have me shot unless I gave him the information he requested. We got nowhere. Then they switched tactics and I got a corporal who had worked in Pittsburg before the war. He tried the soft, persuasive approach. Finally, they gave up.

After a brief period of processing at nearby Dulagluft, a group of us proceeded by train to Stalag Luft I at Barth, north of Berlin on the Baltic Sea. Initially it wasn't so bad. The weather was okay, and we got a Red Cross parcel of food, cigarettes, etc., every week. Then, as the weather got colder, the parcels came less often until by Christmas they stopped altogether. The German guards explained that because of air harassment, they couldn't move anything, much less our food parcels, from the distribution point to our camp. Our diet from Christmas until 30 April '45 consisted of some black bread and a bowl of ersatz (dried vegetable) soup each day. Much of our time passed huddled around our crowded, drafty barracks trying to keep warm in our one outfit of Army wool shirt, pants and field jacket...and trying not to think of good things to eat. Letters from home helped us retain our sanity.

As time went on, we saw our guards change from fit, front-line troops to decrepit retreads who could hardly climb into the guard towers. Suddenly, on 30 April '45, we woke to find no guards and all the gates open. The command decision was made for us to wait for the Americans to come. Later that day the Russians arrived. Finally after what seemed an eternity, the Americans and Russians agreed that B-17s could come in and fly us out.

Diary of a "Short" Tour

by Roland Strong

My first combat mission was the 21 May '44 "Operation Chattanooga Choo Choo" strafing mission to the Leipzig area. I scored an aerial kill that first time out and decided to keep a personal log of my missions. Unfortunately, the result was a "Diary of a Short Tour."

The early missions were to support the invasion of Normandy. Several dive bombing missions were without notable success. Our objective to destroy transportation behind German lines, however, was very successful. I was involved with the destruction of eleven trains during June and July 1944.

On my last missions we lost two of our 505th aces. The mission on July 29th was to Merseberg with a synthetic oil plant our target. After breaking up an attack on the bombers, Blue Section ended up on the deck. Lt C. J. Hanseman, our first ace, was killed during a strafing run. August 4th was our 100th mission. Targets at Hamburg were bombed without opposition. Major Don Larson, our CO, took the 505th to the deck where we destroyed six planes. We were bounced by several Me-109s. Major Larson was killed in a midair collision with Lt Bob Burns while shooting a Me-109 off my tail. My coolant, however, had been shot out by ground fire, and I bailed out at 9,000 feet and landed in a cow pasture.

I was captured in a few minutes and taken to a guard house on a military base at Oldenberg for the night. From there I went by train to the big interrogation center, Auswertestello West. U.S. airmen were picked up at every stop the train made. I found Bob Burns at the interrogation center, and we managed to stay together throughout our captivity. We had our first real meal in about six days at nearby Dulagluft and were given Red Cross packages for the train ride to Stalagluft III. We soon learned the hard way, however, that water was more important to survival. Having had no water during the trip, we finally arrived on the 12th of August at the South Compound of Stalagluft III at Sagan in very poor condition. The South Compound contained 800 American and 2,500 Royal Air Force officers, many who had been POWs for more than four years. They had set up a command structure and were very well organized.

The barracks were prefab, very clean and with no vermin. Our food during the first few weeks was all right, but due to our thorough job on the German transportation system, we were soon cut from one to one half Red Cross parcel per man per week. Our German spud and bread ration was also cut. We were getting about 1,500 calories per day.

Christmas arrived and we had a "bash" of food which had been saved a little at a time. A cake I baked consisted of ground-up black bread crusts, German tooth powder for a rising agent, and diced dried prunes mashed together with sugar cubes. The concoction was put into its own special bake pan which I made and took to the communal kitchen. It baked for eight hours and weighed eleven pounds when finished. Bob Burns got sick and (I think) lost part of it. Burns and I each had an amphetamine tablet which I'd smuggled out of my escape kit. The Germans never did find them. Such was Christmas '44.

By mid January '45 we could hear a steady distant rumbling of artillery from the east. Soon the Germans hastily moved us to the west. We left on foot in the snow, 10,000 men in a marching column (?) which started about 11:00 p.m. We walked about 100 miles over the next few days, sleeping in barns with no hay and piled like pigs to keep from freezing. It was somewhere near the town of Muskow that I fell behind due to an arthritic condition in my left hip. Though I kept moving slowly, I was soon out of sight of anyone. At night a German wagon came from behind. He'd been hired to travel a mile behind the column and pick up stragglers like me.

After being dropped off in the center of town, I gave a Polish slave laborer a package of Chesterfields to help me find "mein comrades, mein brot, mein dekka (blanket)." The guy helped me up a steep hill to a glass factory. The furnaces were going, and the floor was so hot one could hardly walk on it. Nevertheless, I found a place on that delightfully warm floor under a large table and slept the sleep of total fatigue for a least eight hours. Awakening, I no longer had the gimpy leg, and some kind soul gave me a nice slice of black bread.

After another day of marching, they put us on a train for Nuremberg. Then things got mean. They hastily moved out a POW camp of Italians and put us into their quarters which were nothing but filth, lice and fleas. There was no heat and no Red Cross parcels. Our daily diet consisted of a medium sized boiled potato without salt and soup which we called "green death." It was prepared in a communal kitchen in the compound and made of dehydrated bales of green weeds, grass, you name it, plus a half of beef that had been skinned and salvaged following a strafing attack when some of the animals were killed. For the most part they were pretty ripe as evidenced by the generous amount of maggots in the soup. I gave my maggots to a person that really suffered from hunger. I never did feel the pain of hunger as much as some people. There were about 2,000 in this compound, and we got less than 1,000 calories per day while there.

We observed two large air raids on Nuremberg, one R.A.F attack at night, and the next day, a 1,000-plane B-17 raid. We saw a number of British Lancasters go down in flames and eight or ten B-17s the next day.

About 1 April '45 we saw P-47s from the 9th Air Force. A few days later we again heard the distant rumble of artillery in the west. "Hot Dog!" we thought, but too soon. About 10 April the Germans suddenly told us we had to take another walk. The weather was getting tolerable, and our only fear was of being strafed by our own planes. Before leaving we made a cart to haul our possessions. It was priceless to us because we scrounged a five-gallon water container which we filled with any water we could find that was pure. Also, because of our hauling capacity, we gleefully borrowed seed potatoes, a few onions and sugar beets from roadside farms – no repayment intended.

We arrived in Moosburg about 15 April '45 to find a number of large tents set up in a dry river bed. A wagon came through dropping off a bale of hay to be made into beds for the 24 men in each tent. Food here was cooked on a communal basis and served on tables in the same building it was prepared in. It was better than Nuremberg.

By this time the Germans knew that a few days or weeks would mean the end of the war. All day long and through the nights we could hear the Germans retreating, rattling over a wood bridge just east of our position. We could also hear artillery firing from both sides. Projectiles whistled over our camp. About 10:00 a.m. on the 29th of April the Germans came down from the guard towers, many throwing their helmets over the fence – but no weapons. In a few minutes an American tank pulled up to the main gate. After a minute of small arms fire, it was all over.

In a couple of days a convoy of empty supply trucks came through and took us to the jet air base at Landshut. There we lived in German barracks which had the entire water system destroyed. I was in a room with a group of Australians.

After two more days those beautiful birds, C-47s, came in and took us to France and Camp Lucky Strike. I was in Rheims on VE-Day. It had been a long, difficult year in Europe for me.

Prisoner of War

by Allen Young

I was first assigned to the 339th at Rice, California, then transferred to the 76th Tactical Reconnaissance Group and 23rd Tactical Squadron at Thermal, California. From the 23rd some of us were transferred back to Dale Mabry, Tallahassee, Florida, and from there to England.

Again I found myself assigned to the 339th Fighter Group and, more specifically, the 505th Fighter Squadron. This was in June 1944. I arrived there in the afternoon and was immediately given a cockpit check by my Squadron Commander, Major Don Larson, and went on my first mission the following morning. Nothing like a fast orientation.

On the way back from a fighter sweep near Munich, Germany, on 18 November 1944, I was hit by heavy flak in the belly of my P-51 at about 17,000 feet. I lost my oil and coolant, but worst of all, I lost my elevator controls. It felt like a 20-ton tank had hit me. My first attempt at getting out was at about 15,000 feet at an indicated 300 mph. The air stream was so strong that it threw me straight back against the radio section. It seemed an eternity before I was finally thrown free of the plane. Whether I pulled the rip cord or my chute was torn open on the radio or tail, I'll never know, but I probably pulled it after being thrown free. Evidently the chute opened at high speed since three panels were torn from it, causing me to the hit the ground like a ton of lead. Maybe that's why I'm short, or maybe that's why my chest changed places with my waist.

I had a large bruise on my left shoulder and neck, very sore ribs on the right side, and a broken right foot. I struggled out of the chute as best I could and hid in the water and mud of a trench I'd barely missed when landing. The water was cold, so I crawled into a hedgerow a few yards away. A few seconds later a shot whistled through the hedge, and someone shouted, "Stand up!" I lay still, hoping I hadn't been seen. Another shot, closer this time. They knew where I was, so I started to get up. Guess I waited too long. The next shot missed my head by inches, and I hit the ground again. The next shout stood me up in a hurry. There were six soldiers and some young kids, and they had me pretty well surrounded.

It seemed as though the world had come to an end for me. Here I was, a POW and unable to help myself. One soldier had a rifle at my chest as another searched me. They took everything I had – a lighter, watch and knife. A German officer soon arrived and took charge. He spoke a little English and asked me if I was hurt and the old routine of what I was flying, where I'd been and where I was going. They already had parts of my plane. I gave him my name, rank and serial number. I was taken to a small village where I seemed to be regarded more as a curiosity by the civilians than as an enemy. P-47s were dive bombing and strafing nearby, so I was taken to a cellar for shelter, then to Saarlautern. Next I was moved to a church headquarters, followed by a private home and another church.

For the next three or four days I could hardly move my legs or my head. To feed me in the mornings they would come and lift me out of bed. My first interrogator was a non-com who told me he'd worked as a butler in the Hearst Mansion in California. All in all I was taken to eight different headquarters, the last being in a civilian jail in

Saarbrucken. There I was given the good food they'd been promising – black bread and black coffee. I was given a straw bunk and remained in solitary confinement for three days. Sure was getting hungery, but I couldn't stomach the food. While there I learned that a pilot named Van Zandt had been shot down near where I went down and was in a cell next to me. He later said he thought I was a Frenchman.

We were both loaded on a train one morning headed for Frankfurt. We had a very good chance to escape at the station, but Van didn't have his dog tags and I was so banged up I could hardly move. The trip took about sixteen hours during which we got more or less acquainted. At one time during the trip we were threatened by P-51s strafing, but flak drove them away. We arrived in Frankfurt about 1800 hours and were marched through town. We then took a trolley to our first camp – Oberursal.

We were stripped and searched, then assigned to a room. I was interrogated that evening and asked to fill out a Red Cross form. I filled in my name, rank and serial number, then crossed out all other lines on the paper. It made my interrogator quite angry, and he told me I wouldn't leave there until he got all the data he wanted. I was taken to my room, a dinky little hole in the wall with a bed made of bare wooden slats. The room had an electric heater, but I got no heat for three days. I had to keep moving to stay warm.

The food was terrible. Breakfast was two slices of black bread with warm barley water. Lunch consisted of a "weed" soup which was sickening to smell, let alone eat. It looked like grass, leaves, cabbage and sugar beets all boiled together. After eight days of solitary confinement I was called in for more questioning. This time the interrogator placed several books in front of me and told me where I was from, what I was flying, who my CO was, etc. He knew more about the 339th Fighter Group than I did. I was sent back to my cell and was there for three more days.

On 3 December a bunch of us were sent to Wetzlar (Dulag Luft). We were issued a "Joy Box" and some additional clothing, stuff the Red Cross sent in. We were given a shower and some hot food and felt like new men. I was at Dulag Luft for a week. For our trip to Stalag I we were issued half a Red Cross parcel and a tenth of a loaf of bread per day. We got along fairly well although it took us five days to go little more than 300 miles. While going through the marshalling yards of Berlin, we were bombed by the R.A.F. We didn't get a direct hit on the train, but were rocked back and forth by the concussions.

After arriving at Stalag I at Barth on the Baltic Sea north of Berlin, we were given a shower, a de-lousing and then assigned to our compound and barracks. We slept three deep with 24 men to a room. Not like home, but sardines get along and so did we. Colonel Francis Gabreski, the top ace, was Allied Commander. I met Lt Staggers, Lt Moore, Lt Benbow and Capt Mitchell, all from the 339th Fighter Group.

A few more of our pilots from the 339th showed up during the course of my stay at Stalag I, including Lt Col Harvey Henderson (503rd CO) and, can you believe it, Major Fulton, our Fowlmere Mess Officer. On May 1, 1945, the camp came under Allied control, probably one of the happiest days of my life. I feel very fortunate to have come through it all in one piece and in fairly good health.

Happy Birthday

by Harry Ziegler

On 3 March 1945, my birthday, we escorted B-17s to their target in central Germany. I was again flying wing to Jim Starnes who was among those strafing the "piggy-backs" the day before. After the bombers hit their target without interference by fighters, the 505th headed for the Magdeburg area. Jim Starnes led the squadron to the the target area and pointed it out. Joe Thury then radioed that his flight would make the first pass and ordered our flight to tack onto the back of the attacking formation. While we were on our strafing run someone radioed he was hit, and I was asked to escort him home. Upon pulling off my target, however, I felt a sudden jolt from an apparent hit. I announced that I was hit, and Jim ordered our flight to join up. I reported that my engine was rough and temperature was rising rapidly. Jim stated we would head north for the Hannover-Berlin autobahn and try for a "piggy-back" pick-up. He stated that he and I would land while the other two would cover until I could join him in the cockpit of his P-51.

We flew for a few minutes until my plane began losing power. It could no longer sustain altitude. Smoke and flames trailed from the engine. Down below I saw a single large field in an otherwise solid forest area. I immediately dropped my nose toward the clearing and got rid of the canopy. Flames and smoke surged into the cockpit, forcing me into the left rear corner of the cockpit. I dropped full flaps and braced for the crash. The plane dug in upon contact, clods of dirt and grass flying everywhere as the plane came to a screeching halt. The flames made rapid exit imperative, so I unhooked quickly and ran for the nearby woods before she blew. Looking back from the woods, I was surprised to see the fire going out. Seeing no one about, I ran back to the plane and used the incendiary bomb we carried to set it afire again. I placed the sputtering bomb on the left wing tank gauge and ran back into the forest, watching with satisfaction as the plane burned and blew up.

After moving further into the forest for safety, I stopped and took off my "G" suit, removed the radio headset and oxygen mask from my helmet, then buried them. As the odds of my evading capture this deep in enemy territory really never entered my mind, I decided to walk to the autobahn. A short while later I reached the autobahn and began walking in a westerly direction, staying deep enough in the forest to prevent anyone from seeing me, but shallow enough to keep track of any action along the highway. I walked this way all afternoon without incident, only a few times observing vehicular traffic.

Toward late afternoon I found I'd walked through the perimeter of a camouflaged antiaircraft unit. I saw a German soldier working on a halftrack only 30 yards away. He looked toward me, and I waved. He responded with a wave, dropped into the halftrack, then came running at me while shouting in German to other soldiers who began appearing all around.

The soldiers grabbed me and began speaking in German. I gave them my best "Nicht versteh!" and quickly gathered from their "Alles kaput" remarks that I was finished. They took me to a German officer in an underground room who also tried unsuccessfully to question me in German. He finally made a phone call and placed me under guard in another underground room. Sometime later I was turned over in the dark to other soldiers in different uniforms which I assumed were Luftwaffe. They took me to an airbase which I think was the one we'd earlier strafed.

I was put into a large cell with three solid walls. The fourth wall had a door with a small barred window. There were more questions in German, and I continued to say I didn't understand. I understood some German words but couldn't put together what was expected. Later a young soldier came in who spoke English, but I answered only with my name, rank and serial number.

There were four wooden beds in the cell. I lay on one until the door opened and what appeared to be two American lieutenants, dressed in bomber-type clothing, were thrown inside. They said they'd been shot down on a mission that same day and asked who I was and where was I shot down. Remembering the intelligence briefing which described how Germans, dressed to look like American prisoners, were used to extract information, I wasn't very friendly and didn't answer any questions.

After dozing in and out of sleep until midnight, we were awakened by lots of loud noise near the cell door. Shortly, the door opened and five young German pilots pushed their way into the cell and started talking in German. They were laughing and shouting and seemed half-crocked...like a group of ours who'd come in from a night on the town. I was able to make them understand that I was hungry and thirsty. I'd had nothing to eat or drink since breakfast at Fowlmere, so they got the three of us some hot tea and black bread. My first taste of black bread went down quite well. The German pilots seemed to be wishing us well while having a great time of their own. Some time later they left.

The next morning two armed guards started marching us to an unknown destination. We walked most of each day and some nights. Sometimes we rode in electric trolleys and at other times in trucks. I recall we slept on trams or trucks and did not stop for lodging. The eating was always black bread and tea of some sort. The guards were changed periodically along the way. It took about four days to reach Frankfurt. We also picked up more bomber aircrews along the way until we numbered fifteen. I was still wary that anyone could be German "plants" and spoke to no one. They probably felt the same about me, and that made for silence all the way.

The third day enroute we were walking toward a small town when B-26s bombed the town. When things cleared, the guards marched us right through the center of town. The street was lined with civilians armed with clubs, pitch forks, etc., and shouting at us in German. At one point the crowd closed in, but the guards pushed them off until we could get past. That was the first serious incident since I left Magdeburg.

On the rail platform at Frankfurt we heard sirens begin to whine. People from all around, including our group of prisoners and guards, rushed into bomb shelters beneath the bombed-out train station. It was dark, and we had no idea what would happen to us among those people. We could hear the bombs exploding, mostly in another part of Frankfurt. Much later when the "all clear" sounded, we were taken back to the train platform. Again a civilian crowd started pressing toward us, shouting in German. Some of the guards intercepted the crowd while others herded us down the tracks a short distance. There we waited until a trolley picked us up for transport to the interrogation center at Oberursel.

Upon arrival I was placed in solitary confinement and never saw any of that group of prisoners again. As described by other POWs, the cells were very small, dark and dingy. The one bulb in the ceiling stayed lit day and night. My first bed in four nights was wood with slats too far apart and a mattress made of straw biscuits which moved with the slats. Pulling a string on one wall dropped a flag outside informing a guard you needed to relieve yourself. I filled out the complicated forms asking all sorts of information by writing name, rank and serial number, only. On the second day I was escorted to another building for interrogation. Behind the desk sat a well dressed officer crippled in one arm. I saluted and stood at attention. He spoke excellent English, gave his name and volunteered that he had flown Stukas early in the war until wounded. He'd been educated in the States and worked for Anheuser Busch Brewery prior to the war.

After his own introduction, he asked, "Now, who are you?" I gave my name, rank and serial number. "I know that," he said, "but how can I be sure you are not a spy?...and your name? You can't even pronounce your name correctly. It should be *Tsig-ler*. You're German and should be fighting on our side."

"I'm third generation American of German descent," I responded.

The crippled officer said he needed all sort of

information on my outfit to prove I wasn't a spy and that he'd give me more time to think it over.

The following day I was visited in my cell by two civilians who accused me of being a spy and threatened me with abusive language. I was shaken, but rationalized that they were trying to scare me into revealing information.

The third day I was taken back to the interrogation officer who asked, "Are you ready to give me the required information?"

I gave my name, rank and serial number. "It doesn't matter. I know all about you." He handed me a news clipping of my graduation from advanced flying base, my mother's name and address, etc.

"Is that correct?" he asked.

"Yes."

He said they knew about all the fighter and bomber bases in England and pushed a large book across the desk for me to examine. I recalled intelligence briefings about this kind of thing and paged through, stopping on a bomber group. He immediately took the book and looked at the page, then returned it. I stopped at several other bomber and fighter pages. He took the book each time. I passed right over the 339th page without a pause.

He eventually took the book and said, "We know your takeoff times and targets on a daily basis. We've even found your plane and identified the group marking on it."

He never stated the group or squadron, so I felt sure the fire had destroyed the markings.

The officer finished with, "All we need is your station call sign, and then you can proceed to a prisoner of war camp. If you refuse to disclose it, you will remain in solitary confinement for a very long time."

I was sent back to my cell to think about it, but two days later I was escorted to a truck with other POWs on my way to a processing station called "Dulagluft."

After being photographed, fingerprinted, etc., my POW forms were filled out and I was put in a "box car" of the "40 and 8" type with other American British prisoners. We were stacked like sardines with barely enough room to half lay down. The train traveled all night, stopping at a large marshalling yard. The door opened, but none of us moved. A S.S. officer with pistol waving in the air pushed his upper body into the car and started screaming and shouting in German. He kept pointing his pistol at random until two German soldiers came and more or less dragged him from the doorway. We were relieved when the door was closed again.

Later the train moved out and traveled many hours into the next night, stopping at the POW camp at Nurnberg. Prison life here was survival at the most basic level, at least to me it was. I saw my first Red Cross parcel minus the chocolate. It seemed the senior American officer pooled the chocolate and doled it out as a ration. The meals were always "Hot Water Soup" and sometimes some cabbage leaves and at other times beans with a worm or weevil in each bean, plus black bread.

We slept on the floor without beds and without heat in the barracks. Days were spent walking around and talking to other prisoners. Fighting dysentery and lice were part of the routine. One pleasant memory of the Nurnberg camp took place Easter morning 1945 when some of us met with an old Scottish Chaplain in the compound and held an Easter service. Our communion was unique in that each had to bring a piece of black bread saved from our last meal to represent the Body of Christ. Of course we had no wine. The sacrifice that Christ made for us was more real at that moment than ever before in my life.

Toward the middle of April '45 we could hear artillery in the west and were notified that we would be moving out and heading south. The next day the whole Nurnberg POW camp started to move out on foot. We had word that about 34,000 POWs would be on the road when the camp emptied out. It should be noted that depending on where you were along that line of POWs, accounts might differ considerably on what took place on the trip.

Our compound walked out of camp during late morning carrying everything we owned such as tin cans, saved food bits and rag-tag blankets. Our original German guards had been replaced with men that were old and feeble. My best POW friend and I were weak from dysentery at the time, but felt good about being out from behind barbed wire and on the road. Our compound tacked onto the one which had started out ahead of us. Several hours later we had just passed under an autobahn when I looked up and saw four P-47s flying formation directly overhead. I was happy to see friendly planes, but then I saw them start a diving turn straight for us.

Everyone scattered off the road and into ditches. I dove hard into a ground depression among a few trees just as the first machine gun projectiles began striking the ground down the line. The first bomb exploded down and to the left of my position, the next closer and the third even closer amid .50-caliber projectiles striking all around. I figured the fourth bomb would be very close, but it never came. The planes completed their pass and flew off toward the west. For the first time I had that hollow, sinking feeling of fear in my stomach and began to think about the many Germans that had experienced the same feeling when I was strafing them.

After a time all POWs and guards came back on the road and started walking again. I don't know how many were wounded or if anyone was killed and have never heard anything about the incident since. At any rate I came out with only a bruised leg, but considered the action a bad start for a long journey. The "Jug" pilots must've realized their mistake and reported the large column of POWs on the road, because the next morning and every day thereafter we had a P-51 escort fly low, up and down the column. He rocked his wings and appeared to be keeping track of the POW march.

The days and distances of marching have faded, but generally, we walked all day and were supposed to rendezvous with our "Black Bread Wagons" for the evening meal. Sometimes this didn't work out. We slept at night wherever the march stopped. One night I slept in a barn, two nights in fields and one night in a ditch by the roadside with my buddy who refused to move another step that day. The line continued to pass us by until dark, so we just joined at a new place the next morning. On one occasion we walked all day and made contact for the night in a lumber yard. We were informed, however, that we'd have to move on. It was cold and drizzling rain, and it continued raining throughout the night. I walked part of the night in my sleep and occasionally would bump into the person in front of me and wake up, then doze off again while marching. The first break of daylight brought a stop to the rain. We were completely soaked and exhausted, and soon were ordered into a forest to rest and sleep most of the morning.

Over the next few days, we walked the rest of the way to Moosburg under the same conditions. On our arrival, thousands of POWs were pressed into the already crowded Moosburg prison camp.

My friend and I were herded into a completely rundown wooden barracks: no windows, doors or floorboards in some places. Roof holes were everywhere. I did get an upper bunk—the usual wooden slats which were too few and far between for support of the burlap bags filled with straw or grass...and lice. For the next ten days POW life was about the same as before. We heard explosions to our west. They got closer all the time. Word came down that we were again going on the road, south toward the Alps.

Early on 29 April '45, small arms fire and explosions were heard outside our compound. Shortly thereafter a few American tanks came rolling though the fence into camp. General Patton was standing on one of the tanks, waving to the prisoners as the tanks continued on through the camp.

The takeover by American troops did not immediately change the prison routine. The next day the senior American officer set up a process to distribute POW records to anyone who wanted to get in line and wait. I got mine and still have them to this day.

Two days later I was transported to an airfield where I was given a shower, "de-loused" and provided with new Army clothing. The following day I was put aboard a C-47 to Camp Lucky Strike, France, a rehabilitation camp for POWs. There I spent the days lying around and eating in special chow lines where we were well fed but in rationed portions so our stomachs could stretch gradually and not rupture.

A few deaths were reported due to ruptured stomachs of POWs who overate too soon after being released from capture. Egg nog lines were set up around camp between meals. In one of these lines I had a very pleasant reunion with my good friend, Jim Mankie (503rd Fighter Squadron), who'd been shot down over two months before my fateful mission. Eventually I shipped home and docked in New York on 13 June 1945.

PILOT ARTICLES

Recce Escort

by James R. Starnes

Escorting a photo reconnaissance aircraft enroute to take bomb damage assessment photography was usually a routine job. Sometimes it was difficult to keep up with the photo bird, especially a Mosquito. Rarely did the Luftwaffe rise to threaten the recce aircraft, since the Luftwaffe's main goal was to attack the bombers. One of our early recce escort missions proved to be an exception to the rule.

On the morning of 24 May 1944 the 339th escorted bombers to Berlin. That same afternoon we flew a relatively short distance mission escorting B-17s attacking Soissons, France, which is located about thirty miles west of Rheims and only ninety miles from the English Channel. As part of this second mission three P-51s were ordered to escort a P-38 reconnaissance aircraft to assess damage to the Soissons target. The three P-51 pilots performing the recce escort were Jack Price (503), Archie Tower (505) and Hal Everett (505). The bomber escort mission was routine - not so the recce escort. FW-190s approached from several directions with altitude and numerical strength. In the resulting encounter, two FW-190s and one P-51 were downed. The P-38 and the other two Mustangs were fortunate to escape unharmed. The combat action is best recorded in the witness statements attached to the Missing Aircrew Report on Harold M. Everett who scored both FW-190 kills before bailing out from his P-51 #42-106646.

Witness Statement of Lt Archie A. Tower "On 24 May 44 Lts Price, Everett and myself were escorting one P-38 photo airplane to the target area at Soissons. We were flying at 17,000 feet just north of Soissons when I spotted about fifty FW-190s coming in on our tail. We turned into them. I shot at the first four at about 90 degree deflection, and they peeled down. I did a 270-degree turn and observed two FW-190s with Lt Price on their tail. He in turn had two FW-190s on his; Lt Everett was on theirs with two FW-190s on his. I got on the last two with several behind me. I saw one ahead of Lt Everett blow up as the two ahead of me peeled off. One peeled down, rolled right and left, and I followed him to the clouds. The last I saw of Lt Everett was when the FW-190 he was firing on blew up. After that I became separated and continued the rest of the mission alone." (signed) Archie A. Tower, lst Lt., Air Corps.

Witness Statement of Lt Jack B. Price "On 24 May 44 Lts Tower, Everett and I were escorting a P-38 photo ship trailing the rest of the group which was on a bomber escort mission. When we reached the vicinity of Cambrai we were about ten miles behind because the photo ship pilot wanted the smoke to settle before he reached the target area to take photos. I was on the right of the photo ship and Lts Tower and Everett were on the left; altitude approximately 18,000 feet. I saw ten-plus FW-190s at one o'clock (due S) in right echelon about 2000 feet above us. They flew due E, made a 90-degree left turn, then flew N until they got behind us where they made a 180-degree turn. When they completed this turn they were in left echelon. I looked up and there were about fifty more FW-190s overhead. When I looked back at the formation on my left rear the first two had already peeled off to attack me. I called Lt Tower on "C" channel and told him to break, then told the major piloting the photo ship to get out of there as FW-190s were all over us. I then switched to "A" channel and called Armstrong for some help, but he didn't receive me. While transmitting I pushed the throttle and prop pitch full forward, but the first enemy aircraft was closing rapidly on my tail. Lt Everett came over and gave the Jerry a burst which sent him down in flames. Lt Everett was immediately attacked by two more FW-190s, and I still had one on my tail. I nosed down and went into some clouds about 10,000 feet below; in this dive I put some distance between the Jerry and myself, but his tracers were streaming over my left wing. I went into the clouds and did a 180-degree turn to the right. As I broke out, the 190 had done the same thing under the clouds and again got on my tail. I pulled up into a cloud above me, leveled off and lost the E/A on my tail. As I reefed my ship in to return to the flight, my canopy came open. My radio was out also, so I thought I'd been hit and headed for England. The last time I saw Lt Everett, who is now MIA, was immediately after he shot the FW-190 off my tail. I claim one FW-190 destroyed for Lt Everett." (signed) Jack B. Price, 2nd Lt., Air Corps.

Based upon the above reports, Hal Everett was listed as Missing in Action and credited with shooting down one FW-190. The full story of what happened to Hal was not known until three and a half months later when he returned to Fowlmere with a German battle flag, two Lugers and a machine pistol. He was irritated because he had to leave a case of vintage champagne at the forward base in France from where he was flown back to England. Here is the rest of the story.

After Hal downed the FW-190, his aircraft was hit and severely damaged. One 20-mm projectile struck the armor plate behind the cockpit, shattering shrapnel into his shoulder. He headed for home alone, but a couple of minutes later encountered another gaggle of FW-190s. With a shattered shoulder and little more than half a P-51 under him, Everett nevertheless was able to down a second FW-190 before they finished him off. He successfully bailed out with severe injuries and was taken by French police to a collaborationist station for treatment. There, pacing up and down, was a Luftwaffe major whom Everett had shot down moments before. The major was indignant at being shot down by a lone Mustang which was flying through the air like a wounded duck.

He spent the next three months in a German hospital in France where he received the best available treatment, inadequate though it was. Hal explained, "The place was terribly understaffed. The German medics were forced to use paper bandages and the same bandages over and over again." When the Allies broke out of the Normandy Beachhead in August and swept across France, Everett and several other hospitalized Americans were left behind by the retreating German Army. With an immobile shoulder Hal Everett remained grounded until it healed. He then successfully completed his combat tour and went home in December '44. For exceptional valor displayed against great odds in the sky over France on 24 May 1944, Lt Harold M. Everett was awarded the Silver Star and Purple Heart.

Two Wings Are Better

by Jay Marts

It happened August 28th, 1944, on one of my first missions, strafing targets of opportunity with the 505th Fighter Squadron flying out of Fowlmere, England, as part of the 8th Air Force. I was new, flying with a bunch of strangers, some I would never get to know and some who would become friends for life. There was so much to learn, and I sure didn't want to screw up or get someone killed.

The squadron was flying on the deck, spread out, line-abreast along the Luxembourg-German border near Sarrebourg when someone called out, "Targets dead ahead." It appeared the Germans were attempting to hide their tanks and supporting trucks under the trees. I was flying #2 position as wingman to Evan Johnson, covering him from anyone who might jump us from above or behind.

We were approximately 100 feet over the trees when we were engulfed with what looked like fiery golf balls that exploded all around, leaving white puffs of smoke that filled the sky. Fortunately, I was pulling up the nose of my plane when an explosion on the right wing tip blew up the upper panel. Although it remained fastened to the trailing edge of the wing, it stood up vertically like a big flap. I must have rolled four or five times to the right before I could stop the rolling by slowing down the engine and pulling up the nose even more. The flak immediately ceased as if the Germans were sure I was going to crash and had stopped shooting to watch.

Since I couldn't hold the stick to the extreme left side of the cockpit with my arm, I attempted to push my right foot against it while holding the left rudder with my left foot. The trim tabs were full to the left. I began hollering on the radio that I couldn't keep the plane flying much longer, let alone get it back to England. My speed was down to 140; the plane was shaking and beginning to stall. The Mustang was not designed to fly sideways.

A 505th Squadron pilot, Jim Starnes who'd been

PILOT ARTICLES

The Other Enemy

by Harry R. Corey

Weather is a factor in any form of combat. The Romans built roads in Britian, not out of civic pride, but to increase the mobility of their legions. Air combat involves a third dimension because the cloud cover can range from one hundred to over twenty thousand feet. Winds aloft that can reach 70-90 mph are a fourth dimension. We lost eleven pilots (13 planes) due to adverse weather. This was more than we lost to the Luftwaffe. Seven pilots had less than two months of combat experience. Five of these were operational for one month or less. Frequently missions were flown without ever seeing the ground between take-off and landing. If coupled with the loss of radio contact, this could lead to disaster.

We lost two pilots under these same circumstances. It was a long mission (7 hours) to Posnan, Poland. One element became separated from their squadron during combat and were last heard from in the direction of Southampton. They called for a bearing to our base which was forty degrees or northeast. Their transmission was weak and they did not respond. The English Channel is only 110 miles south of our base. A stong wind from the north could easily cause them to drift that far south during a long mission. They went out to sea with very little fuel left.

After an escort mission to Halle, near Leipzig, the bombers returned via a southern route. Our escort left them at Hersfeld, south of Kassel. We made landfall out near Dieppe, on the deck under a 100% cloud cover. This put us on a northerly course for home across the English Channel. All three pilots in one flight were lost when they apparently came upon the cliffs of the Isle of Wight too late to successfully pull up. They must have spun in, as one was found on the Isle, one on the beach at low tide, and the third crashed near Nuthampstead.

The Cliffs of Dover presented a similar hazzard. Most pilots, however, still favored coming home on the deck when the weather was bad. If we let down over East Anglia we would be competing for space with a few hundred bombers and other fighters. If you happened to go past the base before breaking out, you could meet up with a barrage balloon. The most important key was to establish a rate of descent (or climb) before entering the clouds. This relieved pressure on the controls and helped to avoid the very slow, imperceptible movements that can confuse your inner ear, cause vertigo, and put the seat of your pants in conflict with your instruments. Half of our losses can be attributed to vertigo. During the letdown we would call home for a heading from our homing station and get an altimeter setting. In addition to correcting for any change in pressure, it provided a slight margin for

---

leading another flight, appeared off my left wing. He advised I was too low to bail out and said I needed to gain more altitude. For what seemed like hours (in reality only seconds), I nursed the plane upwards, intending to bail out, but knowing the moment I let go of the left rudder and stick, the plane would roll rapidly to the right and spiral into the ground.

The pressure on the controls were becoming impossible to hold, when suddenly, the upright panel tore loose from the plane, allowing me (with much difficulty) to lift the right wing and hold the plane somewhat level and straight. My speed was increased to about 160, but anything higher caused the plane to begin rolling again. Jim Starnes was talking to me, advising me the damage to the wing and aileron, where we were, the direction to England, and helping me avoid the enemy in the air and on the ground. At this point I was sure I had lost my own flight leader Johnson to the same ground fire. I learned later this was not the case. Time dragged. The engine began to heat up. Jim and I talked about how to cool it down - changing the carb mixture and prop speed, etc. The heat stopped climbing. "Junior" was holding together, but I was getting increasingly tired as the French countryside slid slowly by under the wing. I remember wishing I'd gotten into better shape by exercising more when I had the chance.

We finally reached the English Channel - I knew Fowlmere wasn't that far away. My right shoulder and arm ached, but I had to keep that right wing up. I tried repeatedly to get the belt off my pants to tie the stick to the left side of the cockpit. It couldn't be done, jammed into the cockpit as I was.

At last Fowlmere was on the horizon. Someone on the radio (other than Jim) advised me I should head the plane back towards the Channel and bail out. My reply was not exactly acceptable radio language. I told Jim and the Base that I was going to land, straight in, wheels down, with as much flap as possible.

The plane started to shake and stall out at 110 mph. I was afraid the right torn aileron might fail at the last moment or I'd misjudge my approach to the runway. Making a second pass was impossible. I convinced myself I could make a good landing if I concentrated on it.

I pushed the nose down, chopped the throttle, eased the trim tabs to neutral, locked my shoulder harness tight, and aimed for a spot fifty feet short of the runway. The old Mustang, now dropping like an elevator, hit the runway perimeter with so little flareout it seemed more like a controlled crash!

I was still going 100 mph, but the tail was down. Only half of the runway distance remained. At 65 mph I started to tap the brakes very easily, hoping they wouldn't lock. They didn't. "Junior" and I were going to make it!

The plane rolled to a stop off the runway on the last taxi strip. I turned off the switches and just sat there in the cockpit...too tired to move! The crash truck guys, medics and ground crews piled onto the airplane and lifted me out. What a welcome committee! I was HOME!

error because our base was about fifty feet above sea level.

It was also a good idea to have an alternate plan in case the radio failed. My system was to pick up the main road from Norwich to London; turn left down the road until I came to my special roundabout; then hang a hard right due west for two minutes, let down the gear, flaps and look for a green flare. On one occasion I had to warn my flight that there was a "Jug" in our traffic pattern. Once again we were safely down on that good old grass field, except this time, we were at Duxford! Their folks were "kind" enough to point out the direction to Fowlmere, about four miles west.

Of course, one could fly five minutes in any direction in East Anglia and find an air base. This was very helpful on one mission when the ceiling was especially low. Captain Richard Olander led Red Flight, and I had White Flight tucked in behind and below so tightly that I was inside Red Four. We came down from 20,000 feet. Shortly after we made landfall, we came over the end of a paved runway. They were shooting up green flares. Olander called for us to take spacing for landing and no one argued. We made one circle, keeping the field off my left wing tip. When I got back to the flares, we set them down. I was enjoying the roll and the cool breeze when I saw something on my left. The other four planes had landed on the second runway, and we were heading for the intersection. Fortunately, we had good spacing so that a little throttle allowed us to alternate every other plane at the intersection. It was show time at Wormingford, near Colchester, which we subsequently learned was the home of the 55th Fighter Group. After we were inside and the coffee poured, their control tower officer came in with the startling news that we had landed on intersecting runways! Someone in the back of the room said, "We always land that way at a strange field." That plus the hot coffee had reduced the adrenaline levels and chased from our minds any thoughts of what might have been or how narrow the margin between success and disaster can be.

Strategy vs the ME-262 Jet

by Harry R. (Herky) Corey

All historians agree that the contribution of the Me-262 Jet to the outcome of the war was negligible. The several thousand bomber crewmen who were shot down by the Jets, however, would judge otherwise. The jet pilots were among the best and most experienced, and jet fuel was in abundant supply. Their problem was a shortage of planes. There is wide consensus that the Me-262 could have been operational eighteen months earlier with obvious implications relative to air superiority, the timing of D-Day, and the discomfort of all our fighters.

Jet activity, at less than Schwarm (4) levels, was first reported in the fall of 1944. The probability of even seeing a jet along the bomber string was low. It was generally known that jet activity could be expected on missions to the north, including Wilhelmshaven, Bremen, Hamburg, and from Osnabruck to Hanover and Berlin.

There were no intelligence briefings on how we should respond to this new threat. Additional escort fighters flying higher and closer to the bombers was the only game in town for defending the big friends. It made no sense, however, as an offensive strategy for attacking the jets. Faced with a wall of Mustangs, the jets would simply pick out another box of bombers. Their mission was to destroy bombers and demoralize their crews. With their few planes, they could not afford the slightest attrition that might result from aggressively engaging our fighters.

The Me-262 was more than 100 mph faster than the Mustang at altitude. Therefore, the jet could dominate the high ground while the Mustang was more maneuverable and should prevail in any dogfight. The problem was how to force an encounter. We did not know the jet's range, but did know it had to be limited. After hitting the bombers, they probably would let down at low speed to conserve fuel.

The jet was less efficient at low altitude, while the P-51 performed best below 15,000 feet. The jets would probably return individually, not expecting us, and it was easier to see a plane against the sky than against the ground. At low speeds the jet could not accelerate as fast as the propeller-driven P-51. All of these factors suggested to me that the best strategy might be to intercept the jets between their target and their bases. The hope was that, at low altitude and speed, the Mustang's greater acceleration might provide enough time to catch or turn the jet. The viability of this strategy was proven when we shot down the only two jets we saw while on this type of high-speed patrol.

The first of these two jets was shot down by my element leader, Bob Irion, on 20 March 1945. It is significant to note that on this same mission the balance of the 505th Squadron chased thirty jets at altitude over Hamburg for half an hour without success.

My second encounter with a jet came on the 4th of April, 1945. The mission was to Hamburg and Kiel. I was leading the blue section on a sweep ahead of the bombers. We patrolled in a widely spread line abreast formation in the same general area we had swept on the 20th of March. Lee Steiger was #2, Tom Marvel #3, and Jack Rice #4. Bob Irion led the second (green) flight. We patrolled above the clouds which were estimated to be 6/10 to 9/10 from 6,000 feet down to 1,000 feet. Here again, we saw the jet first somewhere southwest of Kummerower Lake. He crossed above and in front of us at about 30 degrees to the right of our course. I pulled up, turned onto him and got off a short burst with a few hits. He broke down to the right into the clouds. I sent green flight above the clouds and we went below. I picked him up again just as he broke left into another cloud. We both broke out into the clear as the jet made a final 180 degree turn to the left. I closed to about 70 yards in the turn and was dead astern for a long burst. He began to break up. I apparently knocked out his left engine, because he snap-rolled twice to the left, fell off into a flat spin and went in. His canopy was jettisoned, but the pilot went down with his plane somewhere in the lake area south of Rostock.

On both missions neither jet got off a shot. We maintained the integrity of the section and formed up for the next possible encounter. Bob Irion still reminds me of how he helped box in the Me-262. It was a team effort on both jet victories, but the prize for effort belongs to Lee Steiger. After I pulled up to avoid the debris, I looked off to my right and there was Lee grinning through a hole in his canopy the size of a basketball.

He had caught some of the debris which also knocked off his goggles. Luckily he was unhurt. During the melee Lee had been glued to my tail protecting my buns from the huns. Lee said that he was following Tom Marvel's advice, "When you see those orange golf balls coming at you, lower your seat!"

Regardless, the day belonged to the 504th Squadron who had strafed planes dispersed near Wismer and Parchim. As the 504th approached Parchim airfield, seven jets had just taken off, and they (the 504th) shot down three of them. It was characteristic of several of these victories that the jets were caught in their most vulnerable attitude. While we can't discount the element of chance, the 339th always acted aggressively and opportunistically. I rate our victories over the twelve Me-262s at the top of our list of records and accomplishments, because they saved at least 1,000 bomber crewmen.

The Luftwaffe wrote their own epitaph on April 7, 1945. "Under the code name 'Wehrwolf' the Me-262 Groups directed their attack for the first time against the fighters instead of the bombers. Without appreciable loss, JG 7 alone claimed as many as 28 Mustangs."*

I believe this was a response to the frustration of veteran pilots fighting a war they knew had been lost a long time ago and who wanted to make a statement about what might have been. While the jets flew a few more missions in April, the bombers forced them to withdraw to other airfields as distant as Prague. We ran out of jets and soon ran out of war. The mission routine that compressed all experience, that crowded out all memory of the past and promised no future beyond tomorrow, was over.

From the Luftwaffe War Diaries

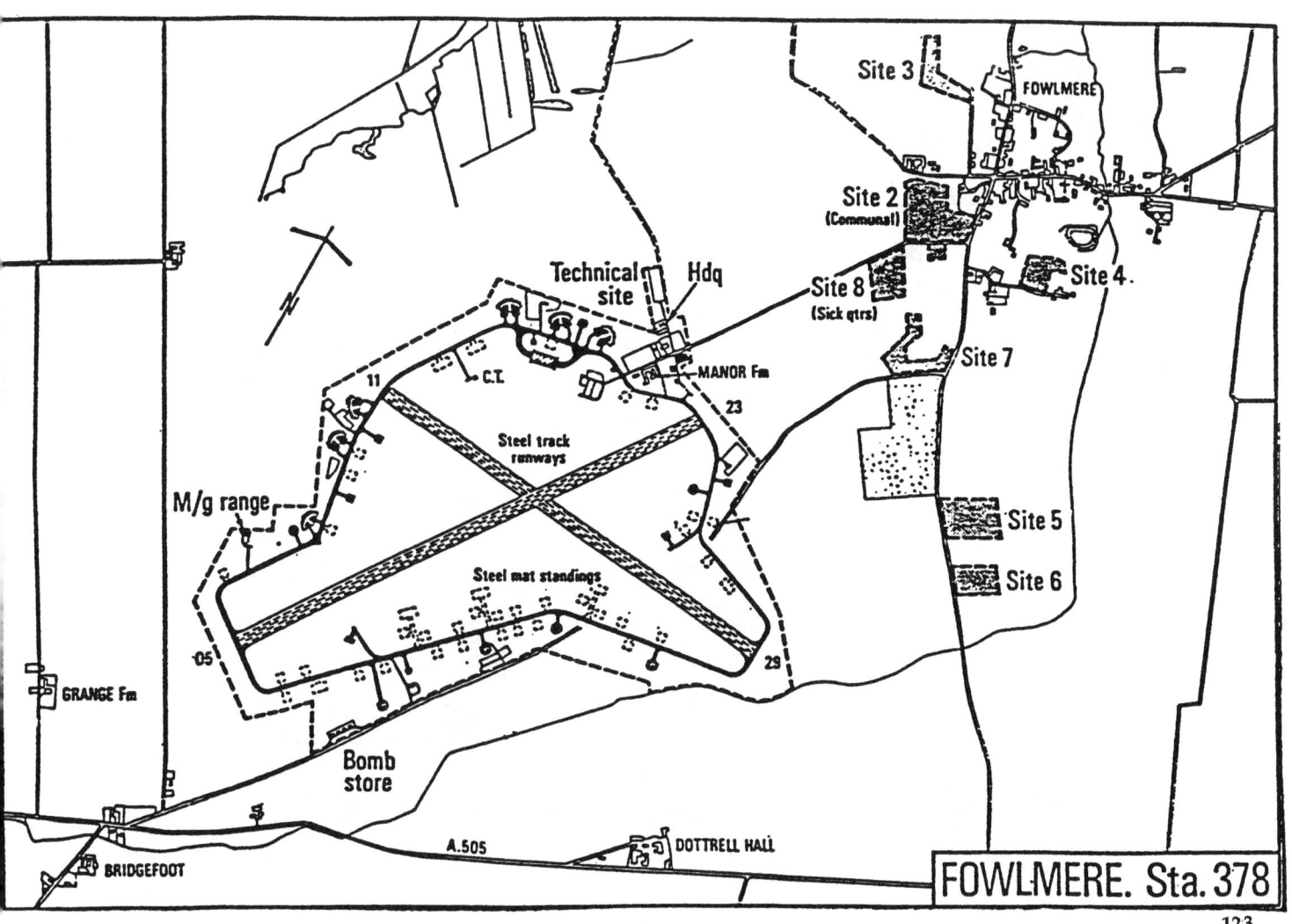

Stephen C Ananian

Leo H Becker

William M Beecher

Oscar K Biggs

J Brooks Bline

Robert W Bloxham

Billy B Booth

Carl H Bundgaard

Harold W Burch

Robert F Burns

Cecil L Byrd

Richard C Cain

Roland E Gousie

Gerald E Graham

William R Guyton

James R Hanson

John G Holloway

Harry F Howard

Waldon E Howard

George J Hrico

Ellis E Hupp

Robert E Irion

William Jaaskelainen

Boyd O Jackson

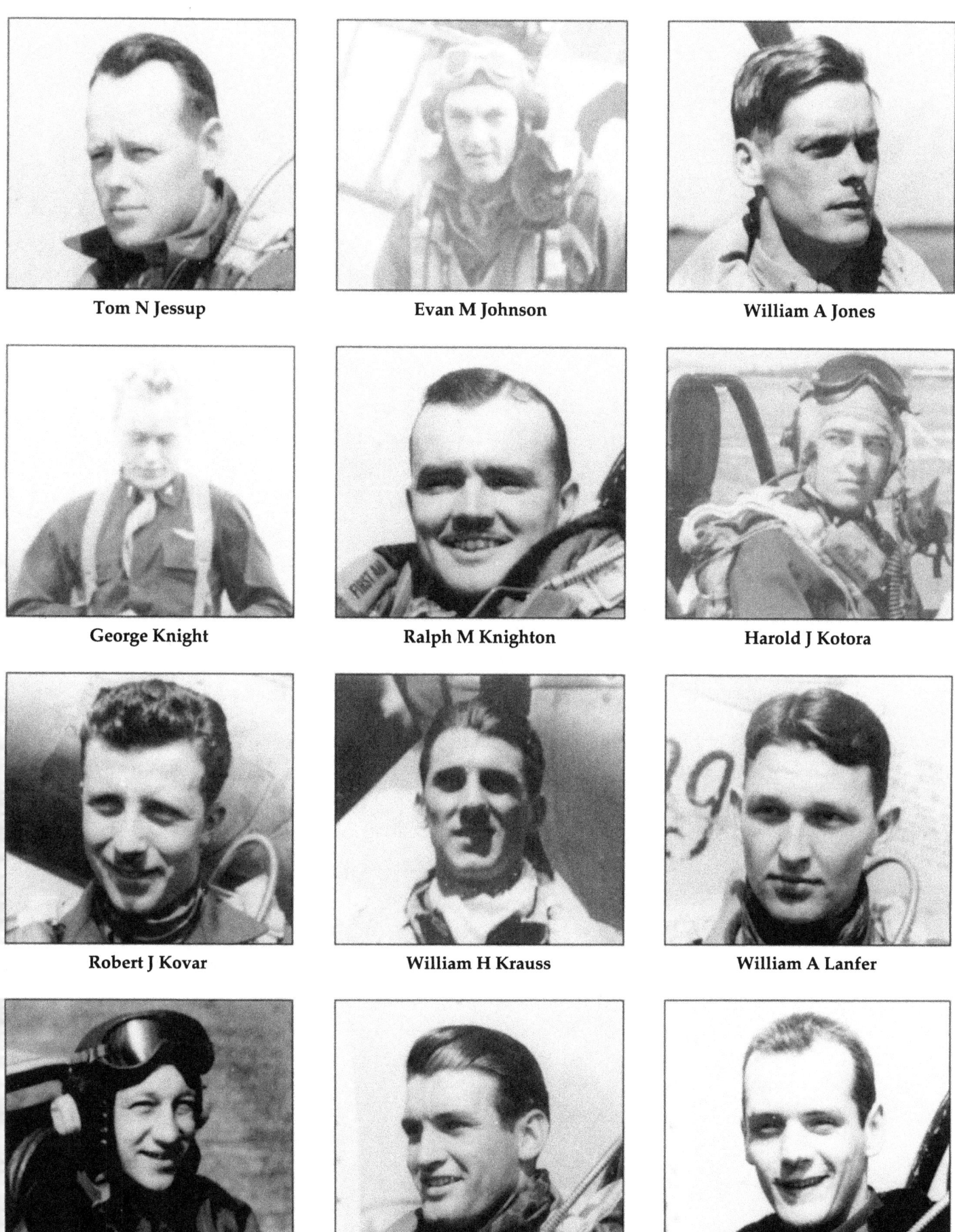

Phillip M Loveless

William Mac Clarence

Chester Malarz

Jay F Marts

Thomas W Marvel

Peter J McMahon

Raymond M Mitchell

William R Moore

William P Mudge

James B Muller

Jerome T Murphy

Martin N Nay

Barnell V Shaw

George W Shepherd

Andrew Sirochman

William R Slovak

Floyd W Smith

Theodore R Staggers

James R Starnes

Leroy A Steiger

Carl R Stewart

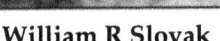
Bert Stiles

Leland M Stoudt

Richard H Tannous

Richard G Thieme

Kessler O Thomas

Joseph L Thury

Archie A Tower

Authur E Tongue

Laird D Travis

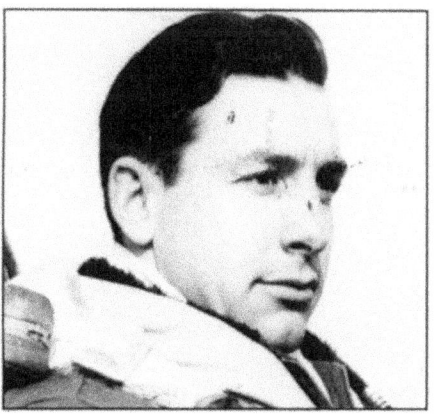
Evergard L Wager

Russell W Wilcox

John C Withers

James C Woolery

Allen D Young

Harry Zeigler

MEMORIAM

To the 339th pilots who flew and fought alone for life and country in the skies of Europe. They left something of themselves in the interest of brotherly concern for their comrades in the vast skies of Europe. These young eagles forged a blazing path across the skies. Some gave the last full measure to the cause of freedom. Together, they helped establish the outstanding record of the 339th Fighter Group. They had that restless spirit of aggression, that passion to be at grips with the enemy. Because of their deeds, the skies were made safer for other men to fly.

Upward, ever upward,
I have climbed above my earthly being
Into a world of cloud and sunshine,
Free of torment, free of toil,
And through the wind, I hear their voices,
And through the clouds, I see their faces.
They are there on my wing, both left and right.
My courageous friends in eternal flight.

Author Unknown

Killed in Action

ATTEBERRY, Ray	504th	JONES, George W., Jr.	505th	SAWICKI, Joseph F.	505th
BAKER, James A.	505th	KURTH, Otis A.	504th	SCHNEIDER, Lewis H.	504th
BALL, Edwin C.	505th	LARSON, Donald A.	505th	SHIVELY, Jack E.	504th
BEAVERS, E. H., Jr.	503rd	LOWERY, Arthur L.	503rd	SLOVAK, William R.	505th
BEECHER, William M.	505th	LUPER, Arch B.	505th	SMITH, Robert C.	503rd
BEHREND, William W.	503rd	LYNCH, James L.	505th	SPAZIANO, Vincent J.	503rd
BLOXAM, Robert W.	505th	MACKENZIE, David A.	503rd	STEIER, Arthur H.	503rd
BROWN, Robert B.	503rd	MAYER, Raymond D.	503rd	STILES, Bert	505th
BROWNSHADEL, Elton J.	504th	McMAHON, Peter J.	505th	STOCKTON, William D.	503rd
CAROTHERS, John M.	503rd	McPHARLIN, M. G. H.	HQ	STOUDT, Leland M.	505th
CROCKETT, James R.	503rd	MEAD, Charles M.	504th	TERRATS, Esteban A.	503rd
DOWELL, Charles W.	HQ	MEYER, Victor W.	503rd	THOMAS, Kessler O.	505th
FLAHERTY, Edward C.	503rd	MONTELL, Richard W.	504th	TONGUE, Arthur E., Jr.	505th
FOWELL, Nathan T.	503rd	MULVEY, Robert F.	503rd	TRAVIS, Laird D.	505th
GIRONE, Felix J.	503rd	MYER, Paul M.	504th	VAN CLEAVE, Ely N.	504th
HANSEMAN, Chris J.	505th	OLANDER, Richard B.	505th	WAGER, Evergard L.	503rd
HAWKINS, Anthony G.	503rd	PALMER, Gerald W.	505th	WHITELAW, Richard S.	503rd
HENEGHAN, Floyd P.	505th	PASTOR, William J.	504th	WILCOX, Russell W.	505th
HERRMANN, Ray F.	504th	PERRY, Gordon F.	505th	WINKELMAN, Myer R.	504th
HOWARD, Waldon E.	505th	PREDDY, William R.	503rd	WOLFORT, Joseph	503rd
HUNTER, Charles M.	504th	REYNOLDS, John R.	505th	WOOD, Robert T.	504th
JACKSON, Boyd O.	505th	REUTER, Raymond F.	503rd		

Killed
(Not in Action)

ALLMAN, Johnnie M.	HQ
BERGUSON, Kenneth V.	504th
COZAD, John W.	503rd
CRUMP, Alan F.	503rd
DEGNAR, Ralph M.	504th
DICKENS, Robert L.	503rd
GILBERT, Kenneth L.	504th
JESSUP, Tom N.	505th
PORTER, George W.	503rd
RIGGS, Gaston H.	503rd
WEST, Rodney C.	503rd

Evaded Capture or Interned

BUNDGAARD, Carl H.	505th	Behind Enemy Lines, Evaded Capture
EWING, Philip H.	505th	Behind Enemy Lines, Evaded Capture
NAY, Martin N.	505th	Behind Enemy Lines, Evaded Capture
SIROCHMAN, Andrew	505th	Behind Enemy Lines, Evaded Capture
TALCOTT, Franklin D.	503rd	Interned in neutral country (killed while interned)

Prisoners Of War

ARMISTEAD, Walter M.	505th	FISH, Wesley G.	505th	MULLER, James B.	505th
ATTEBERRY, Ray N.	504th	GOUSIE, Roland E.	505th	O'SULLIVAN, Walter R.	504th
BALLARD, Jerome J.	504th	HENDERSON, Harvey E.	503rd	POWELL, Lawrence J.	505th
BODEN, Hetzel K.	504th	HOWARD, Harry F.	505th	RUTAN, Frederick S.	504th
BURNS, Robert F.	505th	JONES, William A.	505th	SHAW, Bernell V.	505th
CAIN, Richard C.	505th	LOSKILL, Harry G.	504th	STAGGERS, Theodore B.	505th
CARTER, Walter T.	503rd	MACKENZIE, David A.	503rd	STRONG, Roland W.	505th
COKER, Joseph R.	505th	MANKE, Alfred O.	503rd	THISTLETHWAITE, Edward	504th
CONNER, Bertis A.	505th	MANKIE, James A.	503rd	WYER, Albert L.	503rd
DEAREY, Ralph H.	503rd	MITCHELL, Raymond M.	505th	YOUNG, Allen D.	505th
EVERETT, Harold M.	505th	MOORE, William R.	505th	ZIEGLER, Harry D.	505th
FICKEL, Paul D.	503rd				

Roster of Group Personnel

Including Support Unit Personnel

A

Name	Unit	Rank	Location	Notes
Abadessa, Thomas J.	EM-504		Jamestown, NY	
Abbey, Richard M.	EM-504	Sgt	Feeding Hills, MA	Operations
Abeel, Myron C.	EM-505	Cpl	Sioux City, IA	
Accord, Lewis C.	EM-ATT	Pfc		328 Sv Gp
Acuna, Joe	EM-ATT	Sgt		328 SV Gp
Adams, Ferland	EM-505	Sgt	Vergannes, VT	Communications
Adams, Grady B.	EM-503	SSgt	Lindale, TX	
Adams, John P.	EM-503	SSgt	Ft. Worth, TX	Crew Chief
Addison, Robert	GO-504	1/Lt	Crown Point, IN	Communications
Adler, Abraham A.	EM-503	Pfc	Brooklyn, NY	
Admire, Bert	EM-ATT		Woodland Mills, CA	Crew Chief 863 AES
Aitken, John	P-503	Maj	Elberton, GA	
Aldrich, Richard T.	P-504	1/Lt	Rock Island, IL	
Aleissi, John	EM-505	Sgt	Forrest City, AZ	Asst Crew Chief
Alexander, Oree	EM-ATT	Pfc		989 MP Co.
Allen, Bernie A.	P-503	1/Lt	Interlachen, FL	
Allen, Donald R.	EM-HQ			
Allen, Everett M.	EM-ATT	Pfc		72 SCS
Allers, Lorne W.	P-504		St. Cloud, MN	
Allman, Johnnie M.	P-HQ	2/Lt	Pelly, TX	
Altenhofen, George C.	EM-504			
Althaus, Harry F.	EM-ATT	Pfc		328 SV Gp.
Alverson, Fred B.	EM-ATT	T/5	Itasca, TX	Clerk, 1786 OSM
Amick, Robert L.	EM-ATT	Pfc		328 SV Gp.
Ammerman, Roy W.	P-505	1/LT	Brooklyn, NY	
Ammon, Robert H.	P-503	Capt	Reading, PA	
Ananian, Steve	P-505	1/LT	New York, NY	
Anderson, Afton W.	EM-HQ			
Anderson, Daniel F.	EM-ATT	Cpl		989 MP Co.
Anderson, Francis E.	EM-ATT	Pvt		989 MP Co.
Anderson, Merle E.	EM-503	Sgt	Vancouver, WA	
Anderson, Yeatman	EM-504			
Angione, Charles	EM-503		Yonkers, NY	Asst Crew Chief
Angulo, Adolph E.	EM-505	Cpl	Los Angeles, CA	
Antico, Joseph A.	EM-505	Sgt		
Armistead, Walter M.	P-505	1/Lt	Atlanta, GA	
Arnett, Duff	EM-ATT	Cpl		328 SV Gp.
Arnold, Merlin A.	P-504	2/LT	Tampa, FL	
Ashworth, Carl V.	GO-505	Capt	Richmond, VA	Supply
Atkinson, George T.	EM-503	Sgt	East Orange, NJ	
Atteberry, Ray N.	P-504	2/Lt	Albion, IL	
Azouz, Israel	EM-504			

B

Name	Unit	Rank	Location	Notes
Baietti, Eugene	EM-505	SSgt	Delray Beach, FL	Engineering Clerk
Baird, Hulett C.	EM-503	Cpl	Agra, OK	
Baker, James A.	P-505	2/Lt	Ft Wayne, IN	
Baker, Omer E.	EM-504			
Balbach, Walter E.	EM-503	Cpl	Riverside, CA	
Ball, Charles W.	EM-505	SSgt	Cumberland, KY	Eng. Instruments
Ball, Edwin C.	P-505	1/Lt	Marianna, FL	
Ball, Melville R.	P-504	Capt	Greenwich, CT	
Ball, Sidney	EM-503	SSgt	Swan Lake, NY	
Ballard, Jerome J.	P-504	1/Lt	Detroit, MI	
Ballard, Roy	GO-HQ	Major	San Antonio, TX	Comm. Officer
Balo, James W.	EM-HQ		Port Charlotte, FL	
Bane, John M.	EM-504		Salem, MA	Engineering Clerk
Banks, Ralph E.	P-503		Paxton, MA	
Banks, Steven E.	EM-503	TSgt		Medic
Barbara, William	EM-503	Sgt		Intelligence
Barber, Kenneth G.	EM-ATT	Pfc		464 SV Sq.
Barclay, Harry O.	EM-503	SSgt	Pittsburg, PA	
Bardsley, Earl F.	EM-503	TSgt	Marston, MA	
Bargefrede, Leonard H.	EM-HQ	MSgt	Whitestone, NY	Communications
Barnett, Ray L.	EM-ATT	Pfc		989 MP Co.
Barnes, Alfred	EM-504	SSgt	Conneaut, OH	
Barnes, Walter J.	EM-503	Cpl	Philadelphia, PA	
Barrett, L. Jack	P-504	1/Lt	Watonga, OK	
Barrow, Elijah J.	EM-505	Sgt	Praire du Sac, WI	
Bartle, Richard	EM-503	SSgt		Detroit, MI
Bartlett, Frank D.	EM-ATT	SSgt		989 MP Co.
Barto, Vernon M.	P-504	1/Lt	Depue, IL	
Bateman, William J.	EM-505	Cpl	Morristown, PA	
Bates, Arthur W., Jr.	P-504	1/Lt	Bowling Green, OH	
Bath, William L.	EM-505	Cpl	New Orleans, LA	
Baxley, Clinton O.	EM-ATT	T/4	Gilmore, TX	Hq Sec 1786 OSM
Beadle, Ermy L.	P-504	2/Lt	Shamokin, PA	
Beardon, Sarah	CIV-ATT			Red Cross Assist.
Bears, Alfred L.	EM-ATT	Pfc		989 MP Co.
Beaupre, Albert E.	EM-ATT	Pfc		72 SCS
Beavers, Edward H.	P-503	Capt	Scranton, PA	

ROSTER OF GROUP PERSONNEL

Name	Unit	Rank	Location	Role
Becker, Leo H.	P-505	1/LT	Chicago, IL	
Beckman, Donald G.	EM-505	TSgt	Upr Arlington, OH	Flight Chief
Beecher, William M.	P-505	2/Lt	Brooklyn, NY	
Behner, Norman J.	EM-ATT	SSgt	Rochester, NY	HQ Sec 1786 OSM
Behrend, William W.	P-503	Capt	Trenton, NJ	
Behrendt, Glenn E.	EM-503		Yutan, NE	
Beischal, Frank J.	EM-503	Cpl	Allentown, PA	
Bell, Gerald D.	GO-ATT	Capt		328 SV Gp.
Bell, Thomas W.	EM-ATT	Sgt	Memphis, TN	72 SCS
Bell, William H.	EM-504		High Point, NC	
Belles, James W.	EM-ATT	Pfc		464 SV Sq.
Bellman, Raymond M.	EM-503	SSgt	Manhattan, KS	Crew Chief
Bennett, Carroll W.	P-504	Capt	Burns, OR	
Bennett, Joe L.	GO-ATT	Capt		328 SV Gp.
Bennett, Sam	GO-505	1/Lt	Seal Beach, CA	Armament
Bergen, Arthur F.	EM-ATT	Cpl		38 SV Gp.
Berguson, Kenneth V.	P-504	1/Lt	Cleveland Heights, OH	
Bermudez, Angel L.	EM-504			
Bernberg, Louis P., Jr.	EM-505		Cleveland, OH	Armorer
Bernstein, Harry U.	GO-ATT	1/Lt		989 MP Co.
Berrett, Bernard E.	EM-504			
Berts, Henry J.	EM-505	SSgt	Long Island City, NY	
Bessler, Harry E.	EM-504			
Bevier, William W.	EM-ATT	SSgt		72 SCS
Bewley, Jesse R.	EM-504		Sharon, PA	Engineering Clerk
Bickley, Harry F.	EM-ATT	Pfc		464 SV Sq.
Biggs, Oscar K.	P-505	1/Lt	Wilmington, NC	
Billings	GO-ATT	Maj		863 Air Eng. Sq.
Bingham, John Jr.	EM-504			
Birbiglia, Joseph F.	EM-ATT	TSgt		328 SV Gp.
Bizelia, Jerry A.	EM-505	Cpl	Brooklyn, NY	
Blackford, Charles E.	EM-504			
Blagg, James F.	EM-ATT	Cpl		72 SCS
Bline, J. Brooks	P-505	Capt	Annapolis, IL	
Bliss, Lawrence	EM-ATT	Pvt		Arm Sec, 1786 OSM
Blizzard, R. Vernon	P-504	1/Lt	Los Angeles, CA	
Blockburger, Carl	EM-ATT	Pfc		328 SV Gp.
Bloom, Sidney	EM-504			Radio Maint.
Bloomberg, Stanley S.	EM-504			Asst. Line Chief
Bloxham, Robert W.	P-505	Capt	Arimo, ID	
Boas, Herman L.	EM-ATT	T/4		Arm Section, 1786 OSM
Boatwright, Floyd O.	EM-ATT	Pfc		2120 Eng. F/F
Boccardi, Americo B.	EM-504	Cpl	Lake Hiawatha, NJ	Acft. Mechanic
Boccio, Salvatore V.	EM-ATT	Pfc		989 MP Co.
Bochucinski, Matthew	EM-ATT	Sgt		989 MP Co.
Boden, Hetzel K.	P-504	2/Lt	Cumberland, MD	
Boehl, Robert G.	EM-503	Cpl	Cincinnati, OH	
Bolco, George L.	EM-ATT	Pfc		2120 Eng. F/F
Boland, Raymond E.	EM-HQ	Sgt		
Bolen, William E.	EM-503	Sgt	Denver, CO	
Bono, Joseph	EM-HQ	Pfc		
Booth, Billy B.	P-505	1/Lt	Blanchard, MI	
Borger, Harold N.	GO-ATT	Capt		328 SV Gp.
Borglin, Edgar K.	GO-505	1/Lt	Oakland, CA	Asst. Engineering
Borman, Verrel	EM-503	Sgt	Gipsy, PA	
Borom, Robert C.	GO-505	1/LT	Roswell, NM	Communications
Bova, Pat C.	GO-505	Capt	Oceanside, CA	Engineering
Bowbin, George C.	EM-503	Sgt	Chicago, IL	
Boychuck, Alec	P-503	Capt	New York, NY	
Boyd, John R.	EM-503	SSgt	Petaluma, CA	
Boyd, William H.	P-503	1/Lt	Phoenix, AZ	
Brackett, Lester D.	EM-ATT	SSgt		328 SV Gp.
Bradeen, Donald R.	EM-ATT	Pfc		72 SCS
Bradner, Robert H.	P-504	1/Lt	Chatham, VA	
Brand, Robert O.	EM-ATT	Cpl		72 SCS
Bratton, James T.	EM-ATT	Pfc		72 SCS
Brauer, Siegfried H.	GO-ATT	Major		Med Dr., 328 SV Gp.
Bray, Glenn	EM-ATT	T/4		Auto Sec, 1786 OSM
Breckinridge, Wm. C.	GO-HQ	Capt	Salem, VA	Intel/Pers Officer
Breeden, Albert W.	GO-HQ	Capt	Albany, NY	
Breeden, Melvin L.	EM-ATT	Cpl		72 SCS
Breen, William J.	EM-ATT	Pfc		72 SCS
Brent, Clifton H.	EM-504			
Briggs, Milo E.	EM-505	MSgt	Reno, NV	Line Chief
Bright, Elmer R.	EM-504			
Brignola, James J.	EM-505	SSgt	Troy, NY	Crew Chief
Brock, Thomas C.	P-505	F/O	Chicago, IL	
Brown, Charles N.	EM-504			
Brown, Leonard	EM-505	SSgt	Tampa, FL	Communications
Brown, Melvin O.	EM-505	Pfc	Rotan, TX	
Brown, Robert B.	P-503	1/Lt	Salt Lake City, UT	
Brown, Thomas A.	EM-ATT	Cpl	Charleroi, PA	Photogr., 328 SV Gp.
Brownshadel, Elton J.	P-504	2/Lt	Austin, TX	
Bruce, Alvin	EM-ATT	Sgt		464 SV Sq.
Brundage, Harvey	EM-504	MSgt	Delray Beach, FL	First Sergeant
Brunken, Howard	EM-503	Sgt	Columbus, NE	Food Service
Bryan, Wm. E., Jr.	P-503	Major	Flint, MI	
Bryant, John B.	EM-503	SSgt	Jasper, GA	
Brynar, William R.	EM-ATT	Pfc		989 MP Co.
Bublitz, Wesley T.	EM-503	Cpl	Fond du Lac, WI	
Buchanan, William R.	EM-505	Pvt	Griffin, GA	
Bucheit, Earl R.	EM-ATT	TSgt		328 SV Gp.
Buckbinder, Nathan A.	GO-HQ	1/Lt		
Buckholz, Warren L.	GO-ATT	1/Lt	Linden, NJ	18 WX Sq.
Buergey, Fred	EM-503	Pvt	Long Beach, CA	
Buezing, Arnold A.	EM-503	SSgt	Cretha, NE	
Bunch, John	EM-ATT	Pfc		464 SV Sq.
Bungaard, Carl H.	P-505	1/Lt	Withee, WI	
Burch, Harold W.	P-505	1/Lt	Omaha, NE	
Burkhart, Robert B.	EM-ATT	T/5		2120 Eng. F/F
Burns, Robert C.	EM-503	SSgt	S. Minneapolis, MN	
Burns, Robert F.	P-505	2/Lt	Dearborn, MI	
Burris, Dee R.	EM-ATT	SSgt		72 SCS
Bursey, Raymond A.	EM-ATT	SSgt		328 SV Gp.
Burwell, Elwood N.	EM-ATT	T/4		989 MP Co.
Bush, Jerry P.	P-503	1/Lt	Hulett, WY	
Butler, Frederick	P-503	Capt	Andover, MA	
Butler, Leo C.	EM-504			
Byers, John R.	P-503	1/Lt	St. Louis, MO	
Byrd, Cecil L.	P-505	1/Lt	Polo, IL	
Byrd, Jesse C.	EM-505	Cpl	Asheboro, NC	

C

Name	Unit	Rank	Location	Role
Cabanne, William C.	P-504	1/Lt	Los Angeles, CA	
Cabral, Manuel T.	EM-503	Sgt	Oakland, CA	
Cain, Richard C.	P-505	1/Lt	Gowanda, NY	
Cain, Roy E.	EM-504			
Caldwell, Ben M.	GO-504	1/Lt	Marks, MS	Asst. Intel./Adjutant
Caldwell, Merle F.	P-504	1/Lt	Greenville, PA	
Caler, Rollin C.	P-503/HQ	1/Lt	Humboldt, KS	
Calloa, Vincent	EM-ATT	Pfc		328 SV Gp.
Camarada, Louis A.	EM-503	Ssgt		
Caminiti, Peter	EM-HQ		Ft. Lauderdale, FL	Phys. Trng. Tech.
Campbell, Herbert H.	EM-ATT	Sgt		328 SV Gp.
Campbell, John C., Jr.	P-503	1/Lt	Glenbrook, CT	
Campos, Alfred L.	EM-ATT	Sgt		72 SCS
Canon, James R.	EM-503	TSgt	Pecos, TX	Armament NCO
Cannone, Emanuel F.	EM-504			
Cappuci, Raymond J.	EM-ATT	T/5	Brooklyn, NY	Sup. Sec.,1786 OSM
Carey, Lawrence J.	EM-504			
Carlson, Robert	EM-505	Sgt	Athol, MA	
Carollo, Salvatore A.	GO-503	Capt	Boca Raton, FL	Adjutant/Supply
Carothers, John M.	P-503	1/Lt	Louisville, KY	
Carow, Eldred J.	GO-503	Capt	Sumit, NJ	Intel. Officer
Carr, Clarence M.	EM-505	Sgt	Alpena, MI	Armorer
Carr, Frank M.	EM-ATT	Sgt		72 SCS
Carr, Vernon D.	P-505	1/Lt	Brockton, MA	
Carrol, Albert F.	EM-503	Pvt	Hampton, VA	
Carroll, Edward J.	GO-HQ		Allison Park, PA	
Carroll, John E.	EM-503	Cpl	Los Angeles, CA	
Carson, Francis M.	EM-504			

ROSTER OF GROUP PERSONNEL

Name	Unit	Rank	Hometown	Role
Carter, Alfred J.	GO-505	1/Lt	Elmhurst, NY	Asst. Eng. Officer
Carter, Lyle M.	P-504	1/Lt	Madison, WV	
Carter, Robert A.	EM-503	Pfc	Lucasville, OH	
Carter, Walter T.	P-503	Capt	Prescott, AZ	
Cartera, George C.	EM-ATT	Cpl		328 SV Gp.
Cash, Hugh M.	EM-503	SSgt	Thazton, VA	
Casteele, Frank S.	EM-503	Sgt	Troy, OH	
Catalfamo, Charles P.	EM-505	Sgt	E. Braintree, MA	
Caudel, Donald C.	P-504			
Caufield, Robert J.	EM-ATT	Pfc	Detroit, MI	Supply Sec. 1786 OSM
Caywood, Herbert L.	P-505	1/Lt	Shelton, MO	
Celavecchie, John W.	EM-503	Cpl	Hartford, CT	
Cennell, Eugene O.	EM-504			
Cernicky, Melvin L.	P-504	1/Lt	Arnold, PA	
Chapel, Paul A.	EM-504		Geneva, OH	Armorer
Chaplin, Erford E.	EM-503	SSgt	Gasport, NY	Crew Chief
Chapman, William S.	EM-ATT	Sgt		72 SCS
Charlton, William T.	EM-503	Pvt	Detroit, MI	Armament
Charotte, Joseph M.	EM-505	Sgt	Fall River, MA	
Chastain, Roland B.	EM-HQ	Pfc		
Chemiski, Casmare J.	EM-505	TSgt	Rantramok, MI	
Chenez, Gordon H.	P-504	1/Lt	Detroit, MI	
Chesney, Anthony	EM-503	Sgt	Elizabeth, NJ	
Chetneky, Steve J.	P-503	1/Lt	Trenton, NJ	
Chin, Bak T.	EM-505	Cpl	Los Angeles, CA	
Clair, Harry T.	EM-503	TSgt	Springfield, MO	Personnel Clerk
Claps, Vito S.	EM-505	SSgt	Brooklyn, NY	Crew Chief
Clark, Jack W.	P-503	2/Lt	Jacksonville, FL	
Clark, Neill E.	EM-503	TSgt	Dover, DE	
Clark, William C.	P-HQ	Col	Richmond, VA	
Cleary, John S.	EM-HQ	SSgt	Denville, NJ	Operations Clerk
Cleary, William B., Jr.	EM-503	Sgt	Bronx, NY	
Clements, Floyd M.	EM-505	TSgt	Murrysville, PA	Flight Chief
Clemick, Richard W.	EM-505	Cpl	Philadelphia, PA	
Clifton, Frank A.	P-504	1/Lt	Boise City, OK	
Cloud, Carl E.	P-503	Capt	Norman, OK	
Cobb, J. C.	EM-504			
Cobb, Noble E.	EM-503	Cpl	Louisville, KY	
Cockran, Norval R.	EM-503	Cpl	Jasper, TX	
Coe, Charles S.	P-503	1/Lt	Westbrook, ME	
Coffin, Edward L.	EM-505	Cpl	Mohawk, NY	Asst. Crew Chief
Coggins, James D.	EM-503	Pvt	Redondo Beach, CA	
Cohen, Gilbert G.	P-504	F/O	Indianapolis, IN	
Cohen, Wilbar T.	EM-503		Cincinnati, OH	
Coker, Joseph R.	P-505	F/O	Gardner, FL	
Colburn, Raymond I.	GO-HQ	Capt	New Haven, CT	Stat Con. Off.
Cole, Douglas P.	P-504	1/Lt	Geneva, NY	
Cole, John T.	EM-HQ	Cpl		
Cole, Marshall	GO-ATT		Woodville, TX	Sup Officer, 1178 QM Co
Coll, James J., Jr.	EM-ATT	Sgt		72 SCS
Collins, David A.	EM-505	Cpl	Far Rockaway, NY	
Collins, George E.	EM-503			
Collins, Gleo H.	EM-ATT	Pfc	Bovington, IA	Ammo Sec. 1786 OSM
Collins, Thomas H., Jr.	EM-505	SSgt	Binghamton, NY	Eng. Mech.
Combs, Carl T.	EM-503	Sgt	Crawfordsville, IN	
Conklin, Horace W., Jr.	EM-ATT	Pfc		328 SV Gp.
Conklin, Richard, Jr.	EM-503	SSgt	Lantana, FL	
Conley, Sterling A.	EM-ATT	TSgt	Porterville, CA	Supply, 1786 OSM
Conner, Bertis A.	P-505	1/Lt	Groves, TX	
Connolly, John J.	EM-505	Cpl	Schenectady, NY	
Connors, Arthur F.	P-503	2/Lt	Rockville, NY	
Conroy, Edward B.	EM-503	Cpl	Glouchester, NJ	
Cook, George M.	EM-505	SSgt	Houston, TX	
Coon, Albert S.	EM-503	SSgt	Alliance, OH	
Cooper, Donald	EM-505	Sgt	Boardman, OH	Armorer
Coppela, James A.	EM-503	Sgt	Newark, NJ	
Corbin, Luther L.	P-504	1/Lt	Galion, OH	
Corey, Harry R.	P-505	Capt	Niagra Falls, NY	
Coriz, Frank	EM-504			
Cotter, Michael J.	EM-503	SSgt	West Roxbury, MA	Crew Chief
Courtney, William H.	EM-504		Spokane, WA	Crew Chief
Cox, Fred W.	EM-ATT	MSgt	Vernon, TX	First Sgt, 1786 OSM
Cozad, John W.	P-503	2/Lt	Los Angeles, CA	
Crabtree, Garland M.	EM-HQ	MSgt		
Craiger, Edgar D.	EM-503	MSgt	Waynesburg, KY	First Sergeant
Craigo, Cecil E., Jr.	P-504	Capt	Beckly, WV	
Crapa, Anthony M.	EM-503	SSgt	Jersey City, NJ	
Craven, Elmer T.	GO-504	1/Lt	San Antonio, TX	Adjutant/Supply Off.
Crecelius, Morris W.	EM-504			Armorer
Creswell, Ray	P-504	1/Lt	Des Moines, IA	
Crippen, William P.	EM-ATT	T/5	Rensselaer, NY	Auto Sec. 1786 OSM
Crockett, James R.	P-503	1/Lt	Chattanooga, TN	
Croker, Robert C.	P-504	1/Lt	Whiting, IA	
Crooks, Walter V.	EM-504			
Crouch, Homer L.	EM-ATT	T/5		2120 Eng. F/F
Crowe, Kenneth S.	EM-ATT	TSgt		328 SV Gp.
Crowley, Thomas N.	GO-HQ	Lt Col		
Crump, Alan F.	P-503	2/Lt	Ann Arbor, MI	
Cruz, Carmelo	EM-503	Pfc	Bronx, NY	
Culverwell, John A.	EM-504	Sgt	Wilson, NY	Crew Chief
Cunningham, Robert A.	GO-HQ	Capt	Houston, TX	Dentist
Cunnick, John W.	P-503	1/Lt	Waco, TX	
Curtis, Ernest R.	EM-503	Sgt	Johnson City, TN	
Cutri, Gabriel J.	EM-505	SSgt	Downey, CA	Crew Chief

D

Name	Unit	Rank	Hometown	Role
Dahlstrom, Gustave S.	EM-505	Sgt	Essex, CT	Asst. Crew Chief
Dains, Darwell S.	EM-504			
Damron, James M.	EM-505	Sgt	Greenfield, VA	
Daniell, J. S.	P-505	1/Lt	Birmingham, AL	
Daniel, Sidney R.	EM-505			
Dardel, Sidney P.	EM-505	Sgt	Memphis, TN	
Daubert, Edward J.	EM-505	Pfc	Everett, WA	
Daugherty, Eual	EM-ATT	Pfc		989 MP Co.
Davidson, James R.	EM-503	MSgt	Porterville, CA	Armament NCOIC
Davies, Edwin J.	EM-504			
Davis, Alfred W.	EM-505	Sgt	Ellendale, ND	
Davis, Herbert	EM-503	Sgt	Albany, NY	
Davis, Jersse A.	EM-504			
Davis, J. Clarance, Jr.	GO-ATT	Lt Col		C.O., 328 SV Gp.
Davis, Lee	EM-ATT	Pfc		989 MP Co.
Davis, Solomon	EM-ATT	Sgt		72 SCS
Day, Whitney L.	EM-505	TSgt	New Britian, CT	
Deary, Ralph H.	P-503	2/Lt	Glendale, CA	
Decker, Sidney R.	EM-503	Cpl	New York, NY	
Decourcy, James L.	P-505		Hyannis, MA	
Deering, Joseph J.	EM-504		Staten Island, NY	Armorer
Degner, Ralph M.	P-504	2/Lt		
DeLarye, Woodrow	EM-505	Cpl	Megaunnee, MI	
Delisio, James A.	EM-503	Cpl	Levittown, NY	
DeLorenza, Catello J.	EM-503	Cpl	Thompsonville, CT	
Delson, George	EM-HQ			
DeMaria, James	EM-505	Pfc	Brooklyn, NY	
DeMore, Robert B.	EM-ATT	Cpl		464 SV Sq.
DeNaples, Dominic J.	EM-503	TSgt	Dorchester, MA	
DePalma, Alfonse L.	EM-504		Oceanside, NY	
Derkach, John	EM-505	Sgt	Egg Harbor City, NJ	
Desaules, Joseph M.	EM-503	Pvt	Woonsocket, RI	
DeSimone, Ralph A.	EM-505	Cpl	Middle Village, NY	
DeVerdi, James A.	EM-505	Pfc	Rockford, IL	Crew Chief
DeVoe, Theodore	EM-504			
Dewar, Robert W.	EM-HQ		Central Valley, CA	Mail Clerk
Dey, Russel C.	P-504	2/Lt	Reedville, VA	
Dickens, Robert L., Jr.	P-503	2/Lt	San Antonio, TX	
Diefenbeck, James S.	P-505	Capt	Pottstown, PA	
Doberenz, Ottbert T.	EM-504			
Dodge, Don	EM-504		Clute, TX	Acft Mechanic
Dodge, Franklin N.	EM-ATT	Cpl		72 SCS
Dodson, Trancy C.	EM-505	Pfc	El Dorado, AR	
Doherty, Harry D.	GO-HQ	Capt	Hartford, CT	Pers. Equip. Off.
Donaldson, John C.	EM-503	Sgt	Detroit, MI	

Roster of Group Personnel

Name	Unit	Rank	Location	Notes
Donmoyer, George A.	EM-ATT	Cpl		328 SV Gp.
Donnelly, Adam J.	EM-ATT	SSgt		328 SV Gp
Donovan, Daniel C.	EM-505	Sgt	Atlantic, MA	
Donovan, Walter J.	EM-ATT	Sgt		328 SV Gp.
Doucet, Lucien R.	EM-505	Cpl	Auburn, ME	
Dougherty, James J.	EM-504			
Dowell, Charles W.	GO-505	Capt	San Diego, CA	
Dubin, George L.	EM-503	Pvt	Los Angeles, CA	
Duck, Alvin K., Jr.	EM-503	Sgt	Pasadena, TX	Armorer
Dugrew, John W.	EM-504			
Dujmic, John J.	EM-ATT	Sgt		72 SCS
Duke, Jack E., III	EM-505	Pfc	Alexandria, LA	Asst. Crew Chief
Duncan, William G.	EM-ATT	SSgt	Pine Bluff, AR	Auto Sec. 1786 OSM
Dunlap, Lyle A.	EM-ATT	SSgt		328 SV Gp.
Dunn, John W.	P-504	1/Lt	Wallingford, CT	
Dunn, Robert	P-504	1/Lt	Auburn, NY	
Dunn, Robert F.	EM-503	Sgt	Cleves, OH	
Durett, Earl J., Jr.	EM-505	SSgt	Atlanta, GA	

E

Name	Unit	Rank	Location	Notes
Eagan, Matthew C., Jr.	EM-503	Cpl	Muskegon, MI	
Earnest, John E.	EM-505	SSgt	Wayland, IA	Crew Chief
Eaton, Philip S.	EM-ATT	Sgt		328 SV Gp.
Eavenson, Lee H.	EM-ATT	Pfc		989 MP Co.
Ebersole, Ira R.	EM-505	Sgt	Baltimore, MD	Radio Maint.
Eckstein, Robert L.	EM-ATT	Pfc		989 MP Co.
Edens, Malcomb B.	P-503	Capt	Pickens, SC	
Edminston, Charles J.	EM-HQ	Pfc		
Edwards, James W.	EM-ATT	Cpl		464 SV Sq.
Edwards, Walter D.	EM-503	Pfc	Greenville, SC	Ambulance Driver
Eger, Roy K.	EM-504			
Eisenhart, Lee D.	P-504	Capt	Hellerton, PA	
Eitmer, Donald L.	EM-HQ	SSgt		
Ekiss, Everett J.	EM-HQ			
Elizondo, Rudolph M.	EM-ATT	Cpl		72 SCS
Ellithorpe, Eugene A.	EM-503	Sgt	Clarkston, WA	
Ellis, Lawrence O.	EM-ATT	Sgt		72 SCS
Elmont, Leonard	EM-ATT	Cpl		328 SV Gp.
Emert, Gerald F.	EM-ATT	Cpl	Port Hueneme, CA	Prop. Spec., 464 SV Sq.
Engelhardt, George W.	EM-503	SSgt	Brooklyn, NY	
Engelman, Robert S.	EM-ATT	Cpl		464 SV Sq.
Epp, Edward C.	EM-504	Sgt	Flagler Beach, FL	Homing Sta. Operator
Epstein, Ronald	EM-505	Sgt	Cleveland, OH	Armorer
Erfkammp, Willis R.	EM-503	Cpl	Butler, MO	
Erickson, Earl E.	P-503	1/Lt	Oakwood, MO	
Erickson, Wayne R.	P-503	1/Lt		
Evans, Frank T.	P-505	1/Lt	Indianapolis, IN	
Everett, Harold M.	EM-505	1/Lt	Beverly Hills, CA	
Everson, Kirke B., Jr.	P-504	Capt	Providence, RI	
Ewing, Philip H.	P-505	1/Lt	Easton, MD	

F

Name	Unit	Rank	Location	Notes
Farmer, Owen P., Jr.	P-505	Capt	Ft. Scott, KS	
Farley, Elmer	EM-504			
Farrell, Arthur F.	EM-ATT	Pfc		328 SV Gp.
Farrell, Joseph G.	P-503	Capt	Brooklyn, NY	
Fatica, Mike	GO-ATT	1/Lt		72 SCS
Fernberg, Louis P., Jr.	EM-505	Sgt	Cleveland, OH	Armorer
Ferrace, Frank A.	EM-503	Pfc	Mt. Vernon, NY	
Ferraro, Clem	EM-ATT	Cpl	Franklin, NC	Link Trainer Opr. 72 SCS
Ferrell, Clarence I.	P-503	1/Lt	Knightdale, NC	
Ferszt, Alfred R.	EM-ATT	Pfc		464 SV Sq.
Fetter, Carl C.	EM-504		New Paris, PA	
Ficas, Edward T.	EM-505	SSgt	W. Frankfort, IL	
Fickel, Paul D.	P-503	1/Lt	Ottumwa, IA	
Fields, Derell W.	EM-505	Cpl	Covington, KY	
Filip, Anthony	EM-ATT	Pfc		72 SCS
Filley, Everett R., Jr.	GO-ATT	1/Lt	Houston, TX	
Filmore, Francis P.	EM-ATT	Pfc	Hernando, FL	Ammo. Sec. 1786 OSM
Fiorito, Leonard J.	P-503	Capt	Leroy, NY	
Fish, Robert O.	EM-ATT	Sgt		2120 Engr. F/F
Fish, Wesley G.	P-505	2/Lt	Oakland, CA	
Fisher, Ernest T.	EM-504			
Fisher, George A.	GO-ATT	2/Lt	Medical Admin.,	328 SV Gp.
Fissel, Raymond P.	EM-503	Cpl	Spring Grove, PA	
Fitzgerald, Dale K.	EM-504	MSgt	Salt Lake City, UT	Communications Chief
Flaherty, Edward C.	P-503	2/Lt	Elizabeth, NJ	
Flaming, Virgil O.	EM-504		Perrytown, TX	Armorer
Fleming, Herbert W.	EM-503	Sgt	Sun Cook, NH	
Foard, William M.	P-503	1/Lt	Marion, SC	
Fober, Robert R.	EM-503	TSgt	Freeport, IL	Engineering
Folwell, Nathan T.	P-503	Capt	Allentown, PA	
Fording, Robert L.	EM-504			
Fornal, Nicholas	EM-504			
Fortino, Ross A.	EM-ATT	T/5	Sharpsburg, PA	Auto Sec., 1786 OSM
Fortner, Melvin A.	EM-503	Cpl	Witchita, KS	
Fossum, Chester G.	EM-504			
Fountain, Albert	EM-504			
Fountain, Frank W.	EM-504	TSgt	Plymouth, MA	Eng. Flight Chief
Fox, George, Jr.	EM-504			
France, James L.	P-503	F/O	Miami, FL	
Francis, Luther B.	P-503	1/Lt	Portland, ME	
Frank, Murray	EM-ATT	Cpl		464 SV Sq.
Frankowski, Leonard C.	EM-503	Sgt	Chicago, IL	
Franz, John A.	EM-503	MSgt	Maitland, FL	Maintenance Chief
Fraser, Allan M.	EM-505	Sgt	Bennington, NH	
Fratello, Tom C.	P-503	F/O	Niagra Falls, NY	
Freed, Kenneth	GO-ATT	Capt		Spec. Svcs., 328 SV Gp.
Freeman, Hartwell	EM-505	TSgt	Ocala, FL	Carb. Specialist
French, Bernard J.	P-504	2/Lt	W. Chelmsford, MA	(Trfd to 353 FG)
French, Carl H.	P-503	1/Lt	Loudonville, NY	
French, Lloyd J.	P-503	Capt	West Hartford, CT	
Fresella, Anthony M.	EM-505	SSgt	Bronx, NY	
Frink, James P.	P-505	2/Lt	Charlotte, NC	
Frisch, Robert J.	P-503	1/Lt	Cincinatti, OH	
Fuhrman, Charles E.	EM-505	Sgt	Lake Orion, MI	
Fulton, Baine E.	GO-ATT	Major	Akron, OH	Food Svc. Officer
Fulton, Joseph O., Jr.	P-504	2/Lt	Paoli, PA	
Furrow, James S.	EM-ATT	Cpl		328 SV Gp.

G

Name	Unit	Rank	Location	Notes
Gaertner, Carl W.	EM-504			Radio Maint.
Gager, Andrew B.	EM-505	SSgt	Middleton, MI	Inst. & Elect. Spclst.
Galesky, Frank B.	EM-503	Sgt	Detroit, MI	
Gall, William J.	EM-503	Cpl	Niagra Falls, NY	
Galloway, Walter S.	EM-503	MSgt	Baytown, TX	Line Chief
Ganer, Seymour	P-503	2/Lt	Far Rockaway, NY	
Gant, Allen	EM-505	Cpl	Hopkinsville, KY	
Gapinski, Aloysius V.	EM-ATT	T/5	South Bend, IN	Ammo Sec, 1786 OSM
Garland, Edgar L.	P-504	F/O	Valdosta, GA	
Garneau, Robert A.	EM-505		Lunenberg, MA	
Gates, Leonard R.	EM-505	Cpl	Santa Monica, CA	
Gauger, Henry W.	P-503	1/Lt	Milwaukee, WI	
Gavitt, Daniel E.	EM-503	SSgt	Columbia, SC	
Gelpke, Robert E.	P-505	F/O	Canton, MA	
Generoso, Evie F.	EM-ATT	T/4	Boonton, NJ	Ammo Sec, 1786 OSM
Genshiemer, Theodore B.	EM-503	Sgt	Louisville,	Operations
George, Joseph	EM-503	SSgt	N. Augusta, SC	
Gerard, Francis R.	P-503	Capt	Lyndhurst, NJ	
Gertz, Earl R.	EM-ATT	Cpl	Mesa, AZ	Dental Asst. 72 SCS
Gilbert, Charles H.	EM-503	SSgt	Douglas, A	Engineering
Gilbert, Kenneth L.	P-504	Capt	Middletown, RI	
Gilbert, Kenneth C.	P-505	1/Lt	Jourdanton, TX	
Gilmer, Harry U.	P-505	2/Lt	Birmingham, AL	
Girone, Felix J.	P-503	1/Lt	N. Tarrytown, NY	
Girzi, Henry E., Jr.	P-505	1/Lt	Superior, WI	
Givens, Isdore J.	EM-503	SSgt	Pearlington, MS	Armorer
Glasby, Norman E.	EM-504			
Gleason, Hope W., Jr.	EM-504	Sgt	Ivy, VA	Communications

ROSTER OF GROUP PERSONNEL

Name	Unit	Rank	Location	Notes
Glessner, Walter W.	EM-ATT	Pfc	Alta Vista, KS	Ammo Sec, 1786 OSM
Gluc, Stanley A.	EM-ATT	Cpl		989 MP Co.
Goddard, Michael J.	EM-ATT	MSgt		328 SV Gp.
Goehring, Gustaver H.	EM-504			
Goertz, Allen	EM-503		Wheatland, WY	Medic
Godla, William	EM-ATT	T/5		2120 Eng. F/F
Gokey, John W.	P-503	Capt	Oswego, NY	
Goldenberg, Carl T.	P-HQ	Lt Col	Lynchburg, VA	
Goldstein, Harold M.	EM-ATT	Pfc		464 SV Sq.
Golin, Alfred J.	EM-503	TSgt	Bristol, CT	
Gooch, William D.	P-504	F/O	Winter Park, FL	
Goodwin, Robert L.	EM-504			
Gordon, Stanley	EM-504		Huntington, NY	Control Tower Comm.
Gordon, William R.	P-503	F/O	Miami, FL	
Gousie, Roland E.	P-505	1/Lt	Pawtucket, RI	
Gower, Alton J.	EM-505	Sgt	Bangor, ME	
Grad, Carl E.	P-503	F/O	Spring Hope, NC	
Graham, E. H., Jr.	P-503	1/Lt	Los Angeles, CA	
Graham, Gerald E.	P-505	1/Lt	Grand Rapids, MI	
Grande, Carmen R.	EM-504	SSgt	Trafford, PA	Crew Chief
Grandy, Al J., Jr.	EM-504		Gales Ferry, CT	Homing Station Opr.
Gravel, Roland A.	EM-ATT	Pfc		72 SCS
Gravette, Edgar B.	P-504	Lt Col	Red Bluff, CA	
Greaney, John L.	EM-505	Sgt	Worcester, MA	
Green, Claude W.	P-504	F/O	Fordyce, AR	
Green, Matthew D.	EM-ATT	SSgt		328 SV Gp.
Greenberg, Leonard	EM-504			
Greenberg, Solomon	EM-504			
Greer, Nile C.	P-504	Capt	Blackford, KY	
Gregory, Vincent L.	P-505	2/Lt	Oil City, PA	
Gresh, George	EM-ATT	Cpl		72 SCS
Griffith, Walter B.	P-504	1/Lt	Bridgeport, PA	
Grogan, Stephen J.	EM-504		Jersey City, NJ	Crew Chief
Groteman, Louis S.	EM-ATT	Pfc		72 SCS
Grothendieck, Carl W.	P-503	F/O	Chicago, IL	
Grove, Irving A.	EM-504		Albert Lea, MN	
Guber, Charles	EM-HQ		Aurora, CO	
Guelker, Raymond J.	EM-ATT		St. Louis, MO	
Guernsey, Frank D.	P-504	Major	Orlando, FL	
Gurtner, Edwin H.	EM-503	MSgt	Amherst, NY	Engineering Maint.
Gustke, Richard N.	P-504	F/O	Battle Creek, MI	
Guyton, William R.	P-505	Capt	Pittsburg, PA	

H

Name	Unit	Rank	Location	Notes
Hackett, Paul E.	EM-503	SSgt	Yellow Springs, OH	
Hager, Rose F.	P-HQ	Major	Mercedes, TX	
Hahn, Robert S.	EM-503	Sgt	Oakland, CA	Flight Line Cook
Haidle, Elmer E.	P-503	1/Lt	Greenock, PA	
Haley, R. A.	EM-ATT	Sgt		72 SCS
Hamilton, Clifford H.	EM-ATT	T/5	Plainfield, NJ	Auto Sec, 1786 OSM
Hamilton, George	EM-HQ			
Hammerle, Charles F.	EM-505	Cpl	Syracuse, NY	
Hammond, C. Willis	GO-505	Capt	Lutherville, MO	Intelligence
Hanlon, Arthur A.	EM-ATT	T/5	Sharpsburg, PA	Arm. Sec.,1786 OSM
Hanowitz, Joe	EM-503	TSgt	Memphis, TN	
Hansbury, Bernard P.	EM-505	Sgt	Philadelphia, PA	Photographer
Hanseman, Chris J.	P-505	1/Lt	Mondovi, WI	
Hanson, Albert F.	EM-505	Pfc	Lake Placid, NY	
Hanson, James R.	P-505	1/Lt	Norfolk, VA	
Harbold, Leslie H.	EM-505	SSgt	Toledo, OH	Asst. Crew Chief
Hardee, Davis E., Jr.	GO-504	2/Lt	Savannah, GA	Maint. Officer
Harkey, Fred M.	EM-505	Sgt	Mt. Holly, NC	Armorer
Harlow, Harry W.	EM-503	Sgt	Portland, OR	
Harnack, Kenneth G.	EM-503	SSgt	Janesville, WI	Crew Chief
Harrell, James P.	EM-504			
Harris, Charles H.	EM-ATT	Sgt		328 SV Gp.
Harris, Thomas W.	EM-505	SSgt	Tampa, FL	
Harris, Truman R.	EM-503	Pvt	Dennis, TX	
Harrison, Charles E.	EM-504		Lantana, FL	Maint. Inspector
Harrison, Clyde	EM-ATT	Cpl		72 SCS
Harry, G. P.	P-504/HQ	1/Lt	Garwood, TX	
Hart, Leslie W.	EM-503	TSgt	Spokane, WA	Eng. Flight Chief
Harte, Allan S., Jr.	P-503	Capt	Chestertown, MD	
Hartley, Lennis C.	EM-50	Sgt	Ft. Valley, GA	
Hartman, Howard M.	EM-503	TSgt	Alexandria Bay, NY	Eng. Flight Chief
Haslam, Frederick C.	P-504	1/Lt	Buffalo, NY	
Hatfield, Con	EM-ATT	T/5		2120 Engr. F/F
Hatfield, Thomas R.	EM-HQ			
Hathorn, Vernon B., Jr.	P-HQ	Major	Harvey, LA	Operations
Hauff, John J.	P-503	1/Lt	Milford, NJ	
Haugh, Herbert C.	EM-505	Sgt	Sherman, TX	Armorer
Hauser, Roy J.	EM-ATT	Pvt	San Francisco, CA	Auto Sec, 1786 OSM
Hauss, Howard J.	GO-ATT		Springfield, MO	Dentist, 328 SV Gp.
Havighurst, Robert C.	P-504	1/Lt	Lakewood, OH	
Hawkins, Anthony G.	P-503	Capt	Detroit, MI	
Hawley, Joseph E.	EM-ATT	MSgt	Tuscaloosa, AL	Auto Sec., 1786 OSM
Hayden, James J.	GO-504	Major	Bardstown, KY	
Hayes, Charles F.	EM-503	SSgt	Oklahoma City, OK	
Hayes, James R.	EM-505	SSgt	Muskegon, MI	Elect. Spclst.
Hayes, Kenward R.	EM-ATT	T/5	Castro Valley, CA	Veh. Maint., 1786 OSM
Haynes, Harry E.	P-503	Capt		
Hays, Julian B.	EM-503	SSgt	Bowling Green, KY	Radio Mechanic
Head, Wilbur F.	EM-503	Sgt	Salt Lake City, UT	
Healy, William P.	EM-504			
Heaphy, Russell L.	EM-505	Sgt	Arabi, LA	
Heimerdinger, Milton E.	EM-ATT		Louisville, KY	Radio Maint., 328 SV Gp.
Heinbaugh, Donald O.	EM-503	SSgt	Philippi, WV	
Heinica, Edward	EM-HQ	TSgt		
Helliger, William B.	EM-503	SSgt	Baltimore, MD	
Helsing, Richard V.	EM-504		Baden, PA	Homing Station Opr.
Helton, Fred L.	EM-ATT	T/5	Cape Girardeau, MO	Auto Sec, 1786 OSM
Helzer, Roy	EM-504			
Henderson, Harvey E.	P-503	Lt Col	Tayler, TX	
Hendricks, Charles J.	P-504	2/Lt	Atlanta, GA	
Heneghan, Floyd P.	P-505	2/Lt	Jerseyville, IL	
Henry, Basil D.	EM-504			
Henry, John B., Jr.	P-HQ	Col	San Antonio, TX	Commanding Officer
Herrmann, Ray F.	P-504	Capt	Charleston, WV	
Hermansen, Cephas	P-504	2/Lt	Aldan Station, PA	
Hermanson, Albert J.	EM-505	SSgt	Parma, OH	Crew Chief
Hernandez, Alexander	EM-503	Cpl	Sante Fe Springs, CA	
Hershey, Herbert S.	EM-ATT	Pfc		989 MP Co.
Hicks, Carl L.	EM-505	TSgt	Maryville, TN	
Hild, John F.	GO-ATT	Capt	Arcadia, CA	C.O., 1786 OSM
Hill, Ralph S., Jr.	P-503	1/Lt	Haddonfield, NJ	
Hilton, Frank F.	EM-503	SSgt	Terre Haute, IN	Crew Chief
Hines, Elwood W.	EM-505	SSgt	Columbus, OH	Sheet Metal Spclst
Hintz, Elwood H.	GO-ATT			328 SV Gp.
Hirshout, Matthew	GO-ATT	1/Lt	Wilmington, DE	Adjutant, 72 SCS
Hoar, Robert P.	EM-504			
Hodgens, Ralph M., Jr.	EM-504		Butte, MT	
Hoermann, Leroy F.	EM-ATT	TSgt	Brenham, TX	Radio Maint., 72 SCS
Hoefler, Victor W.	EM-503	SSgt	Denver, CO	Armament Flt Chief
Hoffman, Donald M.	EM-504		Altoona, PA	Radio Mechanic
Hoffman, William R.	P-504	1/Lt	Vanport, OR	
Holbrook, Dan Sq.	EM-ATT	Cpl		Observer (WEA), 18 WX
Holden, Judson R.	GO-ATT	Capt		72 SC
Holland, Lonie E.	EM-504			
Holloway, John G.	P-505	Capt	South Bend, IN	
Holm, Edward W.	EM-505	SSgt	Chicago, IL	Prop Spclst.
Holma, Joseph W.	EM-504			
Hood, Coleman	EM-504			
Horton, Alfred A.	EM-ATT	T/5	Willoughby, OH	Arm Sec.,1786 OSM
Hosler, Galen M.	EM-504		Columbus, OH	
Hotchkiss, Harvey M.	EM-504			
Hovey, Donald R.	EM-505	MSgt	Eden Prairie, MN	Eng. Line Chief
Howard, Charles J.	EM-ATT	Pfc		328 SV Gp.
Howard, Harry F.	P-505	1/Lt	Colorado Springs, CO	
Howard, Walden E.	P-505	1/Lt	Seminole, OK	
Howard, William K.	EM-505	SSgt	Wallins Creek, KY	

Roster of Group Personnel

Name	Unit	Rank	Location	Role
Howell, Stone D.	EM-505	Sgt	Searcy, AR	Assist. Crew Chief
Hrico, George	P-505	Capt	Duquesne, PA	
Hubbell, William R.	P-503	2/Lt	Laurel Springs, NJ	
Hubler, Raymond F.	EM-504			
Huddleston, Ralph L.	EM-503	Pfc	Heavener, OK	
Hudson, Will M.	P-504	1/Lt	Union City, TN	
Hughes, Harris A.	EM-505	Cpl		
Hulett, Harold O.	EM-ATT	T/5	Schenectady, NY	Auto Sec., 1786 OSM
Hull, James F.	P-503	2/Lt	McKeesport, PA	
Hull, William B.	EM-504			
Hulsey, James H.	EM-ATT	Cpl		72 SCS
Hunerwadel, Hugh P.	P-504	2/Lt	Chattanooga, TN	
Hunt, Charlie R.	EM-ATT	Cpl		72 SCS
Hunt, Harlan F.	P-504	1/Lt	Meriden, CT	
Hunter, Charles M.	P-504	1/Lt	Bonham, TX	
Hupp, Ellis E., Jr.	P-505	F/O	Columbus, OH	
Huppert, Leonard V., Jr.	EM-505	Cpl	Mishawaka, IN	Armorer
Hurley, William T.	P-504	Capt	Belmare, NJ	
Husser, Andrew	EM-503	Sgt	Chevy Chase, MD	Armorer
Hutchinson, Sylvester	EM-503	SSgt	Manhasset, NY	NCOC Intelligence
Hutsell, William L.	EM-504			
Hutton, John E., Jr.	P-503	2/Lt	Kingsport, TN	

I

Name	Unit	Rank	Location	Role
Ibello, Ralph F.	EM-505	Cpl	E. Providence, RI	
Iding, Orville R.	EM-504			
Ingeldsby, Bernard M.	EM-503	Sgt	Council Bluffs, IA	
Ippolito, Tony	EM-ATT	Cpl		989 MP Co.
Irion, Robert E.	P-505	Capt	Axtell, KS	
Ivanowski, Theodore	EM-505		Worcester, MA	

J

Name	Unit	Rank	Location	Role
Jaaskelainen, William	P-505	1/Lt	Base Line, MI	
Jackson, Boyd O.	P-505	1/Lt	Harlem, MT	
Jackson, John D.	GO-505	Capt	West Boylston, MA	Adjutant
Jackson, Layton R.	EM-505	SSgt	Newark, NJ	Assist. Crew Chief
Jackson, Samuel H.	EM-ATT	SSgt		464 SV Sq.
Jacob, George	EM-ATT	Cpl		2120 Engr. F/F
Jacobs, John L.	EM-ATT	Pfc		72 SCS
Jacobs, Lewis E.	EM-ATT	Pfc	Minneapolis, MN	Auto Sec., 1786 OSM
James, John R.	GO-504	1/Lt	Sulphur Springs, TX	Armament Officer
Janoski, Joseph J.	EM-504			
Jansen, James S.	EM-HQ			
Jarrait, George E.	EM-504			
Jennings, Carroll L.	EM-505	TSgt	Seattle, WA	Carb. Spclst.
Jensen, Don A.	EM-ATT	TSgt		464 SV Sq.
Jensen, James A.	EM-ATT	Pvt	New York, NY	Auto Sec., 1786 OSM
Jessup, Tom N.	P-505	2/Lt	Atlanta, GA	
Joe, George	EM-503	SSgt	N. Augusta, SC	Communications
Johns, Gaylord T.	EM-504			
Johnson, Albert A.	EM-HQ	MSgt		
Johnson, Allen D.	P-503	2/Lt	Fairfield, CT	
Johnson, Don	EM-504			
Johnson, Donald W.	P-503	Capt	Detroit, MI	
Johnson, Evan M., V	P-505	Capt	Pueblo, CO	
Johnson, George A.	EM-504			
Johnson, George N.	EM-503	Sgt	Chicago, IL	
Johnson, Melvin R.	EM-504			
Johnson, Raymond C.	EM-ATT	MSgt	First Sergeant,	328 SV Gp.
Johnson, Raymond G.	P-503	1/Lt	Clarendon, TX	
Johnson, Robert	EM-504	Cpl	Coneaut Lake, PA	Armorer
Johnson, Robert C.	P-503	Pfc	Minneapolis, MN	
Johnson, William G.	P-503	2/Lt	Columbus, MS	
Johnstone, George J.	P-503	2/Lt	Tarrant, AL	
Jolly, Thomas E.	EM-503	SSgt	Shelby, NC	
Jones, Clifford M.	EM-ATT	Pvt		464 SV Sq.
Jones, George W.	P-505	1/Lt	Lenoir, TN	
Jones, Leslie E.	EM-ATT	Sgt		328 SV Gp.
Jones, William A.	P-505	1/Lt	Phoenix, AZ	
Jones, William A.	EM-504	TSgt		Sheetmetal
Jones, William E.	EM-505	SSgt	Sacramento, CA	Armament
Joppru, Sander	EM-503	Cpl	Thief River Falls, MN	
Jordan, Glen T.	EM-ATT	Cpl		72 SCS
Jordan, John F.	EM-504			
Josefczyk, Rudolph C.	EM-504			
Joseph, Mark J.	EM-505	Sgt	Brazil, IN	
Julian, William H.	P-504	Lt Col	Dallas, TX	
Jurjevic, Sylvester	EM-ATT	Cpl		464 SV Sq.

K

Name	Unit	Rank	Location	Role
Kakarakis, James	EM-ATT		Northfield, IL	Medic, 328 SV Gp.
Kameen, A. J.	GO-504	Capt	Mountaintop, PA	Flight Surgeon
Kaniewski, Eugene N.	EM-504	Cpl	South Bend, IN	Armorer
Kanner, Henry	EM-505	Cpl	New York, NY	
Karhuma, Karl O.	P-505	2/Lt	Detroit, MI	
Karon, Arnold T.	EM-504			
Kass, Sidney C.	EM-503	SSgt	Coral Springs, FL	Engineering Clerk
Kassik, Leonard P.	EM-503	SSgt	Milligan, NE	Tech. Supply
Katz, Calvin E.	EM-505	Sgt	Lake Worth, FL	Gun Camera Tech.
Katz, Charles	EM-503	Cpl	Bronx, NY	
Kaulakis, Stanley A.	EM-504			
Keim, Paul T.	P-503	1/Lt	Greensburg, PA	
Keller, James F.	EM-505	SSgt	Martin, GA	Crew Chief
Kelley, Joseph T.	EM-505	Sgt	Cambridge, MA	
Kellogg, George J.	EM-503	Cpl	Nashville, MI	
Kelly, George P., III	P-503	1/Lt	Houston, TX	
Keniston, Earl F.	EM-505	TSgt	Hudson, NH	
Kennedy, Bennie L.	EM-504			
Kern, Benton W.	EM-503	TSgt	Earlville, PA	Mess Hall Supervisor
Kernan, William W.	EM-505	SSgt		
Kernisky, George	P-504	2/Lt	Monessen, PA	
Kerr, James W.	EM-503	SSgt	Garretsville, OH	
Kerrigan, John S.	P-504	2/Lt	Pontiac, MI	
Keys, Harold J.	EM-504			
Khoury, Samuel A.	EM-HQ	Pfc		
Kibler, Luther E.	EM-504			
Kiesz, Reuben S.	EM-504	Sgt	Moorehead, MN	Asst. Crew Chief
Kilmer, Wilbur B.	EM-505	Cpl	Monticello, IN	Tech. Supply
Kimsey, Arnold E.	EM-505	Cpl	High Point, NC	
King, Carmel L.	EM-505	SSgt	Winston-Salem, NC	Crew Chief
King, James G.	P-504	2/Lt	Waverly, TN	
King, John B.	P-503	2/Lt	Atlanta, IL	
Kinser, Malcomb	EM-503	Cpl	Anderson, IN	
Kissel, Burnas O.	EM-503	TSgt	McCook, NE	
Klatzke, Ray G.	EM-504			
Klein, Homer L.	EM-503	SSgt	Nore, IL	
Kline, Homer L.	EM-HQ	SSgt		
Kliss, Harold F.	EM-504			
Knight, George	P-505	1/Lt	Lakewood, RI	
Knight, Willis A.	EM-503	Pfc	Pittsburg, PA	
Knighton, Ralph M.	P-505	2/Lt	Locust Grove, VA	
Knisely, Lloyd W.	EM-504	MSgt	Beloit, WI	Armorer
Knipper, Robert R.	P-504	2/Lt	Modesto, CA	
Knott, Clarence W.	P-503	Capt	Ventura, CA	
Knox, Walter L.	EM-503	SSgt	Miami, FL	NCOIC Operations
Kollar, Earl W.	EM-505	SSgt	Youngstown, OH	Crew Chief
Komanechy, William	EM-HQ		Lakeland, FL	
Kosmella, Robert B.	EM-503	Cpl	Chicago, IL	
Kotora, Harold J.	P-504	2/Lt	Chicago, IL	
Kotara, Peter B.	EM-503	Cpl	Stockdale, TX	
Kovar, Robert J.	P-505	2/Lt	Pittsburg, PA	
Kowalewski, Anthony J.	EM-505	SSgt	Baltimore, MD	Crew Chief
Kozminski, Sylvester F.	EM-505	Cpl	Milwaukee, WI	
Krausman, Louis A., Jr.	EM-505	Cpl	Collins, IA	
Krauss, Richard E.	P-503	1/Lt	Blue Springs, NE	
Krauss, William H.	P-505	Capt	Altavista, VA	
Krehamer, Gordon	EM-503		Rochester, NY	
Krejci, Peter G.	EM-504			
Krueger, Donald F.	P-504	2/Lt	Lakewood, OH	

ROSTER OF GROUP PERSONNEL

Name	Unit	Rank	Location	Notes
Kruse, Floyd H.	EM-505	Cpl	Council Bluffs, IA	
Ksionzyk, Floryan	EM-505	Pfc	Rochester, NY	
Kuhlman, Robert M.	P-504	Capt	Detroit, MI	
Kuhneert, Warren G.	EM-505	MSgt	Lodi, NJ	Eng. Inspector
Kukura, Frank L.	EM-504			
Kunz, Leonard A.	P-504	1/Lt	St. Louis, MO	
Kurth, Otis A.	P-504	1/Lt	Wichita, KS	
Kurutz, Louis V.	EM-505	Sgt	Chicago, IL	

L

Name	Unit	Rank	Location	Notes
Lackman, Morris W.	EM-504			
LaCombe, Francis W.	EM-ATT	Pfc		464 SV Sq.
Lacy, Jack C.	EM-ATT	SSgt	England	HQ Sec, 1786 OSM
Laderberg, Albert	GO-ATT	1/Lt		72 SCS
Lagocki, Frank L.	EM-ATT	Cpl		72 SCS
Lambert, Cecil L.	EM-505	Cpl	Indianapolis, IN	
Landry, Edmund J.	EM-505	Sgt	Shirley, MA	Asst. Crew Chief
Lane, Joseph K.	P-504			
Lanfer, William A.	P-505	2/Lt	Ft. Worth, TX	
Langlois, Edward J.	EM-505	Cpl	E. Boston, MA	
Langohr, Bill E.	P-504	1/Lt	Columbia City, IN	
Langtry, Charles	EM-505			
Langtry, Edward J.	EM-505	Cpl	Lawrence, MA	Refueling
Lanzo, Sam	EM-504		Scarsdale, NY	
Larnard, Theodore S.	EM-504			
Larson, Donald A.	P-505	Major	Yakima, WA	Commanding Officer
Larson, Duane S.	P-504	1/Lt	Regent, ND	
Larson, Hjalmer E.	EM-505	Sgt	Waterloo, IA	
LaRose, Pete J.	EM-505	Cpl	Akron, OH	
Laskart, Arthur C.	EM-HQ			
Latala, Alvin	EM-505	Pfc	Cheektowaga, NY	
Laubenthal, G. M.	GO-ATT	2/Lt		Weather Offi, 18 WX Sq
Laverick, John H.	P-505	2/Lt	Forty Fort, PA	
LaVoie, Robert	EM-504			
Law, Lyle S.	EM-503	Cpl	Carrell, IL	
Lawes, Bayard F.	P-505	2/Lt	Ferndale, MI	
Lawson, Elmer S.	EM-504			
LeDuc, Charles J.	EM-505	SSgt	Paradise, MI	Crew Chief
Lee, Fitzhugh	EM-504		Wilmington, NC	Supply
Lee, Harry	EM-ATT	TSgt		328 SV Gp.
Lehde, Leonard H.	EM-504			
Leitner, Frank W.	P-503	1/Lt	Aiken, SC	
LeJeune, Edwin J.	EN-505	SSgt	Brusley, LA	Crew Chief
LeJeune, John B.	EM-504			
Lema, John Jr.	EM-505	Cpl	Osterville, MA	Welder
Lemke, Edwin R.	EM-505	Sgt	Orand, CA	
Lettus, Andrew N.	P-503	F/O	Hornell, NY	
Leonard, Kenneth	EM-503	Sgt	Ashtabula, OH	
Lewey, Richard	EM-504		Plantation, FL	Asst. Crew Chief
Lewis, Herbert J.	EM-ATT	Pfc		464 SV Sq.
Lichtash, Ben S.	EM-ATT	Cpl		328 SV Gp.
Lightfoot, James D.	EM-503	Cpl	Sherman, TX	
Liles, Glenn G.	EM-ATT		Spokane, WA	Supply Sec., 1786 OSM
Linder, Bernard	EM-504			
Lindley, George L.	EM-ATT	Cpl		72 SCS
Lindsley, Robert F.	EM-505	Sgt	Hoboken, NJ	
Linger, Claude D.	P-503	1/Lt	Fairmount, WV	
Lingle, Woodrow A.	GO-505	Major	Cordova, SC	Executive Officer
Litecky, Paul A.	EM-504		White Bear Lake, MN	Flight Line Cook
Littlefield, Nervel	EM-503	SSgt	Brownweed, TX	
Litz, William J.	GO-ATT	1/Lt		328 SV Gp.
Lively, Leo C.	EM-ATT	Sgt		72 SCS
Livingston, Joseph D.	EM-HQ	SSgt		
Lockwood, Donald B.	EM-ATT	Pvt	St. Paul, MN	Auto Sec., 1786 OSM
Loesky, Frank	EM-504			
Lohnes, James V.	EM-505	Pfc	Long Beach, CA	
Lombardi, Arthur F.	EM-503	SSgt	Yonkers, NY	Communications
London, Dale L.	EM-503	Sgt	Sacramento, CA	
Long, Hollis E.	EM-ATT	Pvt	Golden, MS	Ammo Sec., 1786 OSM
Long, Michael O.	EM-504			
Long, Robert D.	P-HQ	Lt Col	Coral Gables, FL	
Longo, Sam	EM-505	SSgt	Omaha, NE	
Lopez, Preciliano M.	EM-505	Pfc	Chino, CA	
Loskill, Harry G.	P-504	1/Lt	Chicago, IL	
Loveless, Philip M., Jr.	P-505	Capt	Warren, OH	
Lovett, Doyle D.	EM-504	SSgt		Intelligence
Lowe, Willard	EM-503	Cpl	Middletown, OH	
Lowery, Arthur L.	P-503	1/Lt	Clinton, TN	
Lowra, Frank S.	EM-505	SSgt	Buffalo, NY	
Lubert, Walter M.	EM-505	TSgt	Colonia, NJ	
Luce, Frank L., Jr.	GO-HQ	1/Lt		
Luck, Richard J.	GO-ATT	1/Lt	New Orleans, LA	Arm. Sec., 1786 OSM
Ludzinski, Stanley	EM-505	SSgt	Hempstead, NY	Eng. Mechanic
Lukehart, Forrest W.	EM-505	Cpl	Gallatin, MO	
Luongo, Jerry L.	EM-ATT	Pvt	Mobile, AL	Arm. Sec., 1786 OSM
Luper, Arch B.	P-505	1/Lt	Albuquerque, NM	
Lusky, Gordon P.	EM-504		North Cape May, NJ	
Lynch, James L.	P-505	1/Lt	Ft. H.G. Wright, NY	
Lynch, William A.	EM-HQ		Brooklyn, NY	
Lyons, Joseph K.	EM-504			
Lyons, Michel J.	EM-503	Sgt	Brooklyn, NY	

M

Name	Unit	Rank	Location	Notes
MacClarence, William R.	P-505	1/Lt	N. Plainfield, NJ	
MacGregor, Donald M.	EM-ATT	T/5		2120 Eng F/F
Mack, Paul L.	EM-505	Cpl	E. Orange, NJ	
MacKenzie, David A.	P-503	1/Lt	Medford, MA	
Madden, James S.	EM-ATT	Pvt		989 MP Co.
Madewell, James C.	EM-ATT	Pfc		72 SCS
Madore, Joseph L.	EM-503	Sgt.	Kamouraska, Canada	
Majeska, Harry B.	EM-503	SSgt	Alhambra, CA	
Malarz, Chester	P-505	Capt	Buffalo, NY	
Malashevits, Mike	EM-505	SSgt	Three Bridges, NJ	Crew Chief
Maldonado, Roberto S.	EM-ATT	Pvt		1178 QM Co.
Mallory, Jack K.	EM-505	Cpl	Akron, OH	
Mallow, Lloyd W.	EM-503	MSgt	Walters, OK	Communications Chief
Mammosor, George J.	EM-505	Sgt	Chicago, IL	
Maney, Joseph J.	EM-503	Pfc	Toledo, OH	
Mangan, William H.	EM-503	Sgt	Kingston, PA	
Manke, Alfred O.	P-503	2/Lt	Niles, OH	
Mankie, James A.	P-503	2/Lt	Nutley, NJ	
Mansfield, Joseph J.	EM-505	Sgt	Yonkers, NY	
Marcikonis, John A.	EM-505	Pfc	Hudson, PA	
Markle, Robert T.	EM-503	Sgt	Bowling Green, KY	Armorer
Marsh, Lester C.	P-503	1/Lt	Los Angeles, CA	
Marshall, Hugh S.	EM-503	Sgt	San Antonio, TX	
Martin, Carrol	EM-505	Sgt	Long Beach, CA	Asst. Crew Chief
Martin, Woodrow W.	EM-ATT	Pfc	Columbia, SC	HQ Sec., 1786 OSM
Martinez, Frederico	EM-ATT	Sgt		2120 Eng. F/F
Martinez, Robert	EM-ATT	T/5		2120 Eng. F/F
Marts, Jay F.	P-505	1/Lt	Salem, NJ	
Marvel, Thomas W.	P-505	1/Lt	E. Orange, NJ	
Mason, Clair M.	P-504	Capt	Marshalltown, IA	
Mason, John W., Jr.	GO-ATT	1/Lt	Weather Off.,	18 WX Sq.
Maupin, Daniel B.	EM-505	Sgt	Kansas City, MO	
Mayer, Raymond D.	P-503	1/Lt	Swissvale, PA	
McCabe, William J.	EM-ATT	SSgt		2120 Eng. F/F
McCarty, John T.	EM-ATT	T/4	Willowick, OH	Machinist, 1786 OSM
McClaren, James L.	EM-ATT	Sgt	Observer(WEA),	18 WX Sq.
McClean, Michael V.	EM-ATT	Pfc	Detroit, MI	Auto Sec., 1786 OSM
McClish, Donald E.	P-503	Capt	Akron, OH	
McLure, James M.	P-504	Capt	Alexandria, LA	
McConaghy, James H.	EM-505	Cpl	Brighton, MA	Eng. Mechanic
McCurley, John K.	EM-503	Sgt	Abbeville, AL	
McDonald, James A.	EM-505	Sgt	Chicago, IL	
McDonald, John T.	EM-505	Cpl	Whitestone, NY	Engine Mechanic
McDonald, Joseph P.	EM-ATT	SSgt		989 MP Co.
McElwee, Francis E.	P-503	1/LT	Cranford, NJ	
McFarlane, George	EM-505	Sgt	Abilene, TX	Asst. Crew Chief
McGaha, Robert M.	EM-ATT	T/5	Escondido, CA	Auto Sec., 1786 OSM

ROSTER OF GROUP PERSONNEL

Name	Unit	Rank	Location	Role
McGillivray, John R.	GO-504	Capt	Boston, MA	Intelligence Officer
McGowan, Hubert	GO-504	Capt	Milton, FL	Supply Officer
McHugh, George W.	GO-ATT	Capt	Boston, MA	Cthlc Chp,328 SV Gp.
McKenne, Donald E.	EM-ATT	Sgt		72 SCS
McKinley, Herschel	GO-503	Major	Deming, NM	Executive Officer
McKinney, James E.	EM-505	Cpl	Portland, OR	Armorer
McKnight, George L.	EM-ATT	SSgt		328 SV Gp.
McKnight, John A.	EM-505	Sgt	Newburg, NY	Asst. Crew Chief
McLachlen, Thomas P.	GO-ATT		Rockville, MD	Fin. Off, 328 SV Gp.
McLaughlin, James J.	GO-ATT	1/Lt		328 SV Gp.
McMahan, Bruce D.	P-505	1/Lt	Houston, TX.	
McMahon, Peter J.	P-505	1/Lt	Eldersville, PA	
McMillen, Robert W.	EM-504		Melbourne, FL	Crew Chief
McMillen, Urban S.	EM-504	Sgt	Palacios, TX	Acft Mechanic
McMullen, James P.	P-505	2/Lt	St. Petersburg, FL	
McNally, Richard M.	P-503	2/Lt	Boston, MA	
McNamara, James H.	GO-HQ	Capt	De Ridder, LA	Armament Officer
McPharlin, Michael, G.H.	P-HQ	Major	Toronto, Canada	
Mead, Charles M.	P-504	1/Lt	Phoenix, AZ	
Mealey, Paul E.	EM-ATT			328 SV Gp.
Meier, Clarence B.	EM-504		Aurora, NE	
Meinen, John F.	EM-504	Cpl	Carnegie, PA	Mtr Pl Auto Mec
Meisenbach, Joseph L.	EM-ATT	Cpl		328 SV Gp.
Mele, Raymond R.	P-503	F/O	Manhattan, NY	
Melvin, Morris K.	EM-504		Jackson, MS	Intelligence
Menart, Rudolph	GO-HQ	Capt	Cleveland, OH	
Mendenca, James G.	EM-503	Cpl	New Bedford, MA	
Mendes, Nathan	EM-505	Sgt	Chicago, IL	
Mertz, John R.	EM-ATT	72 SCS		
Messina, Mario M.	EM-503	SSgt	Brooklyn, NY	Crew Chief
Metzelaar, Charles P.	EM-505	Cpl	Salt Lake City, UT	
Meyer, Harold J.	GO-HQ	1/Lt	New York, NY	Eng. Off./Tech. Insp.
Meyer, Herbert T.	EM-ATT	Pfc		328 SV Gp.
Meyer, Victor R.	P-503	1/Lt	Macon, MO	
Meyers, Albert W.	EM-503	SSgt	Stoney Point, NC	
Middleton, John C.	EM-505	Cpl	Corsicana, TX	
Milla, Joseph A.	EM-505	MSgt	Phoenix, AZ	First Sergeant
Miller, Harold	P-503	1/Lt	Detroit, MI	
Miller, John	EM-ATT	Pfc		989 MP Co.
Miller, Robert C.	P-505	Capt	St. Petersburg, FL	
Miller, Ronald E.	EM-505	SSgt	Cohasset, MA	
Miller, Thomas H.	EM-505	SSgt	Houston, TX	Crew Chief
Miller, Weldon J.	EM-503		Dallas, TX	Armorer
Miller, William P.	EM-504			
Mills, Charles L.	EM-504			
Mills, Harry T.	EM-ATT	T/4	Salem, IL	Arm. Sec., 1786 OSM
Mims, Dewey W.	EM-504			
Mintline, Clare D.	EM-ATT	TSgt	Flint, MI	Arm. Sec., 1786 OSM
Mirenburg, Archie	EM-ATT	T/5	Monroe, NY	Auto Sec., 1786 OSM
Mitchell, Arlan E.	EM-504	SSgt		
Mitchell, Ervin L., Jr.	EM-503	Sgt	Elvina, MO	
Mitchell, Ralph	EM-504			
Mobley, Homer E., Jr.	EM-505	Sgt	New Orleans, LA	Asst. Crew Chief
Modjeska, Henry J.	EM-503		Pico River, CA	Radio Maint.
Molnar, John	EM-ATT	Pfc		72 SCS
Mondl, Evan T.	EM-504	SSgt	Norton, OH	Crew Chief
Mondschein, Herman F.	GO-ATT	W/O	Kansas City, MO	St Chf,18 WX Sq.
Monson, Calmar M.	EM-503	Sgt	Elbow Lake, MN	
Montell, Richard W.	P-504	1/Lt	Alameda, CA	
Montgomery, Lyle O.	EM-504		Plattsmouth, N	
Moore, Cecil W.	EM-505	TSgt	Cambridge, MD	Armament Inspector
Moore, Edward J., Jr.	EM-ATT	Sgt		72 SCS
Moore, Paul C., Jr.	EM-ATT	SSgt	WX Forecaster,	18 WX Sq.
Moore, William H.	EM-503	Sgt	Lemay, MO	
Moore, William R.	P-505	1/Lt	Tucson, AZ	
Mootz, William P.	EM-505	SSgt	Sandusky, OH	
Moreland, Kenneth E.	P-503	1/Lt	Fort Dodge, IA	
Morgan, Clifford L.	EM-503	Sgt	Ansley, NE	
Morgan, Cyrus M.	EM-504		Gary, IN	Communications
Morgan, Wilbur L.	EM-504			
Morris, Andy D.	EM-ATT	Cpl		464 SV Sq.
Morrissey, Albert F.	EM-504			
Morrow, James R.	EM-503	Cpl	Ft. Worth, TX	
Morrow, Ralph E., Jr.	P-503	1/Lt	Indianapolis, IN	
Mosenthal, Edward K.	GO-HQ	1/Lt	Redondo Beach, CA	Adjutant
Moser, Gilbert A.	EM-503	SSgt	Brunswick, MO	
Mossburg, Edward G.	EM-503	Pfc	Wheeling, WV	
Mroz, Leon	EM-504		Iron River, MI	
Muchiski, Michael	EM-504			
Mudd, Joseph L.	EM-ATT	Pvt	Washington, DC	Ammo Sec., 1786 OSM
Mudge, William F., Jr.	P-505	1/Lt	Fall River, MA	
Muir, William H.	GO-504	Capt	Olean, NY	Engineering Officer
Mullen, Roy F.	EM-ATT	Pfc		328 SV Gp.
Muller, James B.	P-505	2/Lt	Maplewood, NJ	
Mulvey, Robert F.	P-503	1/Lt	Lowell, MA	
Munch, Earl J.	EM-505	Cpl	Shreveport, LA	
Munneke, Leslie E.	EM-ATT	Sgt	McAllen, TX	Medic, 328 SV Gp.
Murchison, James F.	EM-503	MSgt	Vidalia, GA	
Murphy, Jerome T.	P-505	1/Lt	Brainerd, MN	
Murphy, Thomas J.	EM-505	Cpl	Bronx, NY	
Murray, John D.	EM-505	TSgt	N. Versailles, PA	Armament Chief
Murray, John F.	EM-505	MSgt	Waterlist, NY	
Muto, Alphonse J.	EM-503		Rochester, NY	
Myer, Paul M.	P-504	1/Lt	Arlington, VA	
Myers, Roy A.	EM-505	SSgt	Winston Salem, NC	Crew Chief

N

Name	Unit	Rank	Location	Role
Nap, Bernard H.	EM-503	SSgt	Goodyear, CT	
Nass, John W.	EM-505	SSgt	Schenectady, NY	Tech. Supply
Nay, Martin N.	P-505	1/Lt	Brooklyn, NY	
Neall, Robert W.	EM-505	Cpl	Boston, MA	
Neiswinger, Duane H.	EM-ATT	T/5		989 MP Co.
Nelson, Eugene A.	EM-503	Sgt	Riverside, CA	
Nelson, Gordon R.	EM-504			
Nessler, Ferdinand A.	EM-505	SSgt	W. Yarmouth, MA	Crew Chief
Nethaway, Charles D.	GO-HQ	Capt	Belton, MO	Pub. Relations Off.
Neuman, Charles H., Jr.	EM-ATT	Pfc		464 SV Sq.
Newton, James H.	EM-ATT	Sgt		989 MP Co.
Nicholas, Joseph C.	EM-505	SSgt	Gary, IN	Crew Chief
Nigh, Joseph H.	EM-HQ			
Nine, Myron L.	EM-505	Pfc	Ft. Wayne, IN	
Nissen, Niels Arne	EM-505	SSgt	Cedar Rapids, IA	Crew Chief
North, Yelverton E.	EM-504			
Nowlin, Louis E.	P-504			
Norwood, James P.	GO-HQ	Capt	Satellite Beach, FL	Weather Officer

O

Name	Unit	Rank	Location	Role
O'Brien, Richard C.	P-505	1/Lt	Somerville, MA	
O'Brien, Robert E.	EM-503	Sgt	Butler, PA	Squadron Painter
O'Brien, Roy F.	EM-505		Richardson, TX	
O'Dell, Ralph H.	EM-504			
Offner, Joseph C.	EM-ATT	Pfc		72 SCS
Oglesby, Willie S.	EM-505	Sgt	Hilltonia, GA	
Ohler, Russell B.	EM-ATT	Sgt		2120 Eng. F/F
O'Janen, Kaine A.	EM-505	SSgt	Marquette, MI	Crew Chief
Olander, Richard B.	P-505	Capt	Racine, WI	
Olive, Samuel G.	EM-503	Pvt	Bound Brook, NJ	
Oliver, Bernard J.	P-HQ	Capt		
Olland, Ralph W.	EM-503	Cpl	Union, NJ	
Olsen, Warren L.	EM-ATT	Pvt	Port Charlotte, FL	Auto Sec., 1786 OSM
Olvares, Emil	EM-503	Sgt	San Antonio, TX	
Oostra, Marinus	EM-ATT	Pfc		2120 Eng. F/F
Opitz, William R.	P-505	2/Lt	Spearfish, SD	
Opperman, Henry W.	GO-HQ	Capt	Ontario, Canada	Chaplain
Orcutt, Leon M., Jr.	P-504	1/Lt	Huntington, M	
Oreggia, Louis A.	EM-505	Cpl	Palm Harbor, FL	Armorer
Oser, Edward	EM-505	SSgt	Huntingdon, PA	Armorer
Ossowski, Carl L.	EM-503	Pfc	Omaha, NE	
Ostrow, Nathan	P-503	Capt	Minneapolis, MN	
O'Sullivan, W. R., Jr.	P-504	1/Lt	Harberth, PA	

ROSTER OF GROUP PERSONNEL

Name	Unit	Rank	Location	Role
Ott, Maurice D.	P-504	1/Lt	Kansas City, KS	
Owens, Ernest A.	EM-505	Pfc	San Morando, CA	

P

Name	Unit	Rank	Location	Role
Page, Donald W.	EM-503		Winston-Salem, NC	
Page, Stanley W.	EM-505	SSgt	Lincoln, MA	Control Tower
Pagano, James	EM-504			
Painter, Emery R.	EM-505	Cpl	Export, PA	
Palmer, Arthur J.	EM-ATT	Pfc		989 MP Co.
Palmer, Gerald W.	P-505	2/Lt	Ladysmith, WI	
Palmucci, Sam L.	EM-505	SSgt	Newark, NJ	Acft. Maint.
Panka, Anthony	EM-505	Sgt	Lanoka Harbor, NJ	Acft. Maint.
Panochyk, Ralph G.	EM-ATT	Pfc		72 SCS
Papalko, George R.	EM-503	Cpl	Campbell, OH	Motor Pool
Papi, Agamenone V.	EM-505	SSgt	Portland, ME	Sheet Metal Spclst.
Pappas, S. A. "Jimmy"	EM-HQ	Sgt	Scramento, CA	CO's Driver
Parent, Walter A.	EM-ATT	Pfc		989 MP Co.
Parker, Vince L.	EM-HQ	Cpl		
Parks, Steve C.	GO-ATT	Major		72 SC
Parks, Willard D.	EM-ATT	Pfc		72 SCS
Parton, Robert E.	EM-503	Pfc	Waynesville, NC	
Parodi, Henry	EM-504		Gresskill, NJ	
Pastor, William J.	P-504	2/Lt	Phillipsburg, NJ	
Paterek, Frank	EM-504			
Patterson, Ralph B.	EM-505	SSgt	Jacksonville, FL	Asst. Crew Chief
Patti, Joseph	EM-504			
Patton, William T.	EM-ATT	Pvt		989 MP Co.
Paul, Robert H., Jr.	P-505	1/Lt	Baltimore, MD	
Paxton, Robert W.	EM-505	Cpl	Modesto, CA	
Peace, Fred W.	EM-ATT	Pfc		328 SV Gp.
Peasley, Russell	EM-505	SSgt	E. Lansing, MI	Crew Chief
Peeples, Clyde F.	EM-504			
Pence, Henry E.	GO-503	Capt	Beaver, PA	Engineering Officer
Pennell, Joseph D.	EM-504		S. Portland, M	
Penney, Robert P.	EM-505	SSgt	Lake Worth, F	
Penny, Donald E.	P-504	1/Lt	Columbus, OH	
Penrose, Richard C.	P-504	Capt	Orland, CA	
Per, Joseph J.	EM-505	TSgt	Roseboom, NY	Flight Chief
Perry, Gordon F.	P-505	2/Lt	Sidney, NY	
Perry, John	EM-504		Springfield, PA	Payroll Clerk
Perry, Joseph L.	EM-ATT	Cpl		328 SV Gp
Perry, Stanley E.	EM-503	Sgt	Seymore, IN	
Perry, William W.	P-503	Capt	Independence, KS	
Pesanka, John	P-505	1/Lt	Pittsburgh, PA	
Peter, Lewis S., Jr.	P-504	Major	San Antonio, TX	
Peters, Glenn	EM-503	SSgt	Covington, OK	
Peterson, Donald A.	EM-ATT	Cpl		464 SV Sq.
Petitt, Philip E.	P-503	Capt	New York, NY	
Petrino, William G.	EM-505	SSgt	Bronx, NY	Crew Chief
Petro, John N.	EM-503	Cpl	Toledo, OH	
Petticrew, Stanley S.	P-505	F/O	Springfield, OH	
Pharo, William E.	EM-504			
Phillippi, William R.	P-505	1/Lt	Camden, AL	
Phillips, Donald W.	GO-ATT	1/Lt		72 SCS
Pietrogallo, John J.	EM-ATT	Cpl		328 SV Gp.
Pinkas, Stephen	EM-504			
Pinkerton, Sproul	EM-504	TSgt	Avondale, PA	Armament Supervisor
Pinkos, Frank	EM-504		Bayonne, NJ	Welder
Pirosa, Alfred A.	EM-504			
Placo, Mike A.	EM-ATT	Pfc	Cleveland, OH	Arm. Sec., 1786 OSM
Plant, Robert O.	EM-505	Cpl	Alameda, CA	Armorer
Plaster, Mat J.	EM-504			
Platt, Albert J.	EM-503	Pfc	Colt's Neck, NJ	
Poggi, Thomas P.	EM-503	Cpl	Massapequia, NY	Armorer
Pohl, Jack	EM-505	SSgt	Loch Sheldrake, NY	
Poissant, Raymond L.	EM-ATT	T/5		989 MP Co.
Polich, William W.	EM-ATT	T/5	Great Falls, MT	Auto Sec., 1786 OSM
Pollock, Stuart B.	EM-505	SSgt	Corning, NY	
Pomponio, Paul J.	EM-ATT	Pvt	Brooklyn, NY	Ammo. Sec., 1786 OSM
Porter, George W.	P-503	1/Lt	Los Angeles, CA	
Porter, William E.	EM-504		Pittsburg, PA	Station Homing Oper.
Potthoff, John P.	P-503	1/Lt	Las Vegas, NV	
Potts, Edwin W.	EM-ATT	T/3	Paola, KS	Auto Sec., 1786 OSM
Poutre, Rex Lawrence	P-503	Capt	Concordia, KS	
Powell, Charles, E.	EM-503	SSgt	Milwaukee, WI	
Powell, Lawrence J.	P-505	1/Lt	Southgate, CA	
Praml, Henry W.	EM-505	SSgt	W. Orange, NJ	
Pratt, Francis T.	EM-505	SSgt	Binghamton, NY	Prop Spclst.
Preddy, William R.	P-503	1/Lt	Greensboro, NC	
Presti, James	EM-504		Trenton, NJ	
Price, David E.	EM-ATT	Pfc	Abingdon, VA	72 SCS
Price, Jack B.	P-503	1/Lt	Ada, OK	
Price, William V.	EM-ATT	Cpl	Johnstown, PA	0' Club, 464 SV Sq.
Prine, Louis G.	EM-504			
Profitt, James A.	EM-ATT	SSgt		72 SCS
Propst, John R.	P-HQ	Lt Col	Amarillo, TX	Operations
Puckett, Hollis L.	EM-504			
Purcell, Philip	EM-ATT	Pfc		72 SCS
Purpura, John	EM-504			
Purzycki, Edward J.	EM-ATT		Wilmington, DE	Base Def., 328 SV Gp

Q

Name	Unit	Rank	Location	Role
Quale, Donald H.	G0-503	1/Lt	Reno, NV	Armament Officer
Quinlan, Howard F.	EM-ATT	T/4	Pittsburg, PA	Arm. Sec., 1786 OSM
Quirk, James T.	EM-ATT	Pfc		989 MP Co

R

Name	Unit	Rank	Location	Role
Raca, William P.	EM-503	Pfc	Portsmouth, NH	
Raines, William J.	EM-505	TSgt	Lititz, PA	Control Tower
Rameriz, Larry J.	EM-503		Sacramento, CA	
Rass, Alan J.	EM-503	Cpl	Luxemburg, WI	
Ratte, Leo P.	EM-504			
Rawls, Dennis B., Jr.	P-503	1/Lt	Tampa, FL	
Rea, L. C.	EM-505	Cpl	Broken Bow, OK	Asst. Crew Chief
Redford, Auzie R.	EM-503	TSgt	San Antonio, TX	Ordnance
Reeder, Frank E.	EM-503	Pfc	Portland, Or	
Regan, Kenneth M.	GO-HQ	Capt	Pecos, TX	Asst. Intel. Officer
Register, David H., Jr.	EM-505	SSgt	Houston, TX	Crew Chief
Reichardt, Adolph F.	EM-503	SSgt	Milwaukee, WI	
Reid, Langhorne, Jr.	P-505	Major	Kansas City, MO	
Reid, William G.	EM-503	TSgt	Salt Lake City, UT	
Reidy, Paul A.	EM-ATT	T/5	Worcester, MA	Arm. Sec., 1786 OSM
Reilley, Clemons R.	EM-ATT	Pfc		72 SCS
Reilly, John W.	EM-503	Pfc	Shrewsbury, MA	
Reins, Robert F.	EM-503	Sgt	Cincinnati, OH	Armorer
Resta, Benny	EM-ATT		Bristol, CT	328 SV Gp.
Retherford, Phillip L.	EM-505	SSgt	Limeville, IA	
Reuter, Raymond F.	P-503	Capt	Union, OR	
Reynolds, Gardner H.	P-503	Capt	San Antonio, TX	
Reynolds, John R.	P-HQ	Major	San Antonio, TX	
Rice, John J.	P-505	2/Lt	Hartford, CT	
Rich, George T.	P-505	Capt	Wilmington, NC	
Rickman, William H.	EM-503	Pfc	Clover, VA	
Riddle, Walter J.	EM-ATT	T/5		328 SV Gp.
Riggan, James H.	EM-ATT	T/5	2120 Eng. F/F	
Riggs, Gaston H.	P-503	1/Lt		New Waverly, TX
Rinard, Edward H.	EM-ATT	Pfc		464 SV Sq.
Riotta, Frank	EM-504		Massapequa Park, NY	
Rivera, Alfonso J.	EM-505	SSgt	Santa Fe, NM	Crew Chief
Rizer, Harold W.	EM-ATT	T/4		Auto Sec., 1786 OSM
Robenalt, Ralph L.	EM-ATT	Pfc		989 MP Co.
Roberts, Carl E.	EM-ATT	Pvt	Kingston, PA	Arm. Sec., 1786 OSM
Robinson, Clayton B.	EM-505	Sgt	Waterford, MS	
Robinson, James G.	P-503	Capt	Rocky River, OH	
Robinson, Richard C.	EM-505	Sgt	Helena, MT	Acft. Elect.
Rodenbach, Paul R.	EM-505	Sgt	Slatington, PA	Payroll Clerk
Rogg, Martin	EM-ATT	Sgt		72 SCS
Rogers, Everett I., III	EM-505	Sgt	Providence, RI	Asst. Crew Chief
Rohm, Richard A.	P-505	1/Lt	Los Angeles, CA	

ROSTER OF GROUP PERSONNEL

Name	Unit	Rank	Location	Notes
Romanowicz, Joseph	EM-ATT	Cpl		Obs (WEA)18 WX Sq.
Rooney, John V.	EM-ATT	Sgt		989 MP Co.
Rooney, Raymond E.	EM-503	Sgt	Terre Haute, IN	
Rosati, James J.	EM-505	Sgt	Rochester, NY	Radar Mech.
Rose, Estel	EM-504		Chandler, AZ	Medic
Rosen, George J.	P-504	1/Lt	Schenectady, NY	
Rosen, Herman	EM-ATT	Cpl		72 SCS
Rosenberg, Harry	EM-503	SSgt	Brooklyn, NY	
Rosenberg, Lester D.	EM-505	Cpl	Brooklyn, NY	
Ross, Howard C.	EM-503	Cpl	Portland, OR	
Ross, Roland W.	EM-505	Sgt	Buckholtz, TX	Asst. Crew Chief
Rossiter, Bert E.	EM-ATT	Sgt		72 SCS
Rostad, Ralph E.	EM-503	SSgt	Modesto, CA	Sheet Metal
Roth, John	EM-504			
Roth, Leonard F.	EM-503	Sgt	Hastings, NE	Intelligence
Rothman, Nathan	GO-ATT	Capt		328 SV Gp.
Rountree, James Z.	EM-505	TSgt	Dickson, TN	
Routt, Bill C.	P-504	Major	Nacogdoches, TX	
Ruckman, Gerald R.	EM-ATT	Sgt		2120 Eng. F/F
Ruidoi, Harry H.	EM-505	Cpl	Savannah, GA	
Ruedebusch, Norman F.	EM-504			
Rumpke, Carl E.	EM-503	Cpl	E. Cleveland, OH	
Rupp, Kenneth E.	EM-ATT	Cpl		989 MP Co.
Russell, Jesse L.	EM-504		Conroe, TX	Crew Chief
Rutan, Frederick S., Jr.	P-504	1/Lt	Wallaston, MA	
Ryan, John M.	EM-504			
Ryan, Pat E.	EM-504			

S

Name	Unit	Rank	Location	Notes
Sabine, John W.	EM-503	Sgt	Circleville, OH	
Sabo, Steve	EM-503	SSgt	Brownsville, PA	Engineering
Sadler, Morton P.	EM-503	Sgt	Tipple, WV	Engineering
Safarino, George	EM-505	SSgt	Virginia Beach, VA	Crew Chief
Sahl, Herman	EM-503	SSgt	Orange, CT	Crew Chief
Sainlar, Jerome J.	P-504	1/Lt	Louisville, KY	
Saleem, Albert	P-504	2/Lt	Georgetown, CT	
Salgren, Woodrow K.	EM-504	SSgt	Falls of Rough, KY	Armorer
Salmon, James S., Jr.	GO-HQ	1/Lt	Norwood, MA	
Salter, Alexander P.	EM-ATT		989 MP Co.	
Sams, Thomas G.	P-503	Capt	Taylor, TX	
Sanford, Isaac S.	EM-505	Sgt	Seminary, MS	Parachute Rigger
Santamaria, Antonia	EM-503	Pfc	Waltham, MA	
Santino, Biagio	EM-ATT	Pvt		989 MP Co.
Sargent, Robert F.	P-504	Capt	Youngstown, OH	
Saunders, Randall R.	EM-503	Sgt	Northrup, OH	
Sava, August	EM-504			
Sawicki, Joseph F., Jr.	P-505	2/Lt	Bridgeport, CT	
Schaefer, Richard	EM-HQ			
Schlortt, Quinn	EM-505	Sgt	Smithville, TX	
Schmalried, William C.	EM-503	Pfc	Bellville, TX	
Schmeichel, William	Civ-ATT		Long Beach, CA	Engine Tech. Rep.
Schmidt, Roman F.	EM-ATT	Cpl		328 SV Gp
Schmitz, John W.	EM-HQ			
Schmitz, Leo M.	EM-504	SSgt	Rochester, NY	Crew Chief
Schneider, Edward H.	EM-ATT	Pfc		328 SV Gp.
Schneider, Lewis H.	P-504	2/Lt	Coraopolis, PA	
Schnitker, Clarence	EM-505	SSgt	Nashville, TN	Eng. Mechanic
Schoonover, Martin W.	EM-503	SSgt	Pacific Beach, WA	
Schrull, Arthur W.	EM-ATT			72 SCS
Schuler, Alfred	EM-ATT	Pfc		72 SCS
Schultz, Caroline W.	Civ-ATT		Madison, CT	Red Cross Director
Schultz, Elmer M.	EM-ATT	Pvt	Hubard Lake, MI	Ammo Sec., 1786 OSM
Schwartz, Irving	EM-504			
Scroggin, Frederick R.	GO-505	Capt	Williamstown, KY	Flight Surgeon
Scruggs, Amos	GO-503	Capt	Kingstree, SC	Asst. Intel. Officer
Scruggs, Cecil G.	EM-ATT	Pfc		72 SCS
Scruggs, Harold W.	P-HQ	Lt Col	Hollis, OK	
Sederberg, Lowell	EM-504		Port Orchard, WA	
Segar, John A.	EM-HQ			
Seifts, Dallas	EM-503		Orlando, FL	Medic
Selle, Davis S.	EM-503	Sgt	Barberton, OH	
Semger, Frank M.	EM-505	Cpl	Studley, KS	
Sesco, John	EM-504		Brownsville, PA	
Settle, William C.	EM-503	Cpl	Louisville, KY	
Shafer, Dale E., Jr.	P-503	Lt Col	Dayton, OH	Commanding Officer
Shaffer, James L.	EM-ATT	TSgt		72 SCS
Shake, Charles E.	P-503	2/Lt	Terre Haute, IN	
Shamburg, Dean A.	EM-503	Cpl	Lincoln, NE	Parachute Rigger
Shands, Albert E.	GO-HQ	Lt Col	Miami, FL	Executive Officer
Shannon, Roy E.	EM-ATT	T/5		989 MP Co.
Shaw, Bernell V.	P-505	2/Lt	Brookfield Center, CT	
Shaw, Thomas J.	EM-505	Pvt	Hyde Park, MA	
Sheerman, Dallas M.	EM-ATT	Sgt		72 SCS
Shelnutt, William C.	EM-504	TSgt	Dublin, GA	Communications
Shepard, John L.	EM-HQ			
Shepard, Spencer H.	EM-503	MSgt	Poughquag, NY	Line Chief
Sheperd, David	EM-505	Sgt	Los Angeles, CA	
Shephered, George W.	P-505	F/O	Metairie, LA	
Sheppard, Arthur R.	EM-504			
Shiner, Irvin A.	GO-ATT	1/Lt	New Haven, CT	Transp Off.,1178 QM Co.
Shirey, Elbert E.	EM-503	Cpl	Naples, TX	Medic
Shively, Jack E.	P-504	1/Lt	Saratoga, WY	
Shockley, Clarence B.	EM-505	SSgt	Kansas City, MO	Crew Chief
Shoemaker, Arthur R.	EM-504	Cpl	Hominy, OK	Armorer
Shook, Rex W.	EM-504		Bryan, OH	
Short, Carl L.	EM-503	Sgt	Mangum, OK	
Showker, Fred S.	P-504	Capt	Craigsville, VA	
Siegel, Gordon J. S.	P-504	Capt	Dallas, TX	
Siegel, Joseph C.	EM-503	Sgt	Rankin, PA	
Signet, Wilfred E.	EM-503	Cpl	E. Douglas, MA	
Silberbush, Harold	GO-ATT	Capt	Medical Corps,	328 SV Gp.
Silva, Manuel	EM-HQ			
Silva, Tony J.	EM-505	Cpl	Lawrence, MA	
Simon, Albert G.	EM-503	Pfc	Luzerne, MI	Auto Mech.
Simon, Clifford E.	EM-HQ			
Simpson, Lee B.	EM-503	SSgt	Greensboro, NC	
Sims, Hal	EM-505	Sgt	Atlanta, GA	Eng. Mechanic
Sines, Ulis G.	EM-504			
Sirabella, Ciro	EM-504			
Sirochman, Andrew	P-505	1/Lt	Cleveland, OH	
Skelnar, Eugene W.	EM-503	Cpl	Chicago, IL	
Skouros, Chris	EM-ATT	Sgt		328 SV Gp
Skunda, George	EM-504		Charlotte, NC	
Sloan, Robert J.	EM-505	Cpl	Philadelphia, PA	
Slovak, William R.	P-505	2/Lt	El Campo, TX .	
Smeltzer, Homer	EM-505	Cpl	Ft. Wayne, IN	Painter
Smith, Curtis W.	EM-ATT	Pfc		1178 QM Co.
Smith, Dan W.	EM-ATT	SSgt		72 SCS
Smith, Donald K.	EM-504		Intelligence	
Smith, Donald V.	EM-ATT	Sgt		328 SV Gp
Smith, Dozier B.	EM-ATT		328 SV Gp.	
Smith, Forest B., Jr.	GO-ATT	1/Lt		2120 Eng. F/F
Smith, Frank E.	EM-505	SSgt	Ontario, Canada	Asst. Crew Chief
Smith, Floyd W.	P-505	1/Lt	Bismark, IL	
Smith, George J.	EM-504			
Smith, James, Jr.	GO-ATT	Major		328 SV Gp.
Smith, James A.	EM-504		Eau Claire, WI	
Smith, James C.	EM-503	SSgt	Youngstown, OH	
Smith, Joseph V.	EM-503	Cpl	Wiseman, AR	
Smith, Leland H.	EM-504			
Smith, Lee W.	P-504	2/Lt	Abilene, TX	
Smith, Linwood P.	P-503	2/Lt	Garden City, NY	
Smith, Ray	EM-HQ			
Smith, Ray	EM-505	Cpl	Columbus, OH	Refueling Unit Oper.
Smith, Richard F.	EM-503		Buffalo, NY	
Smith, Robert C.	P-503	1/Lt	Clio, MI	
Smith, Robert H.	P-HQ	Capt		
Smith, Robert W.	GO-ATT	Major		328 SV Gp.
Smith, Roland W.	P-504	F/O	Hastings, NY	
Smith, Shirley K.	P-505	Capt	Williamsport, PA	
Smith, Sidney E.	EM-HQ			

ROSTER OF GROUP PERSONNEL

Name	Unit	Rank	Location	Assignment
Smith, Thomas R.	EM-504		Salt Lake City, UT	
Smith, Vern, Jr.	EM-505	Pfc	Witchita Falls, TX	
Smith, Wallace W.	EM-HQ			
Smith, Walter L.	EM-ATT	Cpl		464 SV Sq.
Sneary, Albert W.	EM-504		Pittsburg, PA	
Snowden, William L.	GO-ATT		Woodhaven, NY	Auto Sec., 1786 OSM
Snyder, Frank, Jr.	EM-505	Pfc	Freehold, NJ	
Snyder, John R.	EM-ATT	Pfc		989 MP Co.
Sobieski, Donald J.	EM-ATT	SSgt		72 SCS
Soderquest, Lowell E.	EM-ATT	Cpl		72 SCS
Solley, George M.	EM-504		Williamsport, PA	Armorer
Soloman, Frederick W.	EM-ATT	SSgt		464 SV Sq.
Somers, Glenwood F.	EM-ATT	Sgt.		464 SV Sq.
Sormanti, Walter A.	EM-ATT	Pfc	Providence, RI	Auto Sec., 1786 OSM
Spade, George	EM-505	SSgt	Troy, OH	Sheet Metal
Spahr, Phil S.	EM-504			
Spainhour, Numa B.	EM-ATT	SSgt		328 SV Gp.
Spallotta, Michael A.	EM-505	Sgt	Irvington, NJ	
Spaziano, Vincent J.	P-503	1/Lt	Providence, RI	
Speckman, Donald	EM-HQ		Sheboygan, WI	
Speckmann, Donald A.	EM-ATT	Cpl		464 SV Sq.
Spence, Ernest C.	EM-504			
Spiess, Eugene J.	EM-505	Cpl	St. Paul, MN	Intelligence
Stachura, Robert M.	P-504	F/O	Leicewater, MA	
Staggers, Theodore R.	P-505	2/Lt	Fairmont, WV	
Stahl, John J.	EM-503	Cpl	London, OH	
Stahoviak, William V.	EM-HQ			
Stanford, William H.	EM-503	Pfc	San Pedro, CA	
Stapp, Glen E.	P-504	F/O	Detroit, MI	
Stark, George	EM-505	Cpl	San Francisco, CA	Carpenter
Starnes, James R.	P-505	Capt	Wilmington, NC	
Staszek, Joseph C.	EM-503	Cpl	Ironwood, MI	
Stavisky, Stephen	GO-ATT	1/Lt		989 MP Co.
Stebbins, Harden E.	EM-ATT	MSgt		First Sgt., 72 SCS
Stedman, Smiley	EM-504			
Steen, Warren R.	EM-505	TSgt	Eagle, ID	
Steffen, Charles J.	EM-503	Sgt	Roanoke, VA	Asst. Crew Chief
Steiger, James A.	P-505	2/Lt	Oceanside, CA	
Steiger, Leroy A.	P-505	2/Lt	East Orange, NJ	
Stein, German W.	EM-503	Cpl	Cuba, MO	
Steier, Arthur H.	P-503	F/O	Los Angeles, CA	
Stemmer, Milton L.	EM-ATT	Pfc		328 SV Gp.
Stephens, Lawrence E.	EM-504	Cpl	Sumner, WA	Radio Mechanic
Stephenson, Enoch B.	P-503	Major	Columbia, TN	
Stern, Edward S.	GO-504	1/Lt	Brooklyn, NY	
Steven, Elmer L.	EM-505	Sgt	Spencer, IA	Teletype Mech.
Stevens, Bradford V.	P-504/503	Capt	Hood River, OR	
Stevens, James M.	EM-503	SSgt	Jackson, MS	
Stevens, Richard C.	P-505	1/Lt	Sunbury, PA	
Stevens, William R.	EM-503	SSgt	Flushing, MI	
Stewart, Carl R.	P-505	1/Lt	Utica, NY	
Stewart, Woodrow W.	EM-503	SSgt	Ft. Worth, TX	
Stiles, Bert	P-505	1/Lt	Denver, CO	
Stillman, Dana W.	EM-503	Sgt	Winterport, ME	
Stillwell, Frank M.	P-503	Capt	Prospect Plains, NJ	
Stockman, Hervey S.	P-504	1/Lt	Andover, NJ	
Stockton, William D.	P-503	1/Lt	Orion, IL	
Stonkus, Joseph C.	EM-505	Cpl	Philadelphia, PA	
Stoudt, Leland	P-505	2/Lt	Reading, PA	
Stouffer, Harold G.	EM-ATT	T/5		989 MP Co.
Stout, Oliver J.	EM-504			
Strachon, Robert	EM-504		Hubbard, OH	Armorer
Stricker, Emil A.	GO-HQ	Major	St. James, MO	Flight Surgeon
Strong, Roland W.	P-505	1/Lt	Bandon, OR	
Stroth, Charles D.	EM-ATT	Pfc	Jamestown, NY	Ammo. Sec., 1786 OSM
Stuhlman, Byron C.	GO-503	Capt	Dayton, OH	Flight Surgeon
Stupp, William J.	EM-503	SSgt	Miamisburg, OH	Ordnance
Sugg, Robert L.	EM-504	Cpl	Salt Lake City, UT	Radio Mechanic
Suggs, Chalmuse	EM-ATT	T/5	Tice, FL	Ammo Sec., 1786 OSM
Sulima, Thaddous M.	EM-505	SSgt	Tucson, AZ	Crew Chief
Sullivan, James L.	EM-503	Cpl	San Diego, CA	Asst. Crew Chief
Sullivan, John W.	EM-ATT	T/5		2120 Eng. F/F
Surdyn, Edward A.	EM-505	Cpl	Pittsburg, PA	
Suter, Joseph	EM-503	TSgt	Lancaster, PA	
Sutton, John L.	P-504	1/Lt	Memphis, TN	
Swan, Thompson	EM-504			Communications
Swank, William L.	EM-HQ			
Sweeney, Walter	EM-ATT	SSgt		328 SV Gp.
Sweezey, Harvey F.	EM-505	Cpl	Falls City, NE	
Swinand, Frank E.	EM-505	Tsgt	Philadelphia, PA	
Sylvester, Kenneth C.	EM-503	TSgt	N. Reading, MA	Acft. Maintenance
Szech, Edward M.	EM-ATT	T/5	Baltimore, MD	Auto Sec., 1786 OSM

T

Name	Unit	Rank	Location	Assignment
Talcott, Franklin D.	P-503	2/Lt	Baltimore, MD	
Tannous, Richard H.	P-505	1/Lt	Pelham Manor, NY	
Tassie, William A.	EM-ATT	Pfc	Tampa, FL	Ammo Sec., 1786 OSM
Taviner, Glenn F.	EM-505	Cpl	Hardin, IL	Tech. Supply
Taylor, Emer F.	EM-ATT	T/5	Portland, OR	Supply Sec., 1786 OSM
Taylor, Frederick E.	EM-HQ			
Taylor, Harold R.	EM-504			Communications
Taylor, James W.	EM-504			
Taylor, Jean C.	GO-HQ	1/Lt	Merced, CA	
Taylor, Vernie F.	EM-503	Sgt	Auburn, NY	
Teagan, Ralph	EM-505	SSgt	Cheboygan, MI	NCOIC Operations
Terrats, Estaban A.	P-503	1/Lt	Santurce, PR	
Teske, Glenn F.	GO-HQ	Capt	Rochester, MN	
Tews, Norman A.	EM-505	Sgt	Appleton, WI	
Thames, Clayton J.	EM-505	Cpl	Frisco City, AL	
Thatcher, John E.	EM-505	SSgt	Salena, IA	
Themascus, George	EM-505	Cpl	Chicago, IL	Armorer
Thibert, Henry G.	P-504	Capt	Detroit, MI	
Thieme, Richard G.	P-505	1/Lt	Sheboygan, WI	
Thistlethwaite, Edward	P-504	2/Lt	Opelousas, LA	
Thomas, J.D.	EM-504			
Thomas, Kessler O.	P-505	1/Lt	Cisco, TX	
Thomas, Walter H.	EM-504			
Thompson, John W.	EM-ATT	Cpl		72 SCS
Thompson, Ralph P.	P-504	1/Lt	Tomales, CA	
Thury, Joseph L.	P-505	Lt Col	St. Paul, MN	Commanding Officer
Timony, James	EM-ATT	Cpl	Observer (WEA),	18 WX Sq.
Tirabasso, Henry J.	EM-505	SSgt	Wicklaffe, OH	Crew Chief
Titus, Robert D.	P-503	1/Lt	Philadelphia, PA	
Todd, Keith A.	EM-505	Sgt	Knoxville, IA	Supply
Todd, William J.	EM-HQ	SSgt		
Todd, William J.	EM-505	Sgt	Webster Groves, MO	
Tolnai, Alexander	EM-ATT	Sgt	Bronx, NY	Supply Sec., 1786 OSM
Tolski, Charles L.	EM-503	Cpl	Torrington, CT	
Tomlinson, Hubert	GO-503	2/Lt		Medical Admin.
Tongue, Arthur E., Jr.	P-505	2/Lt	New York, NY	
Toth, Joseph A.	EM-503	SSgt	Rahway, NJ	Crew Chief
Totten, Ferdinand	EM-HQ			
Tower, Archie A.	P-505	Major	Winthrop, NY	
Trainer, Frederick J.	EM-ATT	Pfc		72 SCS
Travis, Laird	P-505	2/Lt	Smicksburg, PA	
Trester, John R.	P-504	1/Lt	Shorewood, WI	
Tropea, Frank	EM-504	SSgt	Brooklyn, NY	Crew Chief
Tucker, Harry St. G.	GO-HQ	Major	Lexington, KY	Intel. Officer
Turner, Edgar B., Jr.	EM-ATT	T/5	Wichita Falls, TX	HQ Sec., 1786 OSM
Turner, Kermit C.	EM-ATT	T/4	Indianapolis, IN	Auto Sec., 1786 OSM
Tyner, Leon, Jr.	EM-ATT	Pfc		72 SCS

U

Name	Unit	Rank	Location	Assignment
Ulrich, Charles N.	EM-504			
Upchurch, William L.	EM-ATT	Pvt		989 MP Co.

V

Name	Unit	Rank	Location	Assignment
Vacca, Louis N.	GO-ATT	Capt		328 SV Gp.
Valetich, John N.	EM-503	Sgt	Los Angeles, CA	

ROSTER OF GROUP PERSONNEL

Name	Code	Rank	Location	Assignment
Van Auken, Lansing T.	EM-505	Sgt	Greene, NY	
Van Cleave, Ely N.	P-504	1/Lt	Lincoln, NE	
VandeerBosch, Joseph R.	EM-ATT	Pfc		464 SV Sq.
Vasilo, Corrado F.	EM-ATT	Pfc		989 MP Co.
Vaughan, William T.	EM-505	SSgt	Antrim, NH	NCOIC Supply
Veit, Raymond G.	EM-ATT	Cpl	Chicago, IL	Ar. Sec., 1786 OSM
Verna, Dominick J.	EM-505	Sgt	Philadelphia, PA	
Vernon, Robert D.	EM-505	Pfc	Niles, MI	
Vidrino, Nema L.	EM-ATT	Pfc		328 SV Gp.
Vienneau, Doran J. F.	EM-ATT	Pvt	Lyons Park, NY	Auto Sec., 1786 OSM
Vincent, Lacy S.	EM-ATT	T/5	Onley, VA	HQ Sec., 1786 OSM

W

Name	Code	Rank	Location	Assignment
Wager, Evergard L.	P-505	1/Lt	Battle Creek, MI	
Wagner, William R.	EM-ATT	Pfc		72 SCS
Wait, William	EM-505	Cpl	Tech. Supply	
Walbourn, James	EM-504		Sodus, NY	
Walker, George	EM-ATT	Sgt	Observer (WEA),	18 WX Sq.
Wall, Clyde F.	EM-ATT	Cpl		72 SCS
Walley, W. W.	GO-HQ	1/Lt	Richton, MI	Med. Admin. Officer
Walsh, Robert S.	GO-504		Rochester, NY	Armament Officer
Walsh, William J.	EM-ATT	Cpl		72 SCS
Ward, Harold J.	EM-ATT	Pvt	Grand Rapids, OH	Sup Sec.,1786 OSM
Ward, Herbert C.	EM-505	Sgt	Kenosha, WI	Asst. Crew Chief
Wark, Raymond D.	P-505	2/Lt	Camden, NJ	
Warren, Don W.	P-503	1/Lt	Saginaw, MI	
Warren, William R.	EM-503	Sgt	Groten, MA	
Wasser, John J.	EM-503	Cpl	Northglenn, CO	Communications
Waters, Frank T.	P-504	1/Lt	Orange, MA	
Watson, Clyde	EM-ATT	TSgt	Bessemer, AL	Mun Chief, 1786 OSM
Watt, Marvel	EM-504			
Waymire, Harvey R.	P-504	1/Lt	Denver, CO	
Weber, Clyde E.	EM-503	MSgt	Madison, IN	Asst. Line Chief
Webster, George W., Jr.	EM-505	TSgt	Frankfort, KY	
Wehrhan, Harold A.	EM-HQ	TSgt	Mesa, AZ	Intelligence
Weigelk, Charles F.	EM-ATT	Sgt		989 MP Co.
Weinhold, Garry H.	EM-504		Santa Rosa, CA	Armorer
Weirich, Clayton S.	EM-ATT	T/5		989 MP Co.
Welch, Roger	P-504	Capt	Jacksonville, FL	
Welcomer, David C.	EM-503	Sgt	York, PA	
Weller, Richard E.	P-504	Capt	Dayton, OH	
Wells, Arlen W.	P-504	Capt	Corvallis, OR	
Wells, James L., Jr	EM-ATT		Gary, WV	Comm. Ctr Chief, 72 SCS
Wells, John M.	EM-505	T/5	Los Angeles, CA	Auto Sec., 1786 OSM
Wells, John M.	EM-ATT	T/5		989 MP Co.
Wells, Richard G.	P-503	F/O	Williamstown, MI	
West, Rodney C.	P-503	1/Lt	Ponifret, VT	
Westenberger, John H.	EM-HQ			
Weyand, Harry P.	EM-504			
Whatley, Henry	EM-ATT	Pfc		328 SV Gp.
Whatley, James E.	EM-503	Sgt	Mocksville, NC	
Wherry, Wesley J.	EM-ATT	Cpl		328 SV Gp.
Whisman, Norman R.	EM-503	Sgt	Indianapolis, IN	Duty NCO
White, Thomas B.	EM-505	Cpl	Taunton, MA	Armorer
Whitelaw, Richard S.	P-503	Capt	Fillmore, CA	
Whiting, Richard F.	EM-505	Sgt	Vail, IA	Parachute Rigger
Whitney, Olen	EM-505	Pfc	Acworth, GA	
Whitten, William T.	GO-ATT	2/Lt	N. Little Rock, AR	Ammo Sec., 1786 OSM
Wiggins, Russel L.	EM-503	Pfc	Memphis, TN	
Wight, Carroll H.	P-HQ	Major	Temple, TX	Operations
Wilcox, Richard H.	P-504	1/Lt	Skaneateles, NY	
Wilcox, Russell W.	P-505	2/Lt	E. Greenwich, RI	
Willard, Kenneth R.	EM-504	Sgt	Fairport, NY	Armorer
Willey, Carrol	EM-503	SSgt	Cherryfield, ME	
Williams, James E.	EM-505	TSgt	Dudley, NC	
Williams, Mary K.	Civ-ATT		Arlington, VA	Red Cross Director
Wilson, John P.	P-503	Capt	Hurdle Hills, NC	
Wilson, Omar S.	EM-505	TSgt	St. Louis, MO	
Winkelbauer, Donald	EM-HQ		Carroll, NE	
Winkelman, Myer R.	P-504	2/Lt	Baird, TX	
Winklemann, Charles A.	EM-ATT	Cpl		328 SV Gp.
Wincek, Joseph P.	EM-ATT	Pfc		328 SV Gp
Winston, Isaac M.	EM-505	Pfc	Linden, NJ	
Winter, Herbert J.	GO-ATT	1/Lt	Houston, TX	Ph Lab Off., 328 SVGp.
Wirt, Clayborne H.	EM-503	Cpl	Christiansburg, VA	
Wiseman, David	GO-503	1/Lt		Ordnance
Withers, John C.	P-505	1/Lt	Washington, D.C.	
Wojtanowski, Joseph J.	EM-ATT	Pfc		1178 QM Co.
Wolfe, Arthur E.	EM-AT			989 MP Co.
Wolfe, James P.	EM-ATT	Pvt		Ammo Sec., 1786 OSM
Wolfe, John F., Jr.	EM-ATT	Sgt	Baltimore, MD	Ammo Sec., 1786 OSM
Wolfe, Ralph P.	EM-ATT	SSgt		328 SV Gp.
Wolff, William H., Jr.	EM-503	Cpl	Hamilton, OH	
Wolfort, Joseph	P-503	1/Lt	St. Louis, M	
Wood, Jeanne M.	Civ-ATT		Newark, OH	Asst. Red Cross Dir.
Wood, Robert T.	P-504	Capt	Raymond, Canada	
Woodworth, Wilson A.	EM-ATT	T/5		2120 Eng. F/F
Woolery, James C.	P-505	1/Lt	Bloomington, IN	
Woolf, Billy R.	EM-HQ			
Workman, William J.	EM-ATT	Cpl		72 SCS
Worley, Grover H.	EM-503	SSgt	Oklahoma City, OK	
Wreck, John F.	GO-503	1/Lt		Ordnance
Wright, Ellis E., Jr.	P-HQ	Capt		
Wright, Lyle M.	P-503	1/Lt	Buffalo, NY	
Wyatt, Valdee	P-503	Capt	Vernon, TX	
Wyer, Albert L.	P-503	1/Lt	Toledo, OH	

Y

Name	Code	Rank	Location	Assignment
Yaggie, Harold A.	EM-HQ			
Yeselski, Joseph G.	EM-ATT	T/5	Hazelton, PA	Ammo Sec., 1786 OSM
Yosrck, Stanley W.	EM-ATT	Pfc		989 MP Co.
Young, Allen D.	P-505	1/Lt	Salt Lake City, UT	
Young, Jack S.	EM-505		Mt. Vernon, WA	Armorer
Youngbauser, John	EM-505	Cpl	New York, NY	Refueling
Yousko, John	EM-505			

Z

Name	Code	Rank	Location	Assignment
Zacchilli, Alfred	EM-504	Cpl	Milford, MA	Armorer
Zambardo, Primo T.	EM-503	Cpl	Fairfield, CT	Homing Station Oper.
Zane, Arthur C.	EM-503	Sgt	Chemical Warfare	
Zavoda, George	EM-504		Wh Hs, Station, NJ	Crew Chief
Zedak, Leroy F.	EM-503	Sgt	Palo Alto, CA	
Zeine, Donald A.	P-504	1/Lt	Crestone, CO	
Zelno, Joseph S.	EM-ATT	T/5	Eynon, PA	Ammo Sec., 1786 OSM
Zenchak, Stephen	EM-503	Cpl	Hazelton, PA	
Zido, Charles	EM-503			
Ziegler, Harry D.	P-505	1/Lt	Norristown, PA	
Zook, Lloyd A.	EM-ATT	Cpl		328 SV Gp.
Zucker, Milton J.	EM-ATT	Pfc		72 SCS
Zyla, Stanley M.	EM-503	Cpl	Detroit, MI	

Notes:

On 15 April 1945, personnel of units listed below, with the exception of those in the 1786 Ordnance and the 18th Weather SQ (Det), were assigned to the 437th Air Service Group. The 18th WX SQ (Det) was assigned for administrative purposes to the 505th Fighter Squadron.

1178 Quartermaster Company
1786 Ordnance Supply & Maintenance Company (AVN)
HQ and HQ SQ 328 Service Group
2120 Engineer F/F Platoon
72 Station Complement Squadron
Detachment "A" 989th M.P. Company (AVN)
464th Service Squadron, 331 Service Group
863rd Air Engineering Squadron (Mobile Unit #1)
18th Weather Squadron Detachment
437th Air Service Group

339th Fighter Group

Ground Articles

Rememberances By Men Of The 339th Fighter Group Headquarters

Fowlmere Revisited

by G. P. Harry

In June of 1967 Claire and I were on a jaunt to Europe and England. During the visit to England, we visited the old base at Fowlmere. Leaving London on what appeared to be the same train, we arrived in Royston where I think the same station master met us. He said there were still some buildings left at the airfield, but it would probably be a shock to us.

The station master called a young taxi driver who was about 21 years old. The young man could offer very little in the way of information except what he'd heard from his parents, but he did know the location of the airfield. Driving down the same road I had taken many times, we stopped and the driver said, "There it is." All we could see were the remains of the old hanger and some of the Quonset Huts. We went over to the hanger (which was filled with bales of hay) and looked around carefully for anything connected to the 339th. Nothing!

We later had tea with the owners of the property, and they brought us up to date concerning the airfield. There was a great shortage of housing after the war, and nearly all the buildings were utilized as homes for returning veterans. After that, the land returned to farming.

On a dreary, freezing Christmas Day in 1944, I took some toys down to the Fowlmere church. The toys had been sent to me by a girl in New York to give to the children. As I gave them to the reverend, he said, "You will never know what this means to the children." He asked me to sign the church register which I did. In this June of 1967, we revisited the church and turned back a few pages on the same register. There it was - my name which I'd written twenty-three years earlier.

On the way back to the rail station we stopped for one final look at the old airfield. While standing there trying to visualize the layout of the field, I heard a vaguely familiar sound, looked up and saw a Hurricane, a Me-109 and a Ju-88. I turned to the young driver and said, "I could swear I see three old World War Two planes up there."

He glanced up and said, "Oh, yes, they're up there. The Battle of Britain movie is being made at Duxford."

They say time and tide waits for no man. I don't believe that anymore...not after that day in June 1967.

MEMOIRS

by H. J. Meyer

When we arrived in Fowlmere, England, we were assigned quarters. While I was gone, someone moved into my room, and on my return, I looked at the uniform on the rack and noticed a cross on the jacket lapel. My reaction was, "Cripes! I'll be known as the Chaplain's assistant." Well, to be quite honest, this would really not be a title I'd enjoy or be worthy of. My new roommate was Chaplain Henry Opperman. Most Americans learn quickly how to adapt, so I adapted to living with a chaplain.

I was soon to realize that there were benefits associated with having a chaplain as a roommate. The Chaplain definitely had an *IN* with the Mess Sergeant. On those cold winter nights he was able to get bread and cheese which we'd toast over our pot belly stoves. On occasions when we had guests - which was every time they smelled the melted cheese - we'd ask the Chaplain if he had an appropriate drink to go along with the food. It was a ritual we went through many times. Chaplain Opperman would say he didn't have any beverages, but after much pressuring, he'd come up with a bottle of wine. Before getting to drink the wine, we were advised that this was not sacramental wine. It would only become sacramental when the wine was blessed during the religious service. I am happy to say that the wine that was used for religious purposes was twice blessed: once because we didn't get to drink it, and second, it was finally used in a religious service. I hope the good Lord agrees. The Chaplain and I got along so well that when a private room was made available to him, he declined to leave our quarters.

After the war in Europe ended they had to keep us busy somehow. Since we were Army Air Corp, we reverted to Army ways - hikes and bivouacs. We were scheduled to go on a 14-mile hike with *full* pack. Several of us filled our packs with rolled-up newspaper to show bulk, but they were almost weightless. Surprisingly the Chaplain did the same with his pack. We were in formation ready for the hike when suddenly the orders were changed. We were now going to bivouac overnight and were therefore to "prepare for a field inspection." A few of us broke ranks and made a scramble for our field equipment. Chaplain Opperman stayed in ranks. Why, I'll never know. Didn't he know what would happen when he displayed his rolled-up newspaper as field equipment, or was he overcome by religious belief and training and ready to face the consequences, forever repentant?

After several months of rooming together the Chaplain pulled one on me. He started by telling me how he prepared his Sunday sermons a week in advance. On Monday he would jot his thoughts down, on Tuesday he would assemble his sermon, on Wednesday he would read the sermon to his wife and so on. He talked *me* into listening to his sermon on Wednesday. I must say he really had to persuade me, and besides, there was still that wine deal I was thinking about. Well, would you believe? That's right! I was so impressed with the preview of his sermons and thought they were so good that I lifted some of his ideas and sent them to my wife and family via "V" mail.

Before sharing some of my other stories of the war years, let me say I hope Chaplain Opperman recalls the above incidents as I do and can get a laugh out of these memories, because this is the way I remember my good friend and roommate at Fowlmere, England.

At Fowlmere I was asked by the Red Cross gals if I would take charge of the convoy of trucks we used to transport the girls from Cambridge to the enlisted men's Saturday night dance. At first I hesitated, then agreed. What a blast! Every base in our vicinity must have had a Saturday night dance. All the outfits would park their trucks in the square at Cambridge, and the guys would try to talk the girls into coming to *their* base dance. Competition was rough. The girls would promenade around the square, checking the amenities provided at the various bases, conditions of our 2 1/2 ton trucks, size of the orchestra, food provided (hot dogs, ice cream, chocolate cake were sure winners), etc. One outfit even made stairs for the girls to board the tail-end of the trucks. The big sales pitch our guys used was that after the dance we wouldn't just drop them off at the square but would take them to their front doors. This was great for the girls, but tough on the truck drivers and our MPs. Some of our "Romeos" would try to stow away on the trucks (sometimes with the girl's help) that were taking the girls home. One night we found a guy hidden on the truck's canvas roof. Late one dance night we had one girl left in the back of the truck I was in because we couldn't find her house. We brought her up in the truck cab and finally found her street, but she didn't want us to take her to the door of her house. She said, "I don't want you and this noisy truck wakin' up my bybies." That convoy duty was always good for laughs, and I referred to it as the "Passion Run."

I believe the 339th was the first group to be equipped with "G" suits. The pilots wore this suit to give them an advantage in combat. The suit was designed to reduce grayout and blackout and to aide in outmaneuvering enemy aircraft. The suit had rubber bladders on the calves and thighs of the pilot's legs and another bladder across the pilot's stomach.

Air pressure from the exhaust port of the engines vacuum pump was controlled by a check valve that allowed air pressure to inflate the suit bladders, thereby restricting the draining of blood from the pilot's brain when the aircraft was exposed to high "G" loads. We didn't have accelerometers

Ground Articles

installed in the aircraft to indicate what stresses were being imposed on the aircraft during flight maneuvers - as if a pilot would be looking at an accelerometer during aerial combat - so "G" load indicators were mounted in the wheel well of the P-51s as close to the center of gravity (CG) of the aircraft as possible. These were crude indicators consisting of a simple weighted beam with a needle at one end that scratched the surface of a piece of smoked glass. This and information from the pilot gave us an indication of abnormally high loads that were imposed on the aircraft. A more positive indication of excessive stress on the aircraft was popped rivets at the wing root and/or tail section as well as sheet metal buckling. We were replacing so many wings and tail sections that General Doolittle came to our base to personally investigate the problem.

I never did read or hear of a report on the contribution of "G" suits to the success of the war, but I believe they were helpful to the pilots by giving them greater maneuver capabilities when engaged in aerial combat.

The K-14 gun sight was a welcome piece of equipment. To help train the pilots, a K-14 sight was mounted on a Link Trainer while enemy aircraft silhouette models were hung around the room for aiming purposes. The pilot would aim the sight (Link Trainer hood open) on the models while flying the Link. This trainer was a very early flight simulator.

Just prior to the end of hostilities with Germany, we were given a higher octane aircraft fuel (pep fuel) for the P-51s. It was called 140-grade fuel and was for "War Emergency" conditions. It allowed the engines to be operated up to 72" Hg maximum manifold pressure for up to five minutes. To determine if an engine had been run at that condition - if a pilot didn't report it - a piece of .020 brass safety wire was installed across a predetermined position on the throttle quadrant. If the safety wire was broken during flight, we were alerted that the engine had been run above 65" Hg, and a detailed engine inspection was required. In some cases the inspection revealed conditions that required engine replacement. The 140-grade fuel helped, but it also caused engine and related problems. Higher octane fuel was attainable through the addition of lead which would cause spark plug fouling if engines were run at low idle speeds. Engines run at high idling speed caused excessive brake operations during taxiing with greater brake failure and replacement. Improper operations of engines caused valve problems and engine malfunctions.

We were always concerned with engine overheating due to coolant problems. The 1650 Rolls Royce Merlin engine was dependent on a coolant radiator mounted under the fuselage at the mid-wing section. Radiator temperature was controlled by a temperature sensor which would activate an electric motor used to adjust the setting of a coolant radiator door. The electric motor would malfunction, especially at high altitude, and if failure occurred with the door closed, engine overheating and subsequent failure would result. If overheating started, the pilot was unable to do much about it. We did, however, rig a manual control system for radiator door operations. It consisted of a disconnect of the electric motor attachment to the door and a mechanically pre-loaded spring that would force the coolant radiator door fully open. We were never able to solve this problem with a manufacturer's change so we continued to work around it. Pilots would alert each other of faulty radiator door operations during flight when possible, but the problem was never properly corrected.

After the war ended in Europe we modified two 108-gallon fuel drop tanks to carry cargo. The cargo? Wine and champagne from France! The fuel tanks were lined with shock proof material (?) and compartmentalized for various sizes of bottles. It wasn't pretty - looked like a funeral casket lining - but it was effective. When the P-51 carrying this cargo was returning to the base, we all watched the landing with much concern and trepidation. Needless to say we never tried to get this modification approved by 8th Air Force Headquarters.

With the advent of jet fighters being used by the Luftwaffe, we tried to think of ways to increase P-51 performance capabilities. One idea we worked on was the mounting of JATO (Jet Assisted Take Off) rockets on the bomb racks. This would provide a boost in acceleration that would be helpful. Don't know whether we were smart enough *not* to try this or simply not able to work out the many problems with JATO that had to be considered.

In addition to the P-51, the 339th had another aircraft, the Norden Norseman, which was used as a small transport plane. My good friend, Bob Ammon, and I were flying the Norseman to France to pick up five or six of our pilots who were forced to make emergency landings over there. We landed in France and loaded up the pilots and their flight equipment. Bob was in the cockpit's left seat, and I was in the right seat. We took off with some nervous guys as passengers. Soon after leveling off on a course to Fowlmere I noticed our cylinder head temperature rise quite rapidly.

We were now over the Channel. Bob lowered the nose, but the cylinder head temperature was pegged on the high side. We were closer to England than France so Bob decided to try for a landing in England. We called into an American base near the British coast - Manston, I believe - and greased the Norseman in. Things were getting hot now - flames and smoke pouring out from under the engine cowling. Bob cut the landing real short and almost ground looped in front of some emergency vehicles. I never saw a bunch of guys evacuate a plane so fast. The fire truck quickly smothered the fire.

We checked the plane out after things cooled down and found that the short exhaust stack from #1 cylinder to the exhaust collector ring had broken away, and exhaust gas was blasting directly on the cylinder temperature thermocouple leads. The exhaust flame was already hitting the carburetor, and it wouldn't have been very long before the carburetor assembly would have been burned away. This was the only time when flying with Bob that he didn't hand the aircraft controls over to me right after takeoff. I did a lot of flying with Bob Ammon and will always remember him as a great guy, a great pilot and a very good friend.

Weather Support for the 339th Fighter Group

by James P. Norwood

A staff weather concept was used in the 8th Air Force. Each combat unit had a staff weather officer assigned directly to the unit, and his job was to insure that the meteorological requirements of the unit were met. A base weather station (and weather forecast centers at higher levels) was provided to develop the meteorological products (reports, forecasts, etc.) needed by the Staff Weather Officer. These facilities were provided by the 18th Weather Squadron.

An Air Force Forecast Center was located with the 8th Air Force. This center prepared the forecasts for all 8th Air Force missions. These forecasts were distributed (in the detail needed) down to base level and were used by the Staff Weather Officers to prepare their mission briefings. For bomber briefings, no deviation from these forecasts was permitted except for home base conditions. It was mandatory that all units operate from the same data base, otherwise havoc would have reigned.

Staff Weather Officers for fighter groups were permitted much more leeway even when fighters had escort missions. We could make deviations in the forecasts for that part of the route from home base to rendezvous and also for routes and activities after break of escort. We also had great latitude when the fighters were assigned target of opportunity missions.

A high part of our duty was debriefing returning crews to determine how good our forecasts were and to gather data for later missions. I tried to speak with every pilot who returned from a mission. Of course some were more weather conscious and observed better than others, but without exception, I received full cooperation from all of our pilots.

I remember many missions, but the one that sticks most in my mind was one we didn't go on. We and several other groups were authorized to go on target of opportunity missions in the winter of 1944/'45. I recommended we not go because I'd determined that England would be fogged in by return and we would have to land in France. I further forecasted that France would fog in that night, and we wouldn't get home. We didn't go, and my forecasts were accurate. As a result we were available for escort missions from England for the next few days while the groups that went remained stuck in France.

GROUND ARTICLES

Flight Line Chaplain

by H. W. Opperman

As Chaplain of the 339th Fighter Group from its activation to the end of hostilities, I still have fond and happy memories of my associations with the men of the Group. There were the many talks we had together, individually and as groups; the Sunday services on the lines and in the open for each squadron plus the evening services in the Congregational Church - that made five a Sunday. Add to that the "briefing prayers" before each mission, the problems and concerns for which I tried to help them find solutions, hospital visits, flight line visits, etc. I vividly recall a couple of pilots giving me a real dressing down because I was absent for the "briefing prayers" one morning. They told me their mission had not gone well that day because of my absence (necessary, I assure you). We were a very close knit outfit. Yes, the men of the 339th were, still are and always will be a very important part of my life.

The Motor Pool

by S. A. "Jimmy" Pappas

I worked in the motor pool, and most of my duty was at night when I wasn't doing K.P. or guard duty. I was asleep at the pool when I was awakened and told to go to the station to pick up the new C.O. I argued that someone else should go because back in Nashville, Tennessee, I'd had to drive the C.O. who must've been a World War I veteran...and was he strict. That's why I wanted somebody else to go, but there wasn't anyone else. I went to the station and found the 339th C.O. and was quite surprised at how young he was. When I got out to open the door after getting him to his quarters, he said for me to pick him up at 8 o'clock, and suddenly I was the Colonel's driver. A couple of days later I learned that the Colonel had had a driver in the States, so I looked this fellow up and told *him* to drive the Colonel, but he said, "No way!" Well, after putting two and two together, I said okay. As it turned out, that was a good decision. About a week later my sergeant had me on guard duty and K.P. when Colonel Henry had to go to Ajax down near London. I told the Colonel that I couldn't drive him because of these duties. He asked for the sergeant's name and said he'd clear all this up...and he did.

Since I was just a corporal in the service group, I kept asking to be transferred to 339th Headquarters. It took a while, but the Colonel came through for me. I'd pick him up in the mornings to take him to his plane and pick him up when he came in. Oh, another item is everyone had their plane named, and he asked Arnie and me what was a good name. We figured him being from San Antonio, why didn't he name his plane for his hometown, and that's how the plane got its name.

GROUND ARTICLES

Medical Memories

by Dr. Emil A. Stricker

After we had been at Fowlmere a few months, morale on the base was going down; the men were grumpy, sluggish, and not their usual selves. On checking with other group flight surgeons, we found they'd had the same problem until they acquired bicycles to give the men some exercise. Soon our 339th men also had bicycles and were riding all over the back roads - even to Cambridge, nine miles away. Morale improved immediately.

It improved even more when Major Bain "Shorty" Fulton came to our base. He was a pre-war friend of General Jimmy Doolittle. He said if we medics could help with supplies, he could get an ice cream maker for our base. We had hunted all over London with no luck.

One phone call from Fulton to Doolittle, however, and an ice cream freezer was on the next bomber coming over from the U.S. We had some trouble finding enough gelatin, sugar and cream, but we had ice cream twice a week. Morale continued to go up.

With midwinter ice and snow on the roads, bicycling became unsafe, but our men still needed exercise. There was a vacant gas decontamination building next to our dispensary, so I called a meeting of our medical department and, with Major Fulton, discussed making an exercise area in the 40' by 60' building. Ideas started flying high! How about a steam room?...and ultra violet lights??...*AND* a massage parlor??!

What about a furnace? We found one in London. How about fuel? We "liberated" enough paraffin bomb rings from the bomb depots to last the duration. A big thermometer for the steam room? No problem!

When the unit was finished, it could handle about ten men at a time. The routine was for the men to exercise for about fifteen minutes; then go into the "turkish bath" for ten minutes; next, a shower, then time under ultra violet light followed by a massage from our medical personnel. As the men left, there was a basket for "tips" to pay for soap and towels. We soon had plenty of money for expenses and extras. This was the 339th Medical Department's "Hall of Fame." It was the only one of its kind in the E.T.O. and was used *and envied* by pilots and other officers from near-by bases as well.

Another unique project in which the 339th Medical Dept. participated was testing the dosage of penicillin. We received a box of vials of penicillin with the instruction that optimum dose - and interval between doses - be established. The only information we received was that in test tube the drug would kill streptococcus and probably gonoccus. We were to treat *all* infections with the penicillin and report results. We had a page of symptoms to check every day; even the dentist had to check patients' teeth and gums daily.

Due to the urgency of the project, we had only three weeks for completion. We sent in our report that stated 3,000 units every three hours was the effective dose and interval and that the drug was helpful in treating strep throat, gonorrhea, pneumonia, and lymphangitis. The next week all the Air Force units had penicillin with instructions for use as we had suggested. It was a rough treatment. The penicillin at that time was a thick brown liquid; we had to use a size-20 needle, and give it deep in the muscle.

The following month, by coincidence, I was invited to attend a Masonic meeting and banquet in London. At this dinner I met Dr. Fleming, the man who had discovered penicillin. When I congratulated him on this achievement, he was very modest. He said, yes, we discovered it in test tube, but it took you Yanks to develop it into a useful therapeutic medicine.

Chronology

by James L. Wells

During the latter part of January 1944, the 72nd Station Complement Squadron was transferred to Station F-378, Fowlmere, England, in preparation for the arrival of the 339th Fighter Group from the States. The project of readying the base was not an easy task. Prior occupants had left the area in a poor condition. It was necessary to clean, scrub, etc., mess halls, barracks, and clear outside areas of an accumulation of trash and various other tasks.

In setting up for the arrival of the Group, personnel were assigned duties consistent with their MOS. Such duties included mess, communications, motor pool, fire station, airfield control, "Q" site, clerical, etc. I personally was assigned to the Base Message Center-Teletype under a Sergeant Murphy. Shortly after arriving at Fowlmere, Murphy was on TD at the base when the 72nd arrived. Upon the arrival of the 339th Group in 1944, Sergeant Murphy was transferred back to his organization. On May 3, 1944, I was placed on SD with Headquarters 339th Fighter Group and put in charge of the Message Center. I continued in that capacity under 1st Lt Albert Laderborg for the duration. Following the arrival of the 339th Group under Lieutenant Colonel John B. Henry and the base becoming operational, changes were made in the organizational make-up. The 72nd Station Complement Squadron's original commanding officer, Captain Mercer Hicks, was replaced by Captain Steven Parks. The original 1st Sergeant Harden Stebbins was replaced by 1st

Sergeant James Johnson.

Eventually the various squadrons on base were combined into a single unit and became Headquarters and Base Service Group. Captain Steven C. Parks was made commanding officer. Other officer assignments remained essentially the same.

Following the surrender of Germany in May 1945, orientation classes were conducted for base personnel. The purpose thereof was to prepare troops for the eventual return to civilian life. Many possible aspects of the future were related by instructors. Lectures were given by some Allied representatives as to what future course their respective country would follow after the war. In June 1945 our Group received a "Readiness" order to prepare for return to the States. Much elation was in order. "Showdown" inspections were made as the men made preparations, anxious to go home, albeit for only thirty days. Following this, plans were for us to be retrained and shipped to the Pacific Theater of Operations.

Late in July 1945, movement orders were received, and we were transported by train to Greenock, Scotland, where the *Queen Mary* was anchored and being loaded for return to the United States. Our group was one of the last to load. We then departed for the return journey home on July 28, 1945.

The trip home, blessed with beautiful summer weather, was uneventful compared to the trip over in 1943. To me, sleeping on the floor of the Promenade Deck was a pleasure on this trip. Again, as on the trip over in '43, I elected to sleep on the deck rather than change with a partner who slept in the Hold Room 28B.

Arriving in New York Harbor at 3:00 a.m. on August 2, 1945, was a thrill to everyone of the 15,000 service personnel on board. Salutes, whistles, and greetings from many boats in the harbor were really something. The greatest sight of all, however, was that great Lady of the Harbor - the Statue of Liberty - that symbol of freedom.

On docking at Pier 90, from whence we had departed, we were greeted by hundreds of people, one of which was the Mayor of New York City, Fiorello LaGuardia. We were treated to milk and doughnuts. The milk was fresh and the first I'd had in approximately two years.

After debarkation, we were transported to Camp Kilmer, New Jersey, in preparation for transfer to an installation nearest home where leave papers would be given. It was good to be on American soil again. Here we were served steak dinners, with German POWs the waiters. We were offered entertainment, allowed to make calls, etc. In a couple of days, I was transported to Fort Meade, Maryland, where I received leave papers for the 30-day period. Meantime, during my leave, the atom bomb was dropped on Hiroshima, then on Nagasaki. The Japanese then surrendered, unconditionally.

In the interim, with peace declared, conditions changed. The plan to retrain was scuttled, and those with enough points to be eligible for release were discharged. I received my Honorable Discharge on September 25, 1945. Service time was three years, one month and four days.

GROUND ARTICLES

My wartime experiences will never be forgotten. Many of those with whom I served have passed on. One cannot forget the lasting friendship with those whom I served. I am proud to have been able to contribute a small part in the conflict.

One could never forget also the memories of air raids, bombings, and the resulting destruction. The air raid alerts, sirens, searchlights plying the skies with an entire blackout in effect gave one an eerie feeling. I can recall one incident in particular during an air raid involving our "Q" site crew. Each night this unit was stationed in an area quite a few miles from Fowlmere Base. Its function was to simulate an emergency operation during a raid and to decoy the planes away from the actual base locale. On this particular night the German planes "bought" the operation and bombs hit the site area. Sergeant Al Campos reported the next day that the "outhouse" was the only casualty - totally destroyed.

Another incident occurred near the end of the hostilities. Normally "Air Raid Red" messages were given at night. On this occasion a "Red" alert was transmitted in broad daylight. This involved a German V-1 (buzz bomb). It passed directly over the base runway and exploded in a field where British farmers were storing hay. There were no injuries. The farmers took cover behind a large hay stack, protecting them from fragments generated by the explosion.

The tragic effect of air raids on the cities, installations, etc., of Great Britain cannot be described. The loss of lives, destruction of homes and deaths were tragic. Many, many children were orphaned. I remember well on Christmas 1944 when any service person so desiring could "adopt" a child for the day from a local orphanage and take them to Christmas dinner. I, along with many others, did this, and I still remember it with both pleasure and sadness.

Let the chips fall where they may. General Sherman, during the Civil War, stated, "War is hell." It remains true to this day.

Link Trainer

by Clem Ferraro

Two Link Trainers were installed at Fowlmere Air Base in England. Major Bain E. Fulton was in charge with four enlisted men from the base serving as volunteer Link operators. Sergeant Pourchot, 83rd Fighter Squadron, spent about two months instructing us in operation and maintenance of the Link Trainers. We even had a vacuum cleaner to keep dust out of the room because of the instruments in the trainer.

Later on, a new type gun sight was installed on the Link Trainers. We installed a wire around the room with a model airplane that moved so pilots could get practice on using the gun sight. Wonder how many pilots remember practicing with the gun sight during Link Trainer sessions?

339th Headquarters

William C Clark

Carl T Goldenberg

Vernon B Hathorn

John B Henry

Robert D Long

John R Propst

Harold W Scruggs

Carol H Wright

Low pass over Fowlmere

Major Vernon B. Hathorn, Jr., HQ, pursues a Me-262 on 7 April 45.

339th Headquarters

The Group Commander, L/C William C. Clark, strafes a Ju-88 on 16 April 1945.

Fowlmere

Fowlmere flight line coffee, via Red Cross girl.

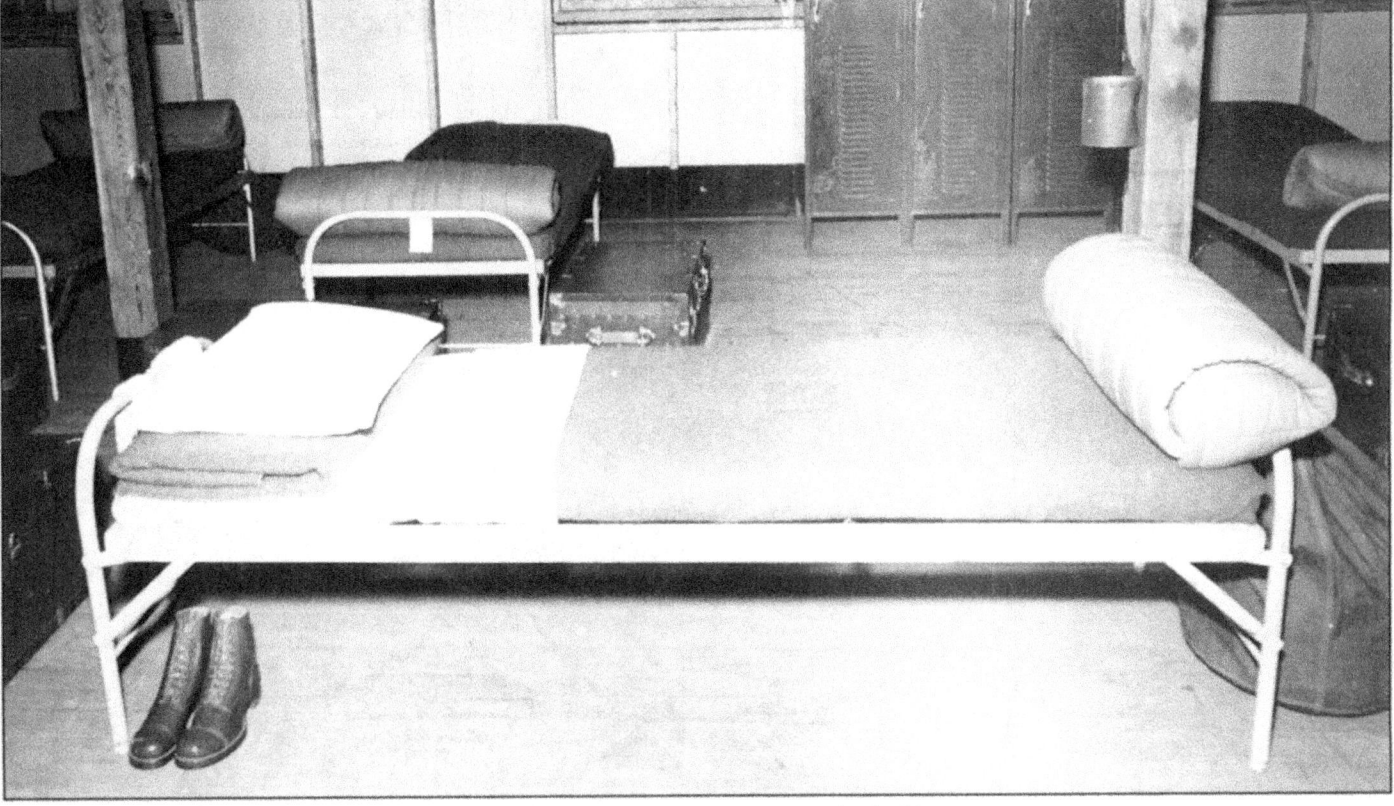

This is the way the room was supposed to look!

339th Headquarters

28 August 44

28 March 45

Lowering of U.S. Flag at Fowlmere September 45
when the base was turned back over to the British

Fowlmere blister hangar

General Partrid, Colonel Henry and General Woodbury

339th Fighter Group

Ground Articles

Rememberances By Men Of The 503rd Fighter Group

"Ode to John B."
(John B. Henry Roast)
by Bill Bryan

I was flying 40s down in Sarasota and having a whale of a time,
Then I got this set of orders that said, "Go to Caroline!"
There you'll fly a 39 –
P.S. Leave your girls behind!

Walterboro — Walterboro — the name didn't ring a bell.
I thought Sarasota was a suburb of Heaven!
And I knew I'd been exiled to Hell.

But I went—and I reported to the base H.Q.
To a Major named Tom Crowley.
I asked, "Are you the leader of this group?" and he said,
"Oh, no, it's a man known as Big John B."

He shoved me thru an imposing door;
A hulk of a Colonel I expected to see.
But there peering over the top of his desk
Was the man known as "Big" John B. (a major!)

We sat and talked for quite a spell
And I felt like a son at his father's knee.
It was plain right away – he was smart for his years,
This man known as "Big" John B.

He said, "We're going to California, my boy,
Where everything's super nice."
Well, you know what happened to his credibility
When our wheels touched down at Rice!

All day long we sifted sand, and at night,
Stared at the walls of our tent.
I told you earlier John was wise for his years,
'Cause off to Parker he went.

We turned those Cobras inside out,
Shooting at jeeps, trucks and tanks.
But the thrill was like kissing your sister,
"Cause the ammo John gave us was blanks!

Ground Articles

No doubt about it, flying was great, but the rest was a bore.
And Rice? It made our butts have a big pain.
Big John recognized the impending mutiny,
So he kicked those aching butts on a train.

It's a well known fact when you coop up a bunch of jocks
There'll be problems no one can foresee.
So they designated a troop train commander.
Yup! You guessed it – none other than Big John B.

Cigarettes and whiskey and wild, wild women
Became more than a song – so help me Hannah!
Big John was a blithering basket case
When we finally rolled into Savannah!

You might think John's problems were then over.
They weren't, and John deserves all your pity.
Before they could herd us onto a ship,
We were loose again, and in New York City.

All of us, yes, all of us should be deeply ashamed
For giving the boss such a hassle.
You just gotta know how relieved he was
When they locked us up on the *Sterling Castle*.

When we finally reached the shore of Jolly Old England,
The nearness of combat was sobering indeed.
Big John sat back smug and complacent,
Thinking his Jocks would become a new breed.

Well, that nice dream soon exploded
As soon as we mastered our "Stangs."
Back to partying in London, Cambridge and even Nissen Huts,
And John had a return case of the "Pangs."

I'm sure what saved John's sanity was that
His group was the best in the Eighth.
He knew all his charges were mavericks,
But not once did he lose faith!

All I've said up to now was in *jest*.
Believe me when I say,
As a commander *and* friend,
John B. was the *BEST*!

Soldier's Medal

by Frank Hilton

Thirty-eight years have clouded my memories, even those of one of the most important days in my life, but with the aid of some barely legible government records and a magnifying glass, I've attempted to reconstruct this story. It happened at Fowlmere where I was a P-51 crew chief.

On the morning of 23 March 1945 I was lumbering along the flight line, headed for my revetment. Most of my day's work was done, and I was thinking about all that had happened since I arrived in England two years before - the blitz and the terrible struggle of the British, the buddies we had lost as well as the ones who made it through the worst of the war unharmed. Most of all I was thinking of going home to my wife and a baby son I hadn't seen, for by now Nazi Germany was about to lose the war. It was almost as if I was in another world, my mind a clutter of thoughts, but soon my serenity was shattered as the war showed its ugly face again.

I heard an almost deafening roar - as if someone had left the throttle of his plane wide open. A split second later I saw a P-51 come streaking down the runway, then slide out of control. As it came to a stop, I noticed thick black smoke rolling out from under the cowling. Next, I expected to see the pilot scrambling away, for such accidents - while not to be taken for granted - were relatively commonplace. This time something went awry. Smoke became thicker and then flames appeared around the fuselage, yet the pilot failed to exit the plane. By now I could tell something was definitely wrong.

There wasn't much time before the entire aircraft would be engulfed in fire, and the pilot would then have no chance to escape. I could see a fire truck in the distance coming down the runway, but there was too little time to wait for the rescue crew. I ran over to the P-51 and forced the canopy open. I yelled at the pilot to see if he was hurt, but he didn't answer. Apparently he was in a state of shock, so I quickly unbuckled his safety harness and pulled him out of the cockpit. As I lowered him to the ground, the rescue squad arrived on the scene. With the aid of a fireman I managed to drag him about fifty feet away before the aircraft erupted into flames. An ambulance then took the pilot to the base hospital, and that was the last I saw of him. To this day, I don't know the man's name, though I would surely like to meet him again under less trying circumstances.

Immediately following the incident, my squadron executive officer, Major McKinley, requested I be given a citation. I was soon awarded the Soldier's Medal and an accompanying citation. The record states that the award was granted in recognition of an act of heroism, but I don't think of it that way. To me a genuine act of heroism occurs when someone is truly aware of the danger of the situation in which he has chosen to involve himself. In my case there was no time to think the situation over and weigh the options. I reacted out of instinct in a manner typical of most American servicemen.

Origin of the 503rd Squadron Insignia

by Bill "Geetus" Knott

It was while we were at the Laguna strip (near Yuma and Imperial Dam) that we 503rd pilots decided we needed a squadron insignia. It had to be something *not* serious, *not* smacking of heraldry, but something that was in vogue at the time - a Disney-type drawing.

Ideas failed to flow from this group of intrepid warriors, so it was decided that we needed help. Help could only come from a comic book and the nearest was at Yuma, a Training Command advanced flying field. With that first decision out of the way, about ten or twelve of us took off in our P-39s and flew to Yuma. The exact number of pilots/aircraft slips my memory - could've been the whole squadron. Anyway, after a short hop we arrived at Yuma and requested transporation to the PX. Let your imagination take over here and visualize the event. Dusty pilots climbing out of dusty aircraft and piling into staff cars and saying, "PX, please."

The PX was a very small building with a low ceiling and typical of all PXs - crowded. Our group of sweat-stained pilots contrasted dramatically with the "spit and polished" aviation cadets. They seemed to hold us in awe because as we moved to the magazine section of the store, the cadets and other "locals" moved away, allowing us ample room for passage. Wonder why? (General Henry would have been proud of the impression we made on those folks.)

We gathered at the magazine rack and began to "graze" through all the comic books with an occasional "How's this?" as someone found a cartoon character that might be suitable. After an interval of scrutinizing all the magazines available, the group decided on a Bugs Bunny book, but now began the painful process of finding the required dime to buy it. I don't know who was stuck with the purchase, but it was comic to see this group of pilots digging through their flight togs in search of a dime. The purchase made, it was back to the staff cars and a return trip to the flight line. A mass formation takeoff from the big concrete landing area ended our quick trip to Yuma.

Back "home" at our maneuver strip at Laguna, we now had completed the research for a likely subject for an insignia. The final concensus was Bugs Bunny riding on a carrot, and it was my job to draw it. You will recall that the pilots got in and out of the P-39 from the right side. The right side was "reserved" for aircraft names and any drawings that the pilot wanted to paint on his aircraft. The Bugs Bunny insignia was painted on the left door. I know I painted some unknown number of Bugs Bunny insignia on the left doors of the aircraft, but I don't have a photograph, only drawings in my sketch book.

Perhaps it needs no reiteration, but the insignia was the result of a whim, something that was "ours" and we could identify with. It was born in the desert, admittedly a steal of an existing cartoon figure, but cartoons were in vogue and we didn't have time for Disney to create one for us. The insignia was very UNOFFICIAL, and for all I knew at the time, had been developed, used and left in the desert on those P-39s.

GROUND ARTICLES

Unplugged

by Lloyd W. Mallow

While this story is rather insignificant when compared to POW stories, it is a remembrance that has stuck with me these forty-four years and points out the many stress stories ground personnel could tell.

It was in the summer of 1944 when the war was in full swing and not long after D-Day that our normal aircraft mission was assembled one morning in preparation for takeoff. The 503rd Squadron was positioned to join the 504th and 505th.

The telephone rang and one of my sergeants came running, wide-eyed and excited. He said, "They want you on the line quick! The Group Leader's radio's out and he's furious!"

As Section Chief, I normally didn't do the actual work on radios since there were many qualified mechanics to do whatever needed to be done. I said, "Well, get on your horse and get down there, quick."

He replied, "No, they said YOU and YOU, only. They want YOU!"

I jumped into a jeep and within one minute drove to the leader's plane. His prop, like all the rest, was spinning, waiting for takeoff. When I climbed up on the wing, I had no tools in my hands, no test equipment, not even a screw driver. The pilot said nothing, but the look on his face said it all. The thought raced through my mind that I was holding up the entire 339th Fighter Group, and that time was of the essence. Holding on with one hand against the spinning prop wash, I started doing what I'd been taught in radio school - always look for the simplest things first.

Was the equipment properly connected? The wires leading from his headset inside his helmet were on the opposite side from where I was positioned, but I began observing at that point and traced the wires and cords down to the floor of the cockpit. The wires seemed to be loose with an overflow on the floor. It was then that I saw a terminal at the end of a cord. I couldn't reach the terminal from my position, so I motioned for him to insert the terminal in the jack. He did it. From the look on his face, I could tell instantly he had radio.

There was never a word spoken. He half-waved to me as I jumped to the ground. I'm sure he was embarrassed when he realized he'd simply forgotten to plug in his radio. He seemed to have sunk a foot lower in the cockpit as he moved his plane out to the proper position for takeoff. In a few short minutes the entire Group was off on their mission.

I could well understand the mistake the Group Leader had made, considering all the stress and strain and responsibility he had to be experiencing. As I stood there that day, however, and watched him lead the Group off to battle, the height of his plane never reached the altitude of my own feelings.

Fowlmere

by Joseph A. Toth

It was at Fowlmere, England, where we experienced both enjoyment and sadness. We in the 503rd were very close. Our friendships were deep because of the war and the daily living together. When our pilots didn't return, we really felt it. And during the Battle of the Bulge when we were fogged in for nearly two weeks, both the ground crews and the pilots were extremely nervous because we couldn't help our troops. I don't think any of us will forget that period of our lives.

I remember when we made furniture - chairs, beds, lounges, etc. - from crates the auxiliary tanks were shipped in. We also rustled up a pot stove. These we put in the bomb shelters and knocked a hole through the roof for a chimney. We had all the comforts of home while we waited for our planes to come back. We even used the old oil from aircraft oil changes for a crude oil burner.

Other memories include afternoon Tea Dances in Cambridge, bike trips to pubs, Red Cross girls, Father McHugh (our Chaplain), the American Cemetery at Cambridge and finally the celebration of V.E. Day at Trafalgar Square in London.

503rd Fighter Squadron

Scruggs

Walter Thomas Carter

Abe Adler putting a radio in a P-51.

Scruggs

Donald W. Johnson

Turning in a reparable propeller.

Henderson

Jim Davidson, armament chief.

Hernandez

503rd Fighter Squadron

Bellman

Charlie Steffen - Rice, California

Pops Rastad

Capt. Jeff French

Capt. Poutre

William R Stevens

Albert L. Wyer

"Conroy"

Lt. Col. Dale Shafer

503rd Fighter Squadron

Vincent J. Spaziano, KIA date unknown

Bill Mangan

Steve Sabo, crew chief

Ed Gurtner & Charlie Steffen's dog Pruney

Capt. Stuhlman, squadron doctor

Bill Bryan

S/Sgt Arthur Lombardi

Luther Francis

Ralph Rostad on a boat trip on Thames.

503rd Fighter Squadron

Rostad repairing landing gear

Nate Ostrow, Dale Shafer and "Fripo" Butler

503rd F. B. Squadron - Rice, California, 1944

R & R in Belfast: Charlie Steffen, Dan Gavitt, Ray Bellman and Jim Kerr

Gilbert, Barr, Fogel and Red

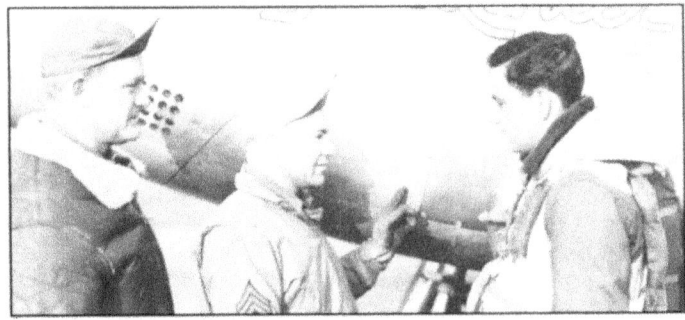
Spencer Shepard, Jim Davidson and unknown pilot

Mike Cotter, Dan Gavitt and Charlie Steffen

503rd Fighter Squadron

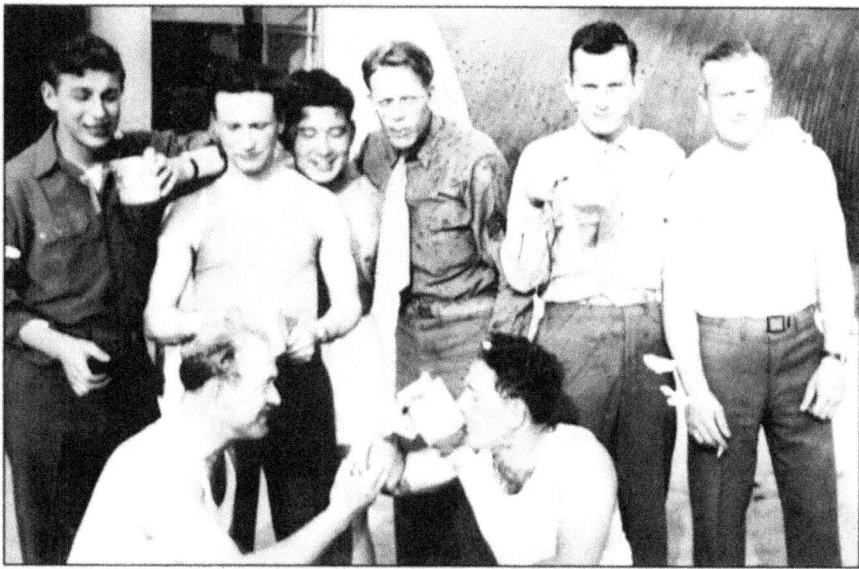

503 enlisted V-E Day party

Pilots of 503rd

Lt. Wyre, Lt. Pence and others at Billy Roses in New York City before going overseas

Al Coon and Ken Sylvester on their day off

Stuhlman and Bryan discussing new "G" suit

Spence Shepard and Ed Gurtner

503rd Fighter Squadron

Maj. Aitken, pilot, points out an interesting feature to his ground crew as they stand by the wing of their North American P-51 of the 339th Fighter Group at 8th AF station F-378, Fowlmere, September 1944

M/Sgt. Ed Gwiztner, M/Sgt. Spencer Shepard and T/Sgt. H. M. Hartman

Friday Night Jewish services at Fowlmere, England 1944

Lt. Scruggs debriefing 503rd

Lt. Steve J. Chetneky DFC presented by Gen. Woodbury

Sgt Lancia, Cpl Angionie and Cpl Taylor

M/Sgt Lloyd Mallow and 2nd Lt David Wiseman making radio adjustments

Jeff French, Bernie Allen and Phil Petit, February 1988

503rd Fighter Squadron

Anthony Hawkins, Lester Marsh, Alec Boychuck and Amos Scruggs

Frank Stilwell & unknown

Spence Shepard and Ed Gurtner in revetment

Lt/Col. Harold Scruggs and Charley Powell

Burns, Kerr, Bellman, Zenechak and Heingbugh

Mario Messina and Peter Caminiti

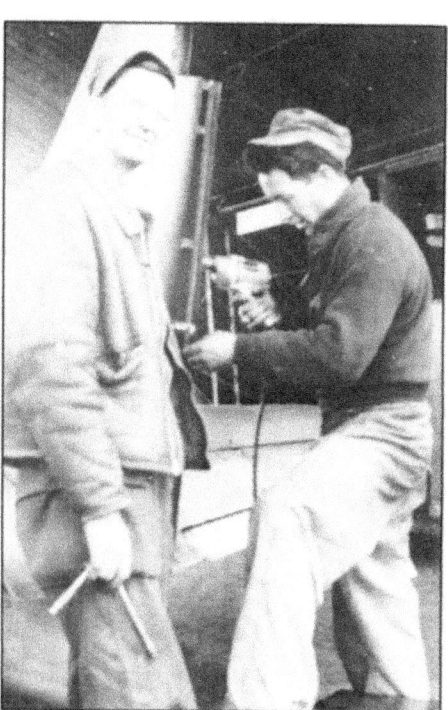

Conroy and Rostad doing a tail job.

503rd Fighter Squadron

Lt/Col Dale Shafer, Capt. Sal Carollo and Maj. William E. Bryan

Exec Off Harold McKinley, 1st Sgt Edgar Craiger and Com Off John Aitken

E. Gray, V. Hoffler, W. Head, G. Adkins, Unknown, Unknown, Unknown, Sanweff, W. Lowe, G. Kellog, Miller, Kissell and C. Brown

Jim Davidson, Burnos Russell, George Atkinson and Unknown

Sal Carrolo, Dale Shafer and Robert Markle

A landing gear job.

Goldberg, Fogel, Adams, Hays, Rostad, Bryant and Gilbert

B. Burns, J. French, R. Bellman & R.B.'s brother

503rd Fighter Squadron

Henry Fober and Jim Davidson

Rosenburg, Kamino, Peters and Ellethorpe.

McKenzie, Ferrell, Krass, Brehend, Pettit, Farrell and Stillwell

Steve Chetneky and Unknown

Knott, Knox and Gensheimer

Carl Brown and Vernie Taylor

Jim Canon and George Atkinson

503rd Fighter Squadron

McKensie, Ray Johnson, Bill Perry, Phil Pettit, Dick Krauss and Mort

Jim Sullivan, Louie Camarda, Mario Messina, Charlie Steffen, Charlie Angione and Arnold Buesina

Arthur Bates (504th), Cecil E. Craigo (504th) and Dale E. Shafer (503rd) by the Officers Club

Harry Rosenburg, Congressman Rooney and Abe Adler.

Bryan, Shafer, Stevens and Carrolo

Lloyd French, Amos Scruggs, William Preddy, Ralph Hill, William Bryan and Alec Boychuck

503rd Fighter Squadron

Miss ETO and Lt. Johnson

Charlie Steffen and Jim Kerr

Dale Shafer, Sal Carollo and Bill Bryan.

Rice Army Air Force Base 1943

Dan Gavitt, crew chief - D7B.

503rd Fighter Squadron

503rd Fighter Squadron

Mess Hall

503d Mess Hall, Rice, CA

503d Ready Room

503rd Fighter Squadron

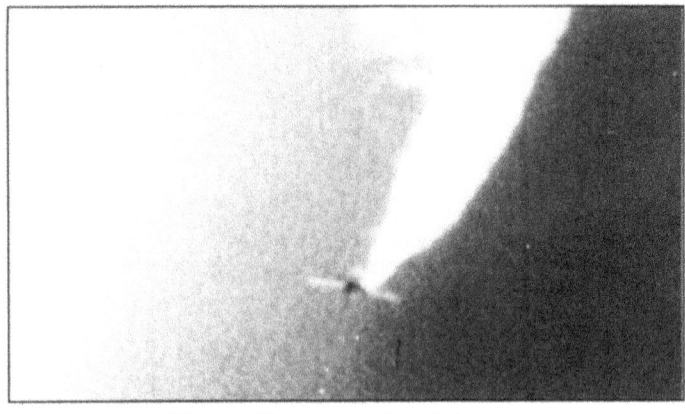

Me-109, one of four enemy aircraft shot down by
1st Lt Francis R. Gerard, on 11 September 44.

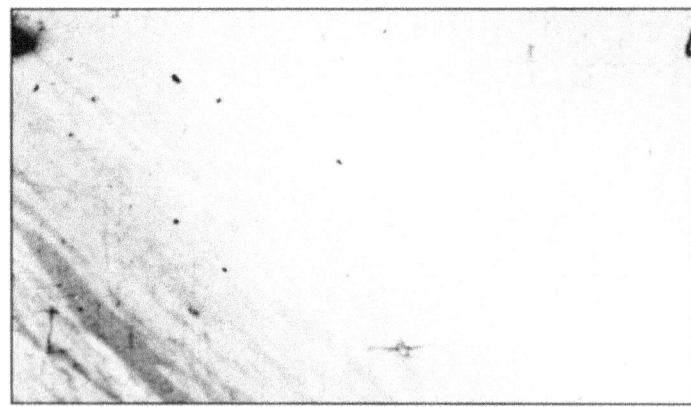

1st Lt Bernie Allen closes on a FW-190 on 31 December 44.

1st Lt William R. Preddy strafing at Krulapy airfield on 16 April 45.

Ar-234 in terminal dive on 18 April 45, shot down by L/C Dale E. Shafer, Jr. This was the last enemy aircraft destroyed in WW2 by the 339th.

Capt. Robert H. Ammon closes in on a parked Ju-88 at Prague/Kebly airfield on 16 April 45. Ammon claimed 11 destroyed, rec'd credit for 9.

1st Lt John C Campbell, Jr. chases the Me-262 he destroyed on 17 April 45. This was southeast of Rokycany, Czechoslovakia.

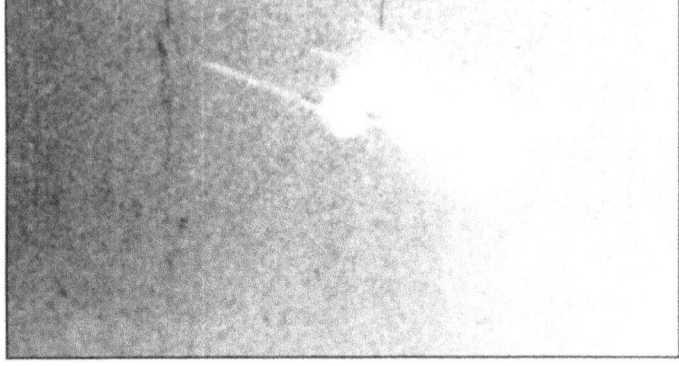

7 April 45 1st Lt Phillip E Pettit destroys a FW-190.

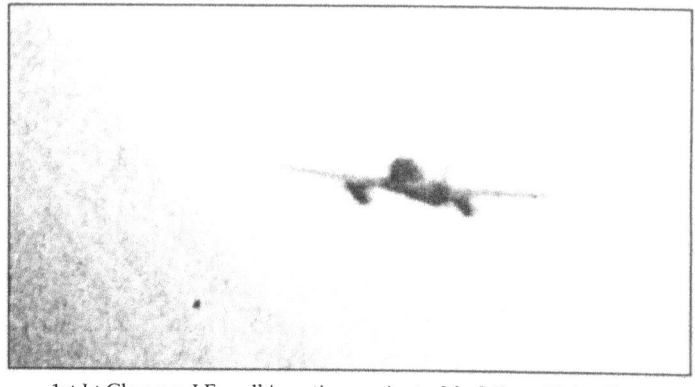

1st Lt Clarence I Ferrell in action against a Me-262 on 17 April 45.

503rd Fighter Squadron

10 April 45, L/C Dale E Shafer, Jr. strafes an enemy aircraft.

1st Lt Bernie Allen fights a FW-190 from JG-301 in the big battle 26 Nov 44.

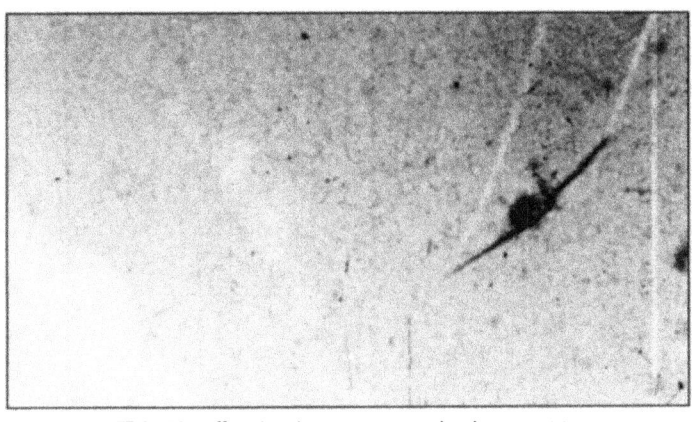
A FW-190 pulls wingtip streamers as it tries to out turn 1st Lt. Bernie Allen on 26 November 1944.

1st Lt Raymond G Johnson pursues a Me-109 over a box of B-17's on a mission to Hamburg on 7 April 45.

Captain Phillip E Pettit hits a FW-190 on an escort mission to Hamburg 7 April 45.

1st Lt Francis R. Gerard shoots down a Me-109 near Polle on an escort mission to Zeitz on 16 August 44. This was his first of eight victories.

2nd Lt Luther B Francis 27 November 44.

8 June 44, 2nd Lt Francis Gerard strafes a vehicle in support of the Normandy invasion

503RD FIGHTER SQUADRON

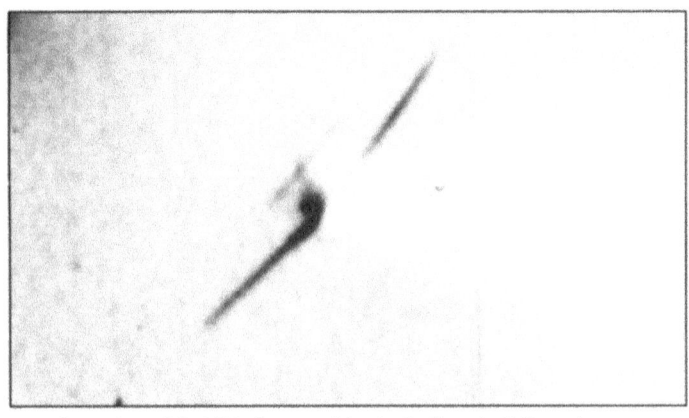

One of two Me-109's destroyed by 1st Lt Francis R Gerard on an escort Mission to Ruhland on 2 March 45.

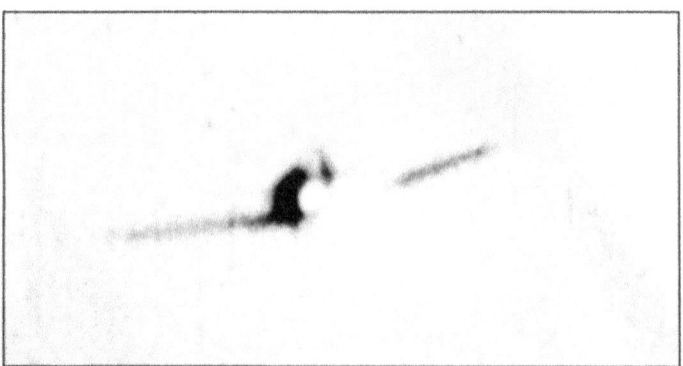

Captain Donald W. Johnson turns with a FW-190 from JG-301 on 26 November 1944. Johnson claimed three of the 503rd's 18 victories.

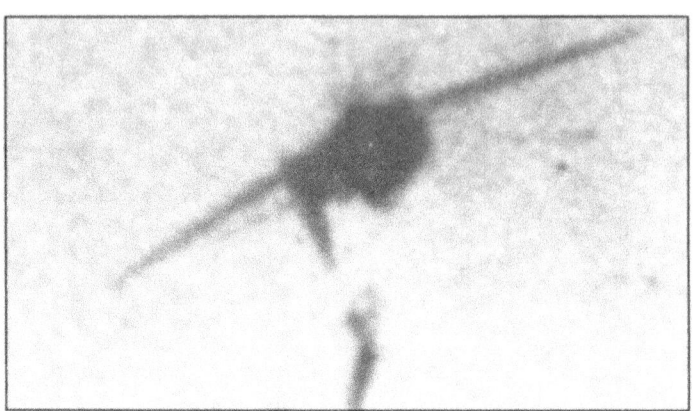

A German pilot drops out of his FW-190 at the top of a loop after being shot up by Capt Donald Johnson in the big battle on 26 November 44.

16 August 1944, 1st Lt Francis R Gerard scores his first victory, a Me-109, on an escort mission to Zeitz.

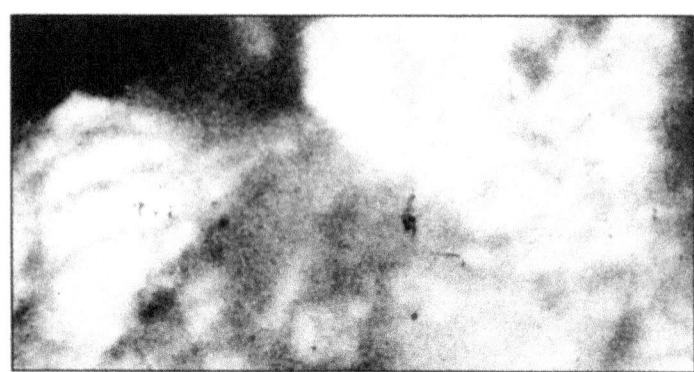

2nd Lt Luther B Francis 27 November 1944.

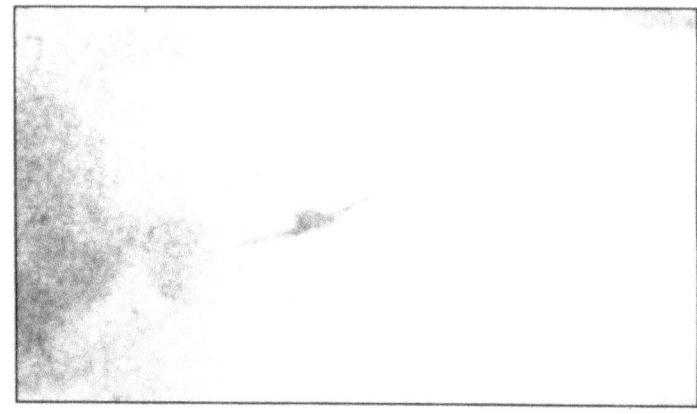

2nd Luther B Francis strafes an ammunition train on 27 November 44.

1st Lt Raymond G Johnson pursues a Me-109 on a mission to Hamburg on 7 April 1945.

339th Fighter Group

Ground Articles

Rememberances By Men Of The 504th Fighter Group

Recollections

by Harvey Brundage

I remember the time we got on a motor pool truck going to Los Angeles. Can't recall how many trucks were in the convoy, but when it was time to return, our truck failed to show and we were stranded. Since we were all late, I decided we'd get back by train. We assembled, and once everyone was accounted for, we got on the train - the sober, the not-too-sober and the noisy. The M.P.s came through and ordered us to quiet down or we'd be thrown off the train at the next station. Fortunately one of our officers was on the train coming back and he was nice enough to vouch that the men had been stranded and that I had been sent to bring them back to base. It was a pretty tight situation, but everything worked out okay since the men had reported to me in time to get back vithout expired passes.

What about our crossing the Atlantic? We finally got settled on ship, but the food was so bad we bought lend-lease food from the ship's store. Remember watching the dock workers when we threw packs of cigarettes to them? Some were pretty handy with their feet, kicking the packs into the air and catching them. We debarked and had to walk to the train with all the equipment on our backs and shoulders. No trucks for us. Some greeting! Guess it was our penalty for complaining about the food on the *H.M.S. Sterling Castle*, that marvelous British "cruise ship."

And then there was the penicillin rumor. One of the men who had had an operation was given penicillin. While he was recovering, he put on a hair piece that fooled everyone that came in to see him. They were so excited about his "newly grown" hair, they all wanted to know, "how come?" He told them the Medics had had an accident and spilled penicillin on his head. He'd been told not to worry; just rub it in and it wouldn't hurt. The result? New hair! The word spread like wildfire, and just about everyone bald or near bald went to the Medics asking for the "cure." What a rumor! We all learned something from that one.

How about an evening pass, a ride on our bikes five or more miles to a country pub, a game of darts and some P-39 beer? Coming back we thought we had kidney problems. That beer was some diuretic. Couldn't make it back to the base without two or three stops.

My brother Roy and I took leave and went up to Edinburgh, Scotland, with thoughts of playing golf on the old St. Andrews course. As we got off the train a gentleman came over and asked if he could buy us a drink. Obviously he was a Scot, for he let us know in a voice loud enough for everyone to hear. Upon learning that we wanted to play golf, he took us to his home and gave us about 25 golf balls. When we offered to pay him, he said he had a friend that worked as a greens keeper on the Edinburgh course and for us to forget about St. Andrews. By the time we reached the 9th hole we had lost all the balls but three. Those fairways were so narrow, if we didn't stay on them it meant 75 to 100 feet down the mountain. It would have been better if one leg had been shorter than the other because most of the walking was on the side of a hill. The greens keeper stopped us at the 9th hole to see how we were doing (his friend had told him to watch out for us). He gave us another bunch of golf balls and told us not to worry, he'd be getting them all back. I'm sure he did. We finished the day, but promptly forgot the scores.

The next day our friend directed us to a private club where the members were mostly ship builders. Since the pro had a couple of young children and we had chocolates and other candy which we willingly shared, the pro arranged clubs for us to use at no charge. When we arrived back at the club around noon time, we were escorted to the dining room, introduced and served a wonderful lunch. Cocktails were served, compliments of "Sandy" or "Jack." I forget which since most of the members were in kilts and had beards.

Oh, yes, we had someone in the squadron that liked chocolate so much that if any was left out, he would eat all of it. I don't remember which hut or who set him up, but one night the gifts from home were left out for everyone to enjoy. A full box of EX-LAX was mixed in with the regular candy, and once again, all the chocolate was cleaned out. I can't recall anymore complaints about someone eating all the chocolates. Guess it must have worked.

We were in London on the way back from leave on V.E. day. Wild is not the word. People were hanging on the lamp posts. Being a Yank, it was almost impossible to get into a pub, and forget about getting a drink. We were just happy to get back to base.

The time to ship home came, and we were put on the *William Cody*. What a ship! A real bronco, bow down, stern up, the propeller coming out of the water and turning in midair. When it came down, the ship shuddered and moaned. The big laugh was when some of our staff saw the four Air Force first sergeants quartered in a steel cage that had only one door handle on the outside. When the door closed, we couldn't get out. We finally wired the door open with a coat hanger. Since that wasn't the solution, we tried a mess kit knife and were able to slide the lock back to let us out.

Most of the men were sea sick, and the quarters were in bad shape. The men were fed saltine crackers and ordered up on deck. That worked, and the quarters became a better place to live.

The Statue of Liberty was a beautiful sight. At last, we were back in the States.

An Overview

by William H. Courtney

It was sometime in the spring of 1943 that I joined the 339th Dive Bomb Group. I was assigned to the 504th Squadron and worked on Douglas Dauntless A-24s and A-25 Curtiss Helldivers. After we moved to Walterboro, South Carolina, on July 3, 1943, we received our P-39s. In late July, four of us were sent by train for a course to learn a little more about P-51s. On August 24th, 1943, I received my diploma from North American Aviation in Inglewood, California.

By the time we made it back to Walterboro, it was time to start packing for our train ride to a secret destination. (Only the girls knew where we were going.) On September 11th, 1943, we arrived at a desolate spot in the middle of the California desert. We trained on our new P-39s, got a suntan, and received a few passes into Los Angeles. On March 4, 1944, we left by train for Camp Shanks, New York. After the preliminaries, we boarded the *Sterling Castle* for overseas. We arrived in Liverpool, England, on April the 4th and went directly to Fowlmere. It was to be our home for a year and a half.

On June 21st, 1944, Evan Mondl and myself were selected to accompany Major Carroll White to the R.A.F. Catfoss Base. We were attached to the R.A.F. for about six weeks. It was very enjoyable duty, but made us appreciate the food back in Fowlmere.

My archives don't seem to tell me when I made buck sergeant. I was a corporal when I went to Catfoss in June '44, but I was a sergeant when I was recommended for the Bronze Star on 10 June 1945. I received the award on August 1, 1945, for maintenance on airplanes 44-14208 and 44-15499. They were flown on sixty-four consecutive missions with a total of 322 hours, 45 minutes without an abortion.

Airplane 15499 was flown mostly by Vernon Blizzard. I know the Bronze Star was easy on that one. I can't ever remember Blizzard bringing an airplane back early. As for airplane 14208, if I had to guess, I would say Gilbert Cohen was the pilot.

After the war in Europe ended, I was sent by ship to Boston, Massachusetts. From there I boarded a train for Fort Lewis, Washington, where I was mustered out on October the 2nd, 1945.

Ground Support
by Elmer T. Craven

On February 4, 1944, I was assigned from the Desert Training Center, Thermal, California, to the 504th Squadron. I almost had to run to catch the troop train bound for Camp Shank, New York. This was our debarkation point for a very cold, fourteen day voyage across the sub-infested North Atlantic. We arrived at the bombed-out port of Liverpool, England, for a country train ride to a peaceful farm in the English countryside, our new home for the next eighteen months.

Though unable to participate in aerial combat, our army of ground support personnel stood solidly behind each pilot as the sorties cleared the steel landing mat and went into daily combat. Victory was great but defeat was hell, and each individual had to deal with the situation. It seems like only yesterday when I returned to a cold, empty hut. None of the pilots sharing my "home" returned from the day's mission.

"Touch Down" at the Homing Station
by Edward C. Epp

Members of runway control stationed themselves at the arriving end of a runway and controlled incoming flights. There was a direct telephone line from our homing station to runway control. During bad weather (low ceilings) the homer operator was aware when a plane passed over the base and would ring up control and ask for a flare to be fired.

I visited the homer and remote transmitter/receiver site in 1978. Both the transmitter and receiver buildings were still standing, but abandoned and gutted. The local farmer told me the R.A.F. operated from the site after the war, but later felled the towers and abandoned the site. I'm not surprised the buildings were still standing (and probably still are). They were constructed of poured concrete and brick with no windows. I'm sure they were constructed to withstand bombing and strafing.

One of the things I remember rather vividly was establishing a mobile homing station at Bassingborne well off the end of a runway on the edge of a grain field. I'm not sure of the date, but I believe it was sometime in November 1944. Al Grandy and I were operating the station that day. We had just homed our last plane and received the okay from the tower to shut down. Power to operate the station was obtained from a gasoline powered generator sitting on a small trailer located about thirty feet from the truck housing the station. Grandy and I went out and shut down the generator in preparation for servicing it. I stood on top of the unit with a 5-gallon can of gas filling the tank while Grandy checked the oil level. Just about that time Bassingborne's B-17s began returning to base.

Fortunately, I look up and noticed that a B-17, wheels down and coming in for a landing, had passed the halfway mark on the runway. It still had not touched down and was losing altitude. I shouted to Grandy that I didn't think this guy was going to make it. Suddenly the pilot gunned the engines, banked to the left and headed straight at us while still losing altitude.

Standing on the trailer, I was about ten feet above the ground and at eye-level with the on-coming B-17. I threw the gas can to the side and dove for the ground. He passed right over the top of us, hit the roof of the truck, tore off our directional antenna and cut a deep gash in the roof.

The plane hit the ground about 100 yards further on, bounced and tore through a hedgerow before coming to rest. Miraculously there was no fire and no explosion. As we ran towards the wreck, all ten crewmen emerged without a scratch. The pilot asked me if that was my truck he hit and then apologized.

Eighteen Months at Fowlmere
by Richard V. Helsing

The following are a few memories of my eighteen months at Station 378 Fowlmere. We who spent our time at the transmitter site, Control Tower, and Homer Station were classed as Spec No. 759 Control Net Systems. I spent the first ten months at the Control Tower recording transmissions and the last eight months at the Homer Station. Some of the more memorable events at the Control Tower were:

- the chilling effect at the end of a mission when the Control Tower Officer would call the call signs of the planes that had not returned and the silence when there was no response;
- the transmission of a pilot who was checking on a group of bombers he was to escort, going in nose first, his plane being hit, and the surprise and dismay in his voice (he was advised to switch to Channel Four and call "May Day" - no further recording as we didn't monitor Channel Four);
- while over half the Group was still on the ground, the excited transmissions of a 339th pilot who had already taken off, asking for permission to land but being told to circle, trying several times to land but having to wait until all planes had taken off, then coming in and crashing near the black and white signal truck (he was badly burned, and I believe several

of the men working at the signal truck received Soldier Medals for their part in the rescue);

- the excitement when a P-51 came back from a mission with a bomb hanging under the wing by only the front support (the important one) and the tension until a smooth landing was completed without dropping the bomb;

- watching a P-51 belly in on the field next to the mess hall while on my way to the E.M. Mess and pedaling my bike across the field, arriving just as the pilot got out (he was unhurt);

- the day a British glider landed at the base after the tow cable broke (I remember getting inside and looking it over).

The only pilot I could recognize on takeoff was General (then Colonel) Henry. He would barely leave the ground when the wheels on his plane would come up. And when the Group was taking off using the up-hill runway past the tower, he would disappear as he dipped out of sight - he never put undue strain on the plane or so it seemed.

The only thing that stands out for me while at the Homer Station (Gas Pump) was on one beautiful day (very few nice days) I was giving steers when a call came in from Upper 20 (Colonel Henry). I immediately gave him a steer, then checked it with the sensing switch. He had passed over the base (180 degrees off). I called back and informed him he had passed over the base and to transmit for a "homing." He did and immediately recognized his position. When I asked him about that at the reunion in Cincinnati, he said he remembered it well. It was a beautiful day, and he was enjoying it a little too much.

The most impressive sight I remember was the Group's fly-by on the last day of operation at the base when the whole Group passed over the field.

Ground Crew

by William Charles Shelnutt, Jr.

I was transferred to the 339th Bomb Group, 483rd B.S., which was activated on 10 August 1942, and shipped to Drew Field, Tampa, Florida. I arrived at Drew Field 10 February 1943 and was the only enlisted man in the communication department. Lt Friedman was my communication officer. We were among the original cadre, but it wasn't long before other enlisted personnel arrived from various radio schools.

From Drew Field we were transferred to Walterboro, South Carolina, arriving on the 4th of July. As the dive bomber had become obsolete, we were re-equipped with P-39s. We were now the 339th Fiqhter Group and assiqned to the 504th Squadron. We were settled in by the time our first shipment of P-39s arrived, and what an arrival! Two collided while landing and were out of service for repairs, essentially cutting our air power of P-39s in half.

In September '43, we were again transferred, this time from Walterboro to Rice Field, California, located in the Mojave Desert. The time passed rather uneventfully, as well as I remember, and it wasn't long before we were packing in preparation for transfer to England. We left Rice Field by troop train on 9 March 1944, arriving at Camp Shanks, New York, on the 14th. On the 22nd of March we boarded the *Sterling Castle* bound for England, offloaded at Liverpool on the 4th of April and went by British troop train directly to Fowlmere, our final destination. Little did I know as I put my gear on the first cot to the right in a Niessen hut that this would be my abode for the next sixteen months and six days.

My crew and I worked around the clock on many occasions keeping the Squadron's planes' radios in working order. Any of you who were stationed at Fowlmere will well remember the blitz of England. The V-ls came whistling in. It was all right as long as you could see them - you prayed the good Lord would make them visible - but the fog factor in England was quite heavy much of the time.

I well remember 5 June 1944 when the first three grades were briefed on preparation for D-Day. Part of the preparations consisted of painting the planes' wings and fuselage with black and white stripes. The last plane we finished didn't have time to dry, and the paint smeared as the pilot took off. The striping was done so that our allies would recognize our planes from a distance. The following day, the 6th of June '44, our pilots flew relentlessy, around the clock. They would return to base, and while the planes were being serviced, they'd grab a cup of coffee and a bite to eat, then off again. My hat was off to our fighter pilots, and we, the ground crew, cheered them on. These young men performed feats well beyond the call of duty. The mighty Nazi siege of Europe was taking a turn, and our group played a major roll in sending Hitler fleeing to his bunker. There were heroics, but there was also despair. We would listen to our radios (SCR-522) for our planes to return, but there were times when there was only silence. Although one would have been too many, we lost several pilots and planes. Our hearts were saddened, but their lives were not lost in vain. Because of them, we redoubled our efforts to bring this ugly thing called war to an end.

As the end of the war in Europe grew closer, I yearned to return to the life I knew, a life that seemed so long ago. I learned I had 94 points - 95 points were needed to be sent home. God bless my crew for they tried to give me one of theirs to make it possible, but the offer was refused by headquarters. I never thought my ability to drive anything except a tank would be a factor in me being sent home, but thank the good Lord it did. After the war in Europe ended, bomber bases all over England were being disassembled, and I was ordered to go to one of these and help in removing all GI equipment. From there I was sent to Stone, England, for return to the States. I waited there six weeks before boarding the *William Patterson*, a Liberty ship, in Barry, Wales, on the 12th of September 1945. We arrived in Boston, Mass, USA, on September the 26th, and I was honorably discharged on 6 October 1945 at Camp Gordon near Augusta, Georgia. I was once again a CIVILIAN in my homeland, reunited with my wife, my son and my loved ones.

My Early Days With The 339th

by Bob Sugg

My first assignment after radio school was to the 84th Bomb Group in Savannah, Georgia, just as they were moving to Drew Field in Tampa, Florida. Soon thereafter the 339th was being formed, and I was transferred to this Group early in 1943. Leaving the 84th meant going from the high rent area of the field with new barracks to the older, tar paper barracks assigned to the 339th.

The Group headquarters installed a telephone switchboard, and I was elected to be an operator since I'd had some switchboard experience. I worked twelve hours and had the following 24 hours off. Every other day I would hitch a ride to Clearwater Beach. It didn't take long to get to know the local talent, and there was a beer stand only 20 feet from the beach. I had visited the area two years earlier as a civilian and paid big bucks for a lesser life style. This is why on payday I felt guilty picking up my pay.

The telephone operator job had one major problem. One squadron had a sergeant who was CQ (Charge of Quarters) almost every night. This man had a bad hangup: he resented telephone operators and took us to task every time he made a call. In the Army you didn't talk back to sergeants. One night Tech Sgt Jacobson from Group headquarters came in to get something from his desk and asked if he could try to work the switchboard. The first call he got was from the bad mouth sergeant. I saw Jake's eyes light up from what he was hearing. Jake let the other sergeant have his say and then told him who he was talking to. The air got blue after that, and Jake ended by saying if he ever heard of him (the other sergeant) talking to an operator like that again, he could expect to clean toilets for the duration plus six.

I remember the time we got a new communications officer fresh out of O.C.S. He was doing fine until he had to pull Officer-of-the-Day. The orderly room clerk knew he was in real trouble when he saw the 2nd Lt walk in slapping leather. The Lt was really proud of his quick draw with the .45 - guess he was reliving the O.K. Corral scene. Anyway, the clerk knew what was coming and dove for the door, but before he got there, the gun went off and blasted the clerk's file cabinet near where he'd been sitting. The rumor went around that the Lt was transferred out and the clerk got a day's combat pay.

At Drew Field I had a chance to fly a few times with Lt Paul M. Myer. Flying the old A-24 with the cockpit open was really super. We knew something was in the wind when all the gunners were fired and we packed for the train ride to Walterboro, South Carolina, in July '43. There we got some A-25s which were really beautiful planes. It looked more powerful than it really was, and I had only one ride in the A-25 before the P-39s started arriving. I was on the ramp with some of the guys looking over a new A-25 when our line chief, M/Sgt Hardy and the engineering officer took us to task. They told us if we damaged the plane by climbing on it, we would have a real problem. M/Sgt Hardy then got into the cockpit to taxi the plane to the parking area. By a bit of bad luck Hardy pulled the wrong lever and dropped the extra gas tank from the bomb bay onto the ramp. The engineering officer just shook his head, but I felt forced to yell, "Bombs away!" I found out then that you just don't mess around with M/Sgts because *few* have a sense of humor and *all* have very long memories.

As the P-39s began to operate from Walterboro, it was not easy for some of our pilots to go from flying Navy dive bombers to Army Air Force fighters. Some would forget to lower the gear before landing. Gear-up landings were hard on the plane as well as the taxpayers. Soon, word got out that Group was looking for a sober, alert person for an important job. (That let me and most of my buddies out.) They put this man in a jeep at the end of the runway with a flare gun. If a plane was about to land gear-up, he would shoot off a flare. Then, if the gear didn't go down, he was to shoot a second flare, but aim at the pilot. In this way the 339th took the first small step toward what is now the high-tech Runway Control Van.

I wonder how many remember our Chemical Warfare Corporal. He insisted that Hitler was out to get us with poison gas, if not that day, then the next day. There was never a G.I. who liked to wear a gas mask. The mask was hot, the air you breathed was stale, and vision was limited. Yet, to prove his point, the Corporal would hide out until he saw a few of us come by, then yell, "Gas attack!" and throw a canister of tear gas at us. He made few friends by this action. Since we were able to outrun the gas in the open, he decided to give us an "attack" while we were dressing for work - in our barracks. This way he would have a captive audience. The idea wasn't bad, but he picked the wrong barracks. He didn't know we had one barracks where the night workers were permitted to sleep until noon. This is the one into which he threw the tear gas. I heard him yell, "Gas attack!", and then all hell broke loose. The night crew didn't know what hit them, and they came stumbling out of the barracks rubbing their eyes. The Corporal saved his life by being fleet of foot and having a good head start. It was quite a sight to see him running for his life with a pack of barefoot, ill-clad, hostile men after him. The Corporal never came around our squadron again. The only good thing to come out of this was it drove some of us to drink.

Our time in South Carolina was short, but it was an important transition for us. Mel Ball told me that the P-39 pilots would fly from Walterboro over to the nearest Navy field to demonstrate the finer points of dogfighting to the newer Navy pilots. We did have some bad luck, though. We lost three good men: a fine pilot whose chute didn't open in time; an officer who had a heart attack on the physical training field; and an enlisted man who made a wrong dive into the city pool and broke his neck.

In September '43 we packed up and went by train to Rice Field, California, taking along Bill Shelnutt's yet-to-be housebroken pet coon. Bill drove to Rice with his wife and didn't have to care for that little monster enroute. He should've at least given us a box of diapers for the thing. How Bill got off without a Statement of Charges from the Pullman Car Company, I'll never know. The coon was disposed of at Rice which was another world, another life style, and another story.

504th Fighter Squadron

Kenneth R. Willard

Kenneth R. Willard

Dutch Eisenhart

Robert T Wood

William C Shelnutt

Kenneth Willard

Gravette

Duane Larson

504th Fighter Squadron

Billy E Langohr

Frank Waters with his plane "Brother Bill".

1st Lt Carroll W. Bennett

Robert Kuhlman

1st Lt Ely N. Van Cleave

Captain Arlen Welles

Bob England putting wing tank's on P-51 fighter.

Anthony J Kameen, flight surgeon

504th Fighter Squadron

Henry G Thibert

Robert V Blizzard

Robert M Kuhlman in Area 5, fall of 1944.

Robert F Sargent

Merle F "Bud" Caldwell

Lt William T Hurley and his P-51 "Dopey Lou". Aircraft is later assigned to Kuhlman

Robert M Kuhlman

John R Trester

504th Fighter Squadron

Ray F Herrman

Donald F Kreuger

Frank Guernsy

Lt Luther Leon Corbin and his plane "Problem"

1/Lt Robert F Blizzard

Queen Mother, Duke of Kent, Wimbledon 1945

Al Zacchilli, Unknown, Unknown and Ken Willard

Frank Guernsy and his plane "Barbara"

504th Fighter Squadron

M Crecelius, R M Kuhlman and J Walbourn

Bradford Stevens, Cecil Craigo, Ray Atteberry, Fred Showker, Frank Waters and Unknown

Pilot Fred Rutan shows souvenier German Helmet picked up after he made an emergency landing.

Hoffman, Smith, Abbey and Anderson

Robert H Ammon, Lawrence J Barrett, Jr, Vernon N Barto and Robert V Blizzard

Chapel, Lawson and Davies

Pilot Frank Waters and John McGillivray

Bill E Langhor, Unknown and Leon M Orcutt, Jr

504TH FIGHTER SQUADRON

Sidney Bloom, Bill Shelnutt, Cy Morgan, Robert Addison, Ralph Hodgens, Robert Sugg, Dale Fitzgerald, Taylor, Adler and Weyment.

Caldwell, Trester, Stevens, Greer, Corbin and Waters

Capt Gurnsey, Lt Col Gravette, Maj Routt and Capt Peters

Cohen, Barrett, Creswell, Agnew, Carter, Allens and Barto.

Dale Fitzgerald and Joe Janosik

Cohen, Carter and Creswell

Dale Fitzgerald, Ralph Mitchell, Robert Radison and Cy Morgan

R O Lewey, "Ikey" Hudson and John Dugrew

504th Fighter Squadron

Robert J Addison, Edward S Stern, Ely Van Cleave, Cecil E Craigo, Bill C Routt, Edgar B Gravette, Hubert McGowan, John L Sutton, Duane S Larson, Charles M Mead, Richard C Penrose, Melvin L Cernicky, William T Hurley, Donald A Zeine, John R James. James J Hayden, Lewis S Peter, Melville R Ball, Richard H Wilcox, William H Muir and Arlen W Wells.

Pinkerton, Chapel, Crecelius, Strachan, Kaulaakis, Dains, Flaming, Solley and Davies

Leon Corbin and unknown

Leon M Orcutt and his plane

William Courtney, Vernon Blizzard and Jesse Russell 1944 - 1955

Capt Craigo, Cpl Schwartz and Sgt Smith

Cephas Hermansen, Unknown and Unknown

504th Fighter Squadron

Richard Abbey and Howard Brent

Bob Irion, Bill Guyton and Tom Rich

Maj Peter, Capt Guernsey and Lt Col Gravette

Corbin, Showker, McClure, McGillivray, Hurley, Harry, Unknown, Waters, Griffith, Greer and Unknown

M Merle Caldwell, E Van Cleave, G P Harry, B Stevens and J Trester

James J Hayden, Donald F Kreuger, Robert C Havighurst, Clair M Mason, Kenneth V Berguson, William T Hurley, Lyle M Carter, Vernon N Barto, William H Muir, Harlan F Hunt, Will M Hudson, Robert V Blizzard, Raymond H Creswell, John R McGillivray, William C Clark, Lewis S Peter, Robert F Sargent, Edward S Stern, Richard C Penrose, Hubert McGowan, Jerome J Ballard, Loren W Allers, Jerome Sainlar, Leonard A Kunz, Robert G Cohen, Carroll W Bennett, Lawrence J Barrett, Billy E Langohr, Leon M Orcutt, Arlen W Wells.

504th Fighter Squadron

Bill E Langhor and Leon M Orcutt, Jr.

Art Shoemaker, E P Ryan, John LeJeune and Lewis S Peter

After breifing, loading for the flight line Harry Corey far left

In line: 1) Unknown, 2) Jerome Sainlar, 3-5) Unknown, 6) Arlen Wells and 7) Roland Smith

Lt Luther Leon Corbin

504th Ready Room at Fowlmere, spring of 1945. There is a card game at the back table, others read.

Richard "Dick" Abbey and Leon M Orcut, Jr.

504th Fighter Squadron

Douglas P Cole, Will M Hudson, Gordon H Chenez, Frank A Clifton and Vernon N Barto.

Lt. Kenneth V. Berguson

Rice, CA

Blizzard and Barto

Pilots Blizzard and Barto

B-17 taking off at Fowlmere after returning 339ers from Scotland

504th Fighter Squadron

Frank Waters in "Brother Bill" over Germany.

Robert Thistlewaite

Ridge O'Sullivan

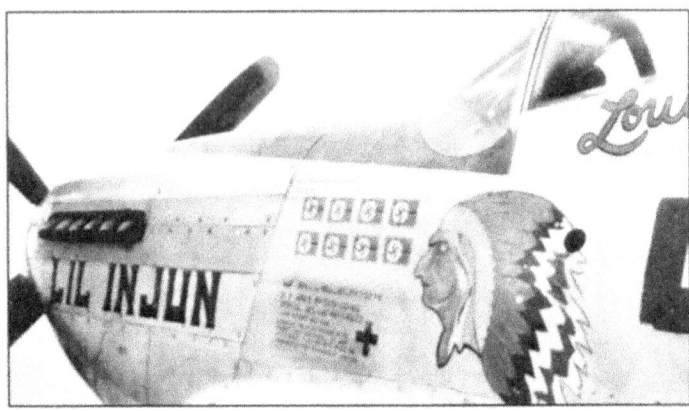
Leon M Orcutt in "LIL INJUN"

The 504th taxis up the runway to the takeoff position.

5Q-E "Beaver Chant" assigned aircraft of Richard C Penrose.

504th Fighter Squadron

Our company street, Tent City, Rice, CA, 1943

Blizzard in "Punkie II"

504FS lined up for take off at Fowlmere, spring 1945.

"LIL INJUN" - painted by Debbie Allen - Leon M Orcutt, pilot

5Q-H assigned to 1st Lt John R Trester.

1st Lt Hervey S Stockman ventilates a locomotive in northern France.

William T Hurley about to take off in 5Q-W.

"LIL INJUN"

504th Fighter Squadron

2t Richard C Penrose strafes a flak car in northern France on 18 August 44.

Pilot Ammon

504FS, 5Q-F assigned to 1st Lt Richard T Aldrich, spring 1945.

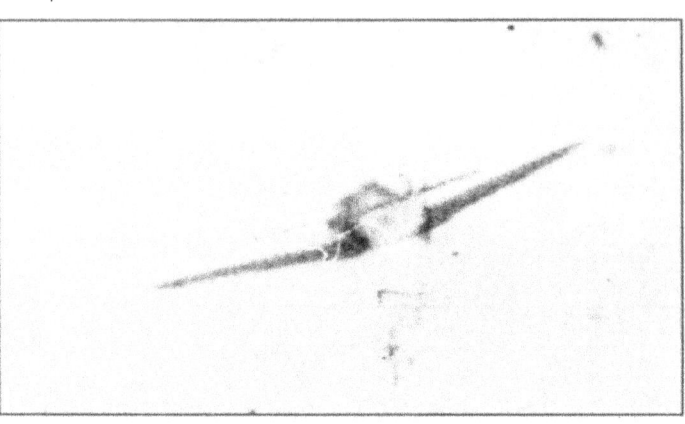
16 August 44, 1st Lt Harvey S Stockman tangles with Lt. Hubert Buschmann, JG-3 (Luftwaffe), before running out of ammunition.

GAF Lt Erich Schulte comes hurtling back toward Capt Robert F Sargent after bail out in their encounter on 30 March 45

10 June 44, 2nd Lt Harvey S Stockman strafes box cars in France.

Two 504th Fighter Squadron P-51's ready for takeoff, spring of 1945.

Parked 504th Fighter Squadron P-51.

504th Fighter Squadron

Original ready room coffee mug and mission scheduling of R C Penrose.

2nd Lt Penrose vs. Lt Hubert Buschman of Staffel 1, I Grupe, JG-3.

At 300 feet GAF Lt Erich Schulte bails out of his crippled Me-262 with Capt Robert F Sargent in close pursuit on 30 March 45.

Captain Robert F Sargent shooting down GAF Lt Erich Schulte on 30 March 45 near Kaltenchirchen Airfield.

18 August 44, 2nd Lt Richard C Penrose makes a pass on a locomotive already steaming from being hit by 1st Lt Duane S Larson.

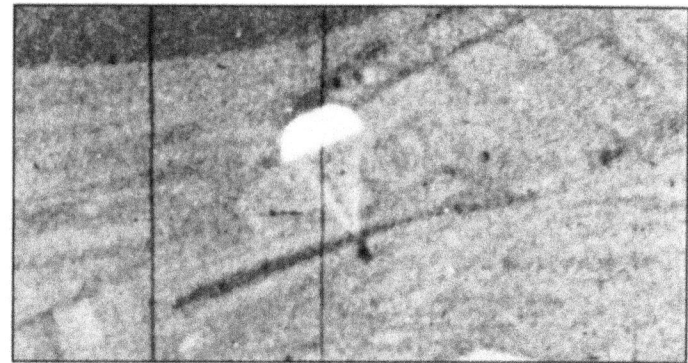
1st Lt Merle F Caldwell photographs Me-109 pilot in his parachute on 7 July 44 during an escort mission to Leipzig.

F/O Roland W Smith strafes the German airfield near Neuruppin.

2nd Lt Richard C Penrose dogfights Lt Hubert Buschmann of 1 Straffel, I Grupe, JG-3 in a wild fight on 16 August 44.

504th Fighter Squadron

Burning German aircraft as seen by 1st Lt Lawrence J Barrett on 16 April 45 at Klatovy Airfield, Czeckoslovakia.

Lt John L Sutton in northeast France on 18 August 44. Burning fuel storage tanks were ignited by Major Vernon B Hathorn, HQ.

2nd Lt Frank T Waters strafing a railroad yard in France on 25 May 44.

Lt John L Sutton strafing railroad cars in northeast France on 18 Aug 44.

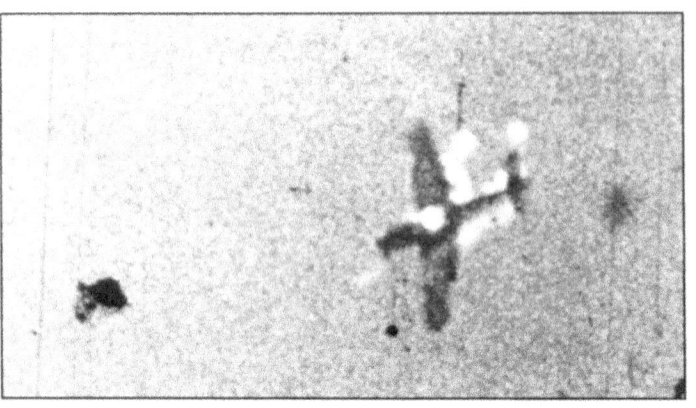

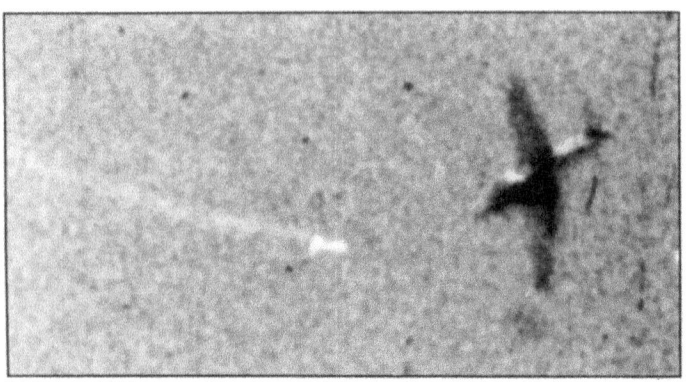

504th Fighter Squadron

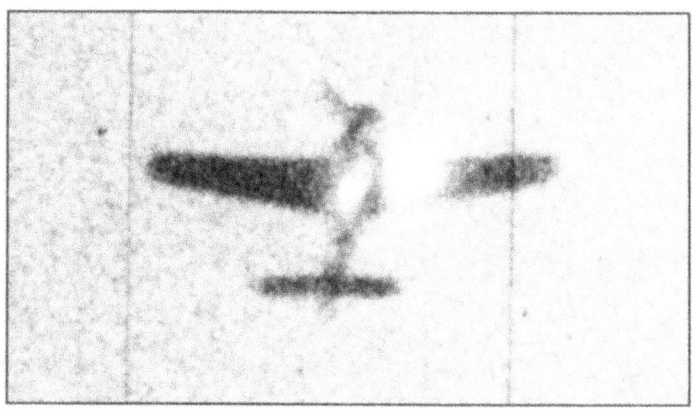

1st Lt Bradford V Stevens hits a FW-190 on an escort mission to Oscherleben on 30 May 44.

1st Lt Bradford V Stevens scores a strike on an FW-190 on 30 may 44. Stevens destroyed two

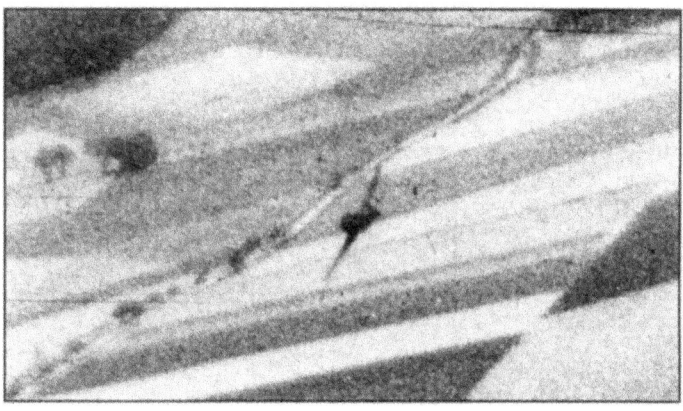

1st Lt Bradford V Stevens pursues a FW-190 on 30 May 44.

1st Lt Bradford V Stevens hits ground targets on D-Day, 6 June 44.

1st Lt Merle F Caldwell strafes a Ju-88 on 13 August 44.

Some strafing obstacles for 2nd Lt Hervey S Stockman on 21 May 44.

Lt Hervey S Stockman strafes a steaming locomotive on 10 June 44.

504th Fighter Squadron

Capt Robert F Sargent trails the smoking Me-262 of GAF Lt Erich Schulte at low altitude near Kaltenkirchen Airfield on 30 March 45.

504th Operations blister hanger, Fowlmere, England.

2nd Lt Richard C Penrose dogfights Lt Hubert Buschmann in the vicinity of Lauenstein on 16 August 1944.

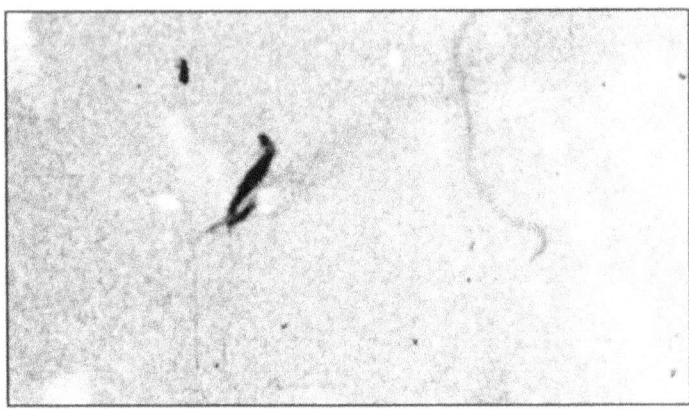

1st Lt Raymond M Cresswell strafing a parked German aircraft on 16 April 1945.

2nd Lt Will M Hudson strafing a Me-109 on a German airfield, 16 April 45.

28 August, 2nd Lt Richard C Penrose strafes a barge hauling coal.

1st Lt Raymond H Cresswell downs a Me-109 on 7 April 45.

2nd Lt Cephas Hermanson after a Me-109 on 7 April 45.

504th Fighter Squadron

1st Lt Hervey S Stockman destroys a Me-109 flown by Feldwebel Richard Karcher of Staffel 1, I Grupe, JG-3, who parachuted (wounded).

28 August 44, 2nd Lt Richard C Penrose strafes a barge hauling coal.

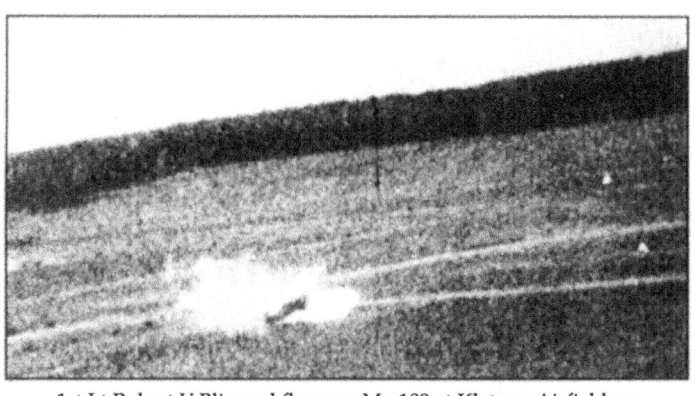

1st Lt Robert V Blizzard flames a Me-109 at Klatovy Airfield on 16 April 45 as the 504th works the field over.

Capt Robert F Sargent shooting down GAF Lt Erich Schulte on 30 March 45 near Kaltenkirchen Airfield.

Pieces fly off the Me-262 of GAF Lt Erich Schulte as Capt Robert F Sargent closes to point blank range on 30 March 45.

1st Lt Robert M Kuhlman strafing a locomotive on 20 February 45.

1st Lt Frank A Clifton strafing a German airfield on 17 April 45.

Capt Kirke B Everson burning hanger, parked aircraft on 16 April 45.

504th Fighter Squadron

1st Lt Robert C Croker photographs GAF Major Rudolf Sinner's parachute on 4 April 45 near Parchim. Croker shared the destruction of Sinner's Me-262 with Capt Kirke B Everson.

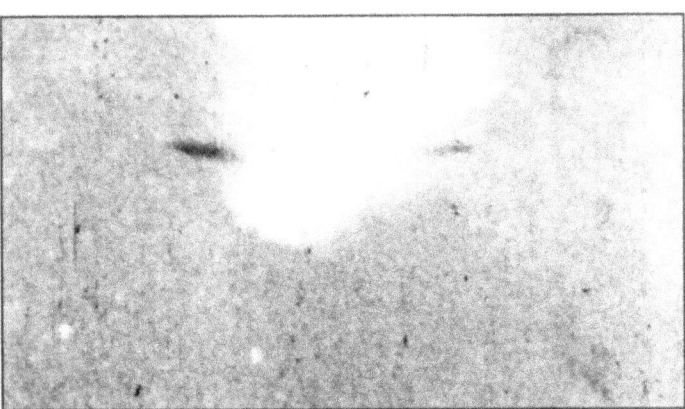

Capt Kirke B Everson destroys a Me-109 on 7 April 45.

2nd Lt Cephas Hermanson follows another P-51 on a strafing run.

Capt Robert F Sargent strafing dispersed German aircraft. Zigzags appear to be trenches, 10 April 45.

13 August 44, 1st Lt Merle F Caldwell strafes a railroad yard.

Capt Lewis S Peter hits a FW-190 on 7 June 44.

1st Lt Robert M Kuhlman strafing a train on 20 February 45.

1st Lt Merle F Caldwell pursues a Me-109 on an escort mission to Leipzig on 7 July 44.

339th Fighter Group

Ground Articles

Rememberances By Men Of The 505th Fighter Group

Remembering When

by John Franz

I have many memories of my service in the 339th. We were blessed with the best fellows whose skills and willingness to serve have never been equaled. For that reason, it's hard to pick a favorite story and put it down on paper, but the story I will tell took place on a cold, rainy day in March 1944 in New York. It might jog a memory of two.

We were transported from our barracks to dock side where we were to board ship for our travel overseas, our "destination unkown." We were all trying to act calm and brave, but down deep inside, the "unknown" was in our thoughts. The mood was very subdued. We had heard stories about strange illnesses and deaths that happened on previous trips, the typical stories that everyone heard before hey were sent overseas. Also, George Jones had received word that his father had passed away the day before. Because our outfit was very close we were all affected very deeply. Although the Red Cross made arrangements for him to go home to Grenola, Kansas, he talked it over with all of us and decided he wouldn't go home. Instead he stayed with his friends and shipped out with the Group. Our outfit was that close. It was a sad night for all, but morning came quickly.

We were all lined up in formation - duffel bags, weapons, and all. The ship looked so big, but as I looked at the hundreds in formation waiting to load as well as the hundreds that had already boarded, I knew it would be crowded. Finally, the signal was given for us to load. I had the roster and papers, so I was first to go up the steps. I had my duffel bag strap over my left shoulder, the strap of my Thompson submachine gun over my right shoulder, the outfit's papers in my left hand, and the little brown Red Cross gift bag in my right. As I reached the first step, my gun slipped off my shoulder and knocked the bag out of my hand. It fell to the pavement and rolled down the ramp. A dockworker scrambled to retrieve it even though I told him to let it go. I continued up the steps to the first platform where the loading officer was waiting at a table. I gave the officer our roster and papers. Now, this is the moment I've never forgotten. As I turned away from the desk, the dockworker was there and handed me the little bag he'd retrieved. As I looked at him face-to-face to thank him, he said, "Good luck, young soldier." I noticed there were tears in his eyes. He added, "You see, I made this trip in 1917." I then turned to face the Squadron, still standing in formation and waiting for the signal to come aboard. I was just a kid, but I knew at that moment that I was in a man's world. I looked at the familiar faces of a bunch of "kid" soldiers who also realized they were in a man's world. It meant taking on a long, hard job, but they were up to it. They were ready to get on with it and get it over.

At that moment, I yelled, "Ship ahoy, Mates," and waved for them to come aboard. It was the response they needed. Smiles appeared on their faces as they gathered their equipment and started up the steps.

I know there will be many good stories written, but I wanted to relate our first big step, leaving the good old U.S.A., a country we'll always be proud to serve.

Fowlmere's Green Hornet

by Bill Hammond and John Franz

Major Bayne "Shorty" Fulton was our Mess Officer, the best in the ETO. He had managed the Akron, Ohio, airport before the war. He was also an aviation pioneer who loved to fly, but, already in his early fifties, he couldn't pass the flight physical. He earned his wings and nickname, "The Green Hornet," flying his motorcycle around the base.

Shorty's yearning for combat mission experience was finally realized. Fate had decreed this before the war in Akron. It was there that Shorty met and befriended Jimmy Doolittle, a barnstorming, "hell for leather airplane driver." He staked the future Eighth Air Force commander to gasoline and assorted airport credits essential to the continuation of Jimmy's barnstorming career and his participation in the Cleveland Air Races. This was characteristic of Shorty Fulton, and characteristically, Jimmy Doolittle did not forget.

General Doolittle was a frequent visitor to our base, often unannounced. He enjoyed the hands-on visits with our aircraft engineering men and reminiscing with Shorty Fulton. Eventually, General Doolittle gave Shorty permission to fly as an observer with the First Air Division. Shorty completed nine missions and was on his way to an Air Medal when his B-17 was clobbered. Shorty was seen to bail out, camera and all. We learned later that he landed in a tree adjacent to a POW camp Commandant's quarters. The thought of a fifty-odd year old mess officer, parachuting from an American bomber, did not fit the Commandant's view of reality. Major Fulton ended up at Stalag 1 near Barth, Germany. As you might expect, Shorty returned to England after VE day in an 8th Air Force Headquarters plane - courtesy of an old friend.

"Where the hell's my booze..."

by William T. Vaughn

As you know, Squadron Supply was not a very colorful activity. On top of this, it was responsible for a sad duty sending our missing pilots' belongings to the Effects Quartermaster. Out of this comes my story.

It seems that General Doolittle had received a lot of complaints about the food on our base. To correct this situation, the General sent us a short, chunky Major by the name of Fulton, better known as "The Green Hornet."

The story comes from the Major's combat activity. I learned about this when Captain Rudy Menart called to inform me that "The Green Hornet" was MIA, and that I should pick up his effects. As Rudy Menart was the 505th Supply Officer for awhile at Rice, we had developed a good rapport which I may have strained by asking, "Why me?" His reply was that I had a lot of experience, which was unfortunately true, and also because he said so!

With that, the 505th Squadron Supply went to work. Frank Semger made a box from an external fuel tank container; Keith Todd went to Quartermaster Supply to make a stencil; Carl Ashworth and I headed to Major Fulton's quarters for his effects. As he was more mature (older, that is) than our young pilots, he didn't have any of the "trading material" some of the others had...like the kind of things we didn't want to send to Mom and Dad or possibly a wife. Instead, the Major had a large supply of liquor and candy!

Major Fulton had a room of his own, and this presented a new problem. When we lost a pilot, I can't recall finding any liquor. Maybe an extra .45, but no liquor. The candy was always left in the barracks along with all other edibles, but liquor? I must admit, I don't know about Carl, but I was secretly tempted. Better judgement prevailed!...and a good thing it did.

A few weeks after we shipped out his effects, I received a phone call that went something like this:

"Hello, Squadron Supply, Sgt. Vaughn." "Sergeant Vaughn, this is Major Fulton." Surprised? You bet! What do I say? "Welcome back."??

No.

Instead, I say, "Yes, sir," as if he'd never been away. "Sergeant Vaughn, what the hell happened to my booze and candy?"

To say the least, I wasn't happy with the tone. My answer, "Major, we gave the whiskey to the Officers Club and the candy to the E.M. Club."

"Good, Sergeant. Thank you." Click! Boy, was I glad we used good judgement. I often wonder if he relayed the incident to his friend, General Doolittle? I also wonder if any other Fighter Groups lost or had its Mess Officer Missing in Action?

505th Fighter Squadron

Roy Myers

Jim Frink on coffee break during a hike.

Cecil L Byrd

Cecil Moore

E. Stevens

Carl Ashworth

Vernon Parr

Gerald E Graham

505th Fighter Squadron

Harry R Corey

James Starnes

Donald Larson

G J Cutri

Dent Stiles

Harry "Herky" R Corey at the tennis court.

Andrew B Gager

Tom Miller

Bill MacClarence

505th Fighter Squadron

Gabe Cutri

Richard Thieme

Herbert C Haugh

John Earnest

Fred Nessler

F Swinand

Briggs and Sam Palmucci

G T Rich

Jay Marts

505th Fighter Squadron

Francis Pratt and James Brignola

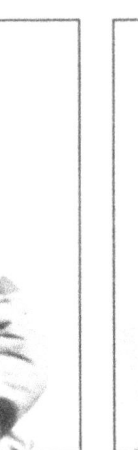
Dave Register

Cecil L Byrd

Progue and White

Russell Peasley

Stan Pattionew, Ed Girzi, Laird Travis, Bob Inion, George Jones and Dick Thieme

Gustave Dahlstrom

Hicks, Ted Sulina and Herbert Ward

505th Fighter Squadron

Tower and Thury

Lt Col Joe Thury Receives Croix De Guerre from French AF General, May 1, 1945

Archie A Tower receiving his Flying Cross from General Woodbury

M Briggs, W Kuhnert, J Franz and P Bova

John Earnest and George Mc Farlane

Lt Johnson and crew

Harbold, Hicks, Per and Nessler

Bert Conners, Charles Hess, Stanley Petticrew

505th Fighter Squadron

Major Turner and Col Thruy

Capt James R Starnes gets Croix De Guerre from French AF General

Hicks, Palmucci, Per, Freeman, Frosella and Popi

George McFarlane, Harry Corey and "Honest" John Earnest

William H Krauss and crew

Cecil L Byrd and maintenance man

505th Fighter Squadron

Milla, Briggs, Miller, Keller, Cabelous, Williams, Donovan, Mamosen, Patterson, Harbold, Kimsey, Langtry, Steen, Runyan, Boere, Page, Collins, Beckman, Franz, Palmucci, Nass, Baudoux, Murray, Rountree, Pollock, Freeman, Smeltzer, Mack, Carlson, Tews, Kelley, Lorwa, Ertle, Haugh, Daniel, Lopez, Raines, Vaughn, Speiss, Whiting, Ross, Myers, Lejeune, Oser, Peasley, Day, Whitley, Todd, Earnest, Panca, Mansfield, Rodenback, Middleton, Neall, Angelo, Webster, Ebersala, Leduc, Huppert, McKinney, Miller, Shockley, Fernberg, Ojanen, Safarino, Dahlstorm, Rivera, Waite, Delarys, Young, Lukehart, Papi, Mobley, Unknown, Kowalenski, Plant, LaRose, Kanner, Catalfamo, Nine, Robinson, Howard, Kuhnert, Brown, Lubert, Charrett, Murray, Steven, Fields, Clemick, Lambert, Kollar, Terabasso, Paxton, White, Nicholas, Jones, Sheppard, Bath, Brock, Borglin, Travis, Thieme, Byrd, Jones, Becker, Stoudt, Marvel, Conner, Bloxman, Petticrew, Irion, Girzi, Corey, Daniel, Everett, Jackson, Stiles, Rich, Cain, Marts, Malarz, Young, Carter, Sirockman, Starnes, Hirco, Holloway, Bova, Tower, Scroggins, Reid, Thury, Lingle, Jackson, Hammond, Johnson, Farmer, Powell, Tannous, Graham, Borom, Bennett and Ashwood

B Irion, D Rich, T Marvel and S Annanian

Bill MacClarence and Unknown

Evan M Johnson and Pat Bova

1st Lt James R Starnes shooting down his fifth aerial victory, a Me-109, on 4 August 44.

17 April 45, Capt Robert E Irion, 505th, flames a parked enemy aircraft near Pocking

G McFarlane, J Earnest, F Pratt and J Brignols

Owen Farmer, William Moore and Allen Young

505th Fighter Squadron

John G Holloway and crew

Runaway control vehicle

6N-1 "Mary Lee" - G E Graham, pilto

Connors, Stoor, Hess Brock, Marvel and 2 Unks

Fred M Harkey, Gabriel J Cutri, James R Starnes and Stone D Howell

"Impatient Virgin" - W A Jones, pilot

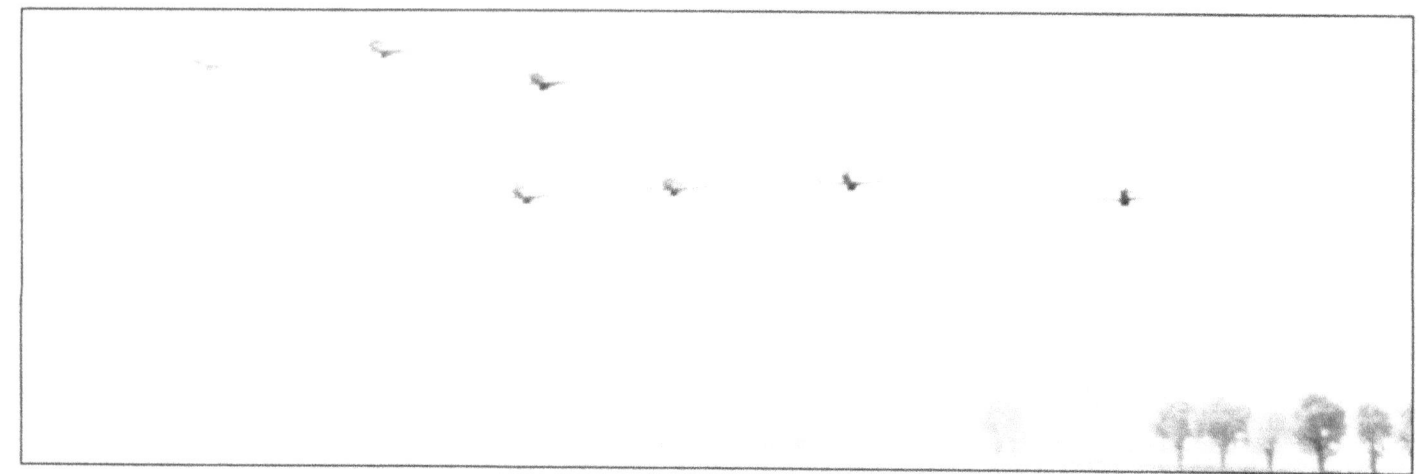

VE DAY FLY OVER - Corey led Group Fly over Base - three passes

505th Fighter Squadron

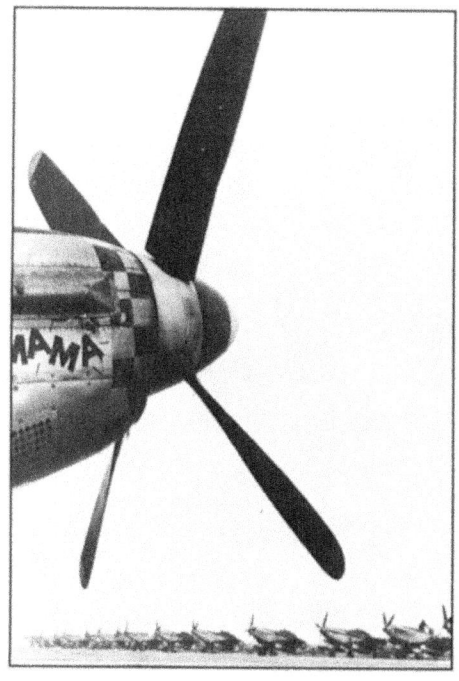

"Jimmy Lee" at Fowlmere on take off.

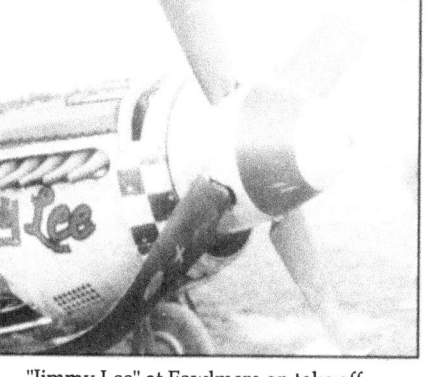

Joe Thury flying his "Pauline"

1 August 44, JU 88 on ground

505th flight line at Fowlmere

"Lone Star Lady", flown by Bert Conner, taxies out for a mission.

"Mary - Queen of Scotts"

505th Fighter Squadron

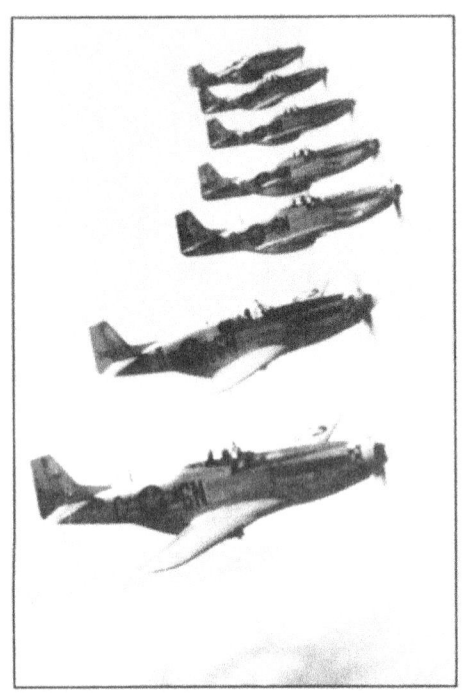

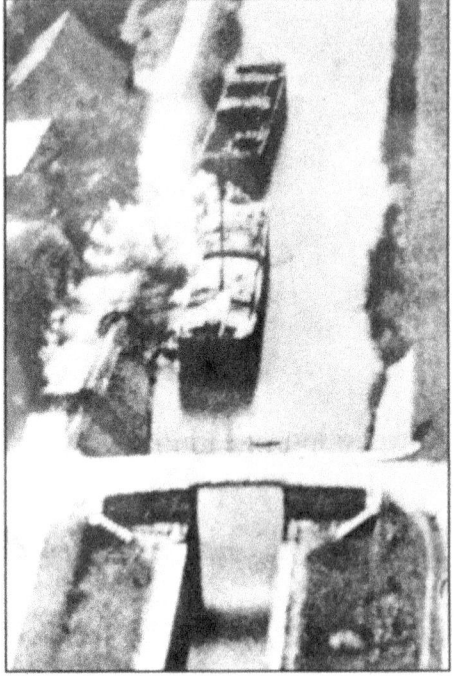

P-51's over Fowlmere, England

Barges in canal

"Junior" - Jay Marts, pilot

2nd Lt Authur E Tongue knocks down a Me-109 south of Hamburg.

505th Fighter Squadron

2nd Lt James R Starnes strafes a train on 7 June 44.

1st Lt Floyd W Smith strafing a parked aircraft, one is burning.

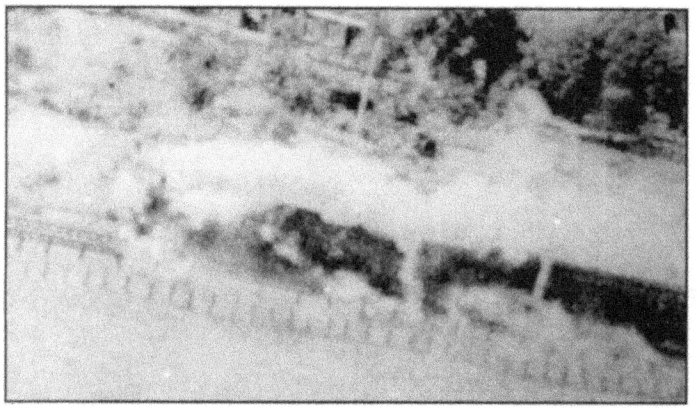

21 June 44, Lt James R Starnes strafes a moving train.

1st Lt Roland W Strong strafes railroad cars on 1 August 44.

F/O Ellis E Hupp, Jr. strafing dispersed parked aircraft on 17 April 45.

2nd Lt James R Starnes strafes a steaming locomotive on 14 June 44.

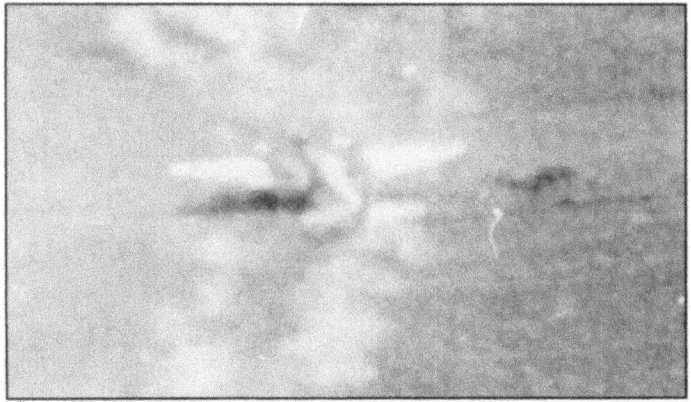

19 July 44, 1st Lt James R Starnes strafing an airfield near Heilbronn.

Capt James A Diefenbeck strafes an airfield near Pocking on 17 April 45.

505th Fighter Squadron

21 June 44, Lt James R Starnes a train on an escort mission to Berlin.

Major Donald A Larson strafing a locomotive on 1 August 44.

10 June 44, 2nd Lt James R Starnes strafes a train.

4 November 44 Lt Robert E Irion strafes a train on an escort mission.

Major Donald A Larson strafing a locomotive.

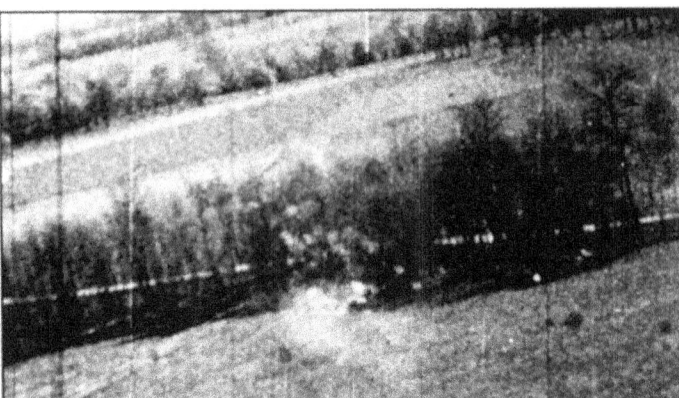

Capt Phillip M Loveless strafing parked German aircraft at the edge of the trees on 17 April 45.

7 June 44, 2nd Lt James R Starnes strafes a train in support of the D-Day landings of the previous day

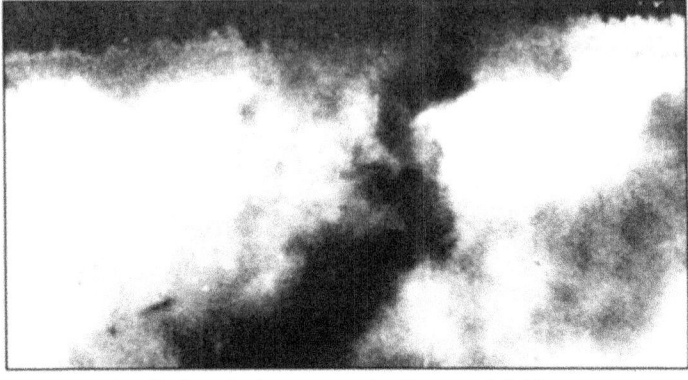

A pall of smoke hangs over the German airfield near Pocking as Capt J Brooks Bline takes another pass.

505th Fighter Squadron

2nd Lt Martin N Nay follows another P-51 on a strafing run on 3 Aug 44.

Capt Phillip M Loveless strafes a FW-190 on 16 April 1945.

1st Lt James R Starnes pursues his fifth aerial victory.

1st Lt Jerome T Murphy scores strikes on a parked aircraft at an airfield near Pocking on 17 April 1945.

2d Lt James R Starnes after his second victory of the day on 8 June 44. He shot down a Me-109 on an earlier mission.

1st Lt Thomas W Marvel tears up the German airfield at Prien, 16 April 45.

2 March 45, Capt James R Starnes shoots down his sixth E/A of the War.

19 July 44, 1st Lt James R Starnes strafes a Ju-188 near Heilbronn.

339th Fighter Group

Ground Articles

Rememberances By Men Of The 1786 Ordnance Supply & Maintenance Company (AVN)

Mission and Functions of the 1786th

by Sterling Conley

General History

On March 1, 1944, the unit received orders to move to a permanent assignment at Station A.A.F. 378, Fowlmere, Cambridgeshire. Upon arriving at Fowlmere there was the usual house cleaning and general preparations to be accomplished before the unit could perform its primary duties - that of the third echelon automotive and armament maintenance and ordnance general and ammunition supply.

After arriving at A.A.F. 378 it was found that the Ordnance Supply and Maintenance Company had to perform many and varied duties because of the limited supplies and equipment of other service units. During the setting-up period prior to the arrival of the fighter group, it was decided to use the 1786th in the general role of Station Ordnance plus duties as a channel for Ordnance General Supply. This proved to be a wise decision. The 1786th performed all duties assigned to it until the early summer of 1945. There was a reorganization of all service units at this time, and the 1786th was integrated into the 687th Air Material Squadron.

In July, 1945, the 687th was alerted to return to the United States. The unit moved directly to Liverpool, boarded the Liberty ship, *Helen Hunt Jackson*, and returned to where they had started - Camp Miles Standish. The men were all given thirty days furlough with orders to return to Drew Field in Tampa, Florida, where they would be deployed to the Pacific.

Fortunately the men never did see action in the Pacific. The war ended in August, the 687th was disbanded and the men were discharged to return home.

Headquarters Section

Headquarters section of the 1786th was under the command of Captain John Hild. Working directly under Captain Hild was 1st Sgt Fred Cox. Captain Hild also served as Base Ordnance Officer, a responsibility requiring a large portion of his time. Consequently, 1st Sgt Cox bore most of the responsibility for the administration of the

Company.

The many duties of the Headquarters Section included the maintenance of all personnel records, sick call, pay, and unit supply records. Files were maintained; Army Air Force Regulation Bulletins were kept up to date; all memos and directives to other section chiefs were distributed for their compliance.

Another responsibility of the section was company supply. This duty was delegated to the capable hands of S/Sgt Norman Behner and Cpl Emer Taylor. All laundry, clothing issues, and other personal needs of the company were handled by these two men.

The payroll records and distribution of cash on payday was handled by Cpl Fred Alverson, another of the many jobs performed so well by this man.

Under the Unit Manning Document (U.M.D.), the Company was authorized to man our own mess. The mess personnel were also under the supervision of the First Sergeant. Upon our arrival at Fowlmere we were informed that the 339th Fighter Group would operate a consolidated mess and that we were to loan our mess personnel to the consolidated mess. This group included S/Sgt Jack Lacey as Mess Sergeant, assisted by Cpl Edgar Turner and Pfc Woodrow Martin. This arrangement proved to be best for the entire base.

As the key administrator of the Headquarters Section it was the duty of the First Sergeant to be responsible for the welfare of the men and serve as a go-between for the enlisted men and other officers in the Company. Sgt Cox would certainly qualify as one of the best First Sergeants in the European Theater of Operations (E.T.O.). In Captain Hild's own words, "I should know! I served under him for three years."

Armament Section

The lives of our pilots depended a great deal on the skill and accuracy of the men in the Armament Section. The task of delivering .50-cal. machine guns in flawless condition to the armament crews of the 503rd, 504th and 505th Fighter Squadrons was the responsibility of Lt Richard Luck and T/Sgt Clare Mintline. These men were assisted by one of the finest group of armorers in the E.T.O. Consequently our pilots felt secure that when their weapons were needed, they wouldn't fail.

The Armament Section performed all Third Echelon armament maintenance for the aircraft and ground weapons, small arms, and all parts and supplies for the armaments. The Armament Section was also assigned an additional duty of having one armorer on the flight line whenever there were any combat planes in the air. The maintenance of weapons on Base F378 was exceptional.

The Armament Section also set up and maintained a skeet range for the pilots. This entailed having a man on duty to check out and maintain the 12-gauge Browning automatic shotguns.

Ammunition Section

The Ammunition Section of any Ordnance Supply and Maintenance Company is probably the least recognized and hardest working section in the entire command. This duty was assigned to Lt William Whitten, assisted by Section Chief T/Sgt Clyde Watson. They were fortunate to have .good men in the section to help them receive, issue, and store all types of ammunition, including bombs and pyrotechnics, for the Fighter Group and all attached units.

Before, on, and after D-Day the demand for ammunition was tremendous. In the period during the Battle of the Bulge and immediately following D-Day this group of men worked around the clock. This was the most urgent job during this time period. To give these men needed rest, all other sections in the Company would send men to relieve them.

As an example of their never-say-quit attitude, on the evening of D minus 3, the 1786 Ammunition Section was ordered to proceed to an army ammunition depot in southwest England to pick up a load of .50-cal. ammunition and 500-1b. bombs. T/Sgt Watson borrowed S/Sgt Gus Duncan from the Automotive Section and they proceeded to the depot. During the return trip to Fowlmere, the weather was so bad they had to alternate walking in front of the truck to stay on the road. They called for permission to stop for the night, but were ordered to continue. They did so, arriving at midnight. Shortly after midnight Sgt. Cox was alerted by base headquarters to have Ordnance start linking ammunition. An exhausted Sgt Watson rounded up his men and began the linking process. They had one linking machine (electric) and several hand machines. As D-Day approached the linking operation turned into a 24-hour shift. Sgt Cox had all sections doing double duty - one shift on their regular job and one shift linking ammunition. At this time most of our P-51s were returning with no ammunition, and in many cases, with machine gun barrels burned out. During this hectic period the electric linking machine broke, and the hand machines couldn't keep up. Deep trouble loomed! Captain Hild finally located a replacement for the electric machine. Sgt Watson made a 36-hour, non-stop trip to Scotland, returned with the new machine, and the men started linking again.

As a matter of interest, 1,200,000 rounds of .50-cal. ammunition were linked and 1,167 bombs were distributed. This was during the first six months of operations with the 339th.

Automotive Section

The Automotive Section was by far the largest section in the Company. This unit consisted of men with many different skills and occupations. Heading this list of mechanics, welders, machinists, sheet metal men and body workers was Lt William Snowden. Lt Snowden had as his key man M/Sgt Joseph Hawley. Sgt Hawley was an excellent leader, organizing his section into one of the best and most efficient units on the base. T/Sgt Ed Szech served as right hand man to Sgt Hawley and was responsible for much of the efficiency.

This section handled all Third Echelon motor maintenance and Second Echelon maintenance for the Company. They also took care of overflow work from the Second Echelon motor maintenance shop and the Base Motor Pool. Their performance was exemplified by the fact that never were there more than three vehicles on the dead line at once. Of all the vehicles serviced and repaired, one received special attention - the Colonel's staff car, kept in A-1 condition at all times.

This group of men were called upon many times for duties other than that of automotive repair and maintenance. Such duties ranged from picking up a load of Pierce planking from a disabled truck in Cambridge and delivering it to Fowlmere for landing mats to freeing a B-17 stuck in the mud. This was indeed a versatile group of men.

Routine work of this section consisted of weekly spot check inspections, 6,000 mile inspection, technical inspections, and major repairs to engine and body. Minor repairs and alterations, devising new tools, and undertaking modifications requested by other organizations on the base were also routine. This section was also called upon to repair and check other vehicles in convoy passing through the Fowlmere area.

Any special jobs involving machine work were given to Sgt John McCarty and his assistant, Cpl William Crippen, who worked in the mobile machine shop nicknamed the "Mechanized Ironmongery." This mobile truck served many purposes: linking machines were made for the ammunition section; gauges for the armament section; paper punches for the supply section; brake drums turned for the automotive section; any work requested by the fighter squadrons. During slack time, Sgt McCarty made adaptors for cameras so that varied size film could be used. Occasionally, during a lull, "Ironmongery" served as a barber shop with Cpl Crippen wielding the shears.

It would be impossible to go into detail about the individual men and their performance. The jobs were done and done well by all.

Supply Section

The Supply Section of the 1786th was under the command of Captain John Hild; working directly under him as section chief was yours truly, T/Sgt Sterling Conley.

Upon arrival in Fowlmere, the Supply Section was given the duty of functioning as Station Ordnance Office in addition to it's regular duties as a channel for Ordnance General Supply. This was an efficient system and worked well for all concerned.

The primary duty of this section was to keep a well supplied warehouse of parts for the other sections of the Company. This required close cooperation with the other section chiefs concerning inventories of parts needed for the present time as well as anticipation of future parts inventories. Often we were caught short and would have to send a special detail to bring in a vehicle, motor parts and weapons parts. Such was the case in December, 1944, when shortly before Christmas it became impossible to keep an adequate supply of .50-cal. machine gun barrels for our pilots. Captain Hild finally located a load at one of our A.F. warehouses on the east coast of England near Ipswich. Cpl Harold (Monk) Ward and I were dispatched to pick up the load of barrels and return to Fowlmere. It was typical English weather - foggy and cold, and the roads were frozen. We managed the trip to Ipswich, but had trouble on the return trip. It was getting dark, and we were coming downhill into a small English village. As we started around a bend, a lady in a cracker-box auto pulled out directly in front of us. There was no chance of stopping due to the ice on the road, and the resulting crash rendered the lady unconscious with considerable damage to her car. We managed to carry her across the street to a pub where, after a little brandy and a cup of tea, she regained consciousness. Fortunately she suffered no serious injury. Once recovered she then turned to us and said, "You bloody Yanks, you come over here and you're killing more of us than the Germans."

In addition to loading gun barrels, we were instructed to pick up an English ambulance on our return trip and drive it to Fowlmere. Cpl Ward drove the ambulance and followed me in the truck. By then the weather was well fogged in and the roads completely frozen. I stopped, but Cpl Ward couldn't.

The result - another crash. We finally accomplished our mission, arriving in Fowlmere about 2 a.m., delivering a truck and trailer load of barrels and one beat-up English ambulance. Our only recognition for this arduous eighteen hours of duty was an accusation of hitting too many pubs plus a reprimand for damaging two vehicles and almost killing an English civilian.

Operating as station ordnance, this section was responsible for maintaining an inventory of all weapons and vehicles on the base. This included the small arms, ammunition, and vehicles issued to each squadron.

Last, but not least, were the !#% bicycles - all 775 of them! The Station Ordnance maintained a complete bicycle shop ably handled by Pfc Serafino Sormanti. This was a full time job. At times Pfc Sormanti was completely swamped. When that happened, he recruited a couple of Italian POWs to help out.

Cpl Paul Reidy was the man in charge of our carpentry shop. All the repair work on buildings and other carpentry alterations that were too difficult for the other men to do were handed to Paul. There wasn't much recognition for this job, but it was a necessary job well done. Station Ordnance also kept a man on duty 24 hours a day. Each man in the section would attend to his assigned duty during the day, and once weekly, stand a 24-hour shift. I think it can safely be said that the Supply Section performed all assigned tasks in a manner to bring credit to each member.

1786th Ordnance Supply & Maintenance Company

Capt John Hild

Lt Richard Luck

Lt William Snowden

Lt William Whitten

1st Sgt Fred Cox

M/Sgt Joseph Hawley

T/Sgt Clyde Watson

T/Sgt Sterling Conley

T/Sgt Clare Mintline

339th at Bassingborn

8th Air Force
Station F-378
Calendar with five plane photos.

Major Vernon B Hathorn on 18 August 44.

Biographical Sketches Of Group And Squadron Comanding Officers

339th Fighter Group

COLONEL
JOHN B. HENRY, JR.
August 1943 - April 1945

John B. Henry was born 15 July 1916 and grew up near Charlotte, Texas. After attending Southwestern University he graduated from flight school at Kelly Field, Texas, in February 1939. He had several assignments in fighter groups in the states and Panama until August 1943 when he assumed command of the newly re-designated 339th Fighter Bomber Group at Walterboro, South Carolina. John took the group to Rice Field, California, for maneuvers and to Fowlmere, England, for combat as part of the Eighth Air Force. He flew two combat tours as Group Commander before being reassigned on 14 April 1945 to the staff of the 45th Bomb Wing in England. He took a P-51 and his crew chief, Arne Nissen, along to the new assignment.

John Henry's post-war assignments included duty in command and staff jobs with the Strategic Air Command, Air Transport Command, Pacific Air Forces, U.S. Air Forces Europe and U.S. Southern Command in Panama. He was stationed in Texas, Kansas, South Dakota, Massachusetts, Colorado, California, Hawaii and twice at the Pentagon in Washington, DC. These tours were interspersed with courses for his military education including the Armed Forces Staff College, Air War College and numerous technical and staff courses. John served as Commandant of the InterAmerican Defense College before his final tour of active duty as Chief of Staff, U.S. Southern Command in Panama, retiring after 36 years of continuous active duty in 1974.

503rd Fighter Squadron

LIEUTENANT COLONEL
HAROLD W. SCRUGGS
August 1943 - May 1944

Harold W. Scruggs was born 2 September 1916 at Hollis, Oklahoma. He graduated from the University of Oklahoma in 1939 and entered flight training in September 1940, graduating at Shreveport, Louisiana, with Class 41-C on 15 March 1941. At graduation ceremonies the new pilots were told that the class would be split down the middle. Those to the right of the center aisle would become bomber pilots, and those on the left would go to fighters. Anyone on the fighter side who preferred bombers could cross the aisle but not vice versa. Hal was on the left and wanted to go to fighters anyway. His first assignment was flying P-40s in the 20th Fighter Group at Hamilton Field, California, under Ira Eaker who later commanded the Eighth Air Force and the Fifteenth Air Force in Europe.

Hal was later assigned to the 338th Fighter Group at Tallahassee, Florida, which was the group responsible for all fighter Replacement Training Unit bases in the southeastern U.S. From there he had temporary duty at Wright Field, Ohio, testing new fighter-type aircraft and later made an exhibition tour demonstrating the P-47 to encourage young men to volunteer for flight training. In August 1943 he joined the 339th Fighter Bomber Group as commander of the 503rd Fighter Bomber Squadron. At Fowlmere, England, he moved up to Deputy Group Commander in May 1944, also serving as acting Group Commander during October through December 1944 while John B. Henry was back in the States on R&R between combat tours. Hal returned to the States in January 1945 to command auxiliary fields at Eglin Field, Florida. Later in his Air Force career he had tours of duty in Panama; Cape Cod, Massachusetts; Chicago, Illinois; Oscoda, Michigan; Taiwan; McChord, Washington; and Reno, Nevada where he retired in 1961.

MAJOR
JOHN AITKEN, JR.
May 1944 - September 1944

John Aitken was born 3 May 1918 in Charlotte, North Carolina, and moved to Elberton, Georgia, in 1936. He completed two years of college at Douglas, Georgia, before transferring to Mercer University where, in April 1941, he took a flight physical for cadet training. He graduated at Victoria Field in Class 42-B on 20 February 1942. His first assignment was to the 52nd Fighter Group in Wilmington, North Carolina, then to Myrtle Beach, South Carolina, for three months in P-40 and P-39 aircraft. He and his fellow pilots were told they were combat-ready fighter pilots even though they had less than 100 hours fighter time.

The 52nd Fighter Group left for England where, upon arrival, the men were informed they and the 31st Fighter Group would be equipped with Spitfires. After four months training they left for Gibraltar by troop transport. They stood two days on alert and then scrambled for Oran, North Africa, on invasion day. The 52nd moved to within 50 miles of German lines and "All hell broke loose!" Although John scored 1 1/2 kills in April '43 in North Affica, he was happy to rotate in July back to the States and to the 339th. He assumed command of the 503rd Fighter Squadron in May 1944 at Fowlmere, England, when Hal Scruggs became Deputy Group Commander.

Upon completion of his tour with the 339th during which he scored three aerial kills to run his total to 4 1/2 confirmed in the air, John returned to the States in October '44. He remained on active duty and received a regular commission. His last fighter assignment was at Neubiberg near Munich, Germany, but he commanded an Air Control and Warning Squadron for three years in Newfoundland, Canada, and also spent several years on the Inspector General Team at Air Defense Command in Colorado. John says the best assignment of his entire Air Force career was with the 339th where it was his privilege to work for the best commander the Air Force ever had - John B. Henry, Jr.

LIEUTENANT COLONEL
HARVEY E. HENDERSON

September 1944 - December 1944

Harvey E. Henderson was born 17 November 1919 near McAllen, Texas. He entered flight training on 29 July 1940 and graduated with Class 41-C on 15 March 1941, remaining at Kelly Field, Texas, as an instructor. He commanded several units, including a P-39 reconnaissance squadron at Thermal, California, and a liaison squadron which he took to England during the summer of 1944. Harvey had unsuccessfully tried to join the 339th at Rice, so he visited Fowlmere to seek a transfer to the 339th in order to fly combat. This was arranged. He arrived in August 1944 and assumed command of the 503rd Fighter Squadron when John Aitken completed his combat tour late in September of that year. After 2 1/2 months as commander he was shot down by a FW-190 near Berlin on the 5th of December, '44, finishing the war as a P.O.W. at Stalagluft I near Barth, Germany.

After the war Harvey remained in the Air Force for a career. In addition to attending the Air War College and the National War College, he commanded a number of combat organizations before retiring from the 363rd Tactical Reconnaissance Wing at Shaw Air Force Base, South Carolina, in March 1967.

LIEUTENANT COLONEL
DALE E. SHAFER, JR.

December 1944 - August 1945

Dale E. Shafer grew up in Dayton, Ohio. He entered flight training in 1941 and graduated from Brooks Field in San Antonio with Class 42-A on 9 January 1942. Two months later he was assigned to the 31st Fighter Group flying P-40s and P-39s before going to England in June 1942. There his group was equipped with Spitfire Vs and became operational in August 1942 as the first fighter group in the Eighth Air Force. In September '42, Dale went to Gibraltar and then participated in the North African, Sicilian and Italian air campaigns. He scored four aerial kills before returning to the U.S. in September 1943. Ten months later he was back in England with the 339th Fighter Group at Fowlmere. Dale was operations officer in the 503rd, but assumed command of the squadron for the remainder of the war when Harvey Henderson went down on 5 December 1944.

During that period he scored three more aerial kills to become an ace with 75 more combat missions in the 339th. He volunteered to take his squadron to fight the Japanese after VE-Day, but that program was cancelled when the Japanese folded after being hit with the A-Bomb.

After the war Dale joined the Ohio Air National Guard and later rose to command that organization with the rank of Major General. He was recognized as one of the finest acrobatic pilots in the Air Force. Few pilots have been more widely admired by their peers than Dale Shafer.

504TH FIGHTER SQUADRON

LIEUTENANT COLONEL
EDGAR BRUCE GRAVETTE

April 1944 - December 1944

Edgar Bruce Gravette was born on 23 August 1919 in Waco, Texas. He grew up in Red Bluff, California, before attending the University of California at Chico from 1937-1941. As the hot breath of the draft was apparent, he decided to fly rather than hit the trenches. In 1940 he took Civilian Pilot Training in college, then entered flight cadet school, graduating in Class 41-I.

Bruce was first assigned to the 54th Fighter Group flying P-39s and P-40s. When it was undecided whether the Japanese would attack California, Midway or Alaska, the 54th left on 4-hours notice in May 1942 and wound up in Alaska a few days later. Bill Routt, Louis Peter and Frank Guernsey were Aleutian buddies. By the time they reached Adak from which missions against Kiska were flown, all Zeroes had been destroyed and they were reduced to strafing Japanese gun emplacements. Bruce returned to the states in 1943 and joined the 339th as Captain and Operations Officer of the 504th Fighter Squadron.

He assumed command of the squadron on arrival at Fowlmere and completed his tour late in December 1944. After being deputy Commanding Officer of a P-51 outfit at Ft. Myers, Florida, until the war was over, he got out of the Air Force in 1946, but was recalled in 1948 after which he commanded various Air Control and Warning squadrons in Japan and the U.S. He was Chief of Operations for the 28th Air Division and Chief of Plans and Requirements for the Air Defense Command. After attending Air War College in 1958 he was Director of Air Defense in

Korea and at the North American Air Defense Command until retirement in 1968.

MAJOR
LEWIS S. PETER
December 1944 - January 1945

Lewis S. Peter was born 29 December 1917 in San Antonio, Texas. He graduated from Texas A & M in 1939 as an engineer. In May 1941 he entered flight school, graduating in Class 41-I on 12 December 1941 at Sacramento, California. Like Bruce Gravette, "Pete" was first assigned to the 54th at Everett, Washington. After several moves they went to Nome, Alaska, and then to Adak Island in the Aleutians. In January 1943 the unit returned to Bartow, Florida, and then Oscoda, Michigan. While at Oscoda, Pete, Bruce Gravette, Bill Routt and Vern Hathorne (later 339th Fighter Group Operations Officer) trained the first black flying unit in the Army Air Forces, the 99th Fighter Squadron, which was commanded by Benjamin O. Davis, Jr. (The 99th became one of the most trained squadrons in the Air Force because no one knew what to do with them. In April 1943 they deployed to Africa and Italy, later becoming the 332nd Fighter Group, the only black fighter group in the Air Force.)

Pete joined the 339th at Walterboro in August 1943 as flight leader in the 504th. At Fowlmere he became Operations Officer when Bill Routt rotated, later assuming command of the squadron in December 1944 when Bruce Gravette rotated to the States. Late in January 1945 he stepped back into the Operations Officer position when Lieutenant Colonel Bill Clark assumed command of the 504th. After returning to the States in the spring of '45, Pete had several short assignments until deciding to leave the service.

LIEUTENANT COLONEL
WILLIAM C. CLARK
January 1945 - March 1945

William C. Clark was born 20 October 1916 in Texas. He graduated from flying school late in 1939 and participated in several fighter type assignments in the states and Panama. After his initial combat experience with the 357th Fighter Group early in January 1945, he joined the 339th on 21 January to command the 504th. When Lieutenant Colonel Carl Goldenberg returned to the States on 23 March '45, Bill Clark moved up to Deputy Group Commander, then assumed command of the Group when John B. Henry was transferred to the 45th Bomb Wing on 15 April 1945. He was credited with one aerial victory and destroyed eight enemy aircraft on the ground. He also damaged a ME-262 jet in the air. Bill saw further combat service in F-86 aircraft in Korea with the 51st Fighter Wing. He was a graduate of the Air Command and Staff College and Armed Forces Staff College before retiring from the Air Force in 1968.

LIEUTENANT COLONEL
WILLIAM H. JULIAN
March 1945 - May 1945

Coming from Dallas, Texas, William H. Julian flew two combat tours with the 78th Fighter Group out of Duxford, England, during which time he shot down five German fighters. He arrived in Fowlmere in late March 1945 where he assumed command of the 504th, scoring three ground victories during his short tenure as 504th commander. Bill returned to the States shortly after the end of hostilities in Europe.

505TH FIGHTER SQUADRON

MAJOR
DONALD A. LARSON
December 1943 - August 1944

Donald A. Larson was born in 1915 in Yakima, Washington. He joined the Army Air Corps in April 1941 and graduated from flying school in December '41. After a series of assignments as instructor in P-40 aircraft at Pinellas County Airport, Florida, Don was assigned to the 339th Fighter Group at Walterboro, South Carolina, in August 1943 as Operations Officer in the 503rd Fighter Squadron.

He assumed command of the 505th in December 1943 and remained in that capacity until killed in action from a mid-air collision with another P-51 during a dogfight on the deck near Hamburg, Germany, on 4 August 1944. Just prior to his death he scored two aerial kills on that final mission to become an ace with six in the air and three on the ground. In 1952 Larson Air Force Base in Grant County, Washington, was named in his honor.

LIEUTENANT COLONEL
JOSEPH L. THURY
August 1944 - June 1945

Joseph L. Thury was born on the 20th of March, 1919, in St. Paul, Minnesota. After three years of college, he entered cadet training in June 1941 and, as a member of Class 42-B, graduated from Luke Field on 6 February 1942. Joe's first duty was with the 10th Pursuit Squadron, Key Field, Mississippi, flying P-40s. He was then transferred to the 57th Pursuit Squadron at Harding Field, Louisiana, and later moved with the squadron to Orlando, Florida. After instructing in P-40s at Drew Field and Pinellas, he joined the 339th Fighter Group at Walterboro, South Carolina, in August 1943, serving as Operations officer for the 505th until assuming command of the squadron after Don Larson was killed in action over Germany a year later. Joe flew two combat tours and remained as squadron commanding officer until the end of the war. Additionally, he was top pilot of the 339th Fighter Group with 2 1/2 kills in the air and 25 1/2 on the ground, an accomplishment which also ranked him in the top ten in the Eighth Air Force. After the end of the war, Joe Thury was offered a regular commission in the Air Force, but declined in order to practice law in the civilian community. He did, however, remain part of the Air Force active reserve program, later retiring from the reserves in the rank of colonel.

EPILOGUE

339th Fighter Group
August 1943 - October 1945

By Harold W. Scruggs

In the beginning, at a small base located in a sleepy little southern town, personnel began to assemble to form a somewhat disorganized and untrained fighter group. Most were young, eager and bright-eyed, and some had brought along even younger brides. All knew they were destined for something... but what? Where? And how would it all end?

The runway was hot enough to fry an egg. Located in the middle of the desert in California, tents were the only shield from the blazing sun. A short distance away was a small desert town whose people were unfamiliar with the type of personnel in a fighter group. The people residing there today still have vivid memories of the day this group descended on their town.

A large Army tank force was also training in the desert. Its commander was destined to become one of the most colorful generals in our time. Some of his company commanders, however, were at a loss to understand the sport of fighter pilots flying their aircraft so low as to clip the antennas on their jeeps.

Intense training was necessary to prepare our pilots to compete against an enemy force whose pilots were already highly trained and experienced in a more deadly sport.

The war in Europe intensified. The situation at Dunkirk was no less than desperate. Only the magnificent heroism of the British fighter pilots made it less so. Churchill spoke of it with words that will long be remembered: "Never, in the history of the British Empire, have so many owed so much to so few!"

The 339th was aboard ship in a large convoy crossing the North Atlantic. It was about midnight. Huge waves were rising several stories high and crashing down on the bow of the ship. As the ship nosed down into the next wave it didn't seem possible for it to rise again. Looking to the stern of the ship, large barrel shaped objects were being hurled some distance aft. As they hit the water and sank, an explosion shot a spout of water high in the sky. It could mean only one thing. We were under attack by submarines! The 339th was asleep several decks below. Would they be awakened by a gush of water through a hole in the side of the ship? Would this be the end?

The many trips to Berlin were much smoother but no less hazardous. The path was easy to follow. The beautiful "con" trails left by the thousands of bombers and fighters stretched all the way from England to the targets in the heart of Germany, but they were marred by huge black explosions laden with sharp pieces of steel which sliced through vital parts of the aircraft and its human contents. The enemy fighters attacked head-on, firing all of their guns as they passed through the formations. Our mission: "To protect the bombers from these attacks." Sometimes, the sky would be filled with exploding aircraft and parachutes. For them, it was the end of the war.

We may never again become involved in a war in which so many aircraft were involved in a conflict and in which individual pilots confronted each other in deadly combat. This was not a one-time affair. It had to be repeated day after day until collapse of the resistance.

Waiting may have been an even more difficult task for those loved ones back home. That official looking letter that arrived in the mail...*O dear God, please don't let it begin with, "We regret to inform you..."*

With bombs dropped and ammunition expended, the scattered elements turned toward home. Straggling wounded bombers were guarded as long as remaining fuel would allow. Would there be enough to make it back? With the fuel gauge flickering near zero, the white object, barely discernible on the distant horizon, was always a welcome sight – the White Cliffs of Dover.

The greatest military invasion force ever assembled was poised and ready to strike. Ike gave the word, "Go!" to the invasion forces. Our call came in the early morning hours. We must help guard this force during its most vulnerable period against the German Luftwaffe. The first report came back in a garbled cable: "1st Force drowned!" Ike must have thought, *is this the end?* The cable should have read: "1st Force ground."

Winter was at hand and weather increasingly became a factor in our operations. Rain caused the sod runway to become a slippery mud path. Instrument conditions became more and more frequent. It was a difficult task to take off and assemble a large number of aircraft under these conditions. On one occasion the bombers were already off the ground and on their way to Berlin when the weather closed in. Visibility was reduced to almost zero.

No fighters were able to take off. The Wing Commander, General Woodbury, sounded very concerned when he called. Was it possible for the 339th to take off? We decided to try and devised a way. Once in the air, the Group assembled on a course to intercept the bombers. We were in the "soup" almost to Berlin. Suddenly we broke out of the clouds near the bomber formations. It appeared as if the entire Luftwaffe was attacking the bombers. When they spotted us they must have thought that all of the 8th Air Force fighters were there. They immediately broke off their attack on the bombers and engaged our group. Although few kills were made that day, the bombers were saved from a devastating loss. Without doubt this was one of the finest missions flown by the 339th Fighter Group.

The 339th also provided ground support for the invasion forces as they gathered strength on the beaches of Normandy. Soon, they would break out and start their march across Europe. The colorful commander of the tank forces we'd trained with in the California desert was making an end run around the right flank of the enemy forces, but weather again became a factor. Air support was not possible and the German forces began a counter attack. The "Battle of the Bulge" was a critical stage in the conduct of the war. We came closer to losing this battle than most people realized. Suddenly, the weather broke, and our air forces were able to take off and provide air support. This enabled the ground forces to cut off the counter attack and prepare for the final onslaught.

One day, Patton sent Ike a very formal report (after being criticized for using some colorful language in a previous report). He added a P.S. to the report: "Today I peed in the Rhine!"

The end was in sight. This was the beginning of the final act. The curtain would soon be drawing to a close.

The accomplishments of the 339th Fighter Group will be long remembered. It is difficult to believe that one group could have accomplished so much in just one year of operations. Those of us who had the opportunity to be a part of this magnificent fighting group should feel honored and beholden. The individual effort and skill exhibited by leaders, the countless acts of bravery, and the support of so many fine people combined to make this group one of the most effective units in the conduct of the war and one which everyone can be proud to have been a member.

As the curtain fluttered to a close on the final act, the end was accomplished simply and without ceremony. It took only the stroke of a pen...."The 339th Fighter Group is inactivated 18 October 1945."

Table One
Missions of the 339th Fighter Group

MISSION #	DATE	MISSION TYPE	FO#	DESTINATION
1.	30 Apr 44	Fighter Sweep	W-59	NW France
2.	1 May 44	Fighter Sweep	FC-322	Belgium & Holland
		Practice Escort		East Anglia
3.	2 May 44	Bomber Escort	FC-324	St. Pol, France
4.	3 May 44	Bomber Escort	325	St. Omar
5.	5 May 44	Bomber Escort	327	Wizerness, France
6.	6 May 44	Bomber Escort	328	St. Pol, France
7.	7 May 44	Bomber Escort	329	Celle
8.	7 May 44	Bomber Escort	330	SW of Leige, Belgium
9.	8 May 44	Bomber Escort	331	W. Germany
10.	9 May 44	Bomber Escort	333	SE Belgium
11.	10 May 44	Bomber Escort	334	NE of Ruhr Valley
12.	11 May 44	Bomber Escort	335	Orleans, France
13.	12 May 44	Bomber Escort	337	Frankfort, Germany
		Bomber Escort		Brussels, Belgium
14.	13 May 44	Bomber Escort	338	NW of Berlin
15.	15 May 44	Fighter Sweep	339	NW France
16.	19 May 44	Bomber Escort	342	Berlin, Germany
17.	20 May 44	Bomber Escort	343-A	N. of Orleans, France
18.	21 May 44	Fighter Sweep	344	Leipzig, Germany
19.	22 May 44	Bomber Escort	346	NW France
20	23 May 44	Bomber Escort	348	SW France
21.	24 May 44	Bomber Escort	349	Berlin
22.	24 May 44	Glide Bombing	W-61	Soissons, France
23.	25 May 44	Bomber Escort	FC-350	Plainville, France
24.	2, May 44	Fighter Sweep	351	Mannheim/Strasbourg
25.	28 May 44	Bomber Escort	352	Lutzendorf, Germany
26.	29 May 44	Bomber Escort	353	E. of Berlin, Germany
27.	30 May 44	Bomber Escort	354	Oscheisleben,Germany
28.	31 May 44	Bomber Escort	355	Colmar, Germany
29.	2 Jun 44	Fighter Sweep	358	Evreux, France
30.	4 Jun 44	Bomber Escort	367	NW France
31.	4 Jun 44	Bomber Escort	368	NW France
32.	5 Jun 44	Bomber Escort	369	NW France
33.	6 Jun 44	Fighter Sweep	371	Beachhead, Normandy
34.	6 Jun 44	Fighter Sweep	371/Stud	SE of Laval, France
35.	6 Jun 44	Fighter Sweep	372-B	Orleans/Janville, France
36.	7 Jun 44	Fighter Sweep	373	Laval Airfield, France
37.	7 Jun 44	Fighter Swp-Patrol	375	Over Laval, France
38.	7 Jun 44	Fighter Sweep	376	Over Nantes, France
39.	8 Jun 44	Dive Bomb	377-1	NW France
40.	8 Jun 44	Dive Bomb	377-2	Rennes, France
41.	8 Jun 44	Dive Bomb	377	Rennes, France
42.	10 Jun 44	Dive Bomb	379	NW France
43.	10 Jun 44	Dive Bomb	381	Rennes, France
44.	10 Jun 44	Dive Bomb	381-3	Chartres, France
45.	11 Jun 44	Fighter Swp-Patrol	FC-382	NW France
46.	11 Jun 44	Dive Bomb	382-3	Alencon, France
47.	12 Jun 44	Fighter Swp-Patrol	383	Rouen, France
48.	12 Jun 44	Bomber Escort	384-2	N. France
49.	13 Jun 44	Fighter Swp-Patrol	386	Evreux AF, France
50.	13 Jun 44	Fighter Swp-Patrol	387	Angers-Saumur, France
51.	14 Jun 44	Fighter Swp-Patrol	388	Orleans, France
52.	15 Jun 44	Bomber Escort	390	Tours, France

Table One (Cont'd.)

53.	16 Jun 44	Bomber Escort	393	NE of St. Pol, France
54.	17 Jun 44	Bomber Escort	394	S. of Paris, France
55.	17 Jun 44	Dive Bm-Bmr Esc	395	N. France
56.	18 Jun 44	Bomber Escort	396	Hamburg, Germany
57.	19 Jun 44	Bomber Escort	399	S. France
58.	20 Jun 44	Bomber Escort	402	Hamburg, Germany
59.	20 Jun 44	Fighter Sweep	404	Rouen/St. Quenten, Fr.
60.	21 Jun 44	Bomber Escort	407	Berlin, Germany
61.	22 Jun 44	Fighter-Swp-Patrol	410	Pas de Calais, France
62.	22 Jun 44	Bomber Escort	412	Paris, France
63.	23 Jun 44	Fighter Swp-Patrol	413	E. of Paris, France
64.	23 Jun 44	Fighter Swp-Patrol	414	NE of Paris, France
65.	24 Jun 44	Bomber Escort	415	Saumur, France
66.	25 Jun 44	Bomber Escort	417	S. France
67.	25 Jun 44	Bomber Escort	418	NW France
68.	27 Jun 44	Dive Bomb	420	N. France
69.	28 Jun 44	Bomber Escort	421	N. France
70.	29 Jun 44	Dive Bm-Bmr Esc	422	Leipzig, Germany
71.	30 Jun 44	Dive Bm-Bmr Esct	424	N. France
72.	2 Jul 44	Fighter Swp Patrol	426	N. France
73.	4 Jul 44	Bomber Escort	427	Tours, France
74.	5 Jul 44	Bomber Escort	430	Citze-Rijer, Holland
75.	6 Jul 44	Bomber Escort	432	Kiel, Germany
76.	6 Jul 44	Fighter Swp-Patrol	435	Saumur-Tours, France
77.	7 Jul 44	Bomber Escort	436	Leipzig, Germany
78.	8 Jul 44	Bomber Escort	437	Paris, France
79.	9 Jul 44	Bomber Escort	FC-438	Tours, France
80.	11 Jul 44	Bomber Escort	441	Munich, Germany
81.	12 Jul 44	Bomber Escort	442-B	Munich, Germany
82.	13 Jul 44	Bomber Escort	444	Saarbucken, Germany
83.	14 Jul 44	Bomber Escort	446	S. France
84.	16 Jul 44	Bomber Escort	450	Munich, Germany
85.	17 Jul 44	Bomber Escort	451	E. France
86.	17 Jul 44	Bomber Escort	453	N. France
87.	18 Jul 44	Bomber Escort	454	Griefswall Bay, Germany
88.	19 Jul 44	Bomber Escort	456	W. of Munich, Germany
89.	20 Jul 44	Bomber Escort	457	Gotha-Erfurt, Germany
90.	21 Jul 44	Bomber Escort	458-A	Kempten, Germany
91.	24 Jul 44	Bomber Escort	461	Normandy
92.	25 Jul 44	Fighter Swp-Patrol	462	N. France
93.	28 Jul 44	Bomber Escort	FC-469	Leipzig, Germany
94.	29 Jul 44	Bomber Escort	470	Merseburg, Germany
95.	30 Jul 44	Fighter Swp-Patrol	471	N. France
96.	31 Jul 44	Bomber Escort	472	Munich, Germany
97.	1 Aug 44	Bomber Escort	473	SE France
98.	2 Aug 44	Bomber Escort	475	N. France
99.	3 Aug 44	Bomber Escort	476	Strasbourg, Germany
100.	4 Aug 44	Bomber Escort	478	Hamburg, Germany
101.	5 Aug 44	Bomber Escort	FC-483	Brunswick, Germany
102.	6 Aug 44	Bomber Escort	487	Muritz Lake, Germany
103.	7 Aug 44	Fighter Swp-Patrol	490	Over Evreux, France
104.	8 Aug 44	Fighter Swp-Patrol	494-A	Over Paris, France
104.	9 Aug 44	Bomber Escort	496	Nurnburg, Germany

(Note: Mission on 8 and 9 August both numbered 104. See CombatNarrative section for explanation)

105.	11 Aug 44	Bomber Escort	503	Paris, France
106.	12 Aug 44	Fight Swp-Dive Bm	506	Luxembourg, Lux.

Table One (Cont'd.)

107.	12 Aug 44	Bomber Escort	507-B	Angouleme, France
108.	12 Aug 44	Bomber Escort	506-A2	Luxembourg, Lux.
109.	12 Aug 44	Bomber Escort	508	Amiens, France
110.	13 Aug 44	Fighter Swp-Patrol	511-A	N. of Paris, France
111.	13 Aug 44	Fight Swp-Dive Bm	511-B	N. of Paris, France
112.	14 Aug 44	Bomber Escort	513	S. of Paris, France
113.	15 Aug 44	Bomber Escort	516	Holland
114.	16 Aug 44	Bomber Escort	518	Chimintz, Germany
115.	17 Aug 44	Bomber Escort	519	La Rochelle, France
116.	18 Aug 44	Fighter Swp-Patrol	520	Over Amiens, France
117.	18 Aug 44	Fighter Swp-Patrol	522	N. of Paris, France
118.	24 Aug 44	Bomber Escort	527	Dresden, Germany
119.	25 Aug 44	Bomber Escort	529	NE Germany
120.	26 Aug 44	Bomber Escort	532	Brest, France
121.	26 Aug 44	Bomber Escort	533	N. France & Belgium
122.	27 Aug 44	Bomber Escort	535	Berlin, Germany
123.	28 Aug 44	Fighter Sweep	538	Nancy, France
124.	30 Aug 44	Bomber Escort	542	Bremen, Germany
125.	1 Sep 44	Bomber Escort	543	Frankfurt, Germany
126.	5 Sep 44	Bomber Escort	550	Stuttgart, Germany
127.	8 Sep 44	Bomber Escort	556	Mainz, Germany
128.	9 Sep 44	Bomber Escort	559	Dusseldorf, Germany
129.	10 Sep 44	Bomber Escort	561	Nurnburg, Germany
130.	11 Sep 44	Bomber Escort	563	Grimma, Germany
131.	12 Sep 44	Bomber Escort	565	Magdeburg, Germany
132.	13 Sep 44	Fighter Sweep	566	Munich, Germany
133.	17 Sep 44	Fighter Swp-Patrol	575	S. Holland
134.	18 Sep 44	Bomber Escort	578	Holland
135.	19 Sep 44	Bomber Escort	579	N & W of Ruhr Valley
136.	20 Sep 44	Fighter Swp-Patrol	580	Over Holland
137.	22 Sep 44	Bomber Escort	583	Kassell, Germany
138.	23 Sep 44	Fighter Swp-Patrol	FC-585	Over NW Germany
139.	25 Sep 44	Bomber Escort	586	Frankfurt, Germany
140.	26 Sep 44	Bomber Escort	588	Bremen, Germany
141.	27 Sep 44	Bomber Escort	590	Ludwigshaven, Germany
142.	28 Sep 44	Bomber Escort	591	Leipzig, Germany
143.	30 Sep 44	Bomber Escort	592	Bielefeld, Germany
144.	2 Oct 44	Bomber Escort	593	Kassell, Germany
145.	3 Oct 44	Bomber Escort	596	Kitzengen, Germany
146.	3 Oct 44	Bomber Escort	598	Munston, Germany
147.	6 Oct 44	Bomber Escort	599	Berlin, Germany
148.	7 Oct 44	Bomber Escort	600	Leipzig, Germany
149.	9 Oct 44	Bomber Escort	603	Frankfort, Germany (Last mission with the 8th Fighter Command)
150.	12 Oct 44	Bomber Escort	1235-A	Bremen, Germany
151.	14 Oct 44	Bomber Escort	1239-A	Cologne, Germany
152.	15 Oct 44	Bomber Escort	1240-A	Cologne, Germany
153.	17 Oct 44	Fighter Swp-Patrol	1245-A	Limburg-Siegen, Germany
154.	18 Oct 44	Bomber Escort	1246-A	Kassell, Germany
155.	19 Oct 44	Bomber Escort	1249-A	Ludwigshaven, Germany
156.	22 Oct 44	Bomber Escort	1254-A	Munster, Germany
157.	24 Oct 44	Fighter Sweep	1261-A	Over SW Bremen, Germany
158.	26 Oct 44	Bomber Escort	1264-A	Hanover, Germany
159.	28 Oct 44	Bomber Escort	1269-A	Hamm, Germany
160.	30 Oct 44	Bomber Escort	1273-A	Merseburg, Germany
161.	2 Nov 44	Bomber Escort	1281-A	Merseburg, Germany
162.	4 Nov 44	Bomber Escort	1286-A	Hanover, Germany

Table One (Cont'd.)

No.	Date	Mission	Code	Location
163.	5 Nov 44	Bmr Escm-Strafing	1288-A	Ruhr Valley, Germany
164.	6 Nov 44	Bomber Escort	1291-A	Nieumunster, Germany
165.	8 Nov 44	Bomber Escort	1296-A	Merseburg, Germany
166.	9 Nov 44	Bomber Escort	1299-A	Metz, Germany
167.	10 Nov 44	Bomber Escort	1301-A	Weisbaden, Germany
168.	11 Nov 44	Bomber Escort	1306-A	Koblenz, Germany
169.	16 Nov 44	Bomber Escort	1314-A	Aachen, Germany
170.	18 Nov 44	Fighter Sweep	1317-A	Mannheim, Germany
171.	20 Nov 44	Bomber Escort	1320-A	Hersfeld, Germany
172.	21 Nov 44	Bomber Escort	1323-A	Merseburg, Germany
173.	25 Nov 44	Bomber Escort	1333-A	Merseburg, Germany
174.	26 Nov 44	Bomber Escort	W-496-A	Hanover, Germany
175.	27 Nov 44	Bmr Esc-Strafing	1343-A	Derben, Germany
176.	29 Nov 44	Bomber Escort	1348-A	E. of Hanover, Germany
177.	30 Nov 44	Bomber Escort	1354-A	Merseburg, Germany
178.	4 Dec 44	Bomber Escort	1370-A	Weisbaden, Germany
179.	5 Dec 44	Bomber Escort	1374-A	Berlin, Germany
180.	6 Dec 44	Bomber Escort	1383-A	Merseburg, Germany
181.	9 Dec 44	Bomber Escort	1397-A	Stuttgart, Germany
182.	10 Dec 44	Bomber Escort	1404-A	Koblenz, Germany
183.	11 Dec 44	Bomber Escort	1408-A	Giessen, Germany
184.	12 Dec 44	Bomber Escort	1412-A	Merseberg, Germany
185.	15 Dec 44	Bomber Escort	1422-A	Hanover, Germany
186.	16 Dec 44	Bomber Escort	1426-A	Stuttgart, Germany
187.	18 Dec 44	Bomber Escort	1430-A	Weisbaden, Germany
188.	28 Dec 44	Bomber Escort	1458-A	Koblenz, Germany
189.	29 Dec 44	Bomber Escort	1463-A	Frankfurt, Germany
190.	30 Dec 44	Bomber Escort	1467-A	Fulda, Germany
191.	31 Dec 44	Bomber Escort	1471-A	Hamburg, Germany
192.	1 Jan 45	Fighter Sweep	1476-A	Hanover, Germany
193.	2 Jan 45	Bomber Escort	1479-A	Metz, Germany
194.	3 Jan 45	Bomber Escort	1485-A	Fulda, Germany
195.	5 Jan 45	Bomber Escort	1491-A	Trier, Germany
196.	7 Jan 45	Bomber Escort	1499-A	Ruthen, Germany
197.	8 Jan 45	Fighter Sweep	1503-A	Aachen, Germany
198.	10 Jan 45	Bomber Escort	1508-A	Cologne, Germany
199.	14 Jan 45	Bomber Escort Escort to PRU Acft	1515-A	Magdeburg, Germany Hamburg, Germany
200.	15 Jan 45	Bomber Escort	1519-A	Kempten, Germany
201.	16 Jan 45	Bomber Escort	1521-A	Leipzig, Germany
202.	17 Jan 45	Fighter Sweep	1525-A	Dummer Lake (Bielfeld), Gmy
203.	20 Jan 45	Bomber Escort	1535-A	Steckrode, Germany
204.	21 Jan 45	Bomber Escort	1539-A	Mannheim, Germany
205.	29 Jan 45	Bomber Escort	1566-A	Kassell, Germany
206.	31 Jan 45	Bomber Escort	1573-A	Bremen, Germany
207.	3 Feb 45	Bomber Escort	1586-A	Berlin, Germany
208.	6 Feb 45	Bomber Escort	1595-A	Leipzig, Germany
209.	7 Feb 45	Bomber Escort	1598-A	Gladbeck, Germany
210.	9 Feb 45	Bomber Escort	1605-A	Leipzig, Germany
211.	14 Feb 45	Bomber Escort	1622-A	Chemnitz, Germany
212.	16 Feb 45	Bomber Escort	1631-A	Hamm, Germany
213.	17 Feb 45	Bomber Escort	1634-A	Koblenz, Germany
214.	19 Feb 45	Bomber Escort	1638-A	Osnabruck, Germany
215.	20 Feb 45	Bomber Escort	1642-A	Nurnberg, Germany
216.	21 Feb 45	Bomber Escort	1647-A	Nurnberg, Germany
217.	22 Feb 45	Bomber Escort	1650-A	Hof-Saalfeld-Eger, Ger.

Table One (Cont'd.)

218.	23 Feb 45	Bomber Escort	1654-A	Neustadt-Ansback, Ger.
219.	24 Feb 45	Bomber Escort	1658-A	Bremen, Germany
220.	25 Feb 45	Bomber Escort	1662-A	Munich, Germany
221.	26 Feb 45	Bomber Escort	1665-A	Berlin, Germany
222.	27 Feb 45	Bomber Escort	1670-A	Leipzig, Germany
223.	28 Feb 45	Bomber Escort	1675-A	Kassell, Germany
224.	1 Mar 45	Bomber Escort	1679-A	Ulm, Germany
225.	2 Mar 45	Bomber Escort	1683-A	Ruhland, Germany
226.	3 Mar 45	Bomber Escort	1690-A	Dallbergen, Germany
227.	4 Mar 45	Bomber Escort	1697-A	Nurnburg, Germany
228.	5 Mar 45	Fighter Sweep	1704-A	Ruhland area, Germany
229.	8 Mar 45	Bmr Esct-Strafing	1721-A	Munster, Germany
230.	10 Mar 45	Bomber Escort	1731-A	Dortmund, Germany
231.	11 Mar 45	Bomber Escort	1738-A	Hamburg, Germany
232.	12 Mar 45	Bomber Escort	1742-A	Swinemunde, Germany
233.	14 Mar 45	Bomber Escort	1752-A	Hanover, Germany
234.	15 Mar 45	Bomber Escort	1761-A	Oranienburg, Germany
235.	17 Mar 45	Bomber Escort	1774-A	Ruhland, Germany
236.	18 Mar 45	Fighter Patrol	1779-A	Brandenburg, Germany
237.	19 Mar 45	Bomber Escort	1785-A	SW of Merseburg, Germany
238.	20 Mar 45	Fighter Sweep	1794-A	Hanover, Germany
239.	21 Mar 45	Bomber Escort	1801-A	Ruhland, Germany
240.	22 Mar 45	Bomber Escort	1810-A	Ruhland, Germany
241.	23 Mar 45	Bomber Escort	1819-A	Dortmund, Germany
242.	24 Mar 45	Fighter Swp-Patrol	1828-A	Siegen-Gerleburg, Ger.
243.	25 Mar 45	Bomber Escort	1838-A	Brunswick, Germany
244.	26 Mar 45	Bomber Escort	1843-A	Plauen, Germany
245.	28 Mar 45	Bomber Escort	1857-A	Hanover, Germany
246.	30 Mar 45	Bomber Escort	1863-A	Hamburg, Germany
247.	31 Mar 45	Bomber Escort	1874-A	Zeitz, Germany
248.	2 Apr 45	Bomber Escort	1882-A	Grove Nidenmark, Ger.
249.	3 Apr 45	Bomber Escort	1887-A	Kiel, Germany
250.	4 Apr 45	Fighter Patrol	1896-A	Over Parchim, Germany
251.	5 Apr 45	Bomber Escort	1903-A	Bayreuth, Germany
252.	6 Apr 45	Bomber Escort	1909-A	Gera, Germany
253.	7 Apr 45	Bomber Escort	1914-A	Hamburg, Germany
254.	8 Apr 45	Bomber Escort	1918-A	Eger, Germany
255.	9 Apr 45	Bomber Escort	1929-A	Munich, Germany
256.	10 Apr 45	Bomber Escort	1936-A	Neuruppin, Germany
257.	11 Apr 45	Bomber Escort	1944-A	Ingolstadt, Germany
258.	16 Apr 45	Bomber Escort	1989-A	Ulm, Germany
259.	16 Apr 45	Fighter Sweep	1997-A	Regensburg, Germany
260.	17 Apr 45	Bmr Esc-Fitr-Swp	2006-A	S. of Pilzen, Germany
261.	18 Apr 45	Bomber Escort	2017-A	NW of Kolin, Germany
262.	19 Apr 45	Freelance Strafing	2024-A	Dresden, Germany
263.	20 Apr 45	Bomber Escort	2039-A	Neuruppin, Germany
264.	21 Apr 45	Freelance Strafing	2053-A	Munich, Germany

Combat duty in ETO closed on this date for this organization.

Table Two
Credits for Enemy Aircraft

PILOT	AIR			GROUND	
	Destroyed	Probable	Damaged	Destroyed	Damaged
Headquarters, 339th Fighter Group					
HATHORN, Vernon B, Jr	0	0	0	3FW190, 16Apr45	0
HENRY, John B, Jr	0	1Me262, 30Mar45	0	0	0
SCRUGGS, Harold W	2FW190, 29Jun44	0	2FW190, 29Jun44	0	0
503rd Fighter Squadron					
AITKEN, John, Jr	3 2FW190, 5Aug44 1Me109, 11Sep44	0	1FW190, 11Sep44	1Ju88, 13Sep44	0
ALLEN, Bernice A.	1FW190, 31 Dec44	0	2 1FW190, 26Nov44 1FW190, 31 Dec44	0	0
AMMON, Robert H.	5 1FW190, 8Jun44 2FW190, 23Sep44 2FW190, 28Sep44	0	2 1FW190, 8Jun44 1Me109, 7Jul44	9 1He111, 16Apr 45 3Ju88, 16 Apr45 1FW190, 16Apr45 4Me109, 16Apr45	0
BEAVERS, Edwards H., Jr.	5 1FW190, 25 Jul44 1FW190, 23Sep44 1Me109, 18Nov44 2FW190, 26Nov44	0	0	0	0
BEHREND, William W.	1Me109, 6Aug44	0	1Me109, 2Mar45	0	0
BOYD, William H.	0	0	0	0	1FW190, 16Apr45
BROWN, Robert B.	1/2Me109, 24May44	0	2Me109, 24May44	0	0
BRYAN, William E., Jr.	7 1/2 1/2FW190, 24May44 2FW190, 30May44 1Me410, 21Jun44 1FW190, 5Aug44 1FW190, 31Dec44 1FW190, 2Mar45 1Me109, 2Mar45	1/2Me109, 21Jun44	1FW190, 2Mar45	2U/ITE, 21May44	0
BUSH, Jerry P.	1/2Me109, 7Jul44	0	0	0	0
BUTLER, Frederick, Jr.	0	1FW190, 2Mar45	1Me109, 2Mar45	0	0
BYERS, John R.	0	0	0	5 3Ju88, 16Apr45 1FW190, 16Apr45 1Me109, 16Apr45	2Ju88, 16Apr45
CAMPBELL, John C. Jr.	1Me262, 17Apr45	0	0	0	0
CARTER, Walter, T.	0	0	0	2Ju88, 21May44	3Do217, 19May44
CHETNEKY, Steve J.	1Me109, 2Mar45	0	1Me109, 2Mar45	6 1He111, 16 Apr45 2Ju88, 16Apr45 3Me109, 16Apr45	3 2Ju88, 16Apr45 1Me109, 16Apr45
CLOUD, Carl E.	1Me109, 11Sep55	0	0	0	0
COE, Charles S.	2 1/2 1 1/2FW190, 11Sep44 1FW190, 26Nov44	0	0	0	0

Table Two (Cont'd)

PILOT	AIR			GROUND	
	Destroyed	Probable	Damaged	Destroyed	Damaged
CROCKETT, James R.	0	0	0	2Ju52, 19May44	0
DEAREY, Ralph H.	0	0	0	1U/ITE, 21May44	2U/ITE, 21May44
EDENS, Malcolm B.	2FW190, 26Nov44	0	0	0	0
ERICKSON, Earl E.	1 1/2 1/2Me109, 9Sep44 1FW190, 11Sep44	1FW190, 11Sep44	0	1U/ITE, 21May44	0
FERRELL, Clarence I.	0	0	0	4Ju88, 16Apr45	2FW190, 16Apr45
FICKEL, Paul D.	1Me109, 6Aug44	0	0	0	0
FIORITO, Leonard J.	2 1Me109, 15Jun44 1FW190, 4Aug44	0	0	1Me110, 21May44	1Ju88, 21May44
FOLWELL, Nathan T.	0	0	0	0	4 3Me109, 19May44 1Trnr, 19May44
FRENCH, Lloyd J.	1FW190, 26Nov44	0	0	0	0
FRENCH, Carl H.	0	0	1Me109, 2Mar45	1Me109, 17Apr45	0
FRISCH, Robert J.	0	0	1Me109, 2Mar45	6 4Ju88, 10Apr45 1Ju88, 17Apr45 1Me262, 17Apr45	3 1Ju88, 10Apr45 1U/IME, 10Apr45 1Me109, 16Apr45
GERARD, Francis R.	8 1Me109, 16Aug 44 3Me109, 11Sep44 1FW190, 11Sep44 2Me109, 2Mar45 1FW190, 18Mar45	0	2 1Me109, 11Sep44 1Me109, 2Mar45	0	0
GOKEY, John W.	1Me109, 2Mar45	0	1FW190, 26Nov44	1Do217, 16Apr45	3U/ITE, 16Apr45
GRAHAM, Ethelbert H., Jr.	1 1/2 1/2Me109, 24May44 1FW190, 11Sep44	0	1Me109, 5Aug44	0	0
HAIDLE, Elmer E.	0	0	0	2FW190, 16Apr45	2 1FW190, 16Apr45 1Me109, 16Apr45
HARTE, Allan S., Jr.	1Me109, 12Sep44	0	0	0	2Ju88, 21May44
HAWKINS, Anthony G.	1FW190, 31Dec44	0	1Me262, 31Dec44	0	0
HENDERSON, Harvey E.	2FW190, 26Nov44	0	0	0	0
HILL, Ralph S. Jr.	0	0	2Me262, 20Mar45	1U/ITE, 16Apr45	1U/ITE, 16Apr45
JOHNSON, Donald W.	3FW190, 26Nov44	0	0	0	0
JOHNSON, Raymond G.	1FW190, 7Apr45	0	1Me262, 2Mar45	0	0
KNOTT, Clarence W.	1 1/2 1/2Me109, 24May44 1FW190, 29Jun44	0	0	0	0
KRAUSS, Richard E.	1Me109, 7Apr45	0	0	0	0
LOWERY, Arthur E.	0	0	0	1U/ITE, 21May44	0
MARSH, Lester C.	5 1FW190, 23Sep44 1Me109, 18Nov44 3FW190, 26Nov44	1FW190, 26Nov44	1FW190, 26Nov44	0	0
MAYER, Raymond D.	3 2Me109, 11Sep44 1FW190, 23Sep44	0	0	0	0
McELWEE, Francis E.	1FW190, 18Mar45	0	0	0	0
McCLISH, Donald E.	1/2Me109, 11Sep44	1FW190, 11Sep44	0	0	0

Table Two (Cont'd)

PILOT	AIR			GROUND	
	Destroyed	Probable	Damaged	Destroyed	Damaged
MEYER, Victor W.	2 1/2 1FW190, 15Jun44 1FW190, 29Jun44 1/2Me410, 29Jun44	0	1Me109, 29Jun44	0	0
OSTROW, Nathan	1 1/2Me109, 5Sep44	0	0	0	0
PETITT, Philip E.	2 1FW190, 26Nov44 1FW190, 7Apr45	0	1Me262, 7Apr45	0	0
POTTHOFF, John R.	0	0	0	0	1Ju88, 17Apr45
POUTRE, Rex L.	4 2Me109, 2Mar45 1FW190, 2Mar45 1Me109, 7Apr45	0	2 1FW190, 18Mar45 1FW190, 7Apr45	0	0
PREDDY, William R.	1FW190, 2Mar45	1Me109, 2Mar45	0	0	1U/ITR, 16Apr45
PRICE, Jack B.	1FW190, 11Sep44	0	0	0	2Ju88, 21May44
REYNOLDS, Gardner H.	0	0	0	1U/ITE, 21May44	0
REYNOLDS, John R. *1/2 credit with 505th	1FW190, 25Jul44	0	0	0*	0
ROBINSON, James G.	1/2FW190, 11Sep44	0	0	0	0
SCRUGGS, Harold W.	1/2FW190, 24May44	0	0	0	0
SHAFER, Dale E., Jr. *4 in MTO	3* 1Me109, 18Nov44 1FW190, 18Mar45 1Ar234, 18Apr45	0	3 1FW190, 5Dec44 1FW190, 18Mar45 1Me262, 25Mar45	2 1Ju88, 10Apr45 1Me109, 10Apr45	4Ju88, 10Apr45
SHAKE, Charles E.	1/2Me109, 24May44	0	0	0	1/2Me109, 24May44
STEPHENSON, Enoch B., Jr.	2 1Me109, 25Jul44 1Me109, 6Aug44	0	1Me110, 11Jul44	0	1 1/2 1/2Ju88, 21May44 1Me109, 24May44
STILWELL, Frank M.	1FW190, 26Nov44	1Me109, 18Nov44	0	0	0
STOCKTON, William D.	0	0	1Me109, 11Sep44	1Ju88, 13 Sep44	0
TALCOTT, Franklin D.	0	1/2Me410, 21Jun44	0	0	0
WEST, Rodney C.	1Me410, 21Jun44	0	0	0	0
WHITELAW, Richard S.	1 1/2 1/2FW190, 24May44 1FW190, 8Jun44	0	0	0	4 3Do217, 19May44 1U/ITE, 21May44
WILSON, John P.	2FW190, 26Nov44	0	0	0	0
WOLFORT, Joseph	1/2Me109, 24May44	0	1Me109, 24May44	1U/ITE, 19May44	0
WRIGHT, Lyle M.	1He111, 21May44	0	1Me109, 29Jun44	0	2 1Ju88, 21May44 1Ju88, 29Jun44
WYATT, Valdee	2 1/2 1FW190, 15Jun44 1/2Me109, 7Jul44 1 Me109, 25Jul44	0	0	0	0

504th Fighter Squadron

PILOT	AIR			GROUND	
	Destroyed	Probable	Damaged	Destroyed	Damaged
ALLERS, Loren W.	1FW190, 31Dec44	0	0	3 2Me410, 10Apr45 1Me109, 16Apr45	3 1Me410, 10Apr45 2Me109, 16Apr45
ATTEBERRY, Ray N.	2 1FW190, 7Jun44 1FW190, 29Jul44	0	0	1FW190, 7Jun44	0
BALL, Melville R.	1FW190, 8Jun44	0	2 1Me109, 24May44 1Me109, 10Jun44	0	0

Table Two (Cont'd)

PILOT	AIR Destroyed	AIR Probable	AIR Damaged	GROUND Destroyed	GROUND Damaged
BALLARD, Jerome J.	1FW190, 18Mar45	0	0	0	0
BARRETT, Lawrence J.	0	0	0	4 1He111, 20Mar45 2Ju88, 10Apr45 1Ju52, 17Apr45	2Me410, 10Apr45
BARTO, Vernon N	11/2 1Me262, 20Mar 45 1/2Me109, 7Apr45	0	1FW190, 31Dec44	3 2Ju88, 10Apr45 1Me109, 16Apr45	1JU88, 10Apr45
BATES, Arthur W.	1FW190, 26Nov44	0	0	0	0
BENNETT, Carroll W.	1Me262, 30Mar45	0	1Me262, 30Mar45	2Me410, 10Apr45	2Me410, 10Apr45
BERGUSON, Kenneth V.	0	0	1Me262, 20Mar45	0	0
BLIZZARD, Robert V.	0	1Me262, 7Apr45	1Me262, 7Apr45	6 2Me410, 10Apr45 4Me109, 16Apr45	2Me410, 10Apr45
CALDWELL, Merle F.	2Me109, 7Jul44	0	0	3 1FW190, 7Jun44 1U/ITE, 13Sep44 1FW190, 13Sep44	0
CARTER, Lyle M.	1Me109, 7Apr45	0	1Me262, 7Apr45	2Me109, 16Apr45	3 1U/IME, 4Apr45 2Me109, 6Apr45
CERNICKY, Melvin L.	0	1FW190, 23Sep44	0	0	0
CHENEZ, Gordon H.	0	0	0	4 2Me410, 10Apr45 2Me109, 16Apr45	3 1Ju52, 20Mar45 2Me410, 10Apr45
CLARK, William C. 1 destroyed air with another FG	0*	0	1Me262, 4Apr45	8 1U/ITE, 20Mar45 1U/IME, 4Apr45 1Ju52, 16Apr45 3FW190, 16Apr45 2Me109, 16Apr45	4 1He111, 20Mar45 1U/ITE, 4Apr45 1FW190, 16Apr45 1Me109, 16Apr45
CLIFTON, Frank A.	0	0	0	6 2Me109, 16Apr45 1FW190, 16Apr45 1Ju88, 17Apr45 1Fi156, 17Apr45 1Me109, 17Apr45	0
CORBIN, Luther L.	0	0	0	1FW190, 7Jun44	0
CRESWELL, Raymond H.	1Me109, 7Apr45	0	0	2 1Me109, 16Apr45 1U/ITE, 16Apr45	2 1FW190, 16Apr45 1U/ITE 16Apr45
CROKER, Robert C.	1/2Me262, 4Apr45	0	0	2Me410, 10Apr45	4Me410, 10Apr45
EISENHART, Lee D.	1FW190, 29Jun44	0	0	1FW190, 21May44	0
EVERSON, Kirke B., Jr.	11/2 1/2Me262, 4Apr45 1Me109, 7Apr45	0	0	13 3Me410, 10Apr45 3FW190, 16Apr45 2Fi156, 17Apr45 2Ju88, 17Apr45 2Me109, 17Apr45 1Me210, 17Apr45	5Me410, 10Apr45
GRAVETTE, Edgar B.	1FW190, 30May44	0	1FW190, 30May44	0	0
GREER, Nile C.	11/2 1/2Me262, 21Mar45 1Me262, Apr45	0	0	0	0
GRIFFITH, Walter B.	1Me109, 24May44	0	0	0	0

Table Two (Cont'd)

PILOT	AIR			GROUND	
	Destroyed	Probable	Damaged	Destroyed	Damaged
GUERNSEY, Frank D., Jr.	1FW190, 7Apr45	0	1Me109, 7Apr45	0	0
HARRY, G. P.	0	0	1U/ISE, 21May44	0	1Ju87, 21May44
HAVIGHURST, Robert C.	1Me262, 4Apr45	0	0	0	0
HERMANSEN, Cephas	0	0	0	5 3Me410, 10Apr45 2Me109, 16Apr45	2Me410, 10Apr45
HERRMANN, Ray A.	3 1FW190, 2Nov44 2FW190, 31Dec44	0	0	0	0
HUDSON, Will M.	0	0	0	4 3FW190, 16Apr45 1Me109, 16Apr45	0
HUNT, Harlan F.	0	0	1Me262, 9Apr45	5 1FW190, 16Apr45 1Me109, 17Apr45 1Ju88, 17Apr45 1FW190, 17Apr45 1Fil56, 17Apr45	1FW190, 16Apr45
HUNTER, Charles W.	1Me109, 16Aug44	0	0	0	0
JULIAN, William H. *5 destroyed air with 78FG	0*	0	0	3 2Me410, 10Apr45 1U/I, 16Apr45	4 2Me410, 10Apr45 1FW190, 16Apr45 1Me109, 16Apr45
KRUEGER, Donald F.	0	0	0	2 1FW190, 16Apr45 1Me109, 16Apr45	2Me410, 10Apr45
KUHLMAN, Robert M.	0	0	0	1FW200, 20Mar45	1Ju52, 20Mar45
KUNZ, Leonard A.	1/2Me109, 7Apr45	0	0	2Me410, 10Apr45	5 3Me410, 10Apr45 2FW190, 16Apr45
LANGOHR, Billy E.	1/2Me262, 21Mar45	0	0	0	0
MASON, Clair M.	0	0	1Me262, 7Apr45	2Me410, 10Apr45	1Me410, 10Apr45
MEAD, Charles M.	1Me109, 18Nov44	0	0	0	0
ORCUTT, Leon M., Jr.	0	0	1Me262, 9Apr45	9 3Ju88, 17Apr45 6Me109, 17Apr45	0
O'SULLIVAN, Walter R.	1FW190, 19May44	0	0	0	0
PENNY, Donald E.	2 1Me109, 6Aug44 1Me109, 2Nov44	0	0	0	0
PENROSE, Richard C.	1Me109, 16Aug44	0	0	0	0
PETER, Lewis S., Jr.	1FW190, 7Jun44	1FW190, 30May44	0	0	0
ROUTT, Bill C.	4 2Me109, 21May44 1Me109, 7Jul44 1Me109, 16Aug44	0	1Me109, 16Aug44	0	0
RUTAN, Frederick S., Jr.	2Me109, 29Jul44	0	0	0	0
SAINLAR, Jerome J.	0	0	1Me262, 9Feb45	0	0
SARGENT, Robert F.	1Me262, 30Mar45	0	0	3Me410, 10Apr45	2Me410, 10Apr45
SMITH, Roland W.	0	0	0	3 1Me410, 10Apr45 2Me109, 16Apr45	1Ju88, 10Apr45
STEVENS, Bradford V.	3 2FW190, 30May44	1Me109, 24May44	2Me109, 24May44	1FW190, 7Jun44	0

Table Two (Cont'd)

PILOT	AIR			GROUND	
	Destroyed	Probable	Damaged	Destroyed	Damaged
STOCKMAN, Hervey S.	1Me109, 12Sep44 2 1Me109, 29Jul44 1Me109, 16Aug44	2 1Me109, 21Jun44 1Me109, 29Jul44	1Me109, 29Jul44	0	0
THIBERT, Henry G.	1Me109, 21Jun44	0	0	0	0
TRESTER, John R.	0	1Me109, 29Jul44	0	0	0
WATERS, Frank T.	0	0	0	1FW190, 7Jun44	0
WAYMIRE, Harvey R.	1Me109, 15Jun44	0	0	0	0
WILCOX, Richard H.	2Me109, 7Jul44	0	0	0	0
WINKELMAN, Myer, R.	1Me109, 6Aug44	0	0	0	0
WOOD, Robert T.	1Me109, 6Aug44	0	0	0	0
ZEINE, Donald E.	1Me109, 6Aug44	0	0	0	0

505th Fighter Squadron

PILOT	AIR			GROUND	
	Destroyed	Probable	Damaged	Destroyed	Damaged
ANANIAN, Stephen C.	1Me262, 9Feb45	0	2 1Me262, 30Mar45 1Me262, 5Apr45	3 2Ju88, 1Mar45 1Ju88, 3Mar45	0
BALL, Edwin C.	0	0	1Me410, 21Jun44	1/2Ju88, 19Jul44	0
BIGGS, Oscar K.	1/2Me109, 7Apr45	0	0	111/2 1/2Ju88, 1Mar45 3Do217, 2Mar45 4Ju88, 10Apr45 1Ju88, 16Apr45 1U/ITE, 16Apr45 1Me109, 16Apr45 1Ju88, 17Apr45	4 2Do217, 2Mar45 2Ju88, 10Apr45
BLINE, J. Brooks	1FW190, 7Apr45	0	0	4 2Ju88, 17Apr45 2Me109, 17Apr45	0
BOOTH, Billy B.	0	0	0	1/2Ju88, 1Mar45	0
BUNDGAARD, Carl H.	2 1Me109, 21Nov44 1FW190, 26Nov44	0	1FW190, 26Nov44	3 2Ju88, 11Sep44 1Ju88, 1Mar45	4 1Me410, 5Sep44 3Ju52, 11 Sep44
BURCH, Harold W.	0	0	0	10 3Do217, 2Mar45 3Me210, 10Apr45 1He111, 10Apr45 1Ju52, 16Apr45 1Ju88, 16 Apr45 1Do217, 17Apr45	3 1Me110, 10Apr45 1U/IME, 10Apr45 1Do217, 17Apr45
CARR, Vernon D.	1/2Me109, 12Mar45	0	0	4 1Ju88, 10Apr45 1Do217, 10Apr45 1Do217, 16Apr45 1Ju88, 17Apr45	3 2Me410, 10Apr45 1Me109, 17Apr45
CAYWOOD, Herbert L.	0	0	.0	7 3Ju88, 10Apr45 3Me109, 16Apr45 1U/ISE, 16Apr45	5 2Ju88, 10Apr45 1Me109, 16Apr45 2Ju88, 16Apr45
COKER, Joseph R.	1Me109, 12Mar45	0	1Me109, 12Mar45	0	0
CONNER, Bertis, A.	0	0	0	2Do17, 2Mar45	0
COREY, Harry R.	1Me262, 4Apr45	0	0	11 4Ju88, 10Apr45 4U/ISE, 16Apr45 2Ju188, 17Apr45 1Me109, 17Apr45	3 1Ju88, 10Apr45 1Ju52, 10Apr45 1FW190, 10Apr45

Table Two (Cont'd)

PILOT	AIR			GROUND	
	Destroyed	Probable	Damaged	Destroyed	Damaged
DANIELL, J. S.	5FW190, 26Nov44	0	0	0	0
DIEFENBECK, James A.	0	0	0	2 1Do217, 17Apr45 1U/ITE, 17Apr45	0
DOWELL, Charles W.	1/2Me109, 18Nov44	0	0	0	0
EVERETT, Harold M.	3 1/2 1Me109, 9May44 1/2Ju88, 21May44 2FW190, 24May44	0	1Me109, 9May44	0	0
EWING, Philip H.	0	0	0	2 1Fil56, 27May44 1U/ITE, 27May44	0
FARMER, Owen P., Jr.	2 1/2FW190, 27Jun44 1 1/2Me109, 12Mar45	0	1Trnr, 21May44	6 1UT/ITE, 10Sep44 3Ju88, 10Apr45 1U/ITE, 16Apr45 1JU88, 16Apr45	3 1Me109, 31Jul44 2U/ISE, 31Jul44
FISH, Wesley G.	1/2 FW190, 27Jun44	0	0	0	0
GIRZI, Henry E., Jr.	1FW190, 26Nov44	0	0	0	0
GRAHAM, Gerald E.	1/2Me410, 29Jun44	0	0	3 1/2Ju188, 19Jul44 1/2Me410, 31Jul44 1Do217, 3Aug44 1Me410, 11Sep44	5 1U/ISE, 31Jul44 1Me410, 5Sep44 1Ju88, 11Sep44 1Do217, 11Sep44 1Me410, 11Sep44
GUYTON, William R.	0	0	0	5 2Ju88, 10Apr45 1Do217, 10Apr45 1Ju88, 16Apr45 1Me109, 16Apr45	0
HANSEMAN, Chris J.	5 1/2JU88, 21May44 2Trnr, 21May44 1 1/2Me109, 24May44 1Me109, 10Jun44	0	0	2 1Ju88, 19Jul44 1U/ITE, 19Jul44	1Ju88, 10Jun44
HANSON, James R.	1 1/2 1Trnr, 21May44 1/2Trnr, 8Jun44	0	0	1Ju88, 19Jul44	0
HOLLOWAY, John G.	2Me109, 4Aug44	0	0	0	0
HOWARD, Harry F.	0	0	0	3Do217, 2Mar45	0
HRICO, George J.	1/2FW190, 25May44	0	0	1/2 Ju52, 29Jul44	2U/ITE, 13Sep44
HUPP, Ellis E., Jr.	0	0	0	2 1Do217, 10Apr45 1Do217, 17Apr45	1Do217, 10Apr45
IRION, Robert E.	1ME262, 20Mar45	0	0	5 1Ju88, 1Mar45 2Ju188, 10Apr45 1Do217, 10Apr45 1Me110, 17Apr45	1ME110, 10Apr45
JAASKELAINEN, William	1FW190, 8Jun44	0	0	1Ju88, 11Sep44	1He111, 11Sep44
JACKSON, Boyd O.	0	0	0	5 1FW190, 31Jul44 2He111, 10Sep44 1Ju88, 10Sep44 1Ju88, 21Nov44	4 1U/ISE, 10Sep44 3U/ITE, 10Sep44

Table Two (Cont'd)

PILOT	AIR			GROUND	
	Destroyed	Probable	Damaged	Destroyed	Damaged
JOHNSON, Evan M., Vth	5 11/1FW190, 19May44 1FW190, 24May44 1/2Ju52, 10Jun44 1/2Me109, 29Jun44 1/2Me410, 29Jun44 1Me109, 18Nov44	0	1Me109, 18Nov44	0	1Me410, 5Sep44
JONES, George W., Jr.	0	0	1Me309, 2Mar45	1 1JU88, 3Mar45	0
JONES, William A.	2 1Me109, 9May44 1FW190, 8Jun44	0	0	4 1/2Ju52, 29Jul44 1/2Me109, 10Sep44 1U/ISE, 10Sep44 1Ju87, 10Sep44 1Ju88, 11Sep44	4 2He111, 10Sep44 1Ju88, 11Sep44 1Ju52, 11Sep44
KNIGHT, George	0	0	0	1/2Ju88, 19Jul44	0
KRAUSS, William H.	1/2Me109, 29Jul44	0	0	41/2 1/2Ju188, 19Jul44 2Me410, 11Sep44 1Ju88, 11Sep44 1Me110, 11Sep44	4 1Ju88, 10Sep44 3Me410, 11Sep44
LARSON, Donald A.	6 1FW190, 13May44 2Me109, 24May44 1FW190, 24May44 1Ju52, 28Jul44 1Me109, 4Aug44	1Me109, 24May44	1FW190, 24May44	3 1Do217, 3Aug44 1FW190, 3Aug44 1Me410, 4Aug44	0
LOVELESS, Phillip M., Jr.	1/2FW190, 26Nov44	0	0	5 1FW190, 16Apr45 3Do217, 17Apr45 1Me109, 17Apr45	3 1Ju87, 16Apr45 1Ju88, 17Apr45 1Do217, 17Apr45
LYNCH, James L.	21/2 11/2Do217, 21May44 1Trnr, 21May44	0	0	1Me109, 24May44	0
MacCLARENCE, William R.	0	0	0	8 1Me410, 4Apr45 3Ju88, 10Apr45 1U/ISE, 16Apr45 1U/ITE, 16Apr45 1He111, 17Apr45 1Ju88, 17Apr45	1Ju88, 17Apr45
MALARZ, Chester	1/2Me109, 21Nov44	0	0	2 1Ju88, 10Sep44 1Me410, 10Sep44	4 1Ju88, 10Sep44 3He111, 10Sep44
MARTS, Jay F.	2Me109, 2Mar45	0	0	3 1Ju88, 28Aug44 2Me410, 10Sep44	4 1Ju88, 10Sep44 2He111, 10Sep44 1U/ITE, 10Sep44
MARVEL, Thomas W.	0	0	0	9 1Ju88, 1Mar45 3Me410, 10Apr45 1Ju88, 16Apr45 1Me109, 16Apr45 1He111, 17Apr45 1Me109, 17Apr45 1U/ITE, 17Apr45	1Me410,. 10Apr45

Table Two (Cont'd)

PILOT	AIR			GROUND	
	Destroyed	Probable	Damaged	Destroyed	Damaged
McMAHON, Peter J.	3 1/2 2Ju87, 6Jun44 1 1/2FW190, 8Jun44	0	0	0	0
MITCHELL, Raymond M.	0	0	0	0	2 1Ju88, 10Sep44 1Do217, 13Sep44
MOORE, William R.	0	0	0	1 1/2 1Ju88, 10Sep44 1/2Ju88, 13Sep44	0
MUDGE, William P., Jr.	2 1/2Ju88, 21May44 1/2FW190, 25May44 1Ju87, 6Jun44	0	0	6 1Ju88, 19Jul44 1FW190, 19Jul44 1Ju52, 29Jul44 1Ju88, 31Jul44 1Me110, 31Jul44 1FW190, 31Jul44	1U/ISE, 31Jul44
MULLER, James B.	1/2Me109, 4Aug44	0	0	2 1Me410, 4Aug44 1Ju88, 10Sep44	0
MURPHY, Jerome T.	0	0	0	7 2Ju88, 10Apr45 3Do217, 10Apr45 1He111, 16Apr45 1Me109, 16Apr45	6 3U/ISE, 10Apr45 2Me109, 17Apr45 1Ju188, 17Apr45
NAY, Martin N.	0	0	0	0	1U/ISE, 31Jul44
OLANDER, Richard B.	1 1/2 1/2FW190, 8Jun44 1Me109, 12Sep44	0	0	5 1Me109, 27May44 1/2Trnr, 11Jul44 1/2Ju88, 19Jul44 1Ju87, 31Jul44 1U/ITE, 31Jul44 1U/ITE, 11Sep44	3 1Trnr, 31Jul44 2U/ITE, 11Sep44
OPITZ, William R.	1/2Do217, 8Jun44	0	0	0	0
PALMER, Gerald W.	1/2Me109, 18Nov44	0	0	0	0
PAUL, Robert H., Jr.	0	0	0	6 2Ju88, 10Apr45 3Do217, 10Apr45 1U/ISE, 17Apr45	3 2Ju52, 10Apr45 1Ju188, 17Apr45
PERRY, Gordon F.	1/2Do217, 21May44	0	0	0	0
PESANKA, John	1Me109, 12Mar45	0	0	3 1U/ISE, 16Apr45 1He111, 17Apr45 1Me109, 17Apr45	0
PHILLIPPI, William R.	1 1/2FW190, 26Nov44	0	0	2Ju88, 10Apr45	0
POWELL, Lawrence J., Jr.	2 1/2 1FW190, 4Aug44 1/2Me109, 4Aug44 1FW190, 23Sep44	0	0	3 1/2 1Me410, 31Jul44 1Me410, 10Sep44 1Do217, 10Sep44 1/2Ju88, 13Sep44	5 1Me109, 31Jul44 4U/ITE, 10Sep44
REID, Langhorne, Jr.	2 1/2Ju88, 21May44 1Ju88, 6Jun44 1/2Ju52, 10Jun44	0	0	0	0
REYNOLDS, John R. *1 destroyed with 503d	0*	0	0	1/2JU88, 28Aug44	0

Table Two (Cont'd)

PILOT	AIR			GROUND	
	Destroyed	Probable	Damaged	Destroyed	Damaged
RICH, George T.	1 1/2 1Me109, 18Nov44 1/2Me109, 21Nov44	0	1Me262, 30Mar45	5 1FW190, 10Sep44 1Me410, 11Sep44 2U/ITE, 11Sep44 1Do217, 4Apr45	1Me410, 11Sep44
ROHM, Richard R.	0	0	0	2 1Fi156, 27May44 1Ju88, 4Aug44	0
RICE, John J.	0	0	1Me262, 7Apr45	5 2Do217, 10Apr45 1Ju88, 16Apr45 2Me109, 16Apr45	2 1Do217, 10Apr45 1Ju88, 16Apr45
SAWICKI, Joseph F., Jr.	0	0	0	1Fl56, 17May44	0
SHAW, Bernell V.	0	0	0	2 1FW190, 3Aug44 1Ju88, 4Aug44	0
SIROCHMAN, Andrew	1 1/2FW190, 8Jun44 1/2Me109, 29Jun44	0	0	2 1/2 1/2Ju188, 19Jul44 1U/ITE, 3Aug44 1Ju88, 4Aug44	1U/ITE, 3Aug44
SMITH, Floyd W.	0	0	0	3 1FW190, 16Apr45 1Ju88, 17Apr45 1Me109, 17Apr45	1U/ISE, 16Apr45
SLOVAK, William R.	0	0	0	2 1Me410, 11Sep44 1U/ITE, 11Sep44	3 1Ju88, 4Aug44 2Me410, 11Sep44
STAGGERS, Theodore R.	0	0	0	2 1U/ISE, 31Jul44 1FW190, 31Jul44	0
STARNES, James R.	6 1/2FW190, 19May44 1/2Trnr, 21May44 1FW190, 29May44 1Me109, 8Jun44 1/2FW190, 8Jun44 1/2Me109, 29Jul44 1Me109, 4Aug44 1Me109, 2Mar45	0	0	6 1/2 1/2Trnr, 11Jul44 1Ju188, 19Jul44 1FW190, 31Jul44 1U/ITE, 31Jul44 1FW190, 3Mar45 1He111, 3Mar45 1Do217, 10Apr45	6 1FW190, 31Jul44 1FW190, 2Mar45 1He111, 2Mar45 3Do217, 10Apr45
STEWART, Carl R.	0	0	0	3 1/2 1U/ISE, 31Jul44 2Ju88, 10Sep44 1/2Me109, 10Sep44	4 1U/ISE, 31Jul44 3Ju88, 10Sep44
STILES, Bert	1FW190, 26Nov44	0	0	0	0
STRONG, Roland W.	1Trnr, 21May44	0	0	1Ju88, 4Aug44	0
TANNOUS, Richard, H.	1FW190, 23Sep44	0	1FW190, 23Sep44	2 1/2 1/2Ju88, 19Jul44 1U/ISE, 10Sep44 1Me410, 10Sep44	6 1U/ISE, 10Sep44 5U/ITE, 10Sep44
THIEME, Richard G.	0	0	0	1Ju88, 3Mar45	0
THURY, Joseph L.	2 1/2 1FW190, 29May44 1FW190, 27Jun44 1/2Me109, 7Apr45	0	1Me262, 18Apr45	25 1/2 1Fi156, 27May44 1He111, 27May44 1Me109, 19Jul44 1U/ITE, 19Jul44	10 1Fi156, 27May44 1U/ITE, 27May44 1U/ISE, 31Jul44 1Me410, 11Sep44

Table Two (Cont'd)

PILOT	AIR			GROUND	
	Destroyed	Probable	Damaged	Destroyed	Damaged
THURY, Joseph L. (Con't)				2U/ISE, 31Jul44 1/2Me 410, 31 Jul44 1Ju88, 10Sep44 2Ju88, 11Sep44 1Ju88, 1Mar45 3Ju88, 3Mar45 1Do217, 3Mar45 3U/ITE, 10Apr45 1Ju88, 10Apr45 1Me109, 16Apr45 2U/ISE, 17Apr45 2Me109, 17Apr45 1He111, 17Apr45 1Ju88, 17Apr45	1He111, 11Sep44 1Me109, 11Sep44 1Ju88, 11Sep44 1Ju88, 3Mar45 1He111, 10Apr45 1U/ITE, 10Apr45
TONGUE, Arthur E., Jr.	2Me109, 4Aug44	0	0	0	0
TOWER, Archie A.	11/2 1/2Do217, 8Jun44 1FW190, 8Jun44	0	0	18 1Ju88, 19Jul44 1Ju88, 10Sep44 1Ju52, 10Sep44 1Me410, 10Sep44 2Ju88, 11Sep44 1Ju87, 11Sep44 1He111, 11Sep44 2Me410, 3Apr45 2Ju88, 10Apr45 2Me410, 10Apr45 2Do217, 10Apr45 2He129, 10Apr45	8 3Ju88, 10Sep44 2He111, 10Sep44 1FW190, 24Mar45 2Do217, 10Apr45
WHITHERS, John C.	1/2Me109, 2Mar45	0	0	1Ju88, 10Apr45	3 1Ju88, 3Mar45 2Ju88, 10Apr45 1Me109, 17Apr45
WOOLERY, James C.	0	0	0	6 1Do217, 1Mar45 2U/ISE, 16Apr45 1FW190, 16Apr45 1Ju88, 17Apr45 1Me109, 17Apr45	
YOUNG, Allen D.	0	0	0	31/2 1/2Ju88, 19Jul44 3U/ITE, 10Sep44	0
ZIEGLER, Harry D.	1/2Me109, 2Mar45	0	0	2 1Ju88, 1Mar45 1Ju88, 3Mar45	0

Table Three
Enemy Aircraft Types Destroyed

A/C TYPE	503RD	504TH	505TH	HQ	TOTAL
Me-109	33	28	31.5	0	90.5
Me-262	1	7	3	0	11
Me-410	2.5	0	1	0	3.5
FW-190	57.5	16	32	2	109.5
Ar-234	1	0	0	0	1
Ju-52	0	0	2	0	2
Ju-87	0	0	3	0	3
Ju-88	0	0	3	0	3
He-111	1	0	0	0	1
Do-217	0	0	3	0	3
Trainer	0	0	6	0	6
	96.0	51.0	84.5	2.0	233.5

Table Four
Original and ReplacementPilot Assignments

EXPLANATION OF CODES

CTD	Completed Tour of Duty	MIA	Missing in Action	EVD	Evaded Capture	POW	Prisoner of War
INJ	Injured	RTD	Returned	INTD	Interned	TRFRD	Transferred
KIA	Killed in Action	VED	Victory in Europe Day	KIT	Killed in Training	WIA	Wounded in Action

ASSIGNMENT			DEPARTURE			
DATE	RANK	NAME	DATE	REASON	RANK	HOMETOWN

Group Pilots

ORIGINAL PILOTS

	Maj.	HATHORN, Vernon B., Jr.	22 Jul 45	CTD	Maj.	Harvey, LA
	Lt. Col.	HENRY, John B., Jr.	11 Apr 45	CTD	Col.	San Antonio, TX
	Maj.	McPHARLIN, Michael G.H.	06 Jun 44	KIA	Maj.	Toronto, Ontario, CAN
	Maj.	SCRUGGS, Harold W.	27 Dec 44	CTD	Lt. Col.	Hollis, OK
	Capt.	WIGHT, Carroll H.	31 Aug 44	TRFRD	Maj.	Temple, TX
	1/Lt.	CALER, Rollin C.	18 Jun 44	Non-Ops	1/Lt.	Humboldt, KS

REPLACEMENT PILOTS

15 Jun 44	Maj.	PROPST, John R.	20 Apr 45	CTD	Lt. Col.	Amarillo, TX
Oct 44	Capt.	DOWELL, Charles W.	21 Nov 44	KIA	Capt.	San Diego, CA
26 Dec 44	Lt. Col.	GOLDENBERG, Carl T.	20 Apr 45	CTD	Lt. Col.	Lynchburg, VA
30 Dec 44	Maj.	LONG, Robert D.	07 Sep 45	CTD	Lt. Col.	Coral Gables, FL
14 Apr 45	Lt. .Col.	CLARK, William C.	07 Sep 45	CTD	Lt. .Col.	Richmond, VA

503RD FIGHTER SQUADRON

	Capt.	AITKEN, John	02 Oct 44	CTD	Maj.	Elberton, GA
	2/Lt.	BROWN, Robert B.	19 Jun 44	KIA	1/Lt.	Salt Lake City, UT
	1/Lt.	BRYAN, William E., Jr.	07 Sep 45	CTD	Maj.	Flint, MI

ASSIGNMENT			DEPARTURE			
DATE	RANK	NAME	DATE	REASON	RANK	HOMETOWN
	2/Lt.	BUSH, Jerry P.	12 Sep 44	CTD	1/Lt.	Hulett, WY
	1Lt.	CARTER, Walter T.	21 May 44	POW	Capt.	Prescott, AZ
	2/Lt.	CLOUD, Carl E.	07 Oct 44	CTD	Capt.	Konawa, OK
	1/Lt.	CROCKETT, James R.	19 May 44	KIA	1/Lt.	Chattanooga, TN
	2/Lt.	FIORITO, Leonard J.	16 Oct 44	CTD	Capt.	LeRoy, NY
	1/Lt.	FOLWELL, Nathan T.	19 Jun 44	KIA	Capt.	Allentown, PA
	2/Lt.	GERARD, Francis R.	27 Apr 45	CTD	Capt.	Lyndhurst, NJ
	2/Lt.	GRAHAM, Ethelbert H., Jr.	20 Sep 44	CTD	1/Lt.	Los Angeles, CA
	1/Lt.	HARTE, Allan S., Jr.	16 Oct 44	CTD	Capt.	Chestertown, MD
	2/Lt.	HAUFF, John J.	17 Oct 44	CTD	1/Lt.	Milford, NJ
	2/Lt.	KELLY, George P. III	14 Oct 44	CTD	1/Lt.	Houston, TX
	2/Lt.	KNOTT, Clarence W.	17 Oct 44	CTD	Capt.	Ventura, CA
	2/Lt.	LOWERY, Arthur L.	22 Jun 44	KIA	1/Lt.	Clinton, TN
	2/Lt.	MULVEY, Robert F.	21 May 44	KIA	1/Lt.	Lowell, MA
	2/Lt.	PRICE, Jack B.	28 Oct 44	CTD	1/Lt.	Ada, OK
	1/Lt.	REYNOLDS, Gardner H.	26 Oct 44	CTD	Capt.	San Antonio, TX
	F/O	STEIER, Arthur H.	21 May 44	KIA	2/Lt.	Los Angeles, CA
	1/Lt.	STEPHENSON, Enoch B., Jr.	19 Oct 44	CTD	Maj.	Columbia, TN
	1/Lt.	WEST, Rodney C.	25 Jun 44	KIA	1Lt.	Ponifret, VT
	1/Lt.	WHITELAW, Richard S.	29 Jun 44	KIA	Capt.	Fillmore, CA
	2/Lt.	WOLFORT, Joseph	24 May 44	KIA	1/Lt.	St. Louis, MO
	2/Lt.	WRIGHT, LYLE M.	02 Dec 44	INJ	1/Lt.	Buffalo, NY
	1/Lt.	WYATT, Valdee	18 Oct 44	WIA	Capt.	Vernon, TX
	2/Lt.	WYER, Albert L.	15 May 44	POW	1/Lt.	Toledo, OH

REPLACEMENT PILOTS

DATE	RANK	NAME	DATE	REASON	RANK	HOMETOWN
13 May 44	2/Lt.	DEAREY, Ralph H.	19 Jun 44	POW	2/Lt.	Glendale, CA
	2/Lt.	ERICKSON, Earl E.	17 Oct 44	CTD	1/Lt.	Oakwood, MO
	2/Lt.	SHAKE, Charles E.	20 Jun 44	TRFRD	2/Lt.	Terre Haute, IN
	2/Lt.	TALCOTT, Franklin D.	05 Aug 44	INTD	2/Lt.	Baltimore, (Sweden)
24 May 44	2/Lt.	AMMON, Robert H.	21 Oct 44	CTD	1/Lt.	Reading, PA
		(flew second tour with the 504th)				
	2/Lt.	DICKENS, Robert L., Jr.	27 May 44	KIT	2/Lt.	San Antonio, TX
	1/Lt.	SMITH, Robert C.	08 Jun 44	KIA	1/Lt.	Clio, MI
06 Jun 44	1/Lt.	MEYER, Victor W.	05 Aug 44	KIA	1/Lt.	Macon, MO
10 Jun 44	1/Lt.	KEIM, Paul T.	29 Oct 44	CTD	1/Lt.	Greensburg, PA
14 Jun 44	2/Lt.	STILLWELL, Frank M.	23 Feb 45	CTD	Capt.	Prospect Plains, NJ
18 Jun 44	1/Lt.	BEHREND, William W.	20 Mar 45	CTD	Capt.	Trenton, NJ
29 Jun 44	2/Lt.	COZAD, John W.	25 Jul 44	KIT	2/Lt.	Los Angeles, CA
	2/Lt.	HAWKINS, Anthony G.	31 Dec 44	KIA	Capt.	Detroit, MI
	2/Lt.	MARSH, Lester C.	11 Dec 44	CTD	1/Lt.	Los Angeles, CA
	2/Lt.	McCLISH, Donald E.	14 Jan 45	CTD	Capt.	Akron, OH
	F/O	OSTROW, Nathan	06 Feb 45	CTD	Capt.	Minneapolis, MN
30 Jun 44	1/Lt.	TITUS, Robert D.	07 Sep 44	TRFRD	1/Lt.	Philadelphia, PA
11 Jul 44	1/Lt.	BEAVERS, Edward H.	27 Nov 44	KIA	Capt.	Scranton, PA
	1/Lt.	FICKEL, Paul D.	26 Sep 44	POW	1/Lt.	Ottumwa, IA
	1/Lt.	JOHNSON, Donald W.	07 Jan 45	CTD	Capt.	Detroit, MI
	2/Lt.	ALLEN, Bernice A.	07 Jan 45	CTD	1/Lt.	Bogue Chitto, MS
	2/Lt.	FLAHERTY, Edward C.	05 Aug 44	KIA	2/Lt.	Elizabeth, NJ
	2/Lt.	MANKE, Alfred O.	23 Sept 44	POW	2/Lt.	Niles, OH
	2/Lt.	REUTER, Raymond F.	10 Sep44	EVD		Union, OR
17 Apr 45				KIA	Capt.	
	2/Lt.	WARREN, Don W.	02 Oct 44	TRFRD	2/Lt.	Saginaw, MI
25 Jul 44	2/Lt.	STOCKTON, William D.	18 Oct 4	KIA	1/Lt.	Orion, IL
31 Jul 44	2/Lt.	CLARK, Jack W.	02 Oct 44	TRFRD	2/Lt.	Jacksonville, FL
	2/Lt.	COE, Charles S.	20 Jan 45	CTD	1/Lt.	Westbrook, ME

ASSIGNMENT			DEPARTURE			
DATE	RANK	NAME	DATE	REASON	RANK	HOMETOWN
04 Aug 44	1/Lt.	CAROTHERS, John M.	27 Aug 44	KIA	1/Lt.	Louisville, KY
09 Aug 44	2/Lt.	BOYCHUCK, Alec	20 Mar 45	CTD	Capt.	New York, NY
	2/Lt.	MAYER, Raymond D.	18 Oct 44	KIA	1/Lt.	Swissvale, PA
	Capt.	ROBINSON, James G.	23 Feb 45	CTD	Capt.	Rocky River, OH
06 Sep 44	1/Lt.	FRENCH, Lloyd J.	05 Apr 45	CTD	Capt.	West Hartford, CT
	1/Lt.	LINGER, Claude D.	02 Oct 44	TRFRD	1/Lt.	Fairmount, WV
	1/Lt.	PETITT, Philip E.	20 Apr 45	CTD	Capt.	New York, NY
22 Sep 44	Maj.	HENDERSON, Harvey E.	05 Dec 44	POW	Lt. Col.	Taylor, TX
26 Sep 44	2/Lt.	CRUMP, Alan F.	Nov 44	KIT	2/Lt.	Ann Arbor, MI
	2/Lt.	FARRELL, Joseph G.	20 Jun 45	CTD	Capt.	Brooklyn, NY
	2/Lt.	GIRONE, Felix J.	27 Nov 44	KIA	1/Lt.	Tarrytown, NY
	2/Lt.	GOKEY, John W.	20 Jul 45	CTD	Capt.	Oswego, NY
	2/Lt.	SPAZIANO, Vincent J.	18 Nov 44	KIA	1/Lt.	Providence, RI
	2/Lt.	WILSON, John P.	20 Jul 45	CTD	Capt.	Hurdle Hills, NC
28 Sep 44	2/Lt.	FRENCH, Bernard J.	02 Oct 44	TRFRD	2/Lt.	West Chelmsford, MA
29 Sep 44	Capt.	SHAFER, Dale E.	07 Sep 45	CTD	Lt. Col.	Dayton, OH
25 Oct 44	2/Lt.	BUTLER, Frederick, Jr.	04 Jun 45	CTD	Capt.	Andover, MA
	2/Lt.	FERRELL, Clarence I.	20 Jul 45	CTD	1/Lt.	Knightdale, NC
	2/Lt.	FRANCIS, Luther B.	20 Jul 45	CTD	1/Lt.	Portland, ME
	2/Lt.	FRENCH, Carl H.	22 Apr 45	CTD	1/Lt.	Loudonville, NY
	2/Lt.	FRISCH, Robert J.	22 Apr 45	CTD	1/Lt.	Cincinnati, OH
	2/Lt.	HAIDLE, Elmer E.	20 Jul 45	CTD	1/Lt.	Greenock, PA
	2/Lt.	HILL, Ralph S., Jr.	22 Apr 45	CTD	1/Lt.	Haddonfield, NJ
	2/Lt.	JOHNSON, Raymond G.	20 Jul 45	CTD	1/Lt.	Clarendon, TX
	2/Lt.	MacKENZIE, Davie A.	07 Apr 45	KIA	1/Lt.	Medford, MA
	2/Lt.	MANKIE, James A.	31 Dec 44	POW	1/Lt.	Nutley, NJ
	Capt.	PERRY, William W.	20 Mar 45	CTD	Capt.	Independence, KS
	1/Lt.	POUTRE, Rex L.	20 Apr 45	CTD	Capt.	Condordia, KS
04 Nov 44	Capt.	EDENS, Malcolm B.	06 Apr 45	CTD	Capt.	Pickens, SC
17 Nov 44	2/Lt.	KRAUSS, Richard E.	20 Jul 45	CTD	1/Lt.	Blue Springs, NE
	2/Lt.	SAMS, Thomas G.	20 Jul 45	CTD	Capt.	Taylor, TX
05 Dec 44	1/Lt.	CHETNEKY, Steve J.	04 Jun 45	CTD	1/Lt.	Trenton, NJ
	1/Lt.	PORTER, George W.	15 Jun 45	KIT	1/Lt.	Los Angeles, CA
	1/Lt.	RAWLS, Dennis B.	04 Jun 45	CTD	1/Lt.	Tampa, FL
13 Feb 45	1/Lt.	TERRATS, Esteban A.	02 Mar 45	KIA	1/Lt.	Santurce, PR
	2/Lt.	BOYD, William H.	05 Aug 45	VED	1/Lt.	Phoenix, AZ
	2/Lt.	CAMPBELL, John G.	22 Jul 45	VED	1/Lt.	Glenbrook, CT
	2/Lt.	McELWEE, Francis E.	20 Jul 45	VED	1/Lt.	Cranford, NJ
	2/Lt.	MORELAND, Kenneth E.	Aug 45	VED	1/Lt.	Fort Dodge, IA
	2/Lt.	PREDDY, William R.	17 Apr 45	KIA	1/Lt.	Greensboro, NC
03 Mar 45	1/Lt.	GAUGHER, Henry W.	20 Jul 45	VED	1/Lt.	Milwaukee, WI
	1/Lt.	POTTHOFF, John P.				Las Vegas, NV
23 Mar 45	2/Lt.	BYERS, John R.	20 Jul 45	VED	1/Lt.	St. Louis, MO
	F/O	GORDON, William R.	20 Jul 45	VED	2/Lt.	Miami, FL
	2/Lt.	SMITH, Linwood P.	20 Jul 45	VED	1/Lt.	Garden City, NY
24 Mar 45	2/Lt.	HULL, James F.	20 Jul 45	VED	2/Lt.	McKeesport, PA
	2/Lt.	HUTTON, John E., Jr.	20 Jul 45	VED	2/Lt.	Kingsport, TN
	2/Lt.	JOHNSON, Allen D.	20 Jul 45	VED	2/Lt.	Fairfield, CT
	2/Lt.	JOHNSON, William G.	20 Jul 45	VED	2/Lt.	Columbus, MS
	2/Lt.	JOHNSTONE, George J.	20 Jul 45	VED	2/Lt.	Tarrant, AL
	2/Lt.	KING, John B.	20 Jul 45	VED	2/Lt.	Atlanta, IL
26 Mar 45	Capt.	AMMON, Robert H.	15 Sep 45	CTD	Capt.	Reading, PA

(flew part of second tour with the 504th)

18 Apr 45	F/O	FRANCE, James L.	08 Sep 45	VED	F/O	Miami, FL
	F/O	FRATELLO, Tom C.	08 Sep 45	VEPD	F/O	Niagara Falls, NY
	2/Lt.	GANER, Seymour	20 Jul 45	VED	2/Lt.	Far Rockaway, NY
	F/O	GRAD, Carl E.	08 Sep 45	VED	F/O	Spring Hope, NC

ASSIGNMENT			DEPARTURE			
DATE	RANK	NAME	DATE	REASON	RANK	HOMETOWN
	F/O	GROTHENDIECK, Carl W.	08 Sep 45	VED	F/O	Chicago, IL
	2/Lt.	KERNISKY, George	08 Sep 45	VED	2/Lt.	Monessen, PA
	F/O	WELLS, Richard G.	08 Sep 45	VED	F/O	Williamstown, MI
Unknown	1/Lt.	RIGGS, Gaston H.	Unknown	KIT	1/Lt.	New Waverly, TX

PILOTS ASSIGNED AFTER VE DAY

22 Jun 45	1/Lt.	William W. FOARD				Marion, SC
	F/O	Andrew N. LETTUS				Hornell, NY
	Maj.	Rose F. HAGER				Mercedes, TX
	F/O	Richard M. McNALLY				Boston, MA
	Capt.	Harry E. HAYNES				Unknown
	F/O	Raymond R. MELE				Manhatten, NY
	1/Lt.	Frank W. LEITNER				Aiken, SC
	1/Lt.	Harold MILLER				Detroit, MI
7 Jul 45	1/Lt.	William R. HUBBEL				Laurel Springs, NJ
8 Jul 45	2/Lt.	Arthur F. CONNORS				Rockville, NY
	1/Lt.	Ralph E. MORROW				Indianapolis, IN
	1/Lt.	John W. CUNNICK				Waco, TX
10 Jul 45	Capt.	Earnest F. DE NEGRIS				New York, NY
12 Jul 45	1/Lt.	Wynne R. GORDON				Ligonier, IN
21 Jul 45	1/Lt.	Davis E. HARDEE				Savannah, GA
25 Jul 45	Capt.	Gordon I. SIEGEL				Dallas, TX

504th Fighter Squadron

ORIGINAL PILOTS

	1/Lt.	BALL, Melville R.	08 Jan 45	CTD	Capt.	Greenwich, CT
	2/Lt.	BROWNSHADEL, Elton J.	06 Jun 44	KIA	1/Lt.	Austin, TX
	2/Lt.	CALDWELL, Merle F.	28 Oct 44	CTD	1/Lt.	Greenville, PA
	2/Lt.	CRAIGO, Cecil E., Jr.	03 Dec 44	CTD	Capt.	Beckly, WV
	2/Lt.	DEGNER, Ralph M.	29 Apr 44	KIT	2/Lt.	Unknown
	1/Lt.	EISENHART, Lee D.	12 Sep 44	CTD	Capt.	Hellertown, PA
	Capt.	GRAVETTE, Edgar B.	28 Dec 44	CTD	Lt. Col	Red Bluff, CA
	2/Lt.	LARSON, Duane S.	02 Nov 44	CTD	1/Lt.	Regent, ND
	2/Lt.	McLURE, James M.	06 Nov 44	CTD	Capt.	Alexandria, LA
	1/Lt.	MYER, Paul M.	30 May 44	KIA	1/Lt.	Arlington, VA
	2/Lt.	O'SULLIVAN, Walter R.	19 May 44	POW	2/Lt.	Harberth, PA
		(Repatriated)				
	1/Lt.	PETER, Lewis S., Jr.	25 Mar 45	CTD	Maj.	San Antonio, TX
	1/Lt.	ROUTT, Bill C.	06 Nov 44	CTD	Maj.	Nacogdoches, TX
	2/Lt.	RUTAN, Frederick S., Jr.	29 Jul 44	POW	1/Lt.	Wallaston, MA
	2/Lt.	SALEEM, Albert	18 Jun 44	TRFRD	2/Lt.	Georgetown, CT
	2/Lt.	SHOWKER, Fred S.	09 Oct 44	CTD	Capt.	Craigsville, VA
	1/Lt.	STEVENS, Bradford V.	20 Jul 45	CTD	Capt.	Hood River, OR
	2/Lt.	STOCKMAN, Hervey S.	13 Sep 44	CTD	1/Lt.	Andover, NJ
	2/Lt.	THIBERT, Henry G.	25 Sep 44	CTD	Capt.	Detroit, MI
	2/Lt.	THISTLETHWAITE, Edward A.	30 May 44	POW	2/Lt.	Opelousas, LA
	F/O	THOMPSON, Ralph P.	28 Nov 44	CTD	1/Lt.	Tomales, CA
	2/Lt.	WATERS, Frank T., Jr.	18 Oct 44	CTD	1/Lt.	Orange, MA
	2/Lt.	WAYMIRE, Harvey R.	02 Nov 44	CTD	1/Lt.	Denver, CO
	1/Lt.	WELLER, Richard E.	13 Sep 44	CTD	Capt.	Dayton, OH
	2/Lt.	WILCOX, Richard H.	12 Oct 44	CTD	1/Lt.	Skaneateles, NY
	2/Lt.	ZEINE, Donald A.	09 Oct 44	CTD	1/Lt.	Glasford, IL

REPLACEMENT PILOTS

13 May 44	2/Lt.	CORBIN, Luther L	02 Nov 44	CTD	1/Lt.	Dalton, TX
	1/Lt.	GRIFFITH, Walter B.	30 Oct 44	CTD	1/Lt.	Bridgeport, PA

ASSIGNMENT			DEPARTURE			
DATE	RANK	NAME	DATE	REASON	RANK	HOMETOWN
	1/Lt.	HARRY, G.P.	28 Jul 44	INJ	1/Lt.	Garwood, TX
24 May 44	2/Lt.	ATTEBERRY, Ray N.	29 Jul 44	POW	2/Lt.	Albion, IL
	2/Lt.	BORDEN, Hetzel, K.	10 Jun 44	POW	2/Lt.	Cumberland, MD
	F/O	HOFFMAN, William R.	14 Dec 44	CTD	1/Lt.	Vanport, OR
06 Jun 44	1/Lt.	HUNTER, Charles, M.	16 Aug 44	KIA	1/Lt.	Bonham, TX
	1Lt	MEAD, Charles M.	29 Dec 44	KIA	1/Lt.	Phoenix, AZ
	1/Lt.	MONTELL, Richard W.	15 Jun 44	KIA	1/Lt.	Alameda, CA
	1/Lt.	PENNY, Donald E.	06 Nov 44	CTD	1/Lt.	Columbus, OH
	1/Lt.	SHIVELY, Jack E.	13 Jun 44	KIA	1/Lt.	Saratoga, WY
10 Jun 44	2/Lt.	CERNICKY, Melvin L.	06 Nov 44	CTD	1/Lt.	Arnold, PA
	2/Lt.	HURLEY, William T.	04 Apr 45	CTD	Capt.	Belmar, NJ
14 Jun 44	2/Lt.	SUTTON, John L.	20 Dec 44	CTD	1/Lt.	Memphis, TN
29 Jun 44	2/Lt.	HASLAM, Frederick C.	05 Apr 45	CTD	1/LT.	Buffalo, NY
11 Jul 44	2/Lt.	HERRMANN, Ray F.	22 Feb 45	KIA	Capt.	Charleston, WV
	2/Lt.	PASTOR, William J.	17 Aug 44	KIA	2/Lt.	Phillipsburg, NJ
	2/Lt.	PENROSE, Richard C.	28 Mar 45	CTD	Capt.	Orland, CA
	2/Lt.	TRESTER, John R.	17 Jan 45	CTD	1/Lt.	Shorewood, WI
	2/Lt.	VAN CLEAVE, Ely N.	26 Nov 44	KIA	1/Lt.	Lincoln, NE
	2/Lt.	WELLS, Arlen W.	28 Mar 45	CTD	Capt.	Corvallis, OR
	2/Lt.	WINKELMAN, Myer R.	13 Aug 44	KIA	2/Lt.	Baird, TX
	2/Lt.	WOOD, Robert T.	22 Feb 45	KIA	Capt.	Raymond, Alberta, CAN
25 Jul 44	2/Lt.	SCHNEIDER, Lewis H.	02 Aug 44	KIA	2/Lt.	Coraopolis, PA
31 Jul 44	2/Lt.	BALLARD, Jerome J.	20 Mar 45	POW	1/Lt.	Detroit, MI
	2/Lt.	BATES, Arthur W., Jr.	12 Mar 45	CTD	1/Lt.	Bowling Green, OH
02 Aug 44	2/Lt.	GREER, Nile C.	13 Apr 45	CTD	Capt.	Blackford, KY
09 Aug 44	2/Lt.	BEADLE, Ermy L.	07 Oct 44	INJ	2/Lt.	Shamokin, PA
06 Sep 44	F/O	KUHLMAN, Robert M.	18 Jul 45	CTD	Capt.	Detroit, MI
	1/Lt.	ROSEN, George J.	02 Oct 44	TRFRD	1/Lt.	Schenectady, NY
28 Sep 44	2/Lt.	ARNOLD, Merlin A.	02 Oct 44	TRFRD	2/Lt.	Tampa, FL
	2/Lt.	FULTON, Joseph O., Jr.	O2 Oct 44	TRFRD	2/Lt.	Paoli, PA
15 Oct 44	Capt.	GUERNSEY, Frank D., Jr.	18 Jul 45	CTD	Maj.	Orlando, FL
25 Oct 44	2/Lt.	ALDRICH, Richard T.	20 Sep 45	CTD	1/Lt.	Rock Island, IL
	2/Lt.	ALLERS, Loren W.	18 Jul 45	CTD	1/Lt.	St. Cloud, MN
	2/Lt.	BARRETT, Lawrence J.	21 Apr 45	CTD	1/Lt.	Watonga, OK
	2/Lt.	BARTO, Vernon N.	21 Apr 45	CTD	1/Lt.	DePue, IL
	2/Lt.	BERGUSON, Kenneth V.	20 Mar 45	KIT	1/Lt.	Cleveland Heights, OH
	2/Lt.	BLIZZARD, Robert V.	18 Jul 45	CTD	1/Lt.	Los Angeles, CA
	2/Lt.	CARTER, Lyle M.	21 Apr 45	CTD	1/Lt.	Madison, WV
	2/Lt.	CHENEZ, Gordon H.	18 Jul 45	CTD	1/Lt.	Detroit, MI
	F/O	COHEN, Gilbert G.	30 May 45	CTD	2/Lt.	Indianapolis, IN
	2/Lt.	CRESWELL, Raymond H.	18 Jul 45	CTD	1/Lt.	Des Moines, IA
	2/Lt.	CROKER, Robert C.	18 Jul 45	CTD	1/Lt.	Whiting, IA
	2/Lt.	LANGOHR, Billy E.	18 Jul 45	CTD	1/Lt.	Columbia City, IN
	1/Lt.	LOSKILL, Harry G.	12 Dec 44	POW	1/Lt.	Chicago, IL
	2/Lt.	MASON, Clair M.	18 Jul 45	CTD	Capt.	Marshalltown, IA
	2/Lt.	ORCUTT, Leon M., Jr.	18 Jul 45	CTD	1/Lt.	Huntington, MA
17 Nov 44	2/Lt.	KREUGER, Donald F.	18 Jul 45	CTD	1/Lt.	Lakewood, OH
	2/Lt.	KUNZ, Leonard A.	18 Jul 45	CTD	1/Lt.	St. Louis, MO
	2/Lt.	KURTH, Otis A.	03 Mar 45	KIA	1/Lt.	Wichita, KS
	2/Lt.	SAINLAR, Jerome J.	18 Jul 45	CTD	1/Lt.	Louisville, KY
27 Dec 44	1/Lt.	BENNETT, Carroll W.	Oct 45	VED	Capt.	Burns, OR
03 Jan 45	2/Lt.	HAVIGHURST, Robert C.	18 Jul 45	VED	1/Lt.	Lakewood, OH
	2/Lt.	HERMANSEN, Cephas	Oct 45	VED	1/Lt.	Alden Station, PA
	2/Lt.	HUDSON, Will M.	Oct 45	VED	1/Lt.	Union City, TN
	2/Lt.	HUNT, Harlan F.	Oct 45	VED	1/Lt.	Meriden, CT
21 Jan 45	1/Lt.	AMMON, Robert H.	26 Mar 45	To 503rd	Capt.	Reading, PA
		(flew first tour with 503rd)				
	Lt. Col.	CLARK, William C.	13 Apr 45	To HQ	Lt. Col	Richmond, VA

ASSIGNMENT			DEPARTURE			
DATE	RANK	NAME	DATE	REASON	RANK	HOMETOWN
13 Feb 45	2/Lt.	HENDRICKS, Charles J.	Unknown	Unknown	2/Lt.	Atlanta, GA
20 Mar 45	1/Lt.	CLIFTON, Frank A.	18 Jul 45	VED	1/Lt.	Boise City, OK
	1/Lt.	COLE, Douglas P.	18 Jul 45	VED	1/Lt.	Geneva, NY
23 Mar 45	Capt.	SARGENT, Robert F.	31 May 45	VED	Capt.	Youngstown, OH
	F/O	SMITH, Roland W.	20 Jul 45	VED	2/Lt.	Hastings, NY
24 Mar 45	Capt.	EVERSON, Kirke B.	18 Jul 45	VED	Capt.	Providence, RI
	2/Lt.	HUNERWADEL, Hugh P.	20 Jul 45	VED	2/Lt.	Chattanooga, TN
	2/Lt.	KING, James C.	20 Jul 45	VED	2/Lt.	Waverly, TN
	F/O	SMITH, Lee W.	20 Jul 45	VED	2/Lt.	Abilene, TX
25 Mar 45	Maj.	JULIAN, William H.	08 Sep 45	CTD	Lt. Col.	Dallas, TX
18 Apr 45	F/O	GARLAND, Edgar L.	08 Sep 45	VED	F/O	Valdosta, GA
	F/O	GOOCH, William D.	08 Sep 45	VED	F/O	Winter Park, FL
	F/O	GREEN, Claude W.	08 Sep 45	VED	F/O	Fordyce, AR
	2/Lt.	KERRIGAN, John S.	08 Sep 45	VED	2/Lt.	Pontiac, MI
	2/Lt.	KLEIN, Frederick, Jr.	08 Sep 45	VED	2/Lt.	Unknown
	2/Lt.	KNAPP, Frank J.	08 Sep 45	VED	2/Lt.	Passiac, NJ
	2/Lt.	KNIPPER, Robert R.	08 Sep 45	VED	2/Lt.	Modesto, CA

PILOTS ASSIGNED AFTER VE DAY

24 Jun 45	1/Lt.	Robert H. BRADNER				Chatham, VA
	Capt.	Warren N. ELLIOTT				Unknown
	1/Lt.	William C. CABANNE				Los Angeles, CAI
	Capt.	Kenneth L. GILBERT				Middletown, RI
	1/Lt.	John F. DUNCAN				Kokomo, IN
	1/Lt.	Delvin G. LARSON				Roseburg, OR
	1/Lt.	Robert DUNN				Auburn, NY
	F/O	Glenn E. STAPP				Detroit, MI
08 Jul 45	1/Lt.	John J. BOYNE				Unknown
	Capt.	Roger WELCH				Jacksonville, FL
	1/Lt.	John W. DUNN				Wallingford, CT

505th Fighter Squadron

Original Pilots

	2/Lt.	BALL, Edwin C.	08 Aug 44	KIA	1/Lt.	Marianna, FL
	2/Lt.	EVANS, Frank T.	15 Sep 44	CTD	1/Lt.	Indianapolis, IN
	2/Lt.	EVERETT, Harold M.	24 May 44	WIA/POW	2/Lt.	Beverly Hills, CA
		Rescued	Nov 44	CTD	1/Lt.	
	2/Lt.	EWING, Philip H.	08 Jun 44	EVD	1/Lt.	Easton, MD
	2/Lt.	FARMER, Owen, P., Jr.	04 Jun 45	CTD	Capt.	Fort Scott, KS
	2/Lt.	GILBERT, Kenneth C.	19 Jul 44	TRFRD	1/Lt.	Jourdanton, TX
	2/Lt.	HANSEMAN, Christ J.	29 Jul 44	KIA	1/Lt.	Mondovi, WI
	2/Lt.	HANSON, James R.	01 Sep 44	CTD	1/Lt.	Norfolk, VA
	2/Lt.	HENEGHAN, Floyd P.	21 May 44	KIA	2/Lt.	Jerseyville, IL
	2/Lt.	HOLLOWAY, John G.	18 Sep 44	CTD	Capt.	South Bend, IN
	2/Lt.	HRICO, George J.	30 Nov 44	CTD	Capt.	Duquesne, PA
	2/Lt.	JAASKELAINEN, William	12 Sept 44	CTD	1/Lt.	Base Line, MI
	2/Lt.	JOHNSON, Evan M., V	27 Nov 44	CTD	Capt.	Pueblo, CO
	2/Lt.	JONES, William A.	11 Sep 44	POW	1/Lt.	Phoenix, AZ
	2/Lt.	KNIGHT, George	12 Sep 44	CTD	1/Lt.	Lakewood, RI
	Capt.	LARSON, Donald A.	04 Aug 44	KIA	Maj.	Yakima, WA
	1/Lt.	LUPER, Arch B.	07 May 44	KIA	1/Lt.	Albuquerque, NM
	2/Lt.	LYNCH, James L.	29 May 44	KIA	1/Lt.	Fort H.G. Wright, NY
	2/Lt.	McMAHON, Peter J.	11 Jul 44	KIA	1/Lt.	Eldersville, PA
	2/Lt.	MUDGE, William F., Jr.	01 Sep 44	CTD	1/Lt.	Fall River, MA
	1/Lt.	OLANDER, Richard B.	17 Jan 45	KIA	Capt.	Racine, WI

ASSIGNMENT			DEPARTURE			
DATE	RANK	NAME	DATE	REASON	RANK	HOMETOWN
	2/Lt.	PERRY, Gordon F.	29 May 44	KIA	2/Lt.	Sidney, NY
	1/Lt.	REID, Langhorne, Jr.	04 Dec 44	CTD	Maj.	Kansas City, MO
	2/Lt.	ROHM, Richard A.	10 Sep 44	CTD	1/Lt.	Los Angeles, Ca
	2/Lt.	SIROCHMAN, Andrew	13 Aug 44	EVD	1/Lt.	Cleveland, OH
			17 Oct 44	CTD		
	2/Lt.	STARNES, James R.	15 Sep 45	CTD	Capt.	Wilmington, NC
	Capt.	THURY, Joseph L.	20 Jul 45	CTD	Lt. Col	St Paul, MN
	1/Lt.	TOWER, Archie A.	07 Sep 45	CTD	Maj.	Winthrop, NY

Replacement Pilots

ASSIGNMENT			DEPARTURE			
DATE	RANK	NAME	DATE	REASON	RANK	HOMETOWN
13 May 44	2/Lt.	FISH, Wesley G.	16 Jul 44	POW	2/Lt.	Oakland, CA
	2/Lt.	SAWICKI, Joseph F.	09 Jun 44	KIA	2/Lt.	Bridgeport, CT
	2/Lt.	STRONG, Roland W.	04 Aug 44	POW	1/Lt.	Bandon, OR
24 May 44	2/Lt.	AMMERMAN, Roy W.	14 Oct 44	CTD	1/Lt.	Brooklyn, NY
	2/Lt.	GRAHAM, Gerald E.	20 Nov 44	CTD	1/Lt.	Grand Rapids, MI
	2/Lt.	OPITZ, William R.	13 Jun 44	INJ	2/Lt.	Spearfish, SD
	2/Lt.	STEWART, Carl R.	23 Sep 44	CTD	1/Lt.	Utica, NY
6 Jun 44	1/Lt.	ARMISTEAD, Walter M.	17 Jun 44	POW	1/Lt.	Atlanta, GA
	1/Lt.	KRAUSS, William H.	06 Dec 44	CTD	Capt.	Altavista, VA
10 Jun 44	2/Lt.	NAY, Martin N.	05 Sep 44	EVD	1/Lt.	Brooklyn, NY
	2/Lt.	POWELL, Lawrence J., Jr.	14 Jan 45	POW	1/Lt.	Southgate, CA
14 Jun 44	2/Lt.	TANNOUS, Richard H.	26 Oct 44	CTD	1/Lt.	Pelham Manor, NY
29 Jun 44	2/Lt.	BUNDGAARD, Carl H.	04 Jul 44	RTD		Withee, WI
			31 Mar 45	CTD	1/Lt.	
11 Jul 44	2/Lt.	BURNS, Robert F.	04 Aug 44	POW	2/Lt.	Dearborn, MI
	F/O	BYRD, Cecil L.	30 May 45	CTD	1/Lt.	Polo, IL
	2/Lt.	DANIELL, J.S.	Mar 45	CTD	1/Lt.	Birmingham, AL
	2/Lt.	JACKSON, Boyd O.	21 Nov 44	KIA	1/Lt.	Harlem, MT
	2/Lt.	MULLER, James B.	23 Sep 44	POW	2/Lt.	Maplewood, NJ
	2/Lt.	SHAW, Bernell W.	24 Aug 44	POW	2/Lt.	Brookfield Center, CT
	2/Lt.	STAGGERS, Theodore R.	11 Sep 44	POW	2/Lt.	Fairmont, WV
	2/Lt.	TONGUE, Arthur E.	06 Aug 44	KIA	2/Lt.	New York, NY
25 Jul 44	2/Lt.	BLOXAM, Robert W.	06 Feb 45	KIA	Capt.	Arimo, ID
	2/Lt.	MALARZ, Chester	09 Feb 45	CTD	Capt.	Buffalo, NY
	2/Lt.	SLOVAK, William R.	13 Sep 44	KIA	2/Lt.	El Campo, TX
31 Jul 44	2/Lt.	BAKER, James A.	05 Dec 44	KIA	2/Lt.	Fort Wayne, IN
	2/Lt.	MOORE, William R.	13 Sep 44	POW	1/Lt.	Harrieta, MI
02 Aug 44	2/Lt.	YOUNG, Allen D.	18 Nov 44	POW	1/Lt.	Salt Lake City, UT
06 Aug 44	Maj.	REYNOLDS, John R.	10 Sep 44	KIA	Maj.	San Antonio, TX
09 Aug 44	2/Lt.	CAIN, Richard C.	04 Dec 44	POW	1/Lt.	Gowanda, NY
	2/Lt.	MARTS, Jay F.	17 Mar 45	CTD	1/Lt.	Salem, NJ
	2/Lt.	RICH, George T.	22 Apr 45	CTD	Capt.	Wilmington, NC
	2/Lt.	WILCOX, Russell W.	29 Aug 44	KIA	2/Lt.	East Greenwich, RI
20 Aug 44	Capt.	MITCHELL, Raymond M., Jr.	23 Sep 44	POW	Capt.	Charlotte, NC
06 Sep 44	2/Lt.	CORREY, Harry R.	20 Jul 45	CTD	Capt.	Niagara Falls, NY
	2/Lt.	GIRZI, Henry E., Jr.	01 Apr 45	CTD	1/Lt.	Superior, WI
	2/Lt.	IRION, Robert E.	20 Jul 45	CTD	Capt.	Axtell, KS
	2/Lt.	JONES, George W., Jr.	03 Mar 45	KIA	1/Lt.	Lenoir City, TN
	2/Lt.	THIEME, Richard G.	22 Mar 45	CTD	1/Lt.	Sheboygan, WI
	2/Lt.	TRAVIS, Laird D.	18 Nov 44	KIA	2/Lt.	Smicksburg, PA
15 Sep 44	1/Lt.	STILES, Bert	26 Nov 44	KIA	1/Lt.	Denver, CO
19 Sep 44	2/Lt.	BECKER, Leo H.	08 Apr 45	CTD	1/Lt.	Chicago, IL
	F/O	BROCK, Thomas C.	02 Oct 44	TRFRD	F/O	Chicago, IL
	2/Lt.	CONNER, Bertis A., Jr.	02 Mar 45	POW	1/Lt.	Groves, TX
	2/Lt.	MARVEL, Thomas W.	20 Apr 45	CTD	1/Lt.	East Orange, NJ
	F/O	PETTICREW, Stanley S.	02 Oct 44	TRFRD	F/O	Springfield, OH

ASSIGNMENT			DEPARTURE			
DATE	RANK	NAME	DATE	REASON	RANK	HOMETOWN
	2/Lt.	STOUDT, Leland M.	21 Nov 44	KIA	2/Lt.	Reading, PA
26 Sep 44	2/Lt.	ANANIAN, Stephen C.	23 Apr 45	CTD	1/Lt.	New York, NY
	2/Lt.	BOOTH, Billy B.	08 Apr 45	CTD	1/Lt.	Blanchard, MI
	2/Lt.	CARR, Vernon D.	20 Jul 45	CTD	1/Lt.	Brockton, MA
	2/Lt.	GILMER, Harry U.	02 Oct 44	TRFD	2/Lt.	Birmingham, AL
	2/Lt.	GOUSIE, Roland E.	15 Apr 45	POW	1/Lt.	Pawtucket, RI
	2/Lt.	PHILLIPPI, William R.	12 Apr 45	CTD	1/Lt.	Camden, AL
25 Oct 44	2/Lt.	CAYWOOD, Herbert L.	20 Apr 45	CTD	1/Lt.	Sheldon, MO
	2/Lt.	HOWARD, Waldon E.	17 Jan 45	KIA	1/Lt.	Seminole, OK
	1/Lt.	LOVELESS, Philip M., Jr.	23 Apr 45	CTD	Capt.	Warren, OH
	F/O	PALMER, Gerald W.	06 Feb 45	KIA	2/Lt.	Ladysmith, WI
	2/Lt.	THOMAS, Kessler O.	06 Feb 45	KIA	1/Lt.	Cisco, TX
	2/Lt.	WITHERS, John C.	17 Apr 45	CTD	1/Lt.	Washington, D.C.
	2/Lt.	WOOLERY, James C.	20 Jul 45	CTD	1/Lt.	Bloomington, IN
	2/Lt.	ZIEGLER, Harry D.	03 Mar 45	POW	1/Lt.	Norristown, PA
17 Nov 44	2/Lt.	O'BRIEN, Richard C.	12 Mar 45	RTD	1/Lt.	Somerville, MA
		(landed behind Russian lines; returned)				
03 Jan 45	Capt.	BLINE, J. Brooks	22 Jul 45	VED	Capt.	Annapolis, IL
	2/Lt.	HOWARD, Harvey F.	02 Mar 45	POW	1/Lt.	Colorado Springs, CO
13 Feb 45	2/Lt.	ALLMAN, Johnnie M.	12 Feb 45	KIT	2/Lt.	Pelly, TX
	2/Lt.	BEECHER, William M.	20 Feb 45	KIA	2/Lt.	Brooklyn, NY
	2/Lt.	BIGGS, Oscar K.	20 Jul 45	VED	1/Lt.	Wilmington, NC
	2/Lt.	BURCH, Harold W.	20 Jul 45	VED	1/Lt.	Omaha, NE
	F/O	COKER, Joseph R.	31 Mar 45	POW	F/O	Gardmer, FL
	Capt.	DIEFENBECK, James A.	23 Apr 45	VED	Capt.	Pottstown, PA
	2/Lt.	MacCLARENCE, William R.	20 Jul 45	VED	1/Lt.	North Plainfield, NJ
	2/Lt.	MURPHY, Jerome T.	20 Jul 45	VED	1/Lt.	Brainerd, MN
	2/Lt.	PAUL, Robert H., Jr.	20 Jul 45	VED	1/Lt.	Baltimore, MD
	F/O	PESANKA, John	20 Jul 45	VED	2/Lt.	Pittsburgh, PA
	1/Lt.	WAGER, Evergard L.	30 Mar 45	KIA	1/Lt.	Battle Creek, MI
20 Mar 45	1/Lt.	GUYTON, William R.	15 Sep 45	VED	1/Lt.	Pittsburgh, PA
	F/O	RICE, John J.	20 Jul 45	VED	F/O	Hartford, CT
	1/Lt.	SMITH, Floyd W.	Aug 45	VED	1/Lt.	Bismarck, IL
	F/O	STEIGER, LeRoy A.	20 Jul 45	VED	F/O	East Orange, NJ
23 Mar 45	F/O	HUPP, Ellis E., Jr.	20 Jul 45	VED	2/Lt.	Zanesville, OH
	2/Lt.	WARK, Raymond D.	20 Jul 45	VED	1/Lt.	Camden, NJ
24 Mar 45	2/Lt.	JESSUP, Tom N.	30 Jun 45	KIT	2/Lt.	Atlanta, GA
	2/Lt.	KNIGHTON, Ralph M.	20 Jul 45	VED	2/Lt.	Locust Grove, VA
	2/Lt.	KOTORA, Harold J.	20 Jul 45	VED	2/Lt.	Chicago, IL
	2/Lt.	KOVAR, Robert J.	20 Jul 45	VED	2/Lt.	Pittsburgh, PA
	2/Lt.	LANFER, William A.	20 Jul 45	VED	2/Lt.	Fort Worth, TX
	2/Lt.	LAVERICK, John H.	20 Jul 45	VED	2/Lt.	Forty Fort, PA
	2/Lt.	LAWES, Bayard F.	20 Jul 45	VED	2/Lt.	Ferndale, MI
	F/O	SHEPHERD, George W., Jr.	20 Jul 45	VED	F/O	Graham, NC
18 Apr 45	2/Lt.	FRINK, James P.	08 Sep 45	VED	2/Lt.	Charlotte, NC
	F/O	GELPKE, Robert E.	08 Sep 45	VED	F/O	Canton, MA
	2/Lt.	GREGORY, Vincent L.	08 Sep 45	VED	2/Lt.	Oil City, PA
	2/Lt.	HILL, Joe S.	08 Sep 45	VED	2/Lt.	Unknown
	2/Lt.	JORGENSON, Loyd N.	08 Sep 45	VED	2/Lt.	Hyrum, UT
	2/Lt.	KARKUMA, Karl O.	08 Sep 45	VED	2/Lt.	Detroit, MI
	1/Lt.	OTT, Maurice	08 Sep 45	VED	1/Lt.	Kansas City, KS

| Capt. | SMITH, Shirley K. | 20 Jul 45 | VED | Capt. | Williamsport, PA |

PILOTS ASSIGNED AFTER VE DAY

22 Jun 45	F/O	Richard N. GUSTKE	St. Petersburg, FL
	Capt.	Robert C. MILLER	Battle Creek, MI
	1/Lt.	Robert L. McINTOSH	Ironton, OH
	1/Lt.	Alfred G. SPRIGGS	Milwaukee, WI
	1/Lt.	Bruce D. McMAHAN	Oceanside, CA
	2/Lt.	James A. STEIGER	Houston, TX
08 Jul 45	2/Lt.	Russell C. DAY	Sunbury, PA
	1/Lt.	Richard C. STEVENS	Reedville, VA
	2/Lt.	James P. McMULLEN	St. Petersburg, FL
01 Aug 45	1/Lt.	Ray C. GORDON	Unknown

Table Five -A
Overall Casualty / Cause Data

EXPLANATION OF CODES

CTD	Completed Tour of Duty	MIA Missing in Action	EVD Evaded Capture	POW	Prisoner of War
INJ	Injured	RTD Returned	INTD Interned	TRFRD	Transferred
KIA	Killed in Action	VED Victory in Europe Day	KIT Killed in Training	WIA	Wounded in Action

339 Fighter Group Headquarters

CAUSE	KIA	POW	EVD	INJ*	INT	WIA*	TOTAL
Enemy Flak	1						1
Unknown (Combat)	1						1
Total Combat	2	0	0	0	00		2

Note: No non-combat casualties

503rd Fighter Squadron

CAUSE	KIA	POW	EVD	INJ*	INT	WIA*	TOTAL
Enemy Aircraft	4	3					7
Enemy Flak	7	2	1			10	
Mechanical Failure	1	2	1	1			5
Weather	2						2
Collision Air/Ground	2						2
Collision Air/Air	1						1
Allied Flak	1						1
B-17	1						1
Unknown	3					3	
Total Combat	22	7	1	0	11		30
Non-Combat (Flying)	4						4
Non-Flying	1						1
Total Non-Combat	5	0	0	0	00		5

504th Fighter Squadron

CAUSE	KIA	POW	EVD	INJ*	INT	WIA*	TOTAL
Enemy Aircraft	4	4					8
Enemy Flak	6	1					7
Mechanical Failure	1	2	1				4

Table Five -A (Cont'd)

CAUSE	KIA	POW	EVD	INJ*	INT	WIA*	TOTAL
Weather	1						1
Unknown	1	1					2
Total Combat	13	8	0	1	0	0	22
Non-Combat (Flying)	2						2

Note: No non-flying casualties

505th Fighter Squadron

CAUSE	KIA	POW	EVD	INJ*	INT	WIA*	TOTAL
Enemy Aircraft	2	3					5
Enemy Flak	12	7	2				21
Mechanical Failure		6	1				7
Weather	5			1			6
Collision Air/Ground	2	2					4
Collision Air/Air	1	1					2
Exploding Train			1				1
Navigation	2						2
P-51		1					1
Unknown	1						1
Total Combat	25	20	4	1	0	0	50
Non-Combat (Flying)	1						1

Note: No non-flying casualties

Serious wounds or injuries - end of combat flying

Table Five -B
KIA / POW Casualty Data

UNIT	ORIGINAL PILOTS ASSIGNED	REPLACEMENT PILOTS ASSIGNED	TOTAL PILOTS ASSIGNED	PILOTS KIA	% OF TOTAL	PILOTS POW	% OF TOTAL	TOTAL KIA / POW	% OF TOTAL
HQ	6	5	11	2	18%	0	0	2	18%
503rd	27	86	113	21	19%	7	6%	28	25%
504th	26	74	100	13	13%	6	6%	19	19%
505th	28	96	124	25	20%	19	15%	44	35%
TOTAL	87	261	348	61	18%	32	9%	93	27%

Table Five -C
Individual Pilot Casualty Information
(COMBAT - DIRECT ENEMY ACTION)

BY ENEMY AIRCRAFT

UNIT PILOT	RANK	ASGMT	DATE	FATE
Robert C. SMITH	1/Lt.	503rd	08 Jun 44	KIA
Victor W. MEYER	1/Lt.	503rd	05 Aug 44	KIA
Alfred O. MANKE	2/Lt.	503rd	23 Sep 44	POW
Harvey E. HENDERSON	Lt. Col.	503rd	05 Dec 44	POW
James A. MANKIE	1/Lt.	503rd	31 Dec 44	POW
Anthony G. HAWKINS	Capt.	503rd	31 Dec 44	KIA
Esteban A. TERRATS	1/Lt.	503rd	02 Mar 45	KIA
Walter R. O'SULLIVAN	2/Lt.	504th	19 May 44	POW
Paul M. MYER	1/Lt.	504th	30 May 44	KIA
Edward A. THISTLETHWAITE	2/Lt.	504th	30 May 44	POW
Richard W. MONTELL	1/Lt.	504th	15 Jun 44	KIA
Frederick S. RUTAN	1/Lt.	504th	29 Jun 44	POW
Ray N. ATTEBERRY	2/Lt.	504th	29 Jul 44	POW
Charles M. HUNTER	1/Lt.	504th	16 Aug 44	KIA
Ely N. VAN CLEAVE	1/Lt.	504th	26 Nov 44	KIA
Harold M. EVERETT	2/Lt.	505th	24 May 44	POW
Joseph F. SAWICKI	2/Lt.	505th	08 Jun 44	KIA
William A. JONES	2/Lt.	505th	11 Sep 44	POW
Raymond M. MITCHELL	Capt.	505th	23 Sep 44	POW
Evergard L. WAGER	1/Lt.	505th	30 Mar 45	KIA

BY ENEMY FLAK

UNIT PILOT	RANK	ASGMT	DATE	FATE
Charles W. DOWELL	Capt.	HQ	21 Nov 44	KIA
Walter T. CARTER	Capt.	503rd	21 May 44	POW
Robert F. MULVEY	1/Lt.	503rd	21 May 44	KIA
Arthur H. STEIER	2/Lt.	503rd	21 May 44	KIA
Joseph WOLFORT	1/Lt.	503rd	24 May 44	KIA
Ralph H. DEAREY	2/Lt.	503rd	19 Jun 44	POW
Arthur F. LOWERY	1/Lt.	503rd	22 Jun 44	KIA
Richard S. WHITELAW	Capt.	503rd	29 Jun 44	KIA
Valdee WYATT	Capt.	503rd	18 Oct 44	WIA
William D. STOCKTON	1/Lt.	503rd	18 Oct 44	KIA
Edward H. BEAVERS	Capt.	503rd	27 Nov 44	KIA
Lewis H. SCHNEIDER	2/Lt.	504th	02 Aug 44	KIA
Myer R. WINKELMAN	2/Lt.	504th	13 Aug 44	KIA
William J. PASTOR	2/Lt.	504th	17 Aug 44	KIA
Ray F. HERRMANN	Capt.	504th	22 Feb 45	KIA
Robert T. WOOD	Capt.	504th	22 Feb 45	KIA
Otis A. KURTH	1/Lt.	504th	03 Mar 45	KIA
Jerome J. BALLARD	1/Lt.	504th	20 Mar 45	POW
Arch B. LUPER	1/Lt.	505th	07 May 44	KIA
Floyd P. HENEGAN	2/Lt.	505th	21 May 44	KIA
Philip H. EWING	1/Lt.	505th	08 Jun 44	EVD
Wesley G. FISH	2/Lt.	505th	16 Jul 44	POW
Roland W. STRONG	1/Lt.	505th	04 Aug 44	POW
Edwin C. BALL	1/Lt.	505th	08 Aug 44	KIA
Russell W. WILCOX	2/Lt.	505th	28 Aug 44	KIA
Martin N. NAY	1/Lt.	505th	05 Sep 44	EVD
John R. REYNOLDS	Maj.	505th	10 Sep 44	KIA

Table Five -C (Cont'd)

Theodore R. STAGGERS	2/Lt.	505th	11 Sep 44	POW
William R. SLOVAK	2/Lt.	505th	13 Sep 44	KIA
William R. MOORE	1/Lt.	505th	13 Sep 44	POW
Allen D. YOUNG	1/Lt.	505th	18 Nov 44	POW
Laird D. TRAVIS	2/Lt.	505th	18 Nov 44	KIA
Boyd O. JACKSON	1/Lt.	505th	21 Nov 44	KIA
Leland M. STOUDT	2/Lt.	505th	21 Nov 44	KIA
Waldon E. HOWARD	1/Lt.	505th	17 Jan 45	KIA
Richard B. OLANDER	Capt.	505th	17 Jan 45	KIA
Bertis A. CONNER	1/Lt.	505th	02 Mar 45	POW
George W. JONES	1/Lt.	505th	03 Mar 45	KIA
Harry D. ZIEGLER	1/Lt.	505th	03 Mar 45	POW

Table Five -D
Individual Pilot Casualty Information
(COMBAT - OTHER THAN ENEMY ACTION)

UNIT PILOT	RANK	ASGMT	DATE	FATE
BY ALLIED FLAK				
Vincent J. SPAZIANO	1/Lt.	503rd	18 Nov 44	KIA
BY B-17				
David A. MacKENZIE	1/Lt.	503rd	07 Apr 45	POW
BY P-51				
James B. MULLER	2/Lt.	505th	23 Sep 44	POW
NAVIGATION - MISSED ENGLAND				
James L. LYNCH	1/Lt.	505th	29 May 44	KIA
Gordon F. PERRY	2/Lt.	505th	29 May 44	KIA
COLLISION - AIR TO AIR				
Edward C. FLAHERTY	2/Lt.	503rd	05 Aug 44	KIA
William R. OPITZ	2/Lt.	505th	13 Jun 44	INJ
Donald A. LARSON	Maj.	505th	04 Aug 44	KIA
Robert F. BURNS	2/Lt.	505th	04 Aug 44	POW
COLLISION - EXPLODING TRAIN				
Andrew SIROCHMAN	1/Lt.	505th	13 Aug 44	EVD
COLLISION - GROUND OBJECTS				
James R. CROCKETT	1/Lt.	503rd	19 May 44	KIA
Raymond D. MAYER	1/Lt.	503rd	18 Oct 44	KIA
Chris J. HANSEMAN	1/Lt.	505th	29 Jul 44	KIA
Bert STILES	1/Lt.	505th	26 Nov 44	KIA
Lawrence J. POWELL	1/Lt.	505th	14 Jan 45	POW
Harry F. HOWARD	1/Lt.	505th	02 Mar 45	POW
WEATHER				
Nathan T. FOLWELL	Capt.	503rd	19 Jun 44	KIA
Robert B. Brown	1/Lt.	503rd	19 Jun 44	KIA

Table Five -D (Cont'd)

UNIT PILOT	RANK	ASGMT	DATE	FATE
Elton J. BROWNSHADEL	1/Lt.	504th	06 June 44	KIA
William R. OPITZ	2/Lt.	505th	13 Jun 44	INJ
Arthur E. TONGUE	2/Lt.	505th	06 Aug 44	KIA
Robert W. BLOXAM	Capt.	505th	06 Feb 45	KIA
Kessler O. THOMAS	1/Lt.	505th	06 Feb 45	KIA
Gerald W. PALMER	2/Lt.	505th	06 Feb 45	KIA
William M. BEECHER	2/Lt.	505th	20 Feb 45	KIA

MECHANICAL FAILURE

UNIT PILOT	RANK	ASGMT	DATE	FATE
Albert L. WYER	1/Lt.	503rd	15 May 44	POW
Franklin D. TALCOTT	2/Lt.	503rd	05 Aug 44	INT
John M. CAROTHERS	1/Lt.	503rd	27 Aug 44	KIA
Raymond F. REUTER	2/Lt.	503rd	10 Sep 44	EVD
Paul D. FICKEL	1/Lt.	503rd	26 Sep 44	POW
Hetzel K. BODEN	2/Lt.	504th	10 Jun 44	POW
Ermy L. BEADLE	2/Lt.	504th	24 Aug 44	INJ
Harry G. LOSKILL	1/Lt.	504th	12 Dec 44	POW
Charles M. MEAD	1/Lt.	504th	29 Dec 44	KIA
Walter M. ARMISTEAD	1/Lt.	505th	17 Jun 44	POW
Carl H. BUNDGAARD	2/Lt.	505th	04 Jul 44	EVD
Bernell W. SHAW	2/Lt.	505th	24 Aug 44	POW
Richard C. CAIN	1/Lt.	505th	04 Dec 44	POW
James A. BAKER	2/Lt.	505th	05 Dec 44	POW
Joseph R. COKER	F/O	505th	31 Mar 45	POW
Roland E. GOUSIE	1/Lt.	505th	15 Apr 45	POW

UNKOWN CAUSES

UNIT PILOT	RANK	ASGMT	DATE	FATE
Michael G. H. McPHARLIN	Maj.	HQ	06 Jun 44	KIA
Felix J. GIRONE	1/Lt.	503rd	27 Nov 44	KIA
Raymond F. REUTER	Capt.	503rd	17 Apr 45	KIA
William R. PREDDY	1/Lt.	503rd	17 Apr 45	KIA
Jack E. SHIVELY	1/Lt.	504th	13 Jun 44	KIA
Peter J. McMAHON	1/Lt.	505th	11 Jul 44	KIA

Table Five -E
Individual Pilot Casualty Information
(NON - COMBAT DEATHS)

UNIT PILOT	RANK	ASGMT	DATE
FLYING			
Robert L. DICKENS	2/Lt.	503rd	27 May 44
John W. COZAD	2/Lt.	503rd	25 Jul 44
Gaston H. RIGGS	1/Lt.	503rd	Unknown
Alan F. CRUMP	2/Lt.	503rd	Nov 44
Ralph M. DEGNER	2/Lt.	504th	29 Apr 44
Kenneth V. BERGUSON	1/Lt.	504th	20 Mar 45
Johnnie M. ALLMAN	2/Lt.	505th	12 Feb 45
NON-FLYING (Jeep Accident)			
Rodney C. WEST	1/Lt.	503rd	25 Jun 44

Table Six
8th Air Force Fighter Command
Enemy Aircraft Destroyed

Fighter Group	Operational Dates	Number of Days	Number of Missions	E/A Dest Air	E/A Dest Ground	Total Destroyed	Spitfire	P-47	P-38	P-51
4	Oct 42-Apr 45	936	529	549	469	1,018	Sep 42-Apr 43	Mar 43-Feb 44		Feb 44-VE Day
20	Dec 43-Apr 45	484	312	210	237	447			Dec 43-Jul 44	Jul 44-VE Day
55	Oct 43-Apr 45	554	413	304	269	572			Sep 43-Jul 44	Jul 44-VE Day
56	Apr 43-Apr 45	739	447	665	311	976		Feb 43-VE Day		
78	Apr 43-Apr 45	739	450	332	359	691		Jan 43-Jan 45		Dec 44-VE Day
339	Apr 44-Apr 45	356	264	234	424	657				Apr 44-VE Day
352	Sep 43-Apr 45	602	420	504	287	791		Jul 43-Apr 44		Apr 44-VE Day
353	Aug 83-Apr 45	615	447	333	414	747		Jul 43-Nov 44		Oct 44-VE Day
355	Sep 43-Apr 45	588	415	339	503	842		Jul 43-Mar 44		Mar 44-VE Day
356	Oct 43-May 45	570	413	201	76	277		Sept 43-Nov 44		Nov 44-VE Day
357	Feb 44-Apr 45	440	313	596	107	702				Feb 44-VE Day
359	Dec 43-Apr 45	494	346	240	98	338		Nov 43-May 44		May 44-VE Day
361	Jan 44-Apr 45	453	341	221	105	326		Dec 43-May 44		May 44-VE Day
364	Mar 44-Apr 45	418	342	263	193	456			Feb 44-Jul 44	Jul 44-VE Day
479	May 44-Apr 45	334	251	154	279	433			May 44-Sep 44	Sep44-VE Day
TOTAL E/A DESTROYED:				5,143	4,128	9,271				

Notes:

1/Compiled from "USAF Historical Study No. 85" except for the 339th which is based on additional confirmation data resulting in a lower figure than "Study No. 85."

2/Taken from The Mighty Eighth by Roger A. Freeman except for the 339th which is based on additional confirmation data resulting in a lower figure than in Mr. Freeman's work.

3/Results of ranking of the 339th Fighter Group among all Eighth Air Force Fighter Groups are: E/A Destroyed (Air).......11th, E/A Destroyed (Ground).....3rd, Total E/A Destroyed...........8th

Table Seven
Enemy Aircraft Destroyed (Air)
by Eighth Air Force Fighter Squadrons

AVG FGTR RANK	SQUADRON/GROUP	TOTAL VICTORIES	TOTAL MISSIONS	VICTORIES PER MISSION
1	364/357	212.0	313	0.677
2	362/357	198.0	313	0.633
3	487/352	235.5	420	0.561
4	61/56	232.0	447	0.519
5	363/357	155.0	313	0.495
6	62/56	219.5	447	0.491
7	63/56	174.0	447	0.389
8	334/4	201.6	529 (est)	0.381
9	434/479	92.5	251	0.369
10	**503/339**	**96.0**	**264**	**0.366**
11	328/352	142.5	420	0.339
12	370/359	111.5	346	0.322
13	**505/339**	**84.5**	**264**	**0.320**
14	354/355	132.0	415 (est)	0.318
15	336/4	161.7	529 (est)	0.306
16	335/4	160.7	529 (est)	0.303
17	38/55	114.0	413 (est)	0.276
18	486/352	115.0	420	0.273
19	357/335	111.5	415 (est)	0.269
20	83/78	120.5	450	0.267
21	338/55	109.0	413 (est)	0.264
22	384/364	89.0	342	0.260
23	385/364	88.5	342	0.259
24	350/353	113.5	447	0.254
25	376/361	83.5	341	0.245
26	77/20	76.0	312	0.243
27	82/78	104.5	450	0.232
28 TIE	84/78	101.5	450	0.226
28 TIE	351/353	101.0	447	0.226
30	369/359	78.0	346	0.225
31	375/361	76.5	341	0.224
32	383/364	76.0	342	0.222
33	361/356	91.0	413	0.220
34	55/20	65.0	312	0.208
35	352/353	87.0	447	0.195
36	**504/339**	**51.0**	**264**	**0.193**
37	358/355	79.5	415 (est)	0.192
38	343/55	76.5	413 (est)	0.185
39	79/20	56.0	312	0.179
40	374/361	53.5	341	0.157
41	368/359	48.5	346	0.140
42	435/479	33.5	251	0.133
43 TIE	359/356	51.0	413	0.123
43 TIE	360/356	51.0	413	0.123
45	436/479	24.0	251	0.096

339th Fighter Group

Visiting congressmen at the 339th Control Tower, 1944.

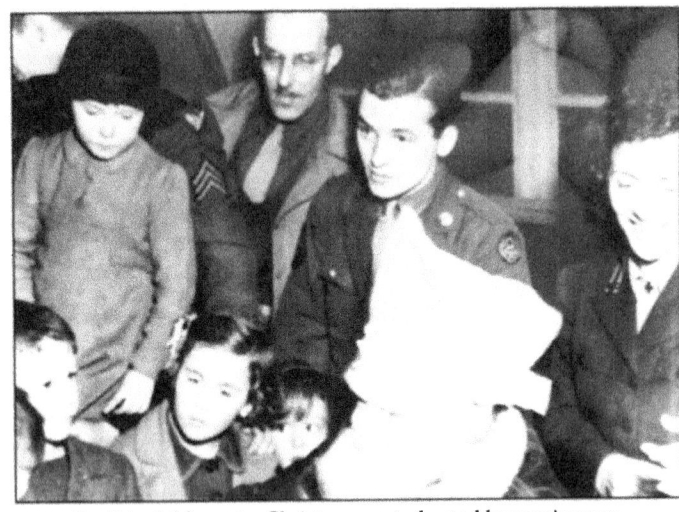
English children at a Christmas party hosted by servicemen.

Bing and Lily Ann Carol sing "I Walk Alone" at Dunford.

Three "gaspump" operators. Left to right, Al Grandy, Primo Zambardo and Eddie Epp.

1st Lt. John W. Mason, Jr. cutting his birthday cake, 1944, at Fowlmere, England.

Colonel John B. Henry with aircraft *Sanantone Rose*.

The first aircraft to crash on Fowlmere Airfield. The plane is a P-51.

Lt. Col. William C. Clark, Hq. Co., 339th Fighter Group.

339th Fighter Group

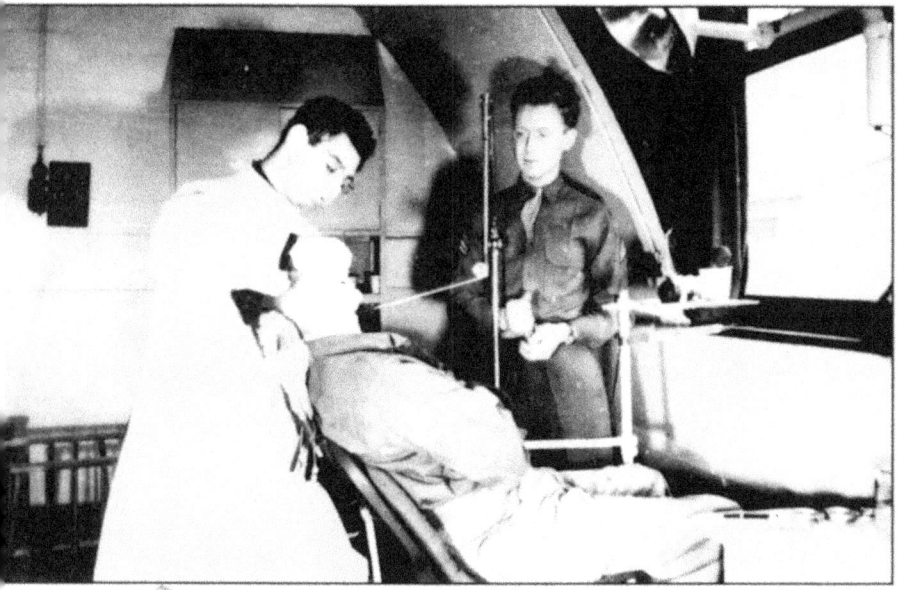

Dentist Howard Hauss and assistant, Earl Gertz. Check-up!

Base weather station, Fowlmere, England. Seated, George Walker. Standing, T/Sgt. Herman F. Mondschein.

Wednesday night dance at the Red Cross Club. Rocketeers is the band.

The 339th Armament Squadron's 50 caliber "greeting."

ARC Club, Fowlmere, England. 339th troops provide entertainment.

Christmas party for Fowlmere children. December 1944.

MISSIONS COMPLETED

Upward, ever upward,
I have climbed above my earthly being
Into a world of cloud and sunshine,
Free of torment, free of toil,
And through the wind, I hear their voices,
And through the clouds, I see their faces.
They are there on my wing, both left and right.
My courageous friends in eternal flight.

Author Unknown

(From the original back cover flap)

BACK COVER

503rd SQUADRON

D7 F "DEE"	Capt. Clarence W. Knott
D7 Z "SHY-ANN"	Lt. Charles E. Shake
D7 W "SALLY"	Capt. Leonard J. Fiorito
D7 0 "MISS MAX"	Lt. Ethelbert H. Graham

*D7 Z was Jerry P. Bush's plane

504th SQUADRON

5Q-Z "Pedunk"	Capt. Claire M. Mason
5Q-R	Lt. Gordon H. Chenez
5Q-D	Lt. Vernon N. Barto
*5Q-T Photo Plane	Lt. Will M. Hudson

505th SQUADRON

6N-C "Pauline"	Capt. Harry R. Corey
6N-Q	Lt. Leo H. Becker
6N-B	Lt. William B. Booth
6N-Y	Lt. Roland E. Gousie

*6N-C was Lt. Col. Joseph L. Thury's plane

www.ingramcontent.com/pod-product-compliance
Lightning Source LLC
Chambersburg PA
CBHW080729230426
43665CB00020B/2671